GERMAN

WARSHIPS

1815–1945

GERMAN

Volume One:

ERICH GRÖNER

WARSHIPS
1815–1945
Major Surface Vessels

Drawings by Erich Gröner, Peter Mickel and Franz Mrva

Revised and Expanded by Dieter Jung and Martin Maass

CONWAY

MARITIME PRESS

First published in West Germany under the title *Die deutschen Kriegsschiffe 1815–1945*

First English language edition published 1990 by

Conway Maritime Press Limited
24 Bride Lane, Fleet Street
London EC4Y 8DR

British Library Cataloguing in Publication Data

Groener, Erich
    German Warships 1815–1945.
    1. Germany. Kriegsmarine. Ships, history
    I. Title   II. Jung, Dieter   III. Maass, Martin

ISBN 0-85177-533-0

Designed by John Leath MSTD

Typeset by Inforum Typesetting, Portsmouth

Printed by Redwood Press Limited, Melksham

Contents

Foreword vii

Notes and abbreviations ix

Armoured vessels 1864–1884
Prinz Adalbert 1
Arminius 1
Friedrich Carl 2
Kronprinz 3
König Wilhelm 3
Hansa 4
Preussen class 5
Kaiser class 6
Sachsen class 7
Oldenburg 8

Coastal battleships 1890–1896
Siegfried class 10
Odin class 11

Battleships 1894–1908
Kurfürst Friedrich Wilhelm class 13
Kaiser Friedrich III class 14
Wittelsbach class 16
Braunschweig class 18
Deutschland class 20

Battleships 1909–1918
Nassau class 23
Helgoland class 24
Kaiser class 25
König class 27
Bayern class 28
Volya 30

Battleships 1939–1941
Scharnhorst class 31
Bismarck class 33
H class 35
H41 class 37
H42 class 38
Foreign battleships 38

Frigates and flush-decked corvettes 1849–1886
Gefion 31
Barbarossa class 39
Hansa 40
Danzig 41
Thetis class 41
Arcona class 42
Leipzig class 43
Bismarck class 44
Charlotte 45

Large cruisers and battlecruisers 1892–1917
Kaiserin Augusta 46

Victoria Louise class 47
Fürst Bismarck 48
Prinz Heinrich 49
Prinz Adalbert class 50
Roon class 51
Scharnhorst class 52
Blücher 53
Von der Tann 53
Moltke class 54
Seydlitz 55
Derfflinger class 56
Mackensen class 57
Ersatz Yorck class 59

Armoured ships 1933–1936
Deutschland/Lützow class 60
D class 63
P1 class 63

Heavy cruisers 1939–1940
Blücher class 65

Battlecruisers (planned) 1939–1940
O class 68

Aircraft carriers 1918–1940
I (ex Ausonia) 70
Graf Zeppelin class 71

Auxiliary aircraft carriers 1942–1943
I (ex Europa) 73
'Jade' class 74
Weser class 75
II (ex De Grasse) 76

Schooners, corvettes, avisos, armed steamers 1816–1886
Stralsund 78
Amazone 78
Preussischer Adler 79
Der Königliche Ernst August class 79
Elbe 80
Bremen class 81
Mercur 81
Nix class 82
Hela class 82
Musquito class 83
Grille 84
Loreley 84
Nymphe class 85
Augusta class 86
Ariadne class 86
Falke 87
Pommerania 88
Zieten 88
Carola class 89

Blitz class 91
Nixe 92

Light cruisers 1887–1918
Greif 93
Schwalbe class 93
Irene class 94
Wacht class 95
Meteor class 96
Bussard class 97
Gefion 98
Hela 99
Gazelle class 99
Bremen class 102
Königsberg class 104
Dresden class 105
Kolberg class 106
Magdeburg class 107
Karlsruhe class 109
Graudenz class 109
Pillau class 110
Wiesbaden class 111
Brummer class 112
Königsberg class 113
Cöln class 114

Fleet cruisers (planned) 1916
FK 1 class 116
FK 2 class 116

Light cruisers 1925–1940
Emden 118
Königsberg class 119
Leipzig class 122
M class 124
KH 1 class (ex-Dutch) 126

Gunboats 1815–1871
Gun sloop No 10 class 127
Danzig 127
Thorn class 128
No 3 class 128
Elmshorn/No 2 class 129
Von der Tann 129
Kiel 130
Bonin 130
Gun yawl No 1 class 130
Oared gunboat No 1 class 131
Jäger class 132
Camäleon class 133
Albatross class 134
ex Avantgarde class (ex-French) 134

Monitors 1872
Rhein class 136

Gunboats 1875–1943

Cyclop   137
Wespe class   137
Otter   138
Wolf class   139
Habicht class   139
Hay   140
Brummer class   140
Eber   141
Loreley   141
Iltis class   142
Meteor   143
Vorwärts   144
Schamien   144
Tsingtau class   145
Otter   145
K1 class (1938 design)   146
KI class (1939 design)   146
K1 class (ex-Dutch)   147
K4/Lorelei (ex-Belgian)   147

Torpedo boats 1872

No I class (Devrient/Waltjen types)   149

Torpeo steamers 1873–1876

Notus class   150
Ulan   150

Torpedo boats 1882–1918

Schütze class   152
Jäger   153
Th 2/No IV   153
I class (White type)   153
No XII class   154
H class   155
S 7 class   156
S 66 class   159
S 82 class   160
A 1 class   161
A 26 class   162
A 56 class   163

Divisional torpedo boats 1887–1896

D 1 class   166

D 7 class   167
D 9   168
D 10   168

Large torpedo boats 1899–1907

S 90 class   169

Large torpedo boats 1907–1919

S 138 class   172
V 1 class   176
V 25 class   178
G 96 class   181

Torpedo boat destroyers 1915–1919

B 97 class   184
S 113 class   185
V 170 class   186

Foreign torpedo boats (up to 1919)

Taku   187
V 105 class   187
G 101 class   188
R 01 class   188
R 04   189
R 10 class   189

Torpedo boats (post-1923)

Möwe class   191
T 1 class   193

Fleet torpedo boats 1942–1944

T 22 class   195
T 43 class   196
T 52 class   196
T 61 class   197

Destroyers 1937–1945

Z 1 class   199
Z 17 class   202
Z 23 class   203
Z 31 class   208
1937 destroyer projects   208
1938–39 destroyer projects   209
Z 51   210

Z 52 class   210
1945 destroyer project   211

Foreign destroyers 1940–1945

ZH 1 class   212
ZH 3   213
ZH 4   213
ZF 2 class   213
ZG 3/Hermes   214

Foreign torpedo boats 1940–1945

ZN 4 class   216
Löwe class   216
Troll   217
Zick class   218
TA 1 class   220
TA 9 class   221
TA 14 class   222
TA 16 class   222
TA 20   223
TA 21 class   223
TA 23 class   224
TA 24 class   225
TA 31   226
TA 32   226
TA 33   227
TA 34 class   228
TA 43   228
TA 44   229
TA 49   229

Fleet escorts 1935–1942

F 1 class   231
G 1 class   232

Fast escort vessels 1942–1945

SG 1   234
SG 10 class   235
SG 14 class   237
SG 18 class   238

Index   240

Foreword

The first edition of Erich Gröner's work was published in 1936 under the title *Die deutschen Kriegsschiffe 1815–1936* (German Warships 1815–1936). He was the first writer to attempt to document a national fleet in its entirety over a long period of time, presenting the technical and historical information in the form of tables, drawings to a standard scale, and details of the fates of individual ships. His book was founded on years of painstaking study of the carefully maintained stocks of documents and plans belonging to the Imperial and Reichs navies.

Since the book was so unusual at the time, it represented a risky project in publishing terms, and it was thought necessary to restrict the extent of the work and the length of the print run. As a result the full manuscript could not be published: the detailed 'ships' diaries' (careers) were omitted, and the vast mass of auxiliary ships had to be treated in a very cursory manner. In 1944 a second edition became necessary, but because of the war it was not possible to expand the work, and the only changes made were those necessary to correct known errors. The unpublished sections of manuscript were destroyed in the war.

In the meantime Gröner's book had become acknowledged as a classic example of this type of reference work. When he resumed his labours in about 1950, however, he found that the state of the source material had changed entirely. About 110 tons of German naval documents had survived the war, but they had been requisitioned and placed in storage by the Admiralty in London, where they lay for the most part in disorder. There were no longer any carefully compiled indices, which had made it possible to follow the course of technical developments. It was also clear that many documents concerning particular technical areas had been destroyed during the war in aerial bombardments. If the book was to be continued up to the year 1945, there remained only one course open: Gröner had to attempt to collect and re-assemble thousands of dispersed and disparate fragments of data, and try to correlate and analyse them. The process of analysis and selection turned out to be essential as many items of information, taken out of their context, proved to be contradictory, and implacably resisted interpretation. A further difficulty was the clear evidence of deliberately incorrect entries in official documents.

The source material remained in this state until 1965, when the process of returning naval documents to Germany began. In the summer of the same year Gröner died, during one of his annual journeys in search of new data. In 1966 we were able to publish the first volume, *Die deutschen Kriegsschiffe 1815–1945 – German Warships 1815–1945 –* including that part of the work which he had completed, and in 1968 the second volume followed, which we completed from the raw material he had left behind.

In addition to completing Erich Gröner's work, we undertook the task of re-checking critically all the data, using as a reference the documents which had become available in the intervening period. This task was carried out continuously. The overall state of the source material can now be summarised as follows.

In the technical area the sequential and unbroken series of documents, by means of which developments could be followed, no longer exists. This makes it impossible to assess the relative importance of particular projects and ideas. In the great air attack on Berlin on the night of 22–23 November 1943 the following were destroyed:

The 9th storey of the OKM in the Shellhaus, including the plan chamber (in particular the stocks of old documents of the Imperial and Reichs navies)

The Naval Wehramt (Defence Office)

The office of the Technical Information Service

All departments of the Naval Artillery office

The Naval Torpedo office

The Research, Invention and Patent office

When the main office for warship building (K-Amt) moved from Berlin in 1945, the official documents and plans were burned. Even the working documents taken to Schleswig-Holstein were destroyed at the end of the war.

In view of this, it is inevitable that the work will remain what it is today: a mosaic assembled from scraps of data, in which every entry has been checked, assessed and selected as accurately as possible. There is no possibility of producing a standard source work, in the sense of a straight reprint of a continuous series of documents, from which a sense of historical development emerges naturally, with no need for interpretation. The stocks of documents which remain include construction plans, project drawings, tests on alternative solutions to technical problems, even price quotations and trials results, all jumbled up together; inevitably the disorder and confusion has already given rise to wild speculation and hypothesis.

In the current edition, now expanded by about 40 percent, we have attempted to include everything which stands up to serious investigation. In some areas we have included projects which contribute to the understanding of technical developments in shipbuilding, but we have excluded the majority of suggestions and ideas which were an inevitable part of the design of almost every new ship type. Such a depth of information could only be provided in a monograph on a ship class or a ship type, not in a work which is intended to provide an overview of all vessels of the German fleet over a period of 130 years, in which the ships were to be treated as equally as possible. We estimate the number of these ships at 10,000. This huge figure brings us to one further important point: we were only able to devote a certain amount of space to any one ship – even the largest. In such cases the book includes construction data and details of important refits, but not every individual modification. One example will make this clear: the continual reinforcement of light AA armament during World War II naturally affected ammunition stocks and crew strengths, but it also affected maximum displacement, maximum weight of fuel, maximum range and much more. A book which intends to summarise cannot encompass the details of such complex interactions; these can also only be covered adequately in a monograph.

We also found it necessary to include large quantities of data relating to the Imperial navy in our critical re-examination. Many of the conclusions of this re-examination are given in notes in the Notes and Abbreviations section, which is completely new. In this regard we owe a debt of gratitude to Prof Dr-Ing E Strohbusch, the last chief officer of the building and maintenance department for large warships and tenders (KIG) in the K-Amt, who suggested a number of fundamental changes. In particular he pointed out to us the problematic and contradictory nature of the information on fuel supplies, fuel consumption, range and trials results. Systematic errors were discovered in some areas, which had slipped in at an earlier stage when complex documents were under assessment. Certain of the contradictions could not be resolved. This is why some of the information which was included in the 1936 edition must now be marked as debatable (?). We would like to emphasise this point here: all amendments which we have made in this text are intentional, including the omissions; the text now represents the true state of current knowledge.

New drawings have been prepared wherever we have been able to discover authentic original plans. Our principal aim here has been to plug obvious gaps and eliminate major errors (eg, distortions of proportion). It has also been possible to include series of drawings relating to certain well-known vessels showing the results of refits. Spatial and financial considerations, and not least the limited time available to our stalwart draughtsmen F Mrva and P Mickel, unfortunately meant that we were unable to satisfy all the wishes of our readers. In particular it proved impossible to provide the depth of detailed information which the builders of large scale models crave. For this type of historical modelling it is best to consider the work as no more than an aid; it can never provide the basis for the actual construction drawings.

After twenty years' work we have now decided to bring our work to an end by issuing a completely new edition, even though we have by no means been able to study all the surviving documents. There are two fundamental reasons for this decision:

1. Categorising accurately the many extant

documents has only been possible with the help of former leading naval officers and naval construction officials, many of whom have died in recent years. Of those still living, more and more are now unable to recall detail, and can no longer provide useful information relating to difficult technical questions. Thus as time goes on we increasingly lose vital clues, without which we cannot hope to piece together the jigsaw of the documents in our hands.

Berlin/Hamburg, July 1982

2. Our work was and is supported by Erich Gröner's circle of friends, whose number is shrinking. The death of Prof Dr-Ing E Strohbusch and Archive Director Dr G Sandhofer hit us particularly hard, as this work would have been inconceivable without their dedication and support on many fronts. Their place can never be filled again. Thus it seems to us that the time is right to present the material once more in a finished form. The work is planned to take 6 years, and we hope that we will be spared to bring it to a conclusion.

We wish to thank Messrs R Wendeler and W Amann of Bernard & Graefe for granting us the opportunity to realise our plans at a time which is by no means easy for publishers. To all those who have supported and continue to support our work, we offer our heartfelt thanks. Their number is so large that we cannot hope to mention everyone individually.

Dr Dieter Jung

Martin Maass

Notes and abbreviations

Vessels are arranged throughout this book by type, and listed chronologically within each type. The drawings of larger ships are generally arranged by ship, and chronologically within the career of each ship. The drawings of smaller ships, particularly in the more numerous classes, are arranged purely chronologically, since often this gives a clearer impression of the modification and development of the class as a whole over time. All drawings are to a constant 1/1250 scale, but note that rigging is generally shown only in a schematic form, and torpedo nets (carried until the Battle of Jutland, 1916) etc are not shown since these would obscure other details of the ships.

All headings and table entries give the name by which each vessel was best known, or under which it served for the longest period in the German navies; full details of changes of name are given in the Career section of the text, and all names and nicknames are cross-referenced in the index.

Major modifications are listed where possible on a separate line in the tables, under the relevant vessel. Where such modifications resulted in changes of specification, the modified figures are listed; where columns remain blank in modification entries, the specifications listed opposite the ship name should be understood to remain unchanged through the modification. Changes to specifications resulting from modifications other than the major modifications listed separately are incorporated in the tables with the specific individual reference 'mod'.

In the text, data relating to modifications are enclosed within square brackets []; in most cases these data may be related directly to modifications noted in the relevant table.

Note that all omissions of information from the tables are deliberate; a blank entry indicates that the relevant information is not available (except as noted above for modification entries). Where a category of information is not applicable, this is indicated in the tables by a dash, —. Parentheses ( ) around a figure in the tables indicate a figure which is uncertain or unconfirmed by all the available entries. Ditto marks '' are generally used in the tables for main ship entries only, and indicate repetition of the figure or group of figures immediately above.

Tables

Building yards (column two) are generally given as an English translation of the contemporary name; variations reflect historical changes in the yards themselves.

Building times (column three) are calculated from the laying of the keel to commissioning. In German practice vessels built in naval dockyards were com-

missioned before the start of running trials, while those built in private yards were commissioned only after the successful conclusion of trials and official acceptance.

Building costs (column four) are given in each case in the German currency in use at the time, unless marked otherwise.

Displacement (column five) includes outer plating and external fittings, bilge keels, rudders, propellers, shaft brackets, shaft fairings and exposed shafts. The specific weight of water is calculated at 1.105 in German practice. Gross tonnage (gt) is given where possible.

Maximum (max) displacement equals type displacement plus full load fuel oil, diesel oil, coal, reserve boiler feed water, aircraft fuel and special equipment.

Design (des) displacement includes 25 to 50 percent full load as above, and has been used in the German navy since 1882 as a basis for performance and speed calculations.

Standard (std) displacement, as defined in the 1922 Washington Treaty and used after 1927 in the German navy, includes hull, armour, main and auxiliary engines, all weapons, water and oil in the engine installations and pipework, fixed ballast (if carried), contents of roll tanks (if fitted), full munitions load for all weapons, maximum consumables, food, drinking and washing water, crew and effects – but not fuel and reserve feed water.

Up to 1933 the displacement figures given here apply in almost every case to the vessel at completion, and thus also at commissioning, since modifications and additional equipment were kept within narrow limits in the interim. Later additions are generally listed separately under modifications. After 1933 the official displacement figures are up to 20 percent too low (up to 35 percent for destroyers). The low official figures arose partly through a deliberate policy of concealing true displacements because of the Washington Treaty, and partly because extra equipment was added after completion to a much greater extent in this period (as in other navies). The additional weight resulted in increased draught, reduced speed, generally inferior stability and poorer seakeeping; in many cases it led to overstressing of the main structural members.

Length (column six) is generally given overall (oa) less jibboom, bowsprit, etc, and at the design waterline (cwl). Length between perpendiculars (bp) was used in the German navy only up to about 1908, and is only given here for vessels taken over from foreign navies or merchant fleets.

Breadth (column seven) is the maximum beam of the hull, over the outer edge of any belt armour or over the

bulkhead edges on ships without belt armour (moulded, that is, less the thickness of the outer plating). Removable fittings, bridge wings, etc, are not included.

Draught (column eight) is generally given forward (fwd) and aft up to about 1920, and as a mean figure for each of the listed displacements after that date. Where one figure only is given, at any period, this is a mean draught at maximum displacement.

Horsepower (column nine) is generally given as maximum (max) and design (des); the former indicates the maximum output of the individual ship under trial conditions, and the latter the design output (generally common to all ships of the class). The design output as given here represents a short-duration forced output; maximum continuous output was about 15 percent less.

Reversing horsepower available from piston steam engines, internal combustion engines and electric motors was approximately equal to forward power, but for steam turbines the figure was only 25 to 35 percent.

Note that where a second horsepower figure is given after a plus sign, this indicates the horsepower of the secondary propulsion machinery (usually diesel engines). Corresponding figures are given where possible in columns ten, eleven and twelve, also with a plus sign.

Revolutions per minute (column ten) as given here relate to the horsepower and speed figures given in columns nine and eleven. Where a single figure only is given, revolutions at maximum horsepower and speed are indicated. For geared installations the figure for primary revolutions of turbines or motors, where known, is given under Propulsion in the text.

Speed (column 11) is generally given in maximum nautical miles per hour (knots – kts) as achieved on trial (max) and design speed at design engine output (des). The maximum figures vary widely from ship to ship due to the external circumstances of the trials. The trials instructions specified wind not above Force 3, no current, and deep water (at least three times the ship's draught), but these conditions could not always be observed, especially in wartime. Machinery was also not forced in wartime to the levels achieved in peacetime, because of the danger of damage. In frontline service horsepower, speed and range were all reduced substantially.

Range (column twelve) is given in nautical miles at the stated speed with full fuel supply. The documentary evidence for these figures shows many variations and leaves many vital questions unanswered about the circumstances in which tests were carried out, and the tables therefore list only those values which seem reasonably probable. In some cases the stated ranges were impossible because of limitations on consumption imposed for reasons of stability. Note also that average values are given where there were several ships in one class.

Text

Construction gives the name under which the ship was built, details of the design and type of construction, and various technical specifications where possible. The extent of any double bottom is given as a percentage of the cwl length of the ship; depth is defined as the height of the ship's hull amidships, measured from the keel to the strength deck, above which the superstructure is generally located; trim moment is short for uniform trim moment, ie, the moment which would produce a 1m change in the ship's trim at the cwl.

Armour thickness is given in millimetres, with a general description of each feature. Belt and main hull (CWL) armour is listed in thickness from the stern forward, with each figure or group of figures connected to the next area forward by a dash (eg, 0–180–350–120mm); this gives an approximate indication of the distribution of this armour. The relative strengths of armour types can be judged from the following comparison:

100mm KC (Krupp Cemented) material = 130mm Harvey = 200mm compound sandwich = 300 wrought iron

The breaking strengths of various armour types and shipbuilding steels are as follows:

Wh material (*Wotan, hart* – hard)	85–96kg/sq mm, expansion 20 percent
Ww material (*Wotan, weich* – soft)	65–75kg/sq mm, expansion 25 percent
Shipbuilding steel St 52 KM	52–64kg/sq mm, expansion 22–24 percent
Shipbuilding steel St 42 KM	42–50kg/sq mm, expansion 25 percent
Shipbuilding steel St 34 KM	34–42kg/sq mm, expansion 30 percent

Propulsion gives details of all propulsion equipment, including sails. Note that the distribution of engine and boiler rooms is indicated by figures connected by plus signs (eg, 1 + 1 + 1 boiler rooms); compartments are counted from the stern forward, interpolated zeros (eg, 1 + 0 + 1 engine rooms) indicate compartments used for other purposes, and multiple figures (eg, 1 + 2 + 1 boiler rooms) indicate side-by-side compartments. Boilers are always fore-and-aft unless tranverse is specified. The distribution of rudders is also indicated: simple numbers, spelt out, indicate parallel rudders, while figures with plus signs indicate rudders in series, counting from the stern. Details of electrical plant are also given in this section.

Reductions in rigging occurred on German ships in distinct historical stages. The first reduction on armoured ships was in 1884–88, and on training ships after the Imperial inspection at Kiel in 1898. Topgallant masts, yards and divided topgallant sails were removed, so that main and topsails only could be set, together with jibs, gaff and staysails. Most ships looked very inelegant in this form, and in 1900 a topgallant mast, an undivided topgallant sail and divided

topsails could be set on training ships. On many smaller ships the original suit of sails was replaced by a simpler set of triangular sails.

The second reduction in rigging occurred after 1900, usually in the course of refits. Semaphores were removed from signal masts in 1905–06, and radio telegraphy equipment was installed from 1900 onwards, necessitating the fitting of radio topmasts and, soon after, radio yards. Antenna spreaders did not become standard until after 1910, first in the large V-form (English) pattern and later in the characteristic German small V-form pattern.

In or around 1909 all large ships (battleships and heavy cruisers) were fitted with new radio topmasts of equal lengths, with reinforced topmast crosstrees intended to carry a spotting top in wartime.

Armament gives details of all weapons, with elevation and corresponding range given for main guns. Torpedo tubes and mines are included, but no details are given of depth charges, minesweeping equipment or weapons such as flamethrowers, rockets, etc. Note that for home duties only about 60 percent of the weapons and munitions was carried.

The following figures give a rough comparison of projectile weight ratings to calibre:

Projectile rating	Calibre (cm)
72pdr, rifled	21.0
68pdr, smoothbore (English)	21.0
60pdr, smoothbore (French)	21.0
36pdr, rifled or smoothbore	17.0
32pdr, smoothbore (English)	16.0
30pdr, smoothbore (French)	16.0
25pdr, rifled (English)	10.5
24pdr, rifled or smoothbore	15.0
18pdr, smoothbore	13.5
12pdr, rifled or smoothbore	12.0
12pdr, rifled (English)	7.6
10pdr, rifled	10.5
3pdr, rifled or smoothbore	6.0
3pdr, rifled (English)	5.7
Shell guns or mortars:	
84pdr (Danish)	23.0
68pdr (Prussian, English)	20.3
60pdr (Danish)	20.1
25pdr (Prussian army)	22.7

Handling gives details of seakeeping, manoeuvrability and turning characteristics. For all vessels turning characteristics became progressively worse at lower speeds, and manoeuvring in canals and restricted waterways was always difficult; with very few exceptions, all vessels were particularly difficult to control when going astern. The fleet rudder angle (close to hard rudder, approximately 35–40 degrees) varied according to the characteristics of the ship in question, but gave an approximately equal turning circle for ships manoeuvring in formation.

Complement figures are given wherever possible in the form officers before the oblique, men after, with additional crew members required for flagship duties in brackets. These nominal crew strengths were subject to wide variations, particularly in wartime when extra weapons crew, technical personnel or others embarked for special purposes were frequently carried. The figures quoted are design complements.

Boats are generally listed in standard categories (under approximate English equivalents). Picket boats and barges were steam or motor-powered, and the smaller types were later fitted with auxiliary motors

and also known as *V-boote* (*Verkehrs* – traffic). Liferafts and similar devices are not listed.

Notes generally cover type characteristics and refits, but particular attention is paid to the identifying features of individual ships. Colour schemes are listed by number only for each ship; details of these colour schemes are as follows:

Colour scheme no 1 (1867 Black) For ships at home and abroad, introduced 21 Jun 1867.

Black	almost overall, except
White	paddle boxes, charthouse, awnings, ventilators, cross-trees, tops, bow and stern ornaments, and a narrow full-length band at the level of the bulwark top edge
Yellow	masts and topmasts
Red	boot topping, or band at the top edge of the coppering or waterline, about 1.5m above cwl

Exceptions were sailing frigates, sailing brigs and flush-decked corvettes, which had a white band level with the gunports; the aviso *Grille*, which had a golden bulwark stripe and yellow yards; the gunboat *Loreley*, which had yellow yards; and all oared gunboats, gun sloops and gun yawls, which were black overall.

Modifications were made on 7 Aug 1867 to the armoured ship *Prinz Adalbert* (red boot topping deleted); and the schooner *Hela* on 8 Apr 1868, the brig *Undine* on 13 Sept 1871, and all other sailing brigs on 28 Jan 1874 (white gunport band deleted).

The modified colour scheme 1874 Black was introduced for all ships on 28 Jan 1874, and specified yellow yards and white boot topping.

Colour scheme no 2 (1878 Black/yellow) For ships at home and abroad, introduced 16 Sept 1878.

Black	hull up to outside edge of upper deck
Yellow	all fittings above the white bulwark stripe (nets, masts, topmasts, yards, davits, ventilators, funnels, etc)
White	Paddle boxes, charhouse, pavilion, crosstrees, tops, bow and stern ornaments and a broad full-length band at the level of the bulwark top edge, also a narrow waterline band at about 0.5m above the cwl

Exceptions were the flush-decked corvette *Niobe*, which had a white gunport stripe, and all turret ships, which had white turrets, ventilators, and funnel and mast mantles.

Colour scheme no 3 (1890 White/yellow) For ships abroad, except for training voyages, and the Imperial yacht and its escort vessel, introduced 10 Jun 1890.

As scheme no 2, except for white hulls with a broad yellow bulwark band.

Schemes 2 and 3 were modified on 31 Jan 1894 to 1894 Black/yellow and 1894 White/yellow respectively, which specified bow and stern ornaments in gold ochre with highlights and heraldic colours.

Colour scheme no 4 (1895 Blue-grey) For ships in home waters, introduced 29 Mar 1895.

Blue-grey overall, except
Yellow-gold bow and stern ornaments (with highlights)

Colour scheme no 5 (1895 Dark grey) For divisional torpedo boats and torpedo boats.

Dark grey overall

Colour scheme no 6 (1895 Black/grey) was applied to dockyard vessels, pilot vessels, barges, barrack ships, etc, not covered in this volume.

Colour scheme no 7 (1895 White/grey) For new vessels (without sails) abroad, the Imperial yacht and its escort vessel.

White hull to the level of the main deck, main deck bulwark or forecastle outside edge, and the extension of this line in way of the enclosed upper deck, also guns, turrets and shields

Blue-grey upper deck, superstructure, funnels, ventilators, masts, etc.

Yellow a half-width band close under the upper edge of the white-painted area, also the bow and stern ornaments.

From 15 Apr 1896 grey was specified in place of blue-grey in this scheme.

Colour scheme no 8 (1895 White/yellow/grey) For older, rigged ships abroad.

White hull as in scheme 7

Yellow upper deck, superstructure where visible from outboard, a narrow to broad band close under the upper edge of the white-painted area, a narrow waterline band about 0.5m above the cwl, and the bow and stern ornaments

Blue-grey funnel, ventilators, masts, etc

Both yellow bands specified in this scheme could also be red or blue.

From 15 Apr 1896 grey was specified in place of blue-grey, and funnels were painted yellow.

Colour scheme no 9 (1896 Grey) For ships in home waters, introduced 15 Apr 1896.

Grey hull up to the level of the main deck or main deck bulwark or forecastle outer edge, and the extension of this line in way of the enclosed upper deck

Light grey upper deck, superstructure, funnels, ventilators, masts, etc, also guns, turrets and shields

Yellow-gold bow and stern ornaments (with highlights)

Torpedo boats covered by colour scheme no 5 and dockyard, etc, vessels by scheme no 6 were excepted from scheme 9. Variations included funnels (usually those with narrow caps, but occasionally up to 1m wide) in black instead of light grey, also masts above the funnels, including crosstrees; main topmasts were also black for a short period.

This scheme was modified on 26 Dec 1902 to specify gold for bow and stern ornaments, except in the case of training, harbour and special-purpose ships. The armoured frigate *König Wilhelm* was painted from 15 Aug 1907 as a dockyard vessel, and mine vessels (apart from the light cruiser *Arcona*) were painted black overall when mobilised after 18 Aug 1911.

Colour scheme no 10 (1898 Black) For torpedo boats in home waters, introduced 14 Dec 1898

Black overall

Colour scheme no 11 (1898 White/yellow) For all ships abroad, the Imperial yacht (up to 1914) and the Imperial yacht escort vessel (up to 1910).

White hull to the level of the main deck, main deck bulwark or forecastle outside edge, and the extension of this line in way of the enclosed upper deck, also guns, turrets and shields.

Yellow upper deck, superstructure, funnels, ventilators, masts, etc, a half-width band close under the upper edge of the white-painted area, and the bow and stern ornaments.

On 17 Aug 1899 this scheme was modified to specify yellow casemate and turret guns, shields and turrets where these were located in areas painted yellow. With the exception of gunboats, training and special-purpose ships, all vessels abroad from 20 Nov 1899 had gold bow and stern ornaments; gold ornaments were specified on gunboats abroad after 26 Dec 1902.

From 14 May 1910 all ships abroad were given grey paintwork overall, matching 1896 Grey, in the following order:
  The East Asia station gunboats and training ships of the *Victoria Louisa* class, after Autumn 1911
  Taku and *S 90*, after mid-1912
  All other vessels at the next opportunity
Loreley, however, retained the 1898 White/yellow scheme (no 11) after 16 Aug 1910.

Colour scheme no 12 (1916 Dark grey) For torpedo boats, introduced 4 Nov 1916.

Dark grey overall

Colour scheme no 13 (Dark brown/olive) For torpedo boats, introduced approximately in 1918–19.

Dark brown/ overall
olive

Wartime colour schemes

Camouflage and special colour schemes were applied according to the conditions of operation, following the booklet *Camouflage Schemes for Ships* (OKM 1942, Korvettenkapitan Dechend), using the camouflage colours white, light grey, dark grey, light green, dark green, olive green, light brown, dark brown, pink, blue and black, and all mixes and combinations of these.

Schemes for boats

Before 1895 all deck boats and boats on davits were black, except that the underbody of boats on davits was white, and gigs and all boats in the tropics were white overall. Sail covers and funnels on steam boats were yellow, though funnels were sometimes black.

After 1895 all boats followed the scheme of the parent ship, except that admiral's barges could be any colour, and life buoys were bright red.

Underbody schemes

Before 1895 the underbody of all vessels, when not coppered, was painted in red antifouling paint. After 1895 this was dark grey, though from 1910 this colour was applied only to a depth of 1m below the cwl (though a wider band was applied to broad ships and those with deep belt armour), with red below.

Deck schemes

Teak-planked upper decks (the forecastle aft of the breakwater, weather deck amidships, and the after deck) had no scheme except natural wood; the superstructure and bridge decks (linoleum-covered in peacetime) were red-brown. Metal decks, with a ridged tin anti-slip surface, were painted in a hard-wearing external deck paint in black, or to match the camouflage scheme (on the light cruiser *Köln*, 1928, destroyers, torpedo boats).

Aircraft recognition schemes

1916–18 Turret decks or forecastle black with a broad white circle (occasionally omitted); also used on manoeuvres up to 1939.

1936–38 Black-white-red bands crosswise on the turrets or shields fore and aft; used in the Spanish Civil War.

1939–45 Black swastika on a white circular field, up to June 1941 on a broad red transverse band on the forecastle, after that on the after deck, also

1940–41 Diagonal red bands on the turrets and shields (eg, on *Prinz Eugen*, *Grille*, T-boats, etc)

from 16 Forecastle, turrets and shields very light
Jun 1941 yellow; used for Operation Barbarossa, the invasion of the Soviet Union.

Career details given here generally relate to the fate of the vessel, rather than to its operational service; no information is given regarding commands or participation in operational groups or formations. The descriptions given of a ship's operational status indicate the whole period in which the ship was considered to belong to that type, before it was reduced to lesser duties; no account is taken of time spent out of commission during these periods. Service abroad indicates ships officially on foreign stations; manoeuvres and training cruises, which were frequent, are not included.

Note that where the date of commissioning is not known, the date of acceptance by the German navy is given. Where ships were purchased or taken as prizes, this information is given before the date of commissioning.

A ship belonged to the German navy from the date of its commissioning to the date of its loss, surrender, or the date at which it was officially stricken. Note that the location of the surrender in 1918–19 is only given here if it differed from the main locations (Harwich for submarines, Firth of Forth for other vessels).

In the case of ships sunk, the site of the loss is given where this is reasonably accurately known (not the site of the wreck at that or a later date).

Brief details are given where possible of the later existence of ex-German navy ships, but the focus of this book is principally on service with the navy.

Abbreviations

AG	*Aktiengesellschaft* (a type of limited company)
cm	centimetre
cu m	cubic metre
cwl	waterline as designed
CWL	belt and main hull armour
des	as designed (see notes)
ehp	effective horsepower, the standard unit for motors, including electric motors
f fl	flotilla flagship
fwd	forward
gt	gross tonnage, derived from the internal volume of a ship's hull
hp/hr	horsepower per hour
ihp	indicated horsepower, the standard unit for expansion (piston) steam engines
KM	*Kaiserliche Marine* up to 1918; *Kriegsmarine* 1934–45
kts	knots
kW	kilowatt
m	metre
M	Mark
max	maximum (see notes)
mod	as modified (see notes)
mm	millimetre
m-t	metre-tonne
nhp	nominal horsepower, a measurement of the internal geometry of an engine by Lloyds formulae
nm	nautical miles
nt	net tonnage, a measurement for merchant ships derived from gross tonnage (qv)
oa	overall
OKM	*Oberkommando der Marine*, the Naval High Command
onv	official new vessel
QF	quick-firing
rpm	revolutions per minute
RM	*Reichsmarine* 1921–34
shp	shaft horsepower, measured at the propellor shaft, the standard unit for turbines
sq fl	squadron flagship
sq m	square metres
std	standard displacement (see notes)
t	tonne
T	ton
Utof	a quickfiring gun in a submarine/torpedo boat anti-aircraft mounting
V	volt
2nd fl	second flagship, flagship of the second in command

Armoured vessels 1864–1884

Prinz Adalbert

Name	Builder	Built	Cost in Marks (000s)	Displacement (t = tonnes T = tons)	Length (m)	Breadth (m)	Draught (m)	Power (hp)	Revs (rpm)	Speed (kts)	Range (nm/kts)	Coal (t)	Oil (t)
PRINZ ADALBERT 779gt	L'Arman Frères, Bordeaux mod: Naval depot Geestemünde	1863–65 1868–69	1863 (=620.9 Thaler)	1560t max 1440t des	56.96 oa 50.48 cwl	9.92	4.94 fwd 5.02 aft	1200ihp max 300nhp des	72	10.1 max 9.5 des	1200/8	96	—

Construction
Laid down as armoured ram *Cheops* (design M L'Arman, 1862). Transverse frame, composite construction in iron and timber, copper sheathed. Wrought iron armour: CWL 127mm, turrets 114mm. Depth 5.78m.

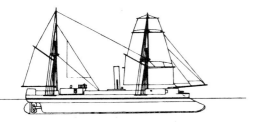

Prinz Adalbert (1870) after refit

Propulsion
Two horizontal 2-cylinder single expansion engines by Mazeline, Le Havre (two 4-bladed screws, 3.6m diameter) in one engine room. Two trunk boilers by Mazeline, Le Havre (1.5 atmospheres forced) in one boiler room. Double stern, two rudders. Brig rig, 740sq m [topsail schooner rig, 677sq m].

Armament
Three rifled 36pdr as designed, one in an integral 5-port bow turret (bow casemate), two in an octagonal non-moving diagonal 2-port turret amidships [after 1865 one 21cm/19 hooped gun (76 rounds) by Krupp in a 3-port bow turret, two 17cm/25 hooped guns (142 rounds) in a turret amidships, one hooped gun on either beam]; turrets uncovered. [Armament removed 1875–76].

Handling
Poor sea-boat, shipping much water (particularly over the ram bow); responsive, with a very tight turning circle.

Complement
Crew: 10/120. Boats: five.

Notes
Colour scheme no 1. First twin-screw ship in the Prussian navy, originally built for the Confederate States of America. Badly constructed [armour correctly mounted later]. Mainmast originally mounted centrally on B turret [later raked as shown in the drawing]. [A breakwater was later mounted on the stem.] The ship leaked very badly throughout her career. Nickname *Der Lahme* (Prinz) – The Lame Prince – refers to the vessel's patron, Prinz Adalbert. Her sister ship *Sphinx* was built for the Confederate States, purchased by Denmark as *Stjerckodder*, not accepted, returned to the Confederacy as *Stonewall Jackson*, taken over, after damage, by the United States and sold on to Japan as *Kotetsu-Kan*, later becoming *Azuma*.

Career
Launched in 1864 as armoured ram *Cheops* for the Confederate States; initial purchase 25 May 1864; stricken, repurchased Jan 1865, delivered 10 Jul 1865. Renamed *Prinz Adalbert* after 29 Oct 1865, in service 9 Jun 1866 with Krupp cannon; guard ship and fleet duties. Out of service 23 Oct 1871 (internal timbers rotted), stricken 28 May 1878 and broken up 1878 at Wilhelmshaven, engines re-used.

Arminius

Name	Builder	Built	Cost in Marks (000s)	Displacement (t = tonnes T = tons)	Length (m)	Breadth (m)	Draught (m)	Power (hp)	Revs (rpm)	Speed (kts)	Range (nm/kts)	Coal (t)	Oil (t)
ARMINIUS 865gt	Samuda Bros, London	1863–65	1887 (=628.9 Thaler)	1829t max 1653t des 1609t mod 1725t onv	63.21 oa 61.60 cwl	10.9	4.32 fwd 4.55 aft 4.25 mod	1440ihp max 1200ihp des 300nhp	87.1	11.2 max 10 des	2000/8	171	—

Construction
Laid down as an armoured monitor (designed by Capt Cowper Coles, 1863). Transverse frame, iron construction (eight watertight compartments). Armour wrought iron on teak: CT 114mm on 229mm timber; CWL 76–114–76mm on 229mm timber; turrets 114–119mm on 406mm timber. Depth 5.67m. Immersion increased by 1cm per 5.556t. Trim moment 1992m-t.

Propulsion

One horizontal 2-cylinder single expansion engine by J Penn & Sons, Greenwich (one 2-bladed screw, 3.96m diameter) in one engine room. Four transverse trunk boilers (sixteen fireboxes, 1.33 atmospheres forced, 510–529sq m) by J Penn & Sons, Greenwich, [Imperial Dockyard, Kiel] in one boiler room. One generator, 1.9kW 55V. One rudder. Topsail schooner rig, 540 sq m [all rigging later removed].

Armament

Initially four rifled bronze 72pdr, refitted after acceptance with four 21cm/19 hooped guns (332 rounds), +12°, range 2800m [4700m]. [After 1881, four machine guns, one 35cm TT (2 rounds) above waterline in bow. Two searchlights, 35Amp.]

Handling

Very crank, with short, fast rolling movements, shipped much water forward, severe roll in beam sea; turned quickly to starboard, very slowly to port (15° port rudder was required for a straight course!).

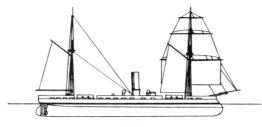

Arminius (1867), first form

Arminius (1888), second form

Complement

Crew: 10/122. Boats: two pinnaces, two cutters, one dinghy.

Notes

Colour scheme no 1, 2, 6. Built speculatively by the dockyard; virtually a sister ship to the Danish monitor *Rolf Krake*. Control under sail alone was impossible. In a competitive trial on 3 Oct 1866 she repeatedly out-ran the American monitor *Miantonomoh*. [From c1870 rig reduced to a foremast only, at the edge of the storm deck.]

Career

Launched 20 Aug 1864, commissioned 22 Apr 1865 as a guard ship, part-financed by voluntary contributions from German public; used as an engineer training ship 1872; used many times at Kiel as an ice breaker after 1881; tender to *Blücher* 1882. Stricken 2 Mar 1901, sold for 72,000M, broken up 1902 at Hamburg.

Friedrich Carl

Name	Builder	Built	Cost in Marks (000s)	Displacement (t = tonnes T = tons)	Length (m)	Breadth (m)	Draught (m)	Power (hp)	Revs (rpm)	Speed (kts)	Range (nm/kts)	Coal (t)	Oil (t)
FRIEDRICH CARL	Societé Nouvelles des Forges et Chantiers La Seyne (Toulon)	1866–67	6453	6932t max 5971t des 5780t mod 5912t onv	94.14 oa 91.13 cwl	16.6	6.90 fwd 8.05 aft 7.00 mod	3550ihp max 3300ihp des 950nhp	64.2	13.5 max 13.0 des	2210/10	624	—
3251gt/2085nt													

Construction

Laid down as armoured frigate *Friedrich Carl* (dockyard design, 1865). Transverse and longitudinal frame iron construction (eight watertight compartments, double bottom 76 percent). Armour wrought iron on teak: CT 114mm on 400mm timber; CWL 127mm, slopes 114 mm on 254mm timber; battery roof 9mm, slopes 114mm on 260mm timber. Depth 9.24m. Immersion increased by 1cm per 11.4t. Trim moment not known.

Propulsion

One horizontal 2-cylinder single expansion engine (one 4-bladed screw, 6.0m diameter) in one engine room. Six trunk boilers (twenty-six fireboxes, 2 atmospheres forced, 1591–1444sq m) in 1 + 1 boiler rooms [new boilers by Imperial Dockyard, Wilhelmshaven]; retractable funnel. [Three generators, 30–36kW 65V.] Barque rig, 2010sq m [1635sq m]. One rudder.

Armament

Twenty-six rifled 72pdr as designed, otherwise as *Kronprinz*. [Armament removed after 1895.]

Handling

Excellent sea-boat, responsive, with a moderate turning circle. Up to 6° port rudder required for straight course. Sails contributed little to performance.

Complement

Crew: 33/498 (plus 6/35 as second flagship). Boats: one large tender, two launches, one pinnace, two cutters, two yawls, one dinghy.

Notes

Colour scheme no 1, 2, 4, 9. All rigging was removed in the war of 1870–71 apart from that to the lower masts; retractable bowsprit. [Torpedo nets fitted 1885–1897.]

Career

Launched 16 Jan 1867, commissioned 3 Oct 1867 into the fleet; served as a torpedo test ship 11 Aug 1895; harbour ship *Neptun* 21 Jan 1902. Stricken 22 Jun 1905, sold Mar 1906 for 284,000M, broken up in Holland.

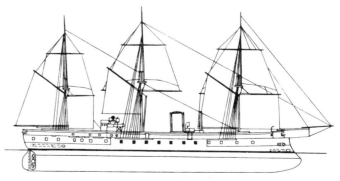

Friedrich Carl (1888)

Kronprinz

Name	Builder	Built	Cost in Marks (000s)	Displacement (t = tonnes T = tons)	Length (m)	Breadth (m)	Draught (m)	Power (hp)	Revs (rpm)	Speed (kts)	Range (nm/kts)	Coal (t)	Oil (t)
KRONPRINZ 3029gt/2096nt	Samuda Bros London mod:Imperial Dockyard, Kiel	1866–67 1901	6297	6760t max 5767t des 5568 mod 5480 onv	89.44 oa 88.20 cwl	15.2	7.85 fwd 7.45 aft 7.38 mod	4870ihp max 4500ihp des 800nhp	69.4	14.7 max 13.5 des	3200/10 max 1730/14 des	646 mas 566 des	—

Construction
Laid down as armoured frigate *Kronprinz* (design Sir Edward Reed, 1866). Transverse and longitudinal frame iron construction (nine watertight compartments, double bottom 43 percent). Armour wrought iron on teak [steel]: [forward CT roof 30mm, sides 50mm]; CWL 76–124–114mm on 254mm timber; battery roof 9mm, slopes 114–121–114mm on 254mm timber. Depth 10.62mm. Immersion increased by 1cm per 10.8t. Trim moment not known.

Propulsion
One horizontal 2-cylinder single expansion engine by J Penn & Sons, Greenwich (one 2-bladed screw, 6.5m diameter) in one engine room. Eight trunk boilers by J Penn & Sons, Greenwich [Eight transverse trunk boilers by Imperial Dockyard, Wilhelmshaven] (thirty-two fireboxes, 2 atmospheres forced, 1688–1778sq m) in 1 + 1 boiler rooms. Funnels retractable. [Three generators, 30kW 65V.] Barque rig, 1980sq m [1409sq m]. One rudder.

Armament
Thirty-two 72pdr as designed. Fitted with two 21cm/22 hooped guns, −5° +13°, range 5900m, and fourteen 21cm/19 hooped guns −8° +14.5°, range 5200m, total 1656 rounds). [Six machine guns, five 35cm TT (12 rounds), one port stern, two lateral, 2 bow, all above water.]

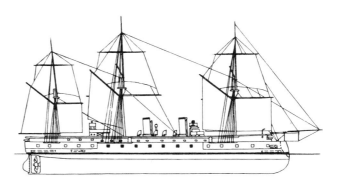
Kronprinz (1888)

Handling
Excellent sea-boat, stiff, responsive to the helm but large turning circle, trimmed by the bow.

Complement
Crew: 33/508. Boats: one large tender, two launches, one pinnace, two cutters, two yawls, one dinghy.

Notes
Colour scheme as *Friedrich Carl*. The ram was sheathed in sheet metal, and carried the bowsprit in a support yoke. Initially masts and funnels were vertical, with projecting steam pipes on the after face. [Torpedo nets fitted 1885–97. After 1901 served as an engineer training ship, with two each Dürr and Thornycroft boilers, two masts, covered upper deck.]

Career
Launched 6 May 1867, commissioned 19 Sept 1867 into fleet. Stricken 22 Aug 1901. Engine hulk at Kiel, sold 3 Oct 1921 to Bonn for 5,000,000M, broken up in Rendsburg-Audorf.

König Wilhelm

Name	Builder	Built	Cost in Marks (000s)	Displacement (t = tonnes T = tons)	Length (m)	Breadth (m)	Draught (m)	Power (hp)	Revs (rpm)	Speed (kts)	Range (nm/kts)	Coal (t)	Oil (t)
KÖNIG WILHELM sq fl 5085gt/2822nt	Thames Iron Works & Sb Co, Blackwall	1865–69	10,103	10,761t max 9757t des 9603t onv	112.2 oa 108.6 cwl	18.3	8.56 fwd 8.12 aft	8440ihp max 8000ihp des	65.3	14.7 max 14.0 des	1300/10	750	—
	mod: Imperial Dockyard, Wilhelmshaven	1878–82		9574t des			8.18	1150nhp			1750/10	893	
	Blohm & Voss, Hamburg	1895–96	603								2240/10 max	1030	
	Imperial Dockyard Wilhelmshaven	1907									1570/14 des	830	

Construction
Laid down as armoured frigate *Fatikh*, later *Wilhelm I* (design, Sir Edward Reed, 1866–67). Transverse and longitudinal frame iron construction (eleven watertight compartments, double bottom 70 percent). Armour wrought iron on teak [steel]: [CT roof 30mm, slopes 50mm to 100mm]; CWL outer layer 152–305–0mm, inner layer 127–178–127mm on 90–250–90mm timber; battery 150mm, slopes 203mm, transverse bulkheads 150mm. Depth 12.94m. Immersion increased by 1cm per 16.5t. Trim moment 10.30m-t.]

Propulsion
One horizontal 2-cylinder single expansion engine by Maudslay, Son & Field, London (one 4-bladed screw,

7.0m diameter) in one engine room. Eight trunk boilers by J Penn & Sons, Greenwich [eight transverse trunk boilers by Imperial Dockyard, Wilhelmshaven] with superheaters (forty fireboxes, 2 atmospheres forced, 2098–2230sq m) in 1 + 1 boiler rooms. Funnels retractable. [Four generators, 60–68kW 65V.] One rudder. Full-rigged ship, 2600sq m [1100sq m, and rig finally removed altogether].

Armament

Thirty-three 72pdr as designed. Fitted with eighteen 24cm/20 hooped guns (1440 rounds), –4° +7.5°, range 4500m, and five 21cm/22 hooped guns, –5° +13°, range 5900m [twenty-two 24cm/20 hooped guns (1426 rounds), –4° +7.5°, range 4500m/ –6° +20°, range 9100m/ –4° +9°, range 5400m; one 15cm/30 hooped gun (109 rounds), range 8900m; eighteen 8.8cm/30 QF guns (4500 rounds); five 35cm TT (13 rounds), one port stern, two lateral, two bow, all above water. As a training ship she was fitted with a total of sixteen 8.8cm/30 QF guns, and after 1915 four 8.8cm/30 QF guns.]

Handling

Satisfactory seakeeping qualities, with severe roll but little pitch; very responsive, with moderate turning circle. Sails contributed little to performance.

Complement

Crew: 36/694 (plus 9/47 as squadron flagship) [36/712 (plus 11/57 as squadron flagship), later 38/1120]. Boats: two picket boats, two launches, one pinnace, two cutters, two yawls, one dinghy.

Notes

Colour scheme no 1, 2, 4, 9, 9. The most powerful ship in the world when newly built. Bowsprit retractable. [Bowsprit removed after 1882, new forecastle added and larger steam pipes fitted to the funnels (see drawing). Mizzen mast removed after 1898. Rigging removed except from lower masts 1870–71. Torpedo nets fitted 1885–97.]

Career

Begun as Turkish *Fatikh*, purchased 6 Feb 1867; renamed *Wilhelm I* 10 Jan 1867, and *König Wilhelm* 14 Dec 1867. Launched 25 Apr 1868, commissioned into fleet 20 Feb 1869; served as a heavy cruiser 25 Jan 1897; harbour ship 3 May 1904; stationary barrack and exercise ship for cadets at Kiel, 1 Oct 1907, and at Mürwik after 1909. Stricken 4 Jan 1921, sold, broken up at Rönnebeck.

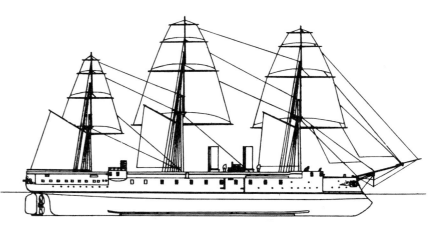

König Wilhelm as an armoured frigate (1879).

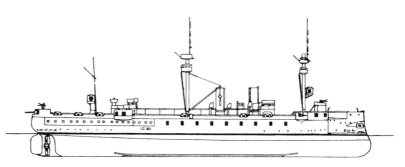

König Wilhelm as a heavy cruiser (1896).

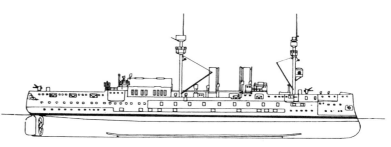

König Wilhelm as a training ship 1908).

Hansa

Name	Builder	Built	Cost in Marks (000s)	Displacement (t = tonnes T = tons)	Length (m)	Breadth (m)	Draught (m)	Power (hp)	Revs (rpm)	Speed (kts)	Range (nm/kts)	Coal (t)	Oil (t)
HANSA 2118gt/1315nt	Royal/Imperial Dockyard,Danzig Fitting out: AG Vulcan, Stettin	1868–75	3665	4404t max 3950t des 3696t onv	73.50 oa 71.73 cwl	14.1	5.74 fwd 6.80 aft	3275ihp max 450nhp des	63.4	12.7 max 12.0 des	1330/10	310	—

Construction

Laid down as armoured corvette *Hansa* (official design, 1868–70). Transverse frame, composite iron-timber construction, copper sheathed (six watertight compartments). Armour wrought iron on teak: casemates slopes 114mm, transverse bulkheads 114mm (armoured transverse bulkheads only at lower battery), CWL 114–152–114mm on 306mm timber. Depth 9.40m. Immersion increased by 1cm per 7.41t. Trim moment 4010m-t.

Propulsion

One horizontal 3-cylinder single expansion engine by AG Vulcan, Stettin (one 3-bladed screw, 6.0m diameter) in one engine room. Four trunk boilers (sixteen fireboxes, 2 atmospheres forced, 1085sq m), one boiler room. Retractable funnel. No electrical system. One rudder. Full-rigged ship, 1760sq m.

Armament

Eight 21cm/19 hooped guns (880 rounds) on upper deck, –8° +14°, range 5700m; in lower casemate –5° +13°, range 3200m.

Handling

Very stiff, with weather helm; control and manoeuvrability were quite good under sail, and under steam manoeuvrability was good, but control poor.

Complement

Crew: 28/371. Boats: two launches, one pinnace, two cutters, one yawl, one dinghy; complement of picket boats and barges not known.

Notes

Colour scheme no 1, 2. Upper deck bulwark drawn inboard to clear guns. Ship quickly became unusable due to very severe corrosion. [Torpedo nets fitted 1885–88.]

Career

Launched 26 Oct 1872, commissioned 19 May 1875 for service abroad; guard ship at Kiel 1884, also engineer and stoker training ship. Stricken 6 Aug 1888, served as a barrack ship at Kiel, and in 1905 as a hulk for stoker training at Mönkeberg, sold March 1906 for 96,000M, broken up at Swinemünde.

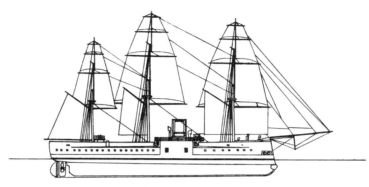

Hansa (1876)

Preussen class

Name	Builder	Built	Cost in Marks (000s)	Displacement (t = tonnes T = tons)	Length (m)	Breadth (m)	Draught (m)	Power (hp)	Revs (rpm)	Speed (kts)	Range (nm/kts)	Coal (t)	Oil (t)
PREUSSEN	AG Vulcan, Stettin Construction no 66	1871–76	7303	7718t max 6821t des 6790t onv	96.59 oa 94.50 cwl	16.3	7.12 fwd 7.18 aft	5471ihp max 850nhp des	66.0	14.0 max 14.0 des	1690/10	565	—
	mod: Imperial Dockyard Wilhelmshaven	1889–90		6770t des						14.1 max 14.0 des			
FRIEDRICH DER GROSSE	Imperial Dockyard, Kiel Construction no 1	1871–77	"	7718t max 6821t des 6790t onv	"	"	"	4998ihp max 900nhp des	72.8		"	"	—
	mod: Imperial Dockyard Wilhelmshaven	1890–91		6770t des									
GROSSER KURFÜRST	Imperial Dockyard Wilhelmshaven Contruction no 2	1869–78	"	7718t max 6821t des 6790t onv	"	"	"	5468ihp max 850nhp des	66.0	14.0 des	"	"	—
3481gt/2224nt													

Construction

Laid down as armoured ships *Borussia, König Friedrich der Grosse, Grosser Kurfürst* (initial official design, 1868, as casemate ships, similar to Austrian *Custoza*; design revised after start of construction of *Grosser Kurfürst* 1869–70 to turret ship, design office Admiralitätsrat Elbertzhagen). Transverse and longitudinal frame iron construction (twelve watertight compartments, double bottom 60 percent). Armour wrought iron on teak [steel]: [forward CT roof 30mm, slopes 50mm]; CWL outer layer 203mm, inner layer 102–229–102mm on 234–260mm timber; turret roof 25mm, slopes 203–254mm on 260mm timber. Depth 10.42 m. Immersion increased by 1cm per 12.7t. Trim moment 6900m-t.

Propulsion

One horizontal 3-cylinder single expansion engine by AG Vulcan, Stettin, and F A Egells, Berlin (4-bladed screw, 6.6m diameter) in one engine room. Six transverse trunk boilers by engine suppliers [by Imperial Dockyard, Wilhelmshaven], (thirty fireboxes, 2 or 3 atmospheres forced [3 atmospheres forced] 1699sq m [1800sq m]) in 1 + 1 boiler rooms. Retractable funnel.

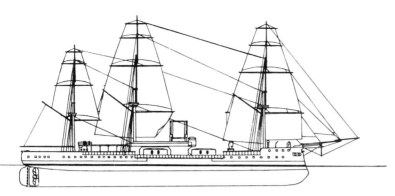

Preussen (1876), *Friedrich der Grosse, Grosser Kurfürst*, first form

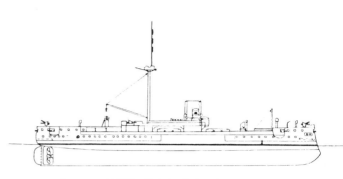

Preussen (1890), *Friedrich der Grosse*, third form

[Three generators, 30kW, later 36kW 65V.] One rudder. Full-rigged ship, 1834–570–0sq m.

Armament

Four 26cm/22 hooped guns (400 [312] rounds), –3° +11°, range 5000m; two 17cm/25 hooped guns (200 [216] rounds), +11°, range 5000m; [six to ten 8.8cm/30 QF guns (2500 rounds); two machine guns; five 35cm TT (13 rounds), one port stern, two lateral, two bow, all above water, except in *Preussen*, where all tubes were under water.]

Handling

Good sea-boat, very sensitive in sea and wind; sea-kindly motion; very responsive, tight turning circle. Crank and slow under sail.

Complement

Crew: 46/454, [34/509]. Boats: one picket boat, two launches, one pinnace, two cutters, two yawls, two dinghies.

Notes

Colour scheme no 1, 2, 4, 9. Flying deck added in 1885. *Grosser Kurfürst* was designed in 1868, as a casemate ship. [Torpedo nets fitted 1885–97.]

Career

Preussen launched 22 Nov 1873, commissioned into fleet 4 Jul 1876; served as a guard ship 1891, harbour ship at Wilhelmshaven 16 Nov 1896; renamed *Saturn* 12 Nov 1903. Stricken 21 May 1906; coal hulk for torpedo boats 1907 (5000t coal); released, sold 27 Jun 1919, broken up 1919 in Wilhelmshaven. Figurehead in Dresden army museum, bow ornament in German Museum, Munich.

Friedrich der Grosse launched 20 Sept 1874, commissioned into fleet 22 Nov 1877; harbour ship 16 Nov 1896. Stricken 21 May 1906, reduced to coal hulk for torpedo boats; stricken again 27 Jan 1919, sold, broken up 1920 at Rönnebeck.

Grosser Kurfürst launched 17 Sept 1875, commissioned into fleet 6 May 1878; sank 31 May 1878 in the Straits of Dover, position 51° 09N, 01° 09E, after collision with armoured ship *König Wilhelm*. Sank excessively quickly because of failure to seal bulkheads; 269 dead.

Kaiser class

Name	Builder	Built	Cost in Marks (000s)	Displacement (t = tonnes T = tons)	Length (m)	Breadth (m)	Draught (m)	Power (hp)	Revs (rpm)	Speed (kts)	Range (nm/kts)	Coal (t)	Oil (t)
KAISER sq fl	Samuda Bros, London	1871–75	8226	8940t max 7645t des 7319t onv	89.34 oa 88.50 cwl	19.1	7.39 max 7.93 des	5779ihp max 800nhp des	61.0	14.6 max 14.0 des	2470/10 1115/14	684 max 680 des	—
	mod: Imperial Dockyard Wilhelmshaven	1891–95		8736t max 7645t des										
DEUTSCHLAND 2nd fl	Samuda Bros, London	1872–75	8240	8940t max 7654t des 7319t onv	,,	,,	,,	5637ihp max 800nhp des	65.5	14.5 max 14.0 des	,,	,,	—
	mod: Imperial Dockyard Wilhelmshaven	1894–97		8736t max 7645t des			7.15 max 7.65 des				3200/10 1440/14	880 max 680 des	
4170gt/1728nt													

Construction

Laid down as armoured frigates (design, Sir Edward Reed, 1869). Tranverse bulkhead – double longitudinal frame iron construction (nine [ten] watertight compartments, double bottom 59 percent). Armour wrought iron on teak [steel]: [CT (*Kaiser*) roof 30mm, sides 50mm (*Deutschland*) roof 30mm, slopes 100mm], deck 38mm–51mm, casemate 178/203/178 on 192–264mm teak, CWL 127–254–254–127mm on 90–226mm timber. Stern shield 216/126 on 384 timber [removed]. Depth 12.46m. Immersion increased by 1cm per 13.27t. Trim moment 6560m-t.

Propulsion

One horizontal 2-cylinder single expansion engine by J Penn & Sons, Greenwich (one 4-bladed screw, 6.86m diameter) in one engine room. Eight trunk boilers by J Penn & Sons, Greenwich, [eight transverse trunk boilers by Imperial Dockyard, Wilhelmshaven and Imperial Dockyard, Danzig and Wilhelmshaven] (forty [forty, later thirty-six] fireboxes, 2 atmospheres forced, 2202sq m [2230, later 2183sq m]) in 1 + 1 boiler rooms. Funnels retractable. [Three generators, 30, later 33kW 65V.] One rudder. Full-rigged ship, 1623sq m, [542sq m, and rig finally removed altogether].

Armament

Eight 26cm/20 hooped guns (768 [636] rounds), –4° +9°, range 5200m, and one 21cm/22 hooped gun, range 5900m [after c1892 six 15cm/22 and one 15cm/30 hooped guns (550 rounds), range 8200–8600m; and finally, for *Kaiser*, one 15cm/30 hooped gun (109 rounds), range 8500m, six 10.5cm/35 QF guns (600 rounds), range 10,800m, and nine 8.8cm/30 QF guns (2200 rounds); for *Deutschland* eight 15cm/35 QF guns (800 rounds), range 12,600m, and eight 8.8cm/30 QF guns (2000 rounds). Both ships had four 37mm machine guns and/or twelve 37mm machine cannon, five 35cm TT

(13 rounds), one port stern under water, two lateral above water (under water in *Deutschland*), two bow above water.]

Handling

Good sea-boats, stable with gentle motion; very responsive, with moderate turning circle.

Complement

Crew: 32/568 (plus 9/47 as squadron flagship, 6/35 as second flagship) [36/620 (plus 11/57 as squadron flagship, 9/48 as second flagship]. Boats: two picket boats, one launch, two pinnaces, two cutters, two yawls, two dinghies.

Notes

Colour scheme no 1, 2, 4, 5, 7, 9, 10, identical before refit; searchlights and searchlight platforms not fitted until 1882. [Torpedo nets fitted 1885–97.]

Career

Kaiser launched 19 Mar 1874, commissioned into fleet 13 Feb 1875; heavy cruiser 25 Jan 1897, abroad until 1899, harbour ship 3 May 1904; renamed *Uranus* 12

Deutschland (1876), *Kaiser*, first form

Oct 1905. Stricken 21 May 1906, barrack ship for *Württemberg* at Flensburg, broken up 1920 at Harburg.

Deutschland launched 12 Sept 1874, commissioned into fleet 20 Jul 1875; converted to a heavy cruiser 25

Jan 1897; abroad 1898–1900; harbour ship 3 May 1904; renamed *Jupiter* 22 Nov 1904. Stricken 21 May 1906, target ship 1907, sold 1908 for 120,000M, broken up at Hamburg-Moorburg 1909.

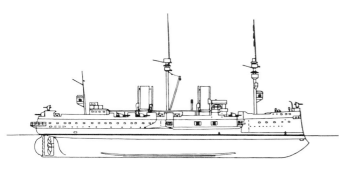

Kaiser (1898), second form

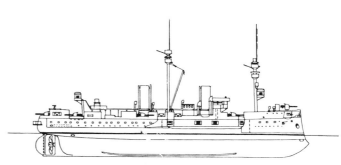

Deutschland (1896), third form

Sachsen class

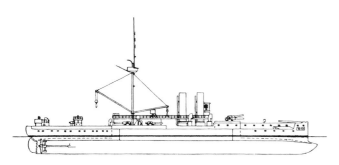

Sachsen (1881), *Bayern, Württemberg, Baden*, first form

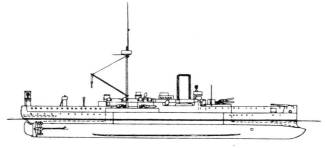

Sachsen (1900), *Bayern*, second form

Württemberg, Baden

Construction

Laid down as armoured ships *B, A, D* and *C* (official design, 1872–1874). Transverse and longitudinal frame iron construction (sixteen watertight compartments, double bottom 60 percent). Armour patent sandwich wrought iron [Krupp armour after conversion]: citadel and CWL, four layers, outer, 0–203mm (sides), 254mm (bulkheads)–0mm on 0–200–0mm teak, inner 0–152mm (sides and bulkheads)–0mm on

0–230–0mm teak; deck 050–075mm; forward CT 140mm [roof 50mm, sides 200mm, aft CT roof 12mm, sides 15mm]; barbettes 254mm on 250mm teak, [centreline longitudinal bulkhead 50mm]. Cork cofferdams. Depth 9.286m. Immersion increased by 1cm per 14.42t. Trim moment 8.68m-t.

Propulsion

Two horizontal 3-cylinder single expansion engines,

in *Bayern* and *Baden* by Märkisch-Schlesischer Maschinenbau und Hütten AG, formerly F A Egells, Berlin (two 4-bladed screws, 5.0m diameter), in two engine rooms. Eight trunk boilers (thirty-two fireboxes, 2 atmospheres forced, 1769sq m) in 2 + 2 boiler rooms. [Two horizontal 4-cylinder double expansion engines (two 4-bladed screws, 4.6m diameter) in two engine rooms; eight Dürr boilers by Düsseldorf-Ratinger Röhrenkesselfabrik (sixteen fireboxes, 13

Name	Builder	Built	Cost in Marks (000s)	Displacement (t = tonnes T = tons)	Length (m)	Breadth (m)	Draught (m)	Power (hp)	Revs (rpm)	Speed (kts)	Range (nm/kts)	Coal (t)	Oil (t)
SACHSEN	AG Vulcan, Stettin Construction no 74	1875–78		7935t max 7635t des	98.20 oa 93.00 oa des	18.4 18.7**	6.32 fwd 6.53 aft	4917ihp max 5600ihp des	78.2	13.6 max 13.0 des	1940/10 max 700/14 des up to	700 max 420 des 576 to	—
	mod: Imperial Dockyard, Kiel	1897–98					6.21 fwd 6.37 aft	6454ihp max	99.4	15.7 max 13.0 des	3000/10 max 1500/14 max	615 + 280*	
BAYERN	Imperial Dock-yard, Kiel Construction no 3	1874–82	9133	7742t max 7635t des	,,	,,	6.32 fwd 6.53 aft	5620ihp max 5600ihp des	85.5	13.8 max 13.0 des	,,	,,	—
	mod: F Schichau, Danzig	1895–98	3786				6.21 fwd 6.37 aft	6373ihp max	115	15.4 max			
WÜRTTEMBERG	AG Vulcan, Stettin Construction no 78	1876–81	8325	7877t max 7635t des	,,	,,	6.32 fwd 6.53 aft	4600ihp max 5600ihp des	84.0	13.5 max 13.0 des	,,	,,	—
	mod: Imperial Dockyard, Kiel	1898–99	4157				6.21 fwd 6.37 aft	6264ihp max	97.9	14.2 max			
BADEN sq fl	Imperial Dock-yard, Kiel Construction no 4	1876–83	8534	7938t max 7635t des	,,	,,	6.32 fwd 6.53 aft	5600ihp max 5600ihp des	79.0	13.9 max 13.0 des	,,	,,	—
	mod: Germania Dockyard, Kiel	1896–97	4303	7690t max 7411t des			6.21 fwd 6.37 aft	6201ihp max 6000ihp des	95.4	14.9 max 14.0 des			

Before refit 3468gt/1840nt; after refit 3474gt/1604nt

* Westfalian Patent fuel deck load as modified   ** Over ejectors

atmospheres forced, 1696sq m), except for *Bayern* – eight Dürr boilers by AG 'Germania', Berlin-Tegel (twenty-four fireboxes, 12 atmospheres forced, 2110sq m), and *Württemberg* – eight transverse Thornycroft boilers by AG 'Germania', Berlin-Tegel (sixteen fireboxes, 13 atmospheres forced, 2000sq m), all in 2 + 2 boiler rooms.] Three generators, 69kW [69–74kW] 65V, [*Württemberg* after 1908, 110V transformer]. One rudder.

Armament
Six 26cm/22 hooped guns (480 rounds), –7° +16.5°, range 7400m, six 8.7cm/24 hooped guns (600 rounds), eight 37mm machine guns [eight 8.8cm/30 QF guns (2000 rounds), four 37mm machine cannon]. After 1886, three 35cm TT (12 [8] rounds), one swivel mounted, stern above water, two bow under water, [two additional 45cm TT (5 rounds), two lateral above water]. [*Württemberg*, after 1906, four to eight 8.8cm/30 QF guns only (later eight 5cm/40 QF guns), seven 45cm TT (14 rounds), one swivel mounted, bow above water, two lateral under water, two lateral above water, on aft outer decks, swivel mounted, and two stern, above water.]

Handling
Poor sea-boats, prone to severe rolling in beam seas and shipping much water; very responsive to helm, with a very tight turning circle. Steering possible by engines only when going astern. Transverse metacentric height 1.88m, longitudinal 102.7m. Maximum stability moment at 21.5°, = zero at 74°.

Complement
Crew: 32/285 (plus 7/34 as second flagship) [33/344 (plus 9/34 as second flagship), later 35/401]. Boats: one picket boat, one launch, one pinnace, two cutters, one yawl, one dinghy.

Notes
Colour scheme no 2, 4, 9. Searchlights, etc, not fitted until 1882, position varied, at times in the tops. Gang-way initially between funnels and approx 1m lower than the later forward bridge deck. [Long steam pipes fitted in 1884, and after superstructure modified to second form shown in drawing, bridge deck also similar to this drawing.] Because of the square central barbette and the initial design of four funnels arranged in a square the ships were popularly known as the *Zement-fabriken* (cement factories). [*Württemberg* fitted with 1.5m higher funnel in final conversion, also covered

barbettes (for use as accommodation rooms, etc); angled stem (see drawing); searchlight fitted 1906 on deckhouse behind funnel. Torpedo nets fitted 1885–1897.

Career
Sachsen launched 21 Jul 1877, commissioned into fleet 20 Oct 1878, fleet duties until 1902. Stricken 19 Feb 1910, used as a target hulk for fleet off Schwansen coast after 1911; stricken 5 May 1919, sold to Hattinger Co, broken up at Wilhelmshaven.

Bayern launched 13 May 1878, commissioned into fleet 4 Aug 1881. Stricken 19 Feb 1910, used as a fleet target ship on Stollergrund after 1911; released 5 May 1919, sold, broken up at Kiel.

Württemberg launched 9 Nov 1878, commissioned into fleet 9 May 1881; used as a torpedo training and test ship 1906; F-boat escort ship Feb 1919. Stricken 20 Oct 1920, sold to Hattinger Co, broken up at Wilhelmshaven.

Baden launched 28 Jul 1880, commissioned into fleet 24 Sept 1883. Stricken 24 Oct 1910, blockade and defence hulk 1912, used as a target hulk at Stollergrund after 1920; sold 23 Apr 1938, broken up 1939–40 at Kiel.

Oldenburg

Construction
Laid down as armoured ship *E* (official design, 1879–81). Transverse and longitudinal frame steel construction with iron stem and stern (twelve water-tight compartments, double bottom 60 percent). Armour compound steel on teak: deck 30mm, forward CT roof 25mm, sides 50mm, aft CT roof 12mm, sides 15mm; CWL outer layer 200–300–200mm, inner layer 180–250–180mm, both on 300–250–300mm timber; casemate sides 150mm, bulkheads 200mm on sides

Name	Builder	Built	Cost in Marks (000s)	Displacement (t = tonnes T = tons)	Length (m)	Breadth (m)	Draught (m)	Power (hp)	Revs (rpm)	Speed (kts)	Range (nm/kts)	Coal (t)	Oil (t)
OLDENBURG

2858gt/1428nt | AG Vulcan, Stettin Construction no 132 | 1883–86 | 8885 | 5743t max 5249t des | 79.80 oa 78.40 cwl | 18.0 18.3* | 6.28 fwd 6.30 aft | 3942ihp max 3900ihp des | 90.5 | 13.8 max 14.0 des | 1770/9 1370/10 980/12 | 450 max 348 des + 120** | — |

* over davits
** patent fuel deck load

250mm, bulkheads 200mm timber. Depth 11.0m. Immersion increased by 1cm per 10.41t. Trim moment 3926m-t.

Propulsion

Two horizontal 4-cylinder double expansion engines (two 3-bladed screws, 4.5m diameter) in two engine rooms. Eight transverse cylinder boilers (twenty-four fireboxes, 5 atmospheres forced, 1296sq m) in 1 + 1 boiler rooms. Three generators, 29kW 65V. One rudder.

Armament

Eight 24cm/30 hooped guns (494 rounds), –5° +8°, range 5700–8800m, temporarily fitted instead with four 15cm/22 hooped guns; two [eight, finally two] 8.7cm/24 hooped guns (300 rounds); six 5cm/40 QF guns; four 35cm TT (10 rounds), one stern above water, two lateral above water, one bow under water.

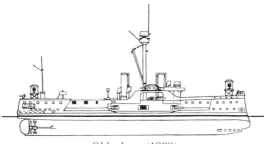

Oldenburg (1898)

Handling

An adequate sea-boat, but subject to severe pitching and with marked weather helm. Serious loss of speed in head sea, up to 25 percent above Beaufort 6; in severe weather steaming was impossible in head sea or cross sea. Transverse metacentric height 0.630m, longitudinal 54.05m. Maximum stability moment at 42°, = zero at 71°.

Complement

Crew: 34/355 [32/401]. Boats: one picket boat, one launch, two pinnaces, two cutters, two yawls, one dinghy.

Notes

Colour scheme no 2, 4, 9. Experimental design, of no real value in combat. 60T ballast fixed permanently in the forepeak. Nicknamed *Bügeleisen* – Flatiron. [Torpedo nets fitted 1885–97.]

Career

Oldenburg launched 20 Dec 1884, commissioned into fleet 8 Apr 1886; served as a guard ship 1900; later harbour ship. Stricken 13 Jan 1912 and used as fleet target ship; released, sold 5 May 1919 to Hattinger Co, broken up 1919 at Wilhelmshaven.

Coastal battleships 1890–1896

Siegfried class

Name	Builder	Built	Cost in Marks (000s)	Displacement (t = tonnes T = tons)	Length (m)	Breadth (m)	Draught (m)	Power (hp)	Revs (rpm)	Speed (kts)	Range (nm/kts)	Coal (t)	Oil (t)
SIEGFRIED	Germania Dockyard, Kiel Construction no 44	1888–90	4770	3741t max 3500t des	79.00 oa 76.00 cwl	14.9*	5.51 fwd 5.74 aft	5022ihp max	141	14.9	1490/10 740/14	220 max 80 des	236 max
	mod: Imperial Dockyard, Danzig	1903–04	2321	4237t max	86.13 oa 84.80 cwl	,,	5.45 fwd 5.47 aft	4724ihp max	147	15.3	3400/10 1940/14	580 max 350 des	500 max 100 des
BEOWULF	AG 'Weser' Bremen Construction no 100	1890–92	5288	3741t max 3500t des	79.00 oa 76.00 cwl	,,	5.51 fwd 5.74 aft	4859ihp max	144	15.1	1490/10 740/14	220 max 80 des	220 max
	mod: Imperial Dockyard, Danzig	1900–02	1881	4320t max	86.13 oa 84.80 cwl	,,	5.42 fwd 5.64 aft	5078ihp max	145	15.4	3400/10 1940/14	580 max 350 des	500 max 100 des
FRITHJOF	AG 'Weser', Bremen Construction no 101	1890–93	5375	3741t max 3500t des	79.00 oa 76.00 cwl	,,	5.51 fwd 5.74 aft	5250ihp max	142	15.0	1490/10 740/14	220 max 80 des	220 max
	mod: Imperial Dockyard, Kiel	1902–03	2805	4367t max	86.13 oa 84.80 cwl	,,	5.59 for 5.59 aft	5023ihp max	142	15.1	3400/10 1940/14	580 max 350 des	500 max 100 des
HEIMDALL	Imperial Dockyard, Wilhelmshaven Construction no 14	1891–94	6110	3741t max 3500t des	79.00 oa 76.00 cwl	,,	5.51 fwd 5.74 aft	4453ihp max	133	14.6	1490/10 740/14	220 max 80 des	220 max
	mod: Imperial Dockyard, Kiel	1901–02	2639	4436t max	86.13 oa 84.80 cwl	,,	5.66 fwd 5.66 aft	5064ihp max	141	15.1	3400/10 1940/14	580 max 350 des	500 max 100 des
HILDEBRAND sq fl	Imperial Dockyard, Kiel Construction no 20	1890–93	5895	3741t max 3500t des	79.00 oa 76.00 cwl	,,	5.51 fwd 5.74 aft	4608ihp max	137	14.8	1490/10 740/14	220 max 80 des	220 max
	mod: Imperial Dockyard Danzig	1901–02	2055	4236t max	86.13 oa 84.80 cwl	,,	5.43 fwd 5.49 aft	5338ihp max	145	15.3	3400/10 1940/14	580 max 350 des	500 max 100 des
HAGEN	Imperial Dockyard, Kiel Construction no 21	1891–94	5921	3741t max 3500t des	79.00 oa 76.00 cwl	,,	5.51 fwd 5.74 aft	4608ihp max	136	14.8	1490/10 740/14	220 max 80 des	220 max
	mod: Imperial Dockyard, Kiel	1898–00	2110	4247t max 4000t des	86.13 oa 84.80 cwl	,,	5.47 fwd 5.45 aft	5332ihp max	143	15.3	3400/10 1940/14	580 max 350 des	500 max 100 des

Before refit 2070gt/1355nt; after refit 2477gt/1550nt

*   without torpedo net booms

Construction

Laid down as fourth rate armoured ships *O, P, Q, U, R* and *S* (official design, 1885–1887–1889). Transverse and longitudinal frame steel construction (eight [nine] watertight compartments, double bottom approx 60 percent). Armour: compound steel and teak: deck 30mm, CT roof 30mm, sides 80mm; CWL upper section 180–240–180mm on 330mm timber, lower section 100–140–100mm on 290mm timber; cupolas and barbettes (Krupp armour used after *Heimdall*) 30 to 200mm on 200mm timber [*Heimdall, Hagen*: Krupp armour, deck 50mm, CT roof 30mm, sides 160mm, CWL (armour plus timber 530mm) upper section 180–240–180mm, lower section 140–140–100mm]. Depth 8.14m. Immersion increased by 1cm per 8.61t. Trim moment 3600m-t.

Propulsion

Two vertical 3-cylinder triple expansion engines (two 3-bladed screws, 3.5m diameter) in two engine rooms. Four locomotive boilers [eight Marine-type, *Hagen* eight Thornycroft boilers] (eight fireboxes, 12 atmospheres forced, 915–1100sq m [1216–1402sq m]) in 1 + 1 boiler rooms. Three generators, 29–36kW [48–60kW] 67V. One rudder. *Siegfried* oil fired until 1903.

Armament

Three 24cm/35 hooped guns (204 rounds), –4° +25°, range 13,000m; eight (*Siegfried* only 6) [ten] 8.8cm/30 QF guns (1500 [2500] rounds); [six machine guns also temporarily fitted]; four 35cm TT (10 rounds), one stern, swivel mounted, above water, two lateral, above water, one bow [three 45cm TT (8 rounds), one stern, swivel mounted, above water, two lateral, under water, plus one 35cm TT (3 rounds) bow, under water]. [Completely or partially disarmed after 1916.]

Handling

Good sea-boats, with gentle motion, but a marked speed loss in head sea and with weather helm. Tendency to lie to in heavy weather. Very responsive, with a tight turning circle.

Complement

Crew: 20/256 (plus 6/22 as second flagship) [20/287 (plus 9/34 as second flagship)]. Boats: one picket boat, one pinnace, two cutters, one yawl, one (plus one) dinghy.

Notes

Colour scheme no 2, 4, 9. Note that *Siegfried* carried

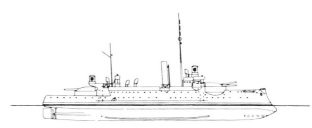

Siegfried (1890); *Beowulf, Frithjof, Heimdall, Hildebrand* and *Hagen* were almost identical.

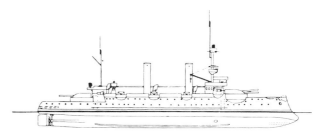

Hagen (1910); *Beowulf, Siegfried, Frithjof, Heimdall, Hildebrand* and *Odin* were almost identical, and *Ägir* was very similar.

only three 8.8cm QF guns on each beam. From *Hildebrand* on Inglefield anchors were fitted and anchor supports dispensed with. *Frithjof, Heimdall* and *Hagen* were fitted with funnels approx 1.20m lower. [Torpedo nets were fitted from 1890 to 1897.]

Career

Siegfried launched 10 Aug 1889, commissioned into fleet 29 Apr 1890 until 1903; fleet 1914; served as a coastal defence ship 1915, barrack ship at Wilhelmshaven 1916. Stricken 17 Jun 1919. Reconstruction as a salvage (raising) ship was planned, but she was instead sold for 425,000M to H Peters, Wewelsfleth, and broken up 1920 at Kiel-Nordmole.

Beowulf launched 8 Nov 1890, commissioned into fleet 1 Apr 1892; coastal defence ship 1915; target ship for submarines 1916; icebreaker in Baltic 1918. Stricken 17 Jun 1919, sold to Norddeutsche Tiefbaugesellschaft, Berlin, broken up 1921 at Danzig.

Frithjof launched 21 Jul 1891, commissioned into fleet 23 Feb 1893; served as a coastal defence ship 1915; barrack ship at Danzig 1916. Stricken 17 Jun

1919, sold to A Bernstein, Hamburg. Reconstructed in 1923 as a freighter by Deutsche Werke, Rüstringen. Broken up 1930 at Danzig.

Heimdall launched 27 Jul 1892, commissioned into fleet 7 Apr 1894; served as a coastal defence ship 1915; barrack ship for submarine crew and Ems Emden coastal defence flotilla 1916. Stricken 17 Jun 1919, reconstruction as a salvage (raising) ship was planned, but instead broken up 1921 by Oltmann at Rönnebeck.

Hildebrand launched 6 Aug 1892, commissioned into fleet 28 Oct 1893; served as a coastal defence ship 1915, barrack and distilling plant ship at Windau 1916. Stricken 17 Jun 1919, sold to Holland for breaking. Stranded on Dutch coast, position 52° 05N, 04° 14E, wreck blown up 1933, broken up.

Hagen launched 21 Oct 1893, commissioned into fleet 2 Oct 1894; barrack ship at Libau, Danzig, Warnemünde from 1916. Stricken 17 Jun 1919, sold to Norddeutsche Tiefbauges, broken up at Berlin.

Odin class

Construction

Built as fourth rate armoured ships *V* and *T* (official design, 1892). Construction details as *Hagen*, except as follows. Krupp armour: deck 70–50mm; CT roof 30mm, sides 120mm; CWL upper section 0–220–0mm, lower section 0–120–0mm armour on teak to make total thickness 400mm. Cork cofferdams. Depth 8.22m. Immersion increased by 1cm per 8.63t. Trim moment 3600m-t.

Propulsion

Odin propulsion machinery as *Siegfried*, *Ägir* same except for eight Thornycroft boilers by Oderwerke, Stettin (eight fireboxes, 12 atmospheres forced, 1500sq m) etc.

Ägir six generators, 243–250kW 120V, *Odin* as *Hildebrand*. One rudder.

Armament

Three 24cm/35 hooped guns (174 rounds), range 13,000m; ten 8.8cm/30 QF guns (2500 rounds); three 45cm TT (8 rounds), two lateral, swivel mounted, above water, one bow, under water, (8 rounds). [Armament as *Siegfried* after refit].

Handling

As *Siegfried*.

Complement

As *Siegfried*.

Notes

Colour scheme no 4, 9. *Odin* was fitted with one funnel only, 42.0m high; her foremast was 1m further aft and she had no davits and no compass platform. *Ägir* was nicknamed *Elektrische Anna* – Electric Anna – on account of her large number of auxiliary electrical machines. All coastal defence ships were notable for the bell-like curvature in their outer hull skin, and their round turret cupolas; hence their nicknames *Meerweibchen* and *Meerschweinen* – mermaids and porpoises – because in a swell they rolled in such a portly manner. Refits resulted in marked improvements in seakeeping

Name	Builder	Built	Cost in Marks (000s)	Displacement (t = tonnes T = tons)	Length (m)	Breadth (m)	Draught (m)	Power (hp)	Revs (rpm)	Speed (kts)	Range (nm/kts)	Coal (t)	Oil (t)
ODIN	Imperial Dockyard, Danzig Construction no	1893–96	6539	3754t max 3550t des	79.00 oa 76.40 cwl	15.2	5.61 fwd 5.47 aft	4650ihp max 4800ihp des	139	14.4 max 15.0 des	2200/10	370 max 270 des	100 tar oil only 1908/09
	mod: Imperial Dockyard, Danzig	1901–03	2170	4376t max 4100t des	86.15 oa 84.80 cwl	15.4	5.59 fwd 5.49 aft	5072ihp max	146	15.5 max	3000/10	580 max 480 des	
ÄGIR sq fl	Imperial Dockyard, Kiel Construction no 22	1892–96	6645	3750t max 3550t des	79.00 oa 76.40 cwl	15.2	5.61 fwd 5.47 aft	5129ihp max 4800ihp des	139	15.1 max 15.0 des	2200/10	370 max 270 des	only 1908/09
	mod: Imperial Dockyard Danzig	1903–04	2280	4292t max 4110t des	86.15 oa 84.80 cwl	15.4	5.60 fwd 5.30 aft	5605ihp max	143	15.5 max	3000/10	580 max 480 des	

and manoeuvring qualities. *Odin* and *Ägir* can be identified by their lack of superstructure for the 8.8cm QF guns and pressure heads; air shafts take their place. *Ägir* was fitted with davits. After 1914 the large semi-circular lower tops were replaced by crows' nests on fore topmasts.

Career

Odin launched 3 Nov 1894, commissioned into fleet 22 Sept 1896; coastal defence ship 1915; tender at Wilhelmshaven 1916. Stricken 6 Dec 1919, reconstructed in 1922 by Deutsche Werke Rüstringen as a freighter for A Bernstein Co, Hamburg; broken up 1935.

Ägir launched 3 Apr 1895, commissioned into fleet 15

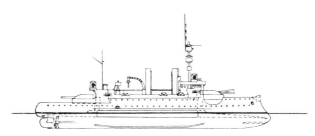

Ägir (1897); *Odin* had one funnel only, without a cap.

Oct 1896; coastal defence ship 1915; barrack hulk at Wilhelmshaven 1916. Stricken 17 Jun 1919, reconstructed in 1922 by Deutsche Werke Rüstringen as a freighter for A Bernstein Co, Hamburg; stranded at Karlsö lighthouse (Gotland) 8 Dec 1929, wrecked. Bow ornament at Laboe naval memorial.

Battleships 1894–1908

Kurfürst Friedrich Wilhelm class

Name	Builder	Built	Cost in Marks (000s)	Displacement (t = tonnes T = tons)	Length (m)	Breadth (m)	Draught (m)	Power (hp)	Revs (rpm)	Speed (kts)	Range (nm/kts)	Coal (t)	Oil (t)
KURFÜRST FRIEDRICH WILHELM sq fl, 2nd fl	Imperial Dockyard, Wilhelmshaven Construction no 13	1890–94		10670t max 10013t des	115.7 oa 13.9 cwl	19.5 19.74*	7.6 fwd 7.9 aft	9686ihp max 10,000ihp des	110	16.9 max 16.5 des	4300/10	1050 max 650 des	110 tar oil only until 1902
	mod: Imperial Dockyard, Wilhelmshaven	1904–05											
BRANDENBURG	AG Vulcan, Stettin Construction no 198	1890–93	15,832	,,	,,	,,	,,	9997ihp max 10,000ihp des	109	16.3 max 16.5 des	,,	,,	,,
	mod: Imperial Dockyard, Wilhelmshaven	1903–04	1318										
WEISSENBURG	AG Vulcan, Stettin Construction no 199	1890–94		,,	,,	,,	,,	10,103ihp max 10,000ihp des	108	16.5 max 16.5 des	,,	,,	,,
	mod: Imperial Dockyard, Wilhelmshaven	1902–04											
WÖRTH	Germania Dockyard, Kiel Construction no 52	1890–93	16,054	,,	,,	,,	,,	10,228ihp max 10,000ihp des	110	16.9 max 16.5 des	,,	,,	,,
	mod: Imperial Dockyard, Wilhelmshaven	1901–03	1340										
5243gt/2619nt													

* with torpedo nets

Construction
Laid down as armoured ships *D, A, C* and *B* (official design, 1888–89). Transverse and longitudinal frame steel construction (thirteen watertight compartments, double bottom 48 percent). Krupp armour (compound steel on *Brandenburg*, barbettes A and B; *Weissenburg*, barbettes A and C; *Kurfürst Friedrich Wilhelm* and *Weissenburg* both sections of the CWL): deck 60mm; CT roof 30mm, sides 300mm; from CWL upward 300–400–300mm, from CWL downward 180–200–180mm (both sections armour plus teak backing total 600mm); cupolas top 50mm, sides 120mm in three layers, each 40mm; barbettes 300mm on 210mm timber, battery 42mm. Cork cofferdams. Depth 11.0m. Immersion increased by 1cm per 17.37t. Trim moment 10,870m-t.

Propulsion
Two vertical 3-cylinder triple expansion engines (two 3-bladed screws, 5.0m diameter) in two engine rooms. Twelve transverse cylindrical boilers (thirty-six fireboxes, 12 atmospheres forced, 2291–2358sq m) in 2 + 2 boiler rooms. Three [four] generators, 72.6–96.5kW 67V [*Kurfürst Friedrich Wilhelm* three generators, 108kW.] One rudder.

Armament
Four 28cm/40 hooped guns, two 28cm/35 hooped guns (total 352 rounds), –4° +25°, range 14,600m [15,900m]; six to eight 10.5cm/35 QF guns (600 [1184] rounds); eight 8.8cm/30 QF guns (2000 [2384] rounds); two 6/8cm boat cannon (machine guns), six 45cm TT (16 rounds), all armoured, four lateral, above water, individually swivel mounted, two bow above water [two 45cm TT (5 rounds), lateral, above water, plus one 45cm TT stern above water, swivel mounted]. [All armament removed after 1916].

Handling
Excellent sea-boat, with easy motion and slight weather helm. Wet at high speed in head sea, with severe pitching. Responsive to helm, with moderate turning circle. Speed loss slight under helm, 30 percent with rudder hard over. Transverse metacentric height 1.05m, longitudinal 180m. Max stability moment at 31.5°, = zero at 57°.

Complement
Crew: 38/530 (plus 9/54 as squadron flagship) [30/561

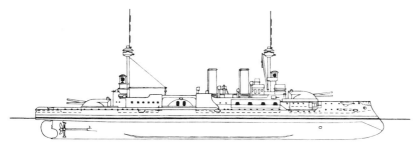

Kurfürst Friedrich Wilhelm (1895, showing the final battery arrangement), *Brandenburg, Weissenburg, Wörth*

(plus 9/48 as second flagship)]. Boats: two picket boats, two launches, one pinnace, two cutters, two yawls, two dinghies.

Notes
Colour scheme no 4, 9. Funnels were 3m and 1.5m lower until 1894 or 1895, and aft superstructure was enclosed. [Major modification involved installation of gangway and conning tower (roof 20mm, sides 120mm armour) aft, forward 10.5cm QF gun (see drawing), also searchlight tops (on roof of battle tops) with one searchlight each; searchlights and their platforms were removed from the lower masts, and anchor supports were removed; after 1908 topmasts were as shown in the drawing. After 1911 *Wörth* had two

searchlights mounted diagonally on the foretop, none at the maintop, one on the upper aft bridge. After 1915 an enclosed spotting top was fitted on the topgallant crosstrees.] *Brandenburg* had steam pipes on the front side of her funnels. [Torpedo nets were fitted 1893–97. In 1900, during a voyage to East Asia, all four vessels were equipped with radio telegraphy – becoming the first ships so fitted in the Imperial Navy. The refit of 1901–05 resulted in weight savings of 500–700t.]

Career
Kurfürst Friedrich Wilhelm launched 30 Jun 1891, commissioned into fleet 29 Apr 1894; service abroad 1900–01. Sold 12 Sept 1910 to Turkey for 9,000,000M and became Turkish ship of the line *Barbaros Hayred-*

din. Sunk 8 Aug 1915 in the Dardanelles, position 40° 27N, 26° 48E, by a torpedo from the British submarine *E11*, 253 dead.

Brandenburg launched 21 Sept 1891, commissioned into fleet 19 Nov 1893; service abroad 1900–01; fleet duties 1901, reduced to coastal defence ship 1915; barrack and distilling plant vessel at Libau 1916–18. Reconstruction as target ship uncompleted, stricken 13 May 1919, sold to Norddeutsche Tiefbauges, Berlin; broken up 1920 at Danzig.

Weissenburg launched 14 Dec 1891, commissioned into fleet 14 Oct 1894; service abroad 1900–01. Sold 12 Sept 1910 to Turkey for 9,000,000M and became Turkish ship of the line *Torgut Reis*; became a Turkish naval training ship 1924; hulk in the Bosporus until 1938, broken up.

Wörth launched 6 Aug 1892, commissioned into fleet 31 Oct 1893; reduced to coastal defence ship 1915, then barrack ship at Danzig. Stricken 13 May 1919, sold to Norddeutsche Tiefbauges, Berlin, broken up at Danzig.

Until this time it was standard practice to carry out running speed measurements as part of the acceptance procedure (dockyard trials), ie before commissioning. After *Wörth* the testing of large ships was carried out afterwards, with certain exceptions.

Kaiser Friedrich III class

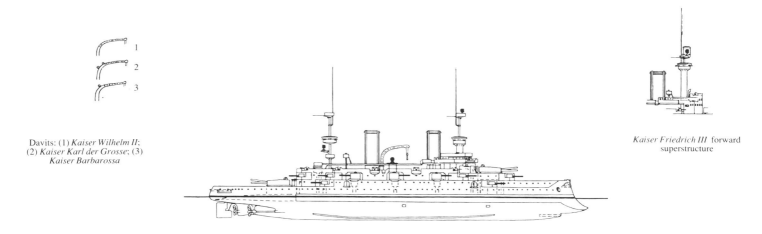

Davits: (1) *Kaiser Wilhelm II*; (2) *Kaiser Karl der Grosse*; (3) *Kaiser Barbarossa*

Kaiser Friedrich III forward superstructure

Kaiser Friedrich III (1903); *Kaiser Wilhelm II, Kaiser Wilhelm der Grosse, Kaiser Karl der Grosse* and *Kaiser Barbarossa* were very similar.

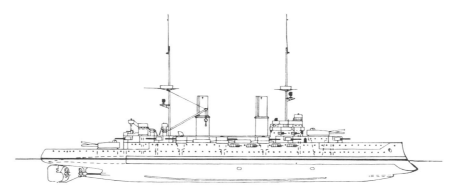

Kaiser Friedrich III (1912); *Kaiser Wilhelm II, Kaiser Wilhelm der Grosse* and *Kaiser Barbarossa* were very similar.

Name	Builder	Built	Cost in Marks (000s)	Displacement (t = tonnes T = tons)	Length (m)	Breadth (m)	Draught (m)	Power (hp)	Revs (rpm)	Speed (kts)	Range (nm/kts)	Coal (t)	Oil (t)
KAISER FRIEDRICH III sq fl	Imperial Dockyard, Wilhelmshaven Construction no 22	1895–98	21,472	11,785t max 11,097t des	125.3 oa 120.9 cwl	20.4	7.89 fwd 8.25 aft	13,053ihp max 13,000ihp des	107	17.3 max 17.5 des	3420/10	1070 max 650 des	200 (only 1908–09)
	mod: Imperial Dockyard, Kiel	1908–09		11,894t max 11,233t des			8.26 fwd 8.25 aft						
KAISER WILHELM II sq fl, 2nd fl	Imperial Dockyard, Wilhelmshaven Construction no 24	1896–1900	20,387	11,785t max 11,097t des	,,	,,	7.89 fwd 8.25 aft	13,922ihp max 13,000ihp des	108	17.6 max 17.5 des	,,	,,	,,
	mod: Imperial Dockyard, Wilhelmshaven	1910	1501	11,894t max 11,233t des			8.26 fwd 8.25 aft						
KAISER WILHELM DER GROSSE	Germania Dockyard, Kiel Construction no 79	1898–1901	20,254	11,785t max 11,097t des	,,	,,	7.89 fwd 8.25 aft	13,658ihp max 13,000ihp des	107	17.2 max 17.5 des	,,	,,	,,
	mod: Imperial Dockyard, Kiel	1908–10	1532	11,894t max 11,233t des			8.26 fwd 8.25 aft						
KAISER KARL DER GROSSE	Blohm & Voss, Hamburg Construction no 136	1898–1902	20,385	11,785t max 11,097t des	,,	,,	7.89 fwd 8.25 aft	13,874ihp max 13,000ihp des	117	17.8 max 17.5 des	,,	,,	,,
KAISER KARL BARBAROSSA	F Schichau Danzig Construction no 640	1898–1901	20,301	11,785t max 11,097t des	,,	,,	7.89 fwd 8.25 aft	13,949ihp max 13,000ihp des	113	17.8 max 17.5 des	,,	,,	,,
	mod: Imperial Dockyard, Kiel	1907–10		11,894t max 11,233t des			8.26 fwd 8.25 aft						

6747gt/3685nt; after refit 6798gt/3959nt

Construction

Laid down as first rate armoured ships *Ersatz Preussen*, *Ersatz Friedrich der Grosse*, *Ersatz König Wilhelm*, ships of the line *B* and *A* (official design, 1892–94). Transverse and longitudinal frame steel construction (twelve watertight compartments, double bottom 70 percent). Krupp armour: deck 65mm, forward CT roof 30mm, sides 250mm; aft, decks 30mm, slopes 150mm; CWL 0–200–300–150mm, lower section 180–100mm, all on 250mm teak; 24cm turrets roof 50mm, sides 250mm; 15cm turrets sides 150mm; shields 70mm; casemates 150mm. Cork cofferdams. Depth 13.1m. Immersion increased by 1cm per 19.2t. Trim moment 13,810 to 13,900m-t.

Propulsion

Three vertical 3-cylinder triple expansion engines, in *Kaiser Wilhelm II* and *Kaiser Wilhelm der Grosse* by AG 'Germania', Berlin-Tegel (three 3-bladed screws, 4.5m diameter, but in *Kaiser Wilhelm II* and *Kaiser Karl der Grosse* two 3-bladed screws, 4.5m diameter and one 4-bladed screw, 4.2m diameter) in 1 + 2 engine rooms. *Kaiser Friedrich III*, four Thornycroft plus eight cylindrical boilers (eight plus thirty-two fireboxes, 12 atmospheres forced, 3390sq m); in *Kaiser Wilhelm II* four Marine-type plus eight cylindrical boilers (eight plus thirty-two fireboxes, 12 atmospheres forced, 3,560sq m); in *Kaiser Wilhelm der Grosse* four Marine-type plus six cylindrical boilers (twelve plus twenty-four fireboxes, 13 atmospheres forced, 3738sq m); in *Kaiser Barbarossa* four Thornycroft plus six cylindrical boilers (twelve plus twenty-four fireboxes, 13.5 atmospheres forced, 3783sq m); and in *Kaiser Karl der Grosse* two Marine-type and two Marine-type double plus six cylindrical boilers (twelve plus eighteen fireboxes, 14.25 atmospheres forced, 3450sq m), all cylindrical boilers mounted transversely in 2 + 2 boiler rooms (in *Kaiser Friedrich III* and *Kaiser Wilhelm II* all mounted transversely in 2 + 2 + 2 boiler rooms). Four generators, 240kW 74V (in *Kaiser Friedrich III* and *Kaiser Wilhelm II* five generators, 320kW 74V). One balanced rudder (one plain rudder in *Kaiser Wilhelm II*); rectangular rudder blade in *Kaiser Friedrich III*, [rudder balance section removed from *Kaiser Wilhelm der Grosse* after damage in 1905].

Armament

Four 24cm/40 QF guns (300 rounds), –4° +30°, range 16,900m; eighteen [fourteen] 15cm/40 QF guns (2160 [1890] rounds), range 13,700m; twelve [fourteen] 8.8cm/30 QF guns (3000 [2100] rounds); twelve machine guns [deleted]; six [five] 45cm TT (16 [13] rounds), one swivel mounted at the stern, above water [deleted], four lateral, under water, one bow, under water. [*Kaiser Karl der Grosse* not refitted; all disarmed after 1916.]

Handling

Excellent sea-boat, with extremely stiff, but not unpleasant motion (rolled up to 15°, period 12 seconds); very responsive, with tight turning circle. Slight speed loss in head sea, and up to 40 percent with hard rudder, at 8° heel. Transverse metacentric height 0.917–1.18m, longitudinal 133.9–142m. Max stability moment 34° and 35° and 39.8°, = zero at 56° and 60.2°.

Complement

Crew: 39/612 (plus 12/51–63 as squadron flagship) [33/589 (plus 2/23 as second command flagship). Boats: two picket boats, two launches, one pinnace [removed], two cutters, two yawls, two [one] dinghies.

Notes

Colour scheme no 9. For *Kaiser Friedrich III* until 1900, see supplementary drawing (note also that the mainmast carried no lower platform at this date; its top was 24m above CWL). After *Kaiser Wilhelm II* the mainmast was as in the drawing of *Wittelsbach*, but with a searchlight mounted on the battle top (in *Kaiser Wilhelm II* a searchlight was mounted on the mainmast platform, 15m above CWL, and on the foremast as in *Kaiser Friedrich III*); until 1901 searchlights were carried instead of the lower davits on the outboard platforms on the upper deck. Until 1901 the bridge was as shown in the supplementary drawing of *Kaiser*

Friedrich III. All ships had the compass platform mounted 17m further forward in 1903. For the davits, see the supplementary drawings. [For identification purposes, note that the funnel cross-sections in *Kaiser Friedrich III* and *Kaiser Wilhelm II* were oval and circular respectively after the refit. Four diagonal steam pipes were fitted on the forward funnel. The refit of *Kaiser Barbarossa* took place in two stages, namely the modifications to the mainmast and davits, and the installation of 8.8cm QF guns after 1907 (see drawing), and the installation of eight 8.8cm QF guns on the upper deck as on the three others after 1910. After 1915 all the ships carried an enclosed spotting top on the forward topgallant crosstrees.]

Career

Kaiser Barbarossa launched 21 Apr 1900, commis- sioned into fleet 10 Jun 1901. Reduced to a prisoner barrack ship at Wilhelmshaven in 1916. Stricken 6 Dec 1919, and broken up 1919–20 at Rüstringen.

Kaiser Friedrich III launched 1 Jul 1896, commis- sioned into fleet 7 Oct 1898. Reduced to a prisoner barrack ship at Kiel 1916; barrack ship at Flensburg 1917, and later at Swinemünde. Stricken 6 Dec 1919, sold to Berlin, broken up 1920 at Kiel-Nordmole. Bow ornament now in Dresden army museum.

Kaiser Karl der Grosse launched 18 Oct 1899, com- missioned into fleet 4 Feb 1902. Reduced to a prisoner barrack ship at Wilhelmshaven 1916. Stricken 6 Dec 1919, sold, broken up 1920 at Rönnebeck.

Kaiser Wilhelm II launched 14 Sept 1897, commis- sioned as fleet flagship 13 Feb 1900 and served as such until 1906; general fleet duties after that, until 1915, after which she served as fleet commander's of- fice ship at Wilhelmshaven. Stricken 17 Mar 1921, sold, broken up 1922 at Hamburg-Altenwärder. Bell now in Dresden army museum.

Kaiser Wilhelm der Grosse launched 1 Jun 1899, commissioned into fleet 5 May 1901. Reduced to har- bour ship 1916; used as a torpedo target ship at Kiel 1917. Stricken 6 Dec 1919, sold to Berlin, broken up 1920 at Kiel-Nordmole.

Wittelsbach class

Name	Builder	Built	Cost in Marks (000s)	Displacement (t = tonnes T = tons)	Length (m)	Breadth (m)	Draught (m)	Power (hp)	Revs (rpm)	Speed (kts)	Range (nm/kts)	Coal (t)	Oil (t)
WITTELSBACH sq fl	Imperial Dockyard, Wilhelmshaven Construction no 25	1899– 1902	22,740	12798t max 11774t des	126.8 oa 125.2 cwl	22.8*	7.95 fwd 8.04 aft	13,900ihp max 14,000ihp des	103	17.0 max 18.0 des	5000/10	1800 max 650 des	200**
	mod: Reichs Dockyard, Wilhelmshaven	1919											
WETTIN	F Schichau, Danzig Construction no 676	1899– 1902	22,597	,,	,,	,,	,,	15,530ihp max 14,000ihp des	114	18.1 max 18.0 des	,,	,,	,,
ZÄHRINGEN	Germania Dockyard, Kiel Construction no 86	1899– 1902	22,275	,,	,,	,,	,,	14,875ihp max 14,000ihp des	107	17.8 max 18.0 des	,,	,,	,,
	mod: Naval Dockyard, Wilhelmshaven	1926–27											
SCHWABEN sq fl	Imperial Dockyard, Wilhelmshaven Construction no 27	1900–04	21,678	,,	,,	,,	,,	13,253ihp max 14,000ihp des	102	16.9 max 18.0 des	,,	,,	,,
	mod: Reichs Dockyard, Wilhelmshaven	1919											
MECKLENBURG	AG Vulcan, Stettin Construction no 248	1900–03	22,329	,,	,,	,,	,,	15,171ihp max 14,000ihp des	112	18.1 max 18.0 des	,,	,,	,,

7346gt/3976nt

* measured over the 15cm QF guns
** tar oil only 1908–09

Construction

Laid down as ships of the line C, D, E, G and F (official design, 1897–99). Transverse and longitudinal frame steel construction (fourteen watertight compartments, double bottom 70 percent). Krupp armour: deck 50mm; slopes 120–75–120mm; forward CT roof 30mm, sides 250mm, aft, roof 30mm, sides 140mm; CWL 0–100–225 (100mm shields)–100mm with 100mm teak; casemate 140mm; citadel 140mm; 24cm turrets roof 50mm, sides 250mm, 15cm turrets 150mm with 70mm shields. Cork cofferdams. Depth 12.77m. Immersion increased by 1cm per 20.50t. Trim moment 14,950m-t.

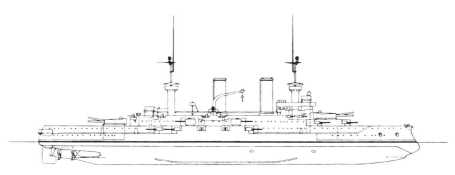

Wittelsbach (1904), *Wettin*, *Zähringen*, *Schwaben*, *Mecklenburg*

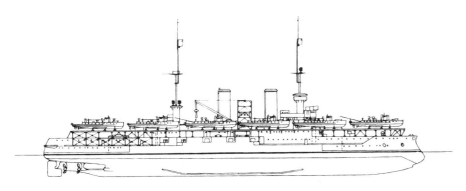

Wittelsbach (1919) as a parent ship for F-boats; *Schwaben* was similar.

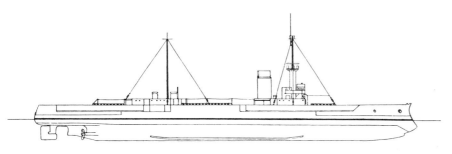

Zähringen (1933) as a target ship

Propulsion

Three vertical 3-cylinder triple expansion engines (two 3-bladed screws, 4.8m diameter, and one 4-bladed screw, 4.5m diameter) in 1 + 2 engine rooms. Six Marine-type boilers (Thornycroft in *Wettin* and *Mecklenburg*) plus six transverse cylindrical boilers (twelve plus twenty-four fireboxes, 13.5 atmospheres forced (14 atmospheres forced in *Zähringen*) 3719–4428sq m) in 2 + 2 boiler rooms. Four generators, 230kW 74V (258kW in *Wittelsbach*). One rudder. [*Schwaben* fitted for supplementary oil firing after winter 1915.] [*Zähringen* (as target ship) fitted with two vertical 3-cylinder triple expansion engines only (two 3-bladed screws, 4.8m diameter) in two engine rooms. Two Marine-type oil-fired boilers (14 atmospheres forced, six fireboxes, 1800sq m) in two boiler rooms. These were fully automatic systems controlled by wireless telegraph.]

Armament

Four 24cm/40 QF guns (340 rounds), –4° +30°, range 16,900m; eighteen 15cm/40 QF guns (2520 rounds), range 13,700m; twelve 8.8cm/30 QF guns (1800 rounds); twelve machine guns (temporary fitting); six 45cm TT (12–16 rounds), one bow, four broadside, one stern, all under water. [Entirely or partially disarmed after 1916.] For wartime mobilisation, *Wittelsbach*, *Wettin* and *Zähringen* were also fitted with one TT aft (above water, swivel mounted) until about 1906. For passing through canals the central 15cm QF casemate gun barrels were retracted, as the casemate recesses would not allow them to be trimmed fore and aft, flush to the sides (see also the notes on the following class).

Handling

Excellent sea-boats, rolling easily but not uncomfortably (roll angle 30°, period 10 seconds). Severe vibration at stern at more than 75rpm (centre engine). Some weather helm, but manoeuvred and turned well on centre screw alone. Speed loss with hard rudder 50 to 60 percent, 9° heel. Very wet in head sea, even at moderate speed. Transverse metacentric height 0.966m, longitudinal 140m. Max stability moment 33.4° = zero at 58.5°.

Complement

Crew 33/650 (plus 13/66 as squadron flagship, 9/44 as second command flagship). [Target ship *Zähringen* crew 67.] Boats: two picket boats, two launches, one pinnace [removed], two cutters, two yawls, two [one] dinghies.

Notes

Colour scheme no 9. *Zähringen* and *Mecklenburg* were fitted with davits as in *Kaiser Barbarossa*, and carried their bow hawses directly on the stem, with reserve anchors in recess to starboard rather than in hawsepipes. [Topmasts and topgallant masts as in the drawing were fitted after 1908. The aft compass platform was moved 15m further aft in 1911. *Wittelsbach*, *Wettin* and *Schwaben* carried two searchlights at the foretop, and two mounted diagonally at the maintop as shown in the drawing, otherwise no searchlights; *Zähringen* and *Mecklenburg*, originally fitted with one searchlight at each masthead, subsequently carried one on each side of the platform adjacent to the forward funnel, otherwise no searchlights. Rangefinders were installed in 1912. One enclosed spotting top was installed on all topgallant crosstrees 1912–14. *Zähringen*'s appearance as a target ship is shown in the drawing; various modifications were involved, including cork filling – displacement was 11,800t and speed 13.5kts. *Wittelsbach* and *Schwaben* were fitted with a new upper deck with supports for twelve F-boats each in 1919.

Career

Wittelsbach launched 3 Jul 1900, commissioned into fleet 15 Oct 1902. Reduced to exercise ship at Kiel 1916, and then to tender at Wilhelmshaven; parent ship for F-boats in the Reichsmarine. Stricken 8 Mar 1921, sold 7 Jul 1921 for 3,561,000M, broken up at Wilhelmshaven.

Wettin launched 6 Jun 1901, commissioned into fleet 1 Oct 1902. Served as an artillery training ship 1911–14; reduced to exercise ship and tender 1916. Stricken 11 Mar 1920, sold 21 Nov 1921, broken up 1922 at Rönnebeck. Bell now in Dresden army museum.

Zähringen launched 12 Jun 1901, commissioned into fleet 25 Oct 1902. Reduced to an exercise ship at Kiel 1916; stoker training ship and target ship, mostly at Kiel 1917. Stricken 11 Mar 1920, hulk at Wilhelmshaven. Reconstructed as a remote controlled target ship for the Reichsmarine and the Kriegsmarine 1926–27. Bombed at Gotenhafen 18 Dec 1944, burnt out and sunk; finally scuttled 26 Mar 1945, at harbour entrance. Broken up where she lay, 1949–50.

Schwaben launched 19 Aug 1901, commissioned 13 Apr 1904 as an artillery training ship, and served until 1911. Joined fleet 1914; reduced to an exercise ship at Wilhelmshaven 1916; served as a parent ship for F-boats under the Reichsmarine. Stricken 8 Mar 1921, sold for 3,090,000M, broken up 1921 at Kiel-Nordmole.

Mecklenburg launched 9 Nov 1901, commissioned into fleet 25 May 1903. Reduced to prisoner barrack ship at Kiel 1916, and then submarine crew barrack ship at Kiel 1918. Stricken 25 Jan 1920, sold 16 Aug 1921 for 1,750,000M, broken up 1921 by Deutsche Werke at Kiel-Nordmole.

Braunschweig class

Name	Builder	Built	Cost in Marks (000s)	Displacement (t = tonnes T = tons)	Length (m)	Breadth (m)	Draught (m)	Power (hp)	Revs (rpm)	Speed (kts)	Range (nm/kts)	Coal (t)	Oil (t)
BRAUNSCHWEIG sq fl	Germania Dockyard, Kiel Construction no 97	1901–04	23,983	14,394t max 13,208t des	127.7 oa 126.0 cwl	25.6* 22.2	8.10 fwd 8.16 aft	16,809ihp max 16,000ihp des	111	18.7 max 18.0 des	5200/10	1670 max 700 des	240 ** max
	mod: Naval Dockyard, Wilhelmshaven	1921–22											
ELSASS	F Schichau, Danzig Construction no 97	1901–04	23,983	,,	,,	,,	,,	16,812ihp max 16,000ihp des	115	18.7 max 18.0 des	,,	,,	,,
	mod: Naval Dockyard Wilhelmshaven	1923–24											
HESSEN	Germania Dockyard, Kiel Construction no 100	1902–05	23,867	,,	,,	,,	,,	16,486ihp max 16,000ihp des	109	18.2 max 18.0 des	,,	,,	,,
	mod: Naval Dockyard, Wilhelmshaven	1923–25 1929–30											
	mod: KM Dockyard, Wilhelmshaven†	1935–37	7200	13,257t max 12,200t des	138.1 max 137.7 des	21.5	7.65	25,000shp des	250	20.3 max	4000/14.5	—	1430
PREUSSEN sq fl	AG Vulcan, Stettin Construction no 256	1902–05	23,990	14,394t max 13,208t des	127.7 oa 126.0 cwl	25.6*	8.10 fwd 8.16 aft	16,980ihp max 16,000ihp des	115	18.5 max 18.0 des	5200/10	1670 max 700 des	240** max
	mod: Reichs Dockyard, Wilhelmshaven	1919											
LOTHRINGEN	F Schichau, Danzig Construction no 716	1902–05	23,801	,,	,,	21.5	,,	16,478ihp max 16,000ihp des	113	18.7 max 18.0 des	,,	,,	,,
	mod: Reichs Dockyard, Wilhelmshaven	1919											

7913gt/4066nt; after refit 8220gt/4119nt

*   measured over the QF guns
** tar oil only 1908–09
†   as a target ship

Construction

Laid down as ships of the line *H, J, L, K* and *M* (official design, 1900–01). Transverse and longitudinal frame steel construction (thirteen watertight compartments, double bottom 60 percent). Krupp armour: deck 40mm; slopes 140–75–140mm; forward CT roof 50mm, sides 300mm, aft, roof 30mm, sides 140mm; CWL 0–100–225 (shields 150mm)–100mm with 100mm teak; casemate 150mm, citadel 140mm; 28cm turrets roof 50mm, sides 250mm; 17cm turrets 150mm, shields 70mm. Cork cofferdams. Depth 12.84m. Immersion increased by 1cm per 21.3t. Trim moment 15,200m-t.

Propulsion

Three vertical 3-cylinder triple expansion engines (two 3-bladed screws, 4.8m diameter, and one 4-bladed screw, 4.5m diameter) in 1 + 2 engine rooms. Eight

	Fuel consumption on test (12–18kn)	Range at cruise speed (average values from extended observation period)
Braunschweig	0.752 to 0.898kg per hp/hr	5200nm/10kts
Elsass	0.770 to 0.847kg per hp/hr	5260nm/10kts
Hessen	0.787 to 0.858kg per hp/hr	4530nm/10kts*
Preussen	0.720 to 0.847kg per hp/hr	5270nm/10kts
Lothringen	0.756 to 0.839kg per hp/hr	5010nm/10kts

* Unstable steering caused an additional distance of 0.5nm per hour to be run; this extra distance should be taken into account in the calculation of fuel consumed per hour (ie, it explains the shorter range).

Marine-type plus six cylinder boilers [supplementary oil firing fitted after winter 1915] (sixteen plus twenty-two fireboxes, 13.5 atmospheres forced, 4500sq m) in 1 + 1 + 1 boiler rooms [*Hessen* eight Marine-type plus two oil-fired Marine-type boilers (sixteen plus two fireboxes, 13.5 atmospheres forced, 4,210sq m). Four generators, 230kW 74V [four turbo-generators, 260kW 110V from *Hessen* onwards]. One rudder.

Davits

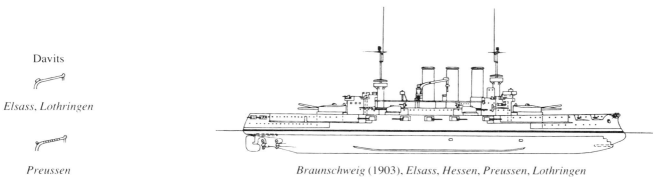

Elsass, Lothringen

Preussen

Braunschweig (1903), *Elsass, Hessen, Preussen, Lothringen*

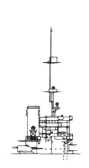

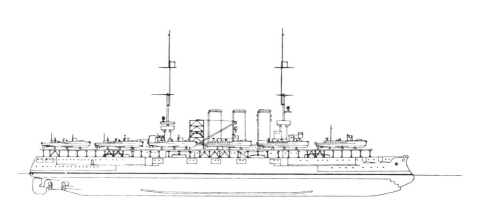

Braunschweig after 1923

Lothringen (1919) as a parent ship for F-boats; *Preussen* was very similar.

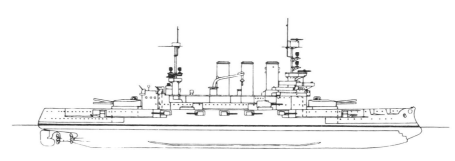

Hessen 1925–1929

Hessen (1932); *Elsass* and *Braunschweig* were very similar.

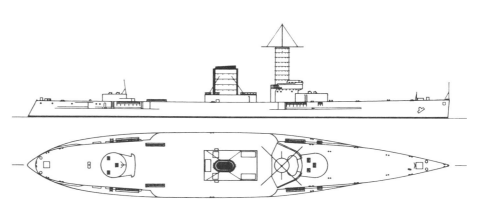

Elsass after 1925

Hessen (1937) as a target ship. *Mrva*

[As a target ship, *Hessen* was fitted with two sets of turbines (two 3-bladed screws, 3.7m diameter), two oil-fired Marine-type boilers plus oil-fired Marine-type double-ended boilers (eight fireboxes, 16 atmospheres forced, surface area not known), fully automatic, in 1 + 1 heating rooms.]

Armament

Four 28cm/40 QF guns (340 rounds), –4° +30°, range 18,800m; fourteen 17cm/40 QF guns (1820 rounds), range 14,500m; eighteen 8.8cm/35 QF guns (2700 rounds); four machine guns temporarily fitted; six 45cm TT (16 rounds), one stern (to port), four lateral, one bow, all under water. [All armament removed 1916–17, except for *Lothringen*, which was fitted with ten 17cm/40 QF guns; these were removed in 1918. In Reichsmarine service, *Braunschweig*, *Elsass* and *Hessen* were fitted with four 28cm/40 QF guns, *Braunschweig* with twelve-, *Elsass* ten-, and *Hessen* fourteen (twelve after 1931) 17cm/40 QF guns, four 8.8cm/45 QF guns (until 1931), four 8.8cm/45 AA guns, four 50cm TT (swivel mounted) on battery deck *Braunschweig* two TT only). *Hessen* as a target ship had one M5 free-firing bow TT (experimental), under water, angled 10° to port.] For passing through canals the three central 17cm QF casemate gun barrels on each beam could be retracted into their pivots, as the casemate recesses did not allow the guns to be trained flush to the sides; with these guns trained normally, the maximum beam was 25.6m – too wide for the canal locks of the time.

Handling

Good sea-boats, crank but with easy motion, given to severe pitching; had weather helm, but responsive, with a tight turning circle at low speed. Speed loss up to 70 percent with hard rudder, at 12° heel. Transverse metacentric height 1.02m, longitudinal 144m. Maximum stability moment at 30.5° = zero at 60.5°.

Complement

Crew 35/708 (plus 13/66 as squadron flagship, 2/23 as second command flagship) [30/697; *Hessen* as target ship 80 crew]. Boats: two picket boats, two launches, one pinnace [removed], two cutters, two yawls, two [one] dinghies.

Notes

Colour scheme no 9. Davits as shown in supplementary drawing. Funnels on *Lothringen* were lowered 2.5m in 1906. [After 1909 topmasts and topgallant masts were fitted as shown in the drawing. Searchlights were fitted as follows: one at the foremast head, one on a new foremast platform 20m above CWL, two mounted diagonally on the roof of the mainmast battle top, one each side on a platform adjacent to the forward funnel; *Hessen*'s searchlights in 1925 were as in 1910, plus one on a mainmast platform 20m above CWL, after 1929 as shown in the drawing. The cover of the fore top was removed in 1909. *Braunschweig* and *Elsass* were fitted in 1923 and 1925 with bridges as shown in the supplementary drawings. *Lothringen* was fitted with torpedo nets 1917–18. *Preussen* was not fitted with new derricks when converted to an F-boat parent ship, but used her existing davits. After 1912–14 one enclosed spotting top was fitted on each topgallant crosstrees.] *Hessen*, lying at Brunsbüttel from 1917–18, was known jokingly as SMS *Kleinste Fahrt* – SMS Shortest Voyage – because of a large warning painted on her hull. [The conversion of *Hessen* to a target ship in 1935–36 involved fitting a new longer bow forward of frame 84 (fifteen watertight compartments), and the removal of all decks and superstructure up to the forward and aft barbettes and bridge. Crew and operating rooms were under the armoured deck and in the aft barbette, with a bow capstan installation in the forward barbette, and more powerful armour in place of cork filling (bow 40mm Wh steel; waterline 100–140–170mm Wh steel).]

Career

Braunschweig launched 20 Dec 1902, commissioned into fleet 15 Oct 1904. Reduced to exercise ship 1916, and after 20 Aug 1917 to a barrack ship at Kiel; fleet duties with the Reichsmarine 1921–26. Stricken 31 Mar 1931, reduced to a hulk at Wilhelmshaven, and broken up.

Elsass launched 26 May 1903, commissioned into fleet 29 Nov 1904. Reduced to exercise ship and barrack ship at Kiel 25 Jul 1916, then to a training ship; fleet duties with the Reichsmarine 1924–30; withdrawn 25 Feb 1930. Stricken 31 Mar 1931, reduced to a hulk at Wilhelmshaven; sold to Technischer Betrieb des Norddeutschen Lloyd, Bremerhaven, 31 Oct 1935, broken up 1936.

Hessen launched 18 Sept 1903, commissioned into fleet 19 Sept 1905. Fleet duties until 1916; reduced to a tender at Brunsbüttel 1917; fleet duties in the Reichsmarine 1925; withdrawn 12 Nov 1934. Stricken 31 Mar 1935; reconstructed as a target ship. Commissioned 1 Apr 1937; remote controlled target ship until 1945. Surrendered 1946 to USSR and renamed *Tsel* in Soviet service.

Preussen launched 30 Oct 1903, commissioned into fleet 12 Jul 1905. Used for sound defence 1916; reduced to a tender at Wilhelmshaven 1917; parent ship for F-boats from 1919 in the Reichsmarine. Stricken 5 Apr 1929, sold 25 Feb 1931 for 216,800M, broken up 1931 at Wilhelmshaven. A 63m long midship section was retained as an explosive target for torpedoes, mines, etc (nicknamed SMS *Vierkant* – SMS Rectangle) at Wilhelmshaven. Bombed and sunk Apr 1945; raised late 1954, broken up.

Lothringen launched 27 May 1904, commissioned into fleet 18 May 1906. Used for sound defence 1916; exercise ship and engineer training ship at Wilhelmshaven 1917; parent ship for F-boats 1919; fleet duties 1922–26 in the Reichsmarine. Stricken 31 Mar 1931, hull less armour sold for 269,650M to Berlin, broken up 1931 by Blohm & Voss, Hamburg.

Deutschland class

Construction

Laid down as ships of the line N, P, O, R and Q (official design for *Deutschland* 1901–02, otherwise 1902–03). Transverse and longitudinal frame steel construction (twelve watertight compartments, except *Pommern* thirteen watertight compartments, double bottom 84 percent). Krupp armour: deck 40mm; slopes 97–67–97mm, CT from roof 80mm, sides 300mm to roof 30mm, sides 140mm; CWL 0–100–240 (shields 170mm)–100mm on 80mm teak; casemate 170mm, citadel 170mm, turrets roof 50mm, sides 280mm; shields 70mm. *Deutschland* CWL max 225/150mm, casemate 160mm, citadel 160mm. All ships had cork cofferdams. Depth 12.84m. Immersion increased by 1cm per 21.18t. Trim moment 14,800m-t.

Propulsion

Engines, etc, as *Braunschweig*. Twelve Marine-type boilers (twenty-four fireboxes, 15 atmospheres forced, 4600–4670sq m) in 1 + 1 + 1 boiler rooms. *Deutschland* boilers as *Braunschweig*. [Supplementary oil firing fitted on *Schlesien* and *Schleswig-Holstein* after winter 1915; eight Marine-type oil-fired boilers were substituted for the same number of coal-fired boilers. After 1938–39 *Schlesien* had no coal-fired boilers, and her forward boiler room was converted to a cadet barracks and instruction room.] Four turbo-generators, 260kW 110V. One rudder.

Armament

Four 27cm/40 QF guns (340 rounds), –4° +30°, range 18,800m; fourteen 17cm/40 QF guns (1820 rounds), range 14,500m; twenty 8.8cm/35 QF guns (2800 rounds); four machine guns temporarily fitted; six

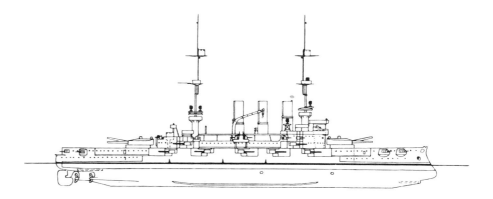

Schlesien (1910), *Deutschland, Hannover, Pommern, Schleswig-Holstein*

Name	Builder	Built	Cost in Marks (000s)	Displacement (t = tonnes T = tons)	Length (m)	Breadth (m)	Draught (m)	Power (hp)	Revs (rpm)	Speed (kts)	Range (nm/kts)	Coal (t)	Oil (t)
DEUTSCHLAND sq fl	Germania Dockyard, Kiel Construction no 109	1903–06	24,481	14,218t max 13,191t des	127.6 oa 125.9 cwl	22.2	8.21 fwd 8.25 aft	16,990ihp max 16,000ihp des	111 max 115 des	18.6 max 18.0 des	4800/10	1540 max 700 des	240*
HANNOVER sq fl	Imperial Dockyard, Wilhelmshaven Construction no 28 mod: Naval Dockyard, Wilhelmshaven	1904–07 1920–21 1929–30	24,253	,,	,,	,,	,,	17,768ihp max 17,000ihp des	114 max 115 des	18.5 max 18.0 des	,,	1750 max 850 des	200*
POMMERN	AG Vulcan, Stettin Construction no 262	1904–07	24,624	,,	,,	,,	,,	17,696ihp max 17,000ihp des	118 max 115 des	18.7 max 18.0 des	,,	,,	,,
SCHLESIEN sq fl 1927	F Schichau, Danzig Construction no 751 mod: Naval Dockyard, Wilhelmshaven mod: KM Dockyard, Wilhelmshaven	1904–08 1926–27 1935	24,920	,,	,,	,,	,,	18,923ihp max 17,000ihp des	119 max 115 des	18.5 max 18.0 des	,, 4000/12**	1380 max	180 max
SCHLESWIG-HOLSTEIN sq fl 1926	Germania Dockyard, Kiel Construction no 113 mod: Naval Dockyard, Wilhelmshaven mod: KM Dockyard, Wilhelmshaven	1905–08 1925–26 1930–31 1936	24,972	,,	,,	,,	,,	19,330ihp max 17,000ihp des 16,000ihp des**	122 max 115 des 112 max	19.1 max 18.0 des 17.0 des	4800/10 5600/12	1750 max 850 des 1340 max 436 max	200* 225 max 1130 max

8048gt/4145nt; after refit 8291gt/4409nt

* tar oil only 1908–9
** data after second refit

45cm TT (16 rounds), one port stern, four lateral, one bow, all under water. [*Deutschland* was disarmed in 1916. In 1918 *Schleswig-Holstein* only was fitted with six 10.5cm/45 Utof guns and four 8.8cm/30 QF guns. In the Reichsmarine *Hannover*, *Schlesien* and *Schleswig-Holstein* carried four 28cm/40 QF guns; *Hannover* fourteen 17cm/40 QF guns, *Schlesien* and *Schleswig-Holstein* fourteen (twelve after 1931, ten after 1935–37, none after 1939) 15cm/45 QF guns; four 8.8cm/45 QF guns until 1931 (*Schlesien* was fitted, 1927–30, with two 8.8cm/45 AA guns only), and, in their place after 1937, six 10.5cm AA guns (1800 rounds); *Schlesien* and *Schleswig-Holstein* were fitted after 1936 with four 3.7cm AA guns and four 2cm AA guns, some in multiples, and after 1944 with ten 4cm Bofors AA guns and twenty-two 2cm AA quadruples and twins; until 1936 four 50cm TT were swivel mounted on the battery deck forward and aft but *Hannover* carried no torpedoes 1921–27, and one 50cm TT forward on each beam on the battery deck 1930–31.]

Handling

Somewhat worse seakeeping qualities than *Braunschweig*. [Even cranker, but less marked weather helm.] Transverse metacentric height 0.98m, longitudinal 130m (*Deutschland* 0.90m and 127m). Maximum stability moment at 31°, = zero at 70°.

Complement

Crew as *Braunschweig* [as a training ship after 1935 *Schlesien*'s crew was 29/559 plus 214 cadets, *Schleswig-Holstein*'s 31/565 plus 175 cadets]. Boats: two picket boats, [one admiral's barge], two launches, one pinnace [removed], two cutters, two yawls, two [one] dinghies.

Notes

Colour scheme no 9. *Deutschland*'s davits are shown in the supplementary drawing. The aft superstructure on *Deutschland* and *Hannover*, with two enclosed decks and the aft conning tower above, are shown in the drawing. The forward conning tower on *Deutschland* and *Pommern* is shown in the supplementary drawing. Searchlights were fitted on *Deutschland* as on *Braunschweig* until 1909, and similarly on the other ships, but one on the roof of the mainmast battle top in place of one at the mainmast head. [After 1909 searchlights were fitted as in the drawing (*Pommern* as in the supplementary drawing of *Deutschland*).] Funnels

	Fuel consumption on test (12–18kn)	Range at cruise speed (average values from extended observation period)
Deutschland	0800 to 0.845kg per hp/hr	4850nm/10kts
Hannover	0.825 to 0.944kg per hp/hr	4520nm/10kts
Pommern	0.723 to 0.789kg per hp/hr	5830nm/10kts
Schlesien	0.794 to 0.836kg per hp/hr	4770nm/10kts
Schleswig-Holstein	0.737 to 0.814kg per hp/hr	5720nm/10kts

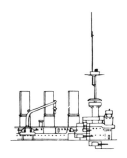

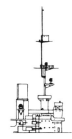

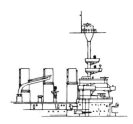

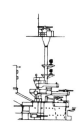

Deutschland until 1909;
Pommern's bridge was similar.

Deutschland after 1911; *Schleswig-Holstein*'s forward funnel was identical.

Schleswig-Holstein
after 1926

Schlesien after 1927

1908–36 are shown in the drawings and supplementary drawings. [All ships after 1912–14 had an enclosed spotting top on all topgallant crosstrees. *Schlesien*'s aft superstructure after 1927 was as the main drawing, her forward superstructure as the supplementary drawing, and she had no forward sponsons; those on *Schleswig-Holstein* were removed in 1936.] *Hannover* was appropriately known as *Qualmpott* – Smoke Pot – because of her coal consumption. Differences between *Schleswig-Holstein* (SX), *Schlesien* (SN) and *Hannover* (HA) during the Reich and war periods are shown below:

Mainmast
SX   tubular mast with with non-extended foretop at all times
SN   tubular mast with extended foretop at all times
HA   Feb 1921 to Mar 1927 (first service period) pole mast with spotting top; Feb 1930 to Sept 1931 (second service period) pole mast as SN

Funnels
SX   initially three separate funnels, after 1928 the two forward funnels were trunked
SN   initially two forward funnels trunked; after 1938 two separate funnels (the forward funnel wider)
HA   three separate funnels at all times

Bow sponsons
SN   none
SX   none after 1936
HA   none after 1930

Career

Deutschland launched 20 Nov 1904, commissioned into fleet 3 Aug 1906. Fleet flagship 1910–13; reduced to barrack ship at Wilhelmshaven Oct 1917. Stricken 25 Jan 1920, broken up 1920–22 at Wilhelmshaven. Bow ornament now in the Eckernförde underwater weapons school, bell now in the Mausoleum of Prince Heinrich, Hemmelmark.

Hannover launched 29 Sept 1905, commissioned into fleet 1 Oct 1907. Used for sound defence 1917; served in Reichsmarine 1921–31. Stricken 1935, target hulk and subject of experiments on effects of ground mines; reconstruction was planned as a remote controlled target ship for aircraft, but not carried out. Broken up May 1944 to October 1946 at Bremerhaven. Bell now in Dresden army museum.

Pommern launched 2 Dec 1905, commissioned into fleet 6 Aug 1907. Sunk 1 Jun 1916 at 0313hrs in the North Sea, position 55° 40N, 06° 35E, by a torpedo from a British 12th flotilla destroyer, 839 dead. Wreck partially broken up after 1957 (armour and non-ferrous

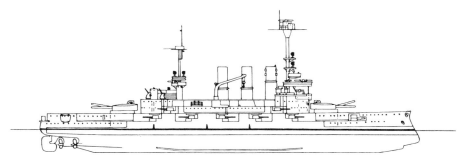

Hannover (1931); *Schleswig-Holstein* was very similar for a short period.

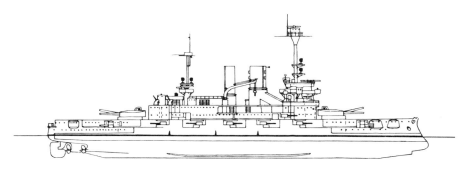

Schleswig-Holstein (1932); *Schlesien* was very similar.

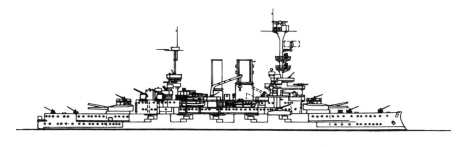

Schlesien (1945); *Schleswig-Holstein* was similar.

material removed). Bow ornament now at Laboe naval memorial.

Schlesien launched 28 May 1906, commissioned into fleet 5 May 1908. Reduced to exercise ship at Kiel and barrack ship 1917; sea cadet training ship 1918; this service continued under the Reichsmarine and the Kriegsmarine. Scuttled 4 May 1945 after being mined on 3 May and bombed by aircraft in the vicinity of Swinemünde, then torpedoed by *T36*. Broken up 1949–70 by an East German company. Her remains were still extant in 1970.

Schleswig-Holstein launched 17 Dec 1906, commissioned into fleet 6 Jul 1908. Tender at Bremerhaven 1917; barrack ship at Kiel 1918; served in Reichsmarine and Kriegsmarine, being converted after 1936 to a sea cadet training ship. Reconstruction as a remote controlled target ship was planned for 1939. Sunk 18 Dec 1944 at Gotenhafen, after being bombed by British aircraft, and finally scuttled 21 Mar 1945. Raised 1945–46, transferred to Kronstadt, and used for a short time as a training hulk (possibly under the name *Borodino*); broken up at Tallinn. Bell now in Dresden army museum.

Battleships 1909–1918

Nassau class

Name	Builder	Built	Cost in Marks (000s)	Displacement (t = tonnes T = tons)	Length (m)	Breadth (m)	Draught (m)	Power (hp)	Revs (rpm)	Speed (kts)	Range (nm/kts)	Coal (t)	Oil (t)
NASSAU	Imperial Dockyard Wilhelmshaven Construction no 30	1907–9	37,399	20,535t max 18,873t des	146.1 oa 145.6 cwl	26.9*	8.57 fwd 8.76 aft	26,244ihp max 22,000ihp des	124	20.0 max 19.0 des	(9400/10) (8300/12) (4700/16) (2800/19)	2700 max 950 des	160 mod
WESTFALEN sq fl	AG 'Weser', Bremen Construction no 163	1907–09	37,615	,,	,,	,,	,,	26,792ihp max 22,000ihp des	121	20.2 max 19.0 des	,,	,,	,,
RHEINLAND	AG Vulcan, Stettin Construction no 287	1907–10	36,916	,,	,,	,,	,,	27,498ihp max 22,000ihp des	123	20.0 max 19.0 des	,,	,,	,,
POSEN 2nd fl	Germania Dockyard, Kiel Construction no 132	1907–10	36,920	,,	,,	,,	,,	28,117ihp max 22,000ihp des	123	20.0 max 19.0 des	,,	,,	,,
10,351gt/6379gt													

* without torpedo nets

Construction

Laid down as ships of the line *Ersatz Bayern, Ersatz Sachsen, Ersatz Württemberg, Ersatz Baden* (official design, 1905–06). Transverse and longitudinal frame steel construction (nineteen watertight compartments, *Nassau* sixteen, double bottom 88 percent). Krupp armour: deck 55mm–80mm; torpedo bulkhead 30mm; forward CT roof 80mm, sides 400mm, aft roof 50mm, sides 200mm; belt 0–90–300–80mm and 0–120–170–100mm; turrets roof 90mm, sides 280mm; casemate 160mm (shields 80mm). Depth 13.25m. Immersion increased by 1cm per 28.92t. Trim moment 24,000m-t.

Propulsion

Three vertical 3-cylinder triple expansion engines (three 3-bladed screws, 5.0m diameter) in three engine

	Fuel consumption on trial (approx 19.5kts)	Distance
Nassau	0.801kg per hp/hr	8100nm/10kts
Westfalen	0.797kg per hp/hr	8380nm/10kts
Rheinland	0.765kg per hp/hr	8380nm/10kts
Posen	0.765kg per hp/hr	9400nm/10kts

rooms. Twelve Marine-type boilers [supplementary oil firing fitted after winter 1915, and hollow grates 1916–17] (twenty-four fireboxes, 16 atmospheres forced, 5040–5076sq m) in 1 + 1 + 1 boiler rooms. Eight turbo-generators, 1280kW 225V. Two rudders.

Armament

Twelve 28cm/45 QF guns (900 rounds), –6° +20°, range 18,900m [20,400m]; twelve 15cm/45 QF guns (1800 rounds), range 13,500m [16,800m after 1915]; sixteen 8.8cm/45 QF guns (2400 rounds) [after 1915, two AA plus fourteen QF guns; after 1916–17, two AA guns]; six 45cm TT (16 rounds), one stern, four lateral, one bow, all under water.

Handling

Indifferent sea-boats, very stiff and with weather helm, but manoeuvrable and with a tight turning circle. Slight speed loss in swell, up to 70 percent with hard rudder; [speed loss due to roll keels (fitted to counter excessive roll as completed) almost 0.8kts. Transverse metacentric height 2.33m, longitudinal 176m, *Nassau* 174m. Maximum stability moment at 33°, = zero at 64°, *Nassau* 62°.

Complement

Crew: 40/968 (plus 13/66 as squadron flagship, 2/23 as second command flagship). Boats: one picket boat, three admiral's barges, two launches, two cutters, two dinghies.

Notes

Colour scheme no 9. The differences in davits and rigging are shown in the supplementary drawings. Recesses for 8.8cm QF guns in the bow and forward superstructure were located differently. [The foremast spotting top was fitted in wartime only. After 1915 the aft compass platform was removed.] Torpedo nets were carried until 1916. [All guns etc were removed from *Rheinland* after stranding.] The foremast was originally intended to be aft of the forward funnel, but this was never implemented.

Career

Nassau launched 7 Mar 1908, commissioned into fleet 1 Oct 1909. Stricken 5 Nov 1919, surrendered as *B*; Japanese prize 7 Apr 1920, sold Jun 1920 to a British company; broken up at Dordrecht.

Westfalen launched 1 Jul 1908, commissioned into

fleet 16 Nov 1909. Used as an artillery training ship after 1 Sept 1918. Surrendered as *D* 5 Aug 1920, British prize; broken up 1924 at Birkenhead.

Rheinland launched 26 Sept 1908, commissioned into fleet 30 Apr 1910. Ran aground in fog at 0730hrs on 11 Apr 1918, in the Ålandsee close to Lagskär, position 59° 51N, 19° 55E, two dead; refloated 9 Jul 1918, after major lightening, but repairs were not undertaken, and she was used as a barrack ship at Kiel. Stricken 5 Nov 1919; sold by allied powers 28 Jun 1920, as *F*, to Dordrecht as a prize; towed there 29 Jul 1928, broken up by 1921 at Dordrecht. Bow ornament now in Dresden army museum.

Posen launched 12 Dec 1908, commissioned into fleet 31 May 1910. Stricken 5 Nov 1919, surrendered as *G*; taken as a British prize 13 May 1920, broken up 1922 at Dordrecht.

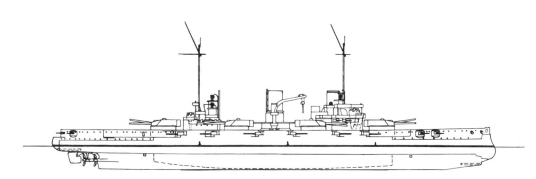

Nassau (1909), *Westfalen, Rheinland, Posen*

Mainmast		Foremast	
Nassau and *Westfalen* after 1911 and 1915	*Rheinland* and *Posen* at all times	*Nassau* and *Westfalen* after 1911 and 1915	*Rheinland* and *Posen* before and after 1915

Helgoland class

Name	Builder	Built	Cost in Marks (000s)	Displacement (t = tonnes T = tons)	Length (m)	Breadth (m)	Draught (m)	Power (hp)	Revs (rpm)	Speed (kts)	Range (nm/kts)	Coal (t)	Oil (t)
HELGOLAND	Howaldtswerke, Kiel Construction no 500	1908–11	46,196	24,700t max 22,808t des	167.2 oa 166.5 cwl	28.5*	8.68 fwd 8.94 aft	31,258ihp max 28,000ihp des	125	20.8 max 20.5 des	5500/10	3200 max 900 des	197 mod
OSTFRIESLAND sq fl	Imperial Dockyard, Wilhelmshaven Construction no 31	1908–11	43,579	,,	,,	,,	,,	35,500ihp max 28,000ihp des	126	21.2 max 20.5 des	,,	,,	,,
THÜRINGEN	AG 'Weser', Bremen Construction no 166	1908–11	46,314	,,	,,	,,	,,	34,944ihp max 28,000ihp des	117	21.0 max 20.5 des	,,	,,	,,
OLDENBURG 12,915gt/7965nt	F Schichau, Danzig Construction no 828	1909–12	45,801	,,	,,	,,	,,	34,394ihp max 28,000ihp des	120	21.3 max 20.5 des	,,	,,	,,

* without torpedo nets

Construction

Laid down as ships of the line *Ersatz Siegfried, Ersatz Oldenburg, Ersatz Beowulf* and *Ersatz Frithjof* (official design, 1907–08). Transverse and longitudinal frame steel construction (seventeen watertight compartments, double bottom 86 percent). Krupp armour: deck 55–80mm; torpedo bulkhead 30mm; forward CT roof 200mm, sides 400mm; aft roof 50mm, sides 200mm; CWL 0–120–300–120mm and 0–100–170–120mm;

turrets roof 100mm, sides 300mm; casemate 170mm (shields 80mm). Depth 13.38m. Immersion increased by 1cm per 34.08t. Trim moment 30,000m-t.

Propulsion

Three vertical 4-cylinder triple expansion engines (three 4-bladed screws, 5.1m diameter) in three engine rooms. Fifteen Marine-type boilers [supplementary oil firing fitted winter 1915, hollow grates 1916–17]

(thirty fireboxes, 16 atmospheres forced, 6480sq m) in 1 + 1 + 1 boiler rooms. Eight turbo-generators, 2,000kW 225V. Two rudders.

Armament

Twelve 30.5cm/50 QF guns (1020 rounds), −8° +13.5°, range 18,000m [−5.5° +16°, range 20,400m]; fourteen 15cm/45 QF guns (2100 rounds), range 13,500m [16,800m after 1915]; fourteen 8.8cm/45 QF guns

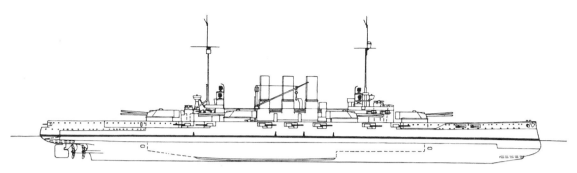

Ostfriesland (1914), *Helgoland, Thüringen, Oldenburg*

(2800 rounds) [two AA plus twelve QF guns after 1914, two AA guns after 1916–17]; six 50cm TT (16 rounds), one stern, four lateral, one bow, all under water.

Handling

Good sea-boats, but stiff and with weather helm. Responsive, with a small turning circle and slight speed loss in swell (speed loss up to 54 percent with hard rudder, heel up to 7°). Transverse metacentric height 2.60m, longitudinal 200m. Maximum stability moment at 21°, = zero at 63°.

Complement

Crew: 42/1071 (plus 13/66 as squadron flagship). Boats: one picket boat, three admiral's barges, two launches, two yawls, two dinghies.

Notes

Colour scheme no 9. Funnel height 18.5m, [*Oldenburg* 21.5m, *Thüringen* 20m after 1913, *Helgoland* and *Ostfriesland* 20m after 1915 and 1917]. Galley outlet pipes and 8.8cm QF gun recesses in the bow and forward superstructure in various configurations. An admiral's bridge was fitted on *Ostfriesland* only. [Foremast spotting top fitted in wartime only. Aft compass platform removed 1915.] Torpedo nets fitted up to 1916.

Career

Helgoland launched 25 Sept 1909, commissioned into fleet 23 Aug 1911. Stricken 5 Nov 1919, surrendered as *K*, 5 Aug 1920 (British prize). Broken up 3 Mar 1921 at Morecambe, after various experiments. Bow coat of arms now in Dresden army museum.

Ostfriesland launched 30 Sept 1909, commissioned into fleet 1 Aug 1911. Stricken 5 Nov 1919, surrendered as *H*, 7 Apr 1920 (US prize). Sunk 1240hrs on 21 Jul 1921 off Cape Henry (Virginia), after experiments, by two very heavy aircraft bombs.

Thüringen launched 27 Nov 1909, commissioned into fleet 10 Sept 1911. Stricken 5 Nov 1919, surrendered as *L*, 29 Apr 1920, at Cherbourg (French prize). Target ship for the French fleet, broken up 1923–33 at Gavres-Lorient.

Oldenburg launched 30 Jun 1910, commissioned into fleet 1 May 1912. Stricken 5 Nov 1919, surrendered as *M*, 13 May 1920 (Japanese prize). Sold Jun 1920 to a British firm, broken up 1921 at Dordrecht.

Kaiser class

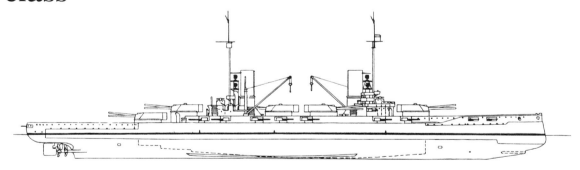

Kaiser (1914), *Friedrich der Grosse, Kaiserin, Prinzregent Luitpold, König Albert*

Prinzregent Luitpold aft superstructure

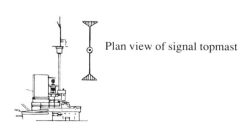

Plan view of signal topmast

Friedrich der Grosse, 1914–18

Kaiser Friedrich der Grosse foremast after 1918

Name	Builder	Built	Cost in Marks (000s)	Displacement (t = tonnes T = tons)	Length (m)	Breadth (m)	Draught (m)	Power (hp)	Revs (rpm)	Speed (kts)	Range (nm/kts)	Coal (t)	Oil (t)
KAISER sq fl	Imperial Dockyard, Kiel Construction no 35	1909–12	44,997	27,000t max 24,724t des	172.4 oa 171.8 cwl	29.0*	9.10 fwd 8.80 aft	55,187shp max 28,000shp des	270 max 270 des	23.4 max 21.0 des	(7900/12) (3900/18) (2400/21)	3600 max 1000 des	200 max
FRIEDRICH DER GROSSE sq fl	AG Vulcan, Hamburg Construction no 310	1910–12	45,802	,,	,,	,,	,,	42,181shp max 28,000shp des	272 max 270 des	22.4 max 21.0 des	,,	,,	,,
KAISERIN	Howaldtswerke, Kiel Construction no 530	1910–13	45,173	,,	,,	,,	,,	41,533shp max 28,000shp des	268 max 270 des	22.1 max 21.0 des	,,	,,	,,
KÖNIG ALBERT	F Schichau, Danzig Construction no 857	1910–13	45,761	,,	,,	,,	,,	39,813shp max 28,000shp des	262 max 270 des	22.1 max 21.0 des	,,	,,	,,
PRINZREGENT LUITPOLD sq fl	Germania Dockyard, Kiel Construction no 167	1910–13	46,374	,,	,,	,,	,,	38,751shp max 26,000shp des +12,000 shp des	272 max 150 des	21.7 max 20.0 des 12.0 des	(7200/12 with diesel; 2000/12 without)	3200 max 750 des	fuel 400 max diesel 100 des
13,629gt/8058nt													

* without torpedo nets

Construction

Laid down as ships of the line *Ersatz Hildebrand, Ersatz Heimdall, Ersatz Hagen, Ersatz Ägir* and *Ersatz Odin*, (official design, 1907–09). Transverse and longitudinal frame steel construction (seventeen watertight compartments, double bottom 88 percent). Krupp armour: deck 60mm to 100mm; torpedo bulkhead 40mm; forward CT roof 150mm, sides 400mm, aft roof 50mm, sides 200mm; CWL 0–180–350–120mm and 0–130–180–120mm; turrets roof 220mm, sides 300mm; casemate 170mm (shields 80mm). Depth 12.18m and 14.40m, immersion increased by 1cm per 36t. Trim moment 34,000m-t.

Propulsion

Kaiser and *Kaiserin*, three sets of Parsons turbines; *Friedrich der Grosse*, three sets of AEG Curtis turbines; *König Albert*, three sets of Schichau turbines (all three 3- bladed screws, 3.75m diameter) in 3 + 3 engine rooms. Sixteen Marine-type boilers for supplementary oil firing (thirty fireboxes, 16 atmospheres forced, 7170–6950sq m). *Prinzregent Luitpold*, two sets of Parsons turbines (two 3-bladed screws, 4.0m diameter) and one Germania 6-cylinder 2-stroke diesel (one 3-bladed screw, 3.75m diameter) in three engine rooms. This large diesel was not yet ready for operational use, and therefore was not installed: the central engine room and shaft were empty. Fourteen Marine-type boilers for supplementary oil firing (twenty-eight fireboxes, 16 atmospheres forced, 5950sq m). On all five ships these were arranged in 3 + 1 + 0 + 3 + 3 boiler rooms [hollow grates fitted to boilers 1916–17]. Four double turbo-generators, two diesel generators, 1800kW 225V. Two rudders.

Armament

Ten 10.5cm/50 QF guns (860 rounds), –8° +13.5°, range 16,200m [–5.5° +16°, range 20,400m]; fourteen 15cm/45 QF guns (2240 rounds), range 13,500m [16,800m after 1915]; eight 8.8cm/45 QF guns [deleted] and four [two] 8.8cm/45 AA guns (2800 rounds); five 50cm TT (19 and 20 rounds), four lateral, one bow, all under water.

Handling

Very good sea-boats, very stiff and with slight weather helm. Speed loss in swell slight; responsive to helm, with fast initial turn but severe torque effects and speed loss with hard rudder up to 66 percent, 8° heel. Transverse metacentric height 2.59m, longitudinal 203m. Maximum stability moment at 28°, = zero at 62°.

Complement

Crew: 41/1043 (plus 14/80 as squadron flagship, 2/23 as second command flagship). Boats: one picket boat, three admiral's barges, two launches, two yawls, two dinghies.

Notes

Colour scheme no 9. On *Friedrich der Grosse* the aft upper bridge was taller and much wider until 1914, and used as a signal and parade bridge [after late 1914 the forward funnel step was 1m higher, and the forward bridge and mast were as shown in the supplementary drawing. The lower foremast platform was nicknamed *Scheers Ruh* – Scheer's Peace.] *Prinzregent Luitpold*'s aft superstructure, etc, were as shown in the supplementary drawing, and her forward funnel step was always 1m higher. *König Albert* carried lateral steam pipes on both funnels. The yards on *Friedrich der Grosse* were as shown in the supplementary drawing at all times [on the other ships after 1915 the foremast yard only was of this type. *Kaiser* and *Friedrich der Grosse* were fitted with a thicker foremast after 1918, as on *König*.] All ships carried torpedo nets until 1916.

Career

Kaiser launched 22 Mar 1911, commissioned into fleet 1 Aug 1912; served abroad until 1914.* Interned at Scapa Flow 25 Nov 1918; scuttled and sunk at 1325hrs on 21 Jun 1919. Raised 20 Mar 1929, broken up by 1930 at Rosyth.

Friedrich der Grosse launched 10 Jun 1911, commissioned as fleet flagship 15 Oct 1912 until 13 Mar 1917. Interned at Scapa Flow 25 Nov 1918; capsized and sank after being scuttled at 1216hrs on 21 Jun 1919. Broken up at Scapa Flow from 1936 to 29 Apr 1937. Her ship's bell was returned to Germany on 30 Aug 1965, and is now in the Fleet Headquarters at Glücksburg-Meierwik.

Kaiserin launched 11 Nov 1911, commissioned into fleet 14 May 1913. Interned at Scapa Flow 25 Nov 1918; capsized and sank after being scuttled at 1400hrs on 21 Jun 1919. Raised 14 May 1936, broken up 1936 at Rosyth.

Prinzregent Luitpold launched 17 Feb 1912, commissioned into fleet 19 Aug 1913. Interned at Scapa Flow 25 Nov 1918; capsized and sank after being scuttled at 1330hrs on 21 Jun 1919. Raised 9 Jul 1931, broken up 1933 at Rosyth.

König Albert launched 27 Apr 1912, commissioned into fleet 31 Jul 1913; served abroad until 1914.* Interned at Scapa Flow 25 Nov 1918; capsized and sank after being scuttled at 1254hrs on 21 Jun 1919. Raised 31 Jul 1935, broken up 1936 at Rosyth.

* These ships participated in the first major trial overseas of a detached division, to South America and South Africa in 1913–14, with the light cruiser *Strassburg*. This exercise had the dual purpose of representation and testing the operational reliability of the turbine installations on large ships.

König class

Name	Builder	Built	Cost in Marks (000s)	Displacement (t = tonnes T = tons)	Length (m)	Breadth (m)	Draught (m)	Power (hp)	Revs (rpm)	Speed (kts)	Range (nm/kts)	Coal (t)	Oil (t)
KÖNIG sq fl Imperial Dockyard, Wihelmshaven Construction no 33	Imperial Dockyard, Wihelmshaven Construction no 33	1911–14	45,000	28,600t max 25,796t des	175.4 oa 174.7 cwl	19.5*	9.19 fwd 9.00 aft	43,300shp max 31,000shp des	251	21.0 max 21.0 des	(8000/12) (4000/18)	3000 max 850 des	600 max 150 des
GROSSER KURFÜRST	AG Vulcan, Hamburg Construction no 4	1911–14	,,	,,	,,	,,	,,	45,100shp max 31,000shp des	254	21.2 max 21.0 des	,,	,,	,,
MARKGRAF sq fl	AG 'Weser', Bremen Construction no 186	1911–14	,,	,,	,,	,,	,,	41,400shp max 31,000shp des	251	21.0 max 21.0 des	,,	,,	,,
KRONPRINZ (WILHELM) 14,630gt/8475nt	Germania Dockyard, Kiel Construction no 182	1912–14	,,	,,	,,	,,	,,	46,200shp max 31,000shp des	256	21.3 max 21.0 des	,,	,,	,,

* without torpedo nets

Construction

Laid down as ships of the line *S*, *Ersatz Kurfürst Friedrich Wilhelm*, *Ersatz Weissenburg* and *Ersatz Brandenburg* (official design, 1909–10). Transverse and longitudinal frame steel construction (eighteen watertight compartments, double bottom 88 percent). Krupp armour: deck 60–100mm; torpedo bulkhead 40mm; forward CT roof 150mm, sides 300mm, aft roof 50mm, sides 200mm; CWL 0–180–350–120mm and 0–130–180–120mm; turrets roof 110mm, sides 300mm; casemate 170mm (shields 80mm). Depth 12.18m and 14.40m, immersion increased by 1cm per 36t. Trim moment 34,000m-t.

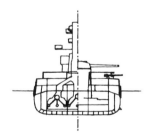

König (1918) midship section

Kronprinz Wilhelm foremast before and after 1918

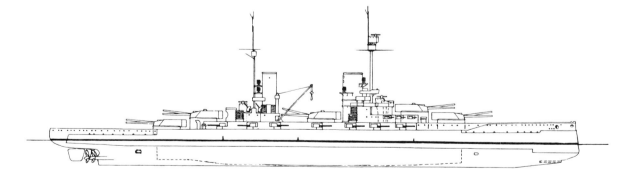

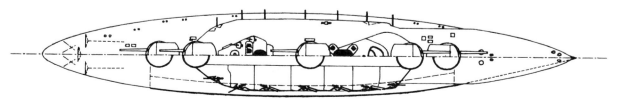

König (1918), *Markgraf*, *Grosser Kurfürst* and *Kronprinz Wilhelm* were very similar.

Propulsion

Three sets of Parsons / AEG Vulcan / Bergmann / Parsons turbines (three 3-bladed screws, 3.8m diameter) in 3 + 3 engine rooms. Three oil-fired Marine-type boilers, twelve Marine-type boilers [hollow grates fitted 1916–17] (three plus twenty-four fireboxes, 16 atmospheres forced, 7420–7550sq m) in 3 + 0 + 3 + 3 boiler rooms. Four turbo-generators, two diesel generators, 2040kW 225V. Two rudders. In 1911 all four ships were to be fitted with one MAN 6-cylinder 2-stroke large diesel as the central engine; this was fitted later, and only to *Grosser Kurfürst* and *Markgraf*. Its specification was: 12,000shp, 150rpm, 12kts, price 1815 million M (one 3-bladed screw, 4.8m diameter).

Armament

Ten 30.5cm/45 QF guns (900 rounds) etc, as *Kaiser*; fourteen 15cm/45 QF guns (2240 rounds), range 13,500m [16,800m after 1915]; six 8.8cm/45 QF guns [removed]; four [two] 8.8cm/45 AA guns (2500 rounds); five 50cm TT (16 rounds), four lateral, one bow, all under water.

Handling

Very good sea-boats, with easy motion, but with severe weather helm. Slight speed loss in swell, speed loss with hard rudder up to 66 percent at 8° heel. Transverse metacentric height 2.59m, longitudinal 203m. Maximum stability moment at 28°, = zero at 62°.

Complement

Crew: 41/1095 (plus 14/68 as squadron flagship, 2/24 as second command flagship). Boats: one picket boat, three barges, two launches, two yawls, two dinghies.

Notes

Colour scheme no 9. *König*, *Grosser Kurfürst* and *Markgraf* were fitted with a foremast as on *Kaiser* until 1917 (though *König* had directors on the foremast) [later as shown in the drawing]. An upper Admiral's bridge was fitted on *König* and [after 1917] *Markgraf* only. [*Grosser Kurfürst* had a temporary straight (emergency) stem fitted after damage from 1917 to 1918.] *Kronprinz Wilhelm* was fitted with a thick foremast after commissioning, and a director as shown in the supplementary drawing. All ships carried torpedo nets until 1916.

Career

König launched 1 Mar 1913, commissioned into fleet 9 Aug 1914. Interned at Scapa Flow 6 Dec 1918; scuttled and sunk at 1400hrs on 21 Jun 1919. Not raised; wreck sold to Britain in 1962.

Grosser Kurfürst launched 5 May 1913, commissioned into fleet 30 Jul 1914. Interned at Scapa Flow 26 Nov 1918; scuttled and sunk at 1330hrs on 21 Jun 1919. Raised 29 Apr 1938, broken up at Rosyth.

Markgraf launched 4 Jun 1913, commissioned into fleet 1 Oct 1914. Interned at Scapa Flow 26 Nov 1918; scuttled and sunk at 1645hrs on 21 Jun 1919. Not raised; wreck sold to Britain in 1962.

Kronprinz launched 21 Feb 1914, commissioned into fleet 8 Nov 1914; renamed *Kronprinz Wilhelm* 15 Jun 1918 (30th anniversary of the Imperial government). Interned at Scapa Flow 26 Nov 1918; scuttled and sunk at 1315hrs on 21 Jun 1919. Not raised; wreck sold to Britain in 1962.

Bayern class

Name	Builder	Built	Cost in Marks (000s)	Displacement (t = tonnes T = tons)	Length (m)	Breadth (m)	Draught (m)	Power (hp)	Revs (rpm)	Speed (kts)	Range (nm/kts)	Coal (t)	Oil (t)
BAYERN	Howaldtswerke, Kiel Construction no 590	1914–16	49,000–50,000	32,200t max 28,530t des	180.0 oa 179.4 cwl	30.0*	9.39 fwd 9.31 aft	55,967shp max 35,000shp des	263 max 265 des	22.0 max 22.0 des	5000/12 4485/15 3740/17	3400 max 900 des	620 max 200 des
BADEN sq fl	F Schichau Danzig Construction no 913	1913–16	,,	,,	,,	,,	,,	56,275shp max 35,000shp des	265 max 265 des	21.0 max 22.0 des	2390/21.5	,,	,,
WÜRTTEMBERG	AG Vulcan, Hamburg Construction no 19	1915–	,,	32,500t max 28,800t des	182.4 oa 181.8 cwl	30.0	9.40 fwd 9.30 aft	48,000shp des	265 des	22.0 des		3100 max 750 des	900 max 360 des
SACHSEN 15,929gt/9550nt	Germania Dockyard, Kiel Construction no 210	1914–	,,	,,	,,	,,	,,	54,000shp des	265 des	22.25 des	2000/12 des**	2700 max 500 des	1300 max 400 des

* without torpedo nets
** diesel engines only

Construction

Laid down as ships of the line *T*, *Ersatz Wörth*, *Ersatz Kaiser Wilhelm II* and *Ersatz Kaiser Friedrich III*, (official design, 1910–1912, design chief Mar. Brt. Paech). Transverse and longitudinal frame steel construction (seventeen watertight compartments, double bottom 88 percent). Krupp armour: deck 60–100mm; torpedo bulkhead 50mm; forward CT roof 170mm, sides 400mm, aft roof 80mm, sides 170mm; belt 0–170–350–200mm and 0–170–250mm; turrets roof 200mm, sides 350mm; casemates 170mm (shields 80mm). Depth 14.8m, immersion increased by 1cm per 38.7t. Trim moment 37,760m-t.

Propulsion

Three sets of Parsons (?) / Schichau / AEG-Vulcan turbines, or two sets of Parsons (?) turbines plus one MAN 6-cylinder 2-stroke diesel (three 3-bladed screws, 3.87m diameter) in 3 + 3 engine rooms. Eleven Marine-type boilers (*Württemberg* nine, *Sachsen* six) fitted with hollow grates 1916–17, and three oil-fired Marine-type boilers (twenty-two plus three fireboxes, 16 atmospheres forced, 7660sq m – for *Bayern* and *Baden*) in 3 + 0 + 3 + 3 boiler rooms. Eight diesel generators, 2400kW 220V. Two rudders. Average fuel consumption 0.531kg per hp/hr, steam consumption 7.5kg. The generator diesel engines from *Sachsen* were installed in *U151*, *U-Bremen*, *U156* and *U157*, see also *Ersatz Gneisenau*, page 31.

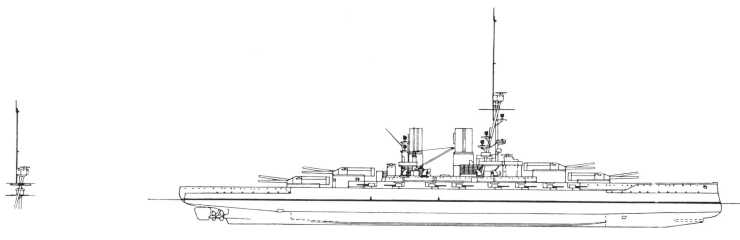

Baden, first form

Bayern (1916); *Baden* was very similar.

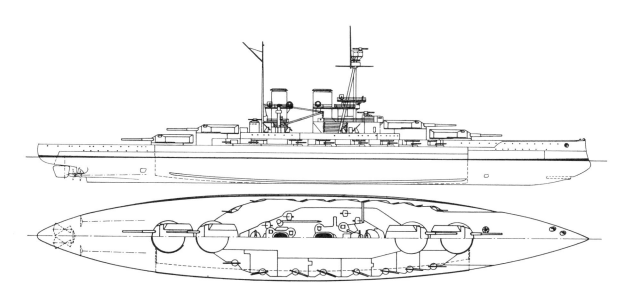

Bayern after 1917

Württemberg (1918)

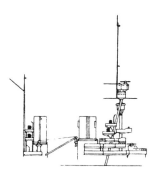

Baden, final form
Bayern's aft mast was the same,
but with the old gaffs.

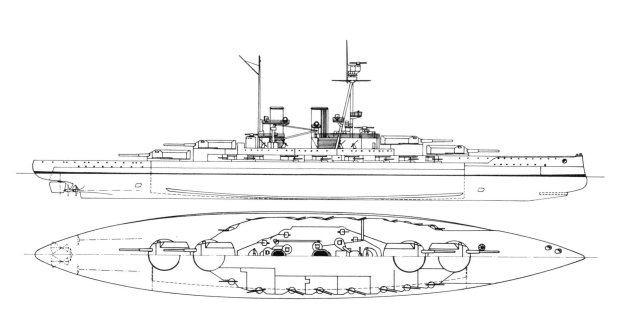

Saschen (1918)

Armament

Eight 38.0cm/45 QF guns (720 rounds), −8° +16°, range 20,400m and −5° +20°, range 23,200m; sixteen 15cm/45 QF guns (2560 rounds), range 16,800m; two 8.8/45 AA guns (800 rounds); five 60cm TT (20 rounds) planned, four lateral, one bow, all under water. *Bayern* and *Baden* were mined in 1917, and lateral torpedo tubes were then removed from both.

Handling

Very good, stable sea-boats, but with severe weather helm, approximately as *Helgoland*. Manoeuvrable and responsive, with slight speed loss in swell and head sea. Speed loss with hard rudder up to 62 percent at 7° heel. Roll period 13.4 seconds; transverse metacentric height 2.53m, longitudinal 206.7m. Maximum stability moment at 31°, = zero at 63°.

Complement

Crew: 42/1129 (plus 14/86 as squadron flagship). Boats: one picket boat, three barges, two launches, two yawls, two dinghies.

Notes

Colour scheme no 9. Details of *Bayern* and *Baden* are shown in the supplementary drawings. [After both ships were mined in 1917 the forward torpedo room was removed and divided as a watertight compartment.] Torpedo nets were fitted until 1916. After 1918 the tripod mast signal topmast was always kept stowed, thus the head of the flagstaff was 44m above CWL.

Career

Bayern launched 18 Feb 1915, trials began 18 Mar 1916, commissioned into fleet 15 Jul 1916. Interned at Scapa Flow 26 Nov 1918; capsized and sank after being scuttled at 1430hrs on 21 Jun 1919. Raised 1 Sept 1934, broken up in 1935 at Rosyth. Ship's bell now in Kiel Fördeklub.

Baden launched 30 Oct 1915, trials began 19 Oct 1916, commissioned 14 Mar 1917 as fleet flagship. Interned at Scapa Flow 14 Nov 1918. Scuttled 21 Jun 1919 and towed aground by British ships to prevent sinking. Raised Jul 1919, used as a Royal Navy target ship, and sunk 16 Aug 1921 southwest of Portsmouth during experiments.

Württemberg launched 20 Jun 1917; construction was halted twelve months before completion, stricken 3 Nov 1919, in accordance with article 186 of the Treaty of Versailles. Sold in 1921, broken up at Hamburg.

Sachsen launched 21 Nov 1916; construction was halted nine months before completion, stricken 3 Nov 1919 as the previous vessel. Sold in 1920, broken up in 1922 at Kiel Arsenalmole.

Volya

Name	Builder	Built	Cost in Marks (000s)	Displacement (t = tonnes T = tons)	Length (m)	Breadth (m)	Draught (m)	Power (hp)	Revs (rpm)	Speed (kts)	Range (nm/kts)	Coal (t)	Oil (t)
VOLYA	Russud, Nikolaev	1911–17		23,900t max 22,600t des	168.8	27.3	8.3	33,200shp max 26,500shp des		21.5 des	1000/21	3000 max 1500 des	720 des

Construction

Laid down as Russian battleship *Imperator Alexander III*. Armour: deck 38–75mm; CT roof 187mm, sides 305mm; CWL 76–203–305–203–187–102mm; 30.5cm turrets 203–305mm, 13cm turrets 127mm.

Propulsion

Four sets of Brown-Curtis turbines (four 4-bladed screws, diameter not known). Twenty Yarrow water-tube boilers.

Armament

Twelve 30.5cm/52 QF guns (range, etc, not known), eighteen 13cm/55 QF guns (range, etc, not known); four 7.6cm AA guns (range, etc, not known); four 45cm TT.

Handling

No details known

Complement

No details known

Notes

No details known

Career

Imperator Alexander III launched 15 Apr 1914; renamed *Volya* and commissioned into Russian Black Sea fleet February 1917. Accepted 1917 as *Imperator*; under German flag after 19 Jun 1918, commissioned for trials 15 Oct 1918; trials halted 11 Nov 1918. Transferred to White Russian control 1919, renamed *General Alexeev*, and became flagship of Wrangel's fleet; interned at Bizerta on 29 Dec 1920; broken up in 1936 in France,

After the arrival of the battlecruiser *Goeben* at Sebastopol, the German flag was also raised on the following Russian ships of the line, from 3 Mar 1918:

Ioann Zlatoust (launched 13 Mar 1906, 12,800t); *Svyatoi Evstafi* (launched 3 Nov 1906, 12,800t); *Borets za Svobodu* (launched October 1900, 12,580t); *Rostislav* (launched September 1896, 8800t); *Tri Svia-*titelia (launched 12 Nov 1893, 12,480t); *Georgi Pobiedonosets* (launched 9 Mar 1892, 10,000t); and *Sinop* (launched June 1878, 10,100t)

However these ships saw no action in the German Imperial Navy, and there were no plans to commission them.

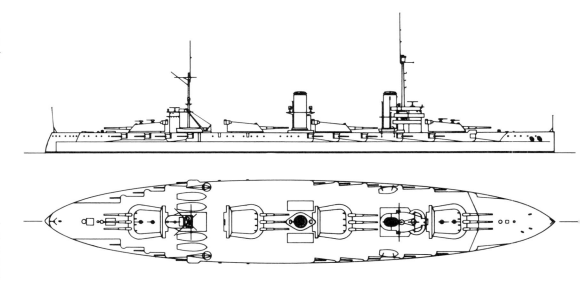

Volya (1918). *Mrva*

Battleships 1939–1941

Scharnhorst class

Name	Builder	Built	Cost in Marks (000s)	Displacement (t = tonnes, T = tons)	Length (m)	Breadth (m)	Draught (m)	Power (hp)	Revs (rpm)	Speed (kts)	Range (nm/kts)	Coal (t)	Oil (t)
SCHARNHORST sq fl	KM Dockyard, Wilhelmshaven Construction no 125	1935–39	143,471	38,100T max 35,540t des 32,100T std	234.9 oa 226.0 cwl	30.0	9.90 max 910 des 8.30 std	165,930 shp max 160,000 shp	280 max 265 des	31.5 max 31.0 des	8200/19* 7100/19**	—	5080 max 2800 des†
GNEISENAU	Deutsche Werke. Kiel Construction no 235	1935–38	146,174	32,100T	229.8 oa 226.0 cwl	,,	,,	,,			31.3 max 31.0 des	8200/19* 6200/19**	—	,,
	mod: KM Dockyard, Gotenhafen	1942–											
19,401gt (Scharnhorst)													

* expected
** achieved
† 6000 carried with additional bunkers

Construction

Laid down as battleships D (*Ersatz Elsass*) and E (*Ersatz Hessen*) (official design, 1932–34 D 1–6, design chief MarObBrt Blechschmidt). Longitudinal frame-stringer steel construction, welded (twenty-one watertight compartments, double bottom 79 percent), bow bulge. Krupp armour: upper deck 50mm; armour deck 20–50–20mm (slopes 105mm); bow and stern 20 and 80mm; all Wh armour. Torpedo bulkhead 45mm Ww armour. Forward CT roof 200mm, sides 350mm; aft CT roof 50mm, sides 100mm (rangefinder 100mm); tops roof 20mm, sides 60mm (rangefinder 20mm); CWL 0–bulkhead 200–350 (shields 170)–bulkhead 150 (shields 70)–0mm; citadel front 45mm, sides 35mm, back 20mm; longitudinal bulkheads 40mm; turrets roof 150mm, sides 200mm, front 360mm (shields 350mm); 15cm turrets roof 50mm, sides 60mm, front 140mm; 15cm shields and 10.5cm AA guns 20mm; all KC armour. Depth 14.00m. Immersion increased by 1cm per 55.1t. Uniform trim moment, *Scharnhorst* 49,295, *Gneisenau* 49,470cu m. Official displacement as new vessels 26,000T standard.

Propulsion

Scharnhorst three Brown, Boveri & Co geared turbines in four housings; *Gneisenau* three Germania geared turbines in three housings (three 3-bladed screws, 4.80m diameter) in 1 + 0 + 2 engine rooms (primary speed at full load 6700rpm high pressure, 3200rpm medium pressure, 2700rpm low pressure; pressure stages grouped around transmission). Reversing power

57,000hp. Twelve Wagner ultra high pressure boilers (58 atmospheres forced, 450°, 42 to maximum 54.5 t/hr steam) in 1 + 0 + 1 + 1 boiler rooms. Five electricity plants with a total of two diesel generators each 150kW, two each 300kW, six turbo-generators each 460kW, two each 230kW (one of the latter connected to a 200kVA AC generator) total 4120kW at 220V. Two rudders. Fuel oil consumption not known.

Armament

Nine 28cm/54.5 QF guns (945–1350 rounds), –8° +40°, range 42,600m; twelve 15cm/55 QF guns (1600–1800 rounds), range 22,000m; fourteen 10.5cm/65 AA guns (5600 rounds), range 17,700m; sixteen 3.7/83 AA guns (32,000–96,000 rounds); ten to thirty-eight 2cm AA guns (32,000 to 76,000 rounds); two, later one, catapults; four Arado 196 seaplanes; six 53.3cm deck-mounted TT (18 rounds) from *Leipzig* and *Nürnberg* were fitted after 1942. The Hein'sches Stau(Lande) sail apparatus for landing seaplanes was carried until 1939 only.

Handling

Poor sea-boats, though with an easy motion, with weather helm and bow-heavy when fully equipped; very wet at the bow as far back as the bridge [seaworthiness at speed in a head sea was somewhat improved after the fitting of an Atlantic bow, but nevertheless turret A was always restricted in use]. Very slow into the turn, though better at high speed; tug assistance was always necessary in shallow waters. Speed loss was greater than 50 percent over a full circle with hard

rudder, and heel more than 10°. The aft deck was also often awash, so the companionways had to be sealed when cruising. During tests she showed about 13° heel with a small load shipped. The rudder location between the screws was particularly inefficient.

Complement

Crew: 56/1613 to 60/1780 (plus 10/61 as a flagship). Boats: two picket boats, two barges, two launches, two pinnaces, two cutters, two yawls, two dinghies.

Notes

Colour scheme no 9 and camouflage schemes; *Scharnhorst* was painted dark grey overall in 1942. Until 1939 *Scharnhorst* had a flat, horizontal funnel cap, black at all times, with a tripod mast on the aft edge [after she was fitted with an angled funnel cap (aluminium-bronze, matt) with steam pipe stubs on a flat plate]. [The Atlantic bow was fitted in August 1939. A catapult was mounted on C turret until March 1940. The Admiral's bridge was enclosed after August 1942. After January 1940 the foretop was fitted with FMG 39 G(go) radar, later FuMO 22. After February 1942 the rangefinder cowls were removed from A turret.]

Gneisenau had a flat, horizontal, silver–grey funnel cap in 1938, no hangar, and a short radio topmast on the foretop rangefinder cowl. [After August 1938 a small aircraft hangar was fitted (see the supplementary drawing). In January 1939 the Atlantic bow was fitted, and a tall, angled, (aluminium–bronze, matt) funnel cap,

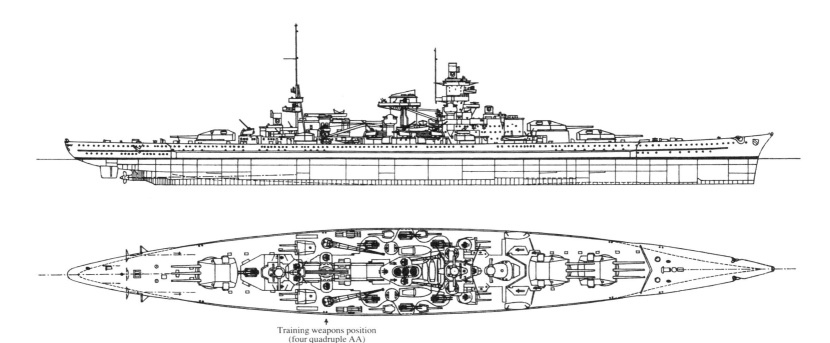

Training weapons position
(four quadruple AA)

Scharnhorst (1942)

without visible steam pipe stubs. In May 1939 the anchor hawses (two port, one starboard) were welded up, and new bar hawses, one on each beam, were fitted, and a new funnel cap, lower, grey, and with steam pipe stubs on a flat plate; at the same time the radio topmast on the foretop was replaced by a large topmast on the tripod mast, and the aircraft hangar was removed. In January 1940 the foretop was fitted with an FMG 39 G(go) radar, and the Admiral's bridge was enclosed. In March 1940 the catapult was removed from C turret. In 1941, while the ship was at Brest, a large aircraft hangar was fitted with an opening for a through-firing catapult, and the rangefinder cowls were removed from A turret.]

It was planned to rearm the ships with six 38cm/47 QF guns later, but this would have required major structural modifications. In any case this calibre was not available until 1940, so the ships were fitted with the 28cm QF guns already in production for other ships, with strengthened turret armour. The conversion to 38cm main armament was planned for 1940–41, on the assumption that the war would be over by then. When *Gneisenau* was bombed at Kiel on 26 Feb 1942 and the bow was burnt out, the following measures were planned: the bow was to be cut off at frame 185.7 and the hull extended by about 10m at the CWL; a new stem without a bulge and sharp almost to the upper deck was then to be fitted.

The planned weight of both ships increased several times during construction, with the result that much freeboard was lost. Eventually the top edge of the CWL armour lay a mere 1.2m above the waterline at maximum displacement. The searchlight platforms on the high catapult were designed to double as lifts; [after 1942 they were fitted with quadruple 2cm AA guns, like those fitted on the forward 15cm turrets. A degaussing loop was fitted after 1940.]

Career

Scharnhorst launched 3 Oct 1936, commissioned into fleet 7 Jan 1939. Sunk at 1945hrs on 26 Dec 1943 in the North Sea, north of North Cape, position 72° 16N, 28° 41E, by shellfire and 14–15 torpedo hits during an engagement with British heavy units and destroyers; 1803 dead.

Gneisenau launched 8 Dec 1936, commissioned into fleet 21 May 1938. Bombed and severely damaged at Kiel 26 Feb 1942, then moved to Gotenhafen; withdrawn from service 1 Jul 1942, disarmed, bow broken up; reconstruction halted 1943. Scuttled and sunk 27 Mar 1945 at Gotenhafen, position 54° 32N, 18° 34E. Raised 12 Sept 1951 by a Polish salvage company (the largest ship raised at that time). C turret was displayed at Trondheim, Norway, as coastal battery *Oerlandet*; Norway offered in 1979 to return it for display in a museum in the Federal Republic of Germany.

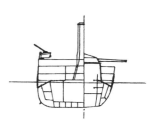

Scharnhorst (1942)
midship section

from Jun 1939
from Feb 1939

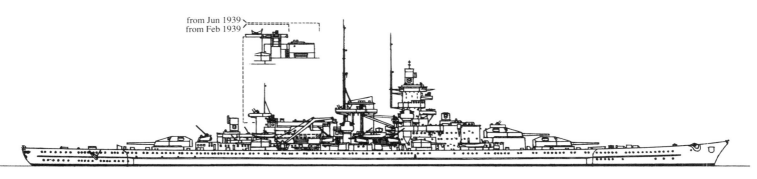

Gneisenau (1942)

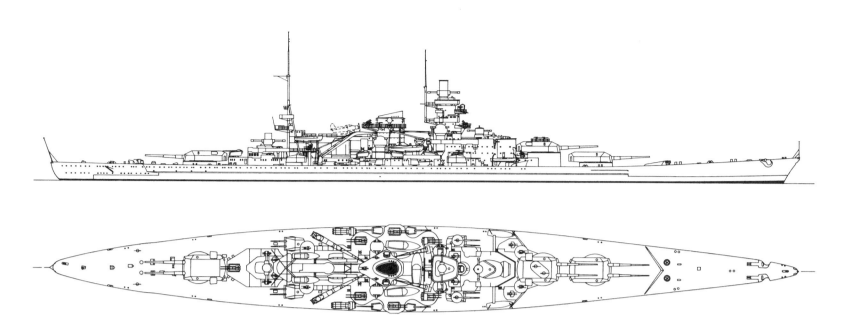

Gneisenau (planned reconstruction 1942–43). Mrva

Bismarck class

Name	Builder	Built	Cost in Marks (000s)	Displacement (t = tonnes T = tons)	Length (m)	Breadth (m)	Draught (m)	Power (hp)	Revs (rpm)	Speed (kts)	Range (nm/kts)	Coal (t)	Oil (t)
BISMARCK	Blohm & Voss, Hamburg Construction no 509	1936–40	196,800	50,300t max 45,950t des 41,700t std	251.0 oa 241.6 cwl	36.0	9.90 max 9.30 des 8.63 std	150,170 shp max 138,000 shp des	265 max 250 des	30.01 max 29.0 des	8525/19	—	7400* 6400 max 3200 des
TIRPITZ	KM Dockyard, Wilhelmshaven Construction no 128	1936–41	181,600	52,600t max 42,900t des	,,	,,	10.6 max 9.0 des	163,026 shp max 138,000 shp des	278 max 250 des	30.8 max 29.0 des	8870/19	—	7780 max* 3000 des

28, 181gt/11,110nt (*Bismarck*) 28,160gt (*Tirpitz*)

* with additional bunkers

Construction

Built as battleships *F* (*Ersatz Hannover*) and *G* (*Ersatz Schleswig-Holstein* (official design, 1933–36, design chief MinRat Burkhardt; during construction the original design of the superstructure, etc, was modified as shown in the lower main drawing. Transverse and longitudinal frame steel construction, more than 90 percent welded (twenty-two watertight compartments, double bottom 83 percent), bow bulge, four bilge keels. Krupp armour: upper deck 50mm; armour deck 100–120mm; bow and stern 60 and 80mm; all Wh armour. Forward CT roof 200mm, sides 350mm (rangefinder roof 100mm, sides 200mm), aft CT roof 50mm, sides 150mm (rangefinder roof 50mm, sides 100mm); CWL 0–bulkhead 220–320 (shields 170)–bulkhead 220 (shields 180)–0mm; citadel 145mm on 50mm teak; turrets roof 130mm, sides 220mm, front 360mm with 220mm shields; 15cm turrets roof 35mm, sides 40mm, front 100mm; 10.5cm shields 20mm; tops roof 20mm, sides 60mm (rangefinder roof 20mm),

sides 50mm; all KC armour. Depth 15.0m. Immersion increased by 1cm per 57.3t. Uniform trim moment 66,903cu m. Official displacement as new vessels 35,000t standard.

Propulsion

Bismarck three sets of Blohm & Voss geared turbines; *Tirpitz* three sets of Brown, Boveri & Co geared turbines, in four housings (three 3-bladed screws, 4.70m diameter) in 1 + 0 + 2 engine rooms; primary revolutions at full load 2825rpm for high and medium pressure turbine, 2390rpm for low pressure turbine, 4130rpm for cruise turbine, pressure stages grouped around transmission. Twelve Wagner ultra high pressure boilers (4560sq m plus 1440sq m superheater, 58 atmospheres forced, 450°) in 3 + 0 + 3 boiler rooms; fuel oil consumption 0.325kg per hp/hr; steam consumption approx 5kg per hp/hr; weight of entire drive installation 20.3kg/hp. (The turbine installation was originally designed for electric transmission, 3 ×

46,000hp. The decision in favour of geared turbines was taken only after the main dimensions, etc, had been established. Their lower unit weight gave a small

Calculated overall performance of the three-shaft turbine installation with twelve boilers, based on a trials displacement of 43,000t

	shp	no of boilers	rpm	kts	fuel consumption
Ahead	3 × 46,000	12	265	29	325g/hp
	3 × 38,350	12	250		320g/hp
	3 × 23,300	9	214		335g/hp
	3 × 13,000	6	176		370g/hp
	3 × 8300	3	151		415g/hp
	3 × 5000	3	128		500g/hp
Astern	3 × 12,000	12	—	—	

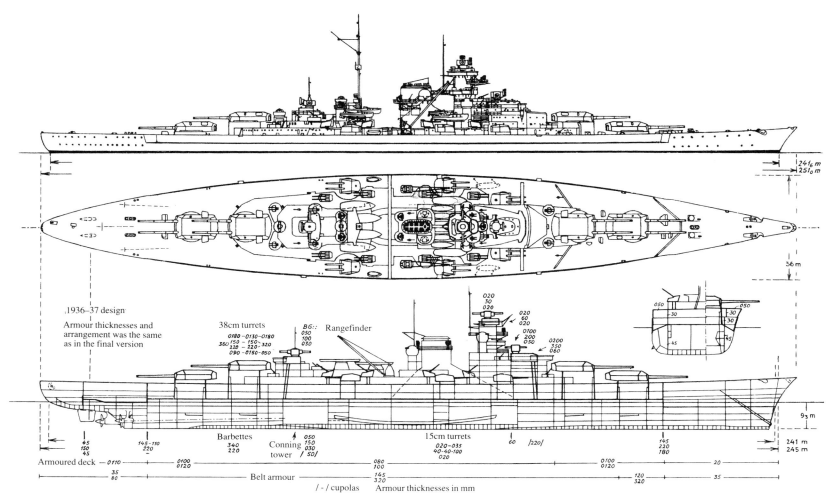

1936–37 design

Armour thicknesses and
arrangement was the same
as in the final version

38cm turrets
0180–0130–0180
360 150 – 150 320
220 – 220
090 –0150–050

BG:: 050
100
030

Rangefinder

020
30
020

020
60
020

0100
200
050

0200
350
060

050   050
30
30   30
45   45

Barbettes
340
220

Conning
tower

050
150
030
/ 50/

15cm turrets
020–035
40-40-100
020

60

/220/

145
220
180

Armoured deck — 0110 —   0100
0120

080
100

0100
0120

20

35
80

Belt armour

145
320

120
320

35

45
150
45

145–110
220

/ - / cupolas   Armour thicknesses in mm

241₆ m
251₀ m

36 m

9₃ m

241 m
245 m

Bismarck (1940); the first design (1936–37) is shown in the lower drawing.

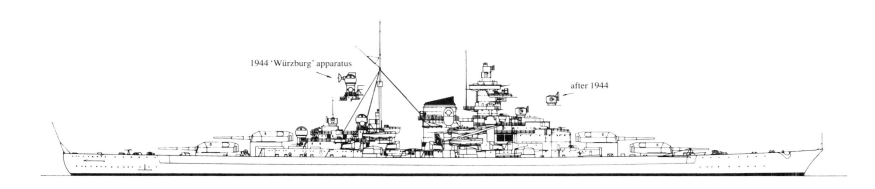

1944 'Würzburg' apparatus

after 1944

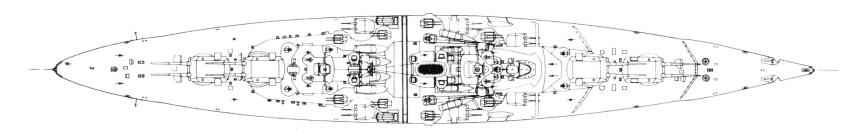

Tirpitz (1942). *Mrva*

Bismark weights (excerpt) at 16 Mar 1940 (tonnes)

Hull	11,691.0
Armour, less rotating turret armour	17,540.0
Main engines	2800.0
Auxiliary engines	1428.0
Main and secondary armament and armour	5973.0
Torpedo armament	–
Aircraft installations	83.0
Defensive weapons	8.0
General equipment, etc	369.4
Nautical instruments	8.6
Rigging	30.0
Displacement, empty, including oil and water in machinery, etc	39,931.2
Artillery ammunition	1510.4
Defensive weapon ammunition	2.5
Consumable materials	155.4
Crew	243.6
Food	194.2
Drinking water	139.2
Washing water	167.0
Type displacement	42,343.5
Feed water (battle cells)	187.5
Fuel oil	3226.0
Diesel oil	96.5
Lubricating oil	80.0
Aircraft fuel	17.0
Design displacement	45,950.5
Feed water	187.5
Fuel oil	3226.0
Diesel oil	96.5
Lubricating oil	80.0
Aircraft fuel reserve	17.0
Fresh water reserve	389.2
Displacement, fully equipped	49.946.7
Extra oil load	1009.0
Displacement, with extra oil load	50,955.7

increase in design performance, but above all a more strongly constructed installation. The overall result was that the projected performance was considerably exceeded on trial.) Four electricity plants, each with two 500kW diesel generators, plus a total of five turbo-generators, each 690kW, and one at 460kW, the latter connected to a 400kVA AC generator; one further 550kVA AC diesel generator; total capacity of electrical installation 7910kW, 220V, in the engine rooms. Two rudders.

Armament

Eight 38cm/47 QF guns (940–960 rounds), –8° +35°, range 36,200m; twelve 15cm/55 QF guns (1800 rounds), –10° +35°, range 23,000m; sixteen 10.5cm/65 AA guns (6720 rounds), +80°; sixteen 3.7cm/83 AA guns (32,000 rounds), twelve 2cm AA guns (24,000 rounds), [*Tirpitz* later sixteen to fifty-eight 2cm AA guns (32,000 to 90,000 rounds)]; one double catapult, six Arado 196 seaplanes. [*Tirpitz* was also fitted after 1942 with eight 53.3cm deck TT (24 rounds) in quadruple tubes.]

Handling

Exceptionally stable sea-boats, with shallow pitching and very slight roll, even in very heavy seas; they also had outstanding directional stability, with no weather helm. Both ships were also very responsive, answering rudder deflections as small as 5°. Heel was only 3° even with the rudder hard over, and speed loss with hard rudder was up to 65 percent. Both ships were difficult to control at low speed or when going astern, and tug assistance was necessary in narrow waters, though frequently not used.

Complement

Crew: 103/1962 plus 27, to about 108/2500. Boats: three picket boats, four barges, one launch, two pinnaces, two cutters, two yawls, two dinghies.

Notes

Colour scheme no 9 and camouflage schemes. A degaussing coil was fitted at the lower edge of the CWL armour. *Bismarck*'s funnel cap was silver–grey or white at all times, and her cranes were mounted 3m further aft and 3.5m further outboard on the upper deck (*Tirpitz*'s cranes were mounted on the superstructure deck). Every second 10.5cm AA shield was 5m further inboard. The potato locker between the turret mast and the funnel was deleted. *Bismarck* was launched with a straight stem, as indicated in the lower drawing. The 1935 design included two standard catapults arranged fore and aft between the funnel and the aft conning tower; this was modified in 1938 to the British pattern, and modifications included an enlarged forward bridge and many changes to the superstructure. A turret lacked a rangefinder. One stand-by hangar was positioned on each side of the funnel, and one large hangar for four seaplanes under the mainmast. The aft AA director was not originally fitted. The mainmast was telescopically retractable. [On *Tirpitz* the configuration of AA quadruples on raised turrets and the forward bridge was altered and their number was increased, and the large searchlight under the splinter guard on the funnel was removed and replaced by an AA gun.]

Career

Bismarck launched 14 Feb 1939, commissioned into fleet 28 Apr 1940. Sunk at 1040hrs on 27 May 1941 in the Atlantic 300nm west of Ouessant, position 48° 10N, 16° 12W. After an aerial torpedo had damaged the rudder, she was overwhelmed by shell and torpedo hits from the British Home Fleet and Force H with five battleships, nine cruisers, two aircraft carriers, etc. The ship was badly damaged and incapable of combat, despite being completely intact below the armoured deck, and was scuttled by her crew; 1977 dead, 115 survivors.

Tirpitz launched 1 Apr 1939, commissioned into fleet 25 Feb 1941. Served in Norway; damaged at Kaafjord at 0912hrs on 22 Sept 1943 by a ground mine, and by British miniature submarines *X6* and *X7*; bombed and damaged at Altafjord in 1944. Sunk at 0845hrs on 12 Nov 1944, capsizing close to Tromsö, position 69° 36N, 18° 59E, after being hit by six 5.45 ton special aircraft bombs dropped by British Lancasters; 1204 dead. Broken up 1948–57 by a Norwegian-German company.

Proportional analysis of weight (19 Oct 1940, figures rounded off)

	tonnes	% of weight
Ship's weight	12,700	27.0
Engine installation	3000	6.4
Auxiliary engines	1400	3.0
Armour	18,700	40.0
Guns	5550	11.8
Equipment	920	2.0
Fuel	4000	8.4
Water	530	1.0
Defensive weapons and equipment	100	0.2
Aircraft and equipment	100	0.2
Design displacement	approx 47,000	100.0

H class

Construction

Designed as battleships (official design, 1937–39). Transverse and longitudinal frame, steel construction, more than 90 percent welded (twenty-one watertight compartments, double bottom 89 percent), four bilge keels. Krupp armour: upper deck 30–50–80mm, armour deck 100–120mm, bow 60–150mm, stern 90–30mm, all Wh armour. Torpedo bulkhead 45mm, Ww armour. KC armour: CT as *Bismarck*; CWL 0–220–300 (bulkhead 180)–220–0mm; citadel 150mm on teak, turrets roof 130mm, sides 240mm, front 385mm (shields 360–240mm); 15cm turrets roof 35mm, sides 40mm, front 100mm; 10.5cm shields 20mm; tops roof 20mm, sides 60mm (rangefinder roof 20mm, 50mm). Depth 15.70m. Uniform trim moment 84,700cu m.

Propulsion

Twelve MAN 9-cylinder double-acting 2-stroke diesel engines, three shafts, four engines per shaft with two gearboxes in 3 + 3 + 3 + 3 + 1 engine rooms (three 3-bladed screws, 4.80m diameter). Two auxiliary oil-fired boilers between the two central transmission rooms, two auxiliary exhaust gas boilers above them over the armour deck. The weight of the entire power installation was 31.4 kg/hp. Four electricity plants, each with two 920kW diesel generators and one 460kW, giving a total of 9200kW at 220V and 110V. Total AC power 1070kVA. 1 + 2 rudders.

Armament

Eight 40.6cm/47 QF guns (960 rounds), –6.5° +30°, range 36,800m; other armament as *Bismarck*, but with the 10.5cm AA guns in rotary turrets rather than open mounts. One fixed, transverse mounted, double catapult. Six Arado 196 seaplanes as originally designed.

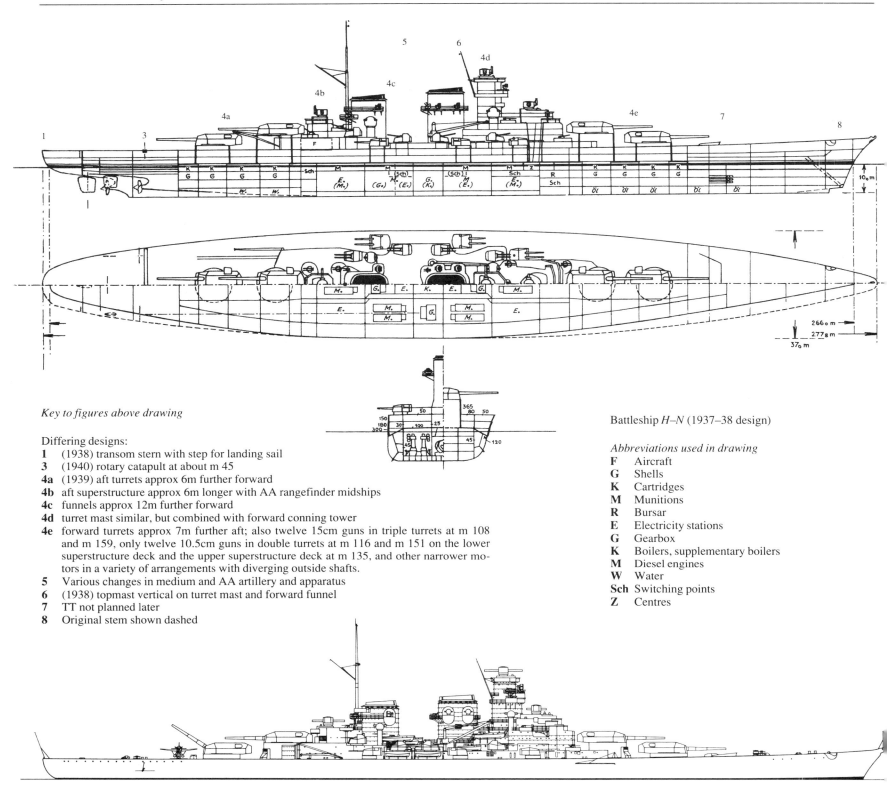

Key to figures above drawing

Differing designs:

1 (1938) transom stern with step for landing sail
3 (1940) rotary catapult at about m 45
4a (1939) aft turrets approx 6m further forward
4b aft superstructure approx 6m longer with AA rangefinder midships
4c funnels approx 12m further forward
4d turret mast similar, but combined with forward conning tower
4e forward turrets approx 7m further aft; also twelve 15cm guns in triple turrets at m 108 and m 159, only twelve 10.5cm guns in double turrets at m 116 and m 151 on the lower superstructure deck and the upper superstructure deck at m 135, and other narrower motors in a variety of arrangements with diverging outside shafts.
5 Various changes in medium and AA artillery and apparatus
6 (1938) topmast vertical on turret mast and forward funnel
7 TT not planned later
8 Original stem shown dashed

Battleship *H–N* (1937–38 design)

Abbreviations used in drawing

F   Aircraft
G   Shells
K   Cartridges
M   Munitions
R   Bursar
E   Electricity stations
G   Gearbox
K   Boilers, supplementary boilers
M   Diesel engines
W   Water
Sch Switching points
Z   Centres

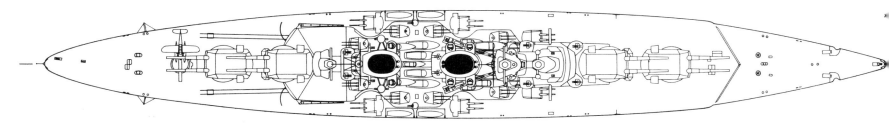

Battleship *H–N* (final plan when the decision was made to build the ship, 1939). *Mrva*

Name	Builder	Built	Cost in Marks (000s)	Displacement (t = tonnes T = tons)	Length (m)	Breadth (m)	Draught (m)	Power (hp)	Revs (rpm)	Speed (kts)	Range (nm/kts)	Coal (t)	Oil (t)
H	Blohm & Voss, Hamburg	1939–	240,500	62,600T max 56,440t des 52,600T std	277.8 oa 266.0 cwl	37.0	11.2 max 10.0 des 9.6 std	165,000 shp des	260 des	30.0 des	19,200/19 7000/28	—	8700 max 4000 des
J	Deschimag, Bremen Construction no 981	1939–	237,600	,,	,,	,,	,,	,,	,,	,,	,,	—	,,
K	Deutsche Werke, Kiel Construction no 264	—	—	,,	,,	,,	,,	,,	,,	,,	,,	—	,,
L	KM Dockyard, Wilhelmshaven Construction no 130												
M	Blohm & Voss, Hamburg Construction no 526					as above							
N	Deschimag, Bremen Construction no 982												

Career

Possible names, eg *Friedrich der Grosse* for *H* or *Grossdeutschland* for *J* are no more than speculation, presumably of British origin. The latter at least is improbable (see the note on the replacement of the name *Deutschland* by *Lützow*, page 60).

H Contract granted 14 Apr 1939, keel laid 15 Jul 1939; construction halted 30 Sept 1939, with 800t material used, 3500t in process, 5800t supplied, and 19,000t ordered. Broken up on stocks after 25 Nov 1941. Projected building time was $4^1/_2$ to 5 years.

J Contract granted 14 Apr 1939, keel laid 1 Sept 1939; construction halted 30 Sept 1939. Broken up on stocks after 25 Nov 1941.

K Contract granted 25 May 1939, cancelled summer 1939. 3500t in process, 6500t supplied, 25,800t material ordered.

M Contract granted in July 1939, cancelled 10 Oct 1939. 3500t in process, 6500t supplied, 25,800t material ordered.

N Contract granted in summer 1939, cancelled 10 Oct 1939. 3500t in process, 6500t supplied, 25,800t material ordered.

H41 class

Name	Builder	Built	Cost in Marks (000s)	Displacement (t = tonnes T = tons)	Length (m)	Breadth (m)	Draught (m)	Power (hp)	Revs (rpm)	Speed (kts)	Range (nm/kts)	Coal (t)	Oil (t)
H 41	intended for Blohm & Voss, Hamburg, Deutsche Werke, Kiel, and KM Dockyard, Wilhelmshaven		—	74,803T max 68,800t des 62,992T std	282.0 oa 275.0 bp	39.0	12.2 max 11.1 des	165,000 shp des		28.8 des	20,000/19	—	

Construction

Designed as a battleship (official design, 1940–41, based on type *H* with improved horizontal protection). Transverse and longitudinal frame steel construction, more than 90 percent welded (triple bottom, percentage not known). Krupp armour: upper deck 50mm; armour deck 200mm, slopes 175mm; stern 135mm, all Wh material. Torpedo bulkhead 45mm, Ww material. CWL 300mm, KC material. Triple bottom, innermost layer 20mm (this was the first time a triple bottom had been used in a design for the German fleet). Depth 18.0m.

Propulsion

Engine installation as *H*. Three rudders.

Armament

Eight 42cm QF guns (calibre not known); twelve 15cm/55 QF guns; sixteen 10.5cm/65 AA guns; sixteen 3.6cm AA guns; thirty-four 2cm AA guns; six 53.3cm TT, under water; four Arado 196 seaplanes.

Career

Replacement design for type *H*, incorporating lessons learned in the war to date and improving on the weaknesses of type *H* (including better positioning of the torpedo bulkhead, repositioning of armour deck with reference to floating plane, and changes to deck height). The plans were based on the assumption of approval for construction six to nine months after

demobilisation at Blohm & Voss and Deutsche Werke, Kiel, and later also the KM dockyard, Wilhelmshaven, after completion of the building dock there. Deschi-

mag could not be considered for a ship of this draught because of the shallow waters of the Weser.

H42 class

Name	Builder	Built	Cost in Marks (000s)	Displacement (t = tonnes T = tons)	Length (m)	Breadth (m)	Draught (m)	Power (hp)	Revs (rpm)	Speed (kts)	Range (nm/kts)	Coal (t)	Oil (t)
H42	—	—		96,555T max 90,000t des 83,268T std	305.0 bp	42.8	12.7 max 11.8 des	280,000 shp des*		32.2 des 24.0*	20,000/ 19**	—	
H43	—	—		118,110T max 111,000t des 103,346T std	330.0 bp	48.0	12.9 max 12.0 des	,,		31.0 des 23.0*	,,	—	
H44	—	—		139,272T max 131,000t des 122,047T std	345.0 bp	51.5	13.5 max 12.7 des	,,		30.1 des 22.5*	,,	—	

* motor only
** raising the range to 25,000nm increased draught at full displacement by about 0.4m

Construction

Designed as battleships (official projects after 1941). Transverse and longitudinal frame steel construction, welded (triple bottom, percentage not known). *H 44* armour: armour deck 330mm, slope 200–150mm, battery deck 140mm, all Wh material. Torpedo bulkhead 45–35mm Ww material. CWL 380mm, KC material. Depth for *H 42* was 19.2m, for *H 43*, 20.0m, and for *H 44*, 21.0m.

Propulsion

Projected designs only, some with pure engine propulsion, others with hybrid engine/turbine system, four 3-bladed screws (the largest projects had five screws). Four rudders.

Armament

H 42 and *H 43*: eight 48cm QF guns (calibre not known); *H 44*: eight 50.8cm QF guns (calibre not known). All, twelve 15cm/55 QF guns; sixteen 10.5cm/65 AA guns; twenty-eight 3.7cm AA guns; forty 2cm AA guns; six 53.3cm TT, under water; six to nine Arado 196 seaplanes.

Notes

Pure study projects by the *Schiffsneubaukommission* (New Ship Construction Committee), not by the actual K-Amt (Warship Building Office), these designs were never approved for implementation. The projects' principal purpose was to establish the size of ship which would result from the armour thickness necessary to counter constantly increasing bomb weights.

Foreign battleships

Sovietskaya Ukraina

Construction

Russian battleship *Sovietskaya Ukraina*, 59,000t, keel laid 1938 in Nikolaev.

Propulsion

264,500hp, turbo-electric propulsion. Turbine contracts granted to Switzerland. Four 3-bladed screws.

Armament

Nine 40.6cm QF (calibre not known) guns; twelve 15.2cm QF (calibre not known) guns; sixteen 10cm AA guns; forty small-calibre AA guns; four seaplanes, two catapults.

Notes

No torpedoes.

Career

Sovietskaya Ukraina was taken as a prize on the stocks at Nikolaev, on 16 Aug 1941, already com-

pleted up to and including the main deck and only slightly damaged by explosions. Construction was not continued at first, since no plans were available, but armour components and medium guns from the ship were used in shore defences at Sebastopol. After 1943 construction continued very slowly. In March 1944 the ship was abandoned on the stocks at Nikolaev, completely destroyed by explosions.

Clemenceau/Gascogne

Construction

Designed as French battleships *Clemenceau* and *Gascogne*. Designed 1938–39, similar to *Jean Bart*; 35,000t.

Armament

Eight 38cm QF guns (calibre not known).

Career

Clemenceau keel laid 17 Jan 1939 at Brest; 10 percent complete by June 1940. The final decision not to complete her for German purposes was taken in December 1941; she was then undocked, and no further construction was undertaken under German management. Used as a torpedo and bomb hulk at anchor off the sub-

marine base, she was sunk by bombs from British aircraft on 27 Aug 1944.

Gascogne preparations for construction were made in late 1939 at Penhöet-Loire, but construction was not started.

Frigates and flush-decked corvettes 1849–1886

Gefion

Name	Builder	Built	Cost in Marks (000s)	Displacement (t = tonnes T = tons)	Length (m)	Breadth (m)	Draught (m)	Power (hp)	Revs (rpm)	Speed (kts)	Range (nm/kts)	Coal (t)	Oil (t)
GEFION	New Royal Dockyard, Conpenhagen Construction no 32	1840–48	262fl	1826t max 1385t des	59.35 oa 52.44 cwl	13.5	5.35 max 5.68 des	—	—	15.0	—	—	—
1360gt	mod: Koninkl. Mij. De Schelde, Vlissingen	1852											

Construction
Laid down as sailing frigate *Gefion* (Danish design, by A Schifter). Transverse frame oak plank carvel construction with copper sheathing. Depth 9.18m.

Propulsion
Full-rigged ship, 1989sq m [rigging removed 1873]. One rudder.

Armament
Two 60pdr; twenty-six long, twenty short 24pdr.

Handling
Good sea-boat, with excellent sailing performance (better than *Thetis* with wind on the quarter).

Complement
Crew: 38/382. Boats: three large, three small.

Notes
Colour scheme no 1.

Career
Gefion launched 27 Sept 1843, completed in 1846 as a Danish frigate. Captured by Schleswig-Holstein batteries off Eckernförde 5 Apr 1849; taken into federal fleet as *Eckenförde*. Transferred to Prussia 1 May 1852 and named *Gefion* as a training ship and for duties abroad; served as a gunnery training ship 1865; barrack ship at Kiel 1870. Stricken 5 May 1880 and used as a coal hulk at Kiel; broken up in summer 1891, at the Imperial Dockyard, Kiel. Figurehead now in Eckernförde Kurpak.

Gefion (1852)

Barbarossa class

Construction
Laid down as Cunard Line steamers *Britannia* and *Acadia* (designed by John Wood, 1838). Transverse frame oak/yellow pine planking, carvel hull with iron knees, bottom copper sheathed; three decks. Hold depth 6.83m; 1135BRT.

Propulsion
Two side beam engines, single-cylinder, by Robert Napier, Glasgow (two wheels, each twenty-four paddles, 8.97m diameter), in one engine and boiler room 23.91m long. Four trunk boilers (1 atmosphere). One rudder. Barque rig [schooner brig rig after 1851; *Barbarossa* brig rig 1851, all rigging removed 1873].

Armament
Nine 68pdr bomb cannon from Woolwich Arsenal.

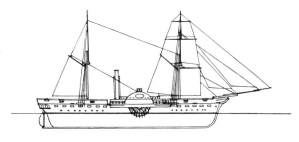

Barbarossa (1851); *Erzherzog Johann* was similar

Name	Builder	Built	Cost	Displacement (t = tonnes T = tons)	Length (m)	Breadth (m)	Draught (m)	Power (hp)	Revs (rpm)	Speed (kts)	Range (nm/kts)	Coal (t)	Oil (t)
BARBAROSSA sq fl	Robert Duncan, Greenock mod: Royal Dockyard, Danzig	1839–40 1853	451fl (bought)	1313t des	64.69 oa 58.68 cwl	16.5 max 9.3 hull	5.10 fwd 5.18 aft	1500ihp max 410nhp des	up to 17	9.5 max 8.0 des		376	—
ERZHERZOG JOHANN	John Wood, Pt Glasgow mod: Trockendock, Brake	1839–40 1849–51	£37 (bought)	,,	,,	,,	,,	,,	,,	,,		,,	—

1135gt; originally 1156gt/619nt

Handling
Extremely good sea-boats, with good performance as paddle steamers, but poor performance as sailing ships owing to insufficient rigging, making severe leeway.

Complement
Crew: 200. Boats: four large, one cutter.

Notes
Colour scheme no 1.

Career
Barbarossa made forty round trips Liverpool–Boston for the Cunard Line as *Britannia* (launched 5 Feb 1840); purchased for £37,000 for the German Federal fleet January 1849, transferred to Bremerhaven 19 Mar 1949 and renamed *Barbarossa*; served as a squadron flagship until 1850; commissioned into the Prussian Navy 1 May 1852 as a barrack and guard ship at Danzig. Engines sold as scrap in 1865; ship served as a barrack hulk at Kiel from 1865 until stricken 5 May 1880; blown up 28 Jul 1880 by a torpedo from *Zieten*; raised 10 Nov 1880, sold for 6000M, and broken up in the same year at the Imperial Dockyard, Kiel.

Erzherzog Johann made more than thirty round trips Liverpool–Boston for the Cunard Line as *Acadia* (launched in April 1840); sold for £37,000 in 1849, stranded on transfer around Terschelling 12 Mar 1849; refloated, transferred to Bremerhaven 25 Mar 1849 and renamed *Erzherzog Johann*. Saw no service, stricken 20 Jan 1853, sold to W A Fritze & Co for C Lehmkuhl, Bremen, 16 Mar 1853 and renamed *Germania*. First voyage Bremerhaven–New York 2 Aug 1853; chartered to Britain from March 1855 to July 1856 as a transport in the Crimean War, under the name Transporter *No 207*; broken up on the Thames (by Marks, Greenwich), 1857.

Hansa

Name	Builder	Built	Cost	Displacement (t = tonnes T = tons)	Length (m)	Breadth (m)	Draught (m)	Power (hp)	Revs (rpm)	Speed (kts)	Range (nm/kts)	Coal (t)	Oil (t)
HANSA sq fl c1800gt	Wm H Webb, New York	1847–48	c $300 (bought)	1650t des	81.90 oa 74.71 des	19.5 max 12.2 hull	4.72	c1800ihp max 750nhp des	up to 17	10.0 des		c 900	—

Construction
Laid down as steamer *United States* for the Black Ball Line (designed by Wm H Webb, 1846). Transverse frame oak/yellow pine carvel hull with Muntz metal sheathing; three decks. Depth 10.06m.

Propulsion
Two side beam engines, single-cylinder, by Secor & Braistatt, New York (two wheels, each twenty-four paddles, 10.97m diameter) in one engine/boiler room, 27.43m long. Four trunk boilers (eight fireboxes, 1 atmosphere). Barque rig. One rudder.

Armament
Three 84pdr bomb cannon; eight 68pdr bomb cannon from Woolwich Arsenal.

Handling
Good sea-boat, very manoeuvrable for a paddle steamer; performance under sail was moderate, and she made severe leeway.

Complement
Crew: 260. Boats: four large, one cutter.

Notes
Colour scheme no 1. Flat transom stern. Various inaccurate models are in existence.

Career
Launched 20 Aug 1847 as *United States*; made one round trip New York–Liverpool after 8 Apr 1848 and four round trips Southampton–Le Havre before 5 Feb 1849 for the Black Ball Line; purchased 17 Feb 1849 for the German Federal Fleet. Transferred to Geestemünde 18 Aug 1849 and renamed *Hansa*. Stricken 20 Jan 1853, sold 16 Mar 1853 to W A Fritze & Co for C Lehmkuhl, Bremen, for whom she made her first voyage Bremerhaven–New York after 30 Aug 1853; chartered to Britain from March 1855 to July 1856 as a transport in the Crimean War, under the name Transporter *No 206*. N Atlantic service resumed in April 1857; chartered to Britain in October 1857 as an India supply transport, then sold to Galway Line on 19 May 1858 as *Indian Empire*. Two round trips Galway–New York, then laid up at Deptford near London after fire damage 24 Jul 1861. She sank after springing a leak on 4 May 1866.

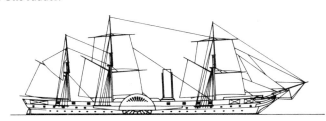

Hansa (1849). *Mrva*

Danzig

Name	Builder	Built	Cost in Marks (000s)	Displacement (t = tonnes T = tons)	Length (m)	Breadth (m)	Draught (m)	Power (hp)	Revs (rpm)	Speed (kts)	Range (nm/kts)	Coal (t)	Oil (t)
DANZIG 1200gt	Royal Dockyard, Danzig/J W Klawitter	1850–53		1920t max 1450t des	75.66 oa 70.18 cwl	16.5 max 10.4 hull	4.27	1800ihp max 400nhp des	26	11.6 max 10.0 des	3500/10	380	—

Construction

Laid down as a paddle corvette (designed by Scott Russell, 1850). Transverse frame oak plank carvel hull with copper sheathing (three watertight compartments). Built on Royal Dockyard land by J W Klawitter.

Propulsion

Two oscillating 2-cylinder single expansion engines by Robinson & Russell, London (two wheels, each eight paddles, 7.75m diameter) in one engine room, housing four trunk boilers (1.33 atmospheres forced) fore and aft of the engines. Barque rig, 1620sq m. One rudder.

Armament

Twelve 68pdr bomb cannon from Woolwich Arsenal [eight 68pdr].

Handling

Excellent sea-boat, moderately handy under steam, though with considerable speed loss in head sea; poor performance under sail.

Complement

Crew: 220. Boats: four large, two small.

Notes

Colour scheme no 1. Engines cost £20,000, plus 27,000 Thaler duty. Dry rot discovered 1856; refit halted because of *Beiräthigkeit der Fonds*, ie, financial considerations.

Career

Danzig launched 13 Nov 1851, commissioned 1 Jun 1853. Taken abroad in 1856, but saw little service. Stricken 1 Sept 1862; sold to England for 56,000 Thaler, in October 1863; renamed *Eagle* in British service; sold to Japan 1864 and renamed *Kwaiten*. Beached near Hakodate during a mutiny in the Shogunate fleet on 6 May 1869; set on fire 20 Jun 1869 and burnt out.

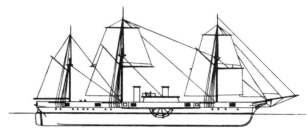

Danzig (1856)

Thetis class

Name	Builder	Built	Cost	Displacement (t = tonnes T = tons)	Length (m)	Breadth (m)	Draught (m)	Power (hp)	Revs (rpm)	Speed (kts)	Range (nm/kts)	Coal (t)	Oil (t)
THETIS	James Graham, Devonport	1844–46	(exchange)	1882t max 1508t des	60.24 oa 50.88 cwl	14.1	5.11 fwd 5.79 aft	—	—	15.0		—	—
NIOBE 1082 and 854gt	Royal Dockyard, Portsmouth	1848–49	180.2 Thaler	1590t max 1270t des	43.29 cwl	12.8	5.05 fwd 5.39 aft	—	—	14.0		—	—

Construction

Laid down as sailing frigates (British design). Transverse frame oak plank carvel hull with copper sheathing.

Propulsion

Full-rigged ships, 2370sq m and 1650sq m.

Armament

Thetis thirty-eight [thirty-six] 68pdr (Swedish). *Niobe* sixteen 68pdr (864 rounds); four 30pdr (332 rounds); six 15cm/22 hooped guns [six 12cm/23 hooped guns].

Handling

Very good sea-boats, but suffered from severe pitching; manoeuvrable, with outstanding performance under sail – *Niobe* sailed well even in light wind. At their best with the wind on the quarter.

Complement

Crew: 35/345 and 34/316. Boats: three large, three small.

Notes

Colour scheme no 1, 2.

Career

Thetis launched 21 Aug 1848 as a British sailing frigate; exchanged 1855 for *Nix* and *Salamander*; served as a training ship for sea cadets and cabin boys 12 Jan 1855; then as an artillery training ship. Stricken 28 Nov 1871, and reduced to a coal hulk at Kiel; sold 1894, broken up at Kiel 1894–95.

Niobe launched 18 Sept 1849, and served in the British navy; bought 1861; served as a training ship for sea cadets from 12 Oct 1861. Stricken 18 Nov 1890 and reduced to a hulk at Kiel; broken up 1919 by Peters, Wewelsfleth. Figurehead in Mürwik Naval School.

Thetis (1856)

Niobe (1862)

Arcona class

Name	Builder	Built	Cost in Marks (000s)	Displacement (t = tonnes T = tons)	Length (m)	Breadth (m)	Draught (m)	Power (hp)	Revs (rpm)	Speed (kts)	Range (nm/kts)	Coal (t)	Oil (t)
ARCONA	Royal Dockyard, Danzig	1855–59	563.7 Thaler	2391t max 1928t des	71.95 oa 63.55 cwl	13.0	5.55 fwd 6.35 aft	1365ihp max 350nhp des	62	12.4 max 8.0 des	1150/11	229 max 176 des	—
GAZELLE	,,	1855–61	599.9 Thaler	,,	,,	,,	,,	1320ihp max 340nhp des	59	12.0 max 8.0 des	,,	,,	—
VINETA	,,	1869–64	576.8 Thaler	2504t max 2113t des	73.32 oa 65.50 cwl	12.9	5.52 fwd 6.53 aft	1580ihp max 400nhp des	66	11.7 max 8.0 des	1350/11	190 max 150 des	—
HERTHA	,,	1860–65	593.7 Thaler	,,	,,	,,	,,	1510ihp max 400nhp des	65	11.5 max 8.0 des	,,	,,	—
ELISABETH	,,	1866–69	2.066 = 688.8 Thaler	2912t max 2454t des	79.30 oa 71.50 cwl	13.2	5.50 fwd 6.40 aft	2440ihp max 650nhp des	72	12.1 max 9.0 des	1900/10 1020/12	240 max 170 des	—

1527gt/1023nt (*Arcona*, *Gazelle*), 1846gt/1076nt (*Vineta*, *Hertha*), 1996gt/1301nt (*Elisabeth*)

Construction

Laid down as screw-driven frigates (design by Gjerling with improvements, 1854). Transverse frame oak plank carvel hull with copper sheathing. Depth 7.48m.

Propulsion

One horizontal 2-cylinder single expansion engine in *Arcona* by John Cockerill, Seraing/Lüttich, 350hp; in *Gazelle* by AG Vulcan, Stettin, 340hp; in *Vineta* and *Hertha* by J Penn & Sons, Greenwich, 400hp; in *Elisabeth* by Maudslay Son & Field, London, 650hp (one 2-bladed screw, 4.8m diameter). Four trunk boilers (sixteen fireboxes, 1.33 atmospheres forced), in an engine and boiler room devoid of bulkheads [four trunk boilers from Imperial dockyard, Danzig (1.5 atmospheres forced, after *Vineta* 2 atmospheres forced)]. Full-rigged ships, about 2200sq m. One rudder.

Armament

Elisabeth and *Gazelle* six 68pdr, plus twenty 36pdr until 1870 [seventeen, finally eight 15cm/22 hooped guns (1692 rounds)]. *Vineta*, *Hertha* and *Arcona* twenty-eight 68pdr until 1869 [seventeen and nineteen 15cm/22 hooped guns, plus two 12.5cm/23 hooped guns on *Vineta* and *Hertha* only].

Handling

Excellent sea-boats, very manoeuvrable and handy under sail with screw raised and ballast at the bow; much sail necessary for best performance. Speed loss severe when steaming in a head sea.

Complement

Crew: 35/345. Boats: one launch, two pinnaces, one cutter, one yawl, two dinghies.

Arcona (1860), *Gazelle*; *Vineta*, *Hertha* and *Elisabeth* were similar.

Notes

Colour scheme no 1, 2. *Arcona* and *Gazelle* had a large steam pipe on the front edge of the funnel. All except *Elisabeth* had a transom stern. *Gazelle*'s engines were very unsatisfactory.

Career

Arcona launched 19 May 1859, commissioned for service abroad 15 Apr 1859; home 1862–69; abroad 1869–71; reduced to a cadet training ship; guard ship at Kiel 1876. Stricken 18 Mar 1884 and used as a target ship; broken up 1884 at the Imperial Dockyard, Kiel.

Gazelle launched 19 Dec 1859, commissioned 15 May 1862; service mostly abroad. Stricken 8 Jan 1884, reduced to a barrack ship at Wilhelmshaven; sold 1906 for 36,000M; broken up.

Vineta launched 4 Jun 1863, commissioned 3 Mar 1864, service mostly abroad. Stricken 12 Aug 1884, reduced to an engine hulk at Wilhelmshaven; sold 1897 for 55,220M; broken up at the Imperial Dockyard, Kiel. Figurehead now in the Mürwik Naval School.

Hertha launched 1 Oct 1864, commissioned 1 Nov 1865, service 1867–82 mostly abroad. Stricken 12 Aug 1884, reduced to a coal hulk for torpedo boats at Kiel-Wik; sold 1902 for 45,600M, broken up at Swinemünde. Figurehead now in the German Maritime Museum.

Elisabeth launched 18 Oct 1869, commissioned 29 Sept 1869; service mostly abroad until 1886. Stricken 20 Sept 1887, reduced to an engine hulk at Kiel for stoker and engineer training; sold 1904 for 83,000M, broken up 1904 at Stettin. Figurehead now in the German Maritime Museum.

Leipzig class

Name	Builder	Built	Cost in Marks (000s)	Displacement (t = tonnes T = tons)	Length (m)	Breadth (m)	Draught (m)	Power (hp)	Revs (rpm)	Speed (kts)	Range (nm/kts)	Coal (t)	Oil (t)
LEIPZIG	AG Vulcan, Stettin Construction no 72	1874–77	4061	4626t max 3980t des	87.50 oa 87.00 cwl	14.0	6.20 for 6.90 aft	6050ihp max 1200nhp des	83.5	15.8 max 14.0 des	2330/10 1580/14	370 max	—
	mod: Imperial Dockyard, Wilhelmshaven	1885–88											
PRINZ ADALBERT	AG Vulcan, Stettin Construction no 73 2627gt/1643nt	1875–77	4130	,,	,,	,,	,,	,,	,,	,,	,,	,,	,,

Construction

Laid down as flush-decked corvettes *Thusnelda* and *A* (official design, 1871–72). Transverse and longitudinal frame iron construction, with two layers of wooden planking and copper sheathing (seven, [nine and ten] watertight compartments, double bottom under engine room only). Depth 9.87m. Immersion increased by 1cm per 9.77t.

Propulsion

One horizontal 3-cylinder single expansion engine (one retractable 2-bladed screw, 6.0m diameter [one 4-bladed screw, 5.8m diameter]) in one engine room. Ten cylinder boilers [new boilers from Imperial Dockyard, Wilhelmshaven]. *Sédan* had six trunk boilers (thirty and twenty-four fireboxes, 5 atmospheres forced, 1609sq m) in one boiler room; retractable funnels [*Leipzig* was fitted with fixed funnels. One generator, 9.1kW 55V.] Full-rigged ships, 2600sq m [1580sq m]. Wooden topmasts, etc, were supplied together with rigging by the Imperial Dockyard, Kiel. One rudder.

Armament

Two 17cm/25 hooped guns plus ten 17cm/20 hooped guns (1226 rounds), range 5000m; [four machine guns;

Leipzig up to 1885; *Prinz Adalbert* had one funnel at all times.

four 35cm TT (10 rounds), two lateral, two bow, all above water].

Handling

Very stiff when bunkers were full, with severe pitch and roll, otherwise not uncomfortable; slow to turn. Performance under sail was very moderate.

Complement

Crew: 39/386. Boats: one picket boat, two launches, one pinnace, one cutter, two yawls, one dinghy.

Notes

Colour scheme no 1, 2. Both ships were designed with a forecastle and a flying deck. The original layout of the midship area is shown in the supplementary drawing. [*Prinz Adalbert* in her final form had first and fourth steam pipes the same length as the funnel.] The bowsprit was retractable.

Career

Leipzig launched 13 Sept 1875, commissioned 1 Jun 1877; service mostly abroad until 1893. Stricken 27 Aug 1894 and reduced to an engine hulk at Wilhelmshaven; sunk 5 Nov 1919 at Wilhelmshaven, raised 1921, sold to Hattinger Co, broken up at Wilhelmshaven.

Prinz Adalbert launched 17 Jun 1876 as *Sédan*, commissioned 28 Aug 1877; renamed *Prinz Adalbert* 1 Sept 1878; served abroad 1878–80 and 1883–88. Stricken 6 May 1890 and reduced to a barrack ship at Wilhelmshaven; sold for 131,000M 7 Jun 1907, broken up 1907 in Holland. Figurehead now in Mürwik Naval School.

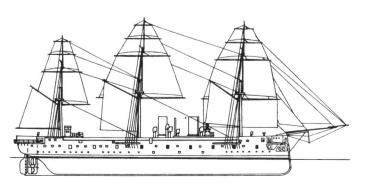

Leipzig (1890); *Prinz Adalbert* was similar.

Bismarck class

Name	Builder	Built	Cost in Marks (000s)	Displacement (t = tonnes T = tons)	Length (m)	Breadth (m)	Draught (m)	Power (hp)	Revs (rpm)	Speed (kts)	Range (nm/kts)	Coal (t)	Oil (t)
BISMARCK	Nordd Schiff AG, Kiel	1875–78	2721	3386t max 2856t des	82.50 oa 72.20 cwl	13.7	5.68 fwd 6.18 aft	2530ihp max 2500ihp des	85.1	12.5 max 12.0 des	2380/9 minimum 1940/10 840/14	270 to 326 max 380 des	
BLÜCHER	Nordd. Schiff AG, Kiel mod: Imperial Dockyard, Kiel	1876–78 1892	2728	,, 2890t max 2756t des	,,	,,	,, 5.28 fwd 6.19 aft	2989ihp max 2500ihp des	94.6	13.9 max 12.0 des	,,	,,	
STOSCH	AG Vulcan, Stettin Construction no 77	1876–78	2521	2994t max 2843t des	82.00 oa 72.18 cwl	,,	5.20 fwd 6.30 aft	2419ihp max 2500ihp des	85.8	12.6 max 12.0 des	,,	,,	
MOLTKE	Imperial Dockyard, Danzig	1875–78	2814	,,	,,	,,	,,	2334ihp max 2500ihp des	92.9	13.9 max 12.0 des	,,	,,	
GNEISENAU	Imperial Dockyard, Danzig	1877–80	3089	,,	,,	,,	,,	2866ihp max 2500ihp des	95.1	13.8 max 12.0 des	,,	,,	
STEIN	AG Vulcan, Stettin Construction no 83	1878–80	2721	,,	,,	,,	,,	2535ihp max 2500ihp des	84.0	13.0 max 12.0 des	,,	,,	

2051gt/1450nt·(*Bismarck*), 2218gt/1212nt (*Blücher*), 2099gt/1305nt (others)

Construction

Laid down as flush-decked corvettes *B*, *C*, *Ersatz Gazelle*, *Ersatz Arcona*, *D*, and *Ersatz Hertha* (official design, 1873–75). Transverse frame iron construction, with one layer of wooden planks with zinc sheathing up to 1m above CWL (nine watertight compartments, double bottom under engine room). Depth 9.18m, immersion increased by 1cm per 8.0t and 8.32t. Trim moment 3567m-t. The class was given the temporary official designation of Third Rate Ship.

Propulsion

One horizontal 3-cylinder single expansion engine (one retractable 2-bladed screw, 5.2m diameter; in *Blücher*, one 3-bladed screw, 4.6m diameter), in *Bismarck*, *Blücher*, *Moltke* and *Gneisenau* by Märkisch-Schlesischer Maschinenbau und Hütten AG, formerly F A Egells, Berlin-Moabit, in one engine room. Four transverse trunk boilers, in *Bismarck*, *Blücher* and *Gneisenau* by Märkisch-Schlesischer Maschinenbau und Hütten AG, etc, Berlin. [*Blücher*, *Stosch* and *Gneisenau* were fitted with new boilers by the Imperial dockyard, Kiel in 1892; *Stein* received new boilers from the Imperial Dockyard, Wilhelmshaven, in 1885; *Moltke* from the Imperial dockyard, Danzig in 1897] (twenty fireboxes, 2 atmospheres forced, approx 1000sq m [959sq m; *Stein*, eighteen fireboxes, 3 atmospheres forced]) in one boiler room. Funnel retractable. [*Bismarck* and *Gneisenau* were fitted with one generator, 1.9kW 55V; *Stosch* and *Moltke* with three generators, 26kW 55V, and later two generators, 20–24kW 67V, as in *Stein*; *Blücher* with three generators 33kW 67V.] Full-rigged ships, 2210sq m [reduced to 1580–1783sq m; *Blücher* 584sq m and all rigging later removed]. One rudder.

Armament

Sixteen 15cm/22 hooped guns (1660 rounds), range 4600–5400m [*Stosch* and *Moltke* were fitted with ten, *Stein* twelve, and *Gneisenau* fourteen 15cm/22 QF guns, two 8.8cm/30 hooped guns, two 8.8cm/30 QF guns, six machine guns; *Blücher* carried no guns other than two to four boat cannons, 8cm/25, plus up to thirteen machine guns; *Blücher* was also fitted with four to seven 35cm TT, one stern, two lateral (all above water), one bow (under water), plus three 45cm TT, one lateral (above water), one – position not known – under water, one bow (under water); *Bismarck* was fitted with two 35cm TT, bow.] All other ships in the class were without torpedoes.

Handling

Fairly good sea-boats, but made severe leeway even in light wind; difficult to manoeuvre, and suffered from considerable loss of speed in a head sea. Performance under sail limited.

Complement

Crew 18/386 [*Stosch*, *Moltke* and *Stein* as training ships carried 20/449, including 50 sea cadets and 210 (*Moltke* finally none) cabin boys; *Gneisenau*, 17/443 including 20 and 230; and *Blücher*, 34/494 to 14/287]. Boats: one picket boat, two launches, one pinnace, two [six] cutters, two yawls, two dinghies; *Blücher*, six [two] picket boats, two launches, one pinnace, two cutters, two yawls, two dinghies [removed].

Notes

Colour schemes: *Bismarck*, no 2; *Blücher*, no 2, 4, 9; after *Stosch*, no 2, 3, 8, 11. All ships initially had no forward bridge and no searchlights. [*Stosch*, *Gneisenau* and *Stein* as training ships were fitted with a flying deck as far aft as the mizzen mast and a searchlight forward of the funnel instead of above the pressure head, on a platform 9m above the CWL.] *Blücher* carried 250t ballast as a stationary training ship.

Career

Bismarck launched 25 Jul 1877, commissioned 27 Aug 1878; served mostly abroad, 1878–88. Stricken 21 Sept 1891 and reduced to a barrack hulk at Wilhelmshaven; broken up 1920 at Rüstringen.

Blücher launched 20 Sept 1877, commissioned 21 Dec 1878; served as a torpedo testing and training ship from 10 Aug 1880, and from Sept 1906 as a training and barrack hulk at Mürwik. Stricken 29 Feb 1908, after a boiler explosion on 6 Nov 1907; sold 1908 to a Rotterdam company for 142,000M, and used as a coal hulk at Vigo, used up.

Stosch launched 8 Oct 1877, commissioned March 1878; served abroad 1881–85, and as a training ship for sea cadets and cabin boys from 1888. Stricken 27 May 1907, sold, broken up.

Moltke launched 18 Oct 1877, commissioned 16 Apr 1878; served abroad 1881–89, and as a training ship for sea cadets and cabin boys from 1891 until 1908. Stricken 24 Oct 1910, became submarine tender *Acheron* at Kiel after 28 Oct 1911; sold 7 Jul 1920 to the submarine administration, but reconstruction was not carried out; broken up.

Gneisenau launched 4 Sept 1879, commissioned 3 Oct 1880; served abroad 1882–86, and as a training ship for sea cadets and cabin boys from 1887. Sunk 16 Dec 1900 near Malaga, position 36° 42N, 04° 26W, after stranding on the Mole in a hurricane, 41 dead.

Stein launched 14 Sept 1879, commissioned 3 Oct 1880; served abroad until 1888; used as a training ship for sea cadets and cabin boys after that date. Stricken 21 May 1908 and reduced to a barrack hulk at Wilhelmshaven, broken up 1920 at Wilhelmshaven.

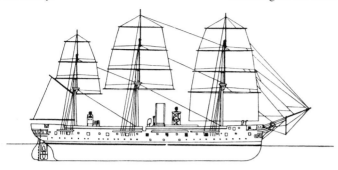

Moltke (1890), *Bismarck*, *Stosch*, *Gneisenau*, *Stein*

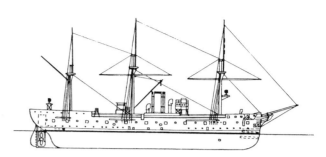

Blücher (1890)

Charlotte

Name	Builder	Built	Cost in Marks (000s)	Displacement (t = tonnes T = tons)	Length (m)	Breadth (m)	Draught (m)	Power (hp)	Revs (rpm)	Speed (kts)	Range (nm/kts)	Coal (t)	Oil (t)
CHARLOTTE	Imperial Dockyard, Wilhelmshaven Construction no 8	1883–86		3763t max 3288t des	83.85 oa 76.85 cwl	14.6	6.04 fwd 6.86 aft	3119ihp max 3000ihp des	92.9	13.5 max 13.0 des	2300/11 2200/13	528	—
2368gt/1963nt	mod: Imperial Dockyard, Kiel	1903-05						1473ihp max 1200ihp des	75.1	11.4 max 11.0 des	4000/12		

Construction

Laid down as flush-decked corvette *Ersatz Victoria* (official design, 1881–82). Transverse frame iron construction, with one layer of wooden planks with Muntz metal sheathing (ten watertight compartments, double bottom under engine room). Depth 9.18m, immersion increased by 1cm per 8.87t. Trim moment 3621m-t.

Propulsion

One plus one coupled horizontal 2-cylinder double expansion engines [one engine eventually removed] (one retractable 2-bladed screw, 5.35m diameter [screw not retractable after 1899; well added]) in one engine room. Eight [six] transverse cylinder recirculating boilers (sixteen [twelve] fireboxes, 5 atmospheres forced, 1064sq m [694sq m]) [new boilers fitted by the Imperial Dockyard, Wilhelmshaven] in 1 + 1 boiler rooms. Funnels retractable. Two generators, 19.5kW 67V. Full-rigged ship, 2360sq m [barque rig 1580sq m]. One rudder.

Armament

Eighteen [twelve] 15cm/22 hooped guns (1868 rounds), range 4600–5500m; two 8.8cm/30 QF guns; six machine guns [after 1899, two 10.5cm/35 QF guns (160 rounds), sixteen 8.8cm/30 QF guns, four machine guns].

Handling

As *Bismarck* class.

Complement

Crew: 20/486 [20/475 including 50 sea cadets and 230 cabin boys]. Boats: one picket boat, two launches, six cutters, one yawl, one dinghy.

Notes

Colour scheme no 2, 3, 8, 11.

Career

Charlotte launched 5 Sept 1885, commissioned 1 Nov 1886; served abroad 1888–89, and as a training ship for sea cadets and cabin boys 1897–1909. Stricken 26 May 1909; used as a barrack ship and tender to *König Wilhelm* from 1910; sold to Hamburg 1921; reported to have been used subsequently as a store ship.

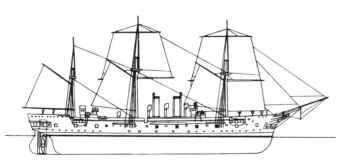

Charlotte (1900)

Large cruisers and battlecruisers 1892–1917

Kaiserin Augusta

Name	Builder	Built	Cost in Marks (000s)	Displacement (t = tonnes T = tons)	Length (m)	Breadth (m)	Draught (m)	Power (hp)	Revs (rpm)	Speed (kts)	Range (nm/kts)	Coal (t)	Oil (t)
KAISERIN AUGUSTA	Germania Dockyard, Kiel Construction no 53	1890–92	8697	6318t max 6056t des	123.2 oa 122.2 cwl	15.6	6.48 fwd 7.40 aft	14,015ihp max 12,000ihp des	124	21.5 max 21.0 des	3240/12	810 max 750 des	—
3371gt/1517nt	mod: Imperial Dockyard, Kiel	1903–07	3037										

Construction

Laid down as cruiser-corvette or Second Rate cruiser *H* (official design, 1887–89). Transverse and longitudinal frame steel construction, with a single layer of timber planks with Muntz metal sheathing up to 0.65m above CWL (ten watertight compartments, double bottom 55 percent). Krupp armour: deck 50mm, slopes 70mm; CT roof 20mm, sides 50mm. Cork cofferdams. Depth 8.03m. Immersion increased by 1cm per 12.84t [12.75t]. Trim moment 7682m-t.

Propulsion

Three vertical 3-cylinder triple expansion engines (two 3-bladed screws, 4.5m diameter, one 3-bladed screw, 4.2m diameter) by AG Germania, Berlin-Tegel, in 1 + 2 engine rooms. Eight cylindrical double boilers (forty-eight fireboxes, 12 atmospheres forced, 3322sq m) by AG Germania, Berlin-Tegel, in 1 + 1 + 1 boiler rooms. Four generators, 48kW 67V [four generators, 124kW 110V]. One balanced rudder.

Armament

Initially temporarily armed with four 15cm/30 hooped guns (292 rounds), eight 10.5cm/35 QF guns (777 rounds), eight 8.8cm/30 QF guns (1361 rounds), four machine guns, and five 35cm TT (13 rounds), four lateral, above water, swivel mounted, one bow, below water. After 1896 armament was twelve 15cm/35 QF guns (1064 rounds), range 12,600m, eight 8.8cm/30 QF guns (1600 rounds), five 35cm TT, etc, and, after 1907, one 35cm TT (3 rounds), one bow, under water. [Armament after 1916 was one 15cm/45 Utof gun, four 10.5cm/45 Utof guns, four 8.8cm/45 QF guns, four 8.8cm/35 QF guns, five 8.8cm/30 QF guns, and one 8.8cm/30 QF gun in a U-boat mounting.]

Handling

Severe pitch and roll, somewhat reduced in wind and beam sea; the forecastle was poorly designed and unable to withstand heavy head seas; she made considerable leeway and was difficult to manoeuvre, though somewhat better at high speed. Transverse metacentric height 0.78m, longitudinal 141.0m. Maximum stability moment at 54°, = zero at >90° with superstructure. Fleet rudder angle 39°.

Complement

Crew: 13/417. Boats: two picket boats, one launch, one pinnace, two cutters, two yawls, two dinghies.

Notes

Colour scheme no 3, 4, 7, 9. Considerable reinforcement was necessary to the main structural components, which were poorly designed and constructed. First ship in the Imperial navy to be fitted with three 3-bladed screws. [In 1905 the bridge was increased to two decks and extended to 4m aft of the foremast; the aft compass platform was moved forward by 10m. One searchlight was fitted on each top. The funnels were 2m higher after 1903.]

Career

Kaiserin Augusta launched 15 Jan 1892, commissioned 17 Nov 1892; served abroad until 1902; used as a gunnery training ship 1914. Stricken 1 Oct 1919, sold to Norddeutsche Tiefbauges, Berlin; broken up 1920 at Kiel-Nordmole.

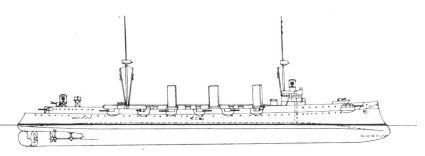

Kaiserin Augusta (1900)

Victoria Louise class

Name	Builder	Built	Cost in Marks (000s)	Displacement (t = tonnes T = tons)	Length (m)	Breadth (m)	Draught (m)	Power (hp)	Revs (rpm)	Speed (kts)	Range (nm/kts)	Coal (t)	Oil (t)
VICTORIA LOUISE sq fl	AG 'Weser', Bremen Construction no 116	1895–98	10,714	6491t max 5660t des	110.6 oa 109.1 cwl	17.4	6.58 fwd 6.93 aft	10,574ihp max 10,000ihp des	136	19.2 max 19.5 des	3412/12	950 max 500 des	—
	mod: Imperial Dockyard, Kiel	1906–08	2552								3300 to 3840/12	840 to 950 max	
HERTHA	AG Vulcan, Stettin Construction no 233	1895–98	9932	,,	,,	,,	6.58 fwd 6.78 aft	10,312ihp max 10,000ihp des	139	19.0 max 19.5 des	3412/12	950 max 500 des	—
	mod: Imperial Dockyard, Danzig	1906–08	2527								3300 to 3840/12	840 to 950 max	
FREYA	Imperial Dockyard, Danzig	1895–98	11,094	,,	,,	,,	6.74 fwd 6.77 aft	10,355ihp max 10,000ihp des	130	18.4 max 19.5 des	3412/12	950 max 500 des	—
	mod: Imperial Dockyard, Wilhelmshaven	1905–07	1777								3300 to 3840/12	840 to 950 max	
	mod: Imperial Dockyard, Danzig	1911–13											
VINETA sq fl	Imperial Dockyard, Danzig	1896–99	10,714	6705t max 5885t des	110.5 oa 109.8 cwl	17.6	7.08 fwd 7.34 aft	10,646ihp max 10,000ihp des	136	19.6 max 18.5 des	3412/12	950 max 500 des	—
	mod: Imperial Dockyard, Danzig	1909–11	2560								3300 to 3840/12	840 to 950 max	
HANSA	AG Vulcan, Stettin Construction no 235	1896–98	10,270	,,	,,	,,	,,	10,388ihp max 10,000ihp des	138	18.7 max 18.5 des	3412/12	950 max 500 des	—
	mod: Imperial Dockyard, Danzig	1907–09									3300 to 3840/12	840 to 950 max	
	mod: Imperial Dockyard, Kiel	1915											

4108 gt/2100nt; after refit 4203gt/2457nt

Construction

Laid down as Second Rate cruisers *L*, *K*, *Ersatz Freya*, *M* and *N* (official design, 1893–95). Transverse and longitudinal frame steel construction, with a single layer of wooden planks with Muntz metal sheathing up to 1m (2m forward) above CWL, [sheathing removed from *Victoria Louise*, *Hertha* and *Freya*] (twelve [later eleven, except *Freya*] watertight compartments, double bottom 60 percent). Krupp armour: deck 40mm, slopes 100mm; forward CT roof 30mm, sides 150mm; aft CT 12mm; 21cm and 15cm turrets, roof 30mm, sides 100mm; casemates 100mm, shields 70mm; cork cofferdams. Depth 11.4m. Immersion increased by 1cm per 13.3t [12.53t]. Trim moment 6695 to 7841m-t [6695 to 6725m-t].

Propulsion

Three vertical 4-cylinder triple expansion engines (three 3-bladed screws, 3.5 to 4.0m diameter) for *Freya* by AG Germania, Berlin-Tegel, in 1 + 2 engine rooms. Boilers were as follows: *Victoria Louise* and *Vineta*, twelve Dürr boilers by Düsseldorf-Ratinger Röhrenkesselfabrik (twenty-four fireboxes, 15 atmospheres forced, 2777sq m); *Freya* (up to 1911), twelve Niclausse boilers (twenty-four fireboxes, 13 atmospheres forced, 2549sq m); *Hertha*, twelve Belleville boilers (twenty-four fireboxes, 13 atmospheres forced, 2400sq m); *Hansa*, eighteen transverse Belleville boilers (eighteen fireboxes, 18 atmospheres forced, 2329sq m). [All refitted with transverse Marine-type boilers (sixteen fireboxes, 14.5 atmospheres forced; *Victoria Louise*, 13 atmospheres forced, 2560sq m, in 1 + 1 boiler rooms*.] Four generators, 271–224kW 110V [after *Hertha*, three generators, 169 to 183kW 110V. One balanced rudder.

* Difficulties in installing the French Niclausse boilers in *Freya* (the ship was not able to commence trials until October 1900) resulted in a policy of installing standard boilers throughout the navy (Thornycroft-Schulz and Marine-type boilers, developed by the Imperial navy).

Armament

Two 21cm/40 QF guns (116 rounds), −5° +30°, range 16,300m; eight [six] 15cm/40 QF guns (960–710 rounds), range 13,700m; ten [eleven] 8.8cm/30 QF guns; [three 8.8cm/35 guns (2500 rounds)]; ten machine cannon [removed]; three 45cm TT (8 rounds), two lateral, one bow, all under water [all ships disarmed after 1916, except for *Freya*, one 15cm/40 QF gun, four 10.5cm/45 QF guns, fourteen 8.8cm/30,35 QF guns].

Handling

Good sea-boats, with easy motion but a tendency to pitch when steaming downwind; dry. Made severe leeway in a sidewind because of the tall superstructure. The centre screw was essential for manoeuvrability. Speed loss in a head sea and with hard rudder was slight – less than 10 percent. Seakeeping abilities deteriorated severely as lower bunkers were emptied (up to 15° more heel at speed with the rudder hard over) [this was improved after reconstruction in all ships of the class]. Transverse metacentric height 0.56 to 0.73m [0.711 to 0.82m], longitudinal 108 to 123m [112 to 123m]. (Maximum) stability moment at 77°, with superstructure at 95°, = zero at 38 to 45° [41 to 46°]. Fleet rudder angle for *Victoria Louise* was 35°, all others 40°.

Complement

Crew: 31/446 (plus 9/41 as second command flagship) [26/658 including 75 sea cadets and 300 cabin boys]. Boats: three [one] picket boats, [one barge], one [two] launches, one pinnace, two [seven] cutters, two yawls, three dinghies [removed].

Notes

Colour scheme no 9, 11. All were very hot ships as designed, and required several improvements to ventilation before and after commissioning, which eased the problem slightly. For identification, note that all ships carried an Inglefield bow anchor, but *Victoria Louise* also carried one to starboard and one to port; *Hertha* and *Hansa*, one Hall anchor to port. *Hertha* and *Hansa* were fitted with non-pierced davits; those on *Freya* and *Vineta* were as shown in the drawing. The searchlight platform was without a roof after *Freya*. Until 1902 a searchlight was carried at the fore masthead and at the casemate deck platforms (refer to the drawing), later on the fore masthead, on the aft conning tower [and above the first 15cm turret on each beam]. On *Hansa* the aft compass platform was 15m further aft. [*Freya*'s hull and masts were as shown in the second drawing, but she retained the earlier three funnels. On all ships after about 1900 the forward bridge was modified; each ship was also fitted with 8.8cm QF sponsons in the forecastle. *Hertha* and *Vineta* were fitted with one compass platform 3m forward of the mainmast and one 1m aft; *Hansa* had one compass platform 3m forward of the mainmast and one on the aft conning tower. After *Hertha* the forward bridge on all ships was rebuilt as shown for *Freya* in 1914.]

Career

Victoria Louise launched 29 Mar 1897, commissioned 20 Feb 1899 into the fleet; served as a training ship for sea cadets and cabin boys after 1908, as a coastal defence ship from 1914, and as a minelayer and barrack ship at Danzig from 1915. Stricken 1 Oct 1919, sold to Norddeutsche Tiefbau Co, Berlin; reconstructed 1920 at Danzig as a freighter, renamed *Flora Sommerfeld*, for Danziger Hoch- und Tiefbau-GmbH; broken up 1923 at Danzig.

Hertha launched 14 Apr 1897, commissioned 23 Jul 1898; served abroad until 1905, as a training ship for sea cadets and cabin boys from 1908, as a coastal defence ship from 1914, and as a barrack ship at the Flensburg seaplane base from 1915. Stricken 6 Dec 1919, and broken up 1920 at Audorf-Rendsburg.

Freya launched 27 Apr 1897, commissioned 20 Oct 1898; served in the fleet from 1900, and from 1907 as a training ship for sea cadets and cabin boys; served as a coastal defence ship in 1914, then reverted to a training ship at Flensburg in 1915. Stricken 25 Jan 1920, and used as a police barrack ship at Hamburg, broken up 1921 at Harburg.

Vineta launched 9 Dec 1897, commissioned 13 Sept 1899; served abroad until 1905, as a torpedo test ship from 1908; used as a training ship for sea cadets and cabin boys from 1911, for coastal defence from 1914, and from 1915 as a barrack ship at Kiel. Stricken 6 Dec 1919, broken up 1920 at Harburg.

Hansa launched 12 Mar 1898, commissioned 20 Apr 1899; served abroad until 1906, as a training ship for sea cadets and cabin boys from 1909, as a coastal defence ship from 1914, and as a barrack ship at Kiel dockyard from 1915. Stricken 6 Dec 1919, broken up 1920 at Audorf-Rendsburg.

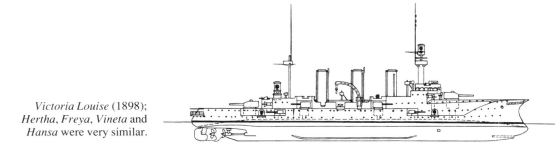

Victoria Louise (1898); *Hertha*, *Freya*, *Vineta* and *Hansa* were very similar.

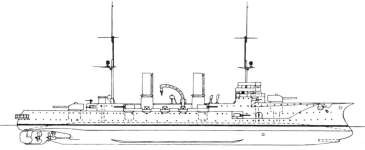

Victoria Louise (1912), second form

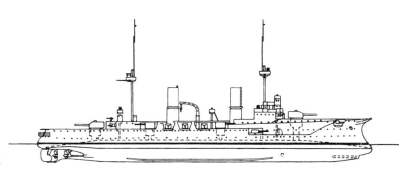

Freya (1914), second form

Fürst Bismarck

Name	Builder	Built	Cost in Marks (000s)	Displacement (t = tonnes T = tons)	Length (m)	Breadth (m)	Draught (m)	Power (hp)	Revs (rpm)	Speed (kts)	Range (nm/kts)	Coal (t)	Oil (t)
FÜRST BISMARK sq fl	Imperial Dockyard, Kiel Construction no 23	1895–00	18,945	11,461t max 10,690t des	127.0 oa 125.7 cwl	20.4	7.80 fwd 8.46 aft	13,622ihp max 13,500ihp des	113 max 115 des	18.7 max 18.7 des	4560/10 3230/12	1400 max 900 des	120 max*
6455gt/3916nt	mod: Imperial Dockyard, Kiel	1910–15											

* tar oil only 1908-09

Construction

Laid down as First Rate cruiser *Ersatz Leipzig* (official design, 1893–95). Transverse and longitudinal frame steel construction, with a single layer of wooden planks with Muntz metal sheathing up to 0.95m above CWL; lower parts of stem and stern bronze (thirteen watertight compartments, double bottom 59 percent). Krupp armour: deck 30mm, slopes 50mm; forward CT roof 30mm, sides 200mm; aft CT roof 30mm, sides 100mm; CWL 100–200 (shields 100)–100mm on 200mm teak; 24cm turrets, roof 40mm, sides 200mm; 15cm turrets 100mm; shields 70mm; casemates 100mm; cork cofferdams. Depth 12.98m. Immersion increased by 1cm per 18.9t. Trim moment 12,064m-t.

Propulsion

Three vertical 4-cylinder triple expansion engines (one plus two 3- bladed screws, 4.4m and 4.8m diameter) in 1 + 2 engine rooms. Four transverse Thornycroft boilers (by AG Germania, Berlin-Tegel) and eight transverse cylindrical boilers (eight plus thirty-two fireboxes, 12 atmospheres forced, 1620sq m and 2112sq m) in 2 + 2 + 2 boiler rooms. Five generators, 325kW 110V. One balanced rudder.

Armament

Four 24cm/40 QF guns (312 rounds), –4° +30°, range 16,900m; twelve [ten] 15cm/40 QF guns (1440 rounds), range 13,700m; ten 8.8cm/30 QF guns (2500 rounds); four machine cannon (temporary); six 45cm TT (16 rounds), one stern above water (swivel mounted), four lateral, under water, one bow, under water. [Disarmed in 1916. The original traverse of the main guns was reduced considerably to avoid damage to the superstructure.]

Handling

Very good sea-boat, with slight lee helm; suffered from slight pitch, but serious roll, though motion was even; very responsive to the helm. Suffered from severe vibration at high speed. Transverse metacentric height 0.72m, longitudinal 138m. Maximum stability moment 38°, = zero at 74°. Fleet rudder angle 40°.

Complement

Crew: 36/585 (plus 14/62 as squadron flagship). Boats: one picket boat, one launch, two pinnaces, two cutters, two yawls, three dinghies.

Notes

Colour scheme no 9, 11. Whaleback forecastle. [After 1901 the searchlights were removed from the aft casemate deck platform, and after 1904 from the forward platform; these were replaced by new units on the aft conning tower. After 1915 new masts were fitted as on *Moltke*; one searchlight was fitted on a foremast platform 20m above CWL, two on a new bridge adjacent to the forward funnel 16.5m above CWL, two on a double platform directly aft of the mainmast 14m above CWL; the crane bridge was removed; the aft 15cm turrets and forward rudder balance were removed, with each rudder carrier now supported by V-shaped struts.]

Career

Fürst Bismarck launched 25 Sept 1897, commissioned 1 Apr 1900; served abroad until 1909, as a coastal defence ship from 1914, and as an engine training ship at Kiel from March 1915; used as an office ship 1919. Stricken 17 Jun 1919, sold to Brand & Son, Audorf, broken up 1919–20 at Audorf-Rendsburg.

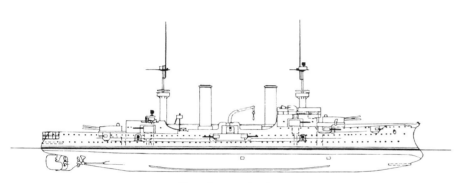

Fürst Bismarck (1900)

Prinz Heinrich

Name	Builder	Built	Cost in Marks (000s)	Displacement (t = tonnes T = tons)	Length (m)	Breadth (m)	Draught (m)	Power (hp)	Revs (rpm)	Speed (kts)	Range (nm/kts)	Coal (t)	Oil (t)
PRINZ HEINRICH sq fl	Imperial Dockyard, Kiel Construction no 26 mod: Imperial Dockyard, Kiel	1898– 1902	16,588	9806t max 8887t des	126.5 oa 124.9 cwl	19.6	7.65 fwd 8.07 aft	15,694ihp max 15,000ihp des	127 max 124 des	19.9 max 20.0 des	4580/10 2290/18	1590 max 900 des	175 max*
6070gt/3087nt		1914											

* 1908-09 only

Construction

Laid down as heavy cruiser *A* (official design, 1896–97). Transverse and longitudinal frame steel construction (thirteen watertight compartments, double bottom 57 percent). Krupp armour: deck 35–40(slopes 50)mm; forward CT roof 30mm, sides 150mm; aft CT 12mm; CWL 80–100–80mm with same thickness of teak; casemate 100mm; citadel 100mm; 24cm turrets, roof 30mm, sides 150mm; 15cm turrets 100mm; shields 70mm; cork cofferdams. Depth 12.00m. Immersion increased by 1cm per 16.81t. Trim moment 10,270m-t.

Propulsion

Three vertical 4-cylinder triple expansion engines (one 4-bladed screw, 4.28m and two 4-bladed screws 4.65m diameter) in 1 + 2 engine rooms. Fourteen Dürr boilers by Düsseldorf-Ratinger Röhrenkesselfabrik (forty-two fireboxes, 15 atmospheres forced, 4197sq m) in 2 + 2 boiler rooms. Four generators, 246kW 110V. One rudder.

Armament

Two 24cm/40 QF guns (150 rounds), –4° +30°, range 16,900m; ten 15cm/40 QF guns (1200 rounds), range 13,700m; ten 8.8cm/30 QF guns (2500 rounds); four machine cannon (temporary); four 45cm TT (11 rounds), one stern, above water (swivel mounted), two lateral, under water, one bow, under water. [Disarmed 1916.]

Handling

Good sea-boat, with slight pitch and severe roll, but gentle motion; responsive to the helm, otherwise similar to *Prinz Adalbert*. Transverse metacentric height 0.731m, longitudinal 128m. Maximum stability moment at 40.5°, = zero at 85°. Fleet rudder angle 40°.

Complement
Crew: 35/532 (plus 9/44 as second command flagship). Boats: two picket boats, one launch, one pinnace, two cutters, two yawls, two dinghies.

Notes
Colour scheme no 9. Whaleback forecastle. [After 1914 one searchlight only was carried on the foretop and one on a platform abaft the mainmast, 14m above CWL; the battle tops were removed except for the foretop; the superstructure deck bulwark was completely removed; and enclosed spotting tops were fitted at half height on the fore topmast and the mainmast crosstrees.]

Career
Prinz Heinrich launched 23 Mar 1900, commissioned 11 Mar 1902 into the fleet; used as an office ship at Kiel 1916, then as a tender, also at Kiel. Stricken 25 Jan 1920, sold, broken up 1920 at Audorf-Rendsburg.

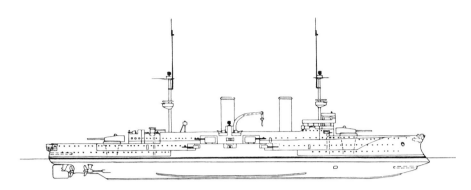

Prinz Heinrich (1900)

Prinz Adalbert class

Name	Builder	Built	Cost in Marks (000s)	Displacement (t = tonnes T = tons)	Length (m)	Breadth (m)	Draught (m)	Power (hp)	Revs (rpm)	Speed (kts)	Range (nm/kts)	Coal (t)	Oil (t)
PRINZ ADALBERT 2nd fl	Imperial Dockyard, Kiel Construction no 27	1900–04	16,371	9875t max 9087t des	126.5 oa 124.9 cwl	19.6	7.43 fwd 7.90 aft	17,272ihp max 16,200ihp des	120 max 118 des	20.4 max 20.0 des	(4970/12) (5080/12)	1630 max 750 des	200*
FRIEDRICH CARL 2nd fl 6070gt/3087nt	Blohm & Voss, Hamburg Construction no 155	1901–03	15,665	,,	,,	,,	7.80 fwd 7.80 aft	18,541ihp max 17,000ihp des	115 max 120 des	20.5 max 20.5 des ,,	,,	,,	

* 1908–09 only

Construction
Laid down as heavy cruisers *B* and *Ersatz König Wilhelm* (official design, 1899–1900). Transverse and longitudinal frame steel construction (fourteen watertight compartments, double bottom 60 percent). Krupp armour: deck 80–40–80mm; slopes 80–50–80mm; forward CT roof 30mm, sides 150mm; aft CT 20mm; CWL 0–80–100–80mm on 50mm teak; casemate 100mm; citadel 100mm; 21cm turrets, roof 30mm, sides 150mm; 15cm turrets 100m with shields 80mm; cork cofferdams. Depth 12.0m. Immersion increased by 1cm per 16.92t. Trim moment 10,410m-t.

Propulsion
Three vertical 3-cylinder triple expansion engines (one 3-bladed screw, 4.5m diameter and two 4-bladed screws, 4.8m diameter) in 1 + 2 engine rooms. Fourteen Dürr boilers by Düsseldorf-Ratinger Röhrenkesselfabrik (forty-two fireboxes, 13.5–14.25 atmospheres forced, 4600sq m) in 1 + 1 + 1 boiler rooms. Four generators, 246kW 110V. One rudder. Fuel consumption on trial: *Prinz Adalbert* 0.905 to 0.865kg per hp/hr; *Friedrich Carl* 0.917 to 0.840kg per hp/hr.

Armament
Four 21cm/40 QF guns (340 rounds), –5° +30°, range 16,300m; ten 15cm/40 QF guns (1500 rounds), range 13,700m; twelve 8.8cm/35 QF guns (1800 rounds); four machine cannon (temporary); four 45cm TT (11 rounds), one stern, port, under water, two lateral, under water, one bow, under water.

Handling
Good sea-boats, with a gentle motion when lower bunkers were full; very slight weather helm was required, and both ships were generally responsive to the helm;

Mainmast 1914–15

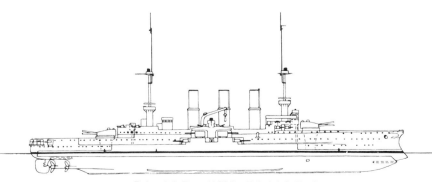

Prinz Adalbert (1906), *Friedrich Carl*

Foremast, *Prinz Adalbert*, 1914–15

speed loss with hard rudder was up to 60 percent, but slight in head seas. The casemate decks and casemate were extremely wet even in a slight swell. Transverse metacentric height 0.734m, longitudinal 126m. Maximum stability moment at 41°, = zero at 88.5°. Fleet rudder angle 40°.

Complement

Crew: 35/551 (plus 9/44 as second command flagship). Boats: two picket boats, one launch, one pinnace, two cutters, two yawls, two dinghies.

Notes

Colour scheme no 9. *Friedrich Carl* was accidentally named *Prinz Friedrich Carl* at her christening. Both ships had a whaleback forecastle. *Friedrich Carl*'s davits were the type shown in the *Yorck* drawing. From 1904–05 *Prinz Adalbert* was fitted with searchlights in the following positions: one at the fore masthead, two diagonally positioned on the foretop roof, one on the mainmast and two on the crane bridge [after 1910 searchlights and a new topmast were fitted as on *Yorck*; *Prinz Adalbert*'s masts from 1915 were as shown in the supplementary drawings]. *Prinz Adalbert*'s funnel design was as in *Wittelsbach*.

Career

Prinz Adalbert launched 22 Jun 1901; served as a gunnery training ship from 12 Jan 1904, and from 1914 in the fleet. Sunk at 0834hrs on 23 Oct 1915 in the Baltic, west of Libau at position 56° 33N, 20° 28E, by a torpedo from the British submarine *E8*; 672 dead.

Friedrich Carl launched 21 Jun 1902, commissioned into the fleet 12 Dec 1903; served as a torpedo training ship from 1 Mar 1909, and as a coastal defence ship from 1914. Sunk at 0715hrs on 17 Nov 1914 in the Baltic, west-southwest of Memel at position 55° 41N, 20° 11E, by a Russian mine; 7 dead.

Roon class

Name	Builder	Built	Cost in Marks (000s)	Displacement (t = tonnes T = tons)	Length (m)	Breadth (m)	Draught (m)	Power (hp)	Revs (rpm)	Speed (kts)	Range (nm/kts)	Coal (t)	Oil (t)
ROON 2nd fl	Imperial Dockyard, Kiel Construction no 28	1902–06	15,345	10,266t max 9533t des	127.8 oa 127.3 cwl	20.2	7.76 fwd 7.73 aft	20,625ihp max 19,000ihp des	118 max 120 des	21.1 max 21.0 des	4200/12	1570 max 750 des	207*
YORCK sq fl 6441gt/3038nt	Blohm & Voss, Hamburg Construction no 167	1903–05	16,241	,,	,,	,,	,,	20,031ihp max 19,000ihp des	119 max 120 des	21.4 max 21.0 des	,,	,,	,,

* tar oil 1908–09 only

Construction

Laid down as heavy cruisers *Ersatz Kaiser* and *Ersatz Deutschland* (official design, 1901). Transverse and longitudinal frame steel construction (twelve watertight compartments, double bottom 60 percent). Krupp armour: deck 40–60mm; slopes 40–50mm; forward CT roof 30mm, sides 150mm; aft CT roof 20mm, sides 80mm; otherwise as *Prinz Adalbert*, but teak backing to belt armour was 55mm. Depth 12.14m. Immersion increased by 1cm per 17.69t. Trim moment 11,500m-t.

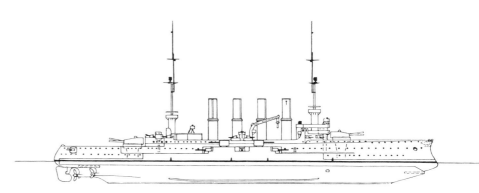

Yorck (1914), *Roon*

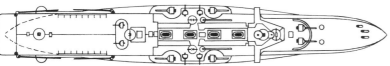

Roon (projected reconstruction 1917–18)

Propulsion

Engines, etc, as *Prinz Adalbert*. Sixteen Dürr boilers by Düsseldorf-Ratinger Röhrenkesselfabrik (forty-eight fireboxes, 15.5 atmospheres forced, 4900sq m) in 1 + 1 + 1 + 1 boiler rooms. Four turbo-generators, 260kW 110V. One rudder. Fuel consumption for *Yorck*, during trials, 0.945 to 0.848kg per hp/hr.

Armament

As *Prinz Adalbert*, but 380 21cm rounds and 1600 15cm rounds, and fourteen 8.8cm/45 QF guns (2100 rounds). [*Roon* was disarmed in 1916, and reconstruction as a seaplane tender was planned; projected armament was: six 15cm/45 QF guns, six 8.8cm/45 AA guns (2400 rounds), four seaplanes in hangars.

Handling

As *Prinz Adalbert*. Transverse metacentric height 1.04m, longitudinal 140m. Maximum stability moment at 39°, = zero at 82°.

Complement

Crew: 35/598 (plus 13/62 as squadron flagship; 9/44 as second command flagship). Boats: two picket boats, one launch, one pinnace, two cutters, two yawls, one dinghy.

Notes

Colour scheme no 9. Whaleback forecastle. Search-

lights and masts up to 1910, and also *Roon*'s davits were as shown in the *Prinz Adalbert* drawing. [In 1914 enclosed auxiliary spotting tops were fitted at half height on the topmast tops.] *Roon* was originally designed with three funnels, to the same design as proposed for *Braunschweig*. [Reconstruction of *Roon* as a seaplane tender was planned for 1917–18 (see drawings); reconstruction time was to be 20 months.]

Career

Roon launched 27 Jun 1903, commissioned 5 Apr 1906 into the fleet; served as a guard ship and barrack ship at Kiel from 1916. Stricken 25 Nov 1920, broken

up 1921 at Kiel-Nordmole.

Yorck launched 14 May 1904, commissioned 21 Nov 1905 into the fleet. Capsized and sank at 0410hrs on 4 Nov 1914 in the Jade, at position 53° 40.2N, 08° 05.2E, after hitting two German mines which had drifted out of position in the current; 336 dead. The wreck was partially cleared 1929–30, 1965, 1982 onwards.

Scharnhorst class

Name	Builder	Built	Cost in Marks (000s)	Displacement (t = tonnes T = tons)	Length (m)	Breadth (m)	Draught (m)	Power (hp)	Revs (rpm)	Speed (kts)	Range (nm/kts)	Coal (t)	Oil (t)
SCHARNHORST sq fl	Blohm & Voss, Hamburg Construction no 175	1905–07	20,319	12,985t max 11,616t des	144.6 oa 143.8 cwl	21.6	8.37 fwd 7.96 aft	28,783ihp max 26,000ihp des	121	23.5 max 22.5 des	5120/12 4800/14	2000 max 800 des	—
GNEISENAU sq fl 8122gt/3657nt	AG 'Weser', Bremen Construction no 144	1904–08	19,243	,,	,,	,,	,,	30,396ihp max 26,000ihp des	126	23.6 max 22.5 des	,,	,,	—

Construction

Laid down as heavy cruisers *D* and *C* (official design, 1903–04). Transverse and longitudinal frame steel construction (fifteen watertight compartments, double bottom 50 percent). Krupp armour: deck 60–35mm; slopes 40–55mm; forward CT roof 30mm, sides 200mm; aft CT roof 20mm, sides 50mm; CWL 0–80–150–80mm with teak backing; casemates 150mm; citadel 150mm; 21cm turrets, roof 30mm, sides 170mm; shields 150mm with 40mm roofs; 15cm shields 80mm; cork cofferdams. Depth 12.65m. Immersion increased by 1cm per 23.69, later 20.91t. Trim moment 14,700m-t.

Propulsion

As *Roon*, but *Scharnhorst* had one plus two 4-bladed screws, 4.7m and 5.0m in diameter, while *Gneisenau* had one plus two 4-bladed screws, 4.6m and 4.8m in diameter. Eighteen Marine-type boilers (thirty-six fireboxes, 16 atmospheres forced, 6300–6315sq m) in 1 + 1 + 1 + 1 + 1 boiler rooms. Electric plant as *Roon*. One rudder.

Armament

Eight 21cm/40 QF guns (700 rounds), –5° +30° and +16°, range 16,300 and 12,400m; six 15cm/40 QF guns (1020 rounds), range 13,700m; eighteen 8.8cm/35 QF guns (2700 rounds); four machine cannon (temporary); four 45cm TT (11 rounds), one stern, port, under water, two lateral, under water, one bow, under water.

Handling

Somewhat better sea-boats than *Prinz Adalbert*. Transverse metacentric height 1.18m, longitudinal 159m.

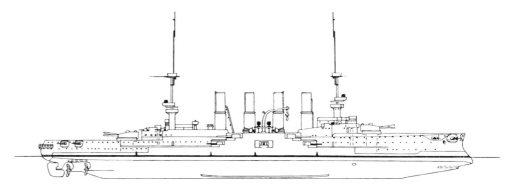

Gneisenau (1909), *Scharnhorst*

Maximum stability moment at 41°, = zero at 81°.

Complement

Crew: 38/726 (plus 14/62 as squadron flagship, 3/25 as second command flagship). Boats: two picket boats, two launches, one pinnace, two cutters, three yawls, one dinghy.

Notes

Colour scheme no 9, 11. Whaleback forecastle. *Scharnhorst* can be identified by her lack of visible steam pipes, and by her davits aft. [After 1912 search-lights were carried as follows: one at the fore masthead, one on the foretop, one each side on platforms over the wings of the lower bridge, 14m above CWL, and two set diagonally on the maintop roof,

those on the crane bridge being removed.]

Career

Scharnhorst launched 23 Mar 1906, commissioned 24 Oct 1907 into the fleet; served abroad after 1909. Sunk at 1617hrs on 8 Dec 1914 in Falklands waters, in position 52° 40S, 55° 51W, by gunfire from the British battlecruisers *Invincible* and *Inflexible*; 860 dead (all crew lost).

Gneisenau launched 14 Jun 1906, commissioned 6 Mar 1908 into the fleet; served abroad from 1910. Sunk at 1802hrs on 8 Dec 1914 in Falklands waters, in position 52° 46S, 56° 04W, by gunfire from the British battlecruisers *Invincible* and *Inflexible*; 598 dead.

Blücher

Name	Builder	Built	Cost in Marks (000s)	Displacement (t = tonnes T = tons)	Length (m)	Breadth (m)	Draught (m)	Power (hp)	Revs (rpm)	Speed (kts)	Range (nm/kts)	Coal (t)	Oil (t)
BLÜCHER sq fl	Imperial Dockyard, Kiel Construction no 33	1907–09	28,532	17,500t max 15,842t des	161.8 oa 161.1 cwl	24.5 25.62*	8.84 fwd 8.56 aft	38,323ihp max 32,000ihp des	123 max 122 des	25.4 max 24.5 des	(6600/12) (3250/18)	2510 max 900 des	—
	mod: Imperial Dockyard, Kiel	1913–14	2670										
9382gt/4222nt													

* over torpedo net booms

Construction

Laid down as heavy cruiser *E* (official design, 1904–05). Transverse and longitudinal steel frame construction (thirteen watertight compartments, double bottom 65 percent). Krupp armour: deck 50–70mm; torpedo bulkhead 35mm; forward CT roof 80mm, sides 250mm; aft CT roof 30mm, sides 140mm; CWL 0–80–180(shields 120)–80mm on 30mm teak; casemate 140mm; citadel 160mm; turrets, roof 80mm, sides 180mm; shields 80mm. Depth 13.8m. Immersion increased by 1cm per 26.19t. Trim moment 21,670m-t.

Propulsion

Three vertical 4-cylinder triple expansion engines (one plus two 4-bladed screws, 5.3 and 5.6m diameter) in three engine rooms. Eighteen Marine-type double boilers (thirty-six fireboxes, 16 atmospheres forced, 7638sq m) in 1 + 1 + 1 + 1 + 1 boiler rooms. Six turbogenerators, 1000kW 225V. One rudder.

Armament

Twelve 21cm/45 QF guns (1020 rounds), –5° +30°, range 19,100m; eight 15cm/45 QF guns (1320 rounds), range 13,500m; sixteen 8.8cm/45 QF guns (3200 rounds); four 45cm TT (11 rounds), one stern, starboard, two lateral, one bow, all under water.

Handling

Good sea-boat, with slight pitch but severe roll, though with gentle motion; slow into the turn with speed loss of up to 55 percent with hard rudder, and up to 10° heel. Transverse metacentric height 1.63m, longitudinal 183m. Maximum stability moment at 37°, = zero at 79°.

Complement

Crew: 41/812 (plus 14/62 as squadron flagship). Boats: two picket boats, three barges, two launches, two yawls, one dinghy.

Notes

Colour scheme no 9. Up to 1913 the foremast was a single pole mast the same as the mainmast; torpedo nets were also carried. *Blücher* was the first ship in the Imperial navy equpped with a tripod mast. Searchlights were finally mounted on a new platform, 6m below the signal cross.

Career

Blücher launched 11 Apr 1908, commissioned 1 Oct 1909 into the fleet; served as a gunnery training ship from 1911, and from 1914 with the fleet. Sunk 1313hrs on 24 Jan 1915 in the North Sea, approx 40nm from Texel in position 54° 20N, 05° 43E, by gunfire from British battlecruisers; 792 dead.

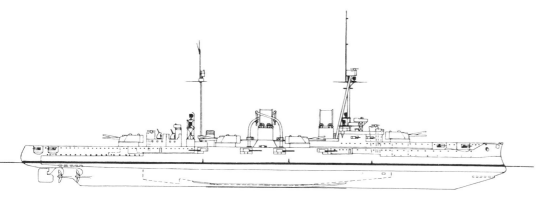

Blücher (1914)

Von der Tann

Name	Builder	Built	Cost in Marks (000s)	Displacement (t = tonnes T = tons)	Length (m)	Breadth (m)	Draught (m)	Power (hp)	Revs (rpm)	Speed (kts)	Range (nm/kts)	Coal (t)	Oil (t)
VON DER TANN sq fl	Blohm & Voss, Hamburg Construction no 198	1908–10	36,523	21,300t max 19,370t des	171.7 oa 171.5 cwl	26.6 27.17*	8.91 fwd 9.17 aft	79,007shp max 42,000shp des	324 max 300 des	27.4 max 24/8 des	4400/14	2600 max 1000 des	—
11,313gt/5091nt													

* over torpedo net booms

Construction

Laid down as heavy cruiser *F* (official design August 1906–July 1907, design officer MarObBrt Konow). Transverse and longitudinal frame steel construction (fifteen watertight compartments, double bottom 75 percent). Krupp armour: deck 50mm, slopes 50mm; torpedo bulkhead 25mm; forward CT roof 80mm, sides 250mm; aft CT roof 50mm, sides 200mm; CWL 0–100–250(shields 150)–120(shields 100)–100mm on 50mm teak; casemate 150mm; citadel 225mm; turrets, roof 90mm, sides 230mm; shields 70mm. Depth 13.28m. Immersion increased by 1cm per 30.58t. Trim moment 28,500m-t.

Propulsion

Two sets of Parsons turbines (four 3-bladed screws, 3.6m diameter) in three engine rooms. Eighteen Marine-type double boilers [fitted with hollow grates after 1916] (fifty-four fireboxes, 16 atmospheres forced, 10,405sq m) in 1 + 1 + 1 + 1 + 1 boiler rooms. Six turbo-generators, 1200kW 225V. Two rudders. Fuel consumption on trial

0.641kg per hp/hr (26.8kts, 68,246shp, 18 boilers, 65mm over pressure); 0.712kg per hp/hr (16.2kts, 12,411shp, 14 boilers, no over pressure); 1.146kg per hp/hr (12kts, 4238shp, 8 boilers, no over pressure).

Armament

Eight 28cm/45 QF guns (660 rounds), –8° +20°, range [20,400m]; ten 15cm/45 QF guns (1500 rounds), range 13,500m [16,800m]; sixteen 12cm QF guns; four 8.8cm/45 AA guns (3200 rounds) [8.8cm QF guns retained for AA use only after 1916]; four 45cm TT (11 rounds), one stern, two lateral, one bow, all under water.

Handling

Very good sea-boats, with slight weather helm, and gentle motion; handy, but tended to run on at speed. Very difficult to steer when running astern. Speed loss was up to 60 percent with hard rudder, and heel up to 8°. Frahm-type roll tanks were fitted [but quickly converted to other uses]. Transverse metacentric height

2.11m, longitudinal 215m. Maximum stability moment at 30°, = zero at 70°.

Complement

Crew: 41/882 (plus 13/62 as squadron flagship). Boats: one picket boat, three barges, two launches, two yawls, two dinghies.

Notes

Colour scheme no 9. *Von der Tann* was the only vessel in the German navy with officers' quarters in the bow. A lattice mast with a square floor area was planned but not fitted. Torpedo nets were carried until 1916. [The foremast was fitted with a spotting top after 1914.]

Career

Von der Tann launched 20 Mar 1909, commissioned 19 Feb 1911 into the fleet. Interned at Scapa Flow after 24 Nov 1918, and sunk there 1415hrs on 21 Jun 1919 after being scuttled; raised 7 Dec 1930, broken up 1934 at Rosyth.

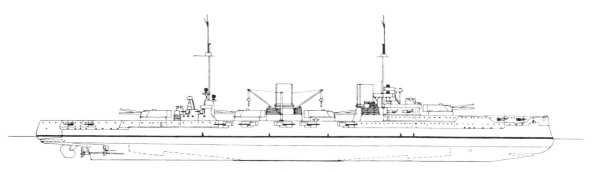

Von der Tann (1914)

Moltke class

Name	Builder	Built	Cost in Marks (000s)	Displacement (t = tonnes T = tons)	Length (m)	Breadth (m)	Draught (m)	Power (hp)	Revs (rpm)	Speed (kts)	Range (nm/kts)	Coal (t)	Oil (t)
MOLTKE sq fl	Blohm & Voss, Hamburg Construction no 200	1909–11	42,603	25,400t max 22,979t des	186.6 oa 186.0 cwl	29.4	8.77 fwd 9.19 aft	85,782shp max 52,000shp des	332	28.4 max 25.5 des	4120/14	3100 max 1000 des	—
GOEBEN sq fl 12,796gt/5758nt	Blohm & Voss, Hamburg Construction no 201	1909–12	41,564	,,	,,	,,	,,	85,661shp max 52,000shp des	330	28.0 max 25.5 des	,,	,,	—

* over torpedo net booms

Construction

Laid down as heavy cruisers *G* and *H* (official design April 1907–September 1908, design officer MarObBrt Dietrich). Transverse and longitudinal frame steel construction (fifteen watertight compartments, double bottom 78 percent). Krupp armour: deck 50mm, slopes 50mm; torpedo bulkhead 30mm, slopes 50mm in KC material; forward CT roof 80mm, sides 350mm; aft CT roof 50mm, sides 200mm; CWL 0–100–270(shields 130)–100mm on 50mm teak; casemate 150mm; citadel 200mm; turrets, roof 90mm, sides 230mm, shields

70mm. Depth 14.08m. Immersion increased by 1cm per 35.64t. Trim moment 31,900m-t.

Propulsion

Two sets of Parsons turbines (four 3-bladed screws, 3.74m diameter) in three engine rooms. Twenty-four Marine-type boilers [hollow grates fitted 1916] (forty-seven and forty-six fireboxes, 16 atmospheres forced, 11,530sq m) in 3 + 3 + 0 + 1 + 1 boiler rooms. Six turbo-generators, 1500kW 225V. 1 + 1 rudders. Fuel consumption on 6-hour forced trial was 0.667kg per

hp/hr at 76,795shp; 0.712kg per hp/hr at 71,275shp.

Armament

Ten 28cm/50 QF guns (810 rounds), –8° +13.5°, range 18,100m [–5.5° +16°, range 19,100m]; twelve 15cm/45 QF guns (1800 rounds), range 13,500m [raised to 16,800m; after 1915 *Goeben* carried only ten 15cm QF guns]; twelve [eight] 8.8cm QF and four 8.8cm/45 AA guns (3000 rounds) [reduced to AA guns only after 1916]; four 50cm TT (11 rounds), one stern, port, lateral, one bow, all under water.

Handling
Good sea-boats, with gentle motion; weather helm was necessary, and manoeuvrability generally was poor. Speed loss with hard rudder was up to 60 percent, with 9° heel. Transverse metacentric height 3.01m, longitudinal 260m, maximum stability moment at 34°, = zero at 68°.

Complement
Crew: 43/1010 (plus 13/62 as squadron flagship; 3/25 as second command flagship). Boats: one picket boat, three barges, two launches, two yawls, two dinghies.

Notes
Colour scheme no 9. *Moltke* had no funnel cap after 1911, and *Goeben* had no mantle on her aft funnel, as on *Seydlitz*. [After 1915 *Goeben*'s third 15cm QF gun on each beam was landed for use in the Dardanelles fortifications; these were never replaced.] Torpedo nets were fitted up to 1916. [A foremast spotting top was added after 1914.]

Career
Moltke launched 7 Apr 1910, commissioned 30 Sept 1911 into the fleet. Interned at Scapa Flow from 24 Nov 1918, and sunk there at 1310hrs on 21 Jun 1919 after being scuttled; raised 10 Jun 1927, broken up 1929 at Rosyth.

Goeben launched 28 Mar 1911, commissioned 2 Jul 1912 into the fleet. Served from 1912 in the Mediterranean division (and was also known, after 16 Aug 1914, by the Turkish name *Jawus Sultan Selim*); she remained battle ready in 1914 despite damage from two mines, though she had to be trimmed to starboard by about 0.80m; transferred permanently to Turkey 2 Nov 1918. Not seaworthy 1919–26; underwent a major overhaul at Ismid by Penhoet, St Nazaire, 1926–30; returned to service as *Jawus Selim*. Renamed *Yavuz* 1963 and retained as a stationary unit at Izmit from 1948. Turkey offered in 1936 to return the vessel to the Federal Republic of Germany, but the offer was declined; she was retained as a Turkish museum ship, out of service, but was broken up by 1976.

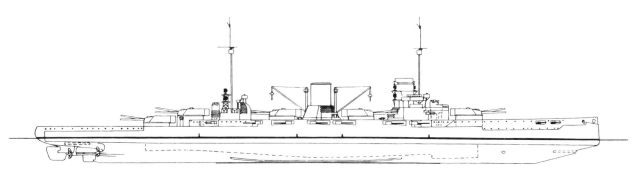

Moltke (1914); *Goeben* was similar.

Seydlitz

Name	Builder	Built	Cost in Marks (000s)	Displacement (t = tonnes T = tons)	Length (m)	Breadth (m)	Draught (m)	Power (hp)	Revs (rpm)	Speed (kts)	Range (nm/kts)	Coal (t)	Oil (t)
SEYDLITZ sq fl 14,342gt/6454nt	Blohm & Voss, Hamburg, Construction no 209	1911–13	44,685	28,550t max 24,988t des	200.6 oa 200.0 cwl	28.5 28.8*	9.29 fwd 9.09 aft	89,738shp max 63,000shp des	329	28.1 max 26.5 des	4200/14	3600 max 1000 des	—

* over torpedo net booms

Construction
Laid down as heavy cruiser *J* (official design March 1909–January 1910, design officer MarObBrt Dietrich). Transverse and longitudinal frame steel construction (seventeen watertight compartments, double bottom 76 percent). Krupp armour: deck 80–30–50mm; torpedo bulkhead 45mm; forward CT roof 200mm, sides 300mm; aft CT roof 50mm, sides 200mm; CWL 0–100–300(shields 150)–100mm on 50mm teak; casemate 150mm; citadel 265mm; turrets, roof 70mm, sides 250mm, shields 70mm. Depth 13.88m. Immersion increased by 1cm per 37.71t. Trim moment 34,200m-t.

Propulsion
Two sets of Marine-type turbines (four 3-bladed screws,

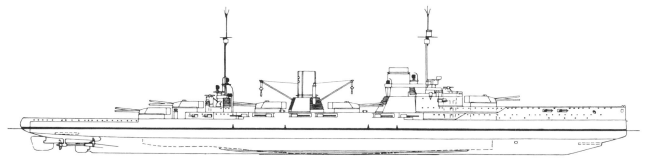

Seydlitz (1918)

3.88m diameter) in three engine rooms. Twenty-seven Marine-type boilers [fitted with hollow grates after 1916] (fifty-two fireboxes, 16 atmospheres forced, 12,500sq m) in 3 + 3 + 0 + 1 + 1 + 1 boiler rooms. Six turbo-generators, 1800kW 220V. 1 + 1 rudders.

Armament

Ten 28cm/50 QF guns (870 rounds) –8° +13.5°, range 18,100m [–5.5° +16°, range 19,100m]; twelve 15cm/45 QF guns (1920 rounds), range 13,500m [raised to 16,800m]; twelve 8.8cm QF guns, or ten 8.8cm QF and two 8.8cm/45 AA guns (3400 rounds) [after 1916 all 8.8cm guns were for AA use]; four 50cm TT (11 rounds), one stern, port, two lateral, one bow, all under water.

Handling

Good sea-boat with gentle motion; required slight lee helm, but manoeuvrability otherwise similar to *Moltke*. Transverse metacentric height 3.12m, longitudinal 278m. Maximum stability moment at 33°, = zero at 72°.

Complement

Crew: 43/1025 (plus 13/62 as squadron flagship). Boats: one picket boat, three barges, two launches, two yawls, two dinghies.

Notes

Colour scheme no 9. Torpedo nets were carried until 1916; [a foremast spotting top was fitted after 1914].

Career

Seydlitz launched 30 Mar 1912, commissioned 22 May 1913 into the fleet. Interned at Scapa Flow from 24 Nov 1918, and sunk there at 1350hrs on 21 Jun 1919 after being scuttled. Raised 2 Nov 1928, broken up 1930 at Rosyth.

Seydlitz returned home after the battlecruiser action at Jutland in spite of extremely grave damage from artillery shells, with over 5300t of water in the ship; freeboard forward was only 2.5m! Turrets C and D were totally burnt out at Doggerbank and Jutland, but no explosion occurred. The ship's bell is now at the Laboe naval memorial.

Derfflinger class

Name	Builder	Built	Cost in Marks (000s)	Displacement (t = tonnes T = tons)	Length (m)	Breadth (m)	Draught (m)	Power (hp)	Revs (rpm)	Speed (kts)	Range (nm/kts)	Coal (t)	Oil (t)
DERFFLINGER	Blohm & Voss, Hamburg Construction no 213	1912–14	56,000	31,200t max 26,600t des	210.4 oa 210.0 cwl	29.0	9.20 fwd 9.56 aft	76,634shp max 63,000shp des	280	25.5 max 26.5 des	5600/14	3500 max 750 des	1000 max 250 des
LÜTZOW sq fl	F Schichau, Danzig Construction no 885	1912–15	58,000	26,741t max 26,600t des	,,	,,	,,	80,988shp max 63,000shp des	277	26.4 max 26.5 des	,,	3700 max 750 des	,,
HINDENBURG c16,700gt	Imperial Dockyard, Wilhelmshaven Construction no 34	1913–17	59,000	31,500t max 26,947t des	212.8 oa 212.5 des	29.0	9.29 fwd 9.57 aft	95,777shp max 72,000shp des	290	26.6 max 27.0 des	6100/14	,,	1200 max 250 des

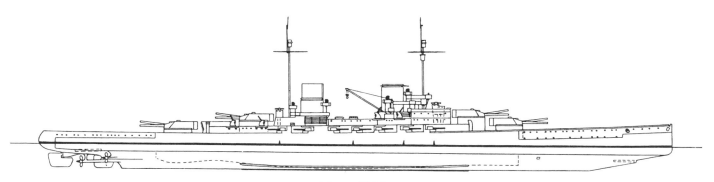

Lützow (1916)

Construction

Laid down as heavy cruisers *K, Ersatz Kaiserin Augusta* and *Ersatz Hertha* (official design, October 1910–June 1911, *Hindenburg* May–October 1912, design officer MarObBrt Dietrich). Longitudinal frame stringer steel construction (sixteen watertight compartments, after *Lützow* seventeen, double bottom 65 percent). Krupp armour: deck 80–30–50mm; torpedo bulkhead 45mm; forward CT roof 130mm, sides 300mm; aft CT roof 50mm, sides 200mm; CWL 0–100–300(shields 150)–120–30mm; casemate 150mm, citadel 270mm, turrets, roof 110mm, sides 270mm (*Hindenburg* roof 150mm, sides 270mm), shields 70mm. Depth 14.75m. Immersion increased by 1cm per 40.1t. Trim moment 39,000m-t.

Propulsion

Two sets of Marine-type turbines (four 3-bladed screws, 3.9m diameter, *Hindenburg* 4.0m diameter) in 2 + 2 engine rooms. Fourteen Marine-type double boilers [fitted with hollow grates after 1916] plus four oil-fired Marine-type double-ended boilers (fifty-six plus eight fireboxes, 16–18 atmospheres forced, 12,270 to 12,450sq m) in 2 + 2 + 2 + 0 + 2 + 2 + 2 boiler rooms, oil-fired boilers forward in compartments 5 and 6, on *Derfflinger* and *Lützow* only in compartment 5 (non divided). Two turbo-, two diesel generators, 1660 and 1520 and 2120kW 220V. 1 + 1 rudders.

Armament

Eight 30.5cm/50 QF guns (720 rounds), –8° +13.5°, range 18,000m [–5.5° +16°, range 20,400m]; .twelve, after *Lützow* fourteen, 15cm/45 QF guns (1920–2240 rounds), range 13,500m [raised to 16,800m]; four 8.8cm/45 QF guns (deleted after *Lützow*) plus eight 8.8cm/45 AA guns (3000–1800 rounds), [of which after 1916 only four (two on *Derfflinger*) 8.8cm/45 AA guns were retained]; four 50cm TT (60cm TT after *Lützow* (12 rounds), one stern, starboard, two lateral, one bow, all under water.

Handling

Excellent sea-boats, with a gentle motion, but somewhat wet at casemate level; weather helm was necessary, and all ships were slow to respond to the helm. Speed loss with hard rudder was up to 65 percent, at 11° heel. Roll angle was 11°, and period 11 seconds; roll tanks were fitted on *Derfflinger* only. Transverse metacentric height 2.60m, longitudinal 296m. Maximum stability moment at 34°, = zero at 74°.

Complement

Crew: 44/1068–1138 (plus 14/62 as squadron flagship). Boats: one picket boat, three barges, two launches, two yawls, two dinghies.

Notes

Colour scheme no 9. Up to 1916 *Derfflinger* was fitted with two signal masts similar to *Seydlitz*, but raked; her forward bridge was smaller [the mainmast was modified, similar to the earlier foremast, and a very wide track tripod was fitted on the foremast itself]. The roll tanks were in the central superstructure. *Lützow* and *Derfflinger* (until 1916) carried a forward searchlight on a platform 16m above CWL on the forward edge of the forward funnel. [*Hindenburg* had no searchlights on the tripod foremast.] Torpedo nets were carried until 1916. [After 1918 the tripod mast signal topmast was always kept stowed; the flag knob was 44m above CWL.]

Career

Derfflinger launched 14 Jun 1913 to 12 Jul 1913, commissioned 1 Sept 1914 into the fleet. Interned from 24 Nov 1918 at Scapa Flow, and sunk there at 1445hrs on 21 Jun 1919 after being scuttled. Raised in 1939, she was anchored, floating keel up, off the island of Risa until 1946, then transferred to the floating dock at Faslane Port until 1948. Her bell was presented to the German Federal Navy on 30 Aug 1965.

Lützow launched 29 Nov 1913, commissioned 8 Aug 1915 into the fleet. Sunk at 0247hrs on 1 June 1916 in the North Sea at position 56° 5N, 05° 53E, by torpedoes from the German *G 38* after heavy damage from British battlecruisers; 116 dead. Partially broken up 1959–62 by Eisen & Metall, Hamburg.

Hindenburg launched 1 Aug 1915, commissioned 10 May 1917 into the fleet. Interned at Scapa Flow from 24 Nov 1918, and sunk there at 1700hrs on 21 Jun 1919 after being scuttled. Several unsuccessful attempts were made to raise her, and a successful attempt on 22 Jul 1930, following which she was broken up 1931–32 at Rosyth. Her bell was presented to the German Federal Navy on 28 May 1959.

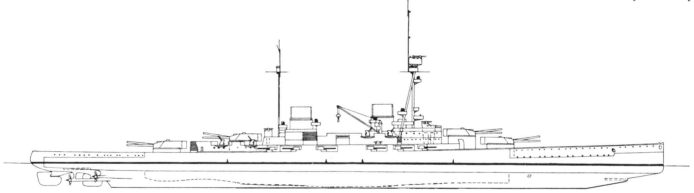

Derfflinger (1918)

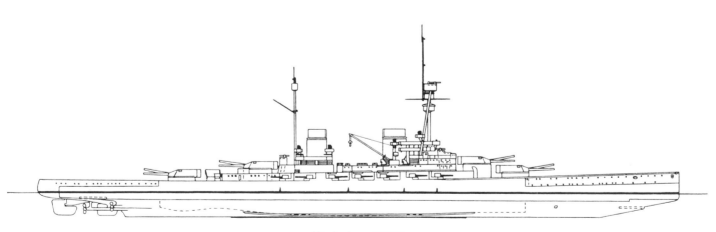

Hindenburg (1918)

Mackensen class

Construction

Designed as heavy cruisers *Ersatz Victoria Louise*, *Ersatz Blücher*, *Ersatz Freya*, and *Ersatz Friedrich Carl* (A) (official design 1913, design officer MarObBrt Ahnhudt); construction not completed. Longitudinal frame stringer steel construction (eighteen watertight compartments, double bottom 92 percent); these were the first German ships designed with a Taylor bulge. The outfit of Krupp armour was similar to that of the *Derfflinger* class. Depth 15.0m.

Name	Builder	Built	Cost in Marks (000s)	Displacement (t = tonnes T = tons)	Length (m)	Breadth (m)	Draught (m)	Power (hp)	Revs (rpm)	Speed (kts)	Range (nm/kts)	Coal (t)	Oil (t)
MACKENSEN	Blohm & Voss, Hamburg Construction no 240	1914–	c 66,000	35,300t max 31,000t des	223.0	30.4	9.3 fwd 8.4 aft	90,000shp des	295	28.0	c 8000/14	4000 max 800 des	2000 max 250 des
GRAF SPEE sq fl	F Schichau, Danzig Construction no 958	1915–	,,	,,	,,	,,	,,	,,	,,	,,	,,	,,	,,
PRINZ EITEL FRIEDRICH	Blohm & Voss, Hamburg Construction no 241	,,	,,	,,	,,	,,	,,	,,	,,	,,	,,	,,	,,
ERSATZ A sq fl	Imperial Dockyard, Wilhelmshaven Construction no 35	,,	,,	,,	,,	,,	,,	,,	,,	,,	,,	,,	,,

Propulsion

Four sets of Marine-type turbines (four 3-bladed screws, 4.2m diameter) in 2 + 2 engine rooms; *Ersatz A* had four sets of turbines with Föltinger fluid transmission, and the remaining ships two sets of direct coupled turbines and additional cruise turbines with gear transmission (which could be de-coupled). Twenty-four coal-fired Marine-type single-ended boilers plus eight oil-fired Marine-type double-ended boilers in 2 + 2 + 0 + 2 + 2 + 2 boiler rooms. Eight diesel generators, 2320kW 220V. Two rudders.

Armament

Eight 35cm/45 QF guns (720 rounds), –8° +16°; fourteen 15cm/45 QF guns (2240 rounds), –8.5° +19°; eight 8.8cm/45 AA guns (3600 rounds), –10° +70°;

five 60cm TT (20 rounds), four lateral, one bow, all under water.

Handling

No roll tanks fitted.

Complement

Crew: 46/1140 (plus 14/62 as squadron flagship). Boats: two picket boats, one barge, two launches, two cutters, three yawls.

Career

Mackensen launched 21 Apr 1917. Stricken 17 Nov 1919, about 15 months before completion; sold, and broken up 1922 at Kiel-Nordmole.

Graf Spee launched 15 Sept 1917. Stricken 17 Nov 1919, about 12 months before completion; hull sold 28 Oct 1921 for 4,400,000M, and broken up 1921–22 at Kiel-Nordmole.

Prinz Eitel Friedrich was the proposed name for *Ersatz Freya*. On 13 Mar 1920, 21 months before completion, an improvised launch was carried out by Hamburg dockyard workers, who named the vessel *Noske*. She was broken up 1921 at Hamburg.

Ersatz A was possibly to have been named *Fürst Bismarck*. Stricken 17 Nov 1919, about 26 months before completion, and broken up; the last parts of the hull were on the stocks in 1922.

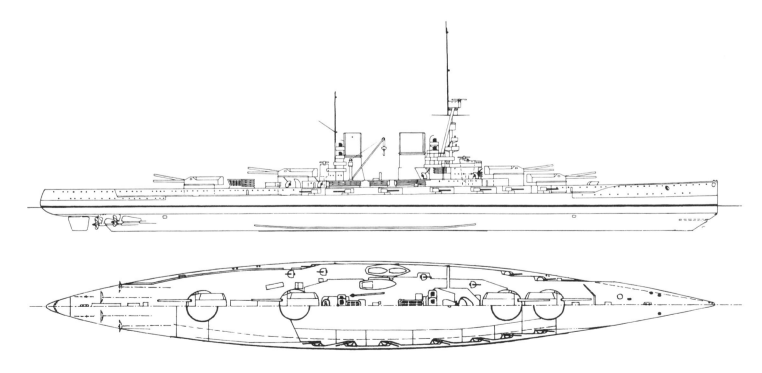

Mackensen (1913 design, not completed); *Graf Spee*, *Prinz Eitel Friedrich* and *Ersatz A* were similar.

Ersatz Yorck class

Name	Builder	Built	Cost in Marks (000s)	Displacement (t = tonnes T = tons)	Length (m)	Breadth (m)	Draught (m)	Power (hp)	Revs (rpm)	Speed (kts)	Range (nm/kts)	Coal (t)	Oil (t)
ERSATZ YORCK	AG Vulcan, Hamburg Construction no 63	1916–	c 75,000	38,000t max 33,500t des	227.8	30.4	9.3	90,000shp des	295	27.3	5500/14	4000 max 850 des	2000 max 250 des
ERSATZ GNEISENAU	Germania Dockyard, Kiel Construction no 250	,,	,,	,,	,,	,,	,,	,,	,,	,,	,,	,,	,,
ERSATZ SCHARNHORST	Blohm & Voss, Hamburg Construction no 246	,,	,,	,,	,,	,,	,,	,,	,,	,,	,,	,,	,,

Construction

Designed as heavy cruisers *Ersatz Yorck*, *Ersatz Gneisenau*, and *Ersatz Scharnhorst* (official design 1915) as a revision of the *Mackensen* design; construction not completed.

Propulsion

Four sets of Marine-type turbines, *Ersatz Yorck* and *Ersatz Gneisenau* as *Ersatz A*, *Ersatz Scharnhorst* as *Mackensen* (four 3-bladed screws, 4.2m diameter) in 2 + 2 engine rooms. Twenty-four coal-fired Marine-type single-ended boilers and eight oil-fired Marine-type double-ended boilers in 2 + 2 + 0 + 2 + 2 + 2 boiler rooms. Generator diesel engines from *Ersatz Gneisenau* were installed in *U151–154*; see *Sachsen*, page 7. Two rudders.

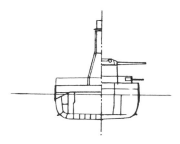

Ersatz Yorck (1915 design) midship section

Armament

Eight 38cm/45 QF guns as *Bayern*; twelve 15cm/45 QF guns; eight 8.8cm/45 AA guns; three 60cm TT (15 rounds), two lateral, one bow, both under water.

Handling

No roll tanks were planned.

Complement

Crew: 47/1180.

Career

Construction continued after 1917 only to keep the workforce occupied; the ships were broken up on the stocks 26 months or more before completion. The design formed the basis for *Scharnhorst* and *Gneisenau*: see page 31.

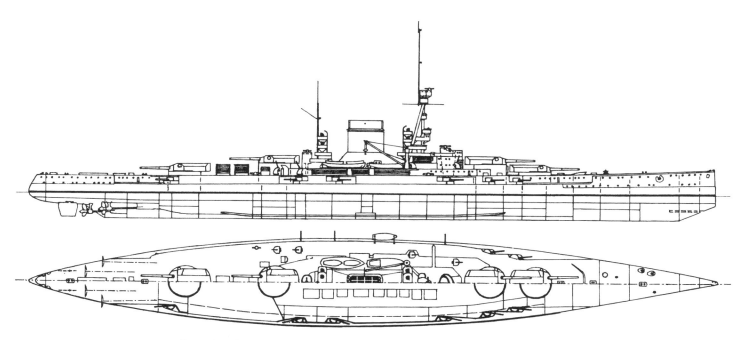

Ersatz Yorck (1915 design, not completed); *Ersatz Gneisenau, Ersatz Scharnhorst*

Armoured ships 1933–1936

Deutschland/Lützow class

Name	Builder	Built	Cost in Marks (000s)	Displacement (t = tonnes T = tons)	Length (m)	Breadth (m)	Draught (m)	Power (hp)	Revs (rpm)	Speed (kts)	Range (nm/kts)	Coal (t)	Oil (t)
LÜTZOW ex DEUTSCHLAND sq fl	Deutsche Werke, Kiel Construction no 219 mod: Deutsche Werke, Kiel	1929–33 1940–41	80,000	14,290T max 12,630t des 10,600T std	186.0 oa 181.7 cwl 187.9 oa mod	20.69	7.25 max 5.78 std	48,390 shp max 54,000 shp des	250 des	28.0 max 26.0 des	10,000/20 16,600/14 17,400/13 (expected: 19,700/13)	—	2750 max
ADMIRAL SCHEER sq fl	KM Dockyard, Wilhelmshaven Construction no 123 mod: KM Dockyard, Wilhelmshaven	1931–34 1940	90,000 6400	15,180T max 13,660t des 11,550T std	186.0 oa 181.7 cwl 187.9 oa mod	21.34	7.25 max 5.78 std	52,050shp max 54,000shp des	,,	28.3 max 26.0 des	9100/20	—	2410 max
ADMIRAL GRAF SPEE sq fl	KM Dockyard, Wilhelmshaven Construction no 125	1932–36	82,000	16,020T max 14,890t des 12,340T std	186.0 oa 181.7 cwl	21.65	7.34 max 5.80 std	54,000shp des	,,	29.5 max 26.0 des	8900/20	—	2500 max

9402gt (*Lützow*), 9445gt (*Admiral Scheer*), 9596gt (*Admiral Graf Spee*)/6299nt

Construction
Laid down as armoured ships *A* (*Ersatz Preussen*), *B* (*Ersatz Lothringen*), and *C* (*Ersatz Braunschweig*) [subsequently designated heavy cruisers] (official designs 1926–28 and 1928–30, design officer MarObBrt Blechschmidt). Longitudinal stringer transverse frame steel construction, more than 90 percent welded; bow and side bulges were included (twelve watertight compartments, double bottom 92 percent). Krupp armour: deck 18–30–40–30mm; upper deck 18mm; top 14mm; torpedo bulkhead 45mm; forward CT roof 50mm, sides 150mm; aft CT roof 20mm, sides 50mm; CWL 0–60–80–60–0mm; turrets, roof 105–85mm, sides 140–85mm; 15cm shields 10mm (*Admiral Scheer* and *Admiral Graf Spee* had deck armour 17–45–40–30mm; upper deck 17mm; top roof 20mm, sides 60mm; torpedo bulkhead 40mm. etc). Depth: *Deutschland* 12.4m, *Admiral Scheer* and *Admiral Graf Spee* 12.2m. Immersion increased by 1cm per 14.2t. Uniform trim moment 23,060, 22,056, 22,661cu m. Official displacement as new vessels was stated as 10,000t standard.

Propulsion
Four sets of double MAN 9-cylinder double acting two-stroke diesels (5.2 atmospheres forced, 450rpm primary revolutions) with, for each set (for *Deutschland* for each two sets) Vulcan transmissions (two 3-bladed screws, 4.40m diameter – *Deutschland* initially 3.97m diameter) in 1 + 1 + 1 + 1 + 1 + 1 rooms. Four electricity plants, each with two diesel generators, total output 2160kW (*Deutschland*), 2800kW (*Admiral Scheer*), and 3360kW (*Admiral Graf Spee*), all 220V. Weight of entire propulsion system for *Deutschland* was 21.96kg/hp. One rudder.

Armament
Six 28cm/52 QF guns (630–720 rounds), –8° +40°, range 42,600m; eight 15cm/55 QF guns (800–1200 rounds), –10° +35°, range 25,700m; three 8.8cm/45 AA guns (rounds not known) [after 1935 six 8.8cm/75 AA guns (3000 rounds), after 1938 (*Admiral Graf Spee*) and 1940 (*Lützow*) six 10.5cm/65 AA guns (2400–3000 rounds), four twin 3.7cm AA guns (8000–24,000 rounds) plus ten to twenty-eight 2cm AA guns (2000 rounds each); AA armament in 1945 was as follows: *Admiral Scheer* six 4.8cm AA, eight 3.7cm AA, thirty-three 2cm AA, and *Lützow* six 4cm AA, ten 3.7cm AA, twenty-eight 2cm AA (planned)]; eight 53.3cm deck TT in quadruple mountings; two Arado 196 seaplanes, one catapult.

Handling
Good sea-boats, with slight roll but wet in a head sea, though less so with the Atlantic bow. In *Admiral Scheer* and *Lützow* the greatly increased bow rake made both vessels much drier. All vessels manoeuvred and steered well, especially with the diesel engines set to the manoeuvring position in which half the engines on each shaft ran ahead and half astern; switching the transmission therefore provided half power on each screw in reverse. Up to 13° heel with hard rudder at high speed when lightly loaded. The low stern was dangerous in a heavy stern sea (all ships suffered from regular loss of all equipment located there, including torpedo supports, fog buoys, companionways, etc). Active roll damping was included, except in *Deutschland*.

Complement
Crew: 33/586, after 1935 30/921–1040 (plus 17/85 as squadron flagship, 13/59 as second command flagship). Boats: two picket boats, two barges, one launch, one pinnace, two dinghies.

Notes
Colour scheme no 9, also dark grey and camouflage schemes 1942–44. Armoured ships of the *Deutschland*

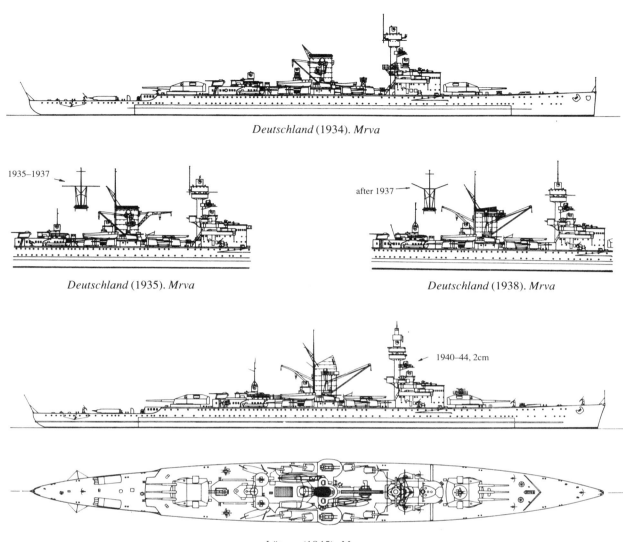

Deutschland (1934). *Mrva*

1935–1937 →

Deutschland (1935). *Mrva*

after 1937 →

Deutschland (1938). *Mrva*

1940–44, 2cm

Lützow (1945). *Mrva*

type were initially scornfully nicknamed 'pocket battleships', but this name soon seemed increasingly appropriate.

Significant differences in appearance between the three ships are as follows: *Graf Spee* and *Scheer* were initially fitted with a turret-type battle mast and *Deutschland* with a tubular mast, with *Scheer* being refitted with a tubular mast in 1940; all three ships were initially without a funnel cap, with *Deutschland* in 1938 and *Scheer* in 1940 being fitted with a flat funnel cap, and both with a high funnel cap in 1942; a catapult was fitted to *Graf Spee* from the beginning, and to *Deutschland* and *Scheer* in 1935 (positioned forward of the funnel on *Deutschland/Lützow* and aft on the other ships); all three ships were built with a straight, almost vertical stem, with Atlantic bows being fitted to *Scheer* in 1940 and *Lützow* in 1941.

Refits were as follows:

[*Deutschland/Lützow*: mid-1934, port loading gear replaced by lattice crane; 1935, funnel crosstrees replaced by mainmast, catapult system installed; 1937, gas pressure deflector fitted before and abaft 15cm battery; mid-1938, low funnel cap fitted; 1940, FMG G(gO) system fitted in a rotating foremast cowl, mine

protection system fitted; early 1941, Atlantic bow fitted; 1942, high funnel cap fitted, FuMo 26 with two antennas fitted (one antenna after 1944).]

[*Admiral Scheer*: 1935, catapult and landing sail system for seaplanes landing on rough water installed; 1936, gas pressure deflector fitted before and abaft 15cm battery; 1938, mainmast yard replaced by gaffs; mid-1939, port crane with straight outrigger replaced by crane with angled outrigger; major reconstruction was carried out in 1940, since fundamental reworking of incorrectly designed engine foundations was found to be unavoidable (new design by MarBrt Strohbusch) – this work involved the installation of new engine foundations, a new auxiliary engine, modification of the bow shape above water and the stem (with a slight rake), the addition of one bow hawse on each beam in place of the former anchor hawses, replacement of the turret mast aft of the navigation bridge by a tubular mast, the installation of an FMG 39 G(gO) system on a rotating foremast cowl, the fitting of a flat funnel cap, the installation of a new tripod mainmast, offset from the funnel, and a new port aircraft crane, the removal of the roll damping system, the replacement of the 8.8cm AA guns by 10.5cm AA guns, reinforcement of

the light AA armament, and the installation of a mine protection system; 1941, FMG 40 G(gO), FuMO 26 systems were installed in a rotating cowl aft; 1942, tall funnel cap fitted, FuMO 26 system with two antennas fitted on foretop (one antenna after 1943).]

[*Admiral Graf Spee*: 1938, FMG G(gO) system installed in a rotating foremast cowl (the antenna was temporarily removable, for security reasons), the angular foretop was rounded off, and one searchlight only was fitted, forward on the turret mast platform at the same height as the two former lateral units (this refit was carried out without de-commissioning).]

Career

Deutschland launched 19 May 1931, commissioned 1 Apr 1933 into the fleet; served at various locations abroad; renamed heavy cruiser *Lützow* 15 Nov 1939. Wrecked at 1720hrs on 16 Apr 1945 at Swinemünde in position 53° 56N, 14° 170E, by three 5.2 ton bombs dropped by British aircraft; she was grounded, with the upper deck approx 2m above the water, and served as a fixed battery in this position until 4 May 1945. Raised by the USSR, she was broken up around 1948–49 at Leningrad.

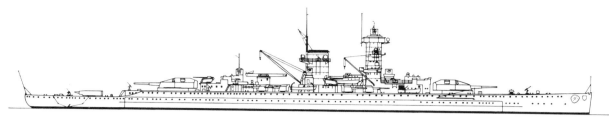

Admiral Scheer (1935). *Mrva*

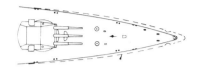

Admiral Scheer (1939). *Mrva*

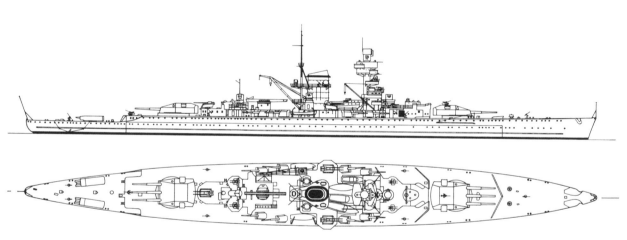

Admiral Scheer (1940), second form. *Mrva*

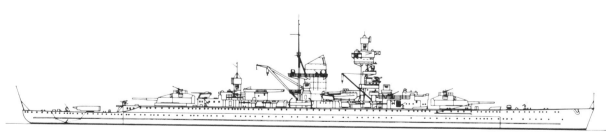

Admiral Scheer (1945). *Mrva*

Admiral Scheer launched 1 Apr 1933, commissioned 12 Nov 1934 into the fleet; served at various locations abroad. Reclassified as a heavy cruiser December 1939. Sunk at 2335hrs on 9 Apr 1945 at the Deutsche Werke, Kiel, dock harbour inlet, position 54° 20N, 10° 08E, after being hit by five bombs dropped by British aircraft

(casualties not known); she was partially broken up and buried under rubble from the explosions.

Admiral Graf Spee launched 30 Jun 1934, commissioned 6 Jan 1936 into the fleet; served at various locations abroad. Sunk at 1956hrs on 17 Dec 1939 in

about 12m of water at La Plata, west-southwest of Montevideo, position 35° 11S, 56° 26W, when scuttled after battle damage, 61 dead. Broken up 1942–43 at the site of the wreck; remains are still visible.

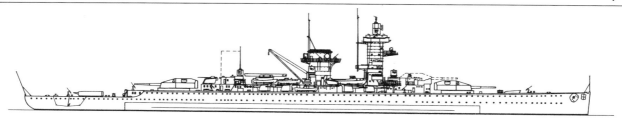

Admiral Graf Spee (1939); the dummy superstructure is shown dashed. *Mrva*

D class

Name	Builder	Built	Cost in Marks (000s)	Displacement (t = tonnes T = tons)	Length (m)	Breadth (m)	Draught (m)	Power (hp)	Revs (rpm)	Speed (kts)	Range (nm/kts)	Coal (t)	Oil (t)
D	KM Dockyard, Wilhelmshaven	1934–		20,000T des	230 oa 225 cwl	25.5	8.5	125,000 shp des		29 des		—	
E	Deutsche Werke, Kiel	,,		,,	,,	,,	,,	,,		,,		—	

Construction

Designed as armoured ships *D* (*Ersatz Elsass*) and *E* (*Ersatz Hessen*) (official designs, 1931–33); construction not completed. Longitudinal frame stringer steel construction, welded. Krupp armour: upper deck 35mm; armour deck 70–80–70(slopes 80)mm; CT 300mm; CWL 220mm; citadel 50mm.

Propulsion

Turbine installation.

Armament

Six 28cm/52 QF guns (900 rounds) – it is possible that eight guns were considered if quadruple turrets were likely to be available; eight 15cm/55 QF guns; eight 10.5cm/65 AA guns; various other AA guns; an unknown number of 53.3cm torpedoes.

Notes

D was to have been fitted with fleet flagship equipment.

Career

D, *E* contract granted 25 Jan 1934, keel laid 14 Feb 1934. Construction work was halted 5 Jul 1934 as a result of a decision to increase the main armament; broken up. The contracts were superseded by those for the construction of the battleships *Scharnhorst* and *Gneisenau* (see page 31), possibly under the same construction number.

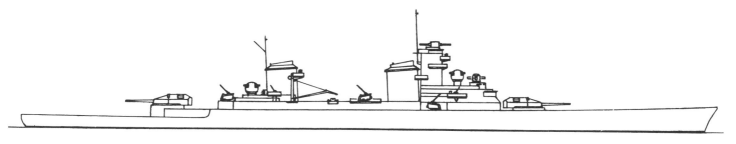

Armoured ship *D* (*Ersatz Elsass*), armoured ship *E* (*Ersatz Hessen*); design A.Kr. 33, 1933.

P1 class

Construction

Designed as armoured ships *P1–P12* (classified after 14 Jan 1939 as Type P cruisers, as also in the Z-plan, for reasons of secrecy) (official design, 1937–39); construction not completed. Longitudinal frame stringer steel construction, welded (thirteen watertight compartments), transom stern. Krupp armour: deck 70mm, slopes 100mm; upper deck 20mm; torpedo bulkhead 30mm; CWL 40–120–40mm; barbettes 100–80mm.

Name	Builder	Built	Cost in Marks (000s)	Displacement (t = tonnes T = tons)	Length (m)	Breadth (m)	Draught (m)	Power (hp)	Revs (rpm)	Speed (kts)	Range (nm/kts)	Coal (t)	Oil (t)
P1	Deutsche Werke, Kiel	—	—	25,689T max 23,700t des 22,145T std	230 oa 223 cwl	26	8.0 max 7.2 des	165,000 shp des	250 des	33 des	25,000/13 15,000/19	—	5000 max 3600 des
P2	Blohm & Voss, Hamburg	—	—	,,	,,	,,	,,	,,	,,	,,	,,	—	,,
P3	KM Dockyard												
P4	Howaldt, Kiel												
P5	Blohm & Voss, Hamburg												
P6	Germania Dockyard, Kiel												
P7	Deutsche Werke, Kiel					as above							
P8	KM Dockyard												
P9	Blohm & Voss, Hamburg												
P10	Deschimag, Bremen												
P11	Blohm & Voss, Hamburg												
P12	Germania Dockyard, Kiel												

Depth 14.2m.

Propulsion

Twelve MAN 9-cylinder V-configuration double acting two-stroke diesels, three working on the geared transmission of each shaft (four screws, 4.30m diameter).

Armament

Six 28cm QF guns (calibre and rounds not known); four 15cm/55 QF guns (rounds not known); four 10.5cm/65 guns (rounds not known); four 3.7cm AA guns (rounds not known); six 53.3cm TT, under water; two Arado 196 seaplanes, two catapults.

Notes

Between March 1938 and December 1939 towing experiments were carried out with at least nine designs, varying slightly in dimensions and in some cases with different gun arrangements (eg, three 28cm triple turrets). Reduction of the Z-plan to eight armoured ships affected dockyard allotment as follows (until the end of 1945): *P2*, KM dockyard; *P3*, Germania; *P5*, Deutsche Werke, Kiel; *P6*, KM dockyard; *P7*, Blohm & Voss; *P8*, AG Weser (otherwise as above).

Career

The first keel was due to be laid 1 Feb 1940; under the 27 Jul 1939 Z-plan this was replaced by battleship *O* (battlecruisers *O*, *P*, *Q*) (see page 68).

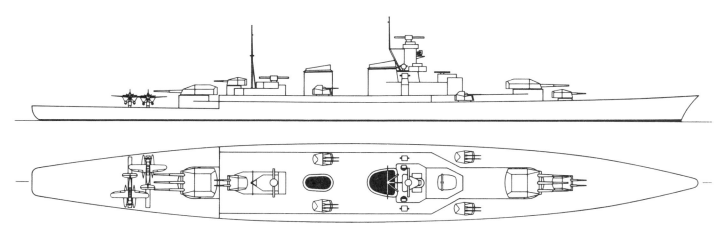

Armoured ships *P1–P2* ('Cruiser type P'); (design A V, 1939). *Mrva*

Heavy cruisers 1939–1940

Blücher class

Name	Builder	Built	Cost in Marks (000s)	Displacement (t = tonnes T = tons)	Length (m)	Breadth (m)	Draught (m)	Power (hp)	Revs (rpm)	Speed (kts)	Range (nm/kts)	Coal (t)	Oil (t)
BLÜCHER	Deutsche Werke, Kiel Construction no 246	1936–39	87,855	18,200T max 16,170t des 14,050T std	203.2 oa 195.0 cwl 205.9 oa mod	22.0	7.2 max 6.5 des 5.7 std	131,821 shp max 132,000 shp des	302 max 320 des	32.8 max 32.0 des	(6800/20) (8000/20 mod)	—	3050 max 1420 des 3700 mod
ADMIRAL HIPPER	Blohm & Voss, Hamburg Construction no 501	1935–39	85,860	18,200T max 16,170t des 14,050T std	202.8 oa 195.5 cwl 205.0 oa mod	21.3	7.2 max 6.5 des 5.8 std	133,631 shp max 132,000 shp des	303 max 320 des	32.6 max 32.0 des	(6800/20 des) 7900/19* 4430/19**	—	3050 max 1420 des 3700 mod
PRINZ EUGEN	Germania Dockyard, Kiel Construction no 564	1936–40	104,490	18,750T max 16,970t des 14,680T std	207.7 oa 199.5 cwl 212 oa mod	21.7	7.2 max 6.6 des 5.9 std	137,500 shp max 132,000 shp des	312 max 320 des	32.2 max 32.0 des	(6800/20 des) (7200/20 mod)	—	3250 max 1460 des 3400 mod
SEYDLITZ	Deschimag, Bremen Construction no 940	1936–	84,090	19,800T max 17,600t des 14,240T std	210.0 oa	21.8	7.9 max 6.9 des	132,000 shp des	320 des	32.0 des		—	4250 max
LÜTZOW	Deschimag, Bremen Construction no 941	1937–	83,590	,,	,,	,,	,,	,,	,,	,,		—	,,

12,053gt (*Admiral Hipper*)

* expected after modification   ** achieved

Construction

Laid down as heavy cruisers G (*Ersatz Berlin*), H (*Ersatz Hamburg*), J, and light (later heavy) cruisers K and L (official designs, 1934–35 and 1934–36). Longitudinal frame stringer steel construction (*Blücher* and *Hipper* fourteen watertight compartments, double bottom 72 percent), side bulges, bow bulge. Krupp armour: upper deck 0–12–30–12–0mm; armour deck 0–50–30(bulkhead 30)–40–20mm, all Wh material; torpedo bulkhead 20mm Ww material; CWL 0–70(bulkhead 70)–80–80(bulkhead 70)–0mm, all W material; forward CT roof 50mm, sides 150mm; aft CT roof 20mm, sides 30mm; all rangefinders and tops 20mm; AA directors 17mm; turrets, roof 70mm, sides 105–70mm. Depth 12.20 and 12.45m. Immersion increased by 1cm per 14.12t. Uniform trim moment *Blücher* 30,942, *Prinz Eugen* 34,390cu m. As new vessels official displacement was given as 10,000t standard.

Propulsion

Three sets of geared turbines (type not known), three housings (three 3-bladed screws, 4.10m diameter, *Admiral Hipper* initially 4.32m diameter) in 1 + 0 + 1 engine rooms (primary revolutions at full load 3840rpm high and medium pressure stage, and 2820rpm low pressure). Twelve ultra high pressure boilers (450°, 58–85 atmospheres forced, 35 to max 50t/h steam), *Seydlitz* and *Lützow* nine double-ended high pressure boilers, in 1 + 0 + 1 + 1 boiler rooms.

Three electricity plants with four diesel generators, each 150kW, four turbo-generators, each 460kW and two at 230kW, with 150kVA AC generators connected; total 2900kW; *Prinz Eugen*, *Seydlitz* and *Lützow* three diesel generators, each 150kW and one similar at 350kW, four turbo-generators, each 460kW and one similar at 230kW with a 150kVA AC generator connected, total 2870kW. All vessels had 220V supply. One rudder. The entire propulsion system was rated at 18.5kg/shp.

	Engine supplier	Boiler type from yard
Blücher	Blohm & Voss turbine	Wagner, 70 atmospheres
Admiral Hipper	Blohm & Voss turbine	La Mont*, 85 atmospheres
Prinz Eugen	Marine turbine (Germaniawerft)	La Mont*, 85 atmospheres
Seydlitz	Deschimag turbine	Wagner, 58 atmospheres
Lützow	Deschimag turbine	Wagner, 60 atmospheres

* Boilers with forced circulation; total optimum fuel oil consumption 0.320kg/hp per hour.

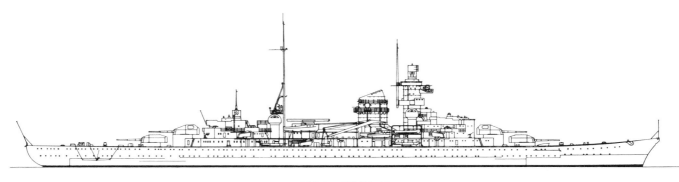

Blücher (1940). *Mrva*

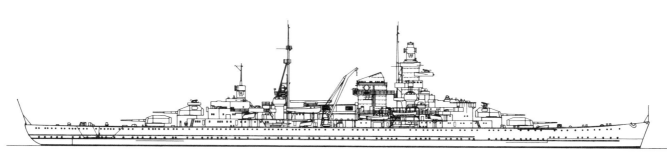

Admiral Hipper (1944). *Mrva*

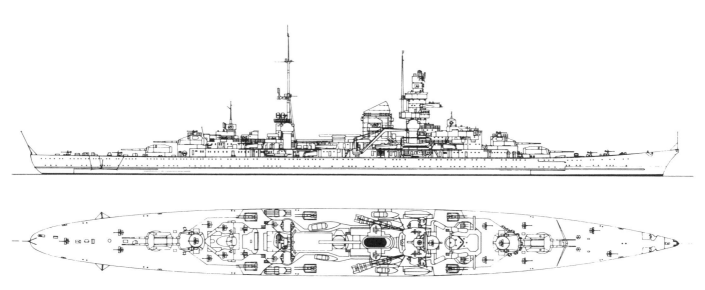

Prinz Eugen (1945). *Mrva*

Armament

Eight 20.3/60 QF guns (960–1280 rounds) –10° +37°, range 36,000m; twelve 10.5cm/65 AA guns (4800 rounds), range 17,600m; twelve [eight] 3.7cm AA guns (4000 rounds); eight [twenty-eight] 2cm AA guns (16,000 [56,000] rounds) [replaced in 1944 by fifteen 4cm AA guns (30,000 rounds); in 1945 *Prinz Eugen* had twenty 4cm AA guns and eighteen 2cm AA guns, and *Admiral Hipper* sixteen 4cm AA guns and fourteen 2cm AA guns]; twelve 53.3cm deck-mounted triple TT (24 rounds); ninety-six EMC mines (*Admiral Hipper* only); three Arado 196 seaplanes, one catapult, and one hangar. The Hein'sches landing sail gear was removed after mid-1939. (The original projected main armament for *Seydlitz* and *Lützow*, of twelve 15cm/55

QF guns in triple turrets (see drawing), was in deference to the London Naval Treaty. The design was completed with this armament, but was converted to a heavy cruiser in a decision dated 14 Nov 1936. The design for the 15cm triple turrets was retained until mid-1941 (!), but with a low production priority.

Handling

Good sea-boats, with a gentle motion, requiring weather helm. Affected unpredictably by wind and current at low speed. Up to 14° heel with hard rudder at high speed, speed loss more than 50 percent. The engine installations were the cause of many complaints, and presented considerable problems, especially in the Atlantic.

Complement

Crew: 42/1340 to 51/1548. Boats: two picket boats, two barges, one launch, one pinnace, two dinghies.

Notes

Colour scheme no 9; but dark grey overall with camouflage from 1944. See the drawings for the major differences in appearance. The Hein'sche Stausegel gear, originally planned for installation on the port beam below the davits, was never installed on *Prinz Eugen*. All cruisers up to *Lützow* were launched with the steeply raked stem. [A degaussing coil was fitted after 1940.]

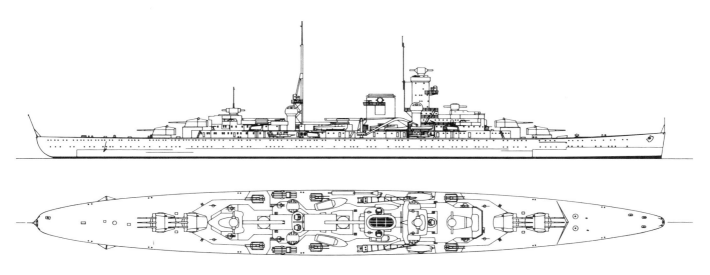

Lützow, Seydlitz; design as a light cruiser, 1936. *Mrva*

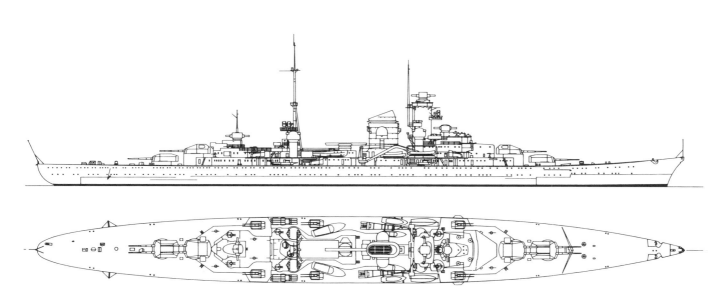

Lützow, Seydlitz; design as a heavy cruiser, not completed, 1936. *Mrva*

Career

Blücher launched 8 Jun 1937, commissioned 20 Sept 1939 into the fleet. Sunk at 0723hrs on 9 Apr 1940 at Dröbak-Enge (Oslofjord), position 59° 44N, 10° 36E, by artillery fire and torpedoes from the Kaaholm battery; casualties not known. The wreck lies at about 45°, at a depth of 90m; the screws were salvaged in 1953, and since 1963 raising the ship has been considered many times, but not carried out to date.

Admiral Hipper launched 6 Feb 1937, commissioned 29 Apr 1939 into the fleet. Sunk at 0425hrs on 3 May 1945 in the dock at Deutsche Werke, Kiel (blown up and scuttled). In July 1945 the wreck was undocked and towed to Heikendorfer Bay, and broken up 1948–52; the bell is now in the National Maritime Museum, Greenwich.

Prinz Eugen launched 22 Aug 1938, commissioned 1 Aug 1940 into the fleet. Surrendered to USA 14 Dec 1945, and used as a test target for the 17 Jun 1946 Bikini atom bomb test; sunk at 1243hrs on 22 Dec 1946 in the Kwajalein lagoon, position 09° 22N, 167° 09E, after capsizing because of leaks. One of the screws was placed in the Laboe naval memorial in August 1979.

Seydlitz launched 19 Jan 1939. Dismantling was begun in 1942, when the ship was 95 percent complete, in preparation for conversion to an aircraft carrier (see page 75). Dismantling was halted in June 1943, and the ship was moved to Königsberg (with the guns and part of the superstructure removed, but the funnel still in place). She was scuttled at Königsberg and blown up on 29 Jan 1945. The wreck became a USSR prize, and cannibalisation was considered to complete *Lüt-zow*; this was not implemented, and *Seydlitz* was broken up after 1958.

Lützow launched 1 Jul 1939; sold to USSR 11 Feb 1940, and towed to Leningrad 15 Apr 1940, where she was renamed *Petropavlovsk*. Served as a floating battery at the Leningrad coal harbour, and was sunk there by German artillery on 17 Sept 1941, coming to rest aground at the wharf on an even keel; hit by a German aircraft bomb in April 1942, she was raised 17 Sept 1942, towed to the Neva, repaired, and in autumn 1943 served as a floating battery under the name *Tallinn*. Further construction work was abandoned 1948–49, and after use as a barrack hulk on the Neva, she was broken up in 1960.

Battlecruisers (planned) 1939–1940

O class

Name	Builder	Built	Cost in Marks (000s)	Displacement (t = tonnes T = tons)	Length (m)	Breadth (m)	Draught (m)	Power (hp)	Revs (rpm)	Speed (kts)	Range (nm/kts)	Coal (t)	Oil (t)
O	Deutsche Werke, Kiel Construction no 265	—		35,400T max 31,650t des 28,900T std	256.0 oa 248.2 cwl	30.0	8.02 des	116,000 shp (turbines) + 60,000 shp (diesels)	300 285	35.0 max 33.5 des	(14,000/ 19)		1000 max 330 des fuel oil + 4610 max 1540 des diesel oil
P	KM Dockyard, Wilhelmshaven Construction no 133	—		″	″	″	″	″	″	″	″		″
Q	Germania Dockyard, Kiel Construction no	—		″	″	″	″	″	″	″	″		″

Construction

Designed as battlecruisers (official design, 1937–40, design officer MarObBrt Hennig); design completed, construction not begun. Longitudinal frame stringer steel construction, welded (twenty watertight compartments, double bottom 78 percent). Krupp armour: upper deck 50mm; armour deck 20–80(shields 60)–20(slopes 110)mm; bow and stern 60mm, all Wh material; torpedo bulkhead 45mm Ww material; forward CT roof 60mm, sides 200mm; aft CT roof 30mm, sides 50mm; tops and rangefinders, roof 20mm, sides 30mm; CWL 0–(bulkhead 80)–100–(bulkhead 100)–190–(bulkhead 110,shields 80)–0mm; citadel 25mm with bulkhead 80mm; turrets, roof 50mm, sides 210mm, shields 180mm; 15cm turrets and all AA guns 14mm, hangars 14mm. Depth 14.35m. Uniform trim moment 61,285cu m.

Propulsion

Eight MAN 24-cylinder V-configuration double acting two-stroke diesels with two Vulcan gearboxes (two 3-bladed screws, 4.85m diameter) in 2 + 2 + 2 engine rooms; aft of these were four Wagner ultra high pressure boilers (temperature not known, 55 atmospheres forced, area not known) in one boiler room, and one set of Brown, Boveri & Co (in O, Blohm & Voss) turbines (one 3-bladed screw, 4.90m diameter) in one engine room. Four diesel generators, 920kW, forward of the main diesels and 2 + 2 diesel generators 920kW, each side of the boiler room, total output 7360kW 220V. 1 + 2 rudders.

Armament

Six 38.1cm/47 QF guns (630 rounds), –8° +35°, range 36,200m; six 15cm/48 QF guns in torpedo boat mounts (900 rounds), range 23,500m; eight 10.5cm/65 AA guns (3200 rounds) +80°; eight 3.7cm/83 AA guns (16,000 rounds); twenty 2cm AA guns (40,000 rounds); six 53.3cm TT (18 rounds), all lateral above water. One double catapult, four Arado 196 seaplanes.

Complement

Crew: 65/1900. Boats: two picket boats, two barges, two launches, etwo pinnaces, two yawls, two dinghies.

Notes

A large hangar was included aft of the forward funnel, with one smaller hangar on either side of the aft funnel.

Career

Design of these battlecruisers was completed, and building contracts placed in spring 1939, but construction did not commence in spite of the short projected building time of 3½ years.

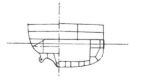

Battlecruisers O–Q
hull section

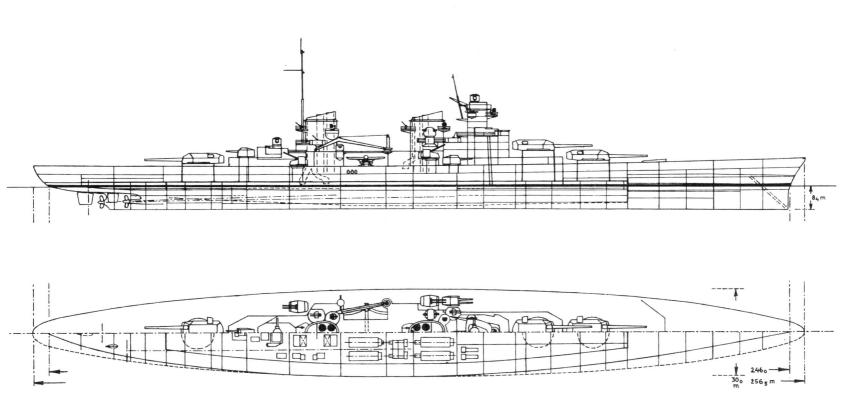

Battlecruisers *O–Q*; preliminary design, 1939

Aircraft carriers 1918–1940

I (ex Ausonia)

Name	Builder	Built	Cost in Marks (000s)	Displacement (t = tonnes T = tons)	Length (m)	Breadth (m)	Draught (m)	Power (hp)	Revs (rpm)	Speed (kts)	Range (nm/kts)	Coal (t)	Oil (t)
I ex AUSONIA	Blohm & Voss Hamburg Construction no 236	(1914–)		12,585t	158.0 oa 149.6 bp	18.8	7.43	18,000shp max 14,000shp des		21 max 20 des		1500	
11,300gt (before rebuild)													

Construction

Designed as an aircraft steamer conversion (design J Reimpell, 1918 for the Commander, Naval Pilots), while *Ausonia* was under construction as a turbine passenger ship; construction not completed. The hangars and flight deck were above the top structural deck. Two hangar decks 82m long were included for wheeled aircraft, and one 128m long for seaplanes, all 18.5m wide; the landing deck was 128.5m long and 18.7m wide. The take-off deck (fighter deck) for wheeled aircraft was 30m long and 10.5m wide. Depth 10.40m.

Propulsion

Two sets of Blohm & Voss geared turbines (two screws, diameter not known), details of boilers not known.

Armament

Thirteen fixed-wing or nineteen folding-wing seaplanes, and about ten wheeled aircraft.

Notes

This was the first German aircraft carrier design, based on reconstruction of the incomplete hull of the Italian turbine-powered passenger ship *Ausonia*. In October 1918 this design led to the projected reconstruction of the armoured cruiser *Roon* into an aircraft support ship (see page 51). In the opinion of the Air Department of the Reichs Navy Office it was 'to be given priority over all other reconstruction projects'. The plan was not implemented due to international negotiations on an armaments moratorium.

Career

I launched 15 Apr 1915 as the turbine-powered passenger ship *Ausonia* for Italian Sitmar; in 1920 the shipping company abandoned the project due to cost increases resulting from the decline in the value of German currency. The hull was broken up in 1922.

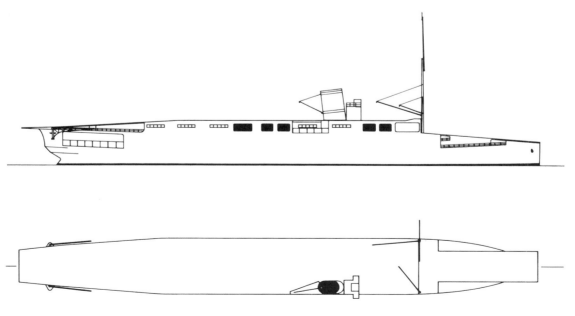

Aircraft steamer *I* (ex *Ausonia*); preliminary design, 1918. *Mrva*

Graf Zeppelin class

Name	Builder	Built	Cost in Marks (000s)	Displacement (t = tonnes T = tons)	Length (m)	Breadth (m)	Draught (m)	Power (hp)	Revs (rpm)	Speed (kts)	Range (nm/kts)	Coal (t)	Oil (t)
GRAF ZEPPELIN	Deutsche Werke, Kiel Construction no 252	1937–	92,700	33,550T max 28,090t des mod 23,200T std	262.5 oa mod 250.0 cwl	36.2* 27.0* 31.5 mod**	8.50 max 7.35 des 6.40 std	200,000 shp des	300 des	33.8 des	8000/19	—	6740 max 3000 des
B	Germania Dockyard, Kiel Construction no 555	1938–	92,400	29,722T max 27,031t des 23,430T std	,,	,,	7.13 des	,,	,,	,,	,,	,,	,,

Originally 19,250T official displacement, including 222t lubricating oil and 119t fuel oil

* over flightdeck   **over bulge

Construction

Designed as aircraft carriers A and B (official design April 1934–April 1939, modifications 1942, design officer MarBrt Hadeler); construction not completed. Transverse and longitudinal frame stringer steel construction (twenty watertight compartments, double bottom 68 percent) [later fitted with side bulges of shipbuilding steel] bow bulge; the flight deck was the top structural deck. Krupp, Wh and Ww armour: flight deck 20–45mm; armoured deck 0–60(bulkhead 60)–40(slope 60)–20mm; Wallgang torpedo bulkhead 20mm Ww; CWL 0–60(bulkheads 80, slopes 80)–100–80(bulkheads 80)–0mm; casemate outer walls 30mm; shields 30mm; crosspieces 20mm; bridgehouse roof 30–150mm; AA directors 14mm. Two hangar decks 183m and 170m long, 16m wide; flight deck 240m long, 27m wide. Depth 22.5m.

Propulsion

Four sets of Brown, Boveri & Co geared turbines (B, Marine-type turbines by Germania dockyard), (four 3-bladed screws, 4.40m diameter) in 1 + 1 + 2 engine rooms, sixteen La Mont ultra high pressure boilers (75 atmospheres forced, 450°) in 1 + 1 + 1 + 1 boiler rooms. Four electricity plants with five diesel generators, each 350kW, five turbo-generators, each 460kW, and one turbo-generator (230kW) with one 200kVA AC generator connected, total output 4280kW 220V. Two rudders; 1 + 1 retractable Voith-Schneider screws in watertight compartments in the bow, each 450hp, = 300kW from the ship's power supply. The total installation weight was 19.23kg/hp.

Armament

Eight [sixteen] 15cm/55 QF guns (1840 rounds), –10° +40°, range 23,000m; ten [twelve] 10.5cm/65 AA guns (4000 and 4800 rounds); twenty-two 3.7cm/83 AA guns (44,000 rounds); seven [finally twenty-eight] 2cm AA guns (14,000 and 56,000 rounds). Two hangar decks, three lifts; two fixed catapults [with under-deck dolly return mechanism for fast launch rate, up to 1 launch/minute], forty-two aircraft in total: twelve [thirty] Ju 87D; ten plus twenty Me 109T or Fi 167 [twelve Me (Bf) 109G]. [In 1941–42 only one 8.8cm AA gun was fitted on board, and in 1943 a few 3.7cm and 2cm AA guns in addition.]

Handling

The ship never steamed under her own power, hence no data is available.

Complement

Crew: 1760 plus flight crew. Boats: two picket boats, two barges, two launches, two pinnaces, two yawls.

Notes

Colour scheme no 9. The vessel was originally designed with a fighter take-off deck above the forecastle, based on the British Courageous. Arrestor cables were planned for 25.5m, 44.5m, 54.2m and 66.0m, calculated from frame zero, 5m forward of the point of the stern. Wind screens were to be 13.5m long and 3.75m high at 122.75m and 194.35m. Drawings show the original planned armament of eight 15cm guns in single turrets. The design officer's suggestion of combining the guns in four double mounts, in order to save space, was misinterpreted in a later planning stage: eight double mounts were planned, although there was insufficient space both for additional ammunition stores and further gun crew accommodation.

Graf Zeppelin; preliminary design, 1937.

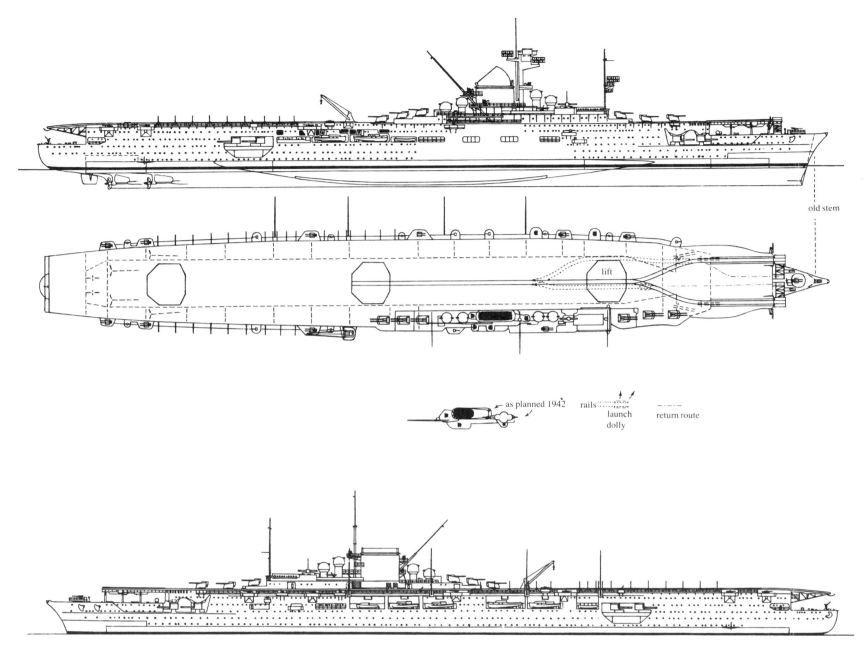

old stem

as planned 1942   rails ·········   launch dolly   —————   return route

Graf Zeppelin; the new vessel *B* is presumed to have been similar.

[After 1942–43 the single Oerlikon AA guns were to be replaced by quads.] The flight deck axis and hangars ran parallel to the midship line, offset 0.5m to port. The outer plating extended 1m further to port than to starboard in order to compensate for weight of island. [In 1939 an Atlantic bow was added, and in 1942–43 a side bulge was added on each side above the roll keel, maximum width 2.4m; normal thickness shipbuilding steel was used on the port side, with thinner material (approx 15–18mm/10–12mm) on the starboard side.]

Career

Graf Zeppelin launched 8 Dec 1938, and was more than 85 percent completed in 1939. Construction was halted 29 Apr 1940, and the ship was transferred to Gotenhafen in July 1940, where she was used as a naval hardwood store; the cover name for this operation was *Zugvogel* – bird of passage. On 16 Mar 1942 the order was issued to resume building; the ship was transferred to Kiel 5 Dec 1942; construction was halted 30 Jan 1943, temporary work continued until March 1943, and the ship was moved to Stettin in April 1943. Sunk 24 Mar 1945 at Stettin, position 53° 26N, 14° 34E, by scuttling. Salvaged by the USSR March 1946,

moved to Swinemünde, and towed to Leningrad in September 1947, during which operation she strayed into a minefield off Finnbusen during a storm and was damaged. Further construction work was abandoned, and she was broken up at Leningrad 1948–49.

B construction begun 1938, and the hull was complete bar the armour deck at the time of cessation of building, 19 Sept 1939. The vessel was broken up within 4 months after 28 Feb 1940 by Eisen & Metall, Essen. The projected name of *Peter Strasser* is an unconfirmed speculation, but not unlikely. The launch was originally planned for 1 Jul 1940.

Auxiliary aircraft carriers 1942–1943

I (ex Europa)

Name	Builder	Built	Cost in Marks (000s)	Displacement (t = tonnes T = tons)	Length (m)	Breadth (m)	Draught (m)	Power (hp)	Revs (rpm)	Speed (kts)	Range (nm/kts)	Coal (t)	Oil (t)
I ex EUROPA 49,746gt	Blohm & Voss, Hamburg Construction no 479 mod: Blohm & Voss, Hamburg	1927–30 —		56,500t max 44,000t des	291.5 oa 280.0 cwl	37.0 max* 31.0 des	10.3 max 8.5 des	100,000 shp des	215 des	26.5 des	5000/27 10,000/19	—	8500 max 6500 des

* over bulge

Construction

Designed as an auxiliary aircraft carrier conversion to a passenger/transport ship (official design, 1942) (sixteen watertight compartments, double bottom, percentage not known); conversion work not begun. No armour, flight deck length 276m, width 30m; hangar length 216m, width forward 25m, aft 30m. Depth to flight deck 24.20m.

Propulsion

Four sets of Blohm & Voss geared turbines, three housings (four 4-bladed screws, 5.00m diameter) in 1 + 1 engine rooms. Twenty-four double-ended narrow water tube boilers (240 point burners, 21 atmospheres forced, area not known) in 1 + 1 + 0 + 1 + 1 boiler rooms. Electricity plant was four diesel generators, each 520kW, and two emergency diesels, each 100kW, total output 2280kW 230V. One rudder.

Armament

Twelve 10.5cm/65 AA guns (4800 rounds) in double mounts; twenty 3.7cm AA guns (40,000 rounds) in double mounts; twenty-eight to thirty-six 2cm AA guns

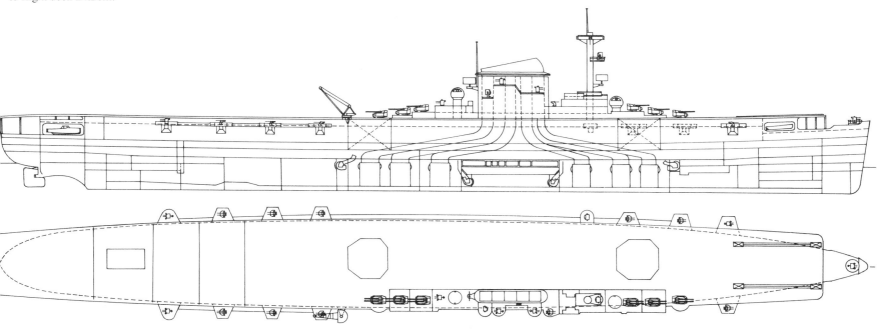

Auxiliary aircraft carrier *I* (ex *Europa*); June 1942 design. *Wünschmann*

(72,000 rounds), quadruples. Two catapults; eighteen Ju 87D aircraft; twenty-four Me (Bf) 109G aircraft.

Notes

This was the most powerful of the planned reconstructions in terms of speed, size and machinery distribution in the engine rooms, but strength remained a problem because the design called for the hangar to be recessed into the main structural deck. Projected fuel consumption remained high, and stability problems persisted in spite of attempts to bulge the hull. The project was abandoned after completion of the design, because many major problems remained unsolved; conversion work on the ship was not started.

Career

I launched 16 Aug 1928 as *Europa*. Severely damaged by a major fire during fitting out 26 Mar 1929; repaired; in service 19 Mar 1930 for the North Atlantic service of Norddeutscher Lloyd, Bremen. Used as a barrack ship at Wesermünde 1939, intended as a transport vessel for Operation Sealion June 1940; conversion to an auxiliary aircraft carrier was planned from May 1942, but the project was abandoned 25 Nov 1942; subsequent planned use was as a tank unit troop transport (including loading gear for 80t tanks). US prize, May 1945; used as a troop transport under the name *AP 177*; awarded to France June 1946; sunk in a storm at Le Havre after being driven against the wreck of *Paris*, on 8 Dec 1946; raised 15 Apr 1947 and repaired; in service 17 Aug 1950 as *Liberté*, on the North Atlantic service of the CGT. Broken up at La Spezia in 1962.

'Jade' class

Name	Builder	Built	Cost in Marks (000s)	Displacement (t = tonnes T = tons)	Length (m)	Breadth (m)	Draught (m)	Power (hp)	Revs (rpm)	Speed (kts)	Range (nm/kts)	Coal (t)	Oil (t)
'JADE'	AG 'Weser', Bremen Construction no 893 mod: KM Dockyard, Wilhelmshaven	1934–35		18,160t des	203.0 oa 191.0 cwl	27.0* 26.8**	8.85 max 5.10 des	26,000shp des	130 des	19.0 max 21.0 des	9000/19	—	4570 max 3400 des†
'ELBE'	Blohm & Voss, Hamburg Construction no 497 mod: Howaldt, Hamburg from 11.42: Blohm & Voss, Hamburg	1934–35 1942–		23,500t max 17,527t des	203.0 oa 189.0 cwl	27.0* 26.8 max** 22.6 des	8.85 max 5.10 des	26,000shp des	160 des	19.0 max 21.0 des	9000/19	—	3145 des†

18,160gt (*Gneisenau*), 17,528gt (*Potsdam*)

* over flightdeck   † + 100t aircraft fuel
** over bulge

Construction

Designed as auxiliary aircraft carrier conversions to passenger/transport ships (official design, 1942), steel construction, welded (twelve watertight compartments, double bottom); the *Elbe* design included a Taylor bulge, the *Jade* design a Maierform bow; neither conversion was completed. Armour (Wh material): aircraft deck 20mm; hangar walls 10–15–10mm. Flight deck 186m long, 27m wide; hangar 148m long, 18m wide. Depth to flight deck 19.05m.

Propulsion

Jade, two sets of geared turbines, Deschimag/Wagner system, three housings (two 3-bladed screws, diameter not known) in one engine room (primary revolutions at full load 7300rpm high and medium pressure stage, 2180rpm low pressure). Four single-ended high pressure boilers (50 atmospheres forced, 450°, 36t/h steam) in one boiler room.

Elbe, two turbo-generators and two electric drive motors from SSW and Blohm & Voss (two 4-bladed screws, 4.9m diameter) in one engine room. Four Benson ultra high pressure boilers (90 atmospheres forced, 450°, steam production not known) in one boiler room.

Both ships had an electricity plant of four turbo-generators, each 760kW, four diesel generators, each 350kW and one emergency diesel, 60kW, total output 4500kW at 220V. One rudder.

Armament

Twelve 10.5cm/65 AA guns (3200 rounds) in double mounts; ten 3.7cm AA guns (20,000 rounds) in double mounts; twenty-four to thirty-two 2cm AA guns (48,000 rounds), quadruples. Two catapults; twelve Ju 87D aircraft, twelve Me (Bf) 109G aircraft.

Complement

Crew: *Jade* 79/804 (including 134 Luftwaffe); *Elbe* approx 900 (including 190 Luftwaffe). Boats not known.

Notes

The hangar was created by removing A deck apart from a strip along the port side. The inadequate stability of the passenger vessels was to be corrected by the addition of side bulges and fixed ballast (known as 'concrete armour', in fact a thick concrete layer on the outer plating below the CWL). An alternative proposal in the *Elbe* IIb design was to solve the stability problem by adding a second outer skin around the entire ship (similar to reconstruction of the light cruiser *Karlsruhe*, see page 109). The names *Jade* and *Elbe* are very probably cover names, since no document has ever been found indicating that these were to be final designations, although all plans, documents, etc, are listed under these names. The various projected reconstructions were designated with Roman numbers, sometimes with additional Arabic letters.

Career

'*Jade*' launched 17 May 1935 as *Gneisenau*; in service from 3 Jan 1936 for the East Asia Service of Norddeutscher Lloyd, Bremen. Taken over as a transporter in June 1940; conversion to an auxiliary aircraft carrier planned from May 1942; project abandoned 25 Nov 1942; served again as a troop transporter (handling gear for heavy loads was briefly planned, as in the case of *Europa*). Sunk at 1202hrs on 2 May 1943, east of Gjedser, position 54° 38N, 12° 25' 01"E, after hitting a mine.

'*Elbe*' launched 16 Jan 1935 as *Potsdam*; in service from 27 Jun 1936 for the East Asia Service of Norddeutscher Lloyd, Bremen. Taken over as a transporter in June 1940; conversion to an auxiliary aircraft carrier planned from May 1942; served as a training carrier from 25 Nov 1942, and conversion work was begun at Kiel in December 1942 with the removal of the passenger fittings; work was halted 2 Feb 1943, and re-conversion to a barrack ship for Gotenhafen was begun. Taken as a British prize 20 Jun 1946; used as a troop transport under the name *Empire Fowey*; became the Pakistani pilgrim ship *Safina-E-Hujjaj* 1960; broken up 1976.

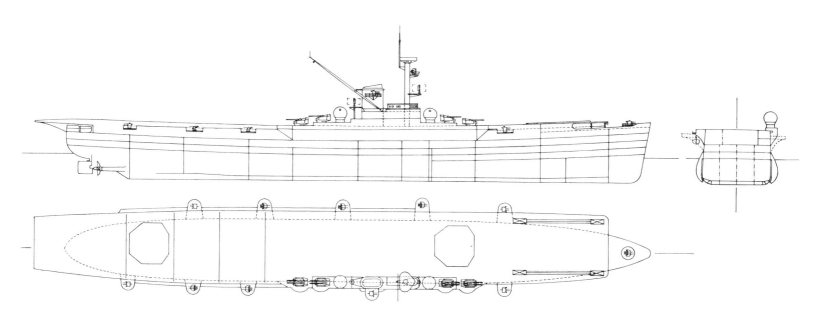

Auxiliary aircraft carrier '*Elbe*' (ex *Potsdam*); design II, June 1942. *Wünschmann*

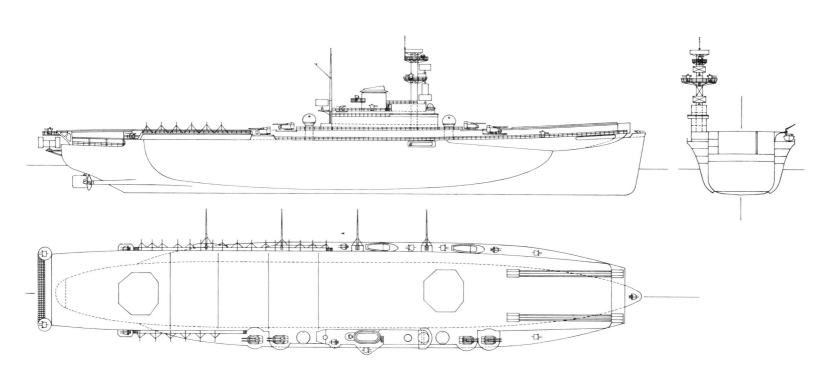

Auxiliary aircraft carrier '*Elbe*'; design IIb, December 1942. *Wünschmann*

Weser class

Construction

Designed as an auxiliary aircraft carrier conversion to the heavy cruiser *Seydlitz* (official design, 1942). Longitudinal frame stringer steel construction (fourteen watertight compartments, double bottom 72 percent); conversion not completed. Flight deck 200m long, 30m wide; hangar 137.5m long, forward width 17m, centre and aft 12m.

Propulsion

Three sets of Deschimag geared turbines, three housings (three 3-bladed screws, 4.0m diameter) in 1 + 0 + 1 engine rooms. Nine double-ended high pressure boilers (450°, 58 atmospheres forced, steam volume not known) in 1 + 0 + 1 + 1 boiler rooms. One rudder.

Name	Builder	Built	Cost in Marks (000s)	Displacement (t = tonnes T = tons)	Length (m)	Breadth (m)	Draught (m)	Power (hp)	Revs (rpm)	Speed (kts)	Range (nm/kts)	Coal (t)	Oil (t)
WESER	Deschimag, Bremen Construction no 940	1936–	84,090	17,139t des	216.0 oa 201.5 cwl	21.8 des	6.65 max 6.08 des	132,000 shp des	320 des	32.0 des	6500/19	—	
	mod: Deschimag, Bremen	1942–											

Armament

Ten 10.5cm/65 AA guns (4000 rounds) in double mounts; ten 3.7cm AA guns (16,000 rounds) in double mounts; twenty-four 2cm AA guns (40,000 rounds), quadruples. Two catapults; ten Ju 87D aircraft; ten Me (Bf) 109G aircraft.

Notes

The cruiser was 95 percent complete, and the following dismantling work carried out: removal of the superstructure above the upper deck as far as the funnel and the immediately adjacent deckhouse section; removal of barbette B; removal of fittings and light walls in battery and tween decks as far as bow section (total removed was 2400t material).

Career

Weser launched 19 Jan 1939 as heavy cruiser *Seydlitz* (see page 55); conversion to an auxiliary aircraft carrier was planned from May 1942; dismantling work was begun in December 1942; dismantling was halted in June 1943, and the ship was transferred to Königsberg. Scuttled and blown up at Königsberg 29 Jan 1945; the wreck became a USSR prize, and cannibalisation to complete *Lützow* was considered, but not carried out; finally broken up.

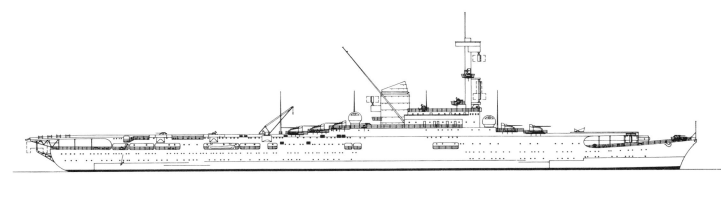

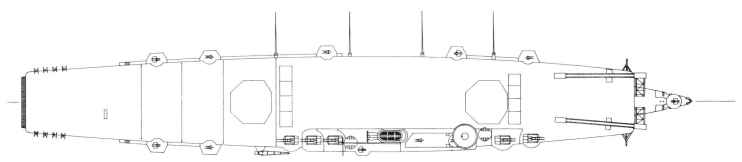

Auxiliary aircraft carrier *Weser* (ex *Seydlitz*); December 1942 design. *Wünschmann*

II (ex De Grasse)

Name	Builder	Built	Cost in Marks (000s)	Displacement (t = tonnes T = tons)	Length (m)	Breadth (m)	Draught (m)	Power (hp)	Revs (rpm)	Speed (kts)	Range (nm/kts)	Coal (t)	Oil (t)
II ex DE GRASSE	State Yard Lorient	(1938– 56)		11,400T des	192.5 oa 180.4 cwl	24.4 des	5.6 des	10,000shp		32 des	7000/19	—	

Construction

Designed as an auxiliary aircraft carrier conversion to a newly built French cruiser; (official design, 1942); conversion not completed. Flight deck 177.5m long, 24m wide; hangar 142m long, 18.6m wide. Depth not known.

Propulsion

Two sets of Rateau-Bretagne geared turbines (two screws, diameter not known), number of engine rooms not known. Four Indret ultra high pressure boilers (pressure not known).

Armament

Twelve 10.5cm/65 AA guns in double mounts; twelve 3.7cm AA guns in double mounts; twenty-four 2cm AA guns, quadruples. Two catapults; twelve Ju 87D aircraft; eleven Me (Bf) 109G aircraft.

Notes

Several alternative plans were prepared for the completion of this new French cruiser as an auxiliary aircraft cruiser, differing in various ways. Data quoted here corresponds with the drawing. The conversion was abandoned because of shortage of labour and materials, danger of air attack at Lorient and major concern regarding the poorly distributed engine installation.

Career

II completion as an aircraft carrier was planned after August 1942; the project was abandoned in February 1943. The ship was launched 11 Sept 1946 as *De Grasse*, and completed as a French AA cruiser 3 Sept 1956.

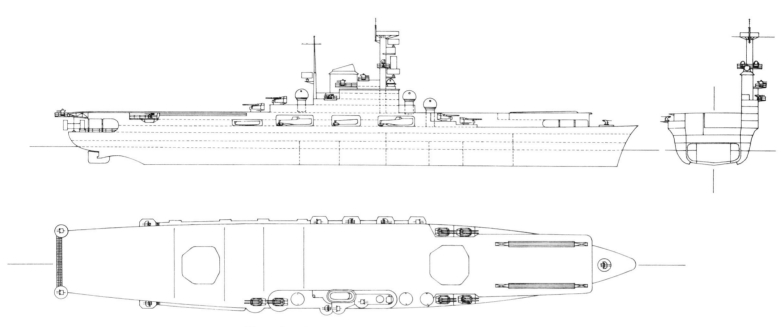

Auxiliary aircraft carrier *II* (ex *De Grasse*); January 1943 design. *Wünschmann*

Schooners, corvettes, avisos, armed steamers 1817–1886

Stralsund

Name	Builder	Built	Cost	Displacement (t = tonnes T = tons)	Length (m)	Breadth (m)	Draught (m)	Power (hp)	Revs (rpm)	Speed (kts)	Range (nm/kts)	Coal (t)	Oil (t)
STRALSUND	J A Meyer, Stralsund	1816–17	10.4 Thaler	c285t max 250t des	24.38 cwl	7.31	1.90 fwd 2.44 aft	—	—	c13		—	—

Construction
Laid down as a schooner (design by Longe, 1816). Transverse frame oak plank carvel hull (seven watertight compartments). Depth not known.

Propulsion
Topsail schooner rig, 583sq m, plus 150sq m studding sails. One rudder.

Armament
Two 24pdr and eight 8pdr, all firing broadside under the rail.

Handling
Seaworthy, fast, tight-turning sailing ship, easy to

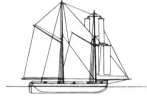
Stralsund (1817)

manoeuvre, tolerating severe weather; little leeway.

Complement
Crew: approx 4/40, accommodated as necessary ashore. Two boats.

Notes
Colour scheme approx no 1.

Career
Stralsund launched 13 Sept 1816; sole commission 12 Feb 1817 for short voyages as a training ship. Stricken 17 Oct 1829, sold 7 Nov 1829 for 1585 Thaler, broken up at Stralsund.

Amazone

Name	Builder	Built	Cost	Displacement (t = tonnes T = tons)	Length (m)	Breadth (m)	Draught (m)	Power (hp)	Revs (rpm)	Speed (kts)	Range (nm/kts)	Coal (t)	Oil (t)
AMAZONE	Carmesins Dockyard, Grabow (Stettin) mod: Royal Dockyard, Danzig	1842–43 / 1852		390t max 348t des	33.49 cwl	8.99	3.14	—	—	c11		—	—

Construction
Laid down as a sailing corvette (design by Elbertzhagen, 1841). Transverse frame oak plank carvel hull, subdivision not known. Freeboard not known.

Propulsion
Full-rigged ship, 876sq m. One rudder.

Armament
Two English 32pdr (planned only); twelve Swedish 18pdr [finally four long guns (size not known) and four short Swedish 24pdr].

Handling
Fast sailing ship in light airs, but able to carry very

little sail above Beaufort 7 wind. Very wet, crank; she was severely over-rigged and suffered continual rigging damage.

Complement
Crew: 6/139. Boats: one large, three small.

Notes

Colour scheme approx no 1. High bulwark. Ammunition was hardly ever shipped, since the guns were for exercise only.

Career

Amazone launched 24 Jun 1843, commissioned 19 May 1844 as a training ship; served abroad 1852–53 as

Amazone (1852)

a cadet training ship. Sunk in the Southern North Sea on about 14 Nov 1861 (probably in the region of the Gallper and Goodwin shallows) during a storm; 114 dead, entire crew lost.

Preussischer Adler

Name	Builder	Built	Cost	Displacement (t = tonnes T = tons)	Length (m)	Breadth (m)	Draught (m)	Power (hp)	Revs (rpm)	Speed (kts)	Range (nm/kts)	Coal (t)	Oil (t)
PREUSSISCHER ADLER	Ditchburn & Mare, London	1846–47	312 Thaler	1430t max 1171t des	62.72 oa 56.60 cwl	16.2* 9.6 **	3.30	990ihp max 900ihp des	25	11.5 max 10.5 des		200 max	—

* over wheelboxes
** over hull

Construction

Laid down as a post steamer for the service from St Petersburg (design by Elbertzhagen, 1846). Transverse frame iron construction with timber decks (subdivision not known). Depth not known.

Propulsion

One horizontal oscillating 2-cylinder single expansion engine (two wheels, each with twenty paddles, 6.34m diameter). Three trunk boilers (1 atmosphere forced). Topsail schooner rig, approx 600sq m. One rudder.

Armament

Two 25pdr bomb cannon; two short 32pdr [four 36pdr; after 1867 two rifled and two smoothbore 24pdr].

Handling

Quite good sea-boat, but slow to manoeuvre and difficult to turn; sails contributed little to performance.

Complement

Crew: 10/100. Boats: one large, four small.

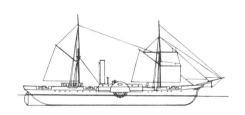

Preussischer Adler (1852)

Notes

Colour scheme approx no 1. As a post steamer she had accommodation for 168 passengers.

Career

Preussischer Adler launched 1846 as a post steamer for the Swinemünde-Kronstadt (St Petersburg) service; requisitioned 1848 for coastal defence; returned 1850–52 to service as a post steamer on the Swinemünde-Kronstadt service, under the control of the Prussian postal administration; abroad from 18 Jun 1863; converted to a Royal yacht 1868. Stricken 27 Nov 1877; blown up in torpedo tests at Kiel-Wik 26 Jun 1879. Bow ornament now in the Mürwik navy school.

Der Königliche Ernst August class

Construction

Laid down as steamers *Cora*, *Inca* and *Cazique* – cover names, in deference to British neutrality – (British designs). Transverse frame oak plank, yellow pine carvel hull with Muntz metal sheathing; two decks. Depth 5.01m and 4.27m.

Propulsion

Two horizontal oscillating single-cylinder expansion engines by Miller & Ravenshill, London (two wheels, twelve paddles each, approx 5.79 to 5.49m diameter). *Der Königliche Ernst August* had three trunk boilers (six fireboxes, approx 1 atmosphere forced) in one en-

gine room, 16.15m long; *Grossherzog von Oldenburg* had four trunk boilers (eight fireboxes, approx 1 atmosphere forced), two forward, two aft of the engines in the non-divided engine room, 20.57m long; *Frankfurt* had two trunk boilers (four fireboxes, approx 1 atmosphere forced) in one engine room, 12.81m long. Schooner brig rig, area not known. One rudder.

Armament

Der Königliche Ernst August had six bomb cannon (68pdr carronades); *Grossherzog von Oldenburg* and *Frankfurt* had two bomb cannon, 68pdr from Woolwich Arsenal, installed by the Arsenal of the

Seezeugmeisterei (Master Mariners), Geestemünde.

Handling

Average seakeeping and manoeuvring characteristics for paddle steamers of the time, with severe leeway and poor sailing qualities.

Complement

Crew: 5/145 and 4/96. Boats: four large, one cutter (or none).

Name	Builder	Built	Cost	Displacement (t = tonnes T = tons)	Length (m)	Breadth (m)	Draught (m)	Power (hp)	Revs (rpm)	Speed (kts)	Range (nm/kts)	Coal (t)	Oil (t)
DER KÖNIGLICHE ERNST AUGUST	Wm Patterson, Bristol	1847–50	150 Thaler	580t des	55.47 oa 49.21 cwl	17.1* 9.72**	3,81 fwd 3.96 aft	c950ihp max 270nhp des	up to 24	c9		200	—
GROßHERZOG VON OLDENBURG	,,	,,	110 Thaler	415t des	50.29 oa 44.40 cwl	14.8* 8.08**	2.95 fwd 3.20 aft	c920ihp max 230nhp des	up to 32	c9	1900/8	150	—
FRANKFURT	,,	,,	,,	448t des	51.02 oa 44.71 cwl	14.4* 8.16**	2.44 fwd 2.74 aft	c700ihp max 180 nhp des	up to 28	c8	1600/8	130	—

900, 600 and 625gt

* over wheelboxes
** over hull

Notes
Colour scheme no 1. *Grossherzog von Oldenburg* had two funnels, the others one.

Career
Der Königliche Ernst August launched 1848 as *Cora*, commissioned into the German Bundesflotte (Federal Fleet) in October 1848, renamed *Der Königliche Ernst August* 27 Nov 1849. Sold to General Steam Navigation Co Ltd, London, 12 Dec 1852; became British ss *Edinburgh* (741BRT) March 1853. Sunk March 1885 at Varna.

Grossherzog von Oldenburg launched 1848 as *Inca*, commissioned in spring 1849 at Bremerhaven as *Grossherzog von Oldenburg* for the German Bundesflotte (Federal fleet). Sold 12 Dec 1852 to General Steam Navigation Co Ltd, London; became British ss *Belgium* in March 1853; rigging removed December 1877, and hulked; used as a floating workshop February 1879; fate unknown.

Frankfurt launched 1848 as *Cazique*; commissioned in spring 1849 at Bremerhaven as *Frankfurt* for the German Bundesflotte (Federal fleet). Sold 12 Dec 1852 to General Steam Navigation Co Ltd, London; became British ss *Holland* in March 1952. Sunk 1 Feb 1860 in the Thames in the vicinity of Deptford, following a collision with ss *Gertrude*; raised and repaired, then finally broken up in December 1878 by Castle & Sons. The total sale price of these ships and *Bremen*, *Hamburg* and *Lübeck* (below) was 238,000 Thaler.

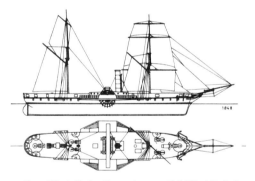

Der Königliche Ernst August (1848). *Mickel*

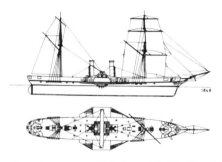

Grossherzog von Oldenburg (1848); *Frankfurt* was similar, but had only one funnel. *Mickel*

Elbe

Name	Builder	Built	Cost	Displacement (t = tonnes T = tons)	Length (m)	Breadth (m)	Draught (m)	Power (hp)	Revs (rpm)	Speed (kts)	Range (nm/kts)	Coal (t)	Oil (t)
ELBE	Marine Dockyard, Nyholm Construction no 27	1832–33		140t	26.0 oa 23.9 bp	6.37	2.27 fwd 2.74 aft	—	—			—	—

Construction
Laid down as a Danish armed schooner (designer not known). Transverse frame oak carvel hull. Depth 3.40m.

Propulsion
Schooner rig, 474sq m. One rudder.

Armament
Eight 12pdr.

Complement
Crew: 12, plus 28 cadets. Boats not known.

Notes
Colour scheme no 1.

Career
Elbe launched 9 Nov 1831 as armed schooner *Elben* for the Danish fleet; laid up in winter quarters at Altona as a guard ship; taken over by Schleswig-Holstein in March 1848. Commissioned as armed schooner *Elbe* 3 Apr 1848, and also served as a training ship for the sea cadet school at Kiel. Returned to the Danish fleet in March 1851; stricken 1858, broken up 1866.

Bremen class

Name	Builder	Built	Cost	Displacement (t = tonnes T = tons)	Length (m)	Breadth (m)	Draught (m)	Power (hp)	Revs (rpm)	Speed (kts)	Range (nm/kts)	Coal (t)	Oil (t)
BREMEN	Johann Marbs Dockyard, Altona-St Pauli	1842	95 Thaler	350t des	55.77 oa 49.35 cwl	12.7 max 6.77 des	2.40 fwd 2.89 aft	c700ihp max 180nhp des	up to 23	c8	2330/8	100	—
HAMBURG	Bernhard Wencke Dockyard, Bremen	1841	,,	380t des	53.34 oa 48.00 cwl	12.1 max 6.91 des	2.89 fwd 3.35 aft	,,	,,	,,	,,	120	—
LÜBECK	S & H Morton & Co, Leith	1844	110 Thaler	335t des	49.99 oa 44.50 cwl	12.6 max 6.48 des	3.35	,,	up to 24	,,	1860/8	100	—

450, 500 and 435gt

Construction
Laid down as steamers (various designs). Transverse frame oak/yellow pine carvel hull with Muntz metal sheathing; two decks. Hold depths 4.57m, 4.88m and 3.96m.

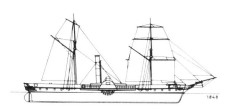

Hamburg (1848); *Bremen* and *Lübeck* were very similar. *Mickel*

Propulsion
Two horizontal oscillating single-cylinder expansion engines by Fawcett, Preston & Co, Liverpool (two wheels, each with twelve paddles, 6.10m diameter). Two trunk boilers (four fireboxes, 1 atmosphere forced) in an engine room 14.32m, 13.42m and 15.03m long. Schooner brig rig, area not known. One rudder.

Armament
One 36pdr bomb cannon (*Bremen*), one 56pdr (*Hamburg*), one 84pdr (*Lübeck*) forward, aft of foremast; one 32pdr aft on the deck saloon; two 18pdr bomb cannon in opposed gunports forward and aft of the wheel box.

Handling
Seakeeping, manoeuvring and sailing qualities were average for paddle steamers of the time.

Complement
Crew: 4/96 (*Hamburg*, 4/116). Boats: two large, plus one cutter (*Bremen* only).

Notes
Colour scheme no 1. Differences between the vessels were very slight, but no authentic sources survive. [*Lübeck*'s overall length was increased from 42.8m to 50.0m in 1847.]

Career
Bremen launched 22 Jun 1842 as *Leeds*, for the Hanseatische Dampfschifffahrts-Ges (Hanseatic Steam Shipping Company), Hamburg; bought by the Hamburg Admiralty for the Hamburg flotilla 23 Jun 1848, and renamed *Bremen*. Taken over by the German Bun-desflotte 15 Oct 1848, in service 15 Dec 1848. Sold 12 Dec 1852 to General Steam Navigation Co Ltd, London; became British ss *Hannover* (519BRT) in March 1853; reduced to a coal hulk by February 1868, fate unknown.

Hamburg launched 6 Apr 1841 for the Hanseatische Dampfschifffahrts-Ges, Hamburg; bought by the Hamburg Admiralty for the Hamburg flotilla 23 Jun 1848. Taken over by the German Bundesflotte 15 Oct 1848, in service 15 Dec 1848. Sold 12 Dec 1852 to General Steam Navigation Co Ltd, London; became British ss *Denmark* in March 1853; broken up in July 1859.

Lübeck launched Sept 1844 as British *Robert Napier*; renamed *Lübeck* 16 Apr 1846 for the Hanseatische Dampfschifffahrts-Ges, Hamburg; bought by the Hamburg Admiralty for the Hamburg flotilla 23 Jun 1848; taken over by the German Bundesflotte 15 Oct 1848, in service 15 Dec 1848. Sold 12 Dec 1852 to General Steam Navigation Co Ltd, London; became British ss *Newcastle* in March 1853; broken up in October 1858. Total sale price of these and *Der Königliche Ernst August*, *Grossherzog von Oldenburg*, and *Frankfurt* was 238,000 Thaler.

Mercur

Name	Builder	Built	Cost	Displacement (t = tonnes T = tons)	Length (m)	Breadth (m)	Draught (m)	Power (hp)	Revs (rpm)	Speed (kts)	Range (nm/kts)	Coal (t)	Oil (t)
MERCUR	J Klawitter, Danzig mod: Marinedepot, Stettin	1847–48 1850–51	36 Thaler	c850t max 580t des	43.25 oa 38.16 des	8.20	2.80	—	—	c9	—	—	—

650gt

Construction
Laid down as a frigate and East Indiaman for the Preussische Seehandlungs Ges – Prussian Maritime Trading Company – (design by Klawitter, 1846). Transverse frame timber carvel hull, subdivision not known.

Propulsion
Full-rigged ship, 805sq m. One rudder.

Armament
Six 26pdr bomb cannon [from 1852 to 1857 seven light field guns were carried in place of the 26pdr; after 1857 the 26pdr were refitted].

Handling
Good sailing ship; initially extremely stiff, later somewhat crank after reduction in ballast; very heavy to work, wet.

Complement
Crew: 12/145 to 5/55. Boats: one large, three smaller.

Mercur (1852)

Notes
Colour scheme no 1. Very long topmast yards were a feature of the merchant rig. Initial trim as a warship, including 200t iron and approx 30t water ballast, had to be reduced considerably due to the danger of mast breakage in violent movements. By 1858 the ship was in poor condition due to dry rot.

Career
Mercur launched 22 Jul 1847; in service from 1848 as a South America and East India ship for the Preussische Seehandlungs Ges, Berlin. Purchased 26 Mar 1850 by the Bundesflotte; served abroad until 1854, and from 1857 as a cadet training ship. Stricken 14 Nov 1860; sold 6 Dec 1860 for 11,950 Thaler to Friedrich Heyn, Danzig, and broken up 1862, at Danzig.

Nix class

Name	Builder	Built	Cost	Displacement (t = tonnes T = tons)	Length (m)	Breadth (m)	Draught (m)	Power (hp)	Revs (rpm)	Speed (kts)	Range (nm/kts)	Coal (t)	Oil (t)
NIX	Robinson & Russell, London	1850–51	£20	430t max 389t des	53.85 oa 53.05 cwl	12.4* 7.2**	2.00	600ihp max 160nhp des	19	13	2500/10	—	—
SALAMANDER 530gt	,,	,,	,,	,,	,,	,,	,,	,,	,,	,,	,,	—	—

* over wheelboxes   ** over hull

Construction
Paddle avisos for coastal waters (design by Prince Adalbert von Preussen/Scott Russell, 1849). Transverse frame iron construction with timber decks (thirteen watertight compartments, double bottom 100 percent). Depth not known.

Propulsion
Two oscillating 2-cylinder single expansion engines (two wheels, each with fourteen paddles, 5.0m diameter) in one engine room. Four trunk boilers (1 atmosphere forced) in 1 + 1 boiler rooms forward and aft of the engines. Two masts with one square topsail and one lower lug sail, also one fore staysail, total rig approx 350sq m. Two rudders, at stem and stern; both could be fixed.

Armament
Four 25pdr bomb cannon; four short 12pdr from Woolwich Arsenal were also planned.

Handling
Good sea-boats, but turned rather less tightly than was expected; totally uncontrollable under sail alone.

Complement
Crew: approx 4/70. Four boats.

Notes
Colour scheme approx no 1. These avisos were hardly ever used, principally because their commanders and crew were not used to steamers (hence the frequent adverse opinions); their classification as suitable for

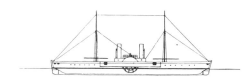

Nix (1854), *Salamander*

coastal waters only underlined their reputation. The timber walls of the stoking room caught fire several times. Great Britain needed small, fast steamers for the Crimean war, and since Prussia required an extra training frigate, the two vessels were exchanged for *Thetis*; the British Admiralty took great advantage of a very one-sided contract, written in English (the 'Prussian' negotiator Kpt z See Hylten Cavallius spoke better English than German).

Career
Nix launched 1850, commissioned 29 Jul 1851; saw very little service; exchanged, with *Salamander*, for *Thetis*, a British sailing frigate, 12 Jan 1855. As British aviso *Recruit* she served abroad until 1861, and was sold 20 Oct 1869 to Sheerness and broken up.

Salamander launched 1850, commissioned 1 Jul 1851; saw very little service; exchanged, with *Nix*, for *Thetis* 12 Jan 1855. As British aviso *Weser* she served abroad until 1865, then as a harbour ship at Malta, and was sold and broken up.

Hela class

Construction
Laid down as armed schooners *Der Urwähler* and *Frauengabe* (design by Klawitter and Lübke, 1853, based on the Dutch *Schorpioon*). Transverse frame timber carvel hull with copper sheathing (subdivision not known). Hold depth 4.90m.

Propulsion
Gaff-rigged schooners, 523sq m [*Hela* as a topsail schooner, 604sq m; brig rig after 1860, 539sq m]. One rudder.

Name	Builder	Built	Cost	Displacement (t = tonnes T = tons)	Length (m)	Breadth (m)	Draught (m)	Power (hp)	Revs (rpm)	Speed (kts)	Range (nm/kts)	Coal (t)	Oil (t)
HELA	Royal Dockyard, Danzig mod:	1853–54 1860	46 Thaler	300t max 271t des	32.60 oa 27.43 cwl	7.85	2.44 fwd 3.66 aft	—	—	c14	—	—	—
FRAUENLOB 77 and 94gt	Lübke, Wolgast	1849–56	43 Thaler	305t max 275t des	32.10 oa 27.66 cwl	8.10	2.61 fwd 3.23 aft	—	—	c13	—	—	—

Armament

One short 30pdr [*Hela* three heavy 24pdr, six light 24pdr].

Handling

These were not ocean-going ships as they could not tolerate swell; in sheltered waters both sailed well.

Complement

Crew: 5/42; *Hela* 5/40 [later 7/75]. Four boats.

Notes

Colour scheme approx no 1. Financed by voluntary

Frauenlob (1857), *Hela* until 1860

contributions from Prussian electors and the women of Germany respectively (hence their construction names 'Primary Elector' and 'Gift of Woman') with State subsidy. Both ships were virtually uninhabitable, especially *Hela* as a training ship.

Career

Hela launched 18 Oct 1853, commissioned 20 Mar 1854 for training purposes; many periods of service. Stricken 28 Nov 1917, broken up.

Frauenlob launched 24 Aug 1855, commissioned 1 May 1856 for service abroad. Sunk 2 Sept 1860 in the Bay of Yeddo in a typhoon; 47 dead, all crew lost.

Musquito class

Name	Builder	Built	Cost in Marks (000s)	Displacement (t = tonnes T = tons)	Length (m)	Breadth (m)	Draught (m)	Power (hp)	Revs (rpm)	Speed (kts)	Range (nm/kts)	Coal (t)	Oil (t)
MUSQUITO	Royal Dockyard, Pembroke	1851	110.0 Thaler = 335.5	627t max 509t des	40.50 oa 34.10 cwl	10.3	4.05 fwd 4.60 aft	—	—	c12	—	—	—
ROVER	,,	1853	117.7 Thaler = 356	,,	,,	,,	,,	—	—	,,	—	—	—
UNDINE 310gt/194nt	Royal Dockyard, Danzig	1869–71	127.4 Thaler = 382.2	624t max 598t des	41.92 oa 35.82 cwl	10.2	4.30	—	—	c10	—	—	—

Construction and Propulsion

Laid down as brig-sloops (English/German design, 1851 and 1860). Transverse frame timber carvel hull. Brig rig 1035sq m. One rudder. Hold depth 7.15m.

Armament

Musquito and *Rover* carried ten smoothbore 24pdr [ten 8cm/23 hooped guns, finally six 8cm/23 hooped guns]; *Undine* carried eight 24pdr [six 8cm/20 hooped guns].

Handling

All three vessels were very unpleasant in heavy swell, with violent movements, and very wet; their sailing performance, however, was good, especially with the wind on the quarter.

Complement

Crew: 8/142. Boats: one fairly large, four smaller.

Undine (1880); *Rover* and *Musquito* were very similar, and *Hela* was similar after 1860, but smaller

Notes

Colour scheme no 1, 2.

Career

Musquito launched 29 Jul 1851 as a British sloop; purchased 1862, and used as a cadet training ship until 1886. Stricken 21 Dec 1891, and reduced to a salvage hulk; sold in March 1906 for 9200M, used as a coal hulk, later broken up at Swinemünde.

Rover launched 21 Jun 1853 as a British sloop; purchased 1861 and used from 19 Oct 1862 as a cadet training ship. Stricken 18 Nov 1890, finally used as a hulk, then broken up. Figurehead now in the Dresden army museum.

Undine launched 8 Dec 1869, commissioned 21 May 1871 as a cadet training ship. Sunk 28 Oct 1884 on the Jütische coast, position 56° 48N, 08° 14E, after stranding in a storm; one dead.

Grille

Name	Builder	Built	Cost in Marks (000s)	Displacement (t = tonnes T = tons)	Length (m)	Breadth (m)	Draught (m)	Power (hp)	Revs (rpm)	Speed (kts)	Range (nm/kts)	Coal (t)	Oil (t)
GRILLE	A Normand, Le Havre	1856–58	648	491t max 350t des	56.86 oa 52.50 cwl	7.38	2.84 fwd 3.20 aft	738ihp max 700ihp des	148	13.2 max 13 des			—
	mod: Imperial Dockyard, Danzig	1885–88		508t max				760ihp max	155	14.4 max	3230/7 2160/10	65	
	mod: Imperial Dockyard, Kiel	1897–98											
326gt/187nt													

Construction

Laid down as an aviso (design by A Normand, 1856). Transverse frame mahogany diagonal carvel hull with copper sheathing (three watertight compartments); the stoking room rear and side walls were iron. Depth 4.12m. Immersion increased by 1cm per 2.66t. Trim moment 652m-t.

Propulsion

One horizontal 2-cylinder single expansion engine by J Penn & Sons, Greenwich [one horizontal 2-cylinder double expansion engine by AG Vulcan, Stettin, fitted 1886] (one 3-bladed screw, 2.74m diameter). Two cylindrical boilers (four fireboxes, 1 atmosphere forced) by J Penn & Sons, Greenwich [two cylindrical boilers (four fireboxes, 7 atmospheres forced, 200sq m) by AG Vulcan, Stettin, then later by Borsig, Berlin-Tegel]. [One generator, 2.3kW, 4.0kW, 2kW, finally 5.0kW 67V.] Three masted schooner rig, 436sq m [reduced to auxiliary sails only]. One rudder.

Armament

Two long 12pdr [after 1879 one 12.5cm/23 hooped gun (140 rounds), range 5200m, and two 8cm/23 hooped guns, plus (in 1882) three machine guns, (in 1898 six machine guns (3000 rounds), and finally two machine guns (1280 rounds) in total].

Handling

Excellent sea-boat, with fast roll but gentle motion; very handy and manoeuvrable, with little speed loss in a head sea or in turns. Sails contributed little to performance.

Complement

Crew: 5/65, 6/72, 7/68. Boats: two yawls, two dinghies.

Notes

Colour scheme no 1, 2, 4, 8, 9. The forward deckhouse was temporary [after 1889 the bow and funnel were as shown in the second drawing, with the deckhouse from 23.0m to 36.0m] but the aft deckhouse was retained. [Three pole masts were fitted at 9.0m, 23.0m and 40.0m, 18–24–24m above CWL, and a bridge forward of the funnel; in from 1880 to 1902 a searchlight was carried on the deckhouse roof.] *Grille* was the longest serving ship in the Imperial navy, with a service life of 62 years, and she was still serviceable when released for sale. The name was suggested by King Friedrich Wilhelm IV, after the well known story *Die Grille –* The Cricket – by the authoress Charlotte Birch-Pfeiffer.

Career

Grille launched 9 Sept 1857, commissioned 3 Jun 1858 as a Royal and Imperial yacht and flagship of gunboats and armoured gunboats; served also in fisheries protection, and in 1889 as a training ship (for Admiral's staff voyages); used as a tender for sea cadet training ship *Freya* July 1915. Stricken 7 Jan 1920, sold, broken up at Hamburg-Moorburg.

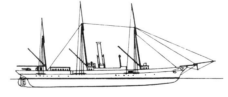

Grille (1857), first form

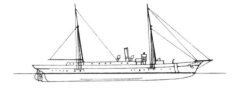

Grille (1898), final form

Loreley

Name	Builder	Built	Cost	Displacement (t = tonnes T = tons)	Length (m)	Breadth (m)	Draught (m)	Power (hp)	Revs (rpm)	Speed (kts)	Range (nm/kts)	Coal (t)	Oil (t)
LORELEY	Royal Dockyard, Danzig	1858–59	103.2 Thaler	470t max 430t des	47.08 oa 43.34 cwl	6.6	2.50 fwd 3.02 aft	350ihp	29	10.5			—
	mod: Imperial Dockyard, Wilhelmshaven Construction no 1	1869–73	151.5 Thaler	450t max 395t des	46.60 oa 42.84 cwl		2.51 fwd 3.05 aft		28	9.1	450/9	34	
290gt/214nt													

Construction

Paddle aviso (official designs 1857 and 1870). Transverse frame timber carvel hull with copper sheathing [transverse frame iron construction with timber planks and copper sheathing] (seven watertight compartments). Freeboard 4.90m. Immersion increased by 1cm per 2.4t.

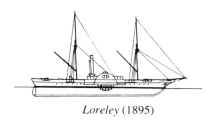

Loreley (1895)

Propulsion

One vertical oscillating 2-cylinder single expansion engine by the engine factory of the Seehandlungs Ges (Maritime Trading Company), Berlin-Moabit (two wheels, each twenty-four paddles, 5.36m diameter) in one engine room. One trunk boiler (two fireboxes, 1.6 atmospheres forced) by AG Vulcan, Stettin [by Frerichs, Osterholz (three fireboxes, 2 atmospheres forced)] in one boiler room. Gaff-rigged schooner, 310sq m, [200sq m]. One rudder.

Armament

Two long 12pdr (240 rounds) [one 12.5cm/23 hooped gun (142 rounds), range 5200m; two 8cm/23 hooped guns (190 rounds).

Handling

Average sea-boat; difficult to steer; little speed loss in a head sea, but considerable speed loss in beam sea.

Sails made only a slight contribution to performance.

Complement

Crew: 4/61, 4/53. Two boats.

Notes

Colour scheme no 1, 2, 3. [The refit, officially termed a reconstruction, involved the removal of timbers only; in 1879 new boilers from the Imperial Dockyard, Wilhelmshaven, were fitted.]

Career

Loreley launched 20 May 1859, commissioned 28 Sept 1859; served abroad 1860–62; [converted 1870 to an aviso under the same name]; relaunched 19 Aug 1871, commissioned 16 Apr 1873 into the fleet; served abroad from 1879. Stricken 7 Sept 1896, sold; fate unknown.

Nymphe class

Name	Builder	Built	Cost	Displacement (t = tonnes T = tons)	Length (m)	Breadth (m)	Draught (m)	Power (hp)	Revs (rpm)	Speed (kts)	Range (nm/kts)	Coal (t)	Oil (t)
NYMPHE	Royal Dockyard, Danzig	1862–63	292.7 Thaler	1202t max 1085t des	64.90 oa 58.54 cwl	10.2	3.92 fwd 4.47 aft	800ihp max 200nhp des	c70	12	1250/12	126 max	—
MEDUSA 728gt/506nt	Royal Dockyard, Danzig	1862–65	296.6 Thaler	,,	,,	,,	,,	,,	,,	8.0	,,	,,	—

Construction

Laid down as flush deck corvettes (official design, 1861). Transverse frame timber carvel hull with copper sheathing. Hold depth approx 7.40m

Propulsion

One horizontal 2-cylinder single expansion engine by J Penn & Sons, Greenwich (one 2-bladed screw, 3.64m diameter) in a common engine and boiler room. Two transverse trunk boilers (six fireboxes, 1.6 atmospheres forced) by J Penn & Sons, Greenwich [(six fireboxes, 2.55 atmospheres forced) by Schichau, Danzig]. The funnel was retractable. Full-rigged ships, 1500sq m. One rudder.

Armament

Ten 36pdr (1100 rounds); six 12pdr (720 rounds); three 24pdr planned as extra armament for mobilisation [seventeen, later nineteen 12cm/23 hooped guns (1900 rounds), range 5900m, fitted after 1869].

Handling

Good, solid sea-boats, with a gentle motion; sailed well, especially with a beam sea and when well ballasted at the stern; tolerated much sail. Speed loss was considerable when steaming in a head sea. Moderately handy under steam, less so under sail.

Complement

Crew: 14/176. Boats: one fairly large, three smaller.

Notes

Colour scheme no 1, 2. *Medusa* had a steam pipe forward of the funnel. By 1880 the internal timbers in both ships were in poor condition.

Career

Nymphe launched 15 Apr 1863, commissioned 25 Nov 1863; served abroad 1865–67 and 1871–85. Stricken 21 Jul 1887; reduced to an engineer training hulk at Kiel; sold 1891, broken up at Hamburg.

Medusa launched 20 Oct 1864, commissioned 10 Apr 1867; served abroad 1867–80. Stricken 5 Apr 1881; reduced to a hulk; sold 1891, broken up at Danzig.

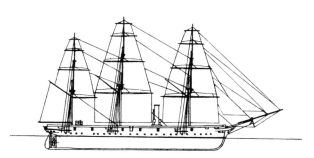

Nymphe (1870), *Medusa*

Augusta class

Name	Builder	Built	Cost in Marks (000s)	Displacement (t = tonnes T = tons)	Length (m)	Breadth (m)	Draught (m)	Power (hp)	Revs (rpm)	Speed (kts)	Range (nm/kts)	Coal (t)	Oil (t)
AUGUSTA	L'Arman Frères, Bordeaux	1863–64	1702 (bought)	2272t max 1827t des	81.50 oa 75.20 cwl	11.1	5.03 fwd 5.62 aft	1300ihp max 400nhp des	56	13.5 max 12.0 des	2500/12	340 max	—
VICTORIA	L'Arman Frères, Bordeaux	,,	1689 (bought)	,,	,,	,,	,,	,,	,,	,,	,,	,,	—

Construction

Laid down as flush deck corvettes *Yeddo* and *Osakka* (design by L'Arman Frères, 1863). Q-timber carvel construction with copper sheathing (three watertight compartments); the standard of construction was poor. Depth not known.

Propulsion

One horizontal 2-cylinder single expansion engine by Mazeline, Le Havre (two 2-bladed screws, 4.28m diameter). Four transverse trunk boilers (eight fireboxes, 1.75 atmospheres forced) by Mazeline, Le Havre [(twelve fireboxes, 2 atmospheres forced) by Imperial Dockyard, Wilhelmshaven] in one engine room. Full-rigged ships, 1600sq m [*Augusta*'s mainsail was removed in 1871; *Victoria* was converted to a barque rig 1879.] One rudder.

Armament

Eight 24pdr; six long 12pdr [after 1872 four 15cm/22 hooped guns (440 rounds), range 5000m; six 12cm/23 hooped guns (660 rounds), range 5900m; one 8cm/23 hooped gun; later six additional machine guns].

Handling

Moderate sea-boats, with severe pitch and extremely wet; severe weather helm was necessary; sailing performance was moderate, but improved when the stern was ballasted. Very handy as a steamer, much less so under sail.

Complement

Crew: 15/215. Boats: one large, five smaller.

Notes

Colour scheme no 1, 2. Both ships were begun by the French dockyard under order for the Confederate States of America, under the (supposedly Japanese) names *Yeddo* and *Osakka*, for the American Civil War; intended names were *Mississippi* and *Louisiana*. Delivery to the CSA was forbidden at the personal intervention of Napoleon III, and the ships were eventually sold to Prussia.

Career

Augusta launched 1864 as *Yeddo*; purchased during construction 13 May 1864; renamed *Augusta* 31 May 1864; served mostly abroad from 3 Jul 1864. Sunk on a voyage home 2 Jun 1885 in the Gulf of Aden, approx position 13°N, 45°E, in a hurricane; 223 dead, total loss, all crew lost.

Victoria launched 1864 as *Osakka*; purchased during construction 13 May 1864; renamed *Victoria* 31 May 1864; served mostly abroad after 14 Sept 1864. Stricken 14 Apr 1891; sold 1892, broken up at Hamburg.

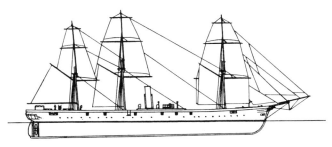

Augusta (1870), *Victoria*

Ariadne class

Ariadne (1880), *Luise*

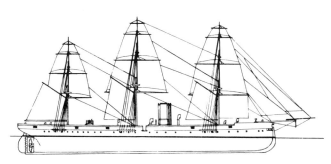

Freya (1880)

Name	Builder	Built	Cost in Marks (000s)	Displacement (t = tonnes T = tons)	Length (m)	Breadth (m)	Draught (m)	Power (hp)	Revs (rpm)	Speed (kts)	Range (nm/kts)	Coal (t)	Oil (t)
ARIADNE	Imperial Dockyard, Danzig	1868–72	1840	2072t max 1692t des	68.16 oa 65.80 cwl	10.8	4.80 fwd 5.70 aft	2260ihp max 2100ihp des	83	14.1 max 14.0 des	1340/10 630/13	168 max	—
LUISE	Imperial Dockyard, Danzig	1871–74	1719	,,	,,	,,	,,	2392ihp max 2100ihp des	85	14.1 max 14.0 des	,,	,,	—
FREYA	Imperial Dockyard, Danzig	1872–76	2137	2406t max 1997t des	85.35 oa 83.60 cwl	,,	4.60 fwd 5.60 aft	2801ihp max 2400ihp des	82.2	15.2 max 14.5 des	2500/10 1060/15	264 max	—

Construction

Laid down as flush deck corvettes *Ariadne*, *Luise* and *Freya* (official designs 1869 and 1871). Transverse frame timber carvel construction with copper sheathing, iron deck beams (*Freya*, four watertight compartments). Depth 7.21m and 7.14m. Immersion increased by 1cm per 5.67t and 6.3t. Trim moment 1974m-t and 2016m-t.

Propulsion

One horizontal 3-cylinder double expansion engine by F A Egells, Berlin-Moabit (one 4-bladed screw, 4.56m diameter, in *Freya* 5.34m diameter). Four trunk boilers (eight fireboxes, 3 atmospheres forced) in one engine room. The funnel was retractable. Full-rigged ships, 1582sq m, *Freya* 1886sq m [barque rig 1049–1261sq m]. One rudder.

Armament

Six 15cm/22 hooped guns (400 rounds), range 5000m; two 12cm/23 hooped guns (200 rounds), range 5900m; [four 4 machine guns after 1882]. [*Freya* had eight, finally seven 15cm/22 hooped guns (760 rounds), range 5000m; four 17cm/25 hooped guns (temporary); plus, after 1881, six additional machine guns.]

Handling

Excellent sea-boats, but with marked weather helm. Sailing performance was much worse than the *Arcona* class, and all ships manoeuvred and steered badly, *Freya* particularly. The screw had a marked braking effect at low speed under sail, as it did not free-wheel below 5kts. Nevertheless, all ships manoeuvred and steered outstandingly well as steamers.

Complement

Crew: 13/220 to 14/234. Boats: two pinnaces, two yawls, three dinghies.

Notes

Colour scheme no 1, 2. *Luise*'s bowsprit was almost horizontal. The bridge on all ships was at first minus a charthouse. *Freya* was the last timber ship in the Imperial Navy. The construction contract for the sister ship *Thusnelda* was converted into a contract for the iron flush decked corvette *Leipzig* (see page 43).

Career

Ariadne launched 21 Jul 1871, commissioned 23 Nov 1872; served abroad 1874–81 as an engine training ship; abroad again 1884–90. Stricken 14 Apr 1891; sold 6 Oct 1891, broken up at Hamburg.

Luise launched 16 Dec 1872, commissioned 4 Jun 1874 for service abroad; used as a training ship from 1885; harbour ship at Kiel from 1891. Stricken 19 Dec 1896; sold 1897 for 54,187M, broken up at Hamburg.

Freya launched 29 Dec 1874, commissioned 1 Oct 1876; served abroad until 1884. Stricken 14 Dec 1896; sold for 65,160M, broken up at Kiel.

Falke

Name	Builder	Built	Cost in Marks (000s)	Displacement (t = tonnes T = tons)	Length (m)	Breadth (m)	Draught (m)	Power (hp)	Revs (rpm)	Speed (kts)	Range (nm/kts)	Coal (t)	Oil (t)
FALKE	Henderson, Coulborn & Co, Renfrew, Glasgow		£12.10.0 (bought)	1230t max 1002t des	78.40 oa 77.50 cwl	11.7* 8.56**	2.60 fwd 2.50 aft	1100ihp max 300nhp des	30	15.0 max 12.0 des	1400/12	200 max	—
779gt/450nt													

* over wheelboxes　　** over hull

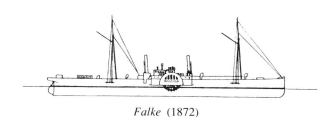

Falke (1872)

Construction

Laid down as a blockade runner, designated paddle aviso *D* at purchase. Transverse frame iron construction (six watertight compartments). Depth not known.

Propulsion

One vertical oscillating 2-cylinder single expansion engine (two wheels, ten paddles each, 6.55m diameter). Two trunk boilers with superheaters (six fireboxes, 1.33 atmospheres forced) in one combined boiler and engine room. Schooner rig, area not known.

Armament

Two 12cm/23 hooped guns (670 rounds), range 5000m; [also five machine guns].

Handling

Good sea-boat, with all the typical disadvantages of a paddle steamer; see *Loreley*.

Complement

Crew: 6/84. Four boats.

Notes

Colour scheme no 1, 2. One of numerous speculative vessels built by Western European dockyards for the Confederate States of America as blockade runners. She was the first ship in the Imperial Navy with searchlights (Siemens Projector), rated at 35 Amp, 50V and 4000NK after 1878.

Career

Falke launched 1865; in service 1866 as the passenger and cattle transport steamer *Heinrich Heister*; laid up at Dordrecht; purchased 25 Aug 1870, and transferred to Emden 4 Sept 1870; renamed *Emden*. After 12 Sept 1870 she reverted to the name *Falke*, and was in service from 4 Oct 1870 as a tender and survey ship. Stricken 18 Nov 1890; sold in September 1892 for 18,000M, broken up.

Pommerania

Name	Builder	Built	Cost in Marks (000s)	Displacement (t = tonnes T = tons)	Length (m)	Breadth (m)	Draught (m)	Power (hp)	Revs (rpm)	Speed (kts)	Range (nm/kts)	Coal (t)	Oil (t)
POMMERANIA 322gt/176nt	AG Vulcan, Stettin Construction no 40	1864	311.4	460t max 391t des	55.20 oa 50.50 cwl	9.70* 6.90**	2.35	700ihp max 200nhp	29	14.5 max 12.0 des	300/14	75 max	—

* over wheelboxes   ** over hull

Construction

Laid down as a post steamer for the Stettin—Stockholm service (design by C A Elbertzhagen, 1863). Transverse frame iron construction (subdivision not known).

Propulsion

As *Falke*, except that wheel diameter was 5.4m, and the boilers were without superheaters (and 1.5 atmospheres forced).

Armament

Two 8cm/23 hooped guns (120 rounds) [two 8.7cm/24 hooped guns (120 rounds), and four machine guns after 1880].

Handling

Good sea-boat, but could not tolerate heavy weather; difficult to work in a head sea, with severe speed loss; very wet. Very handy. Sails contributed little to performance.

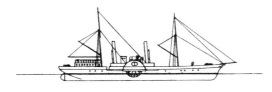

Pommerania (1872)

Complement

Crew: 4/61. Four boats.

Notes

Colour scheme no 1, 2. No other details available.

Career

Pommerania launched September 1894; in service 1 May 1865 as a post steamer for the Stettin–Stockholm service; requisitioned 1870, commissioned 20 Aug 1870; served abroad 1876–79, and as a survey vessel 1880–90, including a period as an Imperial yacht in 1887. Stricken 10 Aug 1890; sold 1892 to a Hamburg company; refitted for Paulsen & Ivers, Kiel, as a sailing schooner; renamed *Adler*. Abandoned by her crew in a storm during her first voyage, 20 Jan 1894, position 49° 45N, 12° 48E, and lost; all crew dead.

Zieten

Name	Builder	Built	Cost in Marks (000s)	Displacement (t = tonnes T = tons)	Length (m)	Breadth (m)	Draught (m)	Power (hp)	Revs (rpm)	Speed (kts)	Range (nm/kts)	Coal (t)	Oil (t)
ZIETEN 716gt/322nt	Thames Iron Works, London	1875–76	1635	1170t max 1001t des	79.40 oa 69.50 cwl	8.56	3.80 fwd 4.63 aft	1807ihp max 2000ihp des 2376ihp*	171	15.9 max 16.0 des 16.3*	1770/9	130 max 129 des	—

* English trial

Construction

Built as a torpedo vessel (English design, 1875). Transverse frame iron construction (eight watertight compartments). Depth 5.64m. Immersion increased by 1cm per 4.4t. Trim moment 1569m-t.

Propulsion

Two horizontal 2-cylinder double expansion engines by J Penn & Sons, Greenwich (two 3-bladed screws, 3.05m [2.75m] diameter) in one engine room. Six cylindrical boilers by J Penn & Sons, Greenwich [replaced in 1891 by the Imperial Dockyard, Kiel] (twelve fireboxes, 5.33 atmospheres forced, 716sq m [699sq m]) in one boiler room. One funnel [circular in cross-section]. [One generator, 10kW 67V.] Schooner rig 355sq m [reduced to auxiliary gaff sail only]. One rudder.

Armament

Six machine guns; two 38cm TT (10 Whitehead torpedoes), one stern, one bow, both under water; [six, finally four (aft only) 5cm/40 QF guns (864 rounds), range 6200m; TT removed; forty-nine mines].

Handling

Good sea-boat, though very crank, but with a gentle motion. Manoeuvred and turned well, but poor in a head sea; dangerous running before a storm, shipping much water and of very light construction.

Complement

Crew: 6/88 [7/99; 7/104 as a fisheries cruiser]. Boats: one picket boat [removed], [two barges], one cutter, two yawls, one dinghy.

Notes

Colour scheme no 1, 2, 4, 9. The bow TT was protected by a folding bottom section of the stem (shown triangular in the drawing). [After 1899 a central superstructure was fitted from 27.0m to 39.0m, beam to beam, with a new bridge on the forward edge, a compass platform on the conning tower, and a charthouse forward of the funnel, the latter with a mantle up to 5.5m above CWL; a long steam pipe was fitted, and the aft and forward bridges were removed and replaced by a platform 6m above CWL, with a searchlight. The foremast was temporarily fitted with a derrick.]

Career

Zieten launched 9 Mar 1876, commissioned 1 Aug 1876 for torpedo experiments, and service as a tender; fisheries protection vessel 1899–1914; coastal guard vessel 1914. Stricken 6 Dec 1919; sold 18 Apr 1921 for 655,000M, broken up at Wilhelmshaven.

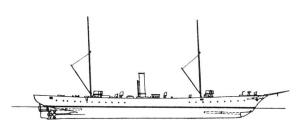

Zieten (1878)

Carola class

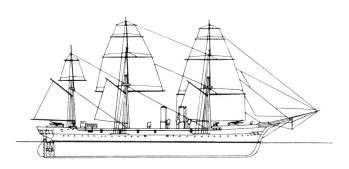

Alexandrine (1890), *Arcona*

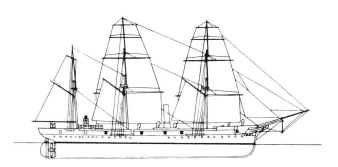

Marie (1895), *Sophie*; *Carola* and *Olga* (after her refit) were similar, but with two funnels.

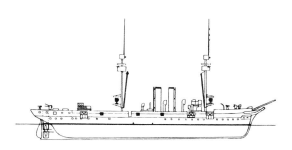

Carola (1897)

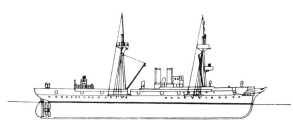

Olga (1902)

Name	Builder	Built	Cost in Marks (000s)	Displacement (t = tonnes T = tons)	Length (m)	Breadth (m)	Draught (m)	Power (hp)	Revs (rpm)	Speed (kts)	Range (nm/kts)	Coal (t)	Oil (t)
CAROLA	AG Vulcan, Stettin Construction no 87	1879–81	2192	2424t max 2147t des	76.35 oa 70.60 cwl	12,5*	4.98 fwd 6.08 aft	2367ihp max 2100ihp des	109	13.7 max 13.5 des	3420/10 1380/14	350 max 297 des 218 mod	—
OLGA	AG Vulcan, Stettin Construction no 88 mod: Imperial Dockyard, Wilhelmshaven	1879–81 1890–92 1900–01	2276	,,	,,	,,	,,	2399ihp max 2100ihp des	106	13.9 max 13.5 des	,,	350 max 297 des	—
MARIE	Reiherstieg, Hamburg Construction no 332	1880–82		,,	,,	,,	,,	2129ihp max 2100ihp des	98	14.0 max 13.5 des	,,	,,	—
SOPHIE	Imperial Dockyard, Danzig	1879–82	2343					2156ihp max 2100ihp des	,,	14.0 max 13.5 des	,,	,,	—
ALEXANDRINE	Imperial Dockyard, Kiel Construction no 9	1881–86	2057	2662t max 2361t des	81.20 oa 71.80 cwl	12.6*	5.00 fwd 6.25 aft	2289ihp max 2400ihp des	86	14.0 max 14.0 des	4180/8.5 1990/13	340 max 270 des	—
ARCONA	Imperial Dockyard, Danzig	,,	2197	,,	,,	,,	,,	2461ihp max 2400ihp des	96.7	14.1 max 14.0 des	,,	,,	—

1278gt/575nt (*Carola, Olga, Marie, Sophie*), 1340gt/739nt (*Alexandrine, Arcona*)

* 13.0 over ejectors

Construction

Laid down as flush deck corvettes *E*, *Ersatz Augusta*, *Ersatz Vineta*, *F*, *G* and *Ersatz Nymphe* (official design, 1875). Upper and longitudinal frame iron-steel construction, with wood planks and zinc sheathing, iron stem and stern (nine watertight compartments, double bottom under engine room); *Alexandrine*, *Arcona*, transverse and longitudinal frame iron-steel construction, with wood planks and copper sheathing, bow wood and iron, stern bronze (eleven watertight compartments, double bottom under engine room. Depth 6.98m. Immersion increased by 1cm per approx 6.35t. Trim moment 2285m-t.

Propulsion

One horizontal 3-cylinder double expansion engine (one 2-bladed screw, 5.02m diameter) in one engine room. Eight cylindrical boilers (sixteen fireboxes, 5 atmospheres forced, 784sq m), transversely in 1 + 1 boiler rooms; but in *Marie* and *Sophie* one 2-cylinder engine (one 2-bladed screw, 4.7m diameter), and only six cylindrical boilers, by Märkisch-Schlesische Maschinen und Hütten AG, formerly F A Egells, Berlin-Moabit (twelve fireboxes, 5 atmospheres forced, 636sq m); and in *Alexandrine* and *Arcona* two horizontal 2-cylinder double expansion engines by AG Germania, Berlin-Tegel, 1 + 1 in one engine room, and, from the same company, eight cylindrical boilers (sixteen fireboxes, 5 atmospheres forced, 790sq m). One generator, 2kW 55V [*Carola*, two generators, 25kW 67V; *Olga*, one generator 12kW 67V. Barque

rig, 1230–1134sq m, but *Carola* and *Olga* had no sails. One rudder.

Armament

One 15cm/22 hooped gun (1000 rounds), range 5000m; two 8.7cm/24 hooped guns (200 rounds); six machine guns [*Carola* six, later four, 15cm/22 hooped guns, two 10.5cm/35 QF guns, eight 8.8cm/30 QF guns and two 5cm/40 QF guns; *Olga* two only 8.8cm/30 QF guns, plus ten machine cannon; *Marie* and *Sophie* ten 15cm/22 hooped guns, two 8.8cm/30 QF guns, plus ten (or six) machine guns]; *Alexandrine* and *Arcona* ten 15cm/30 hooped guns (730 rounds), range 6800m; four 10.5cm/35 hooped guns (400 rounds), range 7300m; six machine guns.

Handling

Moderate sea-boats, but with severe pitch and roll. All vessels required much sail. Speed loss in a head sea was severe; manoeuvrability was good under steam, better under sail. All ships withstood bad weather well.

Complement

Crew: 25/244; *Carola* 10/246; *Olga* 10/265; [*Marie* and *Sophie* 13/285, including 150 cadets]; *Alexandrine* and *Arcona* 25/257 [268]. Boats: *Carola*, *Olga* two picket boats, two cutters, two yawls, one dinghy; remainder one picket boat, one launch, two cutters, two yawls, two dinghies.

Notes

Colour scheme no 2, 3 (except *Olga*), 4, 9 (and for *Sophie* and *Arcona* only, 8, 11). Initially no searchlights were fitted to any ships. *Carola* and *Olga* before refit were as shown in the earlier drawings, but with two funnels as in the later drawings. [*Carola* was fitted with two searchlights on the roof of the forward bridge, in place of searchlights on the mast platform. *Olga* in 1890 carried fore and main yards only, with gaffs and booms, and a 10m long signal topmast on each mast; an enclosed observation platform was fitted on the foretop; from 1900 to 1901 she was reconstructed as a training ship for machine weapons, with battle tops and multiple tuition rooms.] All these ships were obsolete as warships even before construction began.

Career

Carola launched 27 Nov 1880, commissioned 1 Sept 1881 for service abroad; used as an artillery training ship 1893. Stricken 4 Oct 1905; sold in February 1906 for 136,000M, broken up 1906 at Hamburg.

Olga launched 11 Dec 1880, commissioned 10 Sept 1881; served abroad until 1889, then was reduced to a cadet training ship, and then a machine weapon training ship. Stricken 22 Jun 1905; sold in March 1906 for 136,000M, broken up 1908 at Hamburg.

Marie launched 20 Aug 1881, commissioned 12 Sept 1882; served abroad until 1895, then was reduced to a training ship. Stricken 29 Oct 1904; sold 1909 for 116,000M, broken up at Stettin.

Sophie launched 10 Nov 1881, commissioned 10 Aug 1882; served abroad 1883–92, then as a sea cadet training ship; served as a barrack ship at Wilhelmshaven from 21 May 1908, at Helgoland from 1 Aug 1914, and at Emden from 1916. Sold 7 Jul 1920 to the submarine administration, Berlin, and broken up 1921 at Hamburg.

Alexandrine launched 7 Feb 1885, commissioned 6 Oct 1886; served abroad until 1895, and from 1904 as a harbour ship. Stricken 27 May 1907; sold for 148,000M, broken up 1907 at Danzig.

Arcona launched 7 May 1885, commissioned 1 Dec 1886 in the reserve; abroad 1892–99; renamed *Mercur* 11 Jan 1902; served as a harbour ship from 1904. Stricken 22 Jun 1905; sold in December 1905 for 145,000M, broken up 1906 at Danzig.

Blitz class

Name	Builder	Built	Cost in Marks (000s)	Displacement (t = tonnes T = tons)	Length (m)	Breadth (m)	Draught (m)	Power (hp)	Revs (rpm)	Speed (kts)	Range (nm/kts)	Coal (t)	Oil (t)
BLITZ	Nordd Schiffbau AG, Kiel Construction no 1 mod: Imperial Dockyard, Kiel	1881–83 1891–92	1368	1486t max 1381t des	78.43 oa 75.30 cwl	9.90*	4.07 fwd 4.40 aft	2808ihp	146	15.7	2440/9	220 max 185 des	—
PFEIL 815gt/367nt	Imperial Dockyard, Wilhelmshaven Construction no 6 mod: Imperial Dockyard, Wilhelmshaven	1881–84 1892–94	1395	,,	,,	,,	,,	2337ihp max 2700ihp des	144 max	15.6 max 16.0 des	,,	,,	—

* 11.3 over bridge wings

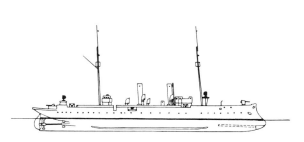

Blitz (1890), *Pfeil*

Construction

Built as avisos *D* and *Ersatz Grille* (official design, 1879). Transverse and longitudinal frame steel construction (eleven watertight compartments, double bottom under engine room). Depth 5.98m. Immersion increased by 1cm per 5.16t. Trim moment 1850m-t.

Propulsion

Two horizontal 2-cylinder double expansion engines, in *Blitz* by Märkisch-Schlesische Maschinenbau und Hütten AG, formerly F A Egells, Berlin-Moabit (two 3-bladed screws, 3.2m diameter) in one engine room. Eight cylindrical boilers (*Blitz*, eight locomotive boilers by Märkisch-Schlesische Maschinenbau und Hütten AG), (sixteen fireboxes, 5 atmospheres forced,

763sq m) [*Blitz*, eight transverse cylindrical boilers by the Imperial Dockyard, Danzig, 934sq m; *Pfeil*, eight cylindrical boilers by the Imperial Dockyard, Danzig (763sq m)] in 1 + 1 boiler rooms. One generator, 10kW 67V [plus two generators, 24–19kW 67V]. Square-rigged schooner rig, 591sq m [auxiliary sails only after 1892 and 1894, 282sq m; 282.5sq m after 1896; sails removed after 1900. One rudder.

Armament

One 12.5cm/23 hooped gun (100 rounds), range 5200m; four 8.7cm/24 hooped guns (400 rounds); four machine guns; one 35cm bow TT (3 rounds) [after about 1890 six 8.8cm/30 QF guns (600 rounds); three 35cm TT (8 rounds), two lateral on deck, one bow, underwater; TT finally deleted].

Handling

Moderate sea-boats, but with severe roll; manoeuvrable, with good response to the helm. Transverse metacentric height 0.968m, longitudinal 110.5m. Maximum stability moment around 34°, = zero at around 78°. Fleet rudder angle 35° and 38°.

Complement

Crew: 7/127, 6/135 (plus 3/16 as flotilla flagship). Boats: one picket boat, [one cutter], one [two] yawls, one [two] dinghies.

Notes

Colour scheme no 2, 4, 9. One searchlight was initially fitted on the forward bridge only; the bridge was without a charthouse, with a bulwark at the aft end. These vessels were amongst the first torpedo cruisers in the world, and the first all-steel vessels in the German fleet.

Career

Blitz launched 26 Aug 1882, commissioned 28 Mar 1883; served as TF1 flotilla flagship until 1900; fleet tender 1903; special-purpose ship 1911; coastal defence ship 1914; tender 1915–19. Stricken 8 Mar 1921; sold for 520,000M and broken up 1921 at Wilhelmshaven.

Pfeil launched 16 Sept 1882, commissioned 25 Nov 1884 as a tender; served abroad 1888–89, and for fisheries protection 1894–99; after 1904 she reverted to service as a tender until 1919, except for a period in 1911 as a special-purpose ship. Stricken 16 Feb 1922, broken up at Wilhelmshaven.

Nixe

Name	Builder	Built	Cost in Marks (000s)	Displacement (t = tonnes T = tons)	Length (m)	Breadth (m)	Draught (m)	Power (hp)	Revs (rpm)	Speed (kts)	Range (nm/kts)	Coal (t)	Oil (t)
NIXE	Imperial Dockyard, Danzig	1883–86	1917	1982t max 1781t des	63.30 oa 54.35 cwl	13.2	5.52 fwd 6.36 aft	724ihp max 700ihp des	88.0	10.4 max 9.0 des	1480/8 1120/10	125 max 105 des	—
	mod: Imperial Dockyard, Kiel	1902–03	598										
1451gt/1036nt													

Construction

Laid down as flush deck (covered) corvette *Ersatz Medusa* (official design, 1882). Transverse frame iron construction, with yellow pine planking and copper sheathing (nine watertight compartments). Depth 9.28m. Immersion increased by 1cm per 5.05t. Trim moment 1683m-t.

Propulsion

One horizontal 2-cylinder double expansion engine (one retractable 2- bladed screw, 3.86m diameter). Two transverse cylindrical boilers (four fireboxes, 5 at- mospheres forced, 240sq m) in one boiler room. The funnel was retractable. One generator, 2kW 55V [two generators 40kW 110V. Full-rigged ship, 1579sq m [reduced]. One rudder.

Armament

Eight [later seven, then six] 12.5cm/23 hooped guns (800 rounds), range 5000m; [two 8.8cm/30 QF guns (300 rounds), range 5000m; four machine guns].

Handling

An extremely poor sea-boat, with a tendency to severe yawing when running before the wind. Speed loss in a head sea was severe; without supporting sails 5–10° lee rudder was required at all times.

Nixe (1890)

Complement

Crew: 27/331 [17/354 including 125 cadets]. Boats: one picket boat, one launch, three [two] cutters, two yawls, two [one] dinghies.

Notes

Colour scheme no 2, 3, 4, 8, 9. A hopeless anachron- ism as a warship even when newly built. She was finally fitted with two derricks on the mainmast, with yards on fore and mainmasts only. [A flying deck was fitted from stern to mizzen mast.]

Career

Nixe launched 23 Jul 1885, commissioned 1 Apr 1886; served abroad until 1894, and as a sea cadet training ship; reduced to a workshop ship 1900; served as a fleet office ship 1901–06, and as a harbour ship at Kiel. Stricken 24 Jun 1911; used as a barrack hulk at Kiel, and 1920–21 as a barrack hulk for the Naval Gunnery School; renamed *Hulk C* 1 Apr 1923, and sold; refitted 1925 as sea-going lighter *Nixe*, for Emil Retzlaff, Stettin; broken up about 1930 at Wewelsfleth.

Light cruisers 1887–1918

Greif

Name	Builder	Built	Cost in Marks (000s)	Displacement (t = tonnes T = tons)	Length (m)	Breadth (m)	Draught (m)	Power (hp)	Revs (rpm)	Speed (kts)	Range (nm/kts)	Coal (t)	Oil (t)
GREIF	Germania Dockyard, Kiel Construction no 27	1885–87	2000	2266t max 2050t des	102.6 oa 99.5 cwl	9.75*	4.22 fwd 4.34 aft	5431ihp max 5400ihp des	105 max	18.2 max 18.0 des	2180/12	350 max 330 des	—
	mod:	1906						5795ihp max	110 max	19.1 max	3960/10	436 max	
1376gt/933nt													

* 10.4 over bridge wings

Construction
Laid down as aviso *Ersatz Loreley* (official design, 1884–85). Transverse frame steel construction, iron stern (twelve watertight compartments). Depth 6.6m. Immersion increased by 1cm per 6.71t. Trim moment 3570m-t.

Propulsion
Two horizontal 2-cylinder double expansion engines by AG Germania, Berlin-Tegel (two 4-bladed screws, 4.0m diameter) in 1 + 1 engine rooms. Six cylindrical double-ended boilers by the Imperial Dockyard, Kiel (twenty-four fireboxes, 7 atmospheres forced, 1245sq m) in 1 + 1 + 1 boiler rooms [refitted in 1906 with eight cylindrical boilers in 1 + 1 boiler rooms]. Two generators, 20kW 67V. One rudder.

Armament
Two 10.5cm/35 hooped guns, range 8200m; ten machine guns [after 1891 eight, later six, 8.8cm/35 QF guns (800–696 rounds), plus six, later four machine guns].

Handling
Tolerable sea-boats, with less pitch than roll; handiness moderate. Transverse metacentric height 0.48m, longitudinal 160m. Maximum stability moment around 44° and 82° with superstructure, = zero above 90°. Fleet rudder angle 40°.

Complement
Crew: 7/163 [178]. Boats: one picket boat, two cutters, one yawl, one dinghy.

Notes
Colour scheme no 2, 4, 9. One searchlight only was fitted until 1890, on the existing galley above the engine room skylight. [After 1896 aft searchlight was removed, as were the tall pressure heads aft of the second funnel.]

Career
Greif launched 29 Jul 1886, commissioned 9 Jul 1887 into the fleet; saw little service; used as a special-purpose ship 21 Jun 1911; reduced to an engine hulk 25 Oct 1912, and in 1917 to a minelayer hulk at Kiel-Heikendorf. Sold 1921 and broken up at Hamburg.

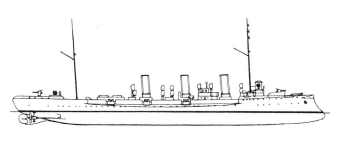

Greif (1889)

Schwalbe class

Construction
Laid down as cruisers *A* and *B* (official design, 1886–67). Transverse frame composite steel/timber/copper construction, timber stem and stern, forestem with bronze ram (eleven watertight compartments). Depth 5.6m. Immersion increased by 1cm per 4.4t. Trim moment 1453m-t.

Propulsion
Two horizontal 2-cylinder double expansion engines (two 3-bladed screws, 2.8m diameter) in 1 + 1 engine rooms. Four cylindrical boilers (eight fireboxes, 7 atmospheres forced, 464sq m) in 1 + 1 boiler rooms. [One generator, 5kW 67V (*Schwalbe* only)]. Schooner barque rig 729sq m, used as auxiliary sails only in *Schwalbe*. One rudder.

Armament
Eight 10.5cm/35 hooped guns (765 rounds), range 8200m; five machine guns.

Name	Builder	Built	Cost in Marks (000s)	Displacement (t = tonnes T = tons)	Length (m)	Breadth (m)	Draught (m)	Power (hp)	Revs (rpm)	Speed (kts)	Range (nm/kts)	Coal (t)	Oil (t)
SCHWALBE	Imperial Dockyard, Wilhelmshaven Construction no 9 mod: Imperial Dockyard, Danzig	1887–88 1903–05	1442	1359t max 1111t des	66.90 oa 62.59 cwl	9.36*	4.40 fwd 4.72 aft	1558ihp max 1500ihp des	152	14.1 max 13.5 des	3290/10 1630/14	240 max 150 des	—
SPERBER 682gt/327nt	Imperial Dockyard, Wilhelmshaven Construction no 10	1888–89	1360	,,	,,	,,	,,	1595ihp max 1500ihp des	155	14.3 max 13.5 des	,,	,,	—

* 10.1 over sponsons

Handling
Very good sea-boats, but with a tendency to roll severely when running before the wind or in a beam sea; severe weather helm, but otherwise handled and manoeuvred outstandingly well. Speed loss was slight in a head sea. The sails performed an auxiliary role only. Transverse metacentric height 0.665m, longitudinal 78m, maximum stability moment 31°, = zero at around 68°. Fleet rudder angle 38°.

Complement
Crew: 9/108. Boats: one picket boat, one cutter, one yawl, one dinghy.

Notes
Colour scheme no 2, 3, 8, 11. [*Schwalbe*'s mainmast was at 17.0m. *Sperber* was finally fitted with tall pressure heads.] Both ships had steel bulwarks.

Career
Schwalbe launched 16 Aug 1887, commissioned 4 May 1888; served abroad until 1893 and 1898–1902, then as a harbour ship; used as a special-purpose ship and barrack ship at Kiel from 26 Oct 1911; target hulk at Kiel 1918. Stricken 6 Dec 1919; sold 7 Aug 1920 to Cuxhaven; broken up 1922 at Hamburg-Moorburg.

Sperber launched 23 Aug 1888, commissioned 2 Apr 1889; served abroad until 1896 and 1902–11; used as a gunboat after 6 Mar 1911. Stricken 16 Mar 1912, used as a target hulk; released and sold to Cuxhaven 7 Aug 1920; broken up 1922 at Hamburg-Moorburg.

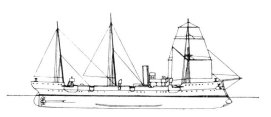

Schwalbe (1890), *Sperber*

Irene class

Name	Builder	Built	Cost in Marks (000s)	Displacement (t = tonnes T = tons)	Length (m)	Breadth (m)	Draught (m)	Power (hp)	Revs (rpm)	Speed (kts)	Range (nm/kts)	Coal (t)	Oil (t)
IRENE	AG Vulcan, Stettin Construction no 175 mod: Imperial Dockyard, Wilhelmshaven	1886–88 1903–05	5115	5027t max 4271t des	103.7 oa 98.9 cwl	14.2*	6.74 fwd 7.63 aft	8223ihp max 8000ihp des	113	18.1 max 18.0 des	2490/9	550 max 400 des	—
PRINZESS WILHELM 2526gt/1137nt	Germania Dockyard, Construction no 30 mod: Imperial Dockyard, Wilhelmshaven	1886–89 1899–02	4536	,,	,,	,,	,,	9732ihp max 8000ihp des	102 max	18.5 max 18.0 des	,,	,,	—

* 15.1 over sponsons

Construction
Laid down as cruiser corvettes *Ersatz Elisabeth* and *Ersatz Ariadne* (official design, 1885–86). Transverse and longitudinal frame steel construction, with wood planks and copper-Muntz metal sheathing, stem bronze below, iron above (ten watertight compartments, double bottom 49 percent). Compound steel armour: deck 20mm plus 30mm with 20mm slopes, plus 55mm; coaming 120mm on 200mm teak; CT roof

20mm; sides 50mm; cork cofferdams. Depth 9.35m. Immersion increased by 1cm per 9.79t. Trim moment 4722m-t [5188m-t].

Propulsion

Two horizontal Wolfsche 2-cylinder double expansion engines, in *Prinzess Wilhelm* by AG Germania, Berlin-Tegel, (two 3-bladed screws, 4.5m diameter, and two 4-bladed screws, 4.7m diameter) in 1 + 1 engine rooms. Four cylindrical double boilers, in *Prinzess Wilhelm* by AG Germania, Berlin-Tegel (twenty-four and thirty-two fireboxes, 7 atmospheres forced, 1744–1900sq m) in 1 + 1 boiler rooms. Two generators, 23kW 67V [*Prinzess Wilhelm*, three generators, 33kW 110V]. One rudder.

Armament

Four 15cm/30 hooped guns (400 rounds), range 8500m; ten 15cm/22 hooped guns (600 rounds), range 5400m; six machine guns [four 15cm/30 hooped guns (rounds not known), range 10,000m, eight 10.5cm/35 QF guns (736 rounds), range 10,800m, six 5cm/10 QF guns (1500 rounds) after 1893]; three 35cm TT (8 rounds), two lateral, deck-mounted, one bow, under water.

Handling

Quite good sea-boats, with moderate roll and pitch; in heavy seas with the wind from ahead only half-speed was possible, due to structural weakness in the forecastle, but both ships ran before the wind very well.

Both ships were very handy, with small speed loss in turns or head seas. Transverse metacentric height 0.72–0.69m, longitudinal 101–104m. Maximum stability moment around 38° and 54° with superstructure, = zero at around 71° and >90°. Fleet rudder angle 40°.

Complement

Crew: 28/337 [17/357]. Boats: two picket boats, one pinnace, two cutters, one yawl, two [one] dinghies.

Notes

Colour scheme no 2, 3, 4, 7, 9, 11. Until 1893 the bulwark was full length, the same height as the forecastle and deckhouse, and the funnels were 2.7m lower. [A foremast searchlight platform was ultimately fitted, 13m above CWL.]

Career

Irene launched 23 Jul 1887, commissioned 25 May 1887 into the fleet; served abroad 1894–1901. Stricken 17 Feb 1914, used as a submarine tender at Kiel, and after 1916 at Wilhelmshaven; released, sold 26 Nov 1921 for 909,000M; broken up 1922 at Wilhelmshaven.

Prinzess Wilhelm launched 22 Sept 1887, commissioned 13 Nov 1889 into the fleet; served abroad 1895–99. Stricken 17 Feb 1914, and used as a mine hulk at Danzig, Kiel and Wilhelmshaven; released, sold 26 Nov 1921 for 909,000M; broken up 1922 at Wilhelmshaven.

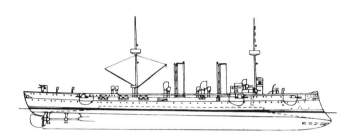

Irene (1895), *Prinzess Wilhelm*

Wacht class

Name	Builder	Built	Cost in Marks (000s)	Displacement (t = tonnes T = tons)	Length (m)	Breadth (m)	Draught (m)	Power (hp)	Revs (rpm)	Speed (kts)	Range (nm/kts)	Coal (t)	Oil (t)
WACHT	AG 'Weser', Bremen Construction no 85	1886–88	1602	1499t max 1246t des	85.50 oa 84.00 cwl	9.66	3.74 fwd 4.67 aft	4000ihp des 3461ihp max mod	149 mod	19.0 des 19.0 max mod	2860/10 1280/18 2720/9 mod	230 max 100 des 220 mod	—
JAGD 873gt/393nt	AG 'Weser', Bremen Construction no 86	1887–89	,,	,,	,,	,,	,,	4000ihp des 3451ihp max mod	158 mod	19.0 des 18.2 max mod	,,	,,	—

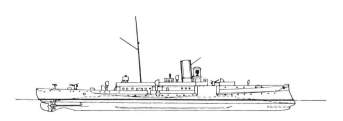

Jagd (1890), *Wacht*

Construction

Laid down as avisos E and *Ersatz Pommerania* (official design, 1885–86). Transverse frame steel construction (ten watertight compartments above armour deck, twelve below). Compound wrought iron armour: deck 10mm plus 10mm with 20mm slopes, plus 20mm; coaming 75mm on 150mm teak; CT roof 10mm, sides 25mm; cork cofferdams. Depth 5.42m [5.10m]. Immersion increased by 1cm per 5.09t. Trim moment 1905m-t.

Propulsion

Two angled 3-cylinder triple expansion engines (two 3-bladed screws, 3.3m diameter) in 1 + 1 engine rooms. Four locomotive boilers (four fireboxes, 10 atmospheres forced, 875sq m) [new boilers by Schichau, Elbing, and the Imperial Dockyard, Wilhelmshaven (eight fireboxes, 872sq m) were fitted in 1891 and 1893] in 1 + 1 boiler rooms. Two generators, 20kW 67V. One rudder.

Armament

Three 10.5cm/35 hooped guns (180 rounds), range

7000m [four 8.8cm/30 QF guns (685 rounds) were fitted in 1891]; three 35cm TT (8 rounds), two lateral above water, one bow, under water.

Handling

Poor sea-boats, with severe roll and pitch; very wet. Manoeuvrability was poor, and both ships required lee helm, but speed loss in a head sea was slight. Transverse metacentric height 0.465m, longitudinal 107m. Maximum stability moment around 31°, = zero around 54°. Fleet rudder angle 40°.

Complement

Crew 7/134. Boats: one picket boat, one cutter, one yawl, one dinghy.

Notes

Colour scheme no 2, 4, 9. [*Wacht* was finally fitted with a 3m higher funnel.]

Career

Wacht launched 27 Aug 1887, commissioned 9 Aug 1888 into the fleet. Sunk 4 Sept 1901 in the Baltic, position 54° 41N, 13° 31E, after collision with the armoured ship *Sachsen*.

Jagd launched 7 Jul 1888, commissioned 25 Jun 1889 into the fleet; served from 3 May 1904 as a harbour ship. Stricken 14 May 1910 and reduced to a hulk and firing platform for the Friedrichsort torpedo workshop; broken up 1920 at Rüstringen.

Meteor class

Name	Builder	Built	Cost in Marks (000s)	Displacement (t = tonnes T = tons)	Length (m)	Breadth (m)	Draught (m)	Power (hp)	Revs (rpm)	Speed (kts)	Range (nm/kts)	Coal (t)	Oil (t)
METEOR	Germania Dockyard, Kiel Construction no 48	1888–91	1639	1078t max 961t des	79.86 oa 78.50 cwl	9.56	3.68 fwd 4.50 aft	4749ihp max 4500ihp des	233 max	20.0 max 19.0 des	960/9	120 max 60 des	—
COMET	AG Vulcan, Stettin Construction no 203	1891–93	1717	1117t max 992t des	79.86 oa 78.70 cwl	9.58	3.68 fwd 3.48 aft	4711ihp max 5000ihp des	228 max	19.5 max 19.5 des	,,	147 max 60 des	—
695 and 728gt/313 and 353nt													

Construction

Laid down as avisos *F* and *G* (official design, 1888). Transverse frame steel construction (six watertight compartments above armour deck, ten below). Steel armour: deck 15mm, slopes 25mm; CT roof 15mm, sides 30mm; cork cofferdams. Depth 5.42m. Immersion increased by 1cm per 4.168t. Trim moment *Meteor* 1500m-t, *Comet* 1450m-t.

Propulsion

Two vertical 3-cylinder triple expansion engines, in *Meteor* by AG Germania, Berlin-Tegel, (two 3-bladed screws, 2.8m diameter) in 1 + 1 engine rooms. Four locomotive boilers, in *Meteor* by AG Germania, Berlin-Tegel, (eight fireboxes, 12 atmospheres forced, 805–850sq m) in 1 + 1 boiler rooms. Two generators, 20–24kW 67V. One rudder.

Armament

Four 8.8cm/30 QF guns (462–680 rounds), range 6900m; three 35cm TT (8 rounds), two lateral, deck-mounted, one bow, under water.

Handling

Very poor sea-boats, very unstable even in moderate weather; superstructure vibration was severe at high speed because of severe cavitation. Manoeuvrability, however, was quite good. Transverse metacentric height 0.41m, longitudinal 96.6m. Maximum stability moment around 48°, = zero >90°. Fleet rudder angle 40°.

Complement

Crew: 7/108–8/110. Boats: one cutter, one yawl, one dinghy.

Notes

Colour scheme no 2, 4, 9. Both ships were unusable except in the most favourable weather conditions, and therefore their period in service was very brief. The design of *Comet* was adapted after a trial run by *Meteor*. *Meteor*'s funnels were initially 1.5m shorter. [After 1901–02 *Meteor* was fitted with an aft wireless telegraphy topmast, as on *Comet*.]

Career

Meteor launched 20 Jan 1890, commissioned 15 May 1891 into the fleet; served for a very short period only; fisheries protection vessel 1895–96; harbour guard vessel after 3 May 1904. Stricken 24 Jun 1911, used as a barrack ship at Kiel; sold 1919, broken up at Audorf/Rendsburg.

Comet launched 15 Nov 1892, commissioned 29 Apr 1893; served for a very brief period only; harbour guard vessel from 3 May 1904 at Danzig. Stricken 24 Jun 1911; used after 1913 as a mine hulk at Emden; broken up 1921 at Hamburg.

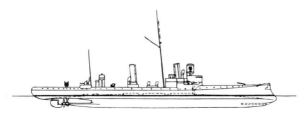

Comet (1893)

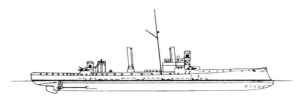

Meteor (1892)

Bussard class

Name	Builder	Built	Cost in Marks (000s)	Displacement (t = tonnes T = tons)	Length (m)	Breadth (m)	Draught (m)	Power (hp)	Revs (rpm)	Speed (kts)	Range (nm/kts)	Coal (t)	Oil (t)
BUSSARD	Imperial Dockyard, Danzig	1888–90	2287	1868t max 1559t des	82.60 oa 79.62 cwl	12.5 max 10.2 des	4.45 fwd 5.63 aft	2806ihp max 2800ihp des	129 max	15.7 max 15.5 des	2990/9	305 max 180 des	—
	mod: Imperial Dockyard, Danzig	1899–1900											
FALKE	Imperial Dockyard, Kiel Construction no 19	1890–91	2475	,,	,,	,,	,,	2910ihp max 2800ihp des	133 max	16.9 max 15.5 des	,,	,,	—
SEEADLER	Imperial Dockyard, Danzig	1890–92	2460	1864t max 1612t des	82.60 oa 79.60 cwl	12.7 max 10.5 des	4.42 fwd 5.35 aft	2881ihp max 2800ihp des	134 max	16.9 max 15.5 des	2950/9	315 max 205 des	—
	mod: Imperial Dockyard, Danzig	1898–99		1887t max							3040/9	340 max	
CONDOR	Blohm Voss, Hamburg Construction no 82	1891–92	2437	1864t max 1612t des 1887t max mod	,,	,,	,,	,,	133 max	16.2 max 15.5 des	2950/9 3040/9 mod	315 max 205 des 340 mod	—
CORMORAN	Imperial Dockyard, Danzig	1890–93	2495	1864t max 1612t des	,,	,,	,,	2857ihp max 2800ihp des	130 max	15.9 max 15.5 des	,,	,,	—
	mod: Imperial Dockyard, Danzig	1907–08		1887t max									
GEIER	Imperial Dockyard, Wilhelmshaven Construction no 21	1893–95	2588	1918t max 1608t des	83.90 oa 79.62 cwl	10.6	4.74 fwd 5.22 aft	2884ihp max 2880ihp des	139 max	16.3 max 15.5 des	3610/9	320 max 170 des	—
	mod: Imperial Dockyard, Danzig	1908–09											

1019gt/458 (*Bussard, Falke*), 1028gt/463nt (*Seeadler, Condor, Cormoran*). After refit: 1049gt/472nt. 1056gt/487nt (*Geier*)

Construction

Laid down as Fourth Rate cruisers *C*, *D*, *Ersatz Adler*, *Ersatz Eber*, *E* and *F* (official design, 1888). Transverse frame steel construction with yellow pine planks as far as upper deck [finally as far as tween decks], and Muntz metal sheathing; the stem was steel/timber, with a bronze ram, the stern steel/timber (ten watertight compartments, double bottom under boiler room). Depth 6.42m. Immersion increased by 1cm per 5.52–5.67t. Trim moment 2191–2320m-t [2570m-t].

Propulsion

Two horizontal 3-cylinder triple expansion engines (two 3-bladed screws, 3.0m diameter) in 1 + 1 engine rooms. Four cylindrical boilers (twelve fireboxes, 12 atmospheres forced, 654–700sq m) [*Cormoran* refitted 1907–8 with new boilers by J W Klawitter, Danzig] in 1 + 1 boiler rooms. Two generators, 24kW 67V. Schooner barque rig 856–877sq m [*Bussard*, *Seeadler* and *Cormoran* were reduced to topsail schooners, approx 600sq m, with a triangular mainsail.] One rudder.

Armament

Eight 10.5cm/35 hooped guns (*Bussard*), or eight 10.5cm/35 QF guns (800 [704] rounds) (after *Falke*), range 8200 and 10,800m; five machine guns [removed]; two 35cm deck TT (5 rounds) except for *Geier*, two 45cm deck TT (5 rounds).

Handling

Quite good sea-boats, with slight pitch but early and severe roll; speed had to be reduced in high seas because the sponsons produced dangerous vibration (except on *Geier*). Manoeuvrability was generally good, except that turning into the wind at low speed was very difficult. Transverse metacentric height 0.54–0.72m, longitudinal 98–106m, maximum stability moment approx 38–45°, = zero at >90°. Fleet rudder angle 40°.

Complement

Crew: 9/152 [157]. Boats: one picket, one cutter, two yawls, two dinghies.

Notes

Colour scheme no 2, 3, 4, 8, 9, 11 (*Geier* 4, 8, 9, 11). *Bussard* and *Falke* were initially fitted with a 2.5m lower funnel, and a searchlight on a platform between the forecastle guns, 4m forward of the foremast, instead of on the charthouse; the pressure heads on these vessels were always smaller than those on the others. *Falke* and *Geier* had an aft compass platform adjacent to the mizzen mast; *Condor* and *Cormoran* a forward compass platform at the forward edge of the bridge. Lateral steam pipes were fitted on *Cormoran* only until 1907; until then this ship had no tall pressure head forward of the funnel, in contrast to all the other ships. The stern and hull were without sponsons on *Geier* (see the drawings).

Career

Bussard launched 23 Jan 1890, commissioned 7 Oct 1890; served abroad until 1910. Stricken 25 Oct 1912; broken up 1913 at Hamburg.

Falke launched 4 Apr 1891, commissioned 14 Sept 1891; served abroad until 1907. Stricken 25 Oct 1912; broken up 1913 at the Imperial Dockyard, Danzig.

Seeadler launched 2 Feb 1892 as *Kaiseradler*, commissioned 27 Jun 1892; renamed *Seeadler* 17 Aug 1892 and served abroad; reclassified as a gunboat 6 May 1914; reduced to a mine hulk at Wilhelmshaven after 1914. Sunk 19 Apr 1917 in the Jade, position 53° 29N, 08° 12E, after an explosion; no casualties.

Condor launched 23 Feb 1892, commissioned 9 Dec 1894; served abroad until 1914; reclassified as a gunboat 8 Jan 1913; reduced to a mine hulk at Kiel Friedrichsort in 1916. Stricken 18 Nov 1920; sold 8 Apr 1921, and broken up in 1921 at Hamburg.

Cormoran launched 17 May 1892, commissioned 25 Jul 1893; served abroad 1894–1903 and 1909–14; reclassified as a gunboat after 24 Feb 1913; fittings unshipped 6 Aug 1914. Scuttled 28 Sept 1914 at Tsingtau, position 36° 03N, 120° 16E.

Geier launched 18 Oct 1894, commissioned 24 Oct 1895; served abroad 1897–1905 and 1911–14; interned 7 Nov 1914 at Honolulu, position 21° 10N, 157° 55W; requisitioned in 1918 by the USA following her entry into the war, and renamed *Carl Schurz*. Sunk 21 Jun 1918 10nm southwest of Cape Lookout (North Carolina coast), after collision with the escorting ss *Fluida*.

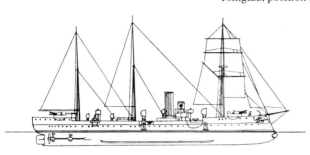

Cormoran (1895); *Bussard*, *Falke*, *Seeadler* and *Condor* were very similar; *Geier* was similar, but without sponsons.

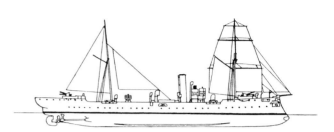

Geier (1914); *Bussard*, *Seeadler* and *Cormoran* were similar, but with differences in the hull.

Gefion

Name	Builder	Built	Cost in Marks (000s)	Displacement (t = tonnes T = tons)	Length (m)	Breadth (m)	Draught (m)	Power (hp)	Revs (rpm)	Speed (kts)	Range (nm/kts)	Coal (t)	Oil (t)
GEFION 2549gt/1147nt	F Schichau, Danzig Construction no 486 mod: Imperial Dockyard, Wilhelmshaven	1892–94 1901–04	5171	4275t max 3746t des	110.4 oa 109.2 cwl	13.2	6.47 fwd 6.27 aft	9827ihp max 9000ihp des	142 max	20.5 max 19.0 des	3500/12	860 max 400 des	—

Construction

Laid down as cruiser corvette (Third Rate cruiser) *J* (official design, 1891). Transverse and longitudinal frame steel construction, stem and stern lower parts bronze, upper parts steel, timber planking and Muntz metal sheathing up to 1m above CWL (ten watertight compartments, double bottom 52 percent). Steel armour: deck 25mm, slopes 30mm; coaming 40mm; engine room coaming 100mm on 180mm teak; CT 30mm; cork cofferdams. Depth 7.87m. Immersion increased by 1cm per 9.58t. Trim moment 5.324m-t.

Propulsion

Two vertical 3-cylinder triple expansion engines (two 3-bladed screws, 4.2m diameter) in two engine rooms. Six transverse cylindrical double boilers (thirty-two fireboxes, 12 atmospheres forced, 2100sq m) in 1 + 1 + 1 boiler rooms. Three generators, 40kW 67V [three generators 58kW 110V]. One rudder.

Armament

Fifteen 10.5cm QF guns were originally planned, but only ten 10.5cm/35 QF guns were fitted (807 rounds), range 10,800m; six 5cm/40 QF guns (1500 rounds), range 6200m; two 45cm deck TT (5 rounds).

Handling

As *Gazelle* class, but making even more severe leeway. Transverse metacentric height 0.55m, longitudinal 131m. Maximum stability moment around 71°, = zero at >90°. Fleet rudder angle 40°.

Complement

Crew: 13/289. Boats: one picket boat, one pinnace, two cutters, two yawls, one dinghy.

Notes

Colour scheme no 4, 7, 9, 11. The whole ship was built very light. [The upper deck was enclosed during the refit, and the 10.5cm QF guns located there were relocated in gunports at 49.0m, 54.0m and 59.0m; the 5cm QF guns at the second funnel position were moved to third funnel.] Even after the refit the ship remained very hot and difficult to ventilate. Funnel cross-sections were rectangular with slightly rounded verticals.

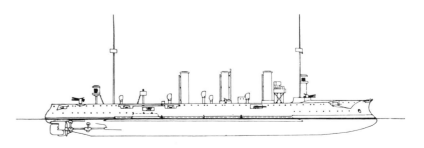

Gefion (1895)

Career

Gefion launched 31 May 1893, commissioned 27 Jun 1894 into the fleet; served abroad 1897–1901, and from 1916 as a barrack ship at Danzig. Stricken 5 Nov 1919, and sold to Norddeutsche Tiefbaugesellschaft, Berlin; converted to the MS *Adolf Sommerfeld* in 1920 at Danzig by Danziger Hoch- und Tiefbau GmbH; broken up 1923 at Danzig.

Hela

Name	Builder	Built	Cost in Marks (000s)	Displacement (t = tonnes T = tons)	Length (m)	Breadth (m)	Draught (m)	Power (hp)	Revs (rpm)	Speed (kts)	Range (nm/kts)	Coal (t)	Oil (t)
HELA	AG Weser, Bremen Construction no 108	1893–95	2703	2082t max 2027t des	105.0 oa 104.6 cwl	11.0	4.46 fwd 4.64 aft	6000ihp des		20.0 des 20.5 max		340 max	—
	mod: Imperial Dockyard, Danzig	1903–06						5982ihp max	176		3000/12	412 max	
1344gt/606nt													

Construction

Laid down as aviso *H* (official design, 1893). Transverse and longitudinal frame steel cosntruction (twenty-two [thirty] watertight compartments above the armour deck, ten below the armour deck, double bottom 35 percent [39 percent]). Steel armour: deck 20mm, slopes 25mm; coaming 40mm; CT 30mm; cork cofferdams. Depth 6.41m. Immersion increased by 1cm per 7.14t. Trim moment 3,390m-t.

Propulsion

Two vertical 3-cylinder triple expansion engines (two 3-bladed screws, 3.25m diameter) in two engine rooms. Six locomotive boilers (twelve fireboxes, 12.5 atmospheres forced, 1161sq m) [eight Marine-type boilers (eight fireboxes, 1515sq m) fitted 1905] in 1 + 1 boiler rooms. Three generators, 36kW 67V. One rudder.

Armament

Four [two] 8.8cm/30 QF guns (800 [312] rounds), range 6900m; six 5cm/40 QF guns (1500 rounds), range 6200m; three 45cm TT (8 rounds), two lateral, deck-mounted, one bow, under water [all relocated under water].

Handling

Good sea-boats, but stiff with severe roll, and extremely wet in a head sea (slightly bow-heavy). Manoeuvrability was average. Transverse metacentric height 0.775m, longitudinal 170m. Maximum stability moment about 42°, = zero at about 73°. Fleet rudder angle 38°.

Complement

Crew: 7/171 [8/187]. Boats: [one picket boat], one barge [removed], one yawl, three dinghies.

Notes

Colour scheme no 4, 7, 9. Refit modifications are shown in the drawings. Examples of estimated building costs, as shown in the main table, are as follows: *Gefion*, 4500 million M; *Hela*, 2267 million M; *Gazelle*, 2535 million M; all these estimates were exceeded.

Career

Hela launched 28 Mar 1895, commissioned 3 May 1896 into the fleet; served abroad 1900–01; fleet tender after 1910; fleet and flotilla patrol boat from 1914. Sunk 13 Sept 1914 in the North Sea, position 54° 03N, 07° 55E, by a torpedo from the British submarine *E9*; 2 dead.

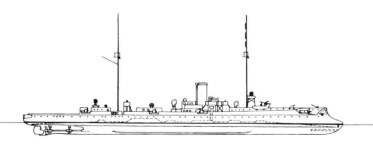
Hela (1899), first form

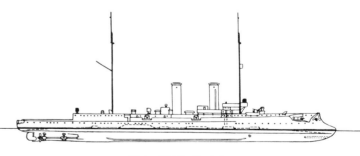
Hela (1914), final form

Gazelle class

Construction

Laid down as Fourth Rate Cruiser *G* and light cruisers *B*; *A, C, D, F* and *E*; *G, H* and *J* (official designs, 1895–96, 1897–1900). Transverse and longitudinal frame steel construction, *Gazelle* and *Niobe* with wooden planks with Muntz metal sheathing up to 1m above CWL (twelve watertight compartments, double bottom 40 percent, after *Frauenlob* 46 percent). Armour (two layers steel, one layer Krupp): deck 20–25(slopes 50)mm, coaming 80mm; (Krupp): CT roof 20mm, sides 80mm; shields 50mm; cork cofferdams. Depth 7.08m. 7.13, 7.50m. Immersion increased by 1cm per 8.44–8.67t. Trim moment 4610–5024m-t.

Propulsion

Original engines and boilers were by the respective building dockyards, but those in *Gazelle*, *Nymphe* and *Amazone* were by AG Germania, Berlin-Tegel; two vertical 4-cylinder triple expansion engines (after *Ariadne* two vertical 3-cylinder triple expansion engines) (two 3-bladed screws, 3.5m diameter) in one (after *Frauenlob* two) engine rooms. *Gazelle*, eight Niclausse boilers (sixteen fireboxes, 13 atmospheres forced, 1454sq m) [eight Marine-type boilers (eight

Name	Builder	Built	Cost in Marks (000s)	Displacement (t = tonnes T = tons)	Length (m)	Breadth (m)	Draught (m)	Power (hp)	Revs (rpm)	Speed (kts)	Range (nm/kts)	Coal (t)	Oil (t)
GAZELLE	Germania Dockyard, Kiel Construction no 76	1897–1900	4611	2963t max 2643t des	105.0 oa 104.4 cwl	12.2 max 11.8 des	4.84 fwd 5.53 aft	6366ihp max 6000ihp des	145 max 143 des	20.2 max 19.5 des	3570/10 2400/14 1400/19	500 max 300 des	—
	mod: Imperial Dockyard, Danzig	1905–07										625 max	
NIOBE	AG 'Weser', Bremen Construction no 120	1898–1900	4534	,,	,,	,,	5.03 fwd 5.31 aft	8113ihp max 8000ihp des	168 max 170 des	22.1 max 21.5 des	,,	500 max 300 des	—
	mod: Deutsche Werke, Kiel	1924–25		2360T std								625 max	
NYMPHE	Germania Dockyard, Kiel	1898–1900	4647	3017t max 2659t des	105.1 oa 104.1 cwl	12.2 max 11.8 des	4.11 fwd 5.44 aft	8486ihp max 8000ihp des	164 max 165 des	21.2 max 21.5 des			
	mod: Marine Dockyard, Wilhelmshaven	1924–25		3139t max 2654t des	108.7 oa 104.4 cwl	12.2 max 11.8 des	5.38 fwd 5.42 aft						
THETIS	Imperial Dockyard, Danzig	1899–01	4487	3005t max 2659t des	105.1 oa 104.1 cwl	12.2 max 11.8 des	4.92 fwd 5.39 aft	8888ihp max 8000ihp des	172 max 165 des	21.9 max 21.5 des	3560/12	560 max 380 des	—
ARIADNE	AG 'Weser', Bremen Construction no 127	1899–01	4799	3006t max 2659t des	105.1 oa 104.1 cwl	12.2 max 11.8 des	4.93 fwd 5.50 aft	8827ihp max 8000ihp des	168 max 165 des	22.2 max 21.5 des	,,	,,	—
AMAZONE	Germania Dockyard, Kiel Construction no 87	1899–1901	4858	3082t max 2659t des	104.8 oa 104.1 cwl	12.2 max 11.8 des	5.12 fwd 5.39 aft	9018ihp max 8000ihp des	165 max 165 des	21.3 max 21.5 des	,,	,,	—
	mod: Reichs Dockyard, Wilhelmshaven	1921–23		3139t max 2654t des 2380T std	108.7 oa 104.4 cwl	12.2 max 11.8 des	5.38 fwd 5.42 aft						
MEDUSA	AG 'Weser', Bremen Construction no 128	1900–01	4739	2972t max 2659t des	105.1 oa 104.1 cwl	12.2 max 11.8 des	4.84 fwd 5.39 aft	7972ihp max 8000ihp des	161 max 165 des	20.9 max 21.5 des	,,	,,	—
	mod: Rickmers, Wesemünde	1939–40											
FRAUENLOB	AG 'Weser', Bremen Construction no 132	1901–03	4596	3158t max 2706t des	105.0 oa 104.4 cwl	12.4 max 12.3 des	4.99 fwd 5.61 aft	8623ihp max 8000ihp des	160 max 165 des	21.5 max 21.5 des	4400/12	700 max 380 des	—
ARCONA	AG 'Weser', Bremen Construction no 133	1901–03	4493	3180t max 2706t des	105.0 oa 104.4 cwl	12.4 max 12.3 des	4.99 fwd 5.62 aft	8580ihp max 8000ihp des	164 max 165 des	21.5 max 21.5 des	,,	,,	—
	mod: Imperial Dockyard, Wilhelmshaven	1911–12											
UNDINE	Howaldtswerke, Kiel Construction no 390	1901–04	4653	3112t max 2706t des	105.0 oa 104.4 cw	12.4 max 12.3 des	4.81 fwd 5.63 aft	8696ihp max 6000ihp des	163 max 165 des	21.5 max 21.5 des	,,	,,	—

1878gt/911nt (*Gazelle, Niobe*); 1918gt/915nt (*Nymphe* to *Medusa*), after refit 2054gt/1052nt; 2152gt/1055nt (*Frauenlob* to *Undine*)

fireboxes, 13 atmospheres forced, 1928sq m)]; *Niobe*, eight Thornycroft boilers (sixteen fireboxes, 15 atmospheres forced, 2020sq m); *Nymphe*, one Marine-type boiler plus nine Marine-type double-ended boilers (eighteen fireboxes, 15 atmospheres forced, 2300sq m); from *Thetis*, nine Marine-type boilers (eighteen fireboxes, 15 atmospheres forced, approx 2300sq m) in 1 + 1 boiler rooms. Three generators, 110kW 110V (*Gazelle*, 73kW, *Niobe* 99kW, *Nymphe* 122kW). One rudder.

Armament

Ten 10.5cm/40 QF guns (1000 rounds, after *Frauenlob* 1500), range 12,200m; fourteen 10cm machine cannon (temporary fitting); *Gazelle*, three 45cm TT (8 rounds), two lateral, deck-mounted, one bow, under water, after *Niobe*, two 45cm TT (5 rounds), two lateral under water; [after 1916 all ships were disarmed except for *Medusa* (six 10.5cm/40 QF guns; *Thetis*, after 1917, nine 10.5cm/45 Utof guns; *Arcona*, after 1912 and

Handling

All ships were crank, with severe roll, and wet in a head sea. All manoeuvred well and turned very tightly, with speed loss in turns up to 65 percent, but slight in a head sea. [Handling after refits was as before but with the added requirement for lee helm.] Transverse metacentric height 0.50–0.63m, longitudinal 155–159m, maximum stability moment about 41.5–45°. Fleet rudder angle 40°, but 38° in *Arcona* and *Undine*.

Complement

Crew: 14/243 (after *Frauenlob* 256) [18/311]. Boats: one picket boat, one pinnace, two cutters, two yawls, one dinghy.

Notes

Colour scheme no 9, 11. The shields for the 10.5cm QF guns in sponsons were reduced approximately by the lower third. The ventilators on *Nymphe* and *Thetis* after their refit were as shown in the drawing (initially

Niobe launched 18 Jul 1899, commissioned 25 Jun 1900 into the fleet; served abroad 1906–09; coastal defence vessel 1914; office and barrack ship at Wilhelmshaven 1917; served in the Reichsmarine. Stricken 26 Jun 1925 and sold for refit as a touring ship; became the Yugoslavian training cruiser *Dalmacija*. Taken over by Italian navy 17 Apr 1941 at Kotor (Cattaro); renamed *Cattaro* in Italian service. Taken over by Germany 11 Sept 1943 at Pola (commissioned 8 Nov 1943), and renamed *Niobe*, with a part-Croat crew. Ran aground at 1900hrs on 19 Dec 1943 on the island of Silba, position 44° 21N, 14° 42E, and abandoned after damage by two torpedoes from the British *MTB 276* and *MTB 298* (19 dead) on 22 Dec 1943. Cannibalised by partisans; raised about 1947; broken up about 1949.

Nymphe launched 21 Nov 1899, commissioned 20 Sept 1900 for fleet and training duties; coastal defence vessel 1914; barrack and exercise ship at Kiel 1916;

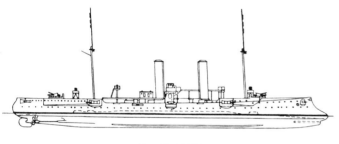
Gazelle (1901)

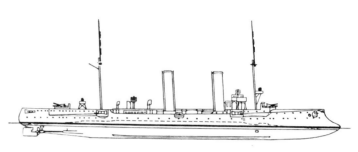
Nymphe (1903), *Thetis, Ariadne, Amazone, Medusa; Niobe* was similar.

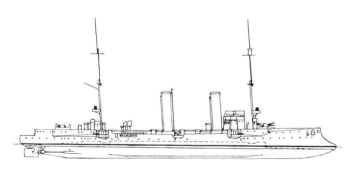
Arcona (1914); *Frauenlob* and *Undine* were very similar.

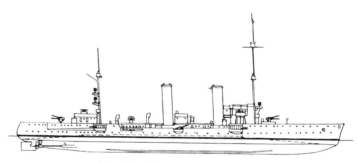
Nymphe (1925); *Amazone*, final form

1914, eight and ten 10.5cm/40 QF guns, two 50cm deck TT, 200 mines]. [In the Reichsmarine *Medusa* and *Arcona* were armed as in 1912; *Niobe*, *Nymphe* and *Amazone* ten 10.5cm/45 Utof guns and two 50cm deck TT; *Thetis* ten 10.5cm/40 Utof guns. *Dalmacija* (see *Niobe* career notes) initially carried no QF guns, but was fitted after 1926 with six Skoda 8.5cm/55 QF guns (1200 rounds), and later an additional four to six 2cm AA guns (8000 rounds). *Medusa* and *Arcona*, after their reconstruction as floating AA batteries in 1940, were fitted with one 10.5cm/45 QF gun (*Arcona*, 4000, *Medusa*, 3200 rounds); two 4cm/56 Bofors AA guns (*Arcona*, 8000, *Medusa*, 4000 rounds); six 2cm AA guns (12,000 rounds); five 10.5cm/65 AA guns (2000 rounds); two 3.7cm AA guns (4000 rounds); and four 2cm AA guns (10,000 rounds); *Niobe* was fitted with six 8.4cm AA guns, four 4.7cm AA guns, four 2cm Oerlikon AA guns, and twenty-six 2cm Breda guns.]

they had been 2m higher). *Frauenlob* and *Undine* were as shown in the drawing, but with stern and armament as on *Ariadne*. [*Medusa* platform with rangefinder on aft deckhouse. *Thetis* 1921 aft superstructure, searchlight and mast as drawing (but with wireless telegraphy topmast). *Amazone* old standard pressure heads at all times, *Niobe* funnel spacing as *Gazelle*.]

Career

Gazelle launched 31 Mar 1898, commissioned 15 Jun 1901 into the fleet, served abroad 1902–04; coastal defence vessel 1914; out of service 22 Feb 1916 after mine damage received 25 Jan 1916 north-northwest of Cape Arkona (screws lost in explosion); reduced to a minelayer hulk at Danzig and Cuxhaven, and from 1918 at Wilhelmshaven. Stricken 28 Aug 1920, broken up at Wilhelmshaven.

served in the Reichsmarine 1924–29. Stricken 31 Mar 1931; sold 29 Aug 1931 for 61,500M; broken up 1932 at Hamburg.

Thetis launched 3 Jul 1900, commissioned 14 Sept 1901; served abroad 1902–06; coastal defence vessel 1914; gunnery training ship 1917; served in the Reichsmarine. Stricken 27 Mar 1929; sold with *V1* and *V6* for 351,000M, broken up 1930 by Blohm & Voss, Hamburg.

Ariadne launched 10 Aug 1900, commissioned 18 May 1901 into the fleet; coastal defence vessel 1914. Sunk at 1600hrs on 28 Aug 1914 in the North Sea north of Norderney, position 54° 09N, 07° 07E, by gunfire from British battlecruisers; 64 dead. Wreck position in 1973 was 54° 08'36"N, 06° 58'57"E.

Amazone launched 6 Oct 1900, commissioned 15 Nov 1901 into the fleet; coastal defence vessel 1914; basic training ship 1916; barrack ship at Kiel 1917; served in the Reichsmarine fleet 1923–30. Stricken 31 Mar 1931, reduced to a barrack hulk for the Submarine Acceptance Commission, Kiel; used as an auxiliary ship for the Warship Construction Test Office, submarine group; used after 1945 as a barrack hulk at Bremen; broken up 1954 at Hamburg.

Medusa launched 5 Dec 1900, commissioned 26 Jul 1901 into the fleet; coastal defence vessel 1914; auxiliary ship for *König Wilhelm* 1917; served in the Reichsmarine fleet 1920–24. Stricken 27 Mar 1929; used as a barrack ship at Wilhelmshaven; converted in

July 1940 to a floating AA battery at Wilhelmshaven for Naval AA Group 222. Scuttled 3 May 1945 at Wilhelmshaven; broken up 1948–50.

Frauenlob launched 22 Mar 1902, commissioned 17 Feb 1903 into the fleet. Sunk at 2335hrs on 31 May 1916 in the North Sea, position 56° 15N, 05° 48E, by a torpedo from the British cruiser *Southampton*; 324 dead.

Arcona launched 22 Apr 1902, commissioned 12 May 1903 into the fleet; served abroad 1907–1910; mine test ship 1913; mine cruiser and coastal defence ship

1914; depot ship for North Sea sweeping fleet 1919–20; Reichsmarine 1921–23. Stricken 15 Jan 1930; used as a barrack ship at Wilhelmshaven and after 1936 at Swinemünde, after 1938 at Kiel; converted in May 1940 into a floating AA battery at Swinemünde, later at Wilhelmshaven for Naval AA Group 233. Scuttled 3 May 1945 at Wilhelmshaven; broken up 1948–49.

Undine launched 11 Dec 1902, commissioned 5 Jan 1904 as a gunnery training ship; coastal defence vessel 1914. Sunk at 1308hrs on 7 Nov 1915 in the Baltic, position 54° 59N, 13° 51E, by two torpedoes from the British submarine *E19*; 14 dead.

Bremen class

Name	Builder	Built	Cost in Marks (000s)	Displacement (t = tonnes T = tons)	Length (m)	Breadth (m)	Draught (m)	Power (hp)	Revs (rpm)	Speed (kts)	Range (nm/kts)	Coal (t)	Oil (t)
BREMEN	AG 'Weser', Bremen Construction no 135	1902–04	4746	3797t max 3278t des	111.1 oa 110.6 cwl	13.3	5.53 fwd 5.53 aft	12,100ihp max 10,000ihp des	144 max 150 des	23.3 max 22.0 des	4270/12	860 max 400 des	—
	mod: Imperial Dockyard, Wilhelmshaven	1914–15											
HAMBURG	AG Vulcan, Stettin Construction no 258	1902–04	4706	3651t max 3278t des	,,	,,	5.28 fwd 5.46 aft	11,582ihp max 10,000ihp des	148 max 150 des	,,	,,	,,	—
BERLIN	Imperial Dockyard, Danzig	1902–05	4545	3792t max 3278t des	,,	,,	5.51 fwd 5.53 aft	12,140ihp max 10,000ihp des	144 max 150 des	,,	,,	,,	—
	mod: Reichswerft, Wilhelmshaven	1921–23		3821t max 3293t des 2970T std	113.8 oa 110.6 des	13.3	5.63 fwd 5.58 aft						
LÜBECK	AG Vulcan, Stettin Construction no 269	1903–05	5436	3661t max 3265t des	111.1 oa 110.6 cwl	13.3	5.40 fwd 5.43 aft	14,035shp max 11,500shp des	663 max 670 des	23.1 max 22.5 des	3800/12	860 max 400 des	—
	mod: AG Vulcan, Stettin	1916											
MÜNCHEN	AG 'Weser', Bremen Construction no 138	1903–05	5054	3780t max 3278t des	,,	,,	5.47 fwd 5.54 aft	12,205ihp max 10,000ihp des	143 max 150 des	23.3 max 22.0 des	(4690/12)	860 max 400 des	—
LEIPZIG	AG 'Weser', Bremen Construction no 143	1904–06	5043	3816t max 3278t des	,,	,,	5.61 fwd 5.60 aft	11,116ihp max 10,000ihp des	136 max 150 des	22.1 max 22.0 des	,,	,,	—
DANZIG	Imperial Dockyard Danzig	1904–07	4828	3783t max 3278t des	,,	,,	5.68 fwd 5.38 aft	12,022ihp max 10,000ihp des	146 max 150 des	22.9 max 22.0 des	,,	,,	—

2421gt/1090nt; after refit 2547gt/1146nt (*Berlin*)

Construction

Laid down as light cruisers *L*, *K*, *Ersatz Zieten*, *Ersatz Mercur*, *M*, *N* and *Ersatz Alexandrine* (official designs, 1901–02 and 1903). Transverse and longitudinal frame

steel construction (twelve watertight compartments, double bottom 56 percent). Armour (two layers steel, one layer Krupp): deck 20–35(slopes 50)–80mm;

coaming 100mm; (Krupp): CT roof 20mm, sides 100mm; shields 50mm; cork cofferdams. Depth 7.75m. Immersion increased by 1cm per 9.63t. Trim moment *Bremen* 5944, *Hamburg* 5820, *Berlin* 5915, *Lübeck* 5855, *München* 5920, *Leipzig* 5790, *Danzig* 5640m-t.

Propulsion

Two vertical 3-cylinder triple expansion engines (two 4-bladed screws, 3.9m diameter), (*Lübeck*, two Parsons turbines by Brown, Boveri & Co, (temporarily eight 4-bladed screws, 1.1m diameter, and four 4-bladed screws, 1.6 and 1.75m diameter) in two engine rooms). Ten Marine-type boilers (twenty fireboxes, 15 atmospheres forced, 2750–2810sq m) in 1 + 1 + 1 boiler rooms. *Bremen, Hamburg* three generators, 111kW 110V; after *Berlin* two turbo-generators, 90kW 110V. One rudder.

Armament

Ten 10.5cm/40 QF guns (1500 rounds), range 12,200m; ten machine cannon (temporary); two 45cm TT (5 rounds), two lateral, under water. [*Bremen* and *Lübeck*, two 15cm/45 QF guns (280 rounds); six 10.5cm/40 and /45 QF guns (900 rounds); *Lübeck*, two 50cm deck TT (4 rounds), plus 50 mines. *Berlin* and *München* were disarmed after 1916. *Hamburg* carried only six 10.5cm/40 QF guns after 1916. In the Reichsmarine *Hamburg* and *Berlin* were fitted with ten and eight 10.5cm/45 QF guns (1650 rounds), and two 50cm deck TT. *Berlin* carried 80 U-mines 1915–16.]

Handling

Good sea-boats, though very crank (up to 20° roll, with pitching), very wet at high speed. Required slight weather helm and always made some leeway, but manoeuvred and turned very well, though slow to initiate turns [*Lübeck* and *Berlin* required hardly any weather helm]; speed loss in turns was up to 35 percent, but slight in a head sea. Transverse metacentric height 0.58–0.61m, longitudinal about 166m. Maximum stability moment about 45°. Fleet rudder angle 40°, except *Lübeck* (to port only) 38°.

Complement

Crew: 14/274–287 [19/330]. Boats: one picket boat, one barge, one pinnace, two cutters, two yawls, one dinghy.

Notes

Colour scheme no 9 (*Bremen, Hamburg* and *Lübeck* no 11). *Berlin* and *München* had stems as shown in the supplementary drawing. *Berlin* had larger forward sponsons than on *Bremen*. *Berlin, Lübeck* and *München* had a single-leg compass platform. [All vessels were fitted with searchlights 1909–10 as in the drawing of *Berlin*'s foremast; *Hamburg* (after 1915) and *München* had an additional large mast platform as shown in the *Danzig* drawing with 1 + 1 searchlights, with the directing platform below it. *Hamburg* was fitted with a gangway to the foremast as shown in the drawing of *Berlin* after 1920.] *Leipzig* was as the drawing of *Danzig* in appearance, but with one aft searchlight only, and also with prominent steam pipes on the aft two funnels up to 1910 (as also on *München* up to 1914). [*Bremen* was not fitted with four searchlights until after 1915 – see the drawing. *Hamburg* was fitted after 1920 with a wireless telegraphy booth between the aft funnels.]

Career

Bremen launched 9 Jul 1903, commissioned 19 May 1904; served abroad until 1914, then with the fleet in 1915. Sunk at 1804hrs on 17 Dec 1915 in the northern Baltic near the Spon Bank, position 57° 31N, 20° 24E, by two mines, along with *V191*; 250 dead.

Hamburg launched 25 Jul 1903, commissioned 8 Mar 1904 into the fleet; second command flagship for UF1 (U-boat Flotilla 1) 1912; served in the fleet and as UF1 flagship 1914, and finally as UF1 squadron flagship and barrack ship for submarine commanders at Wilhelmshaven; served in the Reichsmarine fleet 1920–23, and as a training cruiser 1924–27. Stricken 31 Mar 1931; used after 1936 as a barrack hulk for submarine crews at Kiel. Finally released from service in 1944, towed from Kiel to Hamburg for breaking up 7 Jul 1944; sunk later that year at Hamburg-Harburg by British aircraft bombs. Raised 1949 and 1956, broken up.

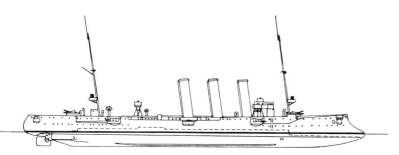

Bremen (1905), *Hamburg, Berlin, Lübeck, München*

Bow, *Berlin* and *München*

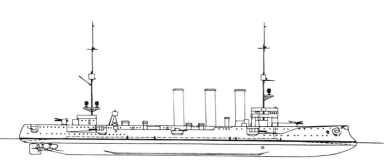

Danzig (1914); *Leipzig* was similar.

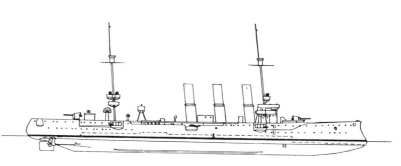

Bremen (1915)

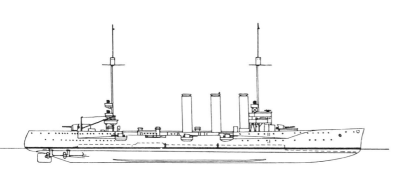

Lübeck (1917)

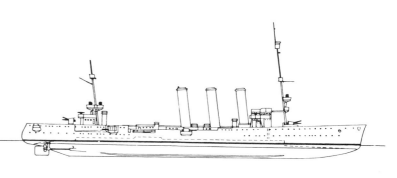

Berlin (1938)

Berlin launched 22 Sept 1903, commissioned 4 Apr 1905 into the fleet; served abroad 1911; with the fleet 1912; coastal defence vessel 1917; training cruiser (on voyages abroad) 1922–1929; tender and barrack ship at Kiel 1935. Scuttled in the Skagerrak with a load of gas shells 31 May 1947.

Lübeck launched 26 Mar 1904, commissioned 26 Apr 1905 into the fleet; coastal defence vessel 1914; basic training and target ship 1917. Stricken 5 Nov 1919;

given up as British prize *P* 3 Sept 1920; broken up 1922–23 in Germany.

München launched 30 Apr 1904, commissioned 10 Jan 1905 for torpedo and wireless telegraphy tests; served with the fleet 1914–15; decommissioned in November 1915 after torpedo damage received on 19 Oct 1915; reduced to a barrack ship for sound guard vessels 1918. Stricken 5 Nov 1919; given up 6 Jul 1920 as British prize *Q*; broken up.

Leipzig launched 21 Mar 1905, commissioned 20 Apr 1906 for service abroad. Sunk at 2123hrs on 8 Dec 1914 near the Falklands, position 53° 55S, 55° 55W, by gunfire from the British cruisers *Cornwall* and *Glasgow*; 315 dead.

Danzig launched 23 Sept 1905, commissioned 1 Dec 1907 into the fleet; gunnery training ship 1910; fleet duties 1914–17. Stricken 5 Nov 1919; given up 15 Sept 1920 as British prize *R*, broken up 1921–23 at Whitby.

Königsberg class

Name	Builder	Built	Cost in Marks (000s)	Displacement (t = tonnes T = tons)	Length (m)	Breadth (m)	Draught (m)	Power (hp)	Revs (rpm)	Speed (kts)	Range (nm/kts)	Coal (t)	Oil (t)
KÖNIGSBERG	Imperial Dockyard, Construction no 31 mod: Imperial Dockyard, Kiel	1905–07 1911–13	5407	3814t max 3390t des	115.3 oa 114.8 cwl	13.2	5.29 fwd 5.20 aft	13,918ihp max 13,200ihp des	144 max 145 des	24.1 max 23.0 des	5750/12 mod	820 max 400 des	—
NÜRNBERG	Imperial Dockyard, Kiel Construction no 32	1906–08	5560	3902t max 3469t des	117.4 oa 116.8 cwl	13.3	5.24 fwd 5.24 aft	13,154ihp max 13,200ihp des	139 max 145 des	23.4 max 23.0 des	(4120/12)	880 max 400 des	—
STUTTGART	Imperial Dockyard, Danzig mod: Imperial Dockyard, Wilhelmshaven	1905–08 1916–18	5488	4002t max 3469t des	,,	,,	5.40 fwd 5.30 aft	13,146ihp max 13,200ihp des	138 max 145 des	23.9 max 23.0 des	,,	,,	—
STETTIN	AG Vulcan, Stettin Construction no 270	1906–07	6398	3822t max 3480t des	,,	,,	5.14 fwd 5.17 aft	21,670shp max 13,500shp des	584 max	25.2 max 24.0 des	4170/12	880 max 400 des	—

2588gt/1165nt (*Königsberg*), 2500gt/1125nt (*Nürnberg, Stuttgart*), 2483gt/1117nt (*Stettin*)

Construction

Laid down as light cruisers *Ersatz Meteor, Ersatz Blitz, O* and *Ersatz Wacht* (official design, 1903–04 and 1904–05). Transverse and longitudinal frame steel construction (thirteen and fourteen watertight compartments, double bottom 47 percent). Armour (two layers steel, one layer Krupp): deck 20–30(slopes 45)–80mm; coaming 100mm; (Krupp): CT roof 20mm, sides 100mm; shields 50mm; cork cofferdams. Depth 7.80m. Immersion increased by 1cm per 10.06–10.38t. Trim moment 6150–6440m-t.

Propulsion

Two vertical 3-cylinder triple expansion engines (two 4-bladed screws, 4.0m diameter) (*Stettin*, two Parsons-system turbines (four 4-bladed screws, 1.9m diameter)) in 1 + 1 engine rooms. Eleven Marine-type boilers (twenty-two fireboxes, 16 atmospheres forced, approx 3050sq m) in 1 + 1 + 1, after *Nürnberg* 1 + 1 + 1 + 1 + 1 boiler rooms. Two, after *Nürnberg* three, turbo-generators, 90 and 135kW 100V. One rudder.

Armament

Ten 10.5cm/40 QF guns (1500 rounds), range 12,200m; ten machine cannon (temporary) and after *Nürnberg* eight 5.2cm/55 QF guns (4000 rounds); two 45cm TT (5 rounds), two lateral, under water. [*Stuttgart* (1918) four 10.5cm/40 QF guns (1242 rounds), two 8.8cm/45 AA guns, two TT as above, three seaplanes.]

Handling

As *Bremen* class, but with poorer turning capability; [*Stuttgart* required severe weather helm, and made severe leeway]. Transverse metacentric height 0.54–0.65m, longitudinal 176–182m. Maximum stability moment approx 37.5°, and 46–48°. Fleet rudder angle 40°.

Complement

Crew: 14/308. Boats: one picket boat, one barge, one cutter, two yawls, two dinghies.

Notes

Colour scheme no 9 (*Königsburg* and *Stettin* no 11). [After 1910–12 searchlights were fitted as follows: two on the foremast platform, 1 + 1 on the mainmast platform, none on the wings of the superstructure deck above central 10.5cm QF guns.] *Nürnberg* and *Stuttgart* had a breakwater on the forecastle and a similar fitting on the deckhouse. [*Stuttgart* was fitted with a large extension on the deckhouse early in 1916. As an aircraft mothership she had double hangars (of lightweight construction), the port hangar further aft than the starboard unit by one-third hangar length, while the port hanger doors opened forward and the starboard doors opened aft (these doors operated like curtains); the port loading gear was at 42.0m, and the third aircraft was carried on the deckhouse roof, uncovered. Only one searchlight remained on the mainmast platform.] The funnel arrangement of the *Stettin* class led to many jokes about the 'detached funnel'.

Career

Königsberg launched 12 Dec 1905, commissioned 6 Apr 1907 into the fleet until 1911; served abroad 1914. Blockaded in the Rufiji delta 30 Oct 1914, and sunk there by scuttling at 1745hrs on 11 Jul 1915, at position 07° 51S, 39° 15E, after coming under fire from British armed forces; 19 dead. The wreck was disarmed and the guns used for the defence of German East Africa; broken up 1963–65.

Nürnberg launched 28 Aug 1906, commissioned 10 Apr 1908; served abroad after 1910. Sunk at 1927hrs on 8 Dec 1914 near the Falklands, position 53° 28S, 55° 04W, by gunfire from the British armoured cruiser *Kent*; 327 dead.

Stuttgart launched 22 Sept 1906, commissioned 1 Feb 1908 as a gunnery training ship; served in the fleet 1914; [reconstructed as a seaplane carrier from February to May 1918]. Stricken 5 Nov 1919; given up 20 Jul 1920 as British prize *S* and broken up.

Stettin launched 7 Mar 1907, commissioned 29 Oct 1907 into the fleet; used as a basic training vessel 1917. Stricken 5 Nov 1919; given up 15 Sept 1920 as British prize *T*; sold and broken up 1921–23 at Copenhagen.

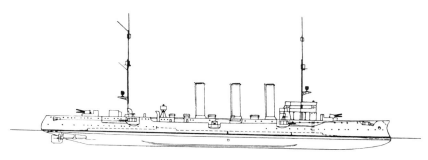

Königsberg (1910)

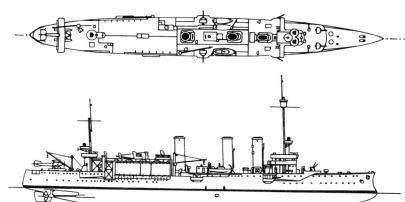

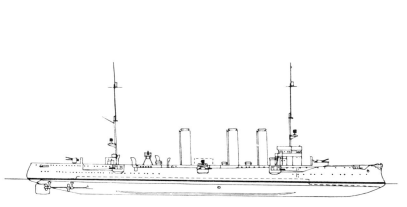

Stettin (1912), *Nürnberg, Stuttgart*

Stuttgart (1918)

Dresden class

Name	Builder	Built	Cost in Marks (000s)	Displacement (t = tonnes T = tons)	Length (m)	Breadth (m)	Draught (m)	Power (hp)	Revs (rpm)	Speed (kts)	Range (nm/kts)	Coal (t)	Oil (t)
DRESDEN	Blohm & Voss, Hamburg Construction no 195	1906–08	7460	4268t max 3664t des	118.3 oa 117.9 cwl	13.5	5.53 fwd 5.54 aft	18,880shp max 15,000shp des	594 max 540 des	25.2 max 24.0 des	3600/14	860 max 400 des	—
EMDEN 2572gt/1157nt	Imperial Dockyard, Danzig	1906–09	5960	„	„	„	„	16,350ihp max 13,500ihp des	144 max 150 des	24.0 max 23.5 des	3760/12	790 max 400 des	—

Construction

Laid down as light cruisers *Ersatz Comet* and *Ersatz Pfeil* (official design, 1905–06). Transverse and longitudinal frame steel construction (thirteen watertight compartments, double bottom 47 percent). Armour (two layers steel, one layer Krupp): deck 20–30(slopes 50)–80mm; coaming 100mm; (Krupp); CT roof 20mm, sides 100mm; shields 50mm. Depth 7.80m. Immersion increased by 1cm per 10.59t. Trim moment 6100m-t.

Propulsion

Two sets of Parsons turbines (four 3-bladed screws, 1.95m diameter) and two vertical 3-cylinder triple expansion engines (two 4-bladed screws, 4.3m diameter)

in 2 + 2 (*Dresden*) and two (*Emden*) engine rooms. Twelve Marine-type boilers (twenty-four fireboxes, 16 atmospheres forced, 3160–3438sq m) in 1 + 1 + 1 + 1 boiler rooms. Three turbo-generators, 125kW 110V. One rudder.

Armament

As *Nürnberg* class.

Handling

As *Bremen* class. Transverse metacentric height 0.59m, longitudinal 179m. Maximum stability moment about 55°. Fleet rudder angle 40°.

Complement

Crew: 18/343. Boats: one picket boat, one barge, one cutter, two yawls, two dinghies.

Notes

Colour scheme no 9, 11. *Dresden* had a breakwater on the forecastle close to the 10.5cm QF guns, with an angled, folding edge; this was absent on *Emden*. *Emden*'s central funnel was minus the steam pipe, and that on the forward funnel was of a different shape. Her mainmast searchlight platform was 2m lower. In her first year of service *Dresden* was fitted with only one searchlight on each mast forward and aft. *Emden* and the submarine *U9* were the only German warships to be awarded the Iron Cross; up to 31 Dec 1933 crew members were entitled to adopt the ship's name as a supplement to their own surnames (this was a unique occurrence in Germany).

Career

Dresden launched 5 Oct 1907, commissioned 14 Nov 1908 into the fleet; served abroad from 1914. Scuttled and sunk at 1115hrs on 14 Mar 1915 at Mas a Tierra, position 33° 37S, 78° 49W, after being fired on by the British cruisers *Kent* and *Glasgow* in a neutral harbour; 7 dead, crew interned in Chile. Her compass and flags were recovered in 1965, and are now in the Mürwik naval college.

Emden launched 26 May 1908, commissioned 10 Jul 1909; served abroad from 1910. Beached at the Cocos Islands, position 11° 50S, 96° 49E, at 1120hrs on 9 Nov 1914 after a fierce exchange of gunfire with the British cruiser *Sydney*; 133 dead. The remains were still in existence in 1963.

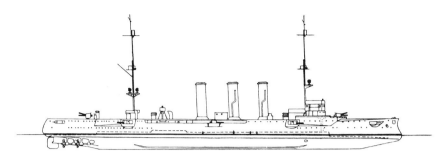

Dresden (1914), *Emden*

Kolberg class

Name	Builder	Built	Cost in Marks (000s)	Displacement (t = tonnes T = tons)	Length (m)	Breadth (m)	Draught (m)	Power (hp)	Revs (rpm)	Speed (kts)	Range (nm/kts)	Coal (t)	Oil (t)
KOLBERG	F Schichau, Danzig Construction no 814	1908–10	8118	4915t max 4362t des	130.5 oa 130.0 cwl	14.0	5.58 fwd 5.38 aft	30,400shp max 19,000shp des	515 max 515 des	26.3 max 25.5 des	3250/14	970 max 400 des	
	mod: Imperial Dockyard, Kiel	1916–17												115
MAINZ	AG Vulcan, Stettin Construction 288	1907–08	8777	4889t max 4362t des	,,	,,	5.60 fwd 5.27 aft	22,040shp max 20,200shp des	316 max 306 des	26.8 max 26.0 des	3630/14	1010 max 400 des	115 mod
CÖLN f fl	Germania Dockyard, Kiel Construction no 141	1908–11	8356	4864t max 4362t des	,,	,,	5.73 fwd 5.56 aft	29,036shp fwd 19,000shp des	307 max 540 des	26.8 max 25.5 des	3500/14	960 max 400 des	,,
AUGSBURG	Imperial Dockyard, Kiel Construction no 34	1908–11	7593	4882t max 4362t des	,,	,,	5.45 fwd 5.36 aft	31,033shp max 19,000shp des	528 max 540 des	26.7 max 25.5 des	,,	940 max 400 des	
	mod: Imperial Dockyard, Kiel	1916–17												115
3113gt/1401nt													

Construction

Laid down as light cruisers *Ersatz Greif*, *Ersatz Jagd*, *Ersatz Schwalbe* and *Ersatz Sperber* (official design, 1906–07). Transverse and longitudinal frame steel construction (thirteen watertight compartments, double bottom 50 per cent). Armour (two layers steel, one layer Krupp): deck 20–40–20(slopes 50)–80mm; coaming 100mm; (Krupp): CT roof 20mm, sides 100mm; shields 50mm. Depth 8.10m. Immersion increased by 1cm per 12.14t. Trim moment 8490–8650m-t.

Propulsion

Kolberg, two sets of Melms & Pfenniger turbines (four 3-bladed screws, 2.25m diameter); *Mainz*, two sets of AEG-Curtiss turbines (two 3-bladed screws, 3.45m diameter); *Cöln*, two sets of Germania turbines (two 3-bladed screws, 2.55m diameter, two 3-bladed screws, 1.78m diameter); *Augsburg*, two sets of Parsons turbines (four 3-bladed screws, 2.25m diameter), all in 2 + 2 engine rooms. Fifteen Marine-type boilers (*Augsburg* thirty, all others twenty-eight fireboxes, 16 atmospheres forced, *Cöln* 17 atmospheres forced, 4500–5070sq m) [after 1916 with supplementary oil firing] in 1 + 1 + 1 + 1 boiler rooms. On *Cöln* the original Zoelly turbines were replaced by Germania turbines before trials started. Three turbo-generators, 135kW 220V. One rudder.

Armament

Twelve 10.5cm/45 QF guns (1800 [2190] rounds), range 12,200m; four 5.2cm/55 QF guns (2000 rounds) (temporary); two 45cm TT (5 rounds), two lateral, under water. [*Kolberg* and *Augsburg*, six 15cm/45 QF guns (900 rounds), range 17,600m. After 1918 each was fitted with two 8.8cm/45 AA guns, plus two additional 50cm deck TT (4 rounds), and 100 mines.

Handling

Good sea-boats, though fairly stiff, and with severe roll; suffered from severe leeway. Not particularly manoeuvrable or handy, poor turning circle. Transverse metacentric height 0.83m, longitudinal 214m. Maximum stability moment at 46°. Fleet rudder angle 40°.

Complement

Crew: 18/349. Boats: one picket boat, one barge, one cutter, two yawls, two dinghies.

Notes

Colour scheme no 9. On *Mainz* the exhaust pipes were entirely exposed, and the upper bridge was originally as long as the lower bridge. *Cöln*'s lower bridge extended to 4m aft of the foremast, with a charthouse above; her engine room ventilators and boiler room ventilators were identical; she had a single-base compass platform. *Augsburg*'s upper bridge was as long as her lower bridge (the latter was enclosed) and the base of the bridge extended beyond the forward sponsons to 91.0m, decreasing slightly in height; her signal topmasts were as shown in the later drawing at all times. [*Kolberg*'s later appearance was as in the drawing, but with ventilators of the earlier type and a wireless telegraphy booth at 55.0m.] The upper forward bridge was originally as shown in the drawing of *Emden* on all ships. After *Cöln* rolled double U-section davits were fitted in place of the standard davits made of curved steel tubing.

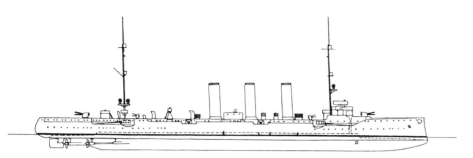

Kolberg (1913), *Mainz, Cöln, Augsburg*

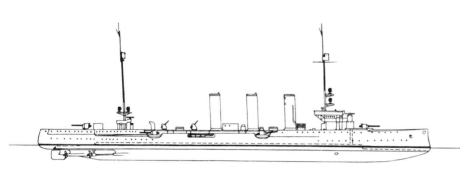

Augsburg (1918), *Kolberg*

Career

Kolberg launched 14 Nov 1908, commissioned 21 Jun 1910 into the fleet; served as a coastal defence vessel 1918. Stricken 5 Nov 1919; taken into the Reichsmarine; surrendered as French prize *W* at Cherbourg 28 Apr 1920; became French cruiser *Colmar*. Stricken 21 Jul 1927; broken up 1929 at Brest.

Mainz launched 23 Jan 1909, commissioned 1 Oct 1909 into the fleet. Sunk at 1410hrs on 28 Aug 1914 in the North Sea, position 53° 58N, 06° 42E, by gunfire and torpedoes from British cruisers and destroyers; 89 dead.

Cöln launched 5 Jun 1909, commissioned 16 Jun 1911 into the fleet; also served as TFI flotilla flagship. Sunk at 1435hrs on 28 Aug 1914 in the North Sea, position 54° 13N, 06° 54E, by gunfire from British battle-cruisers; 507 dead. The wreck was moved in August 1979 to 54° 08'36"N, 06° 58'57"E; salvaged parts are now in the Cuxhaven Shipwreck Museum.

Augsburg launched 10 Jul 1909, commissioned 1 Oct 1910 for torpedo tests; served as a gunnery training ship 1912; coastal defence vessel and fleet unit 1914; surrendered as Japanese prize *Y* 3 Sept 1920; broken up 1922 at Dordrecht.

Magdeburg class

Construction

Laid down as light cruisers *Ersatz Bussard, Ersatz Falke, Ersatz Condor* and *Ersatz Cormoran* (official design, 1908–09, design officer MarObrt Bürkner). Longitudinal frame stringer steel construction (fourteen watertight compartments, *Breslau* sixteen watertight compartments, double bottom 45 percent). Krupp armour: deck 20–40(slopes 40)–60mm; collision bulkhead 40mm; munitions coaming 20mm; CT roof 20mm, sides 100mm; [rangefinder 30mm]; CWL 0–60–18mm; shields 50mm. Depth 8.20m. Immersion increased by 1cm per 13.26t. Trim moment 9250m-t.

Propulsion

Magdeburg, three sets of Bergmann turbines (three 3-bladed screws, 2.75m diameter); *Breslau*, two sets of AEG Vulcan turbines (four 3-bladed screws, 2.47m diameter); *Strassburg*, two sets of Marine-type turbines (two 3-bladed screws, 3.40m diameter); *Stralsund*, three sets of Bergmann turbines (three 3-bladed screws, 2.75m diameter) [after 1916–17 no central turbine and 3-bladed screw]; all in 2 + 2 engine rooms. Sixteen Marine-type boilers initially for coal firing only, later for mixed firing (thirty-two fireboxes, 16 atmospheres forced, 5454–5572sq m) in 1 + 1 + 1 + 1 + 1 boiler rooms. Four (*Breslau* two) turbo-generators, 320kW 220V. Standard cruiser rudder.

Armament

Twelve 10.5cm/45 QF guns (1800 rounds), range 12,200m; two 50cm TT (5 rounds), two lateral, under water [*Breslau* after 1916, two 15cm/45 QF guns (180 rounds), range 17,600m, ten 10.5cm/45 QF guns (1500 rounds), range 12,200m, two 50cm TT (5 rounds), two lateral under water; after 1917, eight 15cm/45 QF guns (741 rounds), two 50cm TT (5 rounds), two lateral, under water; *Strassburg* after 1915, seven 15cm/45 QF guns (980 rounds), two 8.8cm/45 QF guns, two 50cm TT (5 rounds), two lateral, under water plus two 50cm deck-mounted TT; *Stralsund* after 1916, seven 15cm/45 QF guns, two 8.8cm/45 guns, two 50cm deck TT]; all ships carried 120 mines.

Handling

Good sea-boats, with slight weather helm and gentle movements in swell, but made severe leeway. All ships were manoeuvrable, but slow into the turn. Speed loss in a head sea was slight, and in turns up to 60 percent. Transverse metacentric height 0.79m, longitudinal 229m. Maximum stability moment around 58°. Fleet rudder angle 40°.

Complement

Crew: 18/336. Boats: one picket boat, one barge, one cutter, two yawls, two dinghies.

Notes

Colour scheme no 9. These were the first ships with the new cruiser bow in place of a ram bow; they also saw the introduction of the longitudinal frame system to save weight. Steam pipes on the funnels varied as shown in the drawings. [After 1914–15 the lower bridge was extended by 3m aft, and spotting tops were fitted.] *Strassburg* had ventilators aft of the aft funnel, as shown in the *Karlsruhe* drawing; [the mainmast searchlights were side by side on a double platform at the original height; her bridge was as shown in the drawing of *Breslau*].

Career

Magdeburg launched 13 May 1911, commissioned 20 Aug 1912 as a torpedo test ship; served in the Baltic forces 1914. Scuttled and sunk at 0910hrs on 26 Aug 1914 near Odensholm, position 59° 18N, 23° 21N, after stranding in fog; 15 dead. The wreck was cannibalised and finally destroyed by the Russians, but the signal book was salvaged by divers and returned to the British Admiralty.

Breslau launched 16 May 1911, commissioned 10 May 1912 into the fleet; served abroad 1912; after 1914 she was also known by the Turkish name *Midilli*. Sunk at 0910hrs on 20 Jan 1918 in the Aegean Sea, position 40° 05N, 26° 02E, after striking five mines; 330 dead.

Name	Builder	Built	Cost in Marks (000s)	Displacement (t = tonnes T = tons)	Length (m)	Breadth (m)	Draught (m)	Power (hp)	Revs (rpm)	Speed (kts)	Range (nm/kts)	Coal (t)	Oil (t)
MAGDEBURG	AG 'Weser', Bremen Construction no 171	1910–12	8058	4570t max 4535t des	138.7 oa 136.0 cwl	13.5	4.40 fwd 5.16 aft	29,904shp max 25,000shp des	431 max 435 des	27.6 max 27.0 des	(5820/12) (900/25)	1200 max 450 des	106
BRESLAU	AG Vulcan, Stettin Construction no 312 mod: Imperial Ottoman Dockyard, Stenia	1910–12 1915–16 1916–17	7961	5281t max 4564t des	,,	,,	4.93 fwd 5.73 aft	33,482shp max 25,000shp des	484 max 435 des	27.5 max 27.0 des	,,	,,	,,
STRASSBURG	Imperial Dockyard, Wilhelmshaven Construction no 32 mod: Imperial Dockyard Kiel	1910–12 1915	7302	,,	,,	,,	4.25 fwd 5.06 aft	33,742shp max 25,000shp des	442 max 435 des	28.2 max 27.0 des	,,	,,	,,
STRALSUND 2nd fl	AG 'Weser', Bremen Construction no 174 mod: Imperial Dockyard, Kiel 3566gt/1605nt	1910–12 1916	7741	5587t max 4570t des	,,	,,	4.46 fwd 5.10 aft	35,515shp max 25,000shp des	459 max 435 des	28.2 max 27.0 des	,,	,,	,,

Strassburg launched 24 Aug 1911, commissioned 9 Oct 1912 into the fleet; served abroad 1913–14, then with the fleet, and from 1919 with the Reichsmarine. Stricken 10 Mar 1920; surrendered 20 Jul 1920, under the name *O*, as an Italian prize at Cherbourg; became the Italian cruiser *Taranto*. Scuttled at 1400hrs on 9 Sept 1943 at La Spezia internal harbour; raised, planned for use as a block ship; sunk again 23 Oct 1943, by aircraft bombs. Raised again 7 Jan to 13 Apr 1944; sunk for the third time 23 Sept 1944, by aircraft bombs, broken up.

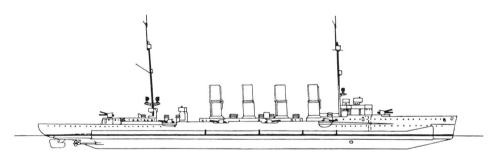

Strassburg (1912); *Magdeburg, Breslau* and *Stralsund* were very similar.

Stralsund (1916), *Strassburg*, final form

Stralsund launched 4 Nov 1911, commissioned 10 Dec 1912 into the fleet; served in the Reichsmarine 1919. Stricken 10 Mar 1920, and surrendered 3 Aug 1920, under the name *Z*, at Cherbourg, as a French prize; became the French cruiser *Mulhouse*. Stricken 15 Feb 1933; broken up at Brest; her bell is now in the Laboe naval memorial.

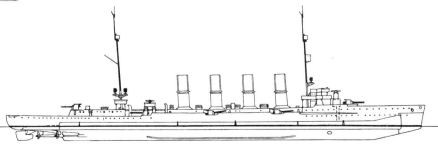

Breslau (1917), final form

Karlsruhe class

Name	Builder	Built	Cost in Marks (000s)	Displacement (t = tonnes T = tons)	Length (m)	Breadth (m)	Draught (m)	Power (hp)	Revs (rpm)	Speed (kts)	Range (nm/kts)	Coal (t)	Oil (t)
KARLSRUHE	Germania Dockyard, Kiel Construction no 181	1911–14	8126	6191t max 4900t des	142.2 oa 139.0 cwl	13.7	5.38 fwd 6.20 aft	37,885shp max 26,000shp des	444	28.5 max 27.8 des	5000/12 900/25	1300 max 400 des	200 max 70 des
ROSTOCK 3874gt/1743nt	Howaldtswerke, Kiel Construction no 560	1911–14	8124	,,	,,	,,	,,	43,628shp max 26,000shp des	449	29.3 max 27.8 des	,,	,,	,,

Construction

Laid down as light cruisers *Ersatz Seeadler* and *Ersatz Geier* (official design, 1910). Longitudinal frame stringer steel construction (fifteen watertight compartments, double bottom 45 percent). Armour: see *Magdeburg* class. Depth 8.50m. Immersion increased by 1cm per 14t. Trim moment 9320m-t.

Propulsion

Two sets of Marine-type turbines (two 3-bladed screws, 3.5m diameter) in 2 + 2 engine rooms. Twelve coal-fired Marine-type boilers plus two oil-fired double-ended Marine-type boilers (twenty-four plus four fireboxes, 16 atmospheres forced, 5800sq m) in 1 + 1 + 1 + 1 + 1 boiler rooms. Two turbo-generators 240 and 200kW 220V. Standard cruiser rudder.

Armament

Approx as *Magdeburg* class.

Handling

Approx as *Magdeburg* class.

Complement

Crew 18/355. Boats: one picket boat, one barge, one cutter, two yawls, two dinghies.

Notes

Colour scheme no 9. [*Rostock* was fitted with spotting tops after 1915. Both vessels had a conning tower on and under the lower bridge.]

Career

Karlsruhe launched 11 Nov 1912, commissioned 15 Jan 1914 for service abroad. Sunk at 1875hrs on 4 Nov 1914 in the West Indies, position 11° 07N, 55° 25W, after what is believed to have been a fuel oil and munitions explosion; 263 dead.

Rostock launched 12 Nov 1912, commissioned 5 Feb 1914 into the fleet; served after 1914 as a torpedo boat flagship. Scuttled and sunk at 0525hrs on 1 Jun 1916 in the North Sea, position 55° 40N, 06° 22E, by five torpedoes from the German *V 71* and *V 73*, after torpedo hits from British destroyers had crippled her; 14 dead.

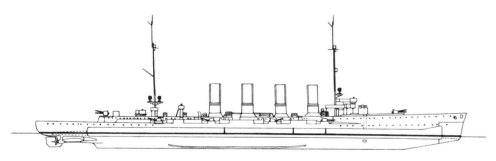

Karlsruhe (1914), *Rostock*

Graudenz class

Construction

Laid down as light cruisers *Ersatz Prinzess Wilhelm* and *Irene* (official design, 1911). Longitudinal frame stringer steel construction (seventeen watertight compartments, double bottom 47 percent). Armour: see *Magdeburg* class. Depth 8.53m. Immersion increased by 1cm per 14.11t. Trim moment not known.

Propulsion

Engines and screws as for *Karlsruhe*. Ten Marine-type coal-fired boilers plus two oil-fired double-ended Marine-type boilers (twenty plus four fireboxes, 16 atmospheres forced, 5560sq m) in 1 + 1 + 1 + 1 boiler rooms. Two turbo, one diesel generator, 260kW 220V. Standard cruiser rudder.

Armament

Twelve 10.5cm/45 QF guns (1800 rounds), range 12,200m; two 50cm TT (5 rounds), two lateral, under water [*Graudenz*, seven 15cm/45 QF guns (980 rounds), range 17,600m, two 8.8cm/45 AA guns, two 50cm TT (5 rounds), two lateral, under water plus two 50cm deck-mounted TT; *Regensburg* seven 15cm/45 QF guns (980 rounds), range 17,600m, two 8.8cm/45 AA guns, four 50cm deck-mounted TT, 120 mines].

Handling

Approx as *Magdeburg* class.

Complement

Crew: 21/364 (plus 3/14 as second command flagship or flotilla flagship). Boats: one picket boat, one barge, one cutter, two yawls, two dinghies.

Notes

Colour scheme no 9. *Graudenz* had grilles on the funnel tops at all times (see the drawing); [she was actually refitted with the aft deck-mounted 50cm TT only, and a lower foremast crow's nest after 1916]. *Regensburg*'s funnels were of the same form as those on *Wiesbaden*, but her funnel tops were never fitted with grilles.

Career

Graudenz launched 25 Oct 1913, commissioned 10 Aug 1914 into the fleet; served from 1916 as TFI flotilla flagship, and from 1919 in the Reichsmarine. Stricken 10 Mar 1920; surrendered 1 Jun 1920, under the name *E*, at Cherbourg as an Italian prize; became the Italian cruiser *Ancona*. Stricken 11 Mar 1937, broken up.

Name	Builder	Built	Cost in Marks (000s)	Displacement (t = tonnes T = tons)	Length (m)	Breadth (m)	Draught (m)	Power (hp)	Revs (rpm)	Speed (kts)	Range (nm/kts)	Coal (t)	Oil (t)
GRAUDENZ 2nd fl, f fl	Imperial Dockyard, Kiel Construction no 36	1912–14	c8800	6382t max 4912t des	142.7 oa 139.0 cwl	13.8	5.75 fwd 6.08 aft	26,000shp des	410 des	27.5 des	5500/12 1000/25	1280 max 380 des	375 max 100 des
	mod: Imperial Dockyard, Kiel	1915											
REGENSBURG 2nd fl, f fl	AG 'Weser', Bremen Construction no 197	1912–15	,,	,,	,,	,,	,,	,,	,,	,,	,,	,,	,,
	mod: Imperial Dockyard, Kiel	1917											
3949gt/1328nt													

Regensburg launched 25 Apr 1914, commissioned 3 Jan 1915 into the fleet; served from 1919 in the Reichsmarine. Stricken 10 Mar 1920; surrendered 4 Jun 1920 under the name *J*, at Cherbourg, as a French prize; became the French cruiser *Strasbourg* and served until 14 Jun 1936; reduced to a barrack ship at Lorient until 1944, then scuttled there to protect the U-boat pen gates against aircraft torpedoes; the wreck was still in existence in 1968.

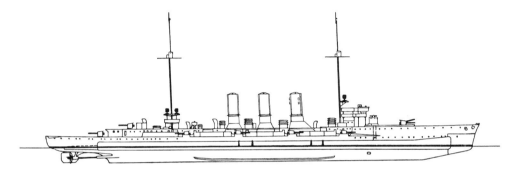

Graudenz (1915), *Regensburg*, first form

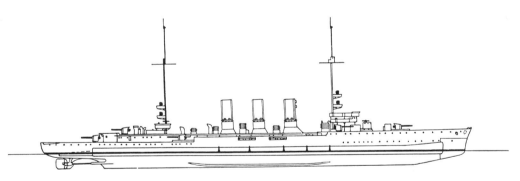

Regensburg (1917), *Graudenz*, final form

Pillau class

Construction
Laid down as the Russian light cruisers *Maraviev Amurskyy* and *Admiral Nevelskoy* (these names were adopted when the keels were laid, according to Russian custom) (Schichau design, 1912). Transverse and longitudinal frame steel construction (sixteen watertight compartments, double bottom 51 percent). Armour (two layers steel, one layer Krupp): deck 20–80(slopes 40)mm; (Krupp): CT roof 50mm, sides 75mm; shields 50mm. Depth 8.15m. Immersion increased by 1cm per 12.37t. Trim moment approx 8800m-t.

Propulsion
Engines and screws as in *Karlsruhe* class. Six Yarrow double boilers plus four oil-fired Yarrow double boilers (twenty-four plus eight fireboxes, 18 atmospheres forced, area not known) in 1 + 1 + 1 + 1 boiler rooms. 1 + 1 + 1 funnels, oval in cross-section. Three turbogenerators, 360kW 220V. One rudder.

Armament
Russian (planned), eight 13cm/55 QF guns and four 6.3cm/55 QF guns. German, eight 15cm/45 QF guns (1024 rounds), range 17,600m; four 5.2cm/55 AA guns [replaced by two 8.8cm/45 AA guns]; two 50cm deck-mounted TT; 120 mines.

Handling
Approx as *Kolberg*, but turning and manoeuvring qualities were similar to *Magdeburg*.

Complement
Crew: 21/421. Boats: one picket boat, one barge, two yawls, two dinghies.

Name	Builder	Built	Cost in Marks (000s)	Displacement (t = tonnes T = tons)	Length (m)	Breadth (m)	Draught (m)	Power (hp)	Revs (rpm)	Speed (kts)	Range (nm/kts)	Coal (t)	Oil (t)
PILLAU	F Schichau, Danzig Construction no 893	1913–14		5252t max 4390t des	135.3 oa 134.3 cwl	13.6	5.98 fwd 5.31 aft	30,000shp des		27.5 des	4300/12	620 max 80 des	580 max 250 des
ELBING 3202gt/1095nt	F Schichau, Danzig Construction no 894	1913–15		,,	,,	,,	,,	,,		,,	,,	,,	,,

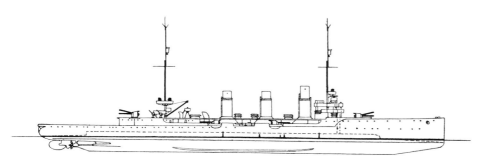

Pillau (1917); *Elbing* was similar

masts were as on *Frankfurt*, the rangefinder was mounted on the CT platform, the forecastle extended to 82.0m and the deckhouse back to 52.0m, and the bulwark was 0.5m higher forward of the deckhouse.

Career

Pillau launched 11 Apr 1914 as *Muraviev Amurskyy*; requisitioned 5 Aug 1914 and renamed *Pillau*, commissioned 14 Dec 1914 into the fleet; served in the Reichsmarine 1919. Stricken 5 Nov 1919, and surrendered 20 Jul 1920, under the name *U*, at Cherbourg as an Italian prize; became the Italian cruiser *Bari*. Sunk early on 28 Jun 1943 at Livorno, by US aircraft bombs; wreck broken up 1944.

Elbing launched 21 Nov 1914; requisitioned 5 Aug 1914 while on the stocks, commissioned 4 Sept 1915 into the fleet. Sunk at approx 0300hrs on 1 Jun 1916 in the North Sea, position 55° 49N, 05° 54E, after colliding with *Posen* at 0030hrs; 4 dead.

Notes

Colour scheme no 9. *Pillau* was fitted with spotting tops initially 4m lower, at the crosstrees, and the rangefinder platform extended 2m further forward [this was later removed and the rangefinder was installed on the CT compass platform; the upper bridge was modified several times]. *Elbing* had a foremast searchlight platform 1.5m lower, the steps of the two aft funnels were 3m lower, and all funnels were 1m higher; the

Wiesbaden class

Name	Builder	Built	Cost in Marks (000s)	Displacement (t = tonnes T = tons)	Length (m)	Breadth (m)	Draught (m)	Power (hp)	Revs (rpm)	Speed (kts)	Range (nm/kts)	Coal (t)	Oil (t)
WIESBADEN	AG Vulcan, Stettin Construction no 357	1913–15		6601t max 5180t des	145.3 oa 141.7 cwl	13.9	5.76 fwd 6.06 aft	31,000shp des		27.5 des	4800/12 1200/25	1280 max 350 des	470 max 150 des
FRANKFURT 4001gt/1331nt	Imperial Dockyard, Kiel Construction no 40	1913–15		,,	,,	,,	,,	,,		,,	,,	,,	,,

Construction

Laid down as light cruisers *Ersatz Gefion* and *Ersatz Hela* (official design, 1912). Construction and armour approx as *Graudenz*. Depth 8.62m. Immersion increased by 1cm per 14.83t. Trim moment 10,320m-t.

Propulsion

Frankfurt was equipped as *Karlsruhe*. *Wiesbaden* was fitted with two sets of Marine-type turbines, one shaft with a Föttinger transformer, one shaft ditto plus a cruise turbine, with gear transmission. Boilers were as in *Graudenz*. Two turbo and one diesel generators, 300kW 220V; *Frankfurt* two turbo-generators, 240kW 220V. Standard cruiser rudder.

Armament

Eight 15cm/45 QF guns (1024 rounds), range 17,600m; four 5.2cm/44 AA guns [two 8.8cm/45 AA guns]; four 50cm TT (8 rounds), two lateral, under water, two deck mounted; 120 mines.

Handling

Approx as for *Magdeburg*.

Complement

Crew: 17/457. Boats: one picket boat, one barge, one cutter, two yawls, two dinghies.

Notes

Frankfurt was fitted with a complete mantle around the central, circular cross-section, funnel up to the top edge, with a step temporarily painted as a disguise; [a foremast crow's nest was fitted 6m below the cross-trees, and two searchlights were mounted on a single platform on each mast, one above the other]. *Frankfurt*'s forward and central funnels, and *Wiesbaden*'s forward funnel were circular in cross-section, all others oval. Steam pipes on all funnels were approx as on *Regensburg*.

Career

Wiesbaden launched 20 Jan 1915, commissioned 23 Aug 1915 into the fleet. Sunk at 0245hrs on 1 Jun 1916 in the North Sea, position 57° 01N, 05° 53E, by gunfire from the British battle fleet; 589 dead.

Frankfurt launched 20 Mar 1915, commissioned 20 Aug 1915 into the fleet; interned at Scapa Flow after 26 Nov 1918; an unsuccessful attempt was made to scuttle the ship on 21 Jun 1919, and she was beached by British ships, and salvaged in July 1919, and became a US prize. Sunk at 1825hrs on 18 Jul 1921 off Cape Henry (Virginia), by heavy aircraft bombs on test.

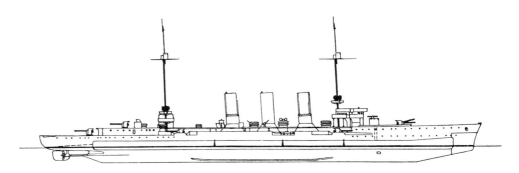

Frankfurt (1916), *Wiesbaden*

Brummer class

Name	Builder	Built	Cost in Marks (000s)	Displacement (t = tonnes T = tons)	Length (m)	Breadth (m)	Draught (m)	Power (hp)	Revs (rpm)	Speed (kts)	Range (nm/kts)	Coal (t)	Oil (t)
BRUMMER	AG Vulcan, Stettin Construction no 422	1915–16		5856t max 4385t des	140.4 oa 135.0 cwl	13.2	6.00 fwd 5.88 aft	42,797shp max 33,000shp des	366	28.0 max 28.0 des	5800/12 1400/25	600 max 300 des	1000 max 500 des
BREMSE 3615gt/1632nt	AG Vulcan, Stettin Construction no 423	1915–16		,,	,,	,,	,,	47,748shp max 33,000shp des	382	28.1 max 28.0 des	,,	,,	,,

Construction

Laid down as mine steamers *C* and *D* (official design 1914, design officer MarObrt Ahnhudt). Longitudinal frame stringer steel construction (twenty-one watertight compartments, double bottom 44 percent). Krupp armour: deck 15mm; CT roof 20mm, sides 100mm; CWL 0–40–0mm; shields 50mm. Depth 8.9m. Immersion increased by 1cm per 12.31t. Trim moment 8650m-t.

Propulsion

Two sets of turbines (requisitioned units intended for the new Russian battlecruiser *Navarin*) (two 3-bladed screws, 3.2m diameter) in 1 + 1 engine rooms. Two coal-fired Marine-type boilers and four oil-fired Marine-type boilers (twelve fireboxes, 18 atmospheres forced, 5600sq m) in 1 + 1 + 1 + 1 + 1 + 1 boiler rooms. Two turbo and one diesel generators, 180kW 110V. Standard cruiser rudder.

Armament

Four 15cm/45 QF guns (600 rounds), range 17,600m; two 8.8cm/45 AA guns; two 50cm deck-mounted TT (4 rounds); 400 mines.

Handling

Extremely good sea-boats, with slight lee helm; very crank, but with gentle motion. Manoeuvrability and turning circle good, speed losses in head sea slight, in turns up to 60 percent; made severe leeway.

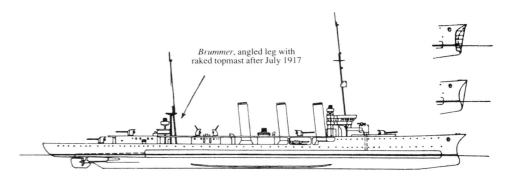

Brummer, angled leg with raked topmast after July 1917

Brummer (1918), *Bremse*

Complement

Crew: 16/293. Boats: one picket boat, one barge, two dinghies.

Notes

Colour scheme no 9. *Bremse* and until July 1917 *Brummer* also had a vertical main topmast, with a mast base without the angled strut and crosstrees; both ships could lower their main topmasts and stow them on superstructure deck, so that their appearance mimicked that of British cruisers of the *Aurora* class. The bow, also mimicking the *Aurora* class, was disguised with sheet metal during construction (see the supplementary drawing). The four turbine sets in both ships were originally built for the Russian battlecruiser *Navarin*, which was requisitioned in 1914. It is alleged that there was a third ship of this class identical to *Lübeck*, whose appearance was matched deliberately to that of *Brummer* during a refit carried out at the same dockyard at the same time (see the drawing of *Lübeck*); but there is no evidence of this. The funnels on both ships were of the same form as those of *Wiesbaden*.

Career

Brummer launched 11 Dec 1915, commissioned 2 Apr 1916 into the fleet; interned at Scapa Flow from 26 Nov 1918. Scuttled and sunk at 1305hrs on 21 Jun 1919.

Bremse launched 11 Mar 1916, commissioned 1 Jul 1916 into the fleet; interned at Scapa Flow from 26 Nov 1918. Scuttled and sunk at 1430hrs on 21 Jun 1919; raised 27 Nov 1929, and broken up 1932–33 at Lyness.

Königsberg class

Name	Builder	Built	Cost in Marks (000s)	Displacement (t = tonnes T = tons)	Length (m)	Breadth (m)	Draught (m)	Power (hp)	Revs (rpm)	Speed (kts)	Range (nm/kts)	Coal (t)	Oil (t)
KÖNIGSBERG 2nd fl	AG 'Weser', Bremen Construction no 210	1914–16		7125t max 5440t des	151.4 oa 145.8 cwl	14.2	5.96 fwd 6.32 aft	45,900shp max 31,000shp des	351	27.8 max 27.5 des	4850/12 1200/27	1340 max 350 des	500 max 150 des
KARLSRUHE	Imperial Dockyard, Kiel Construction no 41	1915–16		,,	,,	,,	,,	55,700shp max 31,000shp des	355	27.7 max 27.5 des	,,	,,	,,
EMDEN 2nd fl, f fl	AG 'Weser', Bremen Construction no 211	1914–16		,,	,,	,,	,,	50,216shp max 31,000shp des	350	27.7 max 27.5 des	,,	,,	,,
NÜRNBERG	Howaldtswerke, Kiel Construction no 595	1915–17		,,	,,	,,	,,						
4557gt/2051nt													

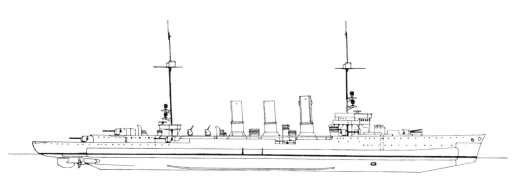

Königsberg (1918), *Emden, Nürnberg; Karlsruhe* was very similar.

Construction

Built as light cruisers *Ersatz Gazelle, Ersatz Niobe, Ersatz Nymphe* and *Ersatz Thetis* (official design, 1913). Longitudinal frame stringer steel construction (eighteen watertight compartments, double bottom 45 percent). Armour as in *Magdeburg*, plus mine hold deck 20mm, sides 30mm. Depth 8.76m. Immersion increased by 1cm per 15.53t. Trim moment 10,690m-t.

Propulsion

Engines, screws and boilers as in *Graudenz* (5740sq m), but *Karlsruhe* was fitted with two sets of Marine-type turbines, whose high pressure turbines worked via gear transmission. Two turbo and one diesel generators, 300kW 220V. Standard cruiser rudder.

Armament

Eight 15cm/45 QF guns (1040 rounds), range 17,600m; two 8.8cm/45 AA guns; four 50cm TT (8 rounds), two lateral, under water, two deck-mounted; 200 mines.

Handling

Approx as *Magdeburg* class, but stern heavy.

Complement

Crew: 17/458 (plus 6/20 as second command flagship). Boats: one picket boat, one barge, one cutter, two yawls, two dinghies.

Notes

Colour scheme no 9. *Karlsruhe* and *Nürnberg* had a 9.8m wide deckhouse on the after deck, and the upper bridge extended to 1.5m aft of the foremast, the command bridge to 5.5m aft of foremast; *Nürnberg* had recessed anchor hawses, to port as shown on *Cöln*, to starboard a vertical experimental pattern. *Königsberg* and *Emden* had a 5.5m wide deckhouse on the after deck, and the upper bridge extended to 3.5m aft of the foremast, the command bridge to 4m aft of foremast. The funnels on all vessels were of the same form as those on *Wiesbaden*.

Career

Königsberg launched 18 Dec 1915, commissioned 12 Aug 1916 into the fleet; served in the Reichsmarine 1919. Stricken 31 May 1920 and surrendered 20 Jul 1920, under the name *A*, at Cherbourg as a French prize; became the French cruiser *Metz*. Stricken 18 Aug 1933; broken up 1936 at Brest.

Karlsruhe launched 31 Jan 1916, commissioned 15 Nov 1916 into the fleet; interned at Scapa Flow from 23 Nov 1918. Scuttled and sunk at 1550hrs on 21 Jun 1919; wreck sold for breaking 1962.

Emden launched 1 Feb 1916, commissioned 16 Dec 1916 into the fleet and as TFI second command flagship; interned at Scapa Flow from 26 Nov 1918. An attempt was made to scuttle the ship on 21 Jun 1919 but she was beached by British ships and salvaged; she became a French prize 11 Mar 1920; used in explosives experiments after 1922; broken up by 1926 at Caën.

Nürnberg launched 14 Apr 1916, commissioned 15 Feb 1917 into the fleet; interned at Scapa Flow from 26 Nov 1918. She was beached 21 Jun 1919 after being scuttled, and salvaged during July 1919. Sunk 7 Jul 1922 off the Isle of Wight during gunnery tests.

Cöln class

Name	Builder	Built	Cost in Marks (000s)	Displacement (t = tonnes T = tons)	Length (m)	Breadth (m)	Draught (m)	Power (hp)	Revs (rpm)	Speed (kts)	Range (nm/kts)	Coal (t)	Oil (t)
CÖLN	Blohm & Voss, Hamburg Construction no 247	1915–18		7486t max 5620t des	155.5 oa 149.8 cwl	14.2	6.01 fwd 6.43 aft	48,708shp max	358	29.3	c6000/12	1100 max 300 des	1050 max 200 des
WIESBADEN	AG Vulcan, Stettin Construction no 433	1915–		,,	,,	,,	,,	31,000shp des		27.5 des	5400/12 1200/25	1100 max 300 des	800 max 200 des
DRESDEN	Howaldtswerke, Kiel Construction no 601	1916–18		,,	,,	,,	,,	49,428shp max 31,000shp des	338	27.8 max 27.5 des	,,	,,	,,
MAGDEBURG	Howaldtswerke, Kiel Construction no 602	1916–		,,	,,	,,	,,	31,000shp des		27.5 des	,,	,,	,,
LEIPZIG	AG 'Weser', Bremen Construction no 235	1915–		,,	,,	,,	,,	,,		,,	,,	,,	,,
ROSTOCK	AG Vulcan, Stettin Construction no 434	1915–											
FRAUENLOB	Imperial Dockyard, Kiel Construction no 42	1915–											
ERSATZ CÖLN	AG 'Weser', Bremen Construction no 236	1916					as above						
ERSATZ EMDEN	AG 'Weser', Bremen Construction no 237	1916–											
ERSATZ KARLSRUHE (A)	Imperial Dockyard, Kiel Construction no 43	1916–											
4650gt/2200nt													

Construction

Laid down as light cruisers *Ersatz Ariadne*, *Ersatz Nürnberg*, *Ersatz Dresden*, *Ersatz Magdeburg*, *Ersatz Leipzig*, *Ersatz Mainz*, *Ersatz Königsberg*, *Ersatz Cöln*, *Ersatz Emden* and *Ersatz Karlsruhe* (A) (official design, 1914). Longitudinal frame stringer steel construction (twenty-four watertight compartments, double bottom 45 percent). Armour as in the *Magdeburg* class. Depth 8.76m.

Propulsion

Engines and screws as in the *Karlsruhe* class. Eight coal-fired Marine-type boilers plus six oil-fired Marine-type boilers (16 atmospheres forced, 5700sq m) in 1 + 1 + 1 + 1 + 1 boiler rooms. Two turbo and one diesel generators, 300kW 220V. Standard cruiser rudder.

Armament

Eight 15cm/45 QF guns (1040 rounds), range 17,600m; three 8.8cm/45 AA guns [reduced to two in 1918]; four 60cm deck-mounted TT (8 rounds); 200 mines.

Handling

Approx as *Magdeburg* class, but slightly stern heavy.

Complement

Crew: 17/542. Boats: one picket boat, one barge, one cutter, two yawls, two dinghies.

Notes

Two 15cm guns were mounted on the forecastle on *Cöln*, and on the upper deck on the other ships; roll damping systems were fitted on *Frauenlob*, *Ersatz Karlsruhe* (A) and *Cöln*.

Career

Cöln launched 5 Oct 1916, commissioned 17 Jan 1918 into the fleet; interned at Scapa Flow from 22 Nov

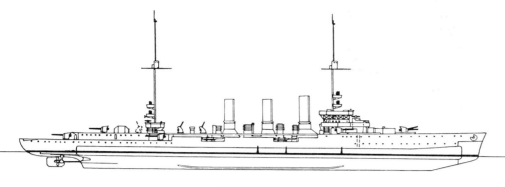

Cöln (1918)

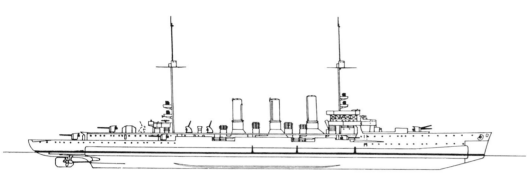

Dresden (1918), *Wiesbaden, Magdeburg, Leipzig, Rostock, Frauenlob, Ersatz Karlsruhe, Ersatz Cöln, Ersatz Emden*

1918. Scuttled and sunk at 1350hrs on 21 Jun 1919.

Wiesbaden launched 3 Mar 1917; construction was halted about 5 months before completion, in December 1918. Stricken 17 Nov 1919; reconstruction plans were produced, but the ship was broken up in 1920.

Dresden launched 25 Apr 1917, commissioned 28 Mar 1918 into the fleet; interned at Scapa Flow from 16 Dec 1918. Beached after being scuttled at 1350hrs on 21 Jun 1919, and later broken up.

Magdeburg launched 17 Nov 1917. Stricken 17 Nov 1919, 9 months before completion; hull sold 28 Oct 1921 for 1,300,000M; broken up 1922 at Kiel-Nordmole.

Leipzig launched 28 Jan 1918. Stricken 17 Nov 1919, 7 months before completion; demilitarised, sold and broken up 1921 at Hamburg.

Rostock launched 6 Apr 1918. Stricken 17 Nov 1919, 7 months before completion; sold 1921, broken up at Hamburg.

Frauenlob launched 16 Sept 1918. Stricken 17 Nov 1919, about 13 months before completion; broken up 1921 at Deutsche Werke, Kiel.

Ersatz Karlsruhe (**A**) contract granted 20 Aug 1915; broken up at frame stage in 1920.

Ersatz Cöln stricken 17 Nov 1919, 13 months before completion; sold 21 Jun 1921 for about 400,000M; broken up 1921 at Hamburg by Köhlbrandwerft.

Ersatz Emden stricken 17 Nov 1919, 10 months before completion; sold 25 Jun 1921 for about 400,000M; broken up 1921 at Hamburg Altenwärder by P Berendsohn.

Fleet cruisers (planned) 1916

FK 1 class

Name	Builder	Built	Cost in Marks (000s)	Displacement (t = tonnes T = tons)	Length (m)	Breadth (m)	Draught (m)	Power (hp)	Revs (rpm)	Speed (kts)	Range (nm/kts)	Coal (t)	Oil (t)
FK 1	—	—		3800t max 3000t des	130 oa 128 cwl	11.6	4.9 fwd 4.1 aft	48,000shp max 35,000shp des		32 max 30 des	2800/17	—	1000 max 200 des
FK 1a	—	—		4850t max 4025t des	136 oa 131 cwl	12.4	4.6 aft	52,000shp des		33 des		—	1150 max 300 des

Construction
Designed as fleet cruisers (official design study, 1916). Longitudinal frame stringer steel construction (fifteen watertight compartments, double bottom approx 52 percent). Krupp armour: deck 15–30(slopes 30)mm; collision bulkhead 30mm; munitions coaming 20mm; CT roof 20mm, sides 80mm; rangefinder 30mm; CWL 0–40–18mm; shields 50mm. Depth 7.85m.

Propulsion
Two sets of Marine-type turbines (two 3-bladed screws, 3.5m diameter) in 1 + 1 engine rooms. Five oil-fired Marine-type boilers (fifteen fireboxes, 18 atmospheres forced, approx 8000sq m) and five oil-fired double-ended Marine-type boilers (in *FK 1a*) in 1 + 1 + 1 + 1 + 1 boiler rooms. Three diesel generators, 300kW 220V. One standard cruiser rudder.

Armament
Five 15cm/45 QF guns (500 and 650 rounds), range 17,600m; two 8.8cm/45 AA guns (200 rounds); four 60cm deck-mounted TT (6 and 8 rounds) in twin mounts; 100 mines (*FK 1a* only).

Complement
Crew: 15/342 or similar. Boats: one picket boat, one barge, two yawls, one dinghy.

Notes
The smallest of a series of design studies for a pure fleet cruiser, a type which had not previously been represented in the German fleet. *FK 1* was a parallel development to the contemporary C class British Light Cruisers (Scouts), at the express wish of Kaiser Wilhelm II.

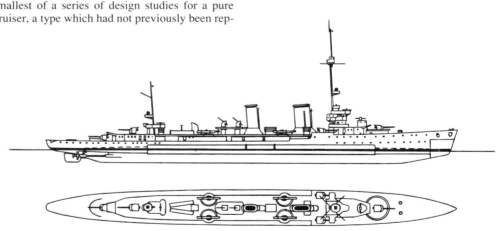

Fleet cruiser *FK 1a*, 1916 design.

FK 2 class

Construction
Designed as fleet cruisers (official design studies, 1916). Longitudinal frame stringer steel construction (double bottom approx 45–50 percent). Krupp armour: deck 20mm; CT sides 100mm; CWL 0–50mm (*FK 4*, 60–0mm).

Propulsion
FK 2, two sets of Marine-type turbines (two screws) in 1 + 1 engine rooms, six oil-fired Marine-type boilers in 1 + 1 + 1 + 1 + 1 + 1 boiler rooms, one standard

Name	Builder	Built	Cost in Marks (000s)	Displacement (t = tonnes T = tons)	Length (m)	Breadth (m)	Draught (m)	Power (hp)	Revs (rpm)	Speed (kts)	Range (nm/kts)	Coal (t)	Oil (t)
FK 2	—	—		5350t max 4500t des	144 oa 139 cwl	13.0	5.5 fwd 4.8 aft	60,000shp max 46,000shp des		32 max 30 des	2800/17	—	1200 max 350 des
FK 3	—	—		6900t max 6000t des	159 oa 155 cwl	14.2	5.8 fwd 5.2 aft	70,000shp max 55,000shp des	,,	,,		—	1400 max 500 des
FK 4	—	—		8650t max 7500t des	170 cwl	15.4	6.0 fwd 5.4 aft	73,000shp max 60,000shp des		32 max 31 des	,,	800	1000 max 650 des

cruiser rudder; *FK 3*, three sets of Marine-type turbines (three screws) in 2 + 0 + 1 engine rooms, thirteen oil-fired Marine-type boilers in 1 + 1 + 1 + 1 + 1 + 1 + 1 boiler rooms, one standard cruiser rudder; *FK 4*, Marine-type turbines, six coal-fired Marine-type boilers plus nine oil-fired Marine-type boilers.

Armament

FK 2, five 15cm/45 QF guns (550 rounds), range 17,600m, two 8.8cm/45 AA guns (200 rounds), four 60cm deck-mounted TT (6 rounds) in twin mounts; *FK 3*, seven 15cm/45 QF guns (840 rounds), range 17,600m, three 8.8cm/45 AA guns (300 rounds), four 60cm deck-mounted TT (6 rounds); *FK 4*, eight 15cm/45 QF guns (1040 rounds), range 17,600m, three 8.8cm/45 AA guns (300 rounds), four 60cm deck-mounted TT (6 rounds).

Notes

These were designs for fleet cruisers, intended to supersede the former type of German light cruisers. *FK 2* had a funnel arrangement as on *Pillau*, but with a short forecastle and gun arrangement as on *Dresden* (1918). *FK 3* had a long forecastle, very similar to that on *Cöln* (1918). Drawings of *FK 4* are not yet available. No evidence has come to light on whether a decision was made on implementing one of these designs.

Light cruisers 1925–1940

Emden

Name	Builder	Built	Cost in Marks (000s)	Displacement (t = tonnes T = tons)	Length (m)	Breadth (m)	Draught (m)	Power (hp)	Revs (rpm)	Speed (kts)	Range (nm/kts)	Coal (t)	Oil (t)
EMDEN	Navy Dockyard, Wilhelmshaven Construction no 100	1921–25		6990T max 6056t des 5300T std	155.1 oa 150.5 cwl	14.2	5.93 max 5.30 des 5.15 std	45,900shp max 46,500shp des	295 max	29.4 max 29.0 des	6700/12 6500/15 5200/18	875 max 300 des	1170 max 200 des
	mod: Navy Dockyard Wilhelmshaven	1933–34									5300/18		1266
4775gt/2464nt													

Construction

Laid down as cruiser *A* (*Ersatz Niobe*) (official design 1921, design officer Rgrat Meienreis (?)). Longitudinal frame stringer steel construction (seventeen watertight compartments, double bottom 56 percent). Krupp armour: deck 20–40(slopes 20)mm; collision bulkhead 40mm; munitions coaming 20mm; CT roof 20mm, sides 100mm, rear 50mm; CWL 0–50–0mm; shields 20mm. Depth 8.96m. Immersion increased by 1cm per 15.6t. Trim moment 12,160m-t.

Propulsion

Two sets of turbines with gear transmission by Brown, Boveri & Co, Mannheim (two 3-bladed screws, 3.75m diameter) in 1 + 2 + 1 engine rooms and two transmission rooms. Four coal-fired Marine-type boilers plus six oil-fired Marine-type boilers (16 atmospheres forced, 1629 plus 3009sq m) [the former replaced by four oil-fired Marine-type boilers (1800sq m) in 1 + 1 + 1 + 1 boiler rooms]. Two electricity plants, with three diesel generators, 420kW 220V. Standard cruiser rudder. Total power installation 25.2kg/shp.

Armament

Eight 15cm/55 QF guns in double mounts midships were planned, but gun manufacture was prevented by the disarmament commission; therefore she was fitted from existing reserve stocks with eight 15cm/45 QF guns (960 rounds), −10° +40°, range 17,600m; two, later three 8.8cm/45 AA guns (900–1200 rounds); four (eight as planned) 50cm deck-mounted TT [after 1934 53.5cm TT] (12 rounds). [After 1938 an additional two, later four, 3.7cm AA guns and up to eighteen 2cm AA guns were fitted, and 120 mines; in 1942 the 15cm QF guns were replaced by 15cm QF guns in torpedo boat mountings, and the 53.5cm TT were reduced to two; AA armament in 1945 was nine 3.7cm and six 2cm guns.]

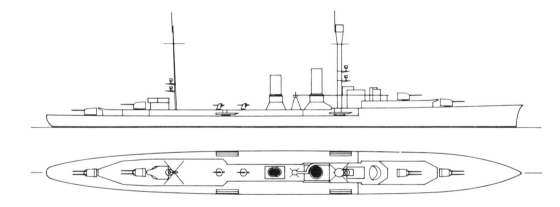

Emden; 1921 design. *Mrva*

Handling

As *Magdeburg*, but with slight lee helm.

Complement

Crew: 19/464 [29/445, plus 162 sea cadets; in 1940, 26/556; in training service, 30/653]. Six boats.

Notes

Colour scheme no 9, plus camouflage schemes and dark grey overall. *Emden* showed considerable differences from all earlier cruisers; the only feature retained from the *Cöln/Ersatz Emden* design was the outline, retained due to the closure of the navy experimental institute and staff shortages in the K-Amt (the principal warship building office). She was the world's first large ship whose main structural components were part-welded. Her range was increased by about 50 percent compared with earlier small cruisers.

During trials the Tulpen (ie, the battle mast) mast

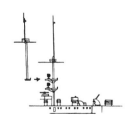

Mainmast before and after 1926

Foremast 1926

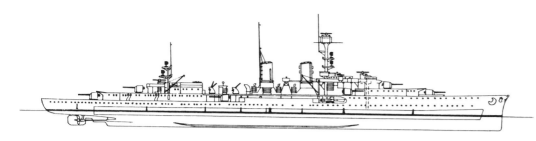

Emden (1936)

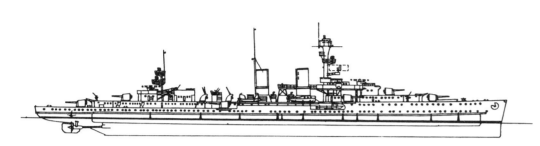

Emden (1944)

was reduced by about 5m in height because of vibration; the lower mainmast was also shortened, but the topmast was extended. After 1929 a navigation platform was fitted on the ventilator at 58m. After the 1934 refit the funnels were about 2m lower, with slightly angled tops, double wireless telegraphy gaffs were fitted on the aft funnel, and a new stem was fitted. After 1937 a large wireless telegraphy topmast was fitted on the aft funnel, with angled struts. After 1940–41 a degaussing coil was fitted at the top edge of the CWL armour, and a radar trials mattress was fitted instead of the lower searchlight on modified platform on the Tulpen mast. The planned 1940 refit to four double 15cm turrets from destroyer 1936 A (designed by MarBrt Strohbusch), and an AA armament increase by one 8.8cm and two 3.7cm guns (176t extra weight) was not carried out because of the war. In 1942 the ship's maximum speed was still 26kts, and continuous speed 24kts.]

Career

Emden launched 7 Jan 1925, commissioned 15 Oct 1925 as a training cruiser; made various voyages abroad; front line service after 1939. Damaged 13–14 Apr 1945 at Deutsche Werke, Kiel, by an aircraft bomb; transferred to Heikendorfer Bay; scuttled and sunk there 3 May 1945, position 54° 22N, 10° 10E; broken up by 1949. Her bow ornament is now in the German Museum, Munich.

Königsberg class

Name	Builder	Built	Cost in Marks (000s)	Displacement (t = tonnes T = tons)	Length (m)	Breadth (m)	Draught (m)	Power (hp)	Revs (rpm)	Speed (kts)	Range (nm/kts)	Coal (t)	Oil (t)
KÖNIGSBERG 2nd fl	Navy Dockyard, Wilhelmshaven Construction no 108	1926–29	38,000	7700T max 6750t des 6000T std	174.0 oa 169.0 cwl	15.2	6.28 max 5.42 des 5.56 std	68,200shp max 65,000shp des + 1800shp	363 max 360 des 900	32.1 max 32.0 des 10.0	(5700/19) (7300/17)	—	1350 max 600 des
KARLSRUHE	Deutsche Werke, Kiel Construction no 207	1926–29	36,000	,,	,,	,,	,,	,,	371 max 360 des 900	,,	,,	—	,,
	mod: KM Dockyard, Wilhelmshaven	1938–39	5700	8350T max 6730T des		16.8	6.20 max		348 max	30.0 max	3340/18		+ 110
KÖLN	Navy Dockyard, Wilhelmshaven Construction no 116	1926–30	36,000	7700T max 6750t des 6000T std	,,	15.2	6.28 max 5.42 des 5.56 std	68,485shp max 65,000shp des + 1800shp	376 max 360 des 900	32.5 max 32.0 des 10.0	(5700/19) (7300/17)	—	1350 max 600 des

5475gt (*Königsberg*), 5443gt (*Karlsruhe*), 5342gt (*Köln*); all 2464nt

Construction

Laid down as cruiser B (*Ersatz Thetis*), C (*Ersatz Medusa*) and D (*Ersatz Arcona*) (official design 1924–25, design officer MarObBrt Ehrenberg). Longitudinal frame stringer steel construction, up to 85 percent welded (nineteen watertight compartments, double bottom 72 percent). Krupp armour: deck 20–40mm (no slope armour); collision bulkhead 20mm; torpedo bulkhead 15mm; CT roof 30mm, sides 100mm, rear 50mm; CWL (bulkhead 70)–50–(bulkhead 70)mm; turrets roof 20mm, sides 20mm, face 30mm, rear 20mm; barbettes, etc, 30mm [*Karlsruhe* was fitted with 10–14mm new outer plating and a new upper deck 16mm, all Wh armour]. Depth 9.25m. Immersion increased by 1cm per 19.98t. Trim moment 15,230m-t, uniform trim moment 16,367cu m/m.

Propulsion

Four sets of Marine-type turbines by Schichau, Elbing, Germania dockyard, Kiel, and Blohm & Voss, Hamburg, with gear transmission, plus two MAN

10-cylinder four-stroke diesels (900rpm primary revolutions) with hydraulic coupling to shafts (two 3-bladed screws, 4.1m diameter; *Köln*, 3.7m diameter) in 1 + 2 + 1 engine rooms and two diesel rooms aft of these. Six Marine-type double-ended oil-fired boilers (16 atmospheres forced, 6540sq m) in 1 + 1 + 1 + 1 boiler rooms. Two electricity plants with three turbo-generators and two diesel generators, 180 and 360kW 220V. One balanced rudder.

Armament

Nine 15cm/60 QF guns (1080 rounds), –10° +40°, range 25,700m; two 8.8cm/45 QF guns (800 rounds), range 10,000m; [from 1933 on (and *Köln* at all times) four 8.8cm/76 AA guns (1600 rounds), range 12,200m (after 1935–36 *Königsberg* two, the others six) and after 1940 six 8.8cm/76 AA guns (2400 rounds); after 1934 all ships had eight 3.7cm AA guns (9600 rounds) and up to eight 2cm AA guns (17,600 rounds); final armament for *Köln* (January 1945) was ten 3.7cm AA guns and twenty-four 2cm AA guns as planned, but only eight 3.7cm AA guns and eighteen 2cm AA guns actually fitted]; twelve [after mid-1940 only nine] 53.3cm deck-mounted TT (24 rounds) in triple mounts (torpedo calibre 50cm up to about 1934); one catapult and two seaplanes after 1935 [the latter was shipped on *Köln* after 1937; in 1939–40 trials were made of a Flettner Fl 265 helicopter on *Köln*, hence the landing platform on turret B]; approx 120 mines.

Handling

Moderately good sea-boats, but very crank, with up to about 20° heel with hard rudder. Very manoeuvrable, but early heel correction was necessary; slight lee helm. Speed loss in a head sea was slight, and in turns usually no more than 30 percent. [*Karlsruhe* was slightly stiffer after the refit.]

Complement

Crew: 21/493 (plus 6/20 as second flagship) [23/588–591, later a total of about 820–850 men]. Boats: two picket boats, two barges, two launches, one cutter, one dinghy.

Notes

Colour scheme no 9; camouflage scheme and, from 1943, overall dark grey for *Köln*. All scantlings were reduced to a minimum in order to maximise the ship's combat capability within the treaty restrictions on ship size; consequent overstressing in heavy seas resulted in fractures and cracks in the midship region (eg *Karlsruhe* required a repair from 7 to 14 Apr 1936 at San Diego, California, because of these problems). Restriction on the ships' use in the North and Baltic Seas was ordered, and also a fuel limit (680t). Reinforcement of longitudinal members to increase strength not carried out until the major reconstruction of *Karlsruhe* (June 1938–November 1939, MarBrt Strohbusch) [in which the beam was increased by new outer plating (in Wh armour), mounted 0.7m outboard of the old outer plating and side armour over about 55 percent of the ship's length, tapering into the old shape forward, aft and below. At the same time the cruise diesels and diesel exhaust pipes were removed, the deckhouses, funnels and searchlight arrangements modified, a new mainmast and a port aircraft crane were installed, and the 8.8cm AA guns were replaced by 10.5 AA guns].

Differences in appearance between the three *K* cruisers were as follows: *Königsberg* and *Köln* always had a single-storey foretop, *Karlsruhe* a two-storey foretop up to 1938 [single-storey after 1939]. *Königsberg* and *Karlsruhe* initially had no deckhouse between the battle mast and the forward funnel [after 1934 *Königsberg* had a single-storey deckhouse, and after 1936 *Karlsruhe* had a two-storey deckhouse]; *Köln* was without this deckhouse throughout her career. All ships initially carried aerials on a tall topmast on the battle mast [this topmast was shortened after 1931 on *Königsberg*; it was mounted on the rear face of the foretop on *Karlsruhe* and *Köln*]. Aerials were also initially carried on the funnel crosstrees; [in *Königsberg* after 1936, and *Karlsruhe* and *Köln* after 1935, a mast was mounted on the aft funnel]. *Karlsruhe* only had funnel caps, and only after the 1938–39 refit.

All ships initially had loading gear on each beam; *Königsberg* and *Karlsruhe* were fitted with a lattice crane after 1934; *Köln* after 1935 with an angled air-craft crane to port, and in 1937 with a loading crane to starboard, and loading gear to port, then after 1939 with a lattice crane to port, and finally after 1942 this was again replaced by loading gear. [*Königsberg* and *Köln* were fitted with a catapult after 1935, *Karlsruhe* after 1936; on *Köln* this was unshipped again after 1937. *Königsberg* and *Karlsruhe* were fitted with a degaussing coil after early 1940, *Köln* after mid-1940.] After 1937 *Königsberg* was temporarily fitted with experimental radio rangefinding equipment aft of the forward command position; *Köln* was fitted after 1942 with a FuMO 24 or FuMO 32 system on the forward command position.

All ships had restricted crew accommodation; crews exceeded design complements as follows: *Königsberg* by 21 percent, *Karlsruhe* and *Köln* by 27.5 percent.

Career

Königsberg launched 26 Mar 1927, commissioned 17 Apr 1929 into the fleet; served as a gunnery training ship 1936, and abroad. Capsized and sunk at 1051hrs on 10 Apr 1940 at the Skoldegrunds quay, Bergen, position 60° 24N, 05° 19E, after being hit by six British aircraft bombs at 0824hrs; 18 dead. Raised 17 Jul 1942, towed away and broken up.

Karlsruhe launched 20 Aug 1927, commissioned 6 Nov 1929 as a training cruiser (abroad); served in the fleet 1936, and again from 13 Nov 1939 after a thorough refit. Hit at 2250hrs on 9 Apr 1940 at Kristiansand South, position 58° 04N, 08° 04E, by a torpedo from the British submarine *Truant* at 1958hrs and then scuttled by two torpedoes from the German torpedo boat *Jaguar*; 11 dead.

Köln launched 23 May 1928, commissioned 15 Jan 1930 into the fleet; served as a training cruiser (abroad) 1932–33. Sunk 30 May 1945 at the Wilhelmshaven construction harbour by an aircraft bomb; settled on an even keel, with the aft artillery turrets still in use; finally blown up 2 May 1945 and broken up after 1946.

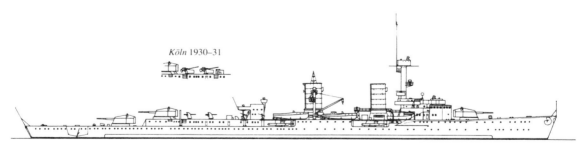

Köln 1930–31

Königsberg (1930); *Köln* and *Karlsruhe* were similar. *Mrva*

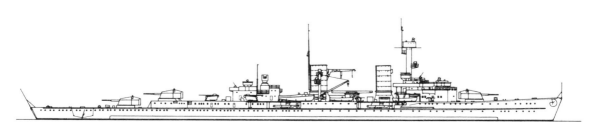

Königsberg (1940), final form. *Mrva*

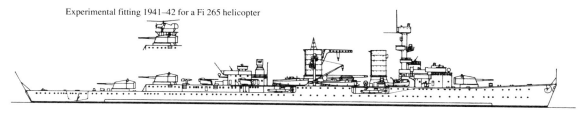

Experimental fitting 1941–42 for a Fi 265 helicopter

Köln (1935). *Mrva*

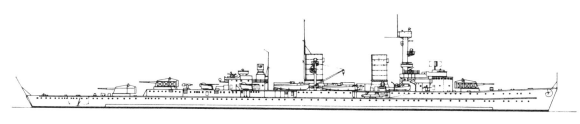

Köln (1942). *Mrva*

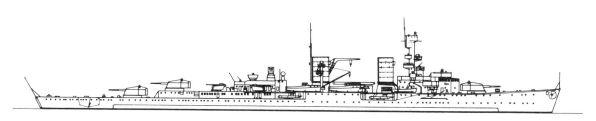

Karlsruhe (1936). *Mrva*

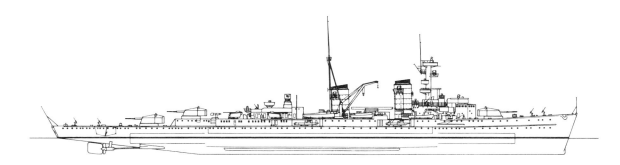

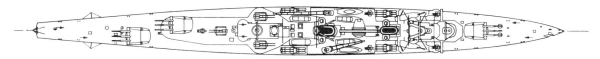

Karlsruhe (1940), final form. *Mrva*

Leipzig class

Name	Builder	Built	Cost in Marks (000s)	Displacement (t = tonnes T = tons)	Length (m)	Breadth (m)	Draught (m)	Power (hp)	Revs (rpm)	Speed (kts)	Range (nm/kts)	Coal (t)	Oil (t)
LEIPZIG 2nd fl	Navy Dockyard, Wilhelmshaven Construction no 117	1928–31	38,000	8100t max 6820t des 6310t std	177.0 oa 165.8 cwl	16.3	5.69 fwd 4.75 aft 4.88 std	65,585shp max 60,000shp des + 12,400shp	309 max 400 des + 600	31.9 max 32.0 des + 16.5	2800/ 16.5* 3900/10**	—	1200† max 550† des +310†† max 75†† des
NÜRNBERG 2nd fl	Deutsche Werke, Kiel Construction no 234	1933–34	40,000	9040t max 8060t des 7150t std	181.3 oa 170.0 des	··	5.74 fwd 4.75 aft 4.90 std	66,075shp max 60,000shp des + 12,400 shp	291 max 400 des + 600	32.3 max 32.0 des +16.5	2800/ 16.5* 3900/10**	—	1100† max 875† des +250†† max

5825gt/1816nt (*Leipzig*), 6264gt/1958nt (*Nürnberg*)

* turbines only   ** motors only
† fuel oil   †† diesel oil

Construction

Laid down as cruiser E (*Ersatz Amazone*) and F (*Ersatz Nymphe*) (official designs 1927 and 1933, design officer MarObBrt Blechschmidt). Longitudinal frame stringer steel construction, more than 90 percent welded (fourteen watertight compartments, double bottom 83 percent), bow and side bulges. Krupp nickel-steel armour (*Nürnberg*, Wh armour): deck 20mm; slope (quarter circle) 25mm; CT roof 50mm, sides 100m, deck 30mm, shaft 50mm; AA director 14mm; CWL 0–(bulkhead 20)35–50–50–35(slope 20)–18mm; turrets, etc, as on *Königsberg*; however on *Nürnberg* the CT shaft was 60mm, forward rangefinder roof 15mm, sides 15mm, AA director 14mm, foretop 20mm decks with 20mm bulkheads, CWL 0–(bulkhead 35)35–50–50–50–18(bulkhead 20)–18mm, turrets roof 20–32mm, face 80mm, sides 35mm, rear 20mm, barbettes 60mm, substructure 30mm. Depth 9.00m. Immersion increased by 1cm per 21.4 and 20.0t. Uniform trim moment 16,057 and 71,619cu m/m.

Propulsion

Two sets of Marine-type turbines by Germania dockyard, Kiel and Deutsche Werke, Kiel, with gear transmission, plus four MAN double-acting 7-cylinder two-stroke diesels with one central Vulcan transmission (*Leipzig* two 3-bladed screws, 4.25m diameter, one 3-bladed screw, 3.00m diameter; *Nürnberg* two 3-bladed screws, 4.0m diameter, one 3-bladed screw, 3.4m diameter) in 1 + 2 + 1 turbine rooms and transmission rooms, with 1 + 1 engine rooms aft of these. Six oil-fired Marine-type double-ended boilers (16 and 17 atmospheres forced, 6700 and 5510sq m) in 1 + 1 + 1 boiler rooms [*Leipzig* had four boilers only in 1 + 1 aft firing rooms after 1940]. Primary revolutions: turbines 2360rpm, motors 600rpm. *Leipzig* had three electricity plants, each with one 180kW turbo-generator, and one 180kW diesel generator, both at 220V, for a total output of 1080kW; *Nürnberg* had four electricity plants with a total of two 300kW turbo-generators and two 350kW diesel generators, all 220V, for a total output of 1300kW. One balanced rudder. The central 3-bladed screw originally had vane-type blades.

Armament

Nine 15cm/60 QF guns (1080–1500 rounds), –10° +40°, range 25,700m; *Leipzig* had two 8.8cm/45 AA guns [after 1934 four, later six, new 8.8cm/76 AA guns (800 and 1600 and 2400 rounds), from 1941 up to October 1944 eight 3.7cm AA guns and fourteen 2cm AA guns, after the collision in 1944 four 3.7cm, eight 2cm AA guns]; *Nürnberg* at all times carried eight 8.8cm/76 AA guns (3200 rounds), eight 3.7cm AA guns (9600 rounds) and various 2cm AA guns (2000 rounds each); twelve [reduced to six after 1941] 53.3cm deck-mounted TT (24 rounds); *Leipzig* carried 50cm torpedoes before 1934, [all TT deleted after 1944, and transferred to *Scharnhorst* and *Gneisenau*]; one catapult, two seaplanes after 1934; approx 120 mines.

Handling

Good sea-boats, with a gentle motion; excellent manoeuvrability at all speeds due to auxiliary manoeuvring gear (see *Lützow*, page 60). Both ships normally tended to lee helm, but weather helm in strong wind and sea. Both made very severe leeway at low speed, especially *Nürnberg* as a result of her large, solid superstructure. Both had active roll damping. At cruise speed the outboard 3-bladed screws were rotated by electric motors for a feathering effect (the resultant power saving was 2500shp). Restrictions were imposed on use and fuel as for *Nürnberg* (150t) for similar reasons to the K class cruisers (see page 119).

Complement

Crew: *Leipzig* 26/508 (plus 6/20 as second flagship) [later 30/628, finally 24/826]; *Nürnberg* 25/648 (plus 17/66 as second flagship) [finally 26/870]. Boats: two picket boats, two barges, two launches, two cutters.

Notes

Colour scheme no 9, light grey overall and camouflage schemes in 1943–44. An attempt was made to improve CWL protection compared to the *K* class by angling the side armour outwards (to reduce the impact angle of shells) and creating a new slope form, as better armour material was not yet available (Wh armour was not available until the construction of *Ersatz Lothringen* (*Admiral Scheer*) was begun). A secondary advantage of the new design was that it permitted a smaller overall length for the main engine installation (and only three boiler rooms, which meant that all smoke pipes could be combined into one funnel); this in turn raised the possibility of accommodating a catapult between the conning tower and the funnel. This overall concept was retained for *Nürnberg*.

Leipzig's arrangement of bridge, conning tower and night director was as on *Königsberg* and *Deutschland*; *Nürnberg*'s conning tower was lower and more restricted in view; she had one position for a 6m rangefinder on the high-set bridge instead of the normal linked forward artillery director stand.

Leipzig was still without the aft rangefinder, the torpedo rangefinder, the navigation antennas and the AA director stand during her trials in 1931–32. [In 1934 the small horizontal gaffs at the front edge of the funnel were replaced by large, angled vertical gaffs on the aft edge, an angled crane was fitted in place of the port loading post, and the deckhouse between the funnel and the battle mast was replaced by a catapult. In 1935 the antenna gaffs were removed, and a topmast with a yard was installed on the aft edge of the funnel. In 1939 the port angled crane was replaced by a lattice crane. In December 1940 a degaussing coil was installed, and the aft torpedo tubes were removed; in 1941 the catapult was removed; in summer 1943 the battle mast was fitted with FuMO 25, and the forward torpedo tubes were removed.]

Nürnberg was still without her enclosed Admiral's bridge, aft rangefinder and navigation antenna on the bridge in 1935. [In mid-1940 a degaussing coil was installed, and the aft torpedo tubes were removed; in 1941 a FuMO 21 was temporarily fitted in place of the rangefinder on the bridge. In 1942–43 the catapult and FuMO 21 were removed, and a FuMO 25 was installed on the mast outrigger; in December 1944 a FuMO 63 Hohentwiel array was fitted on the aft topmast.] New outer plating was planned, in 10–14mm Wh armour from the edge of the bulge to the upper deck (a similar modification to that on *Karslruhe*).

Career

Leipzig launched 18 Oct 1929, commissioned 8 Oct 1931 into the fleet (served abroad); severely damaged in the Skagerrak 13 Dec 1939 by a torpedo from the British submarine *Salmon*; 15 dead. Withdrawn from service 27 Feb 1940 at Kiel, repaired at Danzig. Firing rooms I and II were fitted out as training and living quarters for sea cadets, and maximum speed was reduced to 24kts. Returned to service 1 Oct 1940 as a training cruiser. Severely damaged northeast of Hela 15 Oct 1944 in a collision with *Prinz Eugen*; 27 dead. Served as a stationary training ship at Gotenhafen; surrendered at Apenrade 30 Jun 1945 and transferred to Wilhelmshaven as a barrack ship. Sunk 16 Dec 1946, southwest of Lister, position 57° 53N, 06° 13E, with a cargo of gas munitions, by the British Explosive Command. The ship's bell is now in the Telgte church youth centre.

Nürnberg launched 8 Dec 1934, commissioned 2 Nov 1935 into the fleet (served abroad). Taken as a USSR prize 16 Dec 1945, surrendered at Libau after transfer from Wilhelmshaven on 8 Jan 1946; became the Soviet training cruiser *Admiral Makarov*. Stricken 15 Feb 1961, broken up.

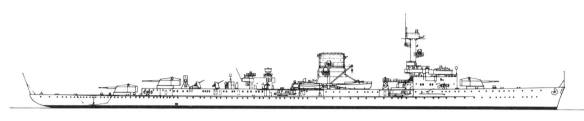

Leipzig (1933). *Mrva*

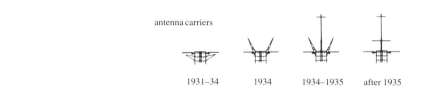

antenna carriers

1931–34   1934   1934–1935   after 1935

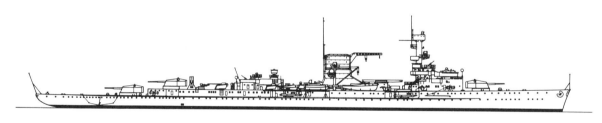

Leipzig (1936). *Mrva*

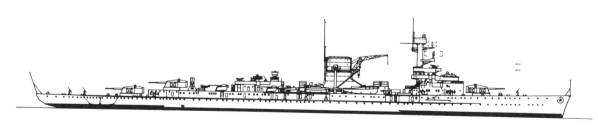

Leipzig (1944). *Mrva*

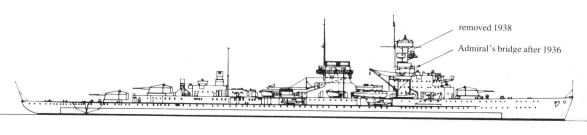

removed 1938

Admiral's bridge after 1936

Nürnberg (1936). *Mrva*

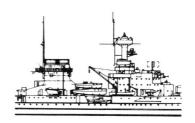

Nürnberg (1940). *Mrva*

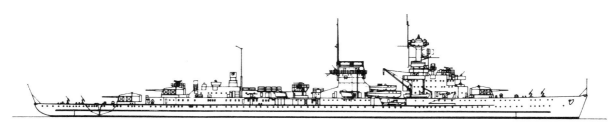

Nürnberg (1942). *Mrva*

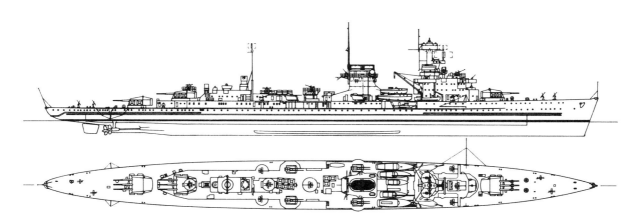

Nürnberg (1945). *Mrva*

M class

Construction

Laid down as 1938 light cruisers (official design 1938 and improved official design 1940, design officer MarBrt Driessen). Longitudinal frame stringer steel construction, about 85 percent welding planned (fifteen watertight compartments, double bottom approx 78 percent). Krupp and Wh armour: deck 20mm with 35mm slope; CT roof 50mm, sides 100mm, deck 20mm, rear 50mm; rangefinder stands 20mm; CWL inner layer 0–50–50–0mm, outer layer 0–30–0mm; turrets, etc, as *Nürnberg*; part of the upper deck and main deck was 20mm Wh. Depth 9.28m and 11.5m.

Propulsion

Two sets of Brown, Boveri & Co and Wagner turbines (*M* and *N*) and Marine-type turbines by Germania dockyard, plus four (*Q*, eight in *R*) MAN double-acting 12-cylinder two-stroke diesels with central Vulcan transmission (three 3-bladed screws, 3.9m diameter, possibly four screws in *Q* and *R*) in one turbine room and 1 + 1 + 1 diesel, transmission and diesel rooms.

Four Wagner ultra high pressure boilers (58 and 70 atmospheres forced, 435 and 465°, size not known) in 1 + 1 boiler rooms. Four electricity plants 2400kW 220V. One balanced rudder.

Armament

Eight 15cm/55 QF guns (960 rounds), −10° +40°, range 23,000m; four 8.8cm/76 AA guns (1600 rounds); eight 3.7cm AA guns (9600 rounds); four 2cm AA guns (2000 rounds each); eight 53.3cm deck-mounted TT (16 rounds); approx 60 mines. One catapult; two Arado 196 seaplanes.

Complement

Crew: 28/892. Boats: one picket boat, one barge, one launch, two cutters.

Notes

The design* bears evidence of French (*La Galisson-nière*) and British influence (*Southampton*), the latter particularly evident in the distribution of side armour.

The stepped arrangement of the armour deck, with a long slope over the transmission room and forward diesel rooms, was not a practical solution in terms of space utilisation, nor realistic in military terms. Reinforcement of the inadequate heavy AA armament, or its replacement by two 10.5cm double turrets, was not possible (or only so with the removal of the catapult) for reasons of strength, munitions storage and firing angle.

* Note on the history of the development of the 1938 cruiser: in autumn 1935 and after, this 8000t Atlantic cruiser, designed solely for the cruiser war, was the focus of fruitless argument between the heads of naval warfare (A IV) and the K-Amt, which considered the set demands (high top speed, relatively high cruise speed, wide radius of action, powerful armament, ability to withstand 15cm shells at 20,000m, all at a displacement of 8000t) to be irreconcilable.

In July 1937 the Ob d M (*Oberbefehlhaber der Marine* – Commander in Chief, naval forces) ordered that the dockyards and navy design officers should all provide quotations for the project. None of the designs (code names *Motorkreuzer* – motor cruiser – for Deutsche Werke, Kiel, Obrt Besch, and *Seeadler*, *Wehr dich*, *Trotz Alledem* and others) was practical in structural terms. For this reason the official design by MarBrt Driessen, which met most of the important formal requirements, was approved for implementation, but its weaknesses quickly became apparent.

Name	Builder	Built	Cost in Marks (000s)	Displacement (t = tonnes T = tons)	Length (m)	Breadth (m)	Draught (m)	Power (hp)	Revs (rpm)	Speed (kts)	Range (nm/kts)	Coal (t)	Oil (t)
M	Deutsche Werke, Kiel Construction no 263	1938–	56,290	10,400T max 8500t des 7800T std	183.0 oa 178.0 cwl	17.0	7.25 fwd 6.03 aft 5.42 std	116,500 shp max 100,000 shp des + 16,500ehp		35.5 des	8000/19	—	1080 +520 max 600 des
N	KM Dockyard, Construction no 129	1938–	55,800	,,	,,	,,	,,	,,		,,	,,	—	,,
O	Germania Dockyard, Kiel Construction no 606 after 8 Aug 1939 at KM Dockyard, Kiel	—	,,	,,	,,	,,	,,	,,		,,	,,	—	,,
P	Germania Dockyard, Kiel Construction no 607	—	,,	,,	,,	,,	,,	,,		,,	,,	—	,,
Q	F Schichau, Danzig	—		9300t des 8568T std	196.0 oa 188.0 cwl	18.0	5.4	90,000shp des + 35,500ehp		36.0 des	12,000/19		
R	Deutsche Werke, Kiel	—		,,	,,	,,	,,	,,		,,	,,		

The design requirement for high speed and great range at low displacement could only be met by fitting smaller main armament and thinner armour. The engine installation was also vulnerable, with both turbines in one room and steam pipes from the forward boiler room routed through the rear boiler room. These cruisers would also probably have been unsuitable for use abroad because of their poor standards of accommodation. All these faults led finally to the planned improvements for *Q* and *R*; these, however, were not carried out.

Career

The two cruisers begun, *M* and *N*, were broken up on the stocks after autumn 1939, following a command to halt construction on 19 and 21 Sept 1939.

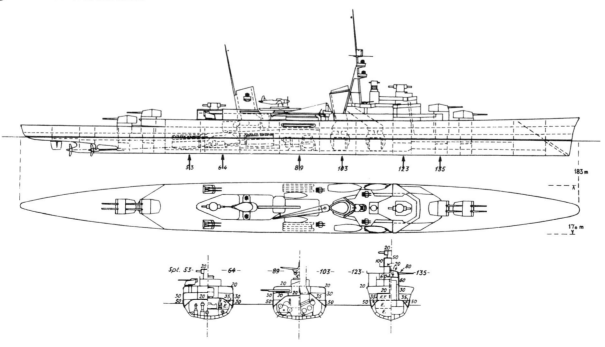

Light cruisers *M, N, O*; 1938–40 design.

KH 1 class (ex-Dutch)

Name	Builder	Built	Cost	Displacement (t = tonnes T = tons)	Length (m)	Breadth (m)	Draught (m)	Power (hp)	Revs (rpm)	Speed (kts)	Range (nm/kts)	Coal (t)	Oil (t)
KH 1	Wilton-Fijenoord, Rotterdam Construction no 670	1939–											
KH 2	Rotterdamse Droogd Mij, Rotterdam Construction no 219	1939–	(20,000) Guilders	8350T des	185.7 oa 182.3 bp 187.3 oa mod	17.25	5.60 max 5.40 des	78,000shp des		32 des		—	1750 max

Construction

Laid down as Dutch cruisers *Ersatz Sumatra* and *Ersatz Java* (Dutch official design by G t'Hooft). Armour: CWL 75–100–75mm; turrets roof 20–32mm, face 80mm, sides 35mm, rear 20mm.

Propulsion

Two sets of Parsons turbines with gear transmissions by the Konigl Mij De Schelde (two screws) in 1 turbine room + 1 transmission room + 1 turbine room. Six and eight (?) Yarrow oil-fired boilers in 1 + 1 boiler rooms. One rudder.

Armament

Eight 15cm/55 QF guns (no of rounds not known), –10° +35°/40°, range 23,000m; twelve 3.7cm AA guns (no of rounds not known); six 53.3cm TT in triple mounts (no of rounds not known). One catapult, two Arado 196 seaplanes.

Complement

Crew: approx 700. Six boats.

Notes

Construction continued as training cruisers *Ersatz Emden* and *Ersatz Königsberg* (?), [including the provision of an Atlantic bow on *KH 1*], initially due for completion mid-1942 to January 1943. In 1941 the turrets from the new cruiser *M* and the medium guns from the battleship *H* were planned as main armament. After August 1941 it was decided that final fitting out was not to be carried out until after demobilisation.

Career

KH 1 keel laid 5 Sept 1939, planned name *De Zeven Provincien*. Taken as a German prize May 1940; construction continued as *KH 1*; after August 1941 minor work only was carried out until the ship's launch on 24 Dec 1944, for planned use as a block ship for the Nieuwe waterway. After 1947 the ship was completely redesigned, and completed for the Dutch navy as *De Ruyter*; commissioned 18 Nov 1953. Stricken 26 Jan 1973; sold to Peru 23 May 1973; renamed *Almirante Grau*.

KH 2 keel laid 19 May 1939, first projected name *Kijkduin*, later *Eendracht*. Taken as a German prize May 1940; construction continued as *KH 2*; after August 1941 minor work only was carried out, and the ship was not launched. After 1947 she was completely redesigned, and construction continued for the Dutch navy as *De Zeven Provincien*, launched 22 Aug 1950, commissioned December 1953. Stricken 17 Aug 1976 and sold to Peru as *Almirante Aguirre*.

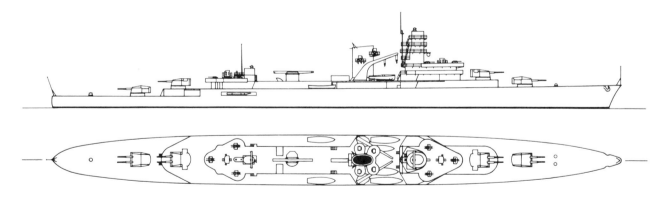

KH 1 (1941 design); *KH 2* was similar. *Mrva*

Gunboats 1815–1871

Gun sloop No 10 class

Name	Builder	Built	Cost	Displacement (t = tonnes T = tons)	Length (m)	Breadth (m)	Draught (m)	Power (hp)	Revs (rpm)	Speed (kts)	Range (nm/kts)	Coal (t)	Oil (t)
Gun sloops Nos 10 and 17	Swedish dockyards at Skäggenäs and Karlshamm	1805–08	750 Swedish Thaler	c60t	19.0	4.2	1.19	—	—	2.5		—	—
No 45	Hultmans'ka Skeppsvarvet, Vestervik	1805	,,	c65t	20.3	4.5	1.26	—	—	,,		—	—
No 48	Skäggenäs	1805											
No 51	Härnösund	1808		as above									
No 116	Karlskrona	1808											

Construction Built to Swedish designs (Oberst Lars Begeman and Vice Admiral F H af Chapman). Timber carvel construction. Depth 0.9m.

Propulsion Designed for rowing, with fourteen (*No 10* and *17*) and fifteen pairs of oars (one per man). One rudder.

Armament Two Swedish iron 24pdr; four Nickhaken (short Swedish 2 to 3pdr).

Handling Only usable in calm seas, with wind strength less than 5.

Complement Crew: 11–13 men, plus 50 soldiers, one officer for each two sloops. With a normal crew all men bar the guard had to bivouac on land at night.

Notes All were accepted in dubious condition, and their timbers quickly rotted away.

Career

Kanonierschaluppen (gun sloops) *No 10*, *17*, *45*, *48*, *51* and *116* launched before 1815; ceded to Prussia as a result of the Congress of Vienna, together with Swedish (outer) Pommerania, in July 1815 at Stralsund, accepted 23 Oct 1815; saw no service. The first vessel (Swedish *No 51*) was stricken 21 Mar 1817, and the remainder on 18 Feb 1819; sold 10 Feb 1820 for 330 Thaler in total.

Danzig

Name	Builder	Built	Cost in Marks (000s)	Displacement (t = tonnes T = tons)	Length (m)	Breadth (m)	Draught (m)	Power (hp)	Revs (rpm)	Speed (kts)	Range (nm/kts)	Coal (t)	Oil (t)
DANZIG	J J Meyer, Stralsund	1824–25	5.28	c70t	19.09	5.81	1.26	—	—	3	8 days	—	—

Construction Laid down as a harbour gunboat (design by Longé, 1824). Timber carvel construction.

Propulsion Designed for rowing, with twenty-four oars (two per man). Lugger rig, approx 100sq m. One rudder.

Armament Two iron 24pdr; one 25pdr mortar; two 12pdr carronades.

Handling Good sea-boat, fairly dry; manoeuvrable, with a tight turning circle (180° in 2¹/₃ minutes under oars); relatively fast under sail (up to about 8kts).

Danzig (1825)

Complement Crew: 2/15, plus 40 soldiers. One boat.

Notes Colour scheme approx no 1, with a white bulwark. The stem and stern were rotted by 1836, and there was much other damage.

Career

Danzig launched 21 May 1825, commissioned 8 Aug 1825; saw very little service. Stricken 23 Apr 1838; sold in May 1838 for 202 Thaler, broken up 1838 at Stralsund.

Thorn class

Name	Builder	Built	Cost in Marks (000s)	Displacement (t = tonnes T = tons)	Length (m)	Breadth (m)	Draught (m)	Power (hp)	Revs (rpm)	Speed (kts)	Range (nm/kts)	Coal (t)	Oil (t)
THORN	J J Klawitter, Danzig	1823	2.99	27.7t	16.33	5.02	0.39	—	—	3		—	—
No 1	J J Meyer, Stralsund	1826	2.73	21.0t	15.86	4.94	,,	—	—	3.2		—	—
No 2	J J Meyer, Stralsund	1827	2.64	,,	,,	,,	,,	—	—	2.5		—	—

Construction Laid down as a river gunboat (design 1819 and 1823, revised in 1827 by Longé). Timber carvel construction. Fittings weighed 7.8 and 6.4t.

Propulsion Designed for rowing, with sixteen, later twelve, oars (one per man). One square sail, approx 40sq m. One rudder.

Armament *Thorn*, two English iron 12pdr, one 10pdr mortar, one 12cm Congreve rocket battery; *No 2*, two English iron 12pdr, one iron 12pdr carronade.

Complement Crew: approx 1/10, plus 30 soldiers. With a normal crew all men bar the guard had to bivouac on land at night.

Notes Colours: brown plus black and yellow. Both *No 1* and *No 2* served on short exercises only.

Career

Thorn launched 21 Jul 1823, commissioned 24 Aug 1823 at Berlin; served at the Garde-Pionier barracks at the Silesian Gate; transferred to the army 24 Apr 1824; served at Stralsund in July 1827, at Thorn in 1828, and at Danzig 1836. Stricken 11 Jul 1840; sold for 50 Thaler and broken up.

No 1 launched 11 Mar 1826, commissioned 3 Sept 1826 at Berlin; served at the Garde-Pionier barracks at the Silesian Gate. Stricken 20 Feb 1841; sold for 60 Thaler and broken up.

No 2 launched 18 Aug 1827, commissioned 14 Nov 1827 at Thorn. Stricken about 1850.

No 3 class

Name	Builder	Built	Cost in Marks (000s)	Displacement (t = tonnes T = tons)	Length (m)	Breadth (m)	Draught (m)	Power (hp)	Revs (rpm)	Speed (kts)	Range (nm/kts)	Coal (t)	Oil (t)
Nos 3, 6, 9, 12	Kiel	1848	11.2	c40t	20.0–20.5	4.55	c0.85	—	—	2.5		—	—
No 8 (NÜBBEL)	Jäger Dockyard, Nübbel	1848–49		,,	21.5	5.00	c0.85	—	—	,,		—	—
No 11 (FRAUENVEREIN)	Jäger Dockyard, Nübbel	,,	16.7	,,	20.6	4.95	c0.85	—	—	,,		—	—

Construction Laid down as Schleswig-Holstein oared gunboats (Danish navy design, 1807) in the old Danish Plattgat (flat stern) style without a deck. Oak carvel hull. Depth of hold 1.40m.

Propulsion 3-masted (French) lugger rig. One rudder.

Armament Two 60pdr bomb cannon in a fixed installation, or one 60pdr and one 32pdr in a fixed installation; plus two 3pdr swivel guns.

Complement Crew: 45–50 men.

Career

No 3 launched 1848, commissioned August 1848. Surrendered 3 Mar 1851 to the Danish fleet; became *Holstensk Kanonchaloup* (gun sloop) *No 3*. Withdrawn from service 1861; scuttled 1864 at Limfjorden.

No 6 launched in August 1848, commissioned August 1848; career as for *No 3*, but became *Holstensk*

Kanonchaloup No 6 in 1853, and *Transportpram* (transport barge) *No 6* in 1861. Stricken 1862.

No 9 launched in November 1848, commissioned November 1848; career as for *No 3*, but became

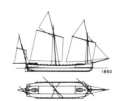

Schleswig-Holstein *Ruderkanonenboote*
Nos 3, 6, 8, 9, 11, 12 (1849). *Mickel*

Holstensk Kanonchaloup No 9 in 1853, and transport barge *No 9* in 1861. Scuttled 1864 at Limfjorden.

No 12 launched in November 1848, commissioned November 1848; career as for *No 3*, but became *Holstensk Kanonchaloup No 12* in 1853, and Transport barge *No 12* in 1861. Broken up 1867.

No 8 launched in 1849, commissioned 1849. Sunk at 0200hrs on 9 Nov 1850 at Maxqueller, in the Elbe estuary, after capsizing in a storm; 42 dead, all crew lost. The wreck was raised and repaired in December 1850 at Glückstadt. Surrendered 3 Mar 1851 to the Danish fleet; became *Holstensk Kanonchaloup No 8* in 1852, and Transport barge *No 8* in 1861. Broken up in 1863.

No 11 launched 1849, commissioned 26 Feb 1849; career as for *No 3*, but became *Holstensk Kanonchaloup No 11* in 1852, and Transport barge *No 11* in 1861. Sold in May 1867.

Elmshorn/No 2 class

Name	Builder	Built	Cost in Marks (000s)	Displacement (t = tonnes T = tons)	Length (m)	Breadth (m)	Draught (m)	Power (hp)	Revs (rpm)	Speed (kts)	Range (nm/kts)	Coal (t)	Oil (t)
No 2 (ELMSHORN)	Kremer, Elmshorn	1848–49		c45t	23.5	4.74	0.95	—	—	2.5		—	—
No 4 (TÖNNING)	Tönning	,,		,,	23.4	4.77	,,	—	—	,,		—	—
No 5 (ECKERNFÖRDE)	Eckernförde	,,		,,	23.6	4.89	,,	—	—	,,		—	—
No 7 (GLÜCKSTADT)	Glückstadt	,,		,,	23.1	4.78	,,	—	—	,,		—	—
No 10 (ARNIS)	Arnis	,,		,,	23.6	4.89	,,	—	—	,,		—	—

Construction Laid down as Schleswig-Holstein oared gunboats (design by Master Shipwright Dryer); the contract was granted by the 'Committee for the building of the German Fleet', and accepted in 1849 by the Schleswig-Holstein Navy Commission. The design was for a new type of gunboat with a round stern and a covered forecastle and quarterdeck. Oak carvel hull. Depth of hold 1.60m.

Propulsion 2-masted lugger rig (with auxiliary mast). One rudder.

Armament Two 60pdr bomb cannon, swivel mounted; two 3pdr swivel guns.

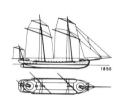

Schleswig-Holstein *Ruderkanonenboote Nos 2, 4, 5, 7, 10* (1849). *Mickel*

Complement Crew: 48 men.

Career
No 2, No 5 launched 1849, commissioned April 1849. Surrendered 3 Mar 1851 to the Danish fleet; became *Holstensk Kanonchaloup No 2* and *No 5* 1852. Stricken 1864; broken up 1871.

No 4, No 7, No 10 launched 1849, commissioned early 1849. Surrendered 3 Mar 1851 to the Danish fleet; became *Holstensk Kanonchaloup No 4, No 7* and *No 10* 1852. Stricken, broken up 1871.

Von der Tann

Name	Builder	Built	Cost in Marks (000s)	Displacement (t = tonnes T = tons)	Length (m)	Breadth (m)	Draught (m)	Power (hp)	Revs (rpm)	Speed (kts)	Range (nm/kts)	Coal (t)	Oil (t)
VON DER TANN	Hilbert'sche Dockyard, Kiel	1848–49	15	c100t	25.1	4.9	1.83	150ihp	10	6	180/6		—
	mod: Bernitt'sche Schiffswerft, Neustadt	1850		c120t	31.3	5.2		150ihp 36nhp					

Construction Laid down as a Schleswig-Holstein screw driven gunboat (engines designed by Master Shipwrights Howaldt, Schau and Hudemann). Oak carvel construction, underwater hull coppered (?). Depth of hold 2.7m.

Propulsion One horizontal oscillating 2-cylinder single acting expansion engine by Schweffel & Howaldt (construction no 1) (one Archimedean screw, diameter not known). Two horizontal locomotive boilers (no of fireboxes and pressure not known, 100sq m). Rigged as a three-masted schooner until July 1850; the foremast and mainmast could be laid flat and the bowsprit was retractable. One rudder.

Armament Two smoothbore 60pdr bomb cannon, swivel mounted (range 1250m).

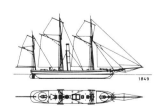

Von der Tann (1849). *Mickel*

Complement Crew: 1/28. Boats: two.

Notes Colour scheme no 1. She was the first screw-driven gunboat designed and built in Germany, and was known colloquially as *De Schruv* – The Screw, in the Plattdeutsch dialect. [During her reconstruction in 1851 she was enlarged and re-rigged as a two-masted schooner.]

Career
Von der Tann launched 1848, accepted 5 Feb 1849. Sunk at 0130hrs on 22 Jul 1850 off Neustadt-Holstein, approx position 54° 08N, 10° 50E, in battle with the Danish battle steamer *Hecla* and corvette *Valkyren*; she was beached and blown up; no casualties. She was salvaged and rebuilt by 6 Oct 1850, then surrendered 25 Mar 1852 to the Danish fleet and renamed *Støren*; broken up 1860. The engine and boiler were used until 1886 in the gunboat *Hauch*.

Kiel

Name	Builder	Built	Cost in Marks (000s)	Displacement (t = tonnes T = tons)	Length (m)	Breadth (m)	Draught (m)	Power (hp)	Revs (rpm)	Speed (kts)	Range (nm/kts)	Coal (t)	Oil (t)
KIEL	England	(1810)		161t	27	12 max 6.5 des	1.6	40nhp		7			—

Construction Laid down as a paddle steamer and Royal yacht. Transverse frame oak carvel hull.

Propulsion One single expansion engine (no of cylinders not known) (two wheels, diameter and no of paddles not known). No details of boilers are known. Square-rigged schooner rig, area not known. One rudder.

Armament Four short 18pdr.

Complement Crew: 35. Boats: two.

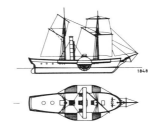

Kiel (1848). *Mickel*

Notes Colour scheme no 1.

Career
Kiel launched between 1810 and 1820 as the British paddle steamer *Eagle*; sold 1824 to the Danish fleet for £4500 as the Royal yacht – *Kongens Skib* – *Kiel*; became a transport ship in 1842, and a passenger ship for the Glückstadt Harbour Commission in 1847; laid up in Altona winter quarters in March 1848, and taken over by Schleswig-Holstein; armed as a gunboat at Glückstadt in 1849. Returned to the Danish fleet in August 1851; engine removed 1853; sold 1865 to the merchant J P Larsen.

Bonin

Name	Builder	Built	Cost in Marks (000s)	Displacement (t = tonnes T = tons)	Length (m)	Breadth (m)	Draught (m)	Power (hp)	Revs (rpm)	Speed (kts)	Range (nm/kts)	Coal (t)	Oil (t)
BONIN	John Wood, Glasgow mod: Kiel	1833 1849	50		45.7	5.8	3.2	180ihp					—

Construction Laid down as a post steamer for the Kiel–Copenhagen service, transverse frame oak carvel hull.

Propulsion One single (?) expansion engine (no of cylinders not known (two wheels, diameter and no of paddles not known). No details of boiler are known. Square rigged schooner rig, area not known. One rudder.

Armament One 84pdr bomb cannon; one 60pdr bomb cannon, two 30pdr bomb cannon.

Complement Crew: 80. Boats: two.

Notes Colour scheme no 1.

Career
Bonin launched 1833 as the British (?) paddle steamer *Vulcan*; later became the Danish post steamer *Christian VIII*, operated by Donner & Schmidt, Kiel; purchased 1848 by the Schleswig-Holstein Naval Commission for 175,000.00 Marks and refitted as a gunboat; in service 4 May 1849. Surrendered in March 1851 to the Danish navy and renamed *Mercur*; used as a barge after 1857; broken up 1867.

Gun yawl No 1 class

Construction *Nos 1–4* were built with an oak carvel hull with two transverse bulkheads and fixed skids for beaching. *Nos 5–8* were of transverse frame iron construction, with one wood and four iron transverse bulkheads.

Propulsion Designed for rowing, with twenty oars (two men per oar [later one shortened oar per man]). Lugger rig, approx 50sq m. One rudder.

Armament One 60pdr bomb cannon.

Handling These vessels were very limited in use, and in good weather only (up to wind strength 4).

Complement Crew: 0/50, plus one officer for each

two yawls. With a normal crew all men bar the guard had to bivouac on land at night.

Notes The wooden yawls proved to be too weak structurally for the armament. All these yawls were intended to advance into battle stern-forward, with a large auxiliary rudder suspended at the actual bow; see the drawing.

Kanonenjollen Nos 1–6 (1849), on passage and in combat.

Career
Kanonenjolle (**Gun yawl**) *No 1* and *No 2* launched 1840–41; saw very little service. Sold 1860–61 at Danzig; finally used as barges or similar.

Gun yawl *No 3* (*Germania*) launched 30 Aug 1848; no further data, but fate as for *No 1*.

Gun yawl *No 4* (*Concordia*) launched 30 Aug 1848; no further data, but fate as for *No 1*.

Gun yawl *No 5* and *No 6* launched 1848; no further data, but fate as for *No 1*.

Gun yawl *No 7* and *No 8* launched 1849; reconstructed at Danzig as water vessels; final fate as for *No 1*.

Name	Builder	Built	Cost in Marks (000s)	Displacement (t = tonnes T = tons)	Length (m)	Breadth (m)	Draught (m)	Power (hp)	Revs (rpm)	Speed (kts)	Range (nm/kts)	Coal (t)	Oil (t)
Gun yawls No 1, No 2	J J Klawitter, Danzig	1840–41		*c*21t	15.0	3.14	0.9	—	—	2.5		—	—
No 3 (GERMANIA)	Schüler	1848		,,	15.39	3.27	0.81	—	—	,,		—	—
No 4 (CONCORDIA)	Stettin-Grabow	,,		,,	,,	,,	,,	—	—	,,		—	—
No 5, No 6	Wöhlert, Berlin	,,	4.98	,,	,,	,,	,,	—	—	,,		—	—
No 7, No 8	Royal Dockyard, Danzig	1849	7.9	*c*26				—	—	,,			

Oared gunboat No 1 class

Name	Builder	Built	Cost in Marks (000s)	Displacement (t = tonnes T = tons)	Length (m)	Breadth (m)	Draught (m)	Power (hp)	Revs (rpm)	Speed (kts)	Range (nm/kts)	Coal (t)	Oil (t)
Oared gunboats Nos 1–8	Various dockyards on the Elbe, Ems, Weser	1848–49			18.8–18.9	4.22–4.98	1.2	—	—	3		—	—
No 9, No 10	Joh Lange, Vegesack Construction nos 184, 185	,,			,,	,,	,,	—	—	,,		—	—
Nos 11–26	Various dockyards on the Elbe, Ems, Weser*	,,			,,	,,	,,	—	—	,,		—	—
No 27 ex *St Pauli*	Johann Marbs, Hamburg	1948			,,	,,	,,	—	—	,,		—	—

* two units at H F Ulrichs Dockyard, Vegesack, construction nos 24 and 25, launched 20 Jun 1848 and 4 Apr 1848; two units Joh Tecklenborg, Bremerhaven

Construction Built with open, uncovered timber carvel hulls, equipped for sailing. Depth of hold 1.75m.

Propulsion Designed for rowing, with thirty oars (two men per oar [later one shortened oar per man]). One rudder.

Armament One 68pdr bomb cannon, one 32pdr bomb cannon; *No 27:* two 32pdr bomb canon.

Complement Crew: 0/60.

Notes Colour scheme no 1.

Career
Ruderkanonenboot (Oared gunboat) *No 1 – No 8* launched after 1840; sold at Vegesack after the dissolution of the fleet to Bremer Schiffsmakler Bödecker for E C Schramm & Co, for 7 percent of the construction cost; fate unknown.

Oared gunboat *No 9* launched 22 Mar 1849; fate as for *No 1*.

Oared gunboat *No 10* launched 31 Mar 1849; fate as for *No 1*.

Oared gunboat *No 11 – No 26* launched after 1840; fate as for *No 1*.

Oared gunboat *No 27* launched 29 Jul 1848 as *St Pauli* in the Hamburg flotilla of 1848, sponsored by the St Pauli suburb; transferred 14 Oct 1848 to the Federal fleet; sold 1853 in Lübeck; fate unknown.

Gun sloop No 1 class

Construction *Prussian types* (design by Gaede), structural timber oak, *No 6, 7, 10* and *11*, transverse frame iron construction, one wood, four iron transverse bulkheads, two iron longitudinal bulkheads; *No 12, 24, 27* and *28*, timber carvel hull with iron frames, two transverse bulkheads and two timber longitudinal bulkheads; *No 8, 9, 13–22, 25, 26* and *29–36*, timber carvel hull, two transverse bulkheads, two longitudinal bulkheads; *Danish types, No 2* and *3*, wood, carvel hull, two transverse, two longitudinal bulkheads; *Swedish types, No 4* and *5*, timber carvel hull, two longitudinal bulkheads; *Dutch types, No 1* and *23*, timber carvel hull, two longitudinal bulkheads. Depth 2.2–2.5m.

Name	Builder	Built	Cost	Displacement (t = tonnes T = tons)	Length (m)	Breadth (m)	Draught (m)	Power (hp)	Revs (rpm)	Speed (kts)	Range (nm/kts)	Coal (t)	Oil (t)
Gun sloops Nos 1–36	*	1848–49	*	c40t	19.2	3.35	1.2	—	—	2.5		—	—

No 1 (Erich, Stralsund) 9.5; *No 2, 3* (Schüler, Grabow); 9.5; *No 4* (Nüske, Stettin) 9.97; *No 5* (Carmesin Dockyard, Grabow) 9.97; *No 6, 7, 10, 11* (Berlin-Moabit Maschinenbauanstalt der Seehandlung) 13.97 – 12.89; *No 8, 9* (Zieske, Stettin) 9.17; *No 12, 24, 27, 28* (Maschinenfabrik der Vereinigten Hamburg-Magdeburger Dampfschiffahrts-Co, Buckau-Magdeburg, construction nos 29–32) 9.72 – 9.6; *No 13, 14* (Wacker, Anklam) 9.56; *No 15, 16* (Wittenburg, Ückermünde) 9.76; *No 17, 18* (Pretzer, Ückermünde) 9.76; *No 19, 20* (Erich & Lübke, Wolgast) 9.74; *No 21, 23* (Gade, Greifswald) 9.37 – 8.18; *No 22, 25* (Juhl, Stralsund) 9.77 – 9.55; *No 26* (Ehmcke, Wollin) 9.76; *No 29, 30* (Dierling, Damgarten) 9.68; *No 31–36* (Moegenburg, Colberg) 9.67 thousand Thaler per boat.

Propulsion Designed for rowing, with twenty-six oars (two men per oar [one shortened oar per man in 1850]). Lugger rig, approx 120sq m; [*No 8* had one mast only, and cutter rig from 1894]. One rudder.

Armament One iron 24pdr; one 25pdr carronade, Swedish [two iron 24pdr; two 12pdr howitzers].

Handling These vessels were of limited military use, in good weather only (up to wind strength 4).

Complement Crew: 0/59 plus one officer for each two sloops. With a normal crew all men bar the guard had to bivouac on land at night, except in the case of the broader (5.22m) *Strelasund*.

Notes Colour scheme no 1. Each vessel towed a tender. *No 22* or *No 25* was fitted out from financial contributions from the Naval Associations of Halle and Rügen (accepted 31 Jul 1849 into the fleet); the vessel temporarily bore the name *Halle–Rügen No 21* or

No 23 was financed in the same manner by the citizens of Greifswald, and temporarily bore the name *Gryphia*.

Career
Kanonenschaluppe (Gun sloop) *No 1* (*Strelasund*) launched 10 Aug 1848, commissioned 25 Oct 1848.

Gun sloop *No 2* launched 20 Oct 1848, commissioned in October 1848.

Gun sloop *No 3* launched 20 Oct 1848, commissioned in October 1848.

Kanonenschaluppen Nos 1–36 (1849), on passage and in combat.

Gun sloop *No 4* launched 20 Oct 1848, commissioned in October 1848.

Gun sloop *No 5* launched in 1848, commissioned in October 1848.

Gun sloop *No 6* launched 12 Oct 1848, commissioned in October 1848.

Gun sloop *No 7* launched in July 1848, commissioned in October 1848.

Gun sloop *No 8–36* launched in 1849, commissioned in 1849.

These vessels were only mobilised in the 1848–49 and 1864 wars; otherwise they served as occasional ferry transports to Rügen. Four sloops were stricken in 1862, and the remainder on 26 Apr 1870. Nine sloops were used until 1890 at Wilhelmshaven as pontoons for the floating bridge over the harbour canal; a few of the Stralsund sloops served as barges for the floating military institute there; two sloops at Kiel were used as barges after 1867; after 1870 these were named *K I* and *K X*.

Jäger class

Construction Laid down as steam gunboats, second rate (official design, 1859). Oak carvel hull with copper sheathing.

Propulsion One pair of horizontal single-cylinder single expansion engines by Borsig, Berlin and F Schichau, Elbing, (*Jäger, Crocodill*) and by AG Vulcan, Stettin, and Möller & Hollberg, Stettin (one 3-bladed screw, 1.88m diameter). Four transverse trunk boilers by the engine manufacturers (four fireboxes, 4 atmospheres forced) in one boiler room. Three-masted schooner rig, approx 300sq m. One rudder.

Armament One rifled 24pdr; two rifled 12pdr; [one 15cm/22 hooped after 1872; *Fuchs*, one 8.7cm/24 hooped gun after 1878, replaced by one machine gun after 1880]. All guns were breech loaders after 1860.

Handling Poor sea-boats, with severe roll, and very wet. Steaming and sailing in a head sea was impossible, and all vessels hove to poorly. Steering and manoeuvrability were moderate.

Complement Crew: 2/38. Boats: two.

Notes Colour scheme no 1, perhaps 2. These vessels spent most of the time laid up on land; the copper sheathing was removed, vent holes were cut in outer planking, the engines, boilers and guns were removed, the masts and funnel were unshipped and a protective

roof was fitted over the hull. The mizzen mast was laid flat during action. [After 1872 all masts were removed except for a signal mainmast.] The vessels' names were announced by AKO on 10 Oct 1859, to allow the Customs authorities to release imported materials for their construction; in the interim Lübke and Wolgast had continued the construction of two boats on their own account under the names *Donner* and *Blitz*. Temporary names planned for the vessels built at Nüscke were *Der Herrscher* (for *Schwalbe*) and *Der Sieger* (for *Salamander*), possibly for the same reason. The nickname *Seeferkel* – sea piglet – probably arose from the tendency of all vessels to dig their bows into the sea.

Career
Jäger launched in January 1860; saw very little service. Stricken 19 Mar 1872, used as a target.

Crocodill launched at the end of 1860; saw little service. Stricken 14 Mar 1867, broken up because of dry rot.

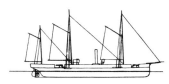

Jäger (1866) Crocodill, Fuchs, Hay, Scorpion, Sperber, Hyäne, Habicht, Pfeil, Natter, Schwalbe, Salamander, Wespe, Tiger, Wolf

Fuchs launched 14 Feb 1860; saw very little service; used as a gunnery tender 1878. Stricken 14 Nov 1882, became mine barge *No 3* at Wilhelmshaven.

Hay launched 14 Feb 1860; saw little service. Stricken 7 Sept 1880; became an inventory barge.

Scorpion launched 14 Feb 1860; saw little service. Stricken 9 Jan 1877; became a barge at Kiel.

Sperber launched 14 Feb 1860; saw very little service. Stricken 12 Nov 1878; became a barge at Kiel.

Hyäne launched in April 1860; saw very little service. Stricken 17 Jul 1873; finally used as a target.

Habicht launched in 1860; saw little service. Stricken 27 Nov 1877; became an inventory barge.

Pfeil launched 14 Feb 1860; saw little service. Stricken 19 Mar 1872; became *Minenprahm* (Mine barge) *No 2* at Wilhelmshaven.

Natter launched 14 Feb 1860; saw little service. Stricken 7 Sept 1880.

Schwalbe launched 14 Feb 1860; saw little service. Stricken 19 Mar 1872; became Mine barge *No 1* at Kiel.

Salamander launched 14 Feb 1860; saw very little service. Stricken 12 Nov 1878; became a barge.

Wespe launched 14 Feb 1860; saw very little service. Stricken 19 Mar 1872; became Mine barge *No 1* at Wilhelmshaven.

Name	Builder	Built	Cost in Marks (000s)	Displacement (t = tonnes T = tons)	Length (m)	Breadth (m)	Draught (m)	Power (hp)	Revs (rpm)	Speed (kts)	Range (nm/kts)	Coal (t)	Oil (t)
JÄGER, CROCODILL	Mitzlaff, Elbing	1859–60	47.4	283t max 237t des	41.2 oa 38.0 cwl	6.69	2.2	220ihp max 60nhp des		9.0		31	—
FUCHS, HAY	J W Klawitter, Danzig	,,	49.0	,,	,,	,,	,,	,,		,,		,,	—
SCORPION, SPERBER	Domcke, Grabow	,,	47.3										
HYÄNE, HABICHT	Keire & Devrient, Danzig	,,	48.7										
PFEIL, NATTER	Lübke, Wolgast	,,	48.5										
SCHWALBE	A E Nüscke, Grabow Construction no 89	,,	48.2					as above					
SALAMANDER	A E Nüscke, Grabow Construction no 88	,,	48.2										
WESPE, TIGER	Zieske, Stettin	,,	48.5										
WOLF	Liegnitz, Grabow	,,	48.4										

164gt/79nt

Tiger launched 14 Feb 1860; saw very little service. Stricken 9 Jan 1877; became Mine barge *No 4* at Wilhelmshaven; broken up.

Wolf launched 29 Apr 1860; saw very little service. Stricken 26 Sept 1875; became a coal barge at Danzig; became Mine barge *No 2* at Kiel 1878. Blown up 5 Aug 1884 in a torpedo experiment; hulk renamed *Blücher*, and finally broken up at Kiel-Wik.

Camäleon class

Name	Builder	Built	Cost in Marks (000s)	Displacement (t = tonnes T = tons)	Length (m)	Breadth (m)	Draught (m)	Power (hp)	Revs (rpm)	Speed (kts)	Range (nm/kts)	Coal (t)	Oil (t)
CAMÄLEON, COMET	Royal Dockyard, Danzig	1859–60	73.9/ 72.6		43.28 oa 41.02 cwl	6.96	2.35 fwd 2.67 aft	250ihp max 80nhp des		9.1		52 max 27 des	
CYCLOP, DELPHIN	,,	,,	74.4/ 71.8		,,	,,	,,	,,				,,	
BLITZ, BASILISK	,,	1861–62	95.3/ 95.5		,,	,,	,,	320ihp max 80nhp des		9.3		,,	
METEOR, DRACHE	,,	1861–65	94.4/ 98.0	422t max 353t des	,,	,,	,,	,,		,,		,,	

203gt/109nt

Construction Laid down as steam gunboats, first rate (official design, 1859). Oak carvel hull with copper sheathing.

Propulsion One pair of horizontal single-cylinder single expansion engines by AG Vulcan, Stettin, and after *Blitz* by F Schichau, Elbing (one 3-bladed screw, 1.9m diameter). Two trunk boilers by engine manufacturers (four fireboxes, 1.66 atmospheres forced) [replaced by the Imperial Dockyards at Kiel and Wilhelmshaven (2 atmospheres forced)] in one boiler room. Three-masted schooner rig, approx 350sq m

[*Delphin* was converted to a schooner barque rig, *Cyclop* to a barque rig]. One rudder.

Armament One rifled 24pdr (15cm) [one rifled 68pdr (21cm) 1865–71]; two rifled 12pdr (12cm); [*Basilisk* was fitted with one 38.1cm deck-mounted TT].

Handling Seakeeping was similar to the *Jäger* class, but slightly better.

Complement Crew: 4/67. Boats: two.

Notes Colour scheme no 1, 2. For details of appearance refer to the drawing; for rigging see the drawing of the *Jäger* class. These vessels were similar to the *Jäger* class with regard to laying up on land, and to naming. [*Delphin* was rebuilt with the upper deck planks replaced higher up, to make the deck below more habitable.]

Career
Camäleon launched 4 Aug 1860; virtually never in service. Stricken 19 Mar 1872 and reduced to a coal hulk; broken up after 1878.

Comet launched 1 Sept 1860; saw little active service; served abroad 1876 to 1879. Stricken 30 Sept 1881, used as a depot hulk; broken up after 1891.

Cyclop launched 8 Sept 1860, and was only temporarily in service. Stricken 19 Mar 1872, reconstructed

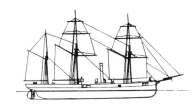

Cyclop (1875); *Camäleon, Comet, Blitz, Basilisk, Meteor* and *Drache*

as the gunboat *Cyclop*, launched 5 Aug 1874; see below.

Delphin launched 15 Sept 1860; served abroad 1864–73, as a survey ship 1874, and as a fisheries protection vessel 1878. Stricken 30 Sept 1881, broken up.

Blitz launched 27 Aug 1862; served abroad 1863 to 1864 and 1866 to 1868. Stricken 28 Dec 1876; reduced to a coal hulk at the Imperial Dockyard, Danzig; broken up 1878.

Basilisk launched 20 Aug 1862; served abroad 1862 to 1864, and as a torpedo gunboat 1873. Stricken 28 Dec 1875; became Mine barge *No 1*; broken up after 1900.

Meteor launched 17 May 1865, commissioned 6 Sept 1869 for service abroad. Stricken 27 Nov 1877; reduced to a coal hulk at Kiel, then used as a target ship.

Drache launched 3 Aug 1865, commissioned 1870; served as a survey ship 1880–86. Stricken 13 Dec 1887; reduced to a coal hulk at Wilhelmshaven; used as a target 1888, and destroyed by a torpedo from the torpedo boat *D 5*; wreck broken up.

Albatross class

Name	Builder	Built	Cost in Marks (000s)	Displacement (t = tonnes T = tons)	Length (m)	Breadth (m)	Draught (m)	Power (hp)	Revs (rpm)	Speed (kts)	Range (nm/kts)	Coal (t)	Oil (t)
ALBATROSS	Imperial Dockyard, Danzig	1869–71	762	786t max 713t des	56.95 oa 51.21 cwl	8.32	3.62 fwd 3.75 aft	491ihp max 601ihp des	104	10.5 max 10.9 des	1270/10	100	—
NAUTILUS 413gt/225nt	,,	1870–73	,,	,,	,,	,,	,,	496ihp max 601ihp des	103	10.0 max 10.9 des	,,	,,	—

Construction Laid down as the gunboat *Ersatz Crocodill* and the aviso *A* (1869). Timber carvel hull with copper sheathing, depth of hull 4.47m.

Propulsion One pair of horizontal single-cylinder single expansion engines by Möller & Hollberg, Stettin (one retractable 2-bladed screw, 3.14m diameter) in an engine room. Two trunk boilers [new cylinders in *Albatross* and trunk boilers in *Nautilus* by the Imperial Dockyard, Kiel] (six fireboxes, 2 atmospheres forced) in a separate boiler room. Barque rig, 710sq m [three-masted schooner rig, 471–415sq m)]. One rudder.

Armament Two 15cm/22 hooped guns (140 rounds), range 4600m; two 12cm/23 hooped guns (180 rounds), range 5500m; [three machine guns. Both vessels were finally disarmed.]

Handling Quite good sea-boats, but with severe speed loss in a head sea; manoeuvred moderately, steered well. Good sailing ships.

Complement Crew: 5/98. Boats: four.

Albatross (1871), *Nautilus*

Notes Colour scheme no 1, 2. [After rigging was removed, one steam pipe was fitted forward of the funnel, 1 + 1 aft of the funnel.] Both vessels had a transom stern.

Career
Albatross launched 11 Mar 1871, commissioned 23 Dec 1871 for service abroad; served as a survey ship 1888. Stricken 9 Jan 1899, and sold as a sea-going lighter; finally became a coal barge. Stranded and destroyed during a storm in March 1906.

Nautilus launched 31 Aug 1871, commissioned 4 Jun 1873; served abroad until 1888, then fulfilled survey duties. Stricken 14 Dec 1896; reduced to a coal hulk at Kiel; sold 1905 for 11,000M and broken up at Swinemünde.

ex Avantgarde class (ex-French)

Construction Laid down as steam gunboats (*canots à vapeur*) on the Loire. Armour: belt 75mm; conning tower 100mm.

Propulsion One screw; no other details of machinery known.

Armament One 12cm muzzle loader (150 rounds) or one 16cm Armstrong breech loader (no of rounds not known).

Name	Builder	Built	Cost in Marks (000s)	Displacement (t = tonnes T = tons)	Length (m)	Breadth (m)	Draught (m)	Power (hp)	Revs (rpm)	Speed (kts)	Range (nm/kts)	Coal (t)	Oil (t)
ex AVANTGARDE	Saint-Denis, Paris	1867–68			12.6	2.85	1.2	12ihp		7			—
ex FRANCTIREUR	,,	,,			,,	,,	,,	,,		,,			—
ex GARDE MOBILE					8.5	2.7	1.0	7ihp		4.4			—
ex BREST					,,	,,	,,	,,		,,			—

Complement Crew: 15 (*Avantgarde* and *Franctireur*), 8 (*Garde Mobile* and *Brest*). Details of boats not known.

Notes Colour scheme no 1. [One boat was fitted with a new engine and new planking by the Imperial Dockyard, Danzig, in 1870.] Their German names and classifications are not known.

Career
All boats were taken as German prizes at Orleans 5 Dec 1870; three boats were then in service. They were transported to Kiel 9 Jan 1871 by water and rail for

Avantgarde, Franctireur (1870), from a contemporary woodcut. *Mrva*

basic repairs. Further use was as follows:

Avantgarde and *Franctireur* were commissioned in the Rhine flotilla 1871, where they were joined after 1874 by *Mosel* and *Rhein* (see below). After 1886 their fate is unknown. *Garde Mobile* and *Brest* became the ferry ships *Clara* and *Sophie* for Norddeutsche Dampfer AG at Kiel (known as 'Jensenstrassen ferries'); they were replaced by new vessels in 1881, and their fate is unknown.

Monitors 1874

Rhein class

Name	Builder	Built	Cost	Displacement (t = tonnes T = tons)	Length (m)	Breadth (m)	Draught (m)	Power (hp)	Revs (rpm)	Speed (kts)	Range (nm/kts)	Coal (t)	Oil (t)
RHEIN, MOSEL 120gt	AG 'Weser', Bremen Construction no 23, 24	1872–74	94.5 Thaler	283t max 200t des	49.60 oa 47.85 cwl	7.85	0.70 fwd 1,07 aft 1.60 max	320ihp des 48nhp	200 des	8.25 max 6.5 des			—

Construction Built as Rhine river monitors (dockyard design, 1872). Transverse frame iron construction, with flooding cells. Wrought iron armour: citadel and turret roof 65mm, sides 55m on 150–200mm teak; CT roof 16mm, sides 40mm. Depth forward 1.30m, aft 1.8m.

Propulsion Two horizontal 2-cylinder single expansion engines (two 3-bladed screws, 0.95m diameter) in one engine room. Two locomotive boilers (four fire-boxes, 7 atmospheres forced) in a separate boiler room. No electrical system.

Armament Two bronze cannon, 12cm/19 (300 rounds).

Handling Manoeuvred slowly, turned very poorly, particularly downstream; turning against the current demanded great skill. Handling when flooded was potentially disastrous.

Complement Crew: 1/22. Boats: one.

Mosel (1872), *Rhein*

Notes Colour unknown, presumably approx no 1. These vessels were built with an obligatory contribution of 300,000 Thaler from the Rhine Railway Company for the defence of the Rhine bridges at Rheinhausen. They were designed to be flooded for action, so that only the upper part of the casemate remained above water; the freeboard was then reduced from 0.6m and 0.75m to 0.05m and 0.20m.

Career
Rhein launched 1872 and *Mosel* launched 1872, commissioned 25 April 1874; transferred after 7 Apr 1875 to the Coblenz defences, based at the Mosel security harbour. Sold late in December for 3500M.

Gunboats 1875–1943

Cyclop

Name	Builder	Built	Cost in Marks (000s)	Displacement (t = tonnes T = tons)	Length (m)	Breadth (m)	Draught (m)	Power (hp)	Revs (rpm)	Speed (kts)	Range (nm/kts)	Coal (t)	Oil (t)
CYCLOP 250gt/144nt	Imperial Dockyard, Danzig	1873–75	340	531t max 411t des	43.30 oa 42.22 cwl	7.00	3.0	380ihp		9.1		82	—

Construction A complete rebuild of the First Rate gunboat *Cyclop* with a transverse frame iron hull and a timber deck.

Propulsion Engines, boilers, etc, were as in *Cyclop*; see above. Barque rig, 510sq m.

Armament Two 12cm/23 hooped guns (165 rounds), range 5500m; she was initially fitted with two 4cm balloon cannon (calibre not known) with hollow-charge si ells for use against air balloons released in Paris in 1870–71, then with two 8.7cm/24 hooped guns (110 rounds); [three machine guns].

Handling Performance was approximately as in *Camaeleon*; the rebuild resulted in no significant improvement at all.

Complement Crew: 5/64. Boats: two.

Notes Colour scheme no 1, 2, 3.

Career
Cyclop launched 5 Aug 1874, commissioned 27 Mar 1875 for service abroad. Stricken 23 Sept 1888; used after 2 Nov 1888 as a hulk in the Cameroons; broken up after 1914.

Wespe class

Name	Builder	Built	Cost in Marks (000s)	Displacement (t = tonnes T = tons)	Length (m)	Breadth (m)	Draught (m)	Power (hp)	Revs (rpm)	Speed (kts)	Range (nm/kts)	Coal (t)	Oil (t)
WESPE, VIPER	AG 'Weser', Bremen Construction nos 31, 32	1875–76	1075	1163t max 1098t des	46.4 oa 45.5 cwl	10.6	3.37 fwd 3.20 aft to 3.24 fwd 3.40 aft	800ihp max 700ihp des	139	10.4	700/7 450/10	40	—
BIENE, MÜCKE	Construction nos 33, 34	1876–77	1257	,,	,,	,,	,,	711ihp max 700ihp des	129	11.0	,,	,,	—
SCORPION, BASILISK	Construction nos 35, 36	1877–80	1161	,,	,,	,,	,,	764ihp max 700ihp des	133	11.0	,,	,,	—
CAMAELEON, CROCODILL	Construction nos 37, 40	1878–80	1145	,,	,,	,,	,,	786ihp max 700ihp des	136	11.2	,,	,,	—
SALAMANDER, NATTER, HUMMEL 473gt/213nt	Construction nos 41, 44, 45	1879–81	1056	,,	,,	,,	,,	756ihp max 700ihp des	136	11.1.1 max 9.0 des	,,	,,	—

Construction Laid down as armoured vessels *A–H*, *J–L* (official design, 1875). Transverse frame iron construction (ten watertight compartments, double bottom 55 percent). Wrought iron armour: deck 22–22 + 28mm; [conning towert 20m]; CWL 102–152–203mm on 210mm teak; barbette 203mm on 210mm teak. Depth 3.9m. Immersion increased by 1cm per 3.99t. Trim moment 1071m-t.

Propulsion Two inclined 2-cylinder double expansion engines (two 4-bladed screws, 2.5m diameter) in an engine room. Four cylindrica! boilers, after *Biene* transverse, (eight fireboxes, 4 atmospheres forced, 294sq m) in a separate boiler room. [One generator, 1.75–1.9kW 55V.] One rudder.

Armament One 30.5cm/22 hooped gun (38 rounds), –5° +20°, range 10,000m; [two 8.7cm/24 hooped guns (200 rounds); two machine guns; two 35cm bow TT (2 rounds), under water, after 1883].

Handling Very poor sea-boats, with violent roll, though with gentle motion at half speed in a head sea; firing was impossible in wind speeds 4–5 and above. The decks shipped much water. All vessels had marked weather helm, and severe turning moment, which made steering difficult and uncertain; a turn, once initiated, was difficult to stop.

Complement Crew: 3/73–3/85 (plus 3/5 [3/8] as second flagship). Boats: two pinnaces, one cutter, one yawl, one dinghy.

Notes Colour scheme no 2, 4, 9. The barbette was semi-circular, open aft; [the open-topped breast protection was only useful against the sea]. These floating gun batteries (eighteen were projected) attracted many nicknames, including *Insektengeschwader* (insect squadron), *Schlickrutscher* (mud sliders) and *Wattwanzen* (mudflat bugs), particularly because, when necessary, they could be left high and dry on mud flats and sands at ebb tide to act as stationary defensive batteries.

Career

Wespe launched 6 Jul 1876, commissioned 26 Nov 1876; saw little service. Stricken 28 Jun 1909; sold 1910 for 52,000M to Düsseldorf; used as a barge.

Viper launched 21 Sept 1876, commissioned 27 Mar 1877; saw little service. Stricken 28 Jun 1909; converted to a navy crane ship at Helgoland, lifting capacity 100t; transferred to Wilhelmshaven and other sites; still in existence in 1962.

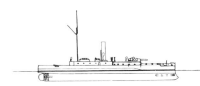

Wespe (1886), *Viper, Biene, Mücke, Scorpion, Basilisk, Camaeleon, Crocodill, Salamander, Natter, Hummel*, first form.

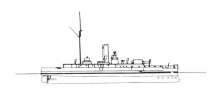

Wespe (1900), *Viper, Biene, Mücke, Scorpion, Basilisk, Camaeleon, Crocodill, Salamander, Natter, Hummel*, final form.

Biene launched 2 Dec 1876, commissioned 20 Aug 1877; saw very little service. Stricken 27 Sept 1910; converted to a floating workshop; sold 1921 to Bremen for 660,000M, broken up 1921 at Wewelsfleth.

Mücke launched 5 May 1877, commissioned 25 Feb 1878; saw very little service; finally used in leakage

experiments. Stricken 18 Mar 1911, used as a stoker ship and for further leakage tests; sold 25 Jun 1921 for 100,000M; broken up 1921 at Wewelsfleth.

Scorpion launched 19 May 1877, commissioned 12 Dec 1877; saw little service. Stricken 18 Mar 1911; converted to a floating firing stand for the torpedo workshop at Flensburg; sold 3 Aug 1919 for 68,000M; used as a floating wrecking workshop at Kiel; broken up at Kiel in 1924.

Basilisk launched 14 Sept 1878, commissioned 20 Aug 1880; saw very little service. Stricken 27 Sept 1910; used in leakage experiments; sold 1919 for 62,660M; broken up 1920 at Hamburg.

Camaeleon launched 21 Dec 1878, commissioned 10 Nov 1879; saw very little service. Stricken 28 Jun 1909, sold 1910 for 52,000M to Düsseldorf; used as a barge.

Crocodill launched 13 Sept 1879, commissioned 7 May 1880; saw very little service. Stricken 18 Mar 1911; used as a target ship, then after 1913 as a floating workshop at Wilhelmshaven; broken up after 1918.

Salamander launched 6 Jan 1880, commissioned 11 Oct 1880; saw little service. Stricken 28 Jun 1909, sold 1910 for 52,000M to Düsseldorf; sunk on transfer in November 1910, west of Castricum, position 52° 33.1N, 04° 36.1E, after stranding in a storm; the superstructure was broken up in 1936, and the rest of the wreck became silted up.

Natter launched 29 Sept 1880, commissioned 20 May 1881; saw very little service. Stricken 18 Mar 1911; converted to *Stromquelle I – Power Source I –* at Wilhelmshaven until 1924, then at Kiel; used as stoker barge *Natter*, 1928; wrecked 1946 at Kiel-Mönckeberg.

Hummel launched 12 Feb 1881, commissioned 28 Aug 1881; saw little service. Stricken 27 Sept 1910; converted to a floating workshop, then used from 1923 as a depot hulk at Swinemünde 194; converted to an AA ship; sunk 4 May 1945 at Swinemünde by an aircraft bomb.

Otter

Name	Builder	Built	Cost in Marks (000s)	Displacement (t = tonnes T = tons)	Length (m)	Breadth (m)	Draught (m)	Power (hp)	Revs (rpm)	Speed (kts)	Range (nm/kts)	Coal (t)	Oil (t)
OTTER 106gt/61nt	F Schichau, Elbing Construction no 110	1877–78		164t max 130t des	31.0 oa 29.1 cwl	6.15	1.13 fwd 1.63 aft	142ihp max 140ihp des	250	8.0	1181/7	15	—

Construction Built as a pirate hunter for China (designed 1878). Transverse frame iron construction (four watertight compartments).

Propulsion Two vertical 2-cylinder single expansion engines (two 4-bladed screws, 1.0m diameter) in one engine room. One cylindrical boiler (two fireboxes, 5 atmospheres forced, 59sq m) in a separate boiler room. Schooner rig, 325sq m [bowsprit later removed]. One rudder.

Armament One 12cm/23 hooped gun in the bow.

Handling Poor sea-boat, making severe leeway; nevertheless, she manoeuvred and steered very well.

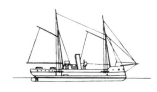

Otter (1888)

Complement Crew: 1/42. Boats: one yawl, one dinghy.

Notes Colour scheme no 1, 2, 4, 9.

Career
Otter launched 7 Jun 1877, commissioned 1 Apr 1878, intended for China, but never left Germany; served as a mine training ship. Stricken 27 May 1907; used as a training hulk, and after 1912 as a coal barge; sold 1913 to a Kiel company; broken up 1926.

Wolf class

Name	Builder	Built	Cost in Marks (000s)	Displacement (t = tonnes T = tons)	Length (m)	Breadth (m)	Draught (m)	Power (hp)	Revs (rpm)	Speed (kts)	Range (nm/kts)	Coal (t)	Oil (t)
WOLF	Imperial Dockyard, Wilhelmshaven Construction no 3	1876–78	487	570t max 490t des	47.2 oa 44.5 cwl	7.66	3.10 fwd 3.40 aft	290ihp max 340ihp des	138	9.4 max 8.5 des	1640/9	95 to 112	—
HYÄNE	Imperial Dockyard, Wilhelmshaven Construction no 4	1876–79	487	,,	,,	,,	,,	373ihp max 340ihp des	145	9.9 max 8.5 des	,,	,,	—
ILTIS 295gt/121nt	Imperial Dockyard, Danzig	1877–80	550	,,	,,	,,	,,	365ihp max 340ihp des	140	9.2 max 8.5 des	,,	,,	—

Construction Laid down as First Rate gunboats *Ersatz Salamander*, *Ersatz Meteor* and *Ersatz Tiger* of the improved *Cyclop* type (official design, 1876). Transverse frame iron construction with timber deck (six watertight compartments). Depth 2.92m. Immersion increased by 1cm per 2.56t. Trim moment 594m-t.

Propulsion Fitted with engines from *Blitz*, *Basilisk* and *Delphin* (see page 133), adapted by the Imperial Dockyard, Wilhelmshaven (one retractable 2-bladed screw, 2.53m diameter) in one engine room. Two trunk boilers with superheaters (four fireboxes, 2 atmospheres forced, 163sq m) [new boilers were fitted in *Wolf*, 1885, by the Imperial Dockyard, Kiel, and in *Hyäne*, 1888, by the Imperial Dockyard, Danzig] in a separate boiler room. No electrical system. Barque rig 541sq m [schooner barque rig 290sq m; *Hyäne* was reduced to auxiliary sails]. One rudder.

Armament Two 12.5cm/23 hooped guns (270 rounds), range 5200m; two 8.7cm/24 hooped guns (200 rounds); three machine guns [*Wolf* was refitted with one 8.7cm/24 hooped gun (113 rounds), one 5cm/40 QF gun in a torpedo boat mount (250 rounds) and two machine guns; *Hyäne* was disarmed in 1897].

Handling Good sea-boats, though with considerable pitch and roll. Ran well before the wind, but could make very little way against a head sea. All vessels were responsive and manoeuvrable, and performed well under sail.

Wolf (1886), *Hyäne*, *Iltis*

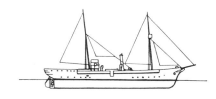

Hyäne (1905)

Complement Crew: 5/80 [*Hyäne*, 5/101]. Boats: one pinnace, two cutters, one yawl, one dinghy [later one barge, one or two cutters, one yawl, one dinghy].

Notes Colour scheme no 2, 3, 4, 8, 9, 11. The initial rig was similar to that shown in the drawing of *Cyclop*. *Iltis* had 1 + 1 steam pipes 6.5m above the CWL and 1m forward of the funnel, instead of on its forward edge. All vessels had a forecastle and flying deck.

Career
Wolf launched 21 Mar 1878, commissioned 1 Oct 1878 for service abroad and as a survey vessel. Stricken 3 Feb 1906; converted to a repair ship at Danzig; sold 26 Apr 1919 to Düsseldorf and broken up.

Hyäne launched 27 Jun 1878, commissioned 15 Aug 1879 for service abroad; became a survey ship 1898; served as a guard ship on the Eider from August 1914; used again as a survey ship from May 1916. Stricken 7 Apr 1920 after being sold 15 Jul 1919 for 200,000M to the Cuxhaven-Brunsbüttel Steamer Company, for whom she became a three-masted steam schooner under the name *Seewolf*. Sunk 2 May 1924 after her cargo caught fire at Dieppe; raised and broken up.

Iltis launched 18 Sept 1878, commissioned 2 Mar 1880 for service abroad. Sunk in the Yellow Sea, position 36° 54N, 122° 30E, during a typhoon; 76 dead.

Habicht class

Construction Laid down as First Rate gunboats *B*, *C* and *Ersatz Comet* (1878). Transverse frame iron construction, timber planking with zinc sheathing, timber deck (nine watertight compartments). Depth 3.63m. Trim moment 1071m-t.

Propulsion One horizontal 3-cylinder double expansion engine (retractable 2-bladed screw, 3.23m diameter, *Adler* 2.8m diameter) in one engine room. Two, *Adler* four, cylindrical boilers (four/eight fireboxes, 6 atmospheres forced, 251–241–360sq m) [new boilers fitted 1895 and 1889 by the Imperial Dockyard, Kiel] in one boiler room. No electrical system. Barque rig, 847sq m [three-masted topsail schooner rig, 601sq m; *Möwe* finally square-rigged schooner rig, 361sq m]. One rudder.

Armament One 15cm/22 hooped gun (115 rounds) plus four 12cm/23 hooped guns (440 rounds) [after 1882 five 12.5cm/23 hooped guns (620 rounds), range 5600m, and five machine guns; *Möwe* was armed with two 12.5cm/23 hooped guns (246 rounds) and five machine guns after 1890, and finally five machine guns only].

Handling Very good sea-boats with good sailing performance; gentle motion and shipped little water. Speed loss in a head sea was severe, but all vessels manoeuvred and steered well.

Complement Crew: 6/121 – 7/126. Boats: one picket boat, one pinnace, two cutters, one yawl, one dinghy.

Name	Builder	Built	Cost in Marks (000s)	Displacement (t = tonnes T = tons)	Length (m)	Breadth (m)	Draught (m)	Power (hp)	Revs (rpm)	Speed (kts)	Range (nm/kts)	Coal (t)	Oil (t)
HABICHT	F Schichau, Elbing Construction no 144	1878–80	661	1005t max 840t des	59.2 oa 53.8 cwl	8.90	3.52 fwd 4.18 aft	801ihp max 600ihp des	124	11.4 max 11.0 des	2010/9 1230/11	100	—
MÖWE	F Schichau, Elbing Construction no 143	,,	668	,,	,,	,,	,,	886ihp max 600ihp des	130	11.7 max 11.0 des	,,	,,	—
ADLER	Imperial Dockyard, Kiel Construction no 7	1882–84	881	1040t max 880t des	61.8 oa 58.1 cwl	8.80	3.11 fwd 4.02 aft	950ihp max 700ihp des	142	11.3 max 11.0 des	2000/9	110	—

569gt/256nt (*Habicht, Möwe*), 583gt/332nt (*Adler*)

Notes Colour scheme no 2, 3, 4, 8, 9, 11. [After re-rigging all vessels had one steam pipe forward of the funnel and one aft of the funnel; the pressure head ventilators were also raised.] All vessels had a fore-castle; *Möwe* also had a flying deck. *Adler* had the same proportions, but was slightly larger than the *Möwe* drawing.

Career
Habicht launched 13 May 1879, commissioned 18 Mar 1880; served mostly abroad. Stricken 24 Mar 1906;

Möwe (1899), *Habicht*; *Adler* was similar.

sold 28 Aug 1906 for 71,000M; broken up at Harburg.

Möwe launched 8 Oct 1879, commissioned 31 May 1880 for service abroad. Stricken 9 Dec 1905; used as a hulk at Tsingtau; sold 1910 and scuttled 1914 at the same location (?).

Adler launched 3 Nov 1883, commissioned 27 May 1885; served abroad 1886–89. Sunk, together with *Eber* (see page 141), in Samoa, position 13° 49S, 171° 46W, after stranding in a hurricane; 20 dead. Wreck still in existence.

Hay

Name	Builder	Built	Cost in Marks (000s)	Displacement (t = tonnes T = tons)	Length (m)	Breadth (m)	Draught (m)	Power (hp)	Revs (rpm)	Speed (kts)	Range (nm/kts)	Coal (t)	Oil (t)
HAY 173gt/74nt	Imperial Dockyard, Danzig	1880–82		247t max 200t des	34.0 oa 31.2 cwl	6.40	2.25 fwd 2.81 aft	202ihp	180	9.3	2400/5 680/9	15	—

Construction Laid down as the gunboat *Ersatz Habicht* (designed 1880). Timber carvel construction with copper sheathing, iron transverse bulkheads (four watertight compartments). Freeboard 1.32m.

Propulsion One vertical 2-cylinder double expansion engine (one 4-bladed screw, 1.7m diameter) in one engine room. Two cylindrical boilers (two fireboxes, 5 atmospheres forced, 70sq m) [new boilers by the Imperial Dockyard, Wilhelmshaven] in a separate boiler room. One generator, 1.75kW 55V. One rudder.

Armament Four 8.7cm/24 hooped guns and four ma-

chine guns [replaced after 1891 by two 8.8cm/30 QF guns (300 rounds)].

Handling Good sea-boat for the size of the vessel. Towing speed in smooth water was 5 to 2kts, depending on the size of the target.

Hay (1900)

Complement Crew: 2/38. Boats: two yawls, one dinghy.

Notes Colour scheme no 2, 4, 9.

Career

Hay launched 28 Sept 1881, commissioned 15 Jun 1882 as tender to *Mars*. Stricken 28 Sept 1906; used as a target barge at Kiel-Friedrichsort; stricken again 5 May 1919; sold for 18,000M; broken up at Wewelsfleth.

Brummer class

Construction Laid down as armoured vessels *M* and *N* (official design, 1883). Transverse frame steel construction (eight watertight compartments). Compound

steel armour on teak; deck two layers, 40–25–0mm; coaming 160mm on 200mm teak; cork and trunk cofferdams. Depth 3.9m. Trim moment 1200m-t.

Propulsion Two inclined 2-cylinder double expansion engines (one 4-bladed screw, 3.6m diameter) in one engine room. Two locomotive boilers (four fireboxes,

Name	Builder	Built	Cost in Marks (000s)	Displacement (t = tonnes T = tons)	Length (m)	Breadth (m)	Draught (m)	Power (hp)	Revs (rpm)	Speed (kts)	Range (nm/kts)	Coal (t)	Oil (t)
BRUMMER	AG 'Weser', Bremen Construction no 52	1883–84		929t max 867t des	64.8 oa 62.6 cwl	8.50	2.68 fwd 4.77 aft	1658ihp max	162	14.1 max	1370/10 max 470/15 des	68	—
BREMSE 538gt/353nt	AG 'Weser', Bremen Construction no 53	"		"	"	"	"	2081ihp max	175	15.2 max	"	"	—

7 atmospheres forced, 510sq m) [Brummer was fitted with new boilers by the Imperial Dockyard, Wilhelmshaven (396sq m)] in a separate boiler room. Two generators, 9.75kW 65V. One rudder.

Armament One 21cm/30 hooped gun (50 rounds), –8° +13°, range 7900m; one 8.7cm/24 hooped gun (75 rounds); two machine guns; one 35cm bow TT (3 rounds), under water [TT and hooped guns finally deleted on Brummer].

Handling Good sea-boats, with little speed loss in head sea, but very wet; beam seas caused sudden severe roll movements (up to 35°). Poor turning circle.

Complement Crew: 5/73 – 3/62. Boats: one picket boat, one launch, one cutter, one yawl, one dinghy.

Notes Colour scheme no 2, 4, 9. Up to 1900 the funnel was 1m lower, and there was no aft platform.

Brummer (1895), *Bremse*

Career
Brummer launched 5 Jan 1884, commissioned 10 Oct 1884 as a torpedo boat flotilla flagship; served as a fisheries protection vessel 1891–94, and as a machine weapon training ship. Stricken 27 May 1907; used as a storage hulk; used in 1914 as a hawser barrier and barrack hulk at Kiel; sold 2 Jul 1921 for 165,000M; broken up 1922 at Wilhelmshaven.

Bremse launched 29 May 1884, commissioned 22 Dec 1884; varied service. Stricken 10 Mar 1903; used as an inventory barge, then as a fuel oil barge; sold 1910 for 52,000M to Düsseldorf as a barge.

Eber

Name	Builder	Built	Cost in Marks (000s)	Displacement (t = tonnes T = tons)	Length (m)	Breadth (m)	Draught (m)	Power (hp)	Revs (rpm)	Speed (kts)	Range (nm/kts)	Coal (t)	Oil (t)
EBER 377gt/222nt	Imperial Dockyard, Kiel Construction no 10	1886–87	732	735t max 582t des	51.7 oa 48.5 cwl	8.00	3.10 fwd 3.80 aft	760ihp	115	11.0	2000/9	78	—

Construction Laid down as the gunboat *Ersatz Albatross* (design 1885). Transverse frame iron construction (five watertight compartments). Depth not known.

Propulsion One horizontal 3-cylinder double expansion engine (one retractable 2-bladed screw, 2.8m diameter) in one engine room. Two cylindrical boilers (four fireboxes, 6 atmospheres forced, 310sq m) in one boiler room. Barque rig 590sq m. One rudder.

Armament Three 10.5cm/35 hooped guns (390

Eber (1888)

rounds), range 8000m; four machine guns.

Handling and **Complement** As *Wolf* class, but crew: 5/76.

Notes Colour scheme no 2.

Career
Eber launched 15 Feb 1887, commissioned 25 Sept 1887 for service abroad. Sunk 16 Mar 1889 in Samoa, position 13° 49S, 171° 46W, in a hurricane; 73 dead.

Loreley

Construction Laid down as the private yacht *Mohican*, purchased and designated as *Ersatz Loreley*. Transverse frame steel construction, timber deck (seven watertight compartments), immersion increased by 1cm per 3.73t. Trim moment 1158m-t.

Propulsion One vertical 3-cylinder triple expansion engine (one 4-bladed screw, 3.66m diameter) in one engine room. One cylindrical boiler (four fireboxes, 9 atmospheres forced, 204sq m) in a separate boiler room. Two generators, 11.4kW 60V. Schooner rig,

435sq m [later with a Bermudan mizzen, 400sq m]. One rudder.

Armament Two 5cm/40 QF guns in torpedo boat mounts (265 rounds), range 4800m.

Name	Builder	Built	Cost in Marks (000s)	Displacement (t = tonnes T = tons)	Length (m)	Breadth (m)	Draught (m)	Power (hp)	Revs (rpm)	Speed (kts)	Range (nm/kts)	Coal (t)	Oil (t)
LORELEY 536gt/313nt	D & W Henderson & Co, Glasgow	1884–86	501	924t max 920t des	68.7 oa 61.0 cwl	8.40	3.78 fwd 4.58 aft	700ihp	97.1	11.9	3900/9	180 max 160 des	—

Handling Good sea-boat, but with severe pitch in a head sea sufficient to endanger the bowsprit, and shipping much water; similar problems were evident in a beam sea, causing severe roll. Ran downwind well, hove to well. Steered well, though more easily to starboard than to port. The sails made a useful contribution to performance.

Complement Crew: 4/57. Boats: one barge, two [one] cutters, one [two] yawls, one dinghy.

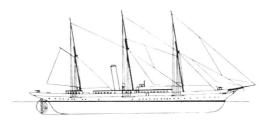

Loreley (1900)

Notes Colour scheme no 8, 11.

Career
Loreley launched 1 Jun 1885 as *Mohican*, a private yacht built by J & W Clark and Family, Glasgow; purchased 6 Aug 1896 and commissioned as *Ersatz Loreley*; renamed *Loreley* 7 Sept 1896 and served abroad. Stricken 2 Nov 1918, and transferred to Turkey; sold in February 1925 to a Turkish shipping company and renamed *Haci Pasa*; lost 1 Jan 1926 in the Black Sea.

Iltis class

Name	Builder	Built	Cost in Marks (000s)	Displacement (t = tonnes T = tons)	Length (m)	Breadth (m)	Draught (m)	Power (hp)	Revs (rpm)	Speed (kts)	Range (nm/kts)	Coal (t)	Oil (t)
ILTIS	F Schichau, Danzig Construction no 630	1897–98	1497	1048t max 894t des	65.2 oa 63.9 cwl	9.10	3.59 fwd 3.63 aft	1378ihp max 1300ihp des	156 max 150 des	14.8 max 13.5 des	3080/9 max	190 max 120 des	—
JAGUAR	F Schichau, Danzig Construction no 631	1898–99	1462	,,	,,	,,	,,	1378ihp max 1300ihp des	157 max 150 des	14.6 max 13.5 des	,,	,,	—
TIGER	Imperial Dockyard, Danzig	1898–1900	1665	1108t max 894t des	65.2 oa 63.9 cwl	,,	3.56 fwd 3.74 aft	1372ihp max 1300ihp des	163	14.0 max 13.5 des	2580/9 max	203 max 165 des	—
LUCHS	Imperial Dockyard, Danzig	,,	1622	,,	,,	,,	,,	1345ihp max 1300ihp des	,,	13.9 max 13.5 des	,,	,,	—
PANTHER	Imperial Dockyard, Danzig	1900–02	1675	1193t max 977t des	66.9 oa 64.1 cwl	9.70	3.54 for 3.62 aft	1344ihp max 1300ihp des	153	13.7 max 13.5 des	3400/9 max	283 max 240 des	—
EBER	AG Vulcan, Stettin Construction no 257	1902–03	1632	,,	,,	,,	,,	1314ihp max 1300ihp des	181	14.3 max 13.5 des	,,	,,	—

726gt/449nt (*Iltis*, *Jaguar*), 758gt/495nt (*Tiger*, *Luchs*), 783gt/525nt (*Panther*, *Eber*)

Construction Laid down as gunboats *Erstaz Iltis*, *Ersatz Hyäne*, *Ersatz Wolf*, *Ersatz Habicht*, *A* and *B* (official design, 1897, 1898). Transverse frame composite steel-timber (Muntz metal) construction (eleven watertight compartments, after *Tiger* double bottom below engine room). Depth *Iltis* and *Jaguar*, 4.86m; *Tiger* and *Luchs*, unknown; *Panther* and *Eber*, 4.71m. Immersion increased by 1cm per 11.42t. Trim moment 1610–1647m-t.

Propulsion Two horizontal (vertical after *Tiger*) 3-cylinder triple expansion engines (two 3-bladed screws, 2.6m diameter (2.4m diameter after *Panther*) in one engine room. Four Thornycroft (Marine-type after *Panther*) boilers (four fireboxes, 13 atmospheres forced, 381sq m, *Panther* 408sq m, *Eber* 366sq m) in one boiler room; *Panther* had two lower boilers with one upper horizontal boiler above each. 1 + 1 funnels, circular in cross-section. Two generators, 16kW 67V;

Panther, three generators, 17.8kW 67V; *Eber* three generators, 20kW 110V. One rudder.

Armament Four 8.8cm/30 QF guns (1124 rounds), range 7300m, plus six machine cannon (9000 rounds); after *Tiger*, two 10.5cm/40 QF guns (482 rounds), range 12,200m, plus six machine cannon (9000 rounds). [*Panther* was disarmed after 1920.]

Handling Very good sea-boats, with gentle motion but severe roll in a beam sea and marked yaw and heel to lee in a quartering sea; reasonably dry. Excellent to manoeuvre and steer, except in shallow water and at high speed; hove to well.

Complement Crew: 9/121. Boats: one barge, one cutter, one yawl, one dinghy; *Panther* and *Eber* carried an extra cutter on the boat on port beam as a surf boat, and an extra two sampans were carried for duty on the China station.

Notes Colour scheme no 9, 11.

Career

Iltis launched 4 Aug 1898, commissioned 1 Dec 1898 for service abroad. Scuttled 28 Sept 1914 at Chiao-chou, position 36° 03N, 120° 16E.

Jaguar launched 19 Sept 1898, commissioned 4 Apr 1899 for service abroad. Scuttled 7 Nov 1914 at Chiao-chou, position 36° 03N, 120° 16E.

Tiger launched 15 Aug 1899, commissioned 3 Apr 1900 for service abroad. Scuttled 29 Oct 1914 at Chiao-chou, position 36° 03N, 120° 16E.

Luchs launched 18 Oct 1899, commissioned 15 May 1900 for serive abroad. Scuttled 28 Sept 1914 at Chiao-chou, position 36° 03N, 120° 16E.

Panther launched 1 Apr 1901, commissioned 15 Mar 1902 for service abroad until 1914; served as a coastal defence vessel, and then in Reichsmarine survey work 1921–26. Stricken 31 Mar 1931, sold 1931 for 37,000M to a Frankfurt company; broken up at Wilhelmshaven.

Eber launched 6 Jun 1903, commissioned 15 Sept 1903 for service abroad. After fitting out the auxiliary cruiser *Cap Trafalgar* (commissioned as an armed merchant cruiser 31 Aug 1914) she sailed for Brazil under the merchant flag, and was interned on 14 Sept 1914. Set on fire and scuttled 26 Oct 1917 at Bahia, position 12° 50S, 38° 30W.

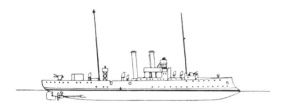

Iltis (1901), *Jaguar*

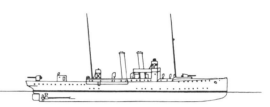

Panther (1910), *Eber*; *Tiger* and *Luchs* were similar.

Meteor

Name	Builder	Built	Cost in Marks (000s)	Displacement (t = tonnes T = tons)	Length (m)	Breadth (m)	Draught (m)	Power (hp)	Revs (rpm)	Speed (kts)	Range (nm/kts)	Coal (t)	Oil (t)
METEOR	Imperial Dockyard, Danzig and Reichs Dockyard, Wilhelmshaven Construction no 101	1914–24		1504t max 1200t des	71.1 oa 67.0 cwl	10.2	3.6 fwd 4.0 aft	1550ihp max 885ihp des	145 des	11.5 des	3650/10 des	440 max 390 des	—
	mod: Deutsche Werke, Kiel	1934						2200ehp		14.5des	1000/9 des	—	44
1168gt/892nt													

Construction Laid down as gunboat *C* (official design 1913, modified 1923). Transverse frame steel construction (ten watertight compartments, double bottom).

Propulsion Two vertical 3-cylinder triple expansion engines (two 3-bladed screws, 2.4m diameter) in one engine room. Two (four planned) Marine-type boilers (four fireboxes, 16 atmospheres forced, 266sq m) in one boiler room. [Her engines and boilers were replaced after 1934 by two MAN 8-cylinder four-stroke diesels.] Schooner-brig rig 463sq m until 1930 (4kts). One rudder.

Armament (Planned 1914) four 10.5cm/45 QF guns (600 rounds); unarmed until 1930; [one 8.8cm/45 AA gun (400 rounds) and two 2cm AA guns (4000 rounds) from 1930].

Handling As *Iltis* class; see above.

Complement Crew: 9/115 [10/128]. Boats: one launch, one cutter, one dinghy.

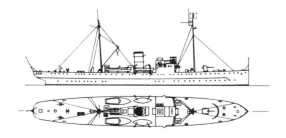

Meteor (1913 design). *Mrva*

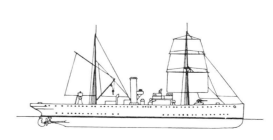

Meteor (1930)

Notes Colour scheme no 9. Planned as an enlarged *Iltis* class ship, with a vent with a coaming forward of the mainmast. Until 1930 she was rigged as a brigantine. The funnel was initially [and after 1934] 2.5m shorter; originally two funnels were planned. [After 1944 the foremast was fitted with two light angled struts, and a rangefinder mattress in place of the searchlight on an extended platform.

Career
Meteor launched 18 Jan 1915, commissioned 15 Nov 1924 for survey work, research and fisheries protection; transferred to the German Hydrographic Institute 27 Sept 1945; taken as a Soviet prize in December 1945; returned to the German Hydrographic Institute 17 Jun 1946; finally taken as a Soviet prize 1 Nov 1946, and renamed *Ekvator*; still in service in 1972 as a barrack ship in the Baltic, named *PKZ-34*.

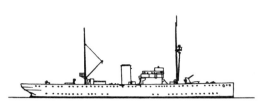
Meteor (1939)

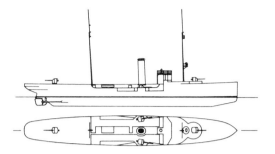
Meteor (1944). *Mrva*

Vorwärts

Name	Builder	Built	Cost in Marks (000s)	Displacement (t = tonnes T = tons)	Length (m)	Breadth (m)	Draught (m)	Power (hp)	Revs (rpm)	Speed (kts)	Range (nm/kts)	Coal (t)	Oil (t)
VORWÄRTS 262gt/156nt	Farnham Boyd & Co, Shanghai	1899		406t	47.0 oa 47.7 cwl	7.50	1.46 fwd 2.20 aft	500ihp		11		68	

Construction Laid down as the merchant steamer *Wuchow*. Transverse frame steel construction (five watertight compartments). Depth 1.52m.

Propulsion Two vertical 2-cylinder double expansion engines (two 4-bladed screws, 1.1m diameter) in one engine room. One cylindrical boiler (three fireboxes, 8.5 atmospheres forced, 119sq m) in a separate boiler room. One generator, 4.8kW 60V. Two rudders.

Armament Two 5cm/40 QF guns (423 rounds) plus two heavy machine guns.

Vorwärts (1900)

Complement Crew: 3/30 plus 3 Chinese. Boats: one yawl, one sampan.

Notes Colour scheme no 11.

Career
Vorwärts launched 1899 as a passenger steamer belonging to the Hongkong, Canton & Macao Steamboat Co Ltd, Hongkong; purchased 1900, and named *Wuchow*; commissioned into the Imperial navy 19 Mar 1901 on the China Yangtze-Kiang station. Stricken 18 Jun 1910; sold 1911 to Shanghai for 50,000M.

Schamien

Name	Builder	Built	Cost in Marks (000s)	Displacement (t = tonnes T = tons)	Length (m)	Breadth (m)	Draught (m)	Power (hp)	Revs (rpm)	Speed (kts)	Range (nm/kts)	Coal (t)	Oil (t)
SCHAMIEN 27gt	China		41.9	36.8t	24.0	3.60	1.4	100ihp		10	450/10	5.5	—

Construction Laid down as the steam boat *Tong Cheong*. Transverse frame steel construction.

Propulsion One vertical 2-cylinder double expansion engine (one 3-bladed screw, 0.7m diameter) in one engine room. One cylindrical boiler in a separate boiler room. One rudder.

Schamien (1900)

Armament One machine gun and two heavy machine guns; one pivot-mounted 6cm/18 boat gun.

Complement Crew 1/10 plus 6 Chinese.

Notes Colour scheme no 11.

Career
Schamien launched as steam boat *Tong Cheong* (date unknown), in the Canton river; purchased from the Kowloon Dock Co 1 Jan 1899; served on the Pearl river station from 20 Oct 1900. Stricken 27 Jan 1904, sold 10 Feb 1904 for 8000 silver dollars to Hongkong; ultimate fate unknown.

Tsingtau class

Name	Builder	Built	Cost in Marks (000s)	Displacement (t = tonnes T = tons)	Length (m)	Breadth (m)	Draught (m)	Power (hp)	Revs (rpm)	Speed (kts)	Range (nm/kts)	Coal (t)	Oil (t)
TSINGTAU	F Schichau, Elbing Construction no 710	1902–04	497	280t max 223t des	50.1 oa 48.0 cwl	8.00	0.93 fwd 0.94 aft	1300ihp	450	13	1630/9 max	up to 85	—
VATERLAND 249gt/67nt	F Schichau, Elbing Construction no 711	1903–04	492	,,	,,	,,	,,	,,	,,	,,	,,	,,	—

Construction Laid down as river gunboats *A* and *B* for the main fleet detachment abroad (design 1902). Transverse frame steel construction (nine watertight compartments consisting of steel pontoons bolted together). Light special steel armour, 8–12mm.

Propulsion Two vertical 3-cylinder triple expansion engines (two 3-bladed screws, 0.95m diameter, in a Yarrow tunnel stern) in engine pontoon no IV. Two Thornycroft-Schulz boilers (four fireboxes, 12 atmospheres forced, 250sq m) in boiler room pontoons V and VI. One generator, 5kW 67V. Two rudders.

Armament One 8.8cm/30 QF gun (100 rounds), range 6900m; one 5cm/40 QF gun (200 rounds); two to three heavy machine guns.

Complement Crew: 3/44 plus 9 Chinese trimmers and cooks plus 2 Chinese pilots. Boats: two yawls, one dinghy.

Notes Colour scheme no 9, 11. Transferred to East Asia in a dismantled state, with nine separate pontoons

Tsingtau (1901), *Vaterland*

and superstructure components, and assembled there. Initially no wireless telegraphy topmasts were carried.

Career
Tsingtau launched 18 Apr 1903, commissioned 3 Feb 1904 on the China Whampoa river station; laid up 2 Aug 1914. Scuttled at Canton, position 23° 06N, 113° 15E, on 21 Mar 1917 after China declared war.

Vaterland launched 26 Aug 1903, commissioned 28 May 1904 on detachment from the main group of fleet units abroad to the China Yangtze-Kiang station; laid up 18 Aug 1914 at Nanking, position 32° 04N, 118° 45E. Apparently sold to a German company and renamed *Landesvater*; requisitioned by China 20 Mar 1917, and became the Chinese gunboat *Li-Sui*; taken over 1932 by the Manchukuo regime, became the Manchurian *Risui*; out of service 1942; ultimate fate unknown.

Otter

Name	Builder	Built	Cost in Marks (000s)	Displacement (t = tonnes T = tons)	Length (m)	Breadth (m)	Draught (m)	Power (hp)	Revs (rpm)	Speed (kts)	Range (nm/kts)	Coal (t)	Oil (t)
OTTER 281gt/96nt	Tecklenborg, Geestemünde Constructon no 232	1909–10	780	314t max 266t des	54.1 oa 53.0 cwl	8.65	0.85 fwd 0.82 aft	1728ihp max 1300ihp des	365 max 350 des	15.2 max	4350/5	87	—

Construction Laid down as river gunboat *C* (dockyard design, 1909). Transverse frame steel construction in special steels (nine watertight compartments; steel pontoons bolted together). Depth not known. Immersion increased by 1cm per 3.48t.

Propulsion Two vertical 3-cylinder triple expansion engines (two 3-bladed screws, 1.4m diameter, in a tun-

Otter (1912)

nel stern) in engine pontoon IV. Two Marine-type boilers (four fireboxes, 16 atmospheres forced, 376sq m) in boiler room pontoons V and VI. One generator, 5.4kW 67V. Two rudders.

Armament Two 5.2cm/55 QF guns (298 rounds), range 7100m; three heavy machine guns.

Handling River gunboats turned very well, but with severe loss of speed; the wind affected steering seriously. *Otter* suffered from severe lee helm, and made severe leeway.

Complement Crew: as *Tsingtau*, see above, plus 3–5 Chinese for the sampans. Boats: two sampans.

Notes Colour scheme no 9, 11. *Otter* was assembled in East Asia in the same manner as *Tsingtau*, see above.

Career
Otter launched 15 Jul 1909, commissioned 1 Apr 1910 on the China Yangtze-Kiang station; laid up at Nanking and apparently sold 18 Aug 1914 to a German company, and renamed *München*; requisitioned by China 20 Mar 1917, and became the Chinese gunboat *Li-Tsieh*. Sunk 19 Oct 1929 at Sungari; wreck broken up.

K1 class (1938 design)

Name	Builder	Built	Cost in Marks (000s)	Displacement (t = tonnes T = tons)	Length (m)	Breadth (m)	Draught (m)	Power (hp)	Revs (rpm)	Speed (kts)	Range (nm/kts)	Coal (t)	Oil (t)
K 1–4	Stücken Sohn, Hamburg Construction nos 747–750	1938	6000	1890T max 1600t des 1390T std	82.5 oa 79.0 cwl	11.4	3.38	4600ihp		18.5	3000/12		176

Construction A design for a gunboat, 1938 (official design). Transverse frame longitudinal stringer construction in steel 45 (eleven watertight compartments). Depth 5.65m.

Propulsion Two vertical 4-cylinder triple expansion engines (two screws, diameter not known) in 1 + 0 + 1 combined engine/boiler rooms. No other details known.

Armament Four 10.5cm/65 QF guns (no of rounds not known); two 3.7cm/83 AA guns (no of rounds not known); four heavy machine guns.

Complement Crew: not known. Boats: one motor cutter, one launch or similar.

Career
The contract was granted 11 Nov 1938, and planned completion dates were as follows: *K1*, 20 May 1941; *K2*, 15 Sept 1941; *K3*, 15 Jan 1942; *K4*, 14 Feb 1942. The contract was cancelled 19 Sept 1939.

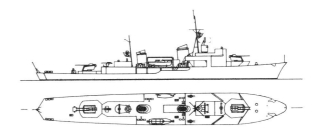

K 1–4 (1938 design). *Mrva*

KI class (1939 design)

Name	Builder	Built	Cost in Marks (000s)	Displacement (t = tonnes T = tons)	Length (m)	Breadth (m)	Draught (m)	Power (hp)	Revs (rpm)	Speed (kts)	Range (nm/kts)	Coal (t)	Oil (t)
K I–IV	—	—		2550T max 2300t des 2100T std	106.4 oa 102.0 cwl	12.3	3.50 fwd	1500ehp		24	11,000/12	—	c380

Construction Designs for colonial gunboats (official designs, 1938–1939). Armour was intended in the region of the engine compartment only; deck 20mm; walls 15mm; CWL 0–15–0mm. Depth 6.50m.

Propulsion Four engines (two screws, diameter not known) in 1 + 0 + 1 engine rooms.

Armament Four 12.7cm/60 QF guns (no of rounds not known); six 3.7cm/83 AA guns (no of rounds not known); four 2cm AA guns (no of rounds not known); four 53.3cm TT (no of rounds not known), deck-mounted twins.

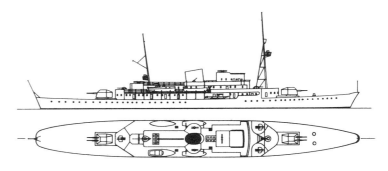

Colonial gunboats *K I–K IV* (1939 design). *Mrva*

Complement Crew: about 165 men. Boats: one motor cutter, one launch, two dinghies or similar.

Career
Six units were included in the Z-plan for stations abroad and commerce protection; the contracts were never granted owing to lack of dockyard capacity.

K1 class (ex-Dutch)

Name	Builder	Built	Cost in Marks (000s)	Displacement (t = tonnes T = tons)	Length (m)	Breadth (m)	Draught (m)	Power (hp)	Revs (rpm)	Speed (kts)	Range (nm/kts)	Coal (t)	Oil (t)
K 1, K 3	P Smit jr, Rotterdam Construction nos 524, 525	1939–42		1420T max 1365t des 1200T std	78 oa 75 cwl	10.2	3.9 fwd 2.9 aft	2770ehp		14.5	6900/12	—	157
K 2	Gusto NV, Schiedam Construction no 750	,,		,,	,,	,,	,,	,,		,,	,,	—	,,

Construction Dutch *Ersatz Brinio* class gunboats taken as prizes (official Dutch design, 1937). Armour: deck 35–20mm; CWL 60–40mm; bridge 20mm; shields 60mm. Depth 5.20m.

Propulsion Designed for two diesel engines, each 3650hp, 18.1kts, but fitted with two quadruple acting Germania diesels (*K3* was fitted with two Humboldt-Klöckner-Deutz submarine diesels) (two 3-bladed screws, diameter not known).

Armament Four 12cm/45 Dutch QF guns (no of rounds not known); four 3.7cm/83 AA guns (no of rounds not known); four, later twelve, 2cm AA guns (no of rounds not known); one 1.3cm Hotchkiss AA gun; 200 mines.

Handling Good sea-boats.

Complement Crew: 161. Boats not known.

Notes Colour: grey. This was a successful design, and more units of the class were recommended.

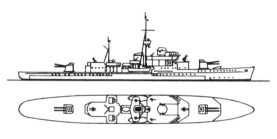

K 2 (1942); K 1 was similar.

K 3 (1945)

Career
K1–3 were taken as prizes during the occupation of Holland, still on the stocks in Rotterdam and Schiedam, and completed under German command.

K1 launched 23 Nov 1940, commissioned 2 Oct 1941. Sunk 5 May 1945 in the vicinity of Aarhus, by an aircraft bomb.

K2 launched 28 Jun 1941. Sunk before completion by enemy action in July 1941; raised, construction continued; in service 14 Nov 1942. Badly damaged 9 Oct 1944 west of Egersund, position 58° 17N, 05° 45E, by an aerial torpedo, and her stern was torn off; she was taken in tow, and the wreck was towed to Holland in July 1945. Sunk at Delfzijl; raised 26 Jul 1948; stricken in October 1947; broken up.

K3 launched 23 Mar 1941, commissioned 24 Jan 1942; returned to Holland in May 1945; became *Van Speyk* after 18 Jun 1946. Stricken 1960; broken up in August 1960 at Amsterdam.

K4/Lorelei (ex-Belgian)

Construction Laid down as the Belgian fisheries protection ship *Ersatz Zinnia*, fitted out as a royal yacht. Transverse frame steel construction in Siemens-Martin steel (eleven watertight compartments, no double bottom). Armour: shields 40mm; depth 5.85m.

Propulsion Two sets of Parsons turbines with geared transmission (two 3-bladed screws, 2.6m diameter) in one engine room. Two Babcock boilers (32 atmospheres forced, 400°) in 1 + 1 boiler rooms. One rudder.

Armament (Belgian design) four 10.2cm AA guns in double shields and two 2cm AA guns; (German design, until 1943) [three 10.5cm/45 QF guns, six 3.7cm/83 QF guns and twelve 2cm AA guns; after

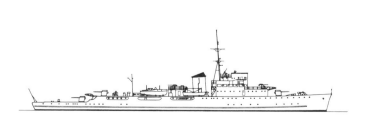

K 4 (Lorelei) (1943). Mrva

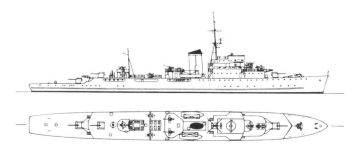

K 4 (Lorelei) (1945). Mrva

Name	Builder	Built	Cost	Displacement (t = tonnes T = tons)	Length (m)	Breadth (m)	Draught (m)	Power (hp)	Revs (rpm)	Speed (kts)	Range (nm/kts)	Coal (t)	Oil (t)
K 4 (LORELEI) 1790gt	Cockerill, Antwerp Construction no 686 completion: Wilton-Fijenoord, Schiedam	1940–43	50,000 Bfr	2270t max 1640t des	98.5 oa 95.7 cwl	10.5	3.8 fwd 3.3 aft	21,700shp max 30,000shp des	500 des	28.5 max 30 des	1200/19	—	680

1943, three 10.5cm/45 QF guns], four 3.7cm/83 QF guns, sixteen 2cm AA guns and 120 mines; (no of rounds not known for any guns).

Complement Crew: 12/168. Boats: one barge, one cutter, two yawls.

Notes Colour scheme no 9. The vessel was rearmed in July 1943, and the hull sub-division was modified to improve stability.

Career
K4 launched 24 Aug 1940 as the Belgian *Artevelde*; requisitioned after launching, towed to Rotterdam, fitted out by 25 Apr 1943. Returned to Belgium in June 1945; renamed *Artevelde*; served from 1950 as a barrack ship. Broken up 22 Nov 1954 at Bruges by J Bakker & Zonen.

Torpedo boats 1872

No I class (Devrient/Waltjen types)

The direct predecessors of the torpedo boats were fourteen small harbour vessels and tugs and seven rowing vessels, which were fitted out temporarily in 1870 to guard the Elbe and Weser estuary as spar torpedo boats for the Freiwillige Seewehr (Voluntary Sea Force). These vessels included the following:

The steam tug *Oscar* built by F L Mathies & Co of Hamburg; launched at Reiherstieg dockyard, Hamburg, in 1866, construction no 134; length 18.3m, beam 4m, approx 65psi.

Two Alster steamers, of which one sank after a collision during transfer to Cuxhaven; 3 dead.

Name	Builder	Built	Cost in Marks (000s)	Displacement (t = tonnes T = tons)	Length (m)	Breadth (m)	Draught (m)	Power (hp)	Revs (rpm)	Speed (kts)	Range (nm/kts)	Coal (t)	Oil (t)
Nos I–III	Devrient, Danzig	1871–72	36 each	34t	20.3	3.30	1.9	250ihp	180	8.0		1.5 mod	1.5
Nos I–III	Waltjen & Co, Bremen Construction nos 14–16	1871	33 each	24	14.6	3.22	1.8	60ihp	,,	7.7		,,	,,

Construction Laid down as Devrient and Waltjen type spar torpedo boats, transverse frame iron construction, galvanised.

Propulsion One vertical 2-cylinder single-acting expansion engine (one 4-bladed screw, 1.7/1.5m diameter) in one engine room. One cylindrical boiler (4 atmospheres forced) in one boiler room. No electrical installation. One rudder.

Armament Spars at the bow carried one 17kg explosive charge with impact fuse. [Devrient type boats carried one 38.1cm torpedo at the bow, above water, after 1881.]

Handling Light coastal vessels.

Complement Crew: 0/8.

Notes Colour scheme no 1 or similar. [After about 1880 these vessels were fitted with one short mast.] Appearance differed according to size; no details are available.

Devrient-type spar torpedo boats *Nr I–III* (1847)

Career
Devrient boats *No I–III* launched 1871, commissioned May to November 1872 as Devrient type torpedo boats for spar experiments; served as minelayers *4–6* for Wilhelmshaven harbour defence from 15 Dec 1875; reclassified as torpedo boats *I–III* for Wilhelmshaven harbour defence 8 Jul 1881. Stricken about 1885; served thereafter as fortification minelayers at Wilhelmshaven.

Waltjen boats *No I–III* launched 1871, commissioned September 1872 as Waltjen type torpedo boats for spar experiments; served as minelayers *1–3* for Wilhelmshaven harbour defence from 15 Dec 1875. Stricken 8 Jul 1881; served thereafter as fortification minelayers at Kiel.

Torpedo steamers 1874–1876

Notus class

Name	Builder	Built	Cost	Displacement (t = tonnes T = tons)	Length (m)	Breadth (m)	Draught (m)	Power (hp)	Revs (rpm)	Speed (kts)	Range (nm/kts)	Coal (t)	Oil (t)
NOTUS ex *No I*	AG 'Vulcan', Stettin Construction no 68	1873–74	78.5 Thaler	308t max 303t des	37.2 oa 35.1 cwl	6.70 max	2.5	500ihp des	30	10.6 max		30	—
ZEPHIR ex *No II*	AG 'Vulcan, Stettin Construction no 69	1873–74	35.0 Thaler	131t max 129t des	30.5 oa 28.9 cwl	5.25 hull	1.65 fwd 1.09 aft	225ihp des	34	9.0 max		10	—
RIVAL ex *No III*	AG 'Vulcan', Stettin Construction no 71	1873–74	38.0 Thaler	131t max 129t des	30.5 oa 28.9 cwl	5.25 hull	1.98	225ihp max 250ihp des	95	6.5 max		10	—
	mod:	1879–80		146t max	,,	,,	,,	250ihp max	36	9.5 max		14	—

308gt (*Notus*), 131gt (*Zephir*), 131gt (*Rival*)

Construction Laid down as torpedo steamers *No I, II* and *III* (dockyard designs). Transverse frame iron construction, in the manner of steam tugs.

Propulsion Two inclined oscillating 2-cylinder single expansion engines (two side paddle wheels, 4.2m and 3.8m diameter; *Rival* was originally powered by Wasserschwallturbinen – water flood turbine-pumps – water being passed to these laterally from the engine room through openings in the hull sides, and pressurised water from the turbine-pumps was thrust out through a tubular duct about 1m in diameter on each side of the sternpost [this system was replaced by side paddle wheels because of its low efficiency] in the engine room. One (*Notus* two) locomotive boilers (1.8 and 2 atmospheres forced, 130 and 256sq m) in the engine room forward of the engine (in a separate boiler room in *Notus*). No electrical installation. One rudder.

Armament Bow spars with 41kg explosive charges.

Handling Light coastal vessels.

Complement Crew: 3/40–25. Boats: two.

Notes Colour scheme no 1 or similar. *Rival* originally had no side paddle wheels.

Zephir (1876)

Career

Notus launched 2 Aug 1873, commissioned 20 Jun 1874 for spar torpedo experiments; served from 15 Dec 1875 as a dockyard steam tug and buoy layer. Stricken 17 Apr 1809; later broken up.

Zephir launched 22 Jun 1874, commissioned 13 Oct 1874 for experiments; served as a steam tug from 1875 to 1907. Broken up at Wilhelmshaven.

Rival launched 2 Sept 1874, commissioned 14 Dec 1874 for spar torpedo experiments and engine tests; later converted to a minelayer at Wilhelmshaven; served as minelayer *4* for harbour defence at Wilhelmshaven from 8 Jun 1871. Stricken 1884; served as a steam tug until 15 Jan 1916; broken up at Wilhelmshaven.

Ulan

Construction Laid down as torpedo steamer *No IV*. Transverse frame iron construction (four watertight compartments, with a collision bulkhead in the reinforced bow). Depth 4.3m. Immersion increased by 4cm per 3.5t.

Propulsion One vertical 2-cylinder single expansion engine (one 4-bladed screw, 3.9m diameter) in one en-

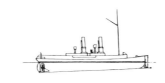

Ulan (1876)

gine room. Four centreline Belleville cylindrical boilers (5.5 atmospheres forced, 382sq m) in one boiler room. No electrical installation. One rudder. [A new engine, and, in 1898, two new boilers per vessel were fitted by the Kiel and Danzig Imperial Dockyards (eight fireboxes, 5.5 atmospheres forced, 382sq m).]

Name	Builder	Built	Cost in Marks (000s)	Displacement (t = tonnes T = tons)	Length (m)	Breadth (m)	Draught (m)	Power (hp)	Revs (rpm)	Speed (kts)	Range (nm/kts)	Coal (t)	Oil (t)
ULAN ex *No IV*	Möller & Hollberg, Grabow b Stetin, Construction no 56	1875–76	437	438t max 374t des	36-38 oa 35.05 cwl	8.00	2.65 fwd 4.57 aft	798ihp max 800ihp des	102 max 106 des	12.2 max 12 des	300/12 470/7	25	—
	mod: Imperial Dockyard, Kiel	1876–79											
222gt/100nt													

Armament Bow spars with 63kg explosive charge [one 38.1cm bow torpedo, under water (three rounds); three 3.7cm machine guns].

Handling Poor sea-boat, with pronounced pitch and roll in wind above force 5.

Complement Crew: 2/39 [1/51].

Notes Initially the spar torpedo had to be attached by divers prior to battle; the automatic launcher shown in the second drawing was fitted in 1878. The method of attack was that within range of the enemy vessel the crew fixed the rudder for a set course, then climbed onto a liferaft. If necessary, the crew could haul themselves back on board from the raft using an overlength

Ulan as a torpedo training tender (1880)

towline, if the ship was still intact; originally there was a simple railing instead of a bulwark. [During the refit in about 1879 the funnels were combined, the mast moved further aft and the storm deck extended as far as the bridge deck.]

Career
Ulan launched 3 Apr 1876, commissioned 8 Oct 1876 for experiments; served as a torpedo and artillery training tender from 1880. Stricken 26 May 1909; used as a barge, then sold on 13 Aug 1919 for 61,500M to Cuxhaven-Brunsbüttel Dampfer AG, and again in 1925 to M Faber & Co, Hamburg; sold again in 1926 H W Ritscher & Co, Hamburg-Moorburg; later broken up.

Torpedo boats 1883–1918

The descriptions of torpedo boats which follow include only the most important modifications. In addition to the identification features noted, each dockyard had characteristic shapes for funnel tops, ventilators, sterns, etc. For example, Schichau boats usually had a spear-shaped, pointed stem in plan view, while Vulcan boats were curved and pointed, and Germania boats blunt and egg-shaped.

Handling notes are applicable to all following torpedo boats up to and including *S 223*, unless otherwise stated. The seakeeping qualities of small boats per-mitted their active use in conditions up to a wind strength of about 6, and of large boats up to a wind strength of about 7 or 8. The small boats were very wet, and the large ones with a waist not much better. Con-version to the extended forecastle design improved seakeeping considerably, but the vessels were corre-spondingly crank, and with more lee helm. The *V* and *S* boats had a tight and fast turning circle; the *G* boats were notably inferior. The latter boats were, however, reputed to be particularly comfortable.

For colour schemes refer to the introductory notes. In peacetime numbers were painted in white on each side of the bow, initially retaining the first digit (hundreds), identification number and name (see the individual de-scriptions). A, B or C painted in white on the second funnel were tactical symbols used for manoeuvres. In the First World War various national identification markings were used, such as a second funnel in yellow or red, and a black–white–red flag on the bridge awn-ings (as in the Battle of the Skagerrak). Further identification markings include the flotilla symbol for 1914–1918 on the main topmast or foremast.

Schütze class

Name	Builder	Built	Cost in Marks (000s)	Displacement (t = tonnes T = tons)	Length (m)	Breadth (m)	Draught (m)	Power (hp)	Revs (rpm)	Speed (kts)	Range (nm/kts)	Coal (t)	Oil (t)
SCHÜTZE ex *No V*, FLINK ex *No VI*, SCHARF ex *No VII*, TAPFER ex *No VIII*, KÜHN ex *No IX*, VORWÄRTS ex *No X*, and SICHER ex *No XI* 54gt	AG 'Weser', Bremen Construction nos 54–60	1882–83		56t max 50t des	32.6 oa 31.5 cwl	3.93	0.87 fwd 2.05 aft	599ihp max 500ihp des	365	17.9	750/10 110/16	8.2	—

Construction Laid down as first class torpedo boats *No V–XI* (dockyard design). Transverse frame steel construction, galvanised (six watertight compartments).

Propulsion One vertical 2-cylinder double expansion engine (*Scharf*, one vertical 3-cylinder double expan-sion engine) (one 3-bladed screw, 1.70m diameter, except *Scharf*, one 4-bladed screw, 1.56m diameter) in an engine room. One locomotive boiler (9 atmospheres forced, size not known, but *Scharf*, 10 atmospheres forced), approx 600psi. One rudder.

Armament One 3.7cm machine gun; two 35cm TT (4 rounds), bow, above water.

Complement Crew: 1/12. Boats: one dinghy.

Notes Two funnels, side by side.

Career
Schütze launched 11 May 1882, commissioned 14 Sept 1883 into the torpedo flotilla as a training boat. Stricken 19 Oct 1891; served as a guard boat at Wil-helmshaven; sold 1900; broken up at Hamburg.

Flink launched 24 May 1882, commissioned 6 Nov 1883 into the torpedo flotilla as a training boat.

Schütze (1883), *Flink, Scharf, Tapfer, Kühn, Vorwärts, Sicher*

Stricken 19 Oct 1891; served as a steam supply boat; sold in 1900 for 5500M; broken up at Hamburg.

Scharf launched 30 May 1882, commissioned 5 Sept 1883 into the torpedo flotilla as a training boat; re-maining career as for *Schütze*.

Tapfer launched 6 Jun 1882, commissioned 5 Aug 1883 into the torpedo flotilla as a minelayer and har-bour torpedo boat. Stricken 19 Oct 1891; served as a target boat; hull sold in 1908 for 90M to Bant.

Kühn launched 12 Jun 1882, commissioned 7 Apr 1883; remaining career as for *Schütze*.

Vorwärts launched 19 Jun 1882, commissioned 7 Apr 1883; remaining career as for *Schütze*.

Sicher launched 26 Jun 1882, commissioned 7 Apr 1883; remaining career as for *Schütze*.

Jäger

Name	Builder	Built	Cost in Marks (000s)	Displacement (t = tonnes T = tons)	Length (m)	Breadth (m)	Draught (m)	Power (hp)	Revs (rpm)	Speed (kts)	Range (nm/kts)	Coal (t)	Oil (t)
JÄGER	AG 'Weser', Bremen Construction no 61	1883	140		34.8 oa 33.5 cwl	5.58	1.8 fwd 2.57 aft	550ihp des	200	15.0	750/10	19	—

Construction Laid down as torpedo gunboat *Ersatz Natter* (dockyard design). Transverse frame steel construction (six watertight compartments).

Propulsion One vertical 2-cylinder double expansion engine (one 4-bladed screw, 1.82m diameter) in an engine room. One locomotive boiler (8 atmospheres forced, size unknown) in a boiler room. One rudder.

Armament Designed for two 8.7cm/24 hooped guns fore and aft, but fitted instead with one Hotchkiss 5-barrel 3.7cm machine gun; two 35cm TT (6 rounds), bow, above water.

Jäger (1885)

Handling Poor sea-boat, unresponsive with unexceptional turning circle.

Complement Crew: 1/21. Boats: one.

Notes Proved ineffective.

Career
Jäger launched 27 Jan 1883, commissioned 24 Jul 1883 as an experimental boat. Stricken 13 May 1889; sold in 1900 for 16,400M; broken up at Hamburg.

Th 2/No IV

Name	Builder	Built	Cost	Displacement (t = tonnes T = tons)	Length (m)	Breadth (m)	Draught (m)	Power (hp)	Revs (rpm)	Speed (kts)	Range (nm/kts)	Coal (t)	Oil (t)
TH 2 (No IV)	John J Thornycroft & Co, London	1883–84	£3600	14.5t max 13.0t des	19.2	2.44	0.46 fwd 1.30 aft	120ihp des	135	14.0		0.4	—

Construction Laid down as second class torpedo boat *No IV* (dockyard design). Transverse frame steel construction.

Propulsion One vertical 2-cylinder double expansion engine (one 3-bladed screw, 1.42m diameter) together with one locomotive boiler (9 atmospheres forced) in the boat hold. One funnel, offset to starboard.

Armament Two 35cm TT (2 rounds), bow, above water. One 3.7cm machine gun.

Handling Only marginally seaworthy above Beaufort 4, similar to tenders.

Th 2 (1883)

Complement Crew: 6

Notes Could also be carried on board larger ships.

Career
Th 2 launched 23 May 1884, commissioned 1 Aug 1884 for experiments; later served as roll gyro test boat *Seebär* at Hamburg. Eventual fate unknown.

I class (White type)

Name	Builder	Built	Cost in Marks (000s)	Displacement (t = tonnes T = tons)	Length (m)	Breadth (m)	Draught (m)	Power (hp)	Revs (rpm)	Speed (kts)	Range (nm/kts)	Coal (t)	Oil (t)
I	J S White & Co, Cowes, Isle of Wight	1885			15.8	2.6				15			—
II	J S White & Co, Cowes, Isle of Wight	1886			17.1	2.8				16			—

Construction Laid down as White type torpedo boats (dockyard design). Timber construction.

Propulsion One vertical expansion engine (one screw, diameter not known). One boiler, in the hold.

Armament One 35cm TT, bow, above water; one 3.7cm machine gun.

Handling Like tenders, only usable in wind strengths up to Beaufort 3–4.

Complement Crew unknown.

Notes Could be carried on board larger ships, and was, in fact, intended for non-autonomous use by larger vessels. In terms of tactical usage and design,

Th 2 and the other non-autonomous torpedo boats were the true predecessors of the fast motor torpedo boats (S-boats).

Career
I and *II* stricken between 1905 and 1910; fate unknown.

No XII class

Name	Builder	Built	Cost in Marks (000s)	Displacement (t = tonnes T = tons)	Length (m)	Breadth (m)	Draught (m)	Power (hp)	Revs (rpm)	Speed (kts)	Range (nm/kts)	Coal (t)	Oil (t)
Nos XII–XVII (W 1–6)	AG 'Weser', Bremen Construction nos 69–74	1884	153	91t max 77t des	34.91 oa	3.92	1.32 fwd 2.38 aft	910ihp max 800ihp des	402 max	19.8 max	1200/10 750/12	11.5	—
Nos XVIII–XXVII (V 1–10)	AG 'Vulcan', Stettin Constructions nos 140–149 mod: AG 'Vulcan', Stettin	1884 1885	156	61t max 54t des	32.75 oa	3.76	0.77 fwd 1.84 aft	590ihp	370	17.9	900/10 120/16	8.5	—
Nos XXVIII–XXXIII (S 1–6)	F Schichau, Elbing Construction nos 235–240	1884–85	206	99t max 84t des	37.72 oa	4.92	1.07 fwd 2.23 aft	870–970 ihp	299 350	19.3	1400/10 250/18	18.2	—
TH 1	John J Thornycroft & Co, Chiswick, London	1884	230	81t max 67t des	37.22 oa	3.82	0.87 fwd 2.07 aft	653ihp	396	17.8	1300/10	20	—
Y	Yarrow, London	1884–85	217	83t max 69t des	36.35 oa	4.02	1.42 fwd 1.79 aft	599ihp	356	18.3	1380/10	21.4	—
G	Germania Dockyard, Kiel Construction no 21	,,	154	86t max 74t des	36.27 oa	4.00	1.00 fwd 2.30 aft	722ihp	417	18.8	1100/10	12.6	—

58gt (*Nos XII–XVII*), 53gt (*Nos XVIII–XXVII*), 82gt (*Nos XXVIII–XXXIII*), 63gt (*TH 1*), 70gt (*G*)

Construction Laid down as first class torpedo boats *No XII–XXXIII* (competitive dockyard designs). Transverse frame steel construction, galvanised, but *S 1–6* and *G* not galvanised (seven/seven/eight/ten/eleven/ten watertight compartments).

Propulsion One vertical 3-cylinder triple expansion engine (*Th 1* and *Y*, one vertical 2-cylinder double expansion engine) in an engine room. One locomotive boiler in a boiler room; details of screws, boilers and sails are given in the table below. The funnel had an oval cross-section on *W 1–6*, *S 1–6* and *G* only, while those on the other boats had a circular cross-section; *Y* had a double funnel. Originally *S 1–6*, *Th 1*, *Y* and *G* were built with two masts with auxiliary sails; [after about 1888 this was reduced to one mast (see *S 7–57*)]. One generator, 2.5kW 67V. One stern rudder [later all boats except *W 1–6* had one bow rudder]. For sail sizes, see the adjacent table.

	Screw, diameter	Boiler pressure (atmospheres forced), area	Sail area
W 1–6	one 3-bladed, 1.71m	10, 115sq m	6.5sq m
V 1–10	one 3-bladed, 1.70 [1.75m]	10, 86sq m	12.0sq m
S 1–6	one 3-bladed, 1.76m	12, 128sq m	22.5sq m
Th 1	one 2-bladed, 1.70m	9, 106sq m	unknown
Y	one 2-bladed, 1.53m	10, 107sq m	24.7sq m
G	one 3-bladed, 1.80m	12, 115sq m	unknown

Armament Two 3.7cm machine guns (180 rounds, *Y* 135 rounds); two 35cm TT (4 rounds), bow, above water; [in addition *S 1–6* were fitted with one 35cm deck TT].

Handling The *S* boats were the best sea-boats, followed by *G*, then *W 1–6* (see the introductory notes to this section).

Complement Crew: 1/13; *W 1–6* and *S 1–6*: 1/14. Boats: [one dinghy].

Notes [*W 1–6* were fitted with a conning tower in place of the aft pair of ventilators. *V 1–4* had no lattice cap on the funnel, and a steam pipe on the funnel itself (the latter was about 0.5m further aft on these boats); the railing extended to the stern, and the rubbing strake round the stern.] *G* was similar to the drawing of *W 1–6* but with a slightly wider funnel, pressure heads at 9.0m and 15.0m, a ram bow; and a balanced rudder.

Career

W 1 launched 22 Apr 1884, commissioned 1884 as *No XII*; renamed *W 1* 25 Nov 1884; finally served as a training and harbour boat. Stricken 30 Jan 1899; used as a target boat; broken up about 1910.

W 2 launched 1 May 1884, commissioned 1884 as *No XIII*; renamed *W 2* 25 Jan 1884; finally served as a training and harbour boat. Stricken 30 Jan 1899; used as a guard boat at Wilhelmshaven; broken up about 1910.

W 3 launched 13 May 1884, commissioned 1884 as *No XIV*; renamed *W 3* 25 Nov 1884; finally served as a training and harbour boat. Stricken 30 Jan 1899; used as a guard boat at Wilhelmshaven; broken up about 1910.

W 4 launched 24 May 1884, commissioned 1884 as *No XV*; renamed *W 4* 25 Nov 1884; finally served as a training and harbour boat. Stricken 30 Jan 1899; used as a guard boat at Wilhelmshaven; broken up about 1910.

W 5 launched 31 May 1884, commissioned 1884 as *No XVI*; renamed *W 5* 25 Nov 1884; finally served as a training and harbour boat. Stricken 30 Jan 1899; used as a guard boat at Wilhelmshaven; broken up about 1910.

W 6 launched 13 Jun 1884, commissioned as *No XVII*; renamed *W6* 25 Nov 1884. Stricken 30 Jan 1899; used as a guard boat at Helgoland 1904, then as a tender to *Helga* from 5 Jul 1904; broken up 1912.

V 1 launched 1 Apr 1884, commissioned 11 Aug 1884 as *No XVIII*; renamed *V 1* 25 Nov 1884; finally served

as a harbour torpedo boat; broken up 1910 at the Imperial Dockyard, Kiel.

V 2 launched 28 Apr 1884, commissioned 3 Sept 1884 as *No XIX*; renamed *V 2* 25 Nov 1884; finally served as a harbour torpedo boat; broken up 1910 at the Imperial Dockyard, Kiel.

V 3 launched 5 May 1884, commissioned 5 Sept 1884 as *No XX*; renamed *V 3* 25 Nov 1884. Sunk at Kiel 9 Sept 1885; raised in October 1885; broken up, engine reused (see torpedo boat *A*, page 156).

V 4 launched 12 May 1884, commissioned 7 Sept 1884 as *No XXI*; renamed *V 4* 25 Nov 1884; finally served as a harbour torpedo boat; broken up 1900 at Hamburg.

V 5 launched 19 May 1884, commissioned 28 Jul 1884 as *No XXII*; renamed *V 5* 25 Nov 1884; finally served as a harbour torpedo boat; broken up 1910 at the Imperial Dockyard, Kiel.

V 6 launched 23 May 1884, commissioned 31 Oct 1884 as *No XXIII*; renamed *V 6* 25 Nov 1884; finally served as a harbour torpedo boat. Stricken 1900; [served as a grain transport lighter at Hameln 1904, and as a landing boat for the Oberweser-Personenschiffahrt (Upper Weser Passenger Shipping Company) in 1908]; converted 1924 to motor ferry *Forelle*. Sunk in the Weser 1 Jul 1955; raised, broken up 1966.

V 7 launched 29 May 1884, commissioned 16 Sept 1884 as *No XXIV*; renamed *V 7* 25 Nov 1884; finally served as a harbour torpedo boat; broken up 1910 at Hamburg.

V 8 launched 6 Jun 1884, commissioned 16 Sept 1884 as *No XXV*; renamed *V 8* 25 Nov 1884; finally served as a tender; broken up 1910 at Hamburg.

V 9 launched 12 Jun 1884, commissioned 24 Oct 1884 as *No XXVI*; renamed *V 9* 25 Nov 1884; finally served as a harbour torpedo boat; broken up 1910 at the Imperial Dockyard, Kiel.

V 10 launched 10 Jul 1884, commissioned 24 Oct 1884 as *No XXVII*; renamed *V 10* 25 Nov 1884, and

V 3 in October 1885. Stricken 30 Jan 1899; used as a target boat for torpedo boats and coastal artillery; broken up 1910 at Hamburg.

V 11–19 New designation planned for *V 1–9* after conversion (during which they were allotted new construction numbers by AG Vulcan, Stettin) but implemented only for a few days on *V 11*.

S 1–6 were designated *No XXVIII–XXXIII* until 25 Nov 1884.

S 1 launched 24 May 1884, commissioned 24 May 1884; finally served as a harbour torpedo boat. Stricken about 1896, engine transferred to the German Museum at Munich, 1905.

S 2 launched 12 Jun 1884, commissioned 24 May 1884; served as a harbour torpedo boat, and as a torpedo retrieval boat from 10 Sept 1904; renamed *T 2* 11 Nov 1910; broken up 1915 at the Imperial Dockyard, Kiel.

S 3 launched 9 Jul 1884, commissioned 9 Jul 1884. Stricken about 1896; used as a steam supply boat, target boat and explosives barge; stricken again 9 Jul 1921; broken up at Wilhelmshaven.

S 4 launched 5 Aug 1884, commissioned 5 Aug 1884. Stricken 1 Jul 1897; used as a target boat for coastal artillery; sold in 1902 for 302M; broken up at Hamburg.

S 5 as above; sold 1909 for 261M.

S 6 as above; sold in 1909 for 311M.

Th 1 launched 13 Jun 1884, commissioned 1 Aug 1884 for experiments; served as a harbour torpedo boat. Stricken 30 Jan 1899; sold 1900; broken up at Hamburg.

Y (also known temporarily as *Y 1*) launched 12 May 1884, commissioned 8 May 1885 as *Th 1*.

G (also known temporarily as *G 1*) launched 20 Dec 1884, commissioned 9 Sept 1885 as an experimental and training boat. Stricken 30 Jan 1899; used as a tender to *Helga* in 1904; finally used as a target boat.

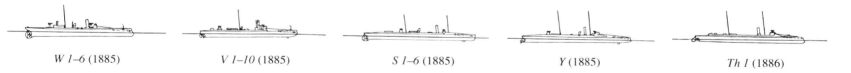

W 1–6 (1885)   V 1–10 (1885)   S 1–6 (1885)   Y (1885)   Th 1 (1886)

H class

Construction *H* (also temporarily known as *H 1*) was of mahogany diagonal carvel construction on steel transverse frames, with a steel deck and copper sheathing (eight watertight compartments); *K* (also temporarily known as *K 1*) was of transverse frame steel construction, galvanised (seven watertight compartments).

Propulsion One vertical 3-cylinder triple expansion engine (*H*, one 3-bladed screw, 1.76m diameter; *K*, one 3-bladed screw – Thornycroft system, with adjustable blades – 1.92m diameter) in an engine room. One locomotive boiler (*H*, 12 atmospheres forced, 154sq m; *K*, 10 atmospheres forced, 135sq m) in a separate boiler room. One generator, 2.5kW 67V. *H*, one stern rudder;

K, one stern rudder [and one bow rudder]. The engine and boiler for *H* were built by F Schichau, Elbing.

Armament Two 3.7cm machine guns (360 rounds); *H*, three 35cm TT (5 rounds), two deck mounted, one bow, under water; *K*, two 35cm TT (4 rounds), bow, above water.

K (1889)

Complement Crew: 1/16. Boats: [one dinghy].

Notes Both boats had a short service life due to the poor quality materials used in their construction. Their appearance was approximately as shown in the drawing of *K*; details are uncertain.

Career

H launched 17 Jul 1886, commissioned 12 Nov 1886 into an experimental division; saw hardly any service. Stricken 12 Nov 1894; finally used as a target boat.

K launched 16 Jul 1887, commissioned in June 1889 into an experimental division. Stricken 30 Jan 1899; sold for 16,000M and broken up at Hamburg.

Name	Builder	Built	Cost in Marks (000s)	Displacement (t = tonnes T = tons)	Length (m)	Breadth (m)	Draught (m)	Power (hp)	Revs (rpm)	Speed (kts)	Range (nm/kts)	Coal (t)	Oil (t)
H	Imperial Dockyard, Wilhelmshaven	1887–89		106t max 89t des	37.92 oa	4.82	1.15 fwd 2.25 aft	950ihp	350	19.0	2120/10	17	—
K	Imperial Dockyard, Kiel Construction no 11	1887–89	240	102t max 86t des	37.58 oa	4.77	1.13 fwd 2.63 aft	996ihp	341	18.8	1490/12	20	—
A	Imperial Dockyard, Danzig mod: Imperial Dockyard, Danzig	1888–89 1898		88t max 70t des	34.63 oa	4.14	1.00 fwd 2.15 aft	591ihp	220	16.5		9	—

Construction *A* (also temporarily known as *A 1*) was of transverse frame steel construction, not galvanised (seven watertight compartments) [55BRT].

Propulsion Engines and boilers were taken from *V 3*, which sank in Kiel harbour 9 Sept 1885 (see pXXX) (one 3-bladed screw 1.46m diameter). One generator, 2.5kW 67V. 1 + 1 stern rudders.

Armament Two 3.7cm machine guns (360 rounds); two 35cm TT (4 rounds), one deck, one bow, under water; [disarmed after about 1892].

Complement Crew: 1/13.

Notes Colour scheme no 1 [as *Schneewittchen*, no

11]. This boat was commissioned without completing trials. Her appearance as a torpedo boat was similar to that shown in the drawing, but the funnel was 1.5m lower and had no ornamental ring; there was also no cabin or planking on the after deck. Two stern rudders

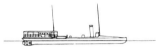

Schneewittchen (1900) as a station yacht for the Baltic.

failed to improve the boat's turning characteristics, and her directional stability was only slightly improved [her handling was not seriously affected by the deckhouse except in that it produced a marked necessity for lee helm].

Career
A launched 20 Dec 1888, commissioned 10 Oct 1889 as a torpedo training boat; renamed *Schneewittchen* 30 Jan 1899 and served as a station yacht in the Baltic and as a guard ship at Kiel. Stricken 21 Sept 1920; broken up 1921 at Kiel for 80,000M.

Experience in the experimental division with various types of torpedo boat designed after the *Schütze* class revealed that the *S* boats were clearly superior; these were systematically developed from that time on.

S 7 class

Construction Transverse frame steel construction, with some partly galvanised up to *S 32*, and all galvanised after *S 33* (eight to nine watertight compartments); *S 32* had double armour plating over the engines and boiler. Depth approx 2.28m.

Propulsion One vertical 3-cylinder triple expansion engine (one 3-bladed screw, 1.76m diameter; *S 24–31* 1.75m, *S 42–57* 1.98m, *S 58–65* 1.99m diameter) in an engine room. One locomotive boiler (12 atmospheres forced; 13 atmospheres forced after *S 33*) in a separate boiler room [in a divided boiler room in *S 32*]; details of the boilers are given in the adjacent table. One generator, 2.5kW [4kW] 67V. One stern and one bow rudder (the latter offset to starboard after *S 42*), but *S 32* had 1 + 1 stern rudders. Sail approx 10sq m.

Armament One 3.7cm machine gun (360 rounds), [after 1893, one 5cm/40 'torpedo gun' (a quick-fire gun with a special torpedo boat mount) (156 rounds)]; three 35cm TT (4 rounds), two deck, one bow, above water (*S 32* and *S 43–65* had two deck, one bow, underwater); [minesweeping apparatus was later fitted].

Complement Crew: 1/15 (*S 32*, 1/19). Boats: One dinghy.

Notes These boats exhibited varying degrees of funnel

Boat	Boiler size (sq m)	Boat (refit)	Refit date	New boiler type	Pressure (atm forced)	Size (sq m)
S 7–23	154	S 7–14	1899–1900	1 locomotive	13	177
		S 15–16	1908	1 marine	12	172
		S 17–19, 23				
		S 20–22	1909	1 marine	13	181
S 24–31	177		1811	1 marine	13	181
S 32	189		1896	2 Yarrow	12	267
S 33–41	180	S 37	1900	1 locomotive	13	177
		S 33, 34, 36, 39	1909	1 marine	13	181
		S 35, 40	1912	1 marine	13	181
S 42	238		1896	1 marine	15	340
S 43–65	238	S 60, 62, 64	1902	1 locomotive	13	294
		S 61	1905	1 marine	13	176
		S 49, 51, 53–56	1909	,,	,,	,,
		S 46, 47	1910	,,	,,	,,
		S 59, 63	1911	,,	,,	,,

rake [after conversion to single-boiler systems the funnels were notably lowered; *S 32* had very narrow funnels. All boats had a vertical mast after 1895]. *S 58–65* had an almost vertical funnel, a mast with a topmast forward of the engine room skylight, and a

derrick (facing aft). [Some boats from *S 43–65* had a long pole mast. A searchlight was fitted (prewar only) on *T 43, 44, 55, 56, 58–60, 63* and *65* on the engine room skylight or forward conning tower. All vessels had an antenna on the (forward) funnel yard.]

Name	Builder	Built	Cost in Marks (000s)	Displacement (t = tonnes T = tons)	Length (m)	Breadth (m)	Draught (m)	Power (hp)	Revs (rpm)	Speed (kts)	Range (nm/kts)	Coal (t)	Oil (t)
S 7–23	F Schichau, Elbing Construction nos 256-272* mod: F Schichau, Elbing	1885	189	98t max 86t des	37.74 oa	4.92	1.20 fwd 2.20 aft	831ihp max 725ihp des	359 max 353 des	20.4 max	2650/10 400/20	17 21	—
S 24–31	F Schichau, Elbing Construction nos 326-333** mod: F Schichau Elbing	1886–87 1911	261	103t max 83t des	37.74 oa	4.80	1.10 fwd 2.34 aft	840ihp max	334	19.1 max	2040/12 740/16	17 21	—
S 32	F Schichau, Elbing Construction no 334 mod: F Schichau, Elbing	1886 1896	311	110t max 104t des	39.12 oa	5.30	1.10 fwd 2.52 aft	900ihp max	344	19.9 max	2050.10	23	—
S 33–41	F Schichau, Elbing Constructions nos 355–363 mod: F Schichau, Elbing S 37, T 35, T 40: others:	1887 1900 1912 1909	177	113t max 94t des	39.88 oa	4.80	1.15 fwd 2.33 aft	1100ihp max	350	20.0 max	2050/10 550/18	17	—
S 42	F Schichau, Elbing Construction no 403 mod: F Schichau, Elbing	1889 1897	261	153t max 123t des	44.20 oa	5.00	1.47 fwd 2.60	1420ihp max	328	22.2 max		18 31	5.7 —
S 43–57	F Schichau, Elbing Construction nos 404-418† mod: F Schichau, Elbing S 46–47, except S 57: T 43–44:	1889–90 1909 1910 1913	261	152t max 127t des	44.20 oa	5.00	1.41 fwd 2.70 aft	1571ihp max	313	21.5 max	2160/10 650/17	30 — 32	— 26†† —
S 58–65	F Schichau, Elbing Construction nos 462–468, 469 mod: F Schichau, Elbing	1891–92 1902–14	308	152t max 132t des	44.31 oa	5.00	1.49 fwd 2.59 aft	1232ihp max	297	20.2 max	1580/12 470/18	30	—

S 60, S 62, S 64 (1902); S 61 (1905); S 59, S63 (1911); S 65 (1912–13); S 58 (1913–14)

* 78gt   ** 78gt   † 194gt   †† S 50–57 only

Career

All torpedo boats and destroyers were allotted to T-Div (torpedo boat divisions), T-Fl (torpedo boat flotillas) Z-Fl or Z-Div (destroyer flotillas and divisions), or (in the case of older boats) held in reserve, unless otherwise stated.

S 7 launched 6 May 1885, commissioned 13 Aug 1885. Stricken 14 Jan 1905; used as a steam supply boat; became defunct.

S 8 launched 13 May 1885, commissioned 4 Nov 1885. Stricken about 1910; used as a target boat; broken up.

S 9 launched 30 May 1885, commissioned 13 Aug 1885. Stricken 14 Jan 1905; hull sold 1906 for 95M.

S 10 launched 8 Jun 1885, commissioned 13 Aug 1885. Stricken 14 Jan 1905; used as a steam supply boat and barrack boat at Wilhelmshaven; broken up.

S 11 launched 18 Jun 1885; commissioned 31 Jul 1885; served as a harbour torpedo boat; renamed T 11 11 Nov 1910; served as an M boat and tender. Stricken 3 Apr 1920; sold 28 Aug 1920 for 26,000M, broken up at Lübeck.

S 12 launched 27 Jun 1885, commissioned 2 Sept 1885. Sunk 13 Mar 1908 in the Elbe estuary, position 53° 56N, 08° 40E, in collision with ss Eduard Gross-

man; 1 dead; raised, broken up.

S 13 launched 7 Jul 1885, commissioned 28 Aug 1885; served as a harbour torpedo boat; renamed T 13 11 Nov 1910; served as a tender and training boat. Stricken and sold, etc, as S 11.

S 14 launched 15 Jul 1885, commissioned 3 Sept 1885; served as a harbour torpedo boat; renamed T 14 11 Nov 1910; served as a tender. Stricken 3 Apr 1920; sold 28 Sept 1920 for 42,000M; broken up at Kiel.

S 15 launched 29 Jul 1885, commissioned 14 Oct 1885; served as a harbour torpedo boat; renamed T 15 11 Nov 1910; served as a tender and training boat.

Stricken 3 Apr 1920; sold 12 Oct 1920 for 25,000M; broken up at Hamburg.

S 16 launched 1 Aug 1885, commissioned 14 Oct 1885; served as a harbour torpedo boat; renamed *T 16* 11 Nov 1910; served as a tender and M boat. Stricken, etc, as *S 11*.

S 17 launched 15 Aug 1885, commissioned 24 Oct 1885. Stricken 18 Jan 1906; used as a target boat; sold 1910; broken up.

S 18 launched 24 Aug 1885, commissioned 24 Oct 1885. Stricken 14 Jan 1905; used as a guard boat, then as a target boat until 1918; broken up.

S 19 launched 4 Sept 1885, commissioned 11 Nov 1885. Stricken 14 Jan 1905; used as a guard boat; sold 1910; broken up.

S 20 launched 8 Sept 1885, commissioned 11 Nov 1885; served as a harbour torpedo boat; renamed *T 20* 11 Nov 1910; served as a tender. Stricken, etc, as *S 11*.

S 21 launched 18 Sept 1885, commissioned 27 Nov 1885; served as a harbour torpedo boat; renamed *T 21* 11 Nov 1910. Sunk at Langeland Belt 16 Aug 1911 after collision with *T 38*; raised 25 Aug 1911; broken up at the Imperial Dockyard, Kiel.

1886; served as a harbour torpedo boat; renamed *T 29* 11 Nov 1910; served as an M boat. Sunk 16 Nov 1916 at Cuxhaven in a collision; raised, repaired; returned to service as a tender. Stricken 3 Apr 1920; sold for 40,000M; broken up at Wilhelmshaven.

S 30 launched 22 Nov 1886, commissioned 15 Jan 1887; served as a harbour torpedo boat; renamed *T 30* 11 Nov 1910; served as an M boat. Stricken, etc, as *S 15*.

S 31 launched 4 Dec 1886, commissioned 13 Apr 1887; served as a harbour torpedo boat; renamed *T 31* 11 Nov 1910; served as an M boat, and as a tender from 1916. Stricken, etc, as *S 15*.

S 32 launched 12 Nov 1886, commissioned 8 Dec 1886. Sunk 17 Aug 1910 in the Baltic, position 54° 30N, 10° 25E, after collision with *S 76*.

S 33 launched 3 May 1887, commissioned 20 Jun 1887; served as a harbour torpedo boat; renamed *T 33* 11 Nov 1910; served as an M boat. Stricken, etc, as *S 15*

S 34 launched 7 May 1887, commissioned 24 Jun 1887; served as a harbour torpedo boat; renamed *T 34* 11 Nov 1910; served as an M boat, also as a tender from 1917. Stricken, etc, as *S 15*.

Oct 1920; sold 6 Jan 1921 for 95,000M; broken up at Wilhelmshaven.

S 43 launched 17 Jun 1889, commissioned 8 Aug 1889; renamed *T 43* 11 Nov 1910; served as an M boat. Sunk 7 Oct 1915 in the North Sea, position 54° 35N, 07° 45E, after hitting a mine; 3 dead.

S 44 launched 30 Oct 1889, commissioned 6 Dec 1889; renamed *T 44* 11 Nov 1910; served as an M boat, as a coastal defence vessel from 1915, and as a tender from 1917; served in the Reichsmarine. Stricken 26 Oct 1920; broken up at Hamburg.

S 45 launched 12 Jul 1889, commissioned 11 Sept 1889; renamed *T 45* 11 Nov 1910; served as an M boat; served in the Reichsmarine. Stricken 10 May 1922; used as a steam supply boat at Kiel arsenal.

S 46 launched 3 Aug 1889, commissioned 2 Nov 1889; renamed *T 46* 11 Nov 1910; served as an M boat. Sunk at 1330hrs on 16 Aug 1915 in the Baltic, position 57° 41N, 21° 50E, by a mine; 17 dead.

S 47 launched 2 Sept 1889, commissioned 30 Oct 1889; renamed *T 47* 11 Nov 1910; served as an M boat. Sunk at 2200hrs on 29 May 1915 in the Baltic, position 55° 03N, 16° 12E, by a mine; 20 dead.

S 7–31 (1894)

T 43–65 (1913) after their conversion to mine hunters

S 22 launched 1 Oct 1885, commissioned 27 Nov 1885; used in the first oil-fired boiler experiments; served as a harbour torpedo boat; renamed *T 22* 11 Nov 1910; served as a tender, M boat and training boat. Stricken 3 Apr 1920; sold 21 May 1921 for 30,000M; broken up at Wilhelmshaven.

S 23 launched 10 Oct 1885, commissioned 21 Dec 1885. Stricken 14 Jan 1905; used as a guard boat; sold 1905 for 16,000M; broken up at Hamburg.

S 24 launched 30 Jul 1886, commissioned 24 Oct 1886; served as a harbour torpedo boat; renamed *T 24* 11 Nov 1910; served as an M boat; career after 1915 as *S 14*.

S 25 launched 4 Aug 1886, commissioned 4 Nov 1886; served as a harbour torpedo boat; renamed *T 25* 11 Nov 1910; served as an M boat. Sunk at 1200hrs on 6 Nov 1914 in the North Sea, position 54° 56N, 07° 55E, after collision with *T 72*.

S 26 launched 21 Aug 1886, commissioned 26 Oct 1886. Sunk 22 Sept 1897 in the Elbe estuary, position 53° 57N, 09° 15E, after capsizing in a storm; 7 dead.

S 27 launched 24 Sept 1886, commissioned 15 Nov 1886; served as a harbour torpedo boat; renamed *T 27* 11 Nov 1910; served as an M boat, and as a submarine training vessel 1914. Stricken, etc, as *S 14*.

S 28 launched 6 Oct 1886, commissioned 3 Dec 1886; served as a harbour torpedo boat; renamed *T 28* 11 Nov 1910; served as an M boat, harbour torpedo boat from 1915, and a tender from 1918. Stricken, etc, as *S 15*.

S 29 launched 19 Oct 1886, commissioned 23 Dec

S 35 launched 25 May 1887, commissioned 26 Jun 1887; remainder of career as *S 34*.

S 36 launched 25 Jun 1887, commissioned 15 Jul 1887; served as a harbour torpedo boat; renamed *T 36* 11 Nov 1910; served as an M boat, and as a tender from 1915. Stricken, etc, as *S 29*.

S 37 launched 9 Jul 1887, commissioned 12 Aug 1887; served as a harbour torpedo boat; renamed *T 37* 11 Nov 1910; served as an M boat, and as a tender from 1915. Stricken, etc, as *S 15*.

S 38 launched 27 Jul 1887, commissioned 29 Jul 1887; served as a harbour torpedo boat; renamed *T 38* 11 Nov 1910; served as an M boat, and as a tender from 1917. Stricken, etc, as *S 15*.

S 39 launched 16 Aug 1887, commissioned 19 Sept 1887; remainder of career as *S 37*.

S 40 launched 27 Aug 1887, commissioned 28 Sept 1887; served as a harbour torpedo boat; renamed *T 40* 11 Nov 1910; served as an M boat, and as a tender from 1916. Stricken, etc, as *S 15*.

S 41 launched 16 Sept 1887, commissioned 12 Oct 1887. Sunk 28 Aug 1895, in the vicinity of Skagen, position approx 57° 30N, 09° 00E, in a storm; 13 dead.

S 42 launched 29 May 1887, commissioned 27 Jun 1889. Sunk 24 Jun 1902 in the Elbe estuary, position 53° 56N, 08° 49E, in a collision with the British SS *Firsby*; 5 dead. Raised, repaired; served as a training boat; renamed *T 42* 11 Nov 1910; served as an M boat, as a coastal defence vessel from 1915, and as a tender from 1917; served in the Reichsmarine. Stricken 26

S 48 launched 20 Sept 1889, commissioned 12 Feb 1890. Sunk 11 Apr 1896 in the Jade, position 53° 35N, 08° 10E, in a collision with *S 46*; 5 dead.

S 49 launched 30 Jan 1890, commissioned 20 Aug 1890; renamed *T 49* 11 Nov 1910; served as an M boat, and from 1916 as a tender; served in the Reichsmarine. Stricken, etc, as *S 44*.

S 50 launched 4 Nov 1889, commissioned 10 Apr 1890; renamed *T 50* 11 Nov 1910; served as an M boat. Sunk 28 Sept 1914 in the Baltic, position 54° 43N, 17° 05E, in a storm.

S 51 launched 28 Nov 1889, commissioned 18 Sept 1890; renamed *T 51* 11 Nov 1910; served as an M boat. Sunk 29 May 1915 at 2200hrs, as for *S 47*.

S 52 launched 20 Dec 1889, commissioned 18 Sept 1890; renamed *T 52* 11 Nov 1910; served as an M boat. Sunk at 0510hrs on 8 Aug 1915 in the Baltic, position 57° 42N, 21° 51E, by a mine.

S 53 launched 18 Jan 1890, commissioned 25 Sept 1890; renamed *T 53* 11 Nov 1910; served as an M boat in the Reichsmarine. Stricken 26 Oct 1920, broken up at Wilhelmshaven.

S 54 launched 30 Jan 1890, commissioned 20 Aug 1890; used in oil-fired boiler experiments; renamed *T 54* 11 Nov 1910; served as an M boat. Sunk at 1405hrs on 6 Oct 1917 in the Baltic, position 57° 38N, 21° 36E, by a mine; 7 dead.

S 55 launched 19 Feb 1890, commissioned 22 Nov 1890; renamed *T 55* 11 Nov 1910; served as an M boat in the Reichsmarine. Stricken 26 Oct 1920; sold 23

Apr 1921 for 110,000M; broken up at Kiel.

S 56 launched 2 Apr 1890, commissioned 6 Oct 1890; renamed *T 56* 11 Nov 1910; served as an M boat. Sunk 16 Oct 1917 in the Baltic, position 58° 42N, 22° 28E, after running aground.

S 57 launched 9 Jun 1890, commissioned 24 Oct 1890; renamed *T 57* 11 Nov 1910; served as an M boat. Sunk 5 Apr 1915 in the Baltic, position 55° 43N, 20° 34E, by a mine.

S 58 launched 3 Dec 1891, commissioned 3 May 1892; renamed *T 58* 4 Sept 1914; served as an M boat. Sunk at 1332hrs on 8 Aug 1915 in the Baltic, position 57° 42N, 21° 55E, by a mine.

S 59 launched 9 Dec 1891, commissioned 29 May 1892; renamed *T 59* 4 Sept 1914; served as an M boat; reduced to a tender 1918. Sunk 25 Jun 1918 in the Baltic, position 54° 35N, 10° 15E, in a collision; 21 dead; raised and repaired; served in the Reichsmarine. Stricken, etc, as *S 15*.

S 60 launched 26 Mar 1892, commissioned 11 Jul 1892; renamed *T 60* 4 Sept 1914; served as an M boat in the Reichsmarine. Stricken 26 Oct 1920; broken up at Hamburg.

S 61 launched 6 Apr 1892, commissioned 23 Jul 1892; renamed *T 61* 4 Sept 1914; remainder of career as for *S 55*.

S 62 launched 7 May 1892, commissioned 29 Jul 1892; renamed *T 62* 4 Sept 1914; remainder of career as for *S 55*.

S 63 launched 28 May 1892, commissioned 12 Aug 1892; renamed *T 63* 4 Sept 1914; remainder of career as for *S 60*.

S 64 launched 28 Jun 1892, commissioned 11 Sept 1892; renamed *T 64* 4 Sept 1914; served as an M boat. Sunk 23 Oct 1916 in the Baltic, position 56° 56N, 21° 00E, by a mine; 10 dead.

S 65 launched 13 Oct 1892, commissioned 10 Nov 1892; renamed *T 65* 4 Sept 1914; served as an M boat. Sunk at 0715hrs on 26 Oct 1917 in the Baltic, position 59° 13N, 22° 37E, by a mine.

S 66 class

Name	Builder	Built	Cost in Marks (000s)	Displacement (t = tonnes T = tons)	Length (m)	Breadth (m)	Draught (m)	Power (hp)	Revs (rpm)	Speed (kts)	Range (nm/kts)	Coal (t)	Oil (t)
S 66	F Schichau, Elbing Construction no 499 mod: F Schichau, Elbing	1892–93 1902	368	172t max 140t des	47.94 oa	5.42	1.50 fwd 2.74 aft	1610ihp max 1600ihp des	310	22.1 max	1560/14	36	—
S 67–73	F Schichau, Elbing Construction nos 500-505 mod: F Schichau Elbing *S 69*: *S 67, 68, 70, 71, 73*: *S 72*: *S 67–73*:	1892–94 1902 1904 1906 1914	346	166t max 137t des	47.94 oa	5.42	1.64 fwd 2.58 aft	1610ihp des	305	21.9 max	1700/12 1010/16	31	—
S 74	F Schichau, Elbing Construction no 550 mod: F Schichau Elbing	1894–95 1905	464	186t max 157t des	49.90 oa 49.90 cwl	5.50	1.58 fwd 2.79 aft	2500ihp des	341	23.7 max		40	—
S 75–81	F Schichau, Elbing Construction nos 551–557 mod: F Schichau, Elbing	1894–96 1909	388	180t max 152t des	49.00 oa	5.30	1.62 fwd 2.85 aft	1744ihp max	319	22.3 max	2070/12 1100/16	43	—

Boat	Screw diameter (m)	Boilers	Pressure (atm forced)	Area (sq m)	Boat (refit)	Refit date	Boilers	Pressure (atm forced)	Area (sq m)
S 66	2.20	2 locomotive	13	343		1902	1 locomotive	13	294
S 67–73	2.20	1 locomotive	13	293		1904	,,	,,	,,
					S 69	1902	,,	,,	,,
					S 72	1906	,,	,,	,,
					S 67–73	1914	2 Marine	13	400
S 74	2.17	2 Thornycroft	14	576		1905	2 Marine	14	497
S 75–81	2.40	2 locomotive	14	343		1909	2 Marine	14	400

Construction Transverse frame steel construction, galvanised (nine watertight compartments). Depth 2.31m to 2.37m.

Propulsion One vertical 3-cylinder (*T 74*, 4-cylinder) triple expansion engine (one 3-bladed screw, see below) in an engine room. Details of boilers are given in the adjacent table. One generator, 2.5kW [4kW] 67V. The funnel cross-section was oval on *T 67–73* only, otherwise circular. One stern rudder, one bow rudder offset to starboard.

Armament One 5cm/40 torpedo gun (156 rounds); three 45cm TT (4 rounds), two deck-mounted, one bow, under water; minesweeping apparatus was also fitted.

Complement Crew: 1/21–23. Boats: one dinghy.

Notes [*S 66* and *S 74–81* were fitted with a searchlight during the war, as in *T 67–73*; these boats had a short port antenna mast]; all boats had a derrick facing forward.

Career

S 66 launched 27 Apr 1893, commissioned 30 Jul 1893; renamed *T 66* 4 Sept 1914; served as an M boat. Sunk at 0930hrs on 18 Oct 1917 in Riga bay, position 58° 18N, 23° 13E, by a mine; 17 dead.

S 67 launched 14 Feb 1893, commissioned 20 May 1903, renamed *T 67* 4 Sept 1914; served as a tender and M boat. Sunk 13 Aug 1918 in the North Sea, position 55° 27N, 06° 46E, by a mine; 2 dead.

S 68 launched 9 Mar 1893, commissioned 1 Jul 1893; renamed *T 68* 4 Sept 1914; served as an M boat. Sunk 4 Jun 1918 in the North Sea, position 55° 28N, 06° 44E, by a mine; 7 dead.

S 69 launched 20 Apr 1893, commissioned 15 Aug 1893; renamed *T 69* 4 Sept 1914; served as an M boat in the Reichsmarine. Stricken 26 Oct 1920; used as a steam supply boat at Wilhelmshaven under the name *W Hz 1*; defunct.

S 70 launched 6 Jun 1893, commissioned 9 Sept 1893; renamed *T 70* 4 Sept 1914; served as a tender and M boat in the Reichsmarine. Stricken 26 Jan 1921; sold 23 Apr 1921 for 110,000M; broken up at Wilhelmshaven.

S 71 launched 2 Aug 1923, commissioned 6 Oct 1893; renamed *T 71* 4 Sept 1914; served as an M boat, and after 1916 as a tender. Stricken 23 Mar 1921; sold 14 Jul 1921 for 110,000M; broken up at Wilhelmshaven.

S 72 launched 20 Jun 1893, commissioned 23 Nov 1893; renamed *T 72* 4 Sept 1914; remainder of career as for *S 70*.

S 73 launched 23 Jun 1893, commissioned 9 Jan 1894; renamed *T 73* 4 Sept 1914; served as an M boat in the Reichsmarine. Stricken 26 Jan 1921; sold 18 May 1921 for 112,000M; broken up at Wilhelmshaven.

S 74 launched 7 Nov 1894, commissioned 25 Oct 1895; renamed *T 74* 4 Sept 1914; remainder of career as for *S 70*.

S 75 launched 22 Jan 1895, commissioned 26 Apr 1895; renamed *T 75* 4 Sept 1914; remainder of career as for *S 70*.

S 76 launched 13 Mar 1895, commissioned 29 May 1895. Sunk 17 Aug 1910 in the Baltic, position 54° 30N, 10° 25E, in collision with *S 32*; raised and repaired; served in TF-1; renamed *T 76* 4 Sept 1914; served as a tender and M boat in the Reichsmarine. Stricken 26 Jan 1921; sold 16 Apr 1921 for 125,000M; broken up at Wilhelmshaven.

S 77 launched 6 May 1895, commissioned 10 Jul 1895; renamed *T 77* 4 Sept 1914; remainder of career as for *S 70*.

S 78 launched 9 Apr 1895, commissioned 1 Jul 1895; renamed *T 78* 4 Sept 1914; served as an M boat. Sunk in the North Sea, position 55° 33N, 17° 15E, by a mine; 26 dead.

S 79 launched 6 Jul 1895, commissioned 1 Sept 1895; renamed *T 79* 4 Sept 1914; served as a tender and M boat (used in 1918 for submarine training) in the Reichsmarine. Stricken 22 Mar 1921; sold in May 1921 for 110,000M; broken up at Kiel.

S 80 launched 14 Jun 1895, commissioned 11 Aug 1895; renamed *T 80* 4 Sept 1914; served as a tender and M boat; remainder of career as for *S 70*.

S 81 launched 30 Sept 1895, commissioned 28 Mar 1896; renamed *T 81* 4 Sept 1914; served as an M boat in the Reichsmarine. Stricken, etc, as *S 76*.

S 67–73 (1894)

S 66 (1896), *S 74–81*

S 67–73 (1914) after their conversion to mine hunters

S 82 class

Name	Builder	Built	Cost in Marks (000s)	Displacement (t = tonnes T = tons)	Length (m)	Breadth (m)	Draught (m)	Power (hp)	Revs (rpm)	Speed (kts)	Range (nm/kts)	Coal (t)	Oil (t)
S 82–87	F Schichau, Elbing Construction nos 599–604 mod: F Schichau, Elbing	1897–98 1904–06	456	170t max 142t des	48.20 oa	5.10	1.62 fwd 2.57 aft	2146ihp max	358	25.3 max	1460/12 680/18 380/20	37	—
G 88–89	Germania Dockyard, Kiel Construction nos 74–75	1897–98	496	177t max 147t des	48.70 oa	5.04	1.65 fwd 2.81 aft	2468ihp max	359	26.0 max	1600/12 420/20	45	—
SCHICHAU EXPERIMENTAL BOAT	F Schichau, Elbing Construction no 450	1890–91		153t des	45.67 oa	5.31	1.83 fwd 2.83 aft	1900ihp des		17.5 des		37	—

Construction Transverse frame nickel-steel construction, *S 82–87* galvanised (twelve and nine watertight compartments). Depth 2.53–2.56m.

Propulsion One vertical 3-cylinder (*Schichau experimental boat* and *G 88–89*, 4-cylinder) triple (quadruple) expansion engine (one 3-bladed screw, 2.11–2.20m diameter) in an engine room amidships between boiler rooms. Two Thornycroft/Marine-type boilers (15 atmospheres forced, 566–540sq m) [*S 82–87* were fitted 1904–06 with two Marine-type boilers (15 atmospheres forced, 491sq m)] in one boiler room forward and one aft. One generator, 4kW 67V. One stern rudder, one bow rudder offset to starboard.

Armament One 5cm/40 torpedo gun (156 rounds); three 45cm TT (3 rounds), two deck-mounted, one bow, above water [the latter removed later]; [mine-sweeping gear was later fitted].

Complement Crew: 1/28–27. Boats: one dinghy.

Notes The Schichau experimental boat was used for testing the use of a quadruple expansion engine on torpedo boats. *G 88–89* had the derrick facing aft. All boats had a round stern. [All were fitted with searchlights as *S 67*, and a short port antenna mast.]

Career

S 82 launched 15 Apr 1897, commissioned 29 Oct 1897; renamed *T 82* 4 Sept 1914; served as an M boat and from 1918 as a tender; served in the Reichsmarine. Stricken 26 Jan 1921; sold 13 May 1921 for 112,000M; broken up at Hamburg-Moorburg.

S 83 launched 26 Jun 1897, commissioned 26 Nov 1897; renamed *T 83* 4 Sept 1914; served as an M boat, and from 1918 as a training boat; served in the Reichsmarine; remainder of career as for *S 82* except for a sale price of 85,000M.

S 84 launched 27 Sept 1897, commissioned 28 Dec 1897; renamed *T 84* 4 Sept 1914; served as a training boat and coastal defence vessel; career as for *S 70* after 1915.

S 85 launched 9 Sept 1897, commissioned 20 Mar 1898. Sunk 1 Sept 1898 at Staber Huk, Fehmarn, position 54° 24N, 11° 21E, after springing a leak after going aground; casualties not known; raised, repaired; renamed *T 85* 4 Sept 1914; served as a training boat and coastal defence vessel, and from 1915 as an M boat; remainder of career as for *S 79*.

S 86 launched 8 Nov 1897; renamed *T 86* 4 Sept 1914; served as a training boat and coastal defence vessel; career after 1915 as for *S 79*.

S 87 launched 10 Dec 1897, commissioned 15 Apr 1898; renamed *T 87* 4 Sept 1914; served as a training boat and coastal defence vessel; career after 1916 as for *S 70*.

S 88 launched 10 Jul 1897, commissioned 2 May 1898; renamed *T 88* 4 Sept 1914; served as a training boat and tender, as an M boat 1916; as a training boat 1918, and in the Reichsmarine; remainder of career as for *S 79*.

S 89 launched 19 Feb 1898, commissioned 18 Aug 1898; renamed *T 89* 4 Sept 1914; remainder of career as for *G 88*.

Schichau experimental boat launched 1891, commissioned 1891; used in dockyard tests 14 Nov 1891 to 12 Feb 1892; laid up. Sold to United States 25 Mar 1898; in service 28 Mar 1898 as US torpedo boat *Somers*; transferred April/May 1899 with ss *Manhattan* to New York. In reserve 1901; renamed *C.T.B 9* 1 Aug 1918. Stricken 7 Oct 1919; transferred 19 Jul 1920 to US Rail and Salvage Co, Newburgh, for breaking up.

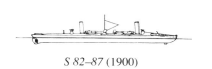

S 82–87 (1900)

A 1 class

Name	Builder	Built	Cost in Marks (000s)	Displacement (t = tonnes T = tons)	Length (m)	Breadth (m)	Draught (m)	Power (hp)	Revs (rpm)	Speed (kts)	Range (nm/kts)	Coal (t)	Oil (t)
A 1–25	AG 'Vulcan', Hamburg Construction nos 20–44	1914–15		137t max 109t des	41.58 oa 41.00 cwl	4.60	1.52 fwd 1.17 aft	1093ihp max 1200ihp des	390	19.0 max 20.0 des	900/12.5 440/19	24.5	—

Construction Laid down as torpedo boats (A-I boats) for use off the Flanders coast (official design, 1914). Transverse frame steel construction (four watertight compartments). Depth not known.

Propulsion One vertical 3-cylinder triple expansion engine (one 3-bladed screw, 1.8m diameter) in an engine room. One Marine-type boiler (17 atmospheres forced, 232sq m) in a separate boiler room. One turbo-generator, 10kW 110V. One stern rudder, one bow rudder.

Armament One 5cm/40 torpedo gun (120 rounds) (*A 1, 2, 17, 18* and *21–25*, one 5.2cm/55 QF gun (100 rounds)); two 45cm TT (2 rounds); four mines; mine-sweeping apparatus.

Complement Crew: 1/27 or 0/28. Boats: one dinghy.

Notes Colour scheme no 10 and grey. In dismantled state *A 2, 4–16, 19* and *20* were transferred by rail to Antwerp-Hoboken and assembled there. The design proved ineffective.

Career

A 1 launched 16 Jan 1915, commissioned 29 Jan 1915; served as a torpedo training boat and guard ship. Stricken 10 May 1922; broken up at Kiel in 1922 for 1,900,000M.

A 2 launched 17 Mar 1915, commissioned 23 Mar 1915; served in Flanders. Sunk at 1800hrs on 1 May 1915 in the North Sea, position 51° 42N, 03° 00E, by gunfire from British destroyers; 12 dead.

A 3 launched 24 Jun 1915, commissioned 13 Jul 1915. Sunk after 7 Nov 1915 en route from Kiel to Danzig; 26 dead (all crew lost)

A 4 launched 26 Jun 1915, commissioned 30 Jun 1915; served in Flanders; scuttled at Antwerp 11 Nov 1918, position 53° 14N, 04° 24E, when Belgium was evacuated; raised; served as Belgian torpedo boat *A 3 PC* in 1926 (also known as *Princesse Marie-José*); renamed *A 4* 1927; sold 1931, broken up.

A 5 launched 5 May 1915, commissioned 10 May 1915; served in Flanders; interned 15 Nov 1918 at Hellevoetsluis, position 51° 42N, 03° 51E, when Belgium was evacuated; transferred to Belgium 25 Jun 1919 as *A 4 PC*; renamed *A 4* 1926; renamed *A 5* 1927, at the dissolution of the Belgian Navy; sold 1931, broken up.

A 6 launched 3 Apr 1915, commissioned 8 Apr 1915; served in Flanders. Sunk at about 1800hrs on 1 May 1915 in the southern North Sea, position 51° 42N, 03° 00E, by gunfire from British destroyers; 1 dead.

A 7 launched 2 Feb 1915, commissioned 19 Apr 1915; served in Flanders. Sunk at about 0600hrs on 21 Mar 1918 off the Flanders coast, position 51° 15N, 02° 40E, by torpedo and gunfire from the French destroyers *Capitaine Mehl* and *Bouclier*; 23 dead.

A 8 launched 25 Apr 1915, commissioned 21 May 1915; served in Flanders until 15 Nov 1918; subsequent career as for *A 5*, but renamed *A 5 PC, A 5,* *A 8*; served 1931 at Oever State Naval School, Ostende; sold 1939.

A 9 launched 4 Aug 1915, commissioned 6 Aug 1915; served in Flanders until 15 Nov 1918; subsequent career as for *A 5*, but renamed *A 6 PC, A 6, A 9*.

A 10 launched 16 Aug 1915, commissioned 23 Aug 1915; served in Flanders. Sunk at 1240hrs on 7 Feb 1918 off the Flanders coast, position 51° 16N, 02° 53E, by a mine; 19 dead.

A 11 launched 4 Jun 1915, commissioned 7 Jun 1915; served in Flanders until 15 Nov 1918; subsequent career as for *A 5*, but renamed *A 7 PC, A 7, A 10*.

A 12 launched 28 Apr 1915, commissioned 2 May 1915; served in Flanders until 15 Nov 1918; subsequent career as for *A 5*, but renamed *A 8 PC, A 2* (*Prince Charles*) etc.

A 13 launched 15 May 1915, commissioned 21 May 1915; served in Flanders. Sunk at 0420hrs on 16 Aug 1917 at Ostende, position 51° 15N, 02° 56E, by an aircraft bomb; 1 dead. Raised; broken up November 1917 at Brügge after further shell damage on 22 Nov 1917.

A 14 launched 22 Jul 1915, commissioned 27 Jul 1915; served in Flanders until 15 Nov 1918; subsequent career as for *A 5*, but renamed *A 1 PC, A 1* (*Prince Leopold*), *A 12*.

A 15 launched 10 Jul 1915, commissioned 15 Jul 1915; served in Flanders. Sunk at 0030hrs on 23 Aug 1915 off the Flanders coast, position 51° 17N, 02° 45E, by gunfire and torpedoes from the French destroyers *Branlebas* and *Oriflamme*; 15 dead.

A 16 launched 16 Jun 1915, commissioned 19 Jun 1915; served in Flanders until 15 Nov 1918; subsequent career as for *A 5*, but renamed *A 8 PC*, *A 8*, *A 16*.

A 17 launched 8 Jun 1915, commissioned 6 Jul 1915 for coastal defence and submarine training. Sunk 13 Mar 1920 off Kiel, position 54° 19.8N, 10° 10E, near Cape Putsch; raised. Stricken 6 Jan 1921; broken up 1922.

A 18 launched 2 Jul 1915, commissioned 20 Jul 1915 for coastal defence. Stricken 21 Jan 1922; broken up 1922 at Kiel.

A 19 launched 9 Sept 1915, commissioned 15 Oct 1915; served in Flanders. Sunk 21 Mar 1918 off the Flanders coast, position 51° 15N, 02° 40E, by gunfire from a British destroyer; 19 dead.

A 20 launched 27 Aug 1915, commissioned 1 Sept 1915; served in Flanders until 15 Nov 1918; subsequent career as for *A 5*, but renamed *A 9 PC*, *A 9* (1927), *A 20* (1927); served from 1931 at West Diep State Naval School, Ostende; taken as a German prize 1940; [converted by Beliard Crighton, Ostende, and served until March 1943 as gunnery training boat *Reiher* for AA training, and from October 1943 as rangefinding training boat *Warendorp*]; taken as a US prize 1945; broken up 1948 at Wilhelmshaven.

A 21 launched 1 Jun 1915, commissioned 29 Jun 1915; served as a coastal defence vessel, in a mine-

A 1–25 (1915)

sweeper flotilla, and as a tender. Sunk 13 Mar 1920 at Kiel, position 54° 19.8E, 10° 10E, near Cape Putsch; raised. Stricken 6 Jan 1921; broken up 1921.

A 22 launched 22 May 1915, commissioned 8 Jun 1915; served in a minesweeper flotilla, and as a coastal defence and submarine training vessel. Stricken 15 May 1922; used as a steam supply boat at Kiel Arsenal.

A 23 launched 5 May 1915, commissioned 29 May 1915; served in a minesweeper flotilla, and as a coastal defence and submarine training vessel. Stricken 15 May 1922; finally used as a target vessel after 1924.

A 24 launched 12 Jun 1915, commissioned 6 Aug 1915; served as a submarine training vessel. Stricken 15 May 1922; used as a steam supply boat at Swinemünde; finally used as a target vessel after 1924.

A 25 launched 13 Jul 1915, commissioned 27 Jul 1915; served as a submarine training vessel. Stricken 15 May 1922; served as a steam supply boat at Kiel Arsenal.

A 26 class

Name	Builder	Built	Cost in Marks (000s)	Displacement (t = tonnes T = tons)	Length (m)	Breadth (m)	Draught (m)	Power (hp)	Revs (rpm)	Speed (kts)	Range (nm/kts)	Coal (t)	Oil (t)
A 26–49	F Schichau, Elbing* Construction nos 959–982	1916–17		250t max 227t des	50.00 oa 49.00 cwl	5.32	2.34 fwd 2.12 aft	3506shp max 3250shp des	515	25.8 max 25.0 des	690/20	—	53
A 50–55	F Schichau, Elbing* Construction nos 988–993	1916–17		252t max 229t des	50.00 oa 49.00 cwl	5.62	2.33 fwd 2.16 aft	,,	,,	,,	,,	—	,,

* Hulls by Sachsenberg yard, RoBlau: *A 35* (construction no 791), *A 38* (792), *A 41* (793)

Construction Laid down as torpedo and mine-seeking boats (A-II boats) (official design, 1915). Transverse frame steel construction (six watertight compartments). Depth not known.

Propulsion One set of Schichau turbines with gear transmission (one 3-bladed screw, 1.88m diameter) in an engine room. One oil-fired Marine-type double boiler (18.5 atmospheres forced, 375sq m) in 1 + 1 boiler rooms. One turbo-generator, 8.5kW 110V. One stern rudder, one bow rudder.

Armament Two 8.8cm/30 torpedo guns (*A 39*, *40*, *42* and *45–55*), two 8.8cm/30 Utof* guns (120 rounds); one 45cm deck TT (1 round); minesweeping gear.

Complement Crew: 1/28 and 0/29. Boats: one torpedo cutter, one dinghy.

Notes Colour scheme no 10 and grey. *A 43*, *44* and *46–50* were transported to Antwerp-Hoboken in dismantled state; *A 51* was taken to Pola by rail and assembled there. Funnel caps were not fitted until 1918; the funnel cross-section was oval.

* A quick-firing gun on a special submarine/torpedo boat anti-aircraft mounting.

Career
A 26 launched 20 May 1916, commissioned 22 Jul 1916; served in a minesweeper flotilla. Stricken 23 Mar 1921; broken up at Kiel.

A 27 launched 27 May 1916, commissioned 12 Aug 1916; served as a coastal defence vessel in Flanders, and as a training boat; released 20 Aug 1920; taken as a British prize; broken up 1922 at Bo'ness.

A 28 launched 10 Jun 1916, commissioned 26 Aug 1916; served as a coastal defence vessel in Flanders, and in a minesweeper flotilla; remainder of subsequent career as for *A 27*.

A 29 launched 15 Jun 1916, commissioned 9 Sept 1916; career as for *A 28*, but broken up 1923 at Bo'ness.

A 30 launched 15 Jul 1916, commissioned 28 Sept 1916; served as a coastal defence vessel in Flanders until 15 Nov 1918; subsequent career as for *A 5*, but renamed *A 29 PC*, and *A 29*; broken up 1927.

A 31 launched 1 Jul 1916, commissioned 30 Sept 1916; subsequent career as for *A 27*, but broken up 1923 at Bo'ness.

A 32 launched 15 Jul 1916, commissioned 14 Oct 1916; served as a coastal defence vessel. Sunk at

0155hrs on 25 Oct 1917 near the Baltic islands, position 58° 38N, 22° 56E, after running aground; raised 1923 and commissioned as Estonian torpedo boat *Sulev*; became Soviet *Ametist* 1940; reduced to a tender 1942; broken up after 1950.

A 33 launched 29 Jul 1916, commissioned 30 Oct 1916; served in a minesweeper flotilla; released 15 Sept 1920; taken as a British prize; broken up 1923 at Bo'ness.

A 34 launched 20 Jul 1916, commissioned 8 Nov 1916; subsequent career as for *A 33*.

A 35 launched 19 Aug 1916, commissioned 1 Dec 1916; served in a minesweeper flotilla; released 20 Aug 1920; subsequent career as for *A 27*.

A 36 launched 14 Aug 1916, commissioned 27 Nov 1916; served in a minesweeper flotilla; released 20 Aug 1920; subsequent career as for *A 27*.

A 37 launched 12 Aug 1916, commissioned 24 Nov 1916; served in a minesweeper flotilla; released 15 Sept 1920; subsequent career as for *A 33*.

A 38 launched 17 Oct 1916, commissioned 14 Mar 1917; served in a minesweeper flotilla; released 15 Sept 1920; subsequent career as for *A 33*.

A 39 launched 12 Sept 1916, commissioned 16 Dec 1916; served in Flanders, then in a minesweeper flotilla; released 20 Aug 1920; subsequent career as for *A 27*.

A 40 launched 2 Sept 1916, commissioned 8 Dec 1916; served in Flanders until 15 Nov 1918; subsequent career as for *A 5*, but renamed *A 22 C*, *A 22*, *A 40*.

A 41 launched 8 Dec 1916, commissioned 16 Mar 1917; served in a minesweeper flotilla; released 20 Aug 1920; subsequent career as for *A 27*.

A 42 launched 1 Nov 1916, commissioned 5 Jan 1917; served in Flanders until 15 Nov 1918; subsequent career as for *A 5*, but renamed *A 23 PC*, *A 23*, *A 42*; renamed *Zand* 1931, and used by the state Naval School, Ostende; sold 1939.

A 43 launched 25 Dec 1916, commissioned 2 Apr 1917; served in Flanders until 15 Nov 1918; subsequent career as for *A 5*, but renamed *A 24 PC*, *A 24* in 1926, *A 43* in 1927, and used by the Wielingen state Naval School, Ostende, 1931; taken as a German prize 1940; broken up 1943 after damage.

A 44 launched 10 Mar 1917, commissioned 30 Apr 1917; served in Flanders, then in a minesweeper flotilla; released 15 Sept 1920; subsequent career as for *A 27*.

A 45 launched 8 Nov 1916, commissioned 15 Jun 1917; served in Flanders, then in the fleet; released 3 Sept 1920; taken as a British prize; broken up 1922 at Bo'ness.

A 46 launched 24 Mar 1917, commissioned 22 May 1917; served in Flanders, then in a minesweeper flotilla; released 3 Sept 1920; subsequent career as for *A 45*.

A 47 launched 23 Apr 1917, commissioned 22 Jun 1917; served in Flanders until 15 Nov 1918; subsequent career as for *A 5*, but renamed *A 25 PC*, *A 25*, *A 47*.

A 48 launched 9 Jun 1917, commissioned 31 Jul 1917; served in Flanders, then in the fleet; released 3 Sept 1920; subsequent career as for *A 45*.

A 26–55 (1917)

A 49 launched 19 May 1917, commissioned 9 Jul 1917; served in Flanders, then in a minesweeper flotilla; commissioned as Belgian *A 26 PC* 1918–20; released 15 Sept 1920; subsequent career as for *A 33*.

A 50 launched 8 Jul 1917, commissioned 20 Aug 1917; served in Flanders. Sunk at 0830hrs on 17 Nov 1917 in the southern North Sea, position 51° 33N, 03° 15E, by a mine; 18 dead.

A 51 launched 16 May 1917, commissioned 26 Jul 1917; served as a tender, and in a Mediterranean submarine flotilla at Pola. Scuttled and sunk 29 Oct 1918 at Fiume, position 45° 21N, 14° 26E; raised; transferred to Italy 1920; broken up; see *A 82*.

A 52 launched 18 Jan 1917, commissioned 1 Apr 1917; served in a minesweeper flotilla; released 30 Sept 1920; taken as a British prize; broken up 1923 at Bo'ness.

A 53 launched 3 Feb 1917, commissioned 7 Apr 1917; served in a minesweeper flotilla; released 15 Sept 1920; subsequent career as for *A 33*.

A 54 launched 22 Feb 1917, commissioned 14 Apr 1917; subsequent career as for *A 52*.

A 55 launched 10 Mar 1917, commissioned 27 Apr 1917; subsequent career as for *A 52*.

A 56 class

Name	Builder	Built	Cost in Marks (000s)	Displacement (t = tonnes T = tons)	Length (m)	Breadth (m)	Draught (m)	Power (hp)	Revs (rpm)	Speed (kts)	Range (nm/kts)	Coal (t)	Oil (t)
A 56–67	AG 'Vulcan', Stettin* Construction nos 476–487	1916–17 1917–18		381t max 330t des	61.10 oa 60.12 cwl	6.41	2.21 fwd 2.24 aft	6008shp max 6000shp des	727	28.2 max 28.0 des	800/20	—	92
A 68–79	F Schichau, Elbing Construction nos 994–1005	1916–17 1917–18		392t max 335t des	60.00 oa 59.30 cwl	6.42	2.34 fwd 2.30 aft	5800shp max 6000shp des	579	26.5 max 28.0 des	,,	—	82
A 80–82	AG 'Vulcan', Stettin Construction nos 514–516	1917–18		381t max 330t des	60.37 oa 60.20 cwl	6.41	2.11 fwd 1.82 aft	5940shp max 5700shp des	704	26.6 max 26.0 des	800/20 790/20	—	92 91
A 83–85	Howaldtswerke, Kiel Construction nos 614–616	,,		,,	,,	,,	,,	,,	,,	,,	,,	—	,,
A 86–91	AG 'Vulcan', Stettin Construction nos 535–540	,,		,,	,,	,,	,,	,,	,,	,,	,,	—	,,
A 92–95	F Schichau, Elbing Construction nos 1019–1022	1917–18		392t max 335t des	61.20 oa 59.40 cwl	6.42	2.12 fwd 2.08 aft	6033shp max 6000shp des	589	26.7 max 26.5 des	800/20	—	82
A 96–113	AG 'Vulcan', Stettin Construction nos 575–592	1918–		381t max 330t des	60.37 oa 60.20 cwl	6.41	2.11 fwd 1.82 aft	5700shp		26.0 des	790/20	—	91

* A 64–67 (construction nos 395–398) had hulls by Seebeck

Construction Laid down as torpedo boats (A-III boats) (official design, 1916). Transverse frame steel construction (seven watertight compartments). Served as prototype for *TF 1-8-24*. Depth 3.10m, but 3.30m after *A 92*.

Propulsion *A 68–79* and *92–95*, two sets of Schichau turbines with gear transmissions (two 3-bladed screws, 1.70m diameter); *A 56–67*, *80–91* and *A 96–113*, two sets of AEG-Vulcan turbines, direct (two 3-bladed screws, 1.60m diameter), in 1 + 1 engine rooms. Two oil-fired Marine-type boilers (18.5 atmospheres forced, 600 and 650 to 684sq m) in 1 + 1 boiler rooms. Two turbo-generators, 12kW 110V. One stern rudder, one bow rudder.

Armament Two (*A 80*, three) 8.8cm/30 Utof guns (140 rounds); one (*A 80*, none) 45cm deck TT (1 round).

Handling Seakeeping qualities were excellent, with equally good manoeuvrability and responsiveness. Transverse metacentric height 0.75–0.65m, longitudinal not known.

Complement Crew: 2/48 (*A 80–91* and *96–113*, 2/53). Boats: one torpedo cutter, one dinghy.

Notes Colour scheme no 10, 12. Differences between the various designs were evident in stern and rudders; the funnels of Schichau boats were oval in cross-section. *A 56–67* initially had no compass platform. *A 80–91* and *96–113* were as shown in the drawing of *A 56*, but with masts as shown in the drawing of *A 92*. *A 82* was transferred to Pola by rail in dismantled state and assembled there. Type A-III boats served in 1939–40 as the prototype for the TF boats (torpedo capture boats) in the Kriegsmarine training flotillas; see *TF 1–4*.

Career
A 56 launched 28 Feb 1917, commissioned 14 Apr 1917; served in a minesweeper flotilla. Sunk 12 Mar 1918 in the North Sea, position 53° 45N, 06° 15E, by a mine; 16 dead.

A 57 launched 28 Feb 1917, commissioned 28 Apr 1917; served in a minesweeper flotilla. Sunk 2 Mar 1918 in the North Sea, position 53° 21N, 04° 57E, by a mine; 12 dead.

A 58 launched 31 Mar 1917, commissioned 19 Mar 1917; served in Flanders. Sunk 15 Aug 1918 off the Flanders coast, position 51° 24N, 03° 16E, by a mine; 3 dead.

A 59 launched 13 Apr 1917, commissioned 9 Jun 1917; served in Flanders, then in a minesweeper flotilla; released 30 Sept 1920; taken as a Polish prize; converted at Rosyth 1921 and served as *Slazak* until 1937. Stricken; broken up.

A 60 launched 15 May 1917, commissioned 23 Jun 1917; served in Flanders. Sunk at 0200hrs on 30 Nov 1917 off the Flanders coast, position 51° 25N, 03° 10E, by a mine; 17 dead.

A 61 launched 15 May 1917, commissioned 11 Jul 1917; served in Flanders, and in a minesweeper flotilla; released 15 Sept 1920; subsequent career as for *A 3*.

A 62 launched 8 Jun 1917, commissioned 25 Jul 1917; served in a minesweeper flotilla; released 15 Sept 1920; subsequent career as for *A 33*.

A 63 launched 16 Jun 1917, commissioned 11 Aug 1917; served in minesweeper and escort flotillas; released 30 Sept 1920; taken as a French prize; broken up 1923 at Bo'ness.

A 64 launched 30 Mar 1918, commissioned 8 Aug 1918; served in an escort flotilla; released 30 Sept 1920; taken as a Polish prize; converted 1921 at Rosyth to *Krakowiak*. Scuttled in Danzig bay 4 Sept 1939.

A 65 launched 30 Mar 1918, commissioned 24 Aug 1918; served in a minesweeper flotilla; released 3 Sept 1920; taken as a Brazilian prize, but sold to England in 1921; broken up 1922 at Queensferry.

A 66 launched 23 Jun 1918, commissioned 20 Sept 1918; served in a minesweeper flotilla; released 30 Sept 1920; subsequent career as for *A 63*.

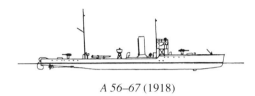

A 56–67 (1918)

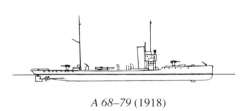

A 68–79 (1918)

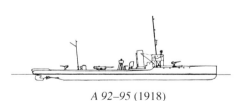

A 92–95 (1918)

A 67 launched 23 Jun 1918, but only 75 percent complete when stricken 3 Nov 1919; broken up 1921 at Hamburg.

A 68 launched 11 Apr 1917, commissioned 13 Jun 1917; served in minesweeper and escort flotillas; released 3 Sept 1920; taken as a Polish prize; converted 1921 at Rosyth to *Kujawiak*. Scuttled at Danzig Bay 4 Sept 1939; raised by the Kriegsmarine minus the boiler; broken up.

A 69 launched 28 Apr 1917, commissioned 4 Jul 1917; served in minesweeper and escort flotillas; released 3 Sept 1920; taken as a Polish prize; broken up 1922 at Queensferry; see also *V 105*.

A 70 launched 19 May 1917, commissioned 23 Jul 1917; served as a submarine training vessel and in the minesweeper flotilla; released 30 Sept 1920; taken as a Japanese prize; broken up 1922 at Bo'ness.

A 71 launched 9 Jun 1917, commissioned 13 Aug 1917; served in minesweeper and escort flotillas. Sunk at 0210hrs on 4 May 1918 in the North Sea, position 54° 39N, 06° 27E, by a mine; 6 dead.

A 72 launched 30 Jun 1917, commissioned 1 Sept 1917; served in minesweeper and escort flotillas. Sunk at 0130hrs on 14 May 1918 in the North Sea, position 55° 34N, 05° 54E, by a mine; 25 dead.

A 73 launched 7 Jul 1917, commissioned 21 Sept 1917; served in a minesweeper flotilla. Sunk 20 Jan 1918 in the North Sea, position 54° 40N, 06° 32E, by a mine; 40 dead.

A 74 launched 4 Aug 1917, commissioned 9 Oct 1917; served in minesweeper and escort flotillas and as a submarine training vessel; released 3 Sept 1920; subsequent career as for *A 65*.

A 75 launched 11 Aug 1917, commissioned 26 Oct 1917; served as a submarine training vessel and in a minesweeper flotilla; released 30 Sept 1920; subsequent career as for *A 63*.

A 76 launched 1 Sept 1917, commissioned 12 Nov 1917; served in a minesweeper flotilla; released 30 Sept 1920; subsequent career as for *A 63*.

A 77 launched 22 Sept 1917, commissioned 27 Nov 1917; served in a minesweeper flotilla. Sunk 20 Jan 1918 in the North Sea, position 54° 40N, 06° 32E, by a mine; 33 dead.

A 78 launched 13 Oct 1917, commissioned 15 Dec 1917; served in an escort flotilla; released 3 Sept 1920; subsequent career as for *A 65*, but broken up 1922 at Bo'ness.

A 79 launched 8 Nov 1917, commissioned 12 Jan 1918; served in an escort flotilla. Sunk at 0015hrs on 11 Jul 1918 in the North Sea, position 54° 47N, 04° 52E, by a mine; 53 dead

A 80 launched 24 Oct 1917, commissioned 21 Dec 1917; served in Flanders and in a minesweeper flotilla; released 30 Sept 1920; taken as a Polish prize, under the name *Goral*; renamed *Podhalanin* after 1922. Stricken 1938; used as a target ship and fuel store; sunk 1 Sept 1939 at Kuznickiej Mulde-Hela by a German aircraft bomb; raised 1939 by Gotenhafen naval salvage group; defunct, broken up.

A 81 launched 27 Nov 1917, commissioned 10 Jan 1918; served in a minesweeper flotilla; released 30 Sept 1920; subsequent career as for *A 65*, but broken up 1921 at Sunderland.

A 82 launched 27 Mar 1918, commissioned 1 Jun 1918; served as a tender for a Mediterranean submarine flotilla at Pola. Scuttled 29 Oct 1918 at Fiume; subsequent fate as for *A 51*.

A 83–85 launched 28 May 1918, commissioned 28 May 1918, 19 Apr 1918, 6 Jun 1918; only 60–40 percent complete when stricken 3 Nov 1919; broken up 1921 at Kiel.

A 86 launched 5 Feb 1918, commissioned 16 Mar 1918; served in an escort flotilla; released 30 Sept 1920; subsequent career as for *A 63*.

A 87 launched 21 Feb 1918, commissioned 8 Apr 1918; served in a minesweeper flotilla; released 15 Sept 1920; subsequent career as for *A 65*, but broken up 1922 at Bo'ness.

A 88 launched 2 Mar 1918, commissioned 27 Apr 1918; served in a minesweeper flotilla; released 30

Sept 1920; taken as a British prize; broken up 1923 at Bo'ness.

A 89 launched 22 Mar 1918, commissioned 14 May 1918; served in an escort flotilla; subsequent career as for *A 88*.

A 90 launched 6 Apr 1918, commissioned 6 Jun 1918; served in an escort flotilla; released 30 Sept 1920; taken as a British prize; broken up 1922 at Bo'ness.

A 91 launched 27 Apr 1918, commissioned 22 June 1918; served in an escort flotilla; subsequent career as for *A 90*.

A 92 launched 16 Mar 1918, commissioned 24 May 1918; served in a minesweeper flotilla; released 15 Sept 1920; subsequent career as for *A 65*, but broken up 1923 at Bo'ness.

A 93 launched 9 Apr 1918, commissioned 18 Jun 1918; served in a minesweeper flotilla; subsequent career as for *A 90*.

A 94 launched 27 Apr 1918, commissioned 19 Jul 1918; served in an escort flotilla; subsequent career as for *A 88*.

A 95 launched 25 May 1918, commissioned 19 Aug 1918; served in an escort flotilla; subsequent career as for *A 88*.

A 96–113 were ships up to 35 percent complete when stricken 3 Nov 1918; broken up on stocks.

Completion was planned for *A 104–A 107* (at the Oder Works), *A 108–110* (at Holtz), and *A 111–113* (at Sachsenberg).

Divisional torpedo boats 1887–1898

D 1 class

Name	Builder	Built	Cost in Marks (000s)	Displacement (t = tonnes T = tons)	Length (m)	Breadth (m)	Draught (m)	Power (hp)	Revs (rpm)	Speed (kts)	Range (nm/kts)	Coal (t)	Oil (t)
D1, D2	F Schichau, Elbing Construction nos 324–325 mod: F Schichau, Elbing (D1): Imperial Dockyard, Kiel (D2):	1886–87 1900–01 1909	466	300t max 249t des	56.05 oa	6.60	1.83 fwd 3.40 aft	2020ihp max 2200ihp des 2036ihp max	265 230	20.6 max	1940/14 660/18 1940/14 660/18	56	—
D3, D4	F Schichau, Elbing Construction nos 365–366 mod: F Schichau, Elbing (D3): D4:	1887–88 1900 1914	,,	,,	57.64 oa	6.80	1.96 fwd 3.23 aft	2200ihp des	235	20.3 max	1940/14 660/18	55	—
D5, D6	F Schichau, Elbing Construction nos 382–385 mod: F Schichau, Elbing (D5): D6:	1888–89 1910 1904	541	406t max 300t des	59.58 oa	7.40	2.18 fwd 3.50 aft	3200ihp des	251	22.6 max	2310/14 1060/18	98	—

231gt (*D1*, *D2*), 215gt (*D3*, *D4*), 264gt (*D5*, *D6*)

Construction

Transverse frame steel construction, galvanised except for *D 1* and initially *D 2* (twelve, after *D 3* eleven, watertight compartments). Depth approx 3.28m.

Propulsion

One vertical 3-cylinder triple expansion engine (one 3-bladed screw, 2.54m/2.80m/2.80m diameter) in an engine room. *D 1–2* had two locomotive boilers (12 atmospheres forced, 406sq m) [*D 1* refitted 1900–01 with two locomotive boilers (13 atmospheres forced, 322sq m); *D 2* refitted 1909 with two Marine-type boilers (13 atmospheres forced, 420sq m)]; *D 3–4* had two locomotive boilers (13 atmospheres forced, 406sq m) [*D 3* refitted 1900 with two Normand boilers (13 atmospheres forced, 492sq m); *D 4* refitted 1914 with two Marine-type boilers (13 atmospheres forced, 460sq m)]; *D 5–6* had two locomotive boilers (13 atmospheres forced, 551sq m) [refitted 1910 and 1904 with two Marine-type boilers (13 atmospheres forced, 640sq m)] in a separate boiler room [new boilers fitted in 1 + 1 boiler rooms on *D 3*, *D 5* and *D 6*]. One generator, 4kW 67V. *D 1* and *D 2* initially had three [later two, as in *D 3–6* from the beginning] raked masts (the foremast 1.5m aft of the conning tower) with sails, 82sq m then 37sq m [finally all boats had one lantern mast and one mast with a topmast, both vertical]; after the refit *D 1* as *Carmen* (see the drawing), *D 2* as *Alice Roosevelt* and *D 4* were fitted with two raked masts with equal height topmasts; *D 3* and *D 5–6* had a wireless telegraphy mast and a foremast with a topmast (mainmast with a topmast on *D 6*). One stern rudder, one bow rudder, the latter offset to starboard after *D 3*.

Armament

Six 3.7cm machine guns (1680 rounds) [after 1893, three 5cm/40 torpedo guns (496 rounds)]; three 35cm TT (4 rounds), two deck-mounted, one bow above water (after *D 3* the bow tube was under water).

Complement

Crew: 7/39 [later *D 1–4* had 1/51–46; *D 5–6* had 4/44]. Boats: one yawl, one dinghy.

Notes

Carmen and *Alice Roosevelt* were painted in colour scheme no 11, all other boats in overall black or grey. All vessels had angled funnel tops as built [later temporarily straightened]. [*Alice Roosevelt*'s deckhouse began 3m aft of the mainmast; after new boilers were fitted, the deckhouse was as on *Carmen*, but the funnel was 2.5m further aft; on both these vessels all additional superstructure and fittings were designed to be removable within 48 hours. *D 1–2* had no deckhouse in wartime; a searchlight was fitted on the enclosed forward bridge. *D 3* was as shown in the drawing, but initially the funnels were of equal height, and no searchlight was fitted.] *D 4* had a wireless telegraphy booth on the funnel (which had an ornamental edge), and a deckhouse approx 6m long immediately aft of the mainmast. *D 5–6* had no forward conning tower, only a breakwater and companionway (as in the drawing of *D 3*, but with the wireless telegraphy booth on the forward edge of the aft funnel, the latter 1m further forward). *D 5*'s funnel was extended forward at all times.

Career

D 1 launched 19 Dec 1886, commissioned 27 Apr 1887 as *D 2*; renamed *D 1* 1 Aug 1887; served as a torpedo boat flotilla flagship; after May 1905 became station yacht *Carmen* in the Baltic (serving as a fleet tender 1907 to 1909); served as a coastal defence vessel 1914. Stricken 2 Aug 1921; broken up 1921 at Wilhelmshaven for 142,000M.

D 2 launched 11 Sept 1886, commissioned 1 May 1887 as *D 1*; renamed *D 2* 1 Aug 1887; served as a torpedo boat flotilla flagship; after March 1902 became station yacht *Alice Roosevelt* in the North Sea; renamed *D 2* and served as a coastal defence vessel 1914. Stricken 7 Dec 1920; broken up 1921.

D 3 launched 1 Oct 1887, commissioned 3 May 1888; served as a torpedo boat flotilla flagship and minesweeper flotilla flagship; served as a coastal defence vessel 1914, and a submarine training vessel 1916; reverted to service with a minesweeper flotilla 1919.

Stricken 7 Dec 1920; broken up 1921 at Wilhelmshaven.

D 4 launched 9 Nov 1887, commissioned 15 Oct 1888; served as a torpedo boat flotilla flagship; fisheries protection vessel 1906; fleet tender 1910–16. Stricken 7 Dec 1920; broken up 1921 at Hamburg.

D 5 launched 20 Oct 1888, commissioned 17 Apr 1889; served as a torpedo boat flotilla flagship; fisheries protection vessel 1905–1906; submarine flotilla flagship 1910; submarine training vessel 1914; minesweeper flotilla 1919. Stricken 7 Dec 1920; broken up 1921 at Hamburg.

D 6 launched 9 Feb 1889, commissioned 28 Jun 1889; served as a torpedo boat flotilla flagship and minesweeper flotilla flagship; patrol flotilla vessel 1915; submarine training vessel 1916. Stricken 7 Dec 1920; broken up 1921.

D 1, D 2 (1896)

Carmen (1905) as a station yacht for the Baltic

D 3 (1914); *D 5* and *D 6* were similar.

D 7 class

Name	Builder	Built	Cost in Marks (000s)	Displacement (t = tonnes T = tons)	Length (m)	Breadth (m)	Draught (m)	Power (hp)	Revs (rpm)	Speed (kts)	Range (nm/kts)	Coal (t)	Oil (t)
D7, D8	F Schichau, Elbing Construction nos 441–442 mod: F Schichau, Elbing (D7): D8:	1890–91 1907 1910	665 each	410t max 320t des	59.72 oa	7.40	2.40 fwd 3.40 aft	3600ihp des	246	22.5	2590/14 1420/18	105	—

Construction

Transverse frame steel construction, galvanised (eleven watertight compartments). Depth 3.44m.

Propulsion

One vertical 3-cylinder triple expansion engine (one 3-bladed screw, 2.80m diameter) in an engine room. Two locomotive boilers (13 atmospheres forced, 561sq m) in a separate boiler room [refitted 1907 and 1910 with new Marine-type boilers (13 atmospheres forced, 642sq m) in 1 + 1 boiler rooms]. One generator, 4kW 67V. Two masts with topmasts [later fitted with a lantern mast and a mainmast with topmast, both vertical; after the refit both boats carried a wireless telegraphy mast forward and a mainmast with topmast aft]. One stern rudder, one bow rudder, offset to starboard.

Armament

Six 3.7cm machine guns (1680 rounds) [after 1893, three 5cm/40 torpedo guns (496 rounds)]; three 45cm TT (4 rounds), two deck-mounted, one bow, under water.

Complement

Crew: 7/39 [4/44]. Boats: one yawl, one dinghy.

D 7, D 8 (1891)

Notes

These boats were similar in appearance to *D 6* but both pressure heads were centrally located between the funnels; the anchor davits were of the earlier form.

Career

D 7 launched 6 May 1891, commissioned 25 Jul 1891; served as a torpedo boat flotilla flagship and minesweeper flotilla flagship until 1908; coastal defence vessel 1914; submarine training vessel 1916. Stricken 7 Dec 1920; broken up 1921 at Hamburg.

D 8 launched 8 Jun 1891, commissioned 25 Oct 1891; subsequent career as for *D 7*, except for use during 1917 in experiments. Stricken 7 Dec 1920; broken up 1921 at Hamburg.

D 9

Name	Builder	Built	Cost in Marks (000s)	Displacement (t = tonnes T = tons)	Length (m)	Breadth (m)	Draught (m)	Power (hp)	Revs (rpm)	Speed (kts)	Range (nm/kts)	Coal (t)	Oil (t)
D9	F Schichau, Elbing Construction no 543	1894	680	458t max 350t des	63.00 oa	7.70	2.36 fwd 3.73 aft	4200ihp des	210	23.5	2600/14 1480/18	106	—
	mod: F Schichau, Elbing	1910									2900/14	119	

Construction

Transverse frame steel construction, galvanised (twelve watertight compartments). Depth 3.86m.

Propulsion

One vertical 3-cylinder triple expansion engine (one 3-bladed screw, 3.21m diameter) in an engine room. Three locomotive boilers (12 atmospheres forced, 807sq m) in a separate boiler room [after 1910, three Marine-type boilers (13 atmospheres forced, 900sq m) in 1 + 1 boiler rooms]. One generator, 4kW 67V. One stern rudder, one bow rudder offset to starboard.

Armament

Three 5cm/40 torpedo guns (496 rounds); three 45cm TT (4 rounds), two deck-mounted, one bow, under water.

Complement

Crew: 7/45 [4/44]. Boats: one yawl, one dinghy.

Notes

The lantern mast was as shown in the earlier drawing, with no searchlight. This boat was nicknamed *Sturm-vogel* – Stormy Petrel.

Career

D 9 launched 3 Sept 1894, commissioned 29 Dec 1894; served as a torpedo boat flotilla flagship; minesweeper flotilla flagship 1907; service after 1914 and eventual fate were as for *D 7*, but she served in a minesweeper flotilla in 1919.

D 9 (1896)

D 9 (1918) after her conversion

D 10

Name	Builder	Built	Cost in Marks (000s)	Displacement (t = tonnes T = tons)	Length (m)	Breadth (m)	Draught (m)	Power (hp)	Revs (rpm)	Speed (kts)	Range (nm/kts)	Coal (t)	Oil (t)
D10	Thornycroft, London mod:	1896–98 1906	1173	371t max 310t des	66.10 oa 64.30 cwl	5.95	2.35	5783ihp	389	27.2	2120/14 810/19 460/22	77 80	—

Construction

Laid down as a sister ship to the British two-funnel 30kts destroyers *Angler*, *Ariel*, *Desperate*, *Fame*, *Foam*, *Cygnet*, *Cynthia*, *Coquette*, *Mallard* and *Stag*; transverse frame steel construction, galvanised (twelve watertight compartments). Depth 3.89m.

Propulsion

Two vertical 4-cylinder triple expansion engines (two 3-bladed screws, 2.14m diameter) in an engine room. Three Thornycroft boilers (15.5 atmospheres forced, 1001sq m) [after 1906, three Yarrow boilers (15.5 atmospheres forced, 1035sq m)] in 1 + 1 + 1 boiler rooms. One generator, 4kW 67V. One rudder at the pointed stern, one bow rudder.

Armament

Five 5cm/40 torpedo guns (826 rounds); three 45cm TT (3 rounds), two deck-mounted, one bow, above water [bow TT removed].

Complement

Crew: 7/40 [4/48]. Boats: one yawl, one dinghy.

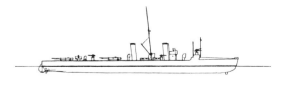

D 10 (1910)

Notes

As built, the funnels were 1.5m lower than shown in the drawing. [The bridge was later enclosed, with a searchlight mounted on top.] This boat was nicknamd *Schlingerpott* – Roll Pot.

Career

D 10 launched 24 Mar 1898, commissioned 13 Oct 1898; served as a submarine acceptance commission tender 1907; coastal defence vessel and submarine flotilla flagship 1914; submarine training vessel and acceptance tender 1915; barrack ship 1919. Stricken 28 Jul 1922; broken up 1922 at Wilhelmshaven.

Large (ocean-going) torpedo boats 1899–1907

S 90 class

Construction

Transverse frame steel construction, galvanised below CWL (ten watertight compartments, eleven after *S 114*, twelve after *G 132*). Depth 3.38m–3.43m.

Propulsion

S 90–107 and *S 114–119*, two vertical 3-cylinder triple expansion engines (two 3-bladed screws, 2.25m diameter); three Thornycroft boilers (15.5 atmospheres forced, 1186–1164sq m) [*S 114–119* fitted with three new Marine-type boilers in 1913 (15.5 atmospheres forced, 1106sq m).]

G 108–113, two vertical 3-cylinder triple expansion engines (two 3-bladed screws, 2.18m diameter); three Marine-type boilers (16 atmospheres forced, 1045sq m).

S 120–124 and *S 126–130*, two vertical 3-cylinder triple expansion engines (two 3-bladed screws, 2.25m diameter); three Marine-type* boilers (15.5 and 16 atmospheres forced, 1100sq m).

G 132–136, two vertical 3-cylinder triple expansion engines (two 3-bladed screws, 2.30m diameter); three Marine-type boilers (17.5 atmospheres forced, 1105sq m).

S 125, one System 7 Parsons turbine (three 3-bladed screws, 1.40m diameter); three Marine-type boilers (15.5 atmospheres forced, 1100sq m).

G 137, one System 6 Parsons turbine (three 3-bladed screws, 1.60m diameter); four Marine-type boilers (17 atmospheres forced, 1735sq m).

From *S 120* these were arranged in 1/1 engine rooms, aft of 1 + 1 + 1 boiler rooms, except that *S 125* and *G 137* had one engine room only, in the latter case with 1 + 1 + 1 + 1 boiler rooms; *S 90–100* had one boiler room forward and two aft of the first engine room, *S 101* two forward and one aft; other details are not known. Trials results on a forced acceptance run are shown in the table above. One or two generators, 4–8kW, 67–110V. One stern rudder, one bow rudder.

Armament

Three 5cm/40 QF guns (252 rounds), but after *G 132*, four 5.2cm/55 QF guns (600 rounds), except for *G 135* (one 8.8cm/35 QF gun plus two 5.2cm/55 QF guns) and *G 137* (one 8.8cm/35 QF gun plus three 5.2cm/55

* *S 124*, three Normand boilers (15.5 atmospheres forced, size not known).

Vessel	Speed (at 386–390t)
S 104	28.95kts
S 107	28.40kts
S 120	27.01kts
S 121	27.09kts
S 122	27.00kts
S 123	28.27kts
S 124	28.38kts
S 125	28.00kts

QF guns [later armament fits were *T 92* and *T 110*, two 8.8cm/30 QF guns; *S 108*, *S 130* and *G 136*, two 8.8cm/45 torpedo guns; *T 113* (and then *T 102–104*), *S 120–123*, *S 126–128* and *S 131*, one 8.8cm/40(35)30 QF (torpedo) gun plus two 5cm/40 torpedo guns; *G 132–134*, one 8.8cm/35 QF gun plus two 5.2cm/55 QF guns; *T 97*, one 5.2cm/55 QF gun plus two 5cm/40 torpedo guns]; all boats had three 45cm deck TT (5 rounds).

Complement

Crew: 2/55; after *S 120*, 2/59; after *G 132*, 2/67; *G 131*, 3/78; half-flotilla staff, 4/11. Boats: one yawl, one dinghy.

Notes

S 90–92 and *S 97* as *Sleipner*, only, colour scheme no 11. All boats were fitted with a lantern mast on the forward edge of the bridge, before searchlights were fitted. [*S 97* as *Sleipner* (see the drawing) had no deckhouse after 1914]; as originally built she had no after mast. *S 102–107* and *S 114–119* had the after funnel and mast 1m closer together than shown in the drawing of *S 90*, and a stern approx as shown in the drawing of *S 120*. *S 125* had a 3-shaft stern.

Career

All torpedo boats and destroyers were allotted as standard to T-Div (torpedo boat divisions), T-Fl (torpedo boat flotillas), Z-Fl or Div (destroyer flotillas or divisions) or, in the case of older boats, held in reserve, unless otherwise stated.

S 90 launched 26 Jul 1899, commissioned 24 Oct 1899; served abroad. Scuttled and sunk 17 Oct 1914, 35nm southwest of Tsingtau, position 35° 32N, 119° 36E, after running aground.

S 91 launched 25 Sept 1899, commissioned 24 Apr 1900; served abroad until 1902; served in a torpedo boat flotilla; renamed *T 91* 4 Sept 1914, and served as a coastal defence vessel; tender 1915; served in the Reichsmarine. Stricken 22 Mar 1921; sold 26 May 1921 to Düsseldorf; broken up.

S 92 launched 15 May 1900, commissioned 27 Jun 1900; served abroad until 1902; served in a torpedo boat flotilla; renamed *T 92* 4 Sept 1914, and served as a minesweeping division flagship; patrol and escort flotilla 1916–18; subsequent career as for *S 91*.

S 93 launched 24 Mar 1900, commissioned 14 Jul 1900; renamed *T 93* 4 Sept 1914, and served as a coastal defence vessel; patrol and escort flotilla 1917–18; served in the Reichsmarine; subsequent career as for *S 91*.

S 94 launched 23 Apr 1900, commissioned 27 Jul 1900; renamed *T 94* 4 Sept 1914; served as a coastal defence vessel; tender 1915; served in the Reichsmarine. Sunk 13 Mar 1920 at Wilhelmshaven during the Kapp Putsch; raised. Stricken 26 Oct 1920; sold 13 May 1921 for 160,000M; broken up at Wilhelmshaven.

S 95 launched 20 Feb 1900, commissioned 29 Aug 1900; renamed *T 95* 4 Sept 1914; served as a coastal defence vessel; tender 1915; served in the Reichsmarine. Stricken 22 Mar 1921; sold 13 May 1921 for 180,000M; broken up at Kiel.

S 96 launched 31 Jan 1900, commissioned 27 Sept 1900; served as a tender; renamed *T 96* 4 Sept 1914; served in the Reichsmarine; subsequent career as for *S 91*.

S 97 launched 16 Dec 1899, commissioned 28 May 1900; after 28 May 1900 served as the dispatch boat *Sleipner* at the service of the Kaiser; renamed *T 97* and served as a coastal defence vessel 4 Sept 1914; served in a patrol and escort flotilla 1917–18; later served in the Reichsmarine; subsequent career as for *S 91*.

S 98 launched 28 Jul 1900, commissioned 4 Nov 1900; served as a tender; renamed *T 98* 4 Sept 1914; served in the Reichsmarine; subsequent career as for *S 91*.

S 99 launched 4 Sept 1900, commissioned 13 Dec 1900; served as a submarine flotilla flagship; renamed *T 99* 4 Sept 1914; served in an escort flotilla 1918; served in the Reichsmarine; subsequent career as for *S 91*.

S 100 launched 13 Nov 1900, commissioned 18 Apr 1901; renamed *T 100* 4 Sept 1914; served as a sub-

Name	Builder	Built	Cost in Marks (000s)	Displacement (t = tonnes T = tons)	Length (m)	Breadth (m)	Draught (m)	Power (hp)	Revs (rpm)	Speed (kts)	Range (nm/kts)	Coal (t)	Oil (t)
S 90-101	F Schichau, Elbing Construction nos 644–649, 670 672–675	1898– 1901	874 1015	394t max 310t des	63.0 oa 62.7 cwl	7.0	2.03 fwd 2.83 aft	5900ihp des	258	26.5 max 27.0 des	830/17 690/20	93	—
S 97	F Schichau, Elbing Construction no 671	1899– 1900	1017	440t max 310t des	,,	,,	2.24 fwd 2.99 aft	,,	,,	,,	,,	,,	—
S 102–107	F Schichau, Elbing Construction nos 679–684	1900–02	1055 1113	406t max 315t des	63.2 oa 63.0 cwl	,,	2.10 fwd 2.68 aft	,,	269	27.5 max 28.0 des	1020/17 870/20	92	—
G 108–113	Germania Dockyard, Kiel Construction nos 91–96	1900–02	1027 1161	440t max 330t des	65.8 oa 65.5 cwl	6.7	2.33 fwd 2.87 aft	6013ihp max 6600ihp des	346	29.2 max 28.0 des	1225/17	112	—
S114–119	F Schichau, Elbing Construction nos 700–705	1902–03	1067 1092	415t max 315t des	63.2 oa 63.0 cwl	7.0	2.17 fwd 2.69 aft	5900ihp des	298	28.0 max 27.0 des	980/17	102	—
S 120–124	F Schichau, Elbing Construction nos 718–722	1903–04	979 994	468t max 391t des	64.7 oa 64.2 cwl	,,	2.33 fwd 2.63 aft	6400ihp des	294	27.5 max 27.5 des	1500/17	115	—
S 125	F Schichau, Elbing Construction no 723	1903–04	1270	454t max 355t des	,,	,,	2.31 fwd 3.17 aft	6600shp des	786	27.7 max 28.0 des		93	—
S 126–131	F Schichau, Elbing Construction nos 737–742	1904–05	1049 1077	482t max 371t des	,,	,,	2.40 fwd 2.76 aft	6497ihp max 6400ihp des	297	28.0 max 28.0 des	1080/17 275/24	117	—
G 132–136	Germania Dockyard, Kiel Construction nos 114–118	1905–07	1175 1198	544t max 412t des	65.7 oa 65.3 cwl	,,	2.63 fwd 2.87 aft	6783ihp max 7000ihp des	287	27.3 max 28.0 des	2000/12 1060/17	132	—
G 137	Germania Dockyard, Kiel Construction no 125	1906–07	1760	693t max 580t des	71.5 oa 68.5 cwl	7.65	2.83 fwd 3.22 aft	10,800shp des	850	33.9 max 30.0 des		168	—
	mod: Imperial Dockyard, Kiel	1914–15										—	108

marine flotilla flagship and as a training boat 1915. Sunk on 15 Oct 1915 in the Baltic, position 54° 30N, 13° 43E in a collision with the ferry *Preussen*; 39 dead. The wreck was blown up 1925–26, then broken up.

S 101 launched 22 Dec 1900, commissioned 30 May 1901; renamed *T 101* 4 Sept 1914; served as submarine flotilla flagship; served in a patrol flotilla 1917 and a torpedo boat flotilla 1918; served in the Reichsmarine; subsequent career as for *S 95*.

S 102 launched 18 Apr 1901, commissioned 18 Jul 1901; renamed *T 102* 4 Sept 1914; served as a coastal defence vessel and training boat, and in a patrol and

escort flotilla 1917–18; served in the Reichsmarine; subsequent career as for *S 95*.

S 103 launched 15 May 1901, commissioned 17 Sept 1901; renamed *T 103* 4 Sept 1914; served as a minesweeper division flagship, and in an escort flotilla 1918; served in the Reichsmarine; subsequent career as for *S 91*.

S 104 launched 22 Jun 1901, commissioned 7 Oct 1901; renamed *T 104* 4 Sept 1914; served as a minesweeper division flagship and in a torpedo boat flotilla 1918; served in the Reichsmarine; subsequent career as for *S 91*.

S 105 launched 7 Aug 1901, commissioned 17 Nov 1901; renamed *T 105* 4 Sept 1914; served as a coastal defence vessel and in a patrol flotilla 1917; served in a torpedo boat flotilla 1918; served in the Reichsmarine; subsequent career as for *S 91*.

S 106 launched 7 Sept 1901, commissioned 9 Dec 1901; subsequent career as for *S 105* and *T 105*.

S 107 launched 17 Oct 1901, commissioned 27 Jan 1902; renamed *T 107* 4 Sept 1914; served as a coastal defence vessel and training boat; served in the Reichsmarine; subsequent career as for *S 95*.

S 108 launched 7 Sept 1901, commissioned 26 Mar 1902; renamed *T 108* 4 Sept 1914; served as a training boat; served in the Reichsmarine. Stricken 22 Mar 1921; broken up at Hamburg.

S 109 launched 9 Nov 1901, commissioned 19 Jun 1902; renamed *T 109* 4 Sept 1914; served as a submarine flotilla flagship 1915, and in a patrol and escort flotilla 1916–18; served in the Reichsmarine; subsequent career as for *S 95*.

S 110 launched 9 Sept 1902, commissioned 21 Jan 1903; renamed *T 110* 4 Sept 1914; served as a coastal defence and training boat, and in a patrol flotilla; served in the Reichsmarine. Stricken 22 Mar 1921; broken up at Hamburg.

S 111 launched 2 Apr 1902, commissioned 21 Jul 1902; renamed *T 111* 4 Sept 1914; served as a training boat, and as a tender 1916; served in the Reichsmarine. Stricken 22 Mar 1920; sold 13 Jun 1921 for 200,000 M; broken up at Kiel.

S 112 launched 19 Jun 1902, commissioned 6 Sept 1902; renamed *T 112* 4 Sept 1914; served as a coastal defence vessel, and in patrol and escort flotillas; served in the Reichsmarine; subsequent career as for *G 111*.

S 113 launched 9 Aug 1902, commissioned 16 Oct 1902; renamed *T 113* 4 Sept 1914; served as a coastal defence vessel, and in patrol and escort flotillas; served in the Reichsmarine. Stricken 22 Mar 1921; sold 8 Jun 1921 for 260,000M; broken up at Wilhelmshaven.

S 114 launched 9 Aug 1902, commissioned 25 Oct 1902; served as a coastal defence vessel after 1915; renamed *T 114* 4 Sept 1916; served in patrol and escort flotillas; served in the Reichsmarine. Stricken 9 Nov 1920; sold 7 Jul 1921 for 170,000M; broken up at Kiel.

S 115 launched 10 Sept 1902, commissioned 22 Feb 1903. Sunk 17 Oct 1914 in the North Sea, position 52° 48–50N, 03° 49–50E, by gunfire from the British light cruiser *Undaunted* and four British destroyers; 55 dead.

S 116 launched 14 Oct 1902, commissioned 28 Mar 1903. Sunk at 0120hrs on 6 Oct 1914 in the North Sea, position 53° 42N, 06° 09E, by a torpedo from the British submarine *E 9*; 9 dead.

S 117 launched 4 Feb 1903, commissioned 21 May 1903; fate as for *S 115*; 64 dead.

S 118 launched 21 Mar 1903, commissioned 9 Jul 1903; fate as for *S 115*; 52 dead.

S 119 launched 8 Jul 1903, commissioned 6 Sept 1903; fate as for *S 115*; 47 dead.

S 120 launched 10 Feb 1904, commissioned 7 May 1904; served as a coastal defence vessel after 1915; renamed *T 120* 27 Sept 1916; served as a patrol and training boat; served in the Reichsmarine. Stricken 22 Mar 1921; sold 28 May 1921 for 210,000M; broken up at Wilhelmshaven.

S 121 launched 3 Mar 1904, commissioned 17 Jun 1904; renamed *T 121* 27 Sept 1916; served as a training and patrol boat; served in the Reichsmarine; subsequent career as for *G 111*.

S 122 launched 23 Apr 1904, commissioned 5 Aug 1904; served as a submarine flotilla flagship 1914; coastal defence vessel 1915; renamed *T 122* 27 Sept 1916; served as a training boat, and in patrol and escort flotillas 1916–18. Sunk at 0700hrs on 5 Oct 1918 in the North Sea, position 54° 40N, 05° 57E, by a mine; 12 dead.

S 123 launched 25 Jun 1904, commissioned 23 Aug 1904; was a member of the wreck destruction command. Sunk at 2040hrs on 1 May 1916 in the North Sea, position 55° 04N, 08° 23E, by a mine; 23 dead.

S 124 launched 3 Aug 1904, commissioned 8 Oct 1904; served as a coastal defence vessel. Sunk 30 Nov 1914 in the Baltic 54° 22N, 12° 11E, in a collision with the Danish ss *Anglodane*; 1 dead. Salvaged; broken up 1915 at Kiel.

S 125 launched 19 May 1904, commissioned 4 Apr 1905; served as a coastal defence vessel 1914; renamed *T 125* 27 Sept 1916; served in patrol and escort flotillas 1917–18; served in the Reichsmarine. Stricken 26 Oct 1920; sold 13 May 1921 for 215,000M; broken up at Hamburg-Moorburg.

S 126 launched 26 Nov 1904, commissioned 30 Apr 1905. Sunk 17 Nov 1905 in the Baltic, position 54° 30N, 10° 20E, in a collision with the light cruiser *Undine*, in which she was broken in two; 33 dead. The front section was raised 8 May 1906, the stern 18–20 May 1906; the boat was repaired during 1908 and returned to service; renamed *T 126* 27 Sept 1916; served as a training boat; served in the Reichsmarine; subsequent career as for *G 111*.

S 127 launched 12 Jan 1905, commissioned 7 Jun 1905; renamed *T 127* 27 Sept 1916; served as a patrol flotilla flagship and in an escort flotilla; served in the Reichsmarine; subsequent career as for *S 120*.

S 128 launched 25 Feb 1905, commissioned 8 Jul 1905; renamed *T 128* 27 Sept 1916; served as a patrol flotilla flagship, and as an escort and training boat; served in the Reichsmarine; subsequent career as for *G 111*.

S 129 launched 4 Mar 1905, commissioned 10 Aug 1905; served as a coastal defence vessel. Sunk 5 Nov 1915 in the North Sea, position 53° 59N, 08° 21E, after running aground; no casualties.

S 130 launched 27 Apr 1905, commissioned 17 Sept 1905; renamed *T 130* 27 Sept 1916; served as a training boat, coastal defence vessel and tender; served in the Reichsmarine; subsequent career as for *S 120*.

S 131 launched 25 May 1905, commissioned 6 Oct 1905; served as a training boat after 1915; renamed *T 131* 27 Sept 1916; served in patrol and escort flotillas, served in the Reichsmarine; subsequent career as for *S 120*.

G 132 launched 12 May 1906, commissioned 22 Aug 1906; renamed *T 132* 27 Sept 1916; served in submarine flotilla and as a minesweeper flotilla flagship; served in the Reichsmarine; subsequent career as for *S 120*.

G 133 launched 30 Jun 1906, commissioned 10 Dec 1906; renamed *T 133* 27 Sept 1916; subsequent career as for *S 120*.

G 134 launched 23 Jul 1906, commissioned 6 Mar 1907; renamed *T 134* 27 Sept 1916; served as a training boat; served in the Reichsmarine. Stricken 9 Nov 1920; sold 13 May 1921 for 185,000M; broken up at Hamburg-Moorburg.

G 135 launched 7 Sept 1906, commissioned 24 Jan 1907; served as a coastal defence vessel 1915; renamed *T 135* 27 Sept 1916 and served in patrol and escort flotillas; served in the Reichsmarine. Stricken 25 May 1921; sold 10 Oct 1921; broken up at Wilhelmshaven.

G 136 launched 25 Aug 1906, commissioned 16 Mar

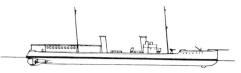

Sleipner as a dispatch boat

G 108–113 (1902)

S 114–119 (1903)

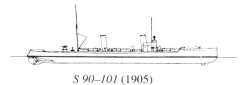

S 90–101 (1905)

S 120–131 (1906)

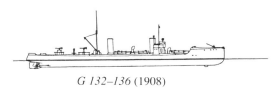

G 132–136 (1908)

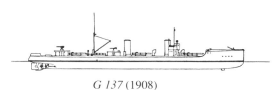

G 137 (1908)

1907; renamed *T 136* 27 Sept 1916; served as a minesweeper division flagship, and in an escort flotilla 1918; served in the Reichsmarine. Stricken 21 Jul 1921; sold 20 Aug 1921; broken up at Wilhelmshaven.

G 137 launched 24 Jan 1907, commissioned 24 Jul 1907; served as a training boat 1914, and submarine flotilla flagship 1915; renamed *T 137* 27 Sept 1916; served in the Reichsmarine; subsequent career as for *S 120*.

Large torpedo boats 1907–1919

S 138 class

Name	Builder	Built	Cost in Marks (000s)	Displacement (t = tonnes T = tons)	Length (m)	Breadth (m)	Draught (m)	Power (hp)	Revs (rpm)	Speed (kts)	Range (nm/kts)	Coal (t)	Oil (t)
S 138–149	F Schichau, Elbing Construction nos 777–788	1906–08	1458 1478	684t max 533t des	70.7 oa 70.2 cwl	7.8	2.75 fwd 2.95 aft	11,000ihp des	320	30.3 max 30.0 des	1830/17 390/24	194	—
V 150–160	AG 'Vulcan', Stettin Construction nos 274–284	1907–08	1473 1523	691t max 558t des	72.5 oa 72.5 cwl	″	2.84 fwd 3.03 aft	10,900ihp des	″	31.1 max 30.0 des	895/17	158	—
	mod: Navy Dockyard, Wilhelmshaven (T151, 153, 155–158)	1922–24		796t max 670 des	73.8 oa 72.2 cwl		3.22 fwd 3.15 aft	10,600 ihp	″	29.9 max	3500/17 1450/20	—	181
V 161	AG 'Vulcan', Stettin Construction no 285	1907–08	1780	687t max 596t des	72.5 oa 72.2 cwl	7.8	2.94 fwd 2.98 aft	14,800shp des	670	33.0 max 32.0 des	1520/14	166	—
V 162–164	AG 'Vulcan', Stettin Construction nos 289–291	1908–09	1801 1857	739t max 639t des	73.9 oa 73.6 cwl	7.85	3.02 fwd 3.12 aft	16,020shp max 15,100shp des	626	33.4 max 32.0 des	2140/12 960/17	134	60
S 165–168	F Schichau, Elbing Construction nos 819–822, 853–856	1908–11	1666 1690	765t max 665t des	74.2 oa 74.0 cwl	7.9	3.04 fwd 3.03 aft	17,700shp max 17,500shp des	753	33.6 max 32.0 des	975/17 450/27	116	74
G 169–172	Germania Dockyard, Kiel Construction nos 138, 139, 142, 143	1908–09	1785 1816	777t max 670t des	74.0 oa 74.0 cwl	″	2.82 fwd 3.25 cwl	16,610shp max 15,000shp des	817	32.7 max 32.0 des	1250/17 460/30	125	84
G 173	Germania Dockyard, Kiel Construction no 144	1908–09	1800	778t max 700t des	74.0 oa 74.0 cwl	″	2.78 fwd 3.28 aft	15,820shp max 15,000shp des	648	31.4 max 32.0 des	1250/17 460/30	″	″
G 174–175	Germania Dockyard, Kiel Construction nos 145, 146	1909–11	1830	824t max 700t des	74.0 oa 74.0 cwl	″	3.04 fwd 3.28 aft	15,000shp des		31.5 max 32.0 des	920/17	145	80
S 176–179	F Schichau, Elbing Construction nos 839–842	1909–11	1726	781t max 566t des	74.2 oa 74.0 cwl	″	3.06 fwd 3.10 aft	17,840shp max 17,600shp des	727	32.9 max 32.0 des	1025/17	117	75

continued opposite

V 180–185	AG 'Vulcan', Stettin Construction nos 295–300	1909–10	1979 2021	783t max 650t des	73.9 oa 73.6 cwl	7.85	3.12 fwd 3.22 aft	17,640shp max 18,000shp des	686	33.3 max 32.0 des	2360/12 1250/17	121	76
	mod: Navy Dockyard, Wilhelmshaven (T 185)	1925–26		858t max 761t des			3.23 fwd 3.27 aft				2800/12 1400/17	—	198
V 186–191	AG 'Vulcan', Stettin Construction nos 304–309	1910–11	1844 1856	775t max 666t des	73.9 oa 73.9 cwl	,,	3.07 fwd 3.17 aft	18,060shp max 18,000shp des	693	33.5 max 32.0 des	1170/17 480/32	136	67
	mod: Navy Dockyard, Wilhelmshaven (T 190)	1923–24 1927		861t max 766t des			3.21 fwd 3.22 aft				2800/12 1400/17	—	198
G 192–197	Germania Dockyard, Construction nos 151–156	1910–11	1801 1810	810t max 660t des	74.0 oa 73.6 cwl	7.9	3.02 fwd 3.25 aft	19,130shp max 18,200shp des	654	33.9 max 32.0 des	2590/12 1150/17 420/30	145	76
	T 196 mod: Navy Dockyard, Wilhelmshaven	1923 1927–28		875t max 766t des			3.23 fwd 3.31 aft	11,200shp	606	27.3	1850/19		204

450gt/157nt (*T 138–149*), 461gt/161nt (*T151–160*), 506gt/163nt (*T151, 153, 155–158*), 505gt/178nt (*T 165–168*)

Construction

Transverse frame steel construction in special torpedo boat steels (thirteen watertight compartments, twelve after *V 150*). Depth 4.15m.

Propulsion

Details of engines and boilers are given in the table below. After reboilering *T 185*, *190* and *196* had two oil-fired Marine-type boilers plus one oil-fired Marine-type double boiler (18.5–18 atmospheres forced, 1906–1921sq m). [The forward funnel of the double boiler was oval in cross-section.] Two generators, 17kW 110V; after *V 186* see *V 1*. One stern rudder, one retractable bow rudder.

Vessel	Machinery	Screws No	Diam	Boilers	Pressure (atm forced)	Area
S 138–149	2 vertical 3-cyl triple expansion engines	2	2.35m	4 Marine	19	1685
V 150–160	,,	2	2.40m	,,	19	1677
V 161	2 sets AEG turbines, direct	2	2.10m	,,	19	1679
V 162–164	,,	2	2.25m	3 Marine, 1 Marine oil	18.5	1815
V 163	2 sets AEG-Vulcan turbines, direct	2	2.25m	,,	18.5	1815
S 165–168	2 sets Schichau turbines, direct	2	2.15m	,,	18.5	1871
G 169–172	1 system 6 Parsons turbines, direct	3	1.65m	,,	17	1834
G 173	2 sets Zoelly turbines, direct	2	2.25m	,,	17.5	1833
G 174–175	2 sets Parsons turbines, direct	2	2.25m	,,	18	1833
S 176–179	2 sets Schichau turbines, direct	2	2.25m	,,	17	1871
V 180–185	2 sets AEG Vulcan turbines, direct	2	2.20m	,,	18.5	1815
V 186–191	,,	2	2.25m	,,	18.5	1815
G 192–197	2 sets Germania turbines, direct	2	2.25m	,,	18.5	1833

All machinery in 1 + 1 engine rooms; all boilers in 1 + 1 + 1 + 1 boiler rooms.

Armament

S 138–149, one 8.8cm/35 QF gun (100 rounds) plus three 5.2cm/55 QF guns (450 rounds); *V 150–155*, two 8.8cm/35 QF guns (200 rounds); *V 156* onwards, two 8.8cm/30 torpedo guns (200 rounds) [*S 138–141, 143, 145* and *147–149* were rearmed with two 8.8cm/35 QF guns and one 5.2cm/55 QF gun; *S 142* and *144* with two 8.8cm/35 QF guns; *S 153* and *155*, two 8.8cm/45 QF guns; *G 170, 172–175, S 146, 165, 168, 176, 178, 179, V 180–186, 189, 190* and *G 192–197*, two 8.8cm/45 torpedo guns (280 rounds); *T 168*, two 8.8cm/45 torpedo guns plus one 8.8cm/30 Utof gun; after 1920 *T 139, 141, 143, 144, 146, 148, 149* and *154* were fitted with two 8.8cm/45 torpedo guns; *T 151, 153* and *155–158* with two 8.8cm/45 Utof guns; *T 185, 190* and *196* with two 10.5cm/45 Utof guns]; three 45cm deck TT (4 rounds), but from *G 174* onwards four 50cm deck TT (5 rounds) [after refit *T 151, 153* and *155–158* had two 50cm deck TT in double V-tubes; *T 185, 190* and *196* had four 50cm deck TT in double V- tubes]. *Blitz* had two 2cm AA guns [*Claus von Bevern*, (from July 1944) one 10.5cm/45 Utof gun and two 2cm AA guns; also two 50cm TT. *Eduard Jungmann* (from September 1940) one 8.8cm/45 Utof gun].

Handling

Relatively good sea-boats for their size, but crank and with severe roll; responsive, especially the turbine boats; very tight turning circle, even at low speeds and when running astern, especially against the current. Strong sidewinds made all manoeuvres difficult, and tended to make lee helm a necessity. The waist between the forecastle and bridge rendered the weapons mounted there unusable in wind speeds above 6/7 because of spray, and this also severely hindered navigation; all weapons were extremely difficult to use above Beaufort 7.

Complement

Crew: 3/77; from *V 150* onwards, 3/81 (with half-flotilla staff 4/9) [after refit, 4/94–4/95 (with half-flotilla staff 5/14); after 1935, 4/87–88; *Eduard Jungmann* 1/74; *Claus von Bevern* 2/83–1/76; *Blitz* 0/78–0/56; TF boats 1/60]. Boats: one yawl, one dinghy [later up to three yawls, one dinghy].

Notes

[*T 139, 141, 143, 144, 146, 148*, and *149* had the lower bridge extended aft by 1m and the upper bridge by 3m after 1919; the compass platform was also moved forward of the after mast, and both funnels had caps; two masts were fitted, as in the drawing of *T 185*. *V 150–161* had a cap on the forward funnel during war service. *T 152* and *154* had masts as in the drawing of *T 185* after 1919, and a very tall funnel cap. *T 151, 153* and *155–158* had a starboard derrick after 1935; *T 153* as a rangefinder training boat was as in the drawing. *V 162–165* had the bridge and forward funnel raised, as in the drawing of *G 169*. *S 165–168* were similar to

V 162, etc, but with a mainmast 1m further forward.] *S 168*'s forward funnel was 1m higher from the beginning [a cap was later fitted on this funnel]; *G 169–175* [also later fitted with a forward funnel cap] had a forward funnel 1m lower initially, and a bridge as shown in the drawing of *V 164*. *G 173* was similar in appearance to the drawing of *G 174*, but the bridge shape and torpedo mount were as in the drawing of *V 164*. [*S 176–179* were refitted with a bridge, forward funnel and wireless telegraphy booth as in the drawing of *G 174* (with a cap on the forward funnel).] *V 180–185* were generally as shown in the drawing of *T 185*, but with a bridge, forward funnel and torpedo mount as on *S 176* [with a cap on the forward funnel]. [*T 183*, *c*1917, had a forward funnel with a cap, and a dummy third funnel in sailcloth in the space between the real funnels. *T 185* after 1926 had a long forecastle and after bridge, as in the drawing; previously the bridge, funnel and masts were as in the drawing of *G 7* (second appearance), but without a derrick on the after mast, this being replaced by a similar pole-type derrick on the after edge of the forecastle; after 1929 this boat had a characteristic box-shaped forward bridge. *V 186–191* had the bridge and forward funnel raised, as in the drawing of *G 174* (with a cap on forward funnel); after 1924 *T 190* was similar to *T 185*, and after 1926 it was similar to the drawing of *T 185*, but the forward funnel was approx 0.7m higher, with angled top edges and flat caps on both funnels.] *V 187* retained the English bridge arrangement after trials. *G 192–197* had a low forward funnel and bridge as built; see the drawing of *V 186*. [After 1922 *T 196* appeared as in the drawing, and after 1928 as in the later drawing, but with no searchlight platforms on the masts until 1931, and one searchlight where the rangefinder was fitted later; the superstructure after 1935 is shown by a dotted line in the drawing, replacing the TT. *T 185*, *190* and *196* had a new stern shape and stem as shown in the drawing of *T 196*, but not until after about 1932–33. All boats were fitted with depth charge launchers at the stern. After January 1943 *Claus von Bevern* had a fishing steamer KDB installation.]

Career

S 138 launched 22 Sept 1906, commissioned 7 May 1907; served in patrol and escort flotillas 1916–18; renamed *T 138* 24 Sept 1917. Sunk at 0106hrs on 7 Jul 1918 in the North Sea, position 54° 26N, 04° 32E, by a mine; 32 dead.

S 139 launched 12 Nov 1906, commissioned 6 Jul 1907; renamed *T 139* 24 Sept 1917; served in the Reichsmarine. Stricken 3 Aug 1927; converted to fast tug and remote control boat *Pfeil*; taken out of service 28 Sept 1937, and converted to a *TF* boat; still in service in 1944 with the 24th submarine flotilla; ultimate fate not known.

S 140 launched 22 Dec 1906, commissioned 3 Aug 1907; renamed *T 140* 24 Sept 1917; served in the Reichsmarine; subsequent career as for *G 113*.

S 141 launched 7 Feb 1907, commissioned 9 Sept 1907; served as a coastal defence vessel 1916; renamed *T 141* 24 Sept 1917; served in the Reichsmarine. Stricken 3 Aug 1927; converted to fast tug and remote control boat *Blitz*; sold 28 Apr 1933; broken up at Wilhelmshaven.

S 142 launched 6 Mar 1907, commissioned 20 Sept 1907; served as a coastal defence vessel 1916–18 and in training and escort flotillas; renamed *T 142* 24 Sept 1917; served in the Reichsmarine. Stricken 2 Dec 1920; subsequent career as for *G 111*, but sold for 260,000M.

S 143 launched 6 Apr 1907, commissioned 12 Oct 1907; served as a coastal defence vessel 1914. Sunk at 1700hrs on 3 Aug 1914 in the Baltic, position 54° 30N, 12° 06E, by a boiler explosion; 24 dead. Raised and repaired; served in a torpedo boat flotilla; renamed *T 143* 24 Sept 1917; served in the Reichsmarine. Stricken 10 May 1927; sold 25 Mar 1930 for 61,500M; broken up at Hamburg-Moorburg.

S 144 launched 27 Apr 1907, commissioned 3 Dec 1907; served as a coastal defence vessel 1915, and as a tender 1918; renamed *T 144* 24 Sept 1917; served in the Reichsmarine. Stricken 8 Oct 1928; sold 10 Apr 1929 for 81,000M to Essen, then broken up.

S 145 launched 8 Jun 1907, commissioned 17 Dec 1907; renamed *T 145* 24 Sept 1917; served in the Reichsmarine; subsequent career as for *G 113*.

S 146 launched 27 Jun 1907, commissioned 20 Nov 1907; served as a tender 1916–18 and as a training boat; renamed *T 146* 24 Sept 1917; served in the Reichsmarine; subsequent career as for *S 144*.

S 147 launched 3 Aug 1907, commissioned 10 Apr 1908; served in patrol and escort flotillas from 1916; renamed *T 147* 24 Sept 1917; served in the Reichsmarine. Stricken 2 Dec 1920; sold 21 May 1921 for 120,000M; broken up at Wilhelmshaven.

S 148 launched 11 Sept 1907, commissioned 8 Mar 1908; served in a patrol flotilla; renamed *T 148* 24 Sept 1917, and served in an escort flotilla; served in the Reichsmarine. Stricken 8 Oct 1928, broken up 1935 at Wilhelmshaven.

S 149 launched 19 Oct 1907, commissioned 27 Jul 1908; served as a minesweeper flotilla flagship from 1916; renamed *T 149* 24 Sept 1917; served in the Reichsmarine. Stricken 16 May 1927, then broken up.

V 150 launched 1 Aug 1907, commissioned 20 Nov 1907. Sunk at 0020hrs on 18 May 1915 in the Jade, position 54° 24N, 07° 45E, in a collision with *V 157*; 60 dead.

V 151 launched 14 Sept 1907, commissioned 29 Feb 1908; renamed *T 151* 24 Sept 1917; served in the Reichsmarine and Kriegsmarine; converted to fast tug *Comet* 12 Mar 1937, then to a *TF* boat in April 1939; served in minesweeping group (W) 20 Nov 1945; taken as a USA prize 4 Jan 1946. Transferred to Bremer Vulkan 1948, and broken up.

V 152 launched 11 Oct 1907, commissioned 10 Apr 1908; renamed *T 152* 24 Sept 1917; served in the Reichsmarine. Stricken 31 Mar 1931; broken up 1935.

V 153 launched 13 Nov 1907, commissioned 9 May 1908; served as a submarine flotilla flagship 1916–18; renamed *T 153* 24 Sept 1917; served in the Reichsmarine and Kriegsmarine, as the rangefinding training boat *Eduard Jungmann* from 29 Aug 1938; taken as a USA prize 22 Dec 1945, and used as a GM/SA buoy boat until 1947. Broken up 1949 in the Netherlands.

V 154 launched 19 Dec 1907, commissioned 5 Jun 1908; renamed *T 154* 24 Sept 1917; served in the Reichsmarine. Stricken 8 Oct 1928; broken up 1935.

V 155 launched 28 Jan 1908, commissioned 25 Jun 1908; renamed *T 155* 24 Sept 1917; served in the Reichsmarine and Kriegsmarine; served as a tender and *TF* boat from October 1936. Scuttled and sunk 22 Apr 1945 at Swinemünde, position 53° 56N, 14° 17E; broken up.

V 156 launched 29 Feb 1908, commissioned 21 Jul 1908; served as a training boat 1916–18; renamed *T 156* 24 Sept 1917; served in the Reichsmarine and Kriegsmarine; served as a *TF* boat from 1936; renamed *Bremse* 1944 in the K-Verband Norway. Scuttled 3 May 1945 at Kiel; broken up.

V 157 launched 29 May 1908, commissioned 27 Aug 1908; renamed *T 157* 24 Sept 1917; served in the Reichsmarine and Kriegsmarine, as a *TF* boat from 1936. Sunk at 1725hrs on 22 Oct 1943 at Neufahrwasser, position 54° 25N, 18° 43E, by a mine; casualties not known; later raised and broken up.

V 158 launched 23 Jun 1908, commissioned 8 Oct 1908; renamed *T 158* 24 Sept 1917; served in the Reichsmarine and Kriegsmarine, as a *TF* boat from 1936; taken as a Soviet prize 15 Jan 1946; renamed *Prozorlivyy*; broken up 1950.

V 159 launched 18 Jul 1908, commissioned 2 Nov 1908; served as a submarine flotilla flagship 1916–18; renamed *T 159* 24 Sept 1917; served in the Reichsmarine. Released 20 Aug 1920; taken as a British prize; broken up 1922 at Granton.

V 160 launched 12 Sept 1908, commissioned 15 Dec 1908; renamed *T 160* 24 Sept 1917; served in the Reichsmarine; subsequent career as for *T 159*.

V 161 launched 21 Apr 1908, commissioned 17 Sept 1908; served as a submarine flotilla flagship 1916–18; renamed *T 161* 24 Sept 1917; served in the Reichsmarine. Released 3 Sept 1920; taken as a British prize; broken up 1922.

V 162 launched 9 May 1909, commissioned 28 May 1909 as a coastal defence vessel. Sunk at 2230hrs on 15 Aug 1916 in the Baltic, position 57° 35N, 21° 35E, by a mine; 15 dead.

V 163 launched 24 May 1909, commissioned 22 Jul 1909; served as a training boat 1916–18; renamed *T 163* 24 Sept 1917; served in the Reichsmarine; subsequent career as for *S 161*, but broken up 1921 at Dordrecht.

V 164 launched 27 May 1909, commissioned 20 Aug 1909; served as a submarine flotilla flagship 1916–18; renamed *T 164* 24 Sept 1917; served in the Reichsmarine. Released 5 Aug 1920; subsequent career as for *V 161*.

*S 165** launched 20 Mar 1909, commissioned 1910 as *Muavenet-i-Milleye*. Laid up after 1918; broken up at Istanbul about 1921.

*S 166** launched 24 Apr 1909, commissioned 1910 as *Yadagar-i-Millet*. Sunk 10 Jul 1917 in the Bosporus, position 39° 56N, 29° 10.5E, by a bomb from a British aircraft; 29 Turkish dead. Raised October 1917; broken up 1924.

*S 167** launched 3 Jul 1909, commissioned 1910 as *Numune-i-Hamiyet*. Laid up after 1918; broken up at Istanbul about 1921.

*S 168** launched 30 Sept 1909, commissioned 1910 as *Gayret-i-Vataniye*. Run onto rocks and sunk 30 Oct 1916 in the Black Sea near Varna.

S 165† launched 26 Nov 1910, commissioned 27 Apr 1911; served in an escort flotilla until 1918; renamed

---

* These boats, modern at the time, were included as part of the 1910 contract with Turkey to purchase *Kurfürst Friedrich Wilhelm* and *Weissenburg*.

† Replacements for boats sold to Turkey in 1910, *before* commissioning; dimensions, etc, exactly identical.

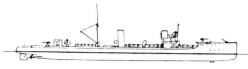

V 150–155 (1908)

V 156–160 (1908)

S 138–149 (1909)

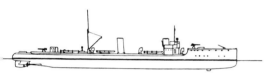

V 164 (1910); *V 162* and *V 163* were similar.

V 186 (1911), *V 188–191*

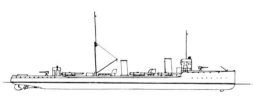

V 187 (1912)

S 176–179 (1912)

G 192–197 (1912)

G 174, G 175 (1914)

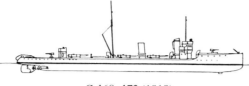

G 169–172 (1918)

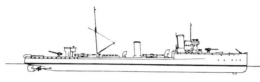

T 196 (1923)

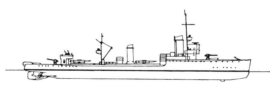

T 185 (1932)

T 156; T 151, T 153, T 155, T 157 and *T 158* were similar.

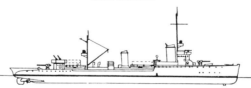

T 196 (1934; dotted line, 1936)

Claus von Bevern (ex *T 190*) (1938)

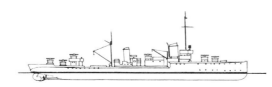

Eduard Jungmann (ex *T 153*) (1939)

T 158 (1944) as a TF boat; *T 151* and *T 155* were similar.

T 165 24 Sept 1917; served in the Reichsmarine. Released 15 Sept 1920; taken as a British prize; broken up 1922 at Montrose.

S 166† launched 27 Dec 1910, commissioned 7 Jul 1911; served as a training boat until 1916; renamed *T 166* 24 Sept 1917; served in the Reichsmarine. Released 5 Aug 1920; taken as a British prize; broken up 1922 at Dordrecht.

S 167† launched 15 Feb 1911, commissioned 26 Aug 1911; served as a training boat until 1917; renamed *T 167* 24 Sept 1917; served in the Reichsmarine. Stricken 22 Mar 1921; sold 3 Sept 1921 for 250,000M; broken up at Kiel.

S 168† launched 16 Mar 1911, commissioned 1 Sept 1911; served as a training boat until 1917; renamed *T 168* 24 Sept 1917; served as a tender 1918; served in the Reichsmarine. Stricken 8 Jan 1927; sold for 63,000M; broken up at Hamburg.

S 169 launched 29 Dec 1908, commissioned 29 Apr 1909; renamed *T 169* 24 Sept 1917; served in an escort flotilla 1918; served in the Reichsmarine; subsequent career as for *S 166*.

G 170 launched 3 Mar 1909, commissioned 14 Sept 1909; renamed *T 170* 24 Sept 1917; served in an escort flotilla 1918; served in the Reichsmarine. Stricken 22 Mar 1921; sold 27 Sept 1921; broken up at Wilhelmshaven.

G 171 launched 28 May 1909, commissioned 4 Jan 1910; served in a torpedo boat flotilla. Sunk while on manoeuvres, 14 Sept 1912, in the North Sea, position 54° 10N, 08° 05E, in a collision with the battleship *Zähringen*; 7 dead; wreck blown up later in 1912.

G 172 launched 10 Jul 1909, commissioned 4 Jan 1910; renamed *T 172* 24 Sept 1917; served in escort flotilla. Sunk at 0428hrs on 7 Jul 1918 in the North Sea, position 54° 26N, 04° 35E, by a mine; 16 dead.

G 173 launched 28 Jul 1909, commissioned 24 Jan 1910; served as a training boat 1917; renamed *T 173* 24 Sept 1917; served in the Reichsmarine. Released 3 Sept 1920; taken as a British prize; broken up 1922 at Montrose.

G 174 launched 8 Jan 1910, commissioned 6 Jul 1910; renamed *T 174* 22 Feb 1918; served in the Reichsmarine; subsequent career as for *V 159*.

G 175 launched 24 Feb 1910, commissioned 4 Dec 1910; served as the dispatch boat *Sleipner* February–March 1912; returned as *G 175*; served in a torpedo boat flotilla 1913–1917, and an escort flotilla; renamed *T 175* 22 Feb 1918; served in the Reichsmarine. Stricken 23 Sept 1926; sold for 63,000M; broken up at Hamburg.

S 176 launched 12 Apr 1910, commissioned 23 Sept 1910; renamed *T 176* 22 Feb 1918; served in the Reichsmarine; subsequent career as for *S 165*.

S 177 launched 21 May 1910, commissioned 16 Feb 1911. Sunk at 0946hrs on 23 Dec 1915 in the Baltic, position 57° 30N, 21° 27E, by a mine; 7 dead.

S 178 launched 14 Jul 1910, commissioned 9 Dec 1910. Sunk 4 Mar 1913 in the North Sea, position 54° 11N, 07° 56E, in a collision with the heavy cruiser *Yorck*; 69 dead. Raised in two sections May–June 1913, repaired; served in a torpedo boat flotilla 1915; renamed *T 178* 22 Feb 1918; served in the Reichsmarine; subsequent career as for *S 166*.

S 179 launched 27 Aug 1910, commissioned 8 Mar 1911; renamed *T 179* 22 Feb 1918; served in the Reichsmarine; subsequent career as for *S 166*, but broken up 1921.

V 180 launched 15 Oct 1909, commissioned 4 Jan 1910; renamed *T 180* 22 Feb 1918; served in the Reichsmarine. Released 5 Aug 1920; taken as a Brazilian prize; broken up 1921 at Dordrecht.

V 181 launched 6 Nov 1909, commissioned 11 Mar 1910; served in an escort flotilla 1918; renamed *T 181* 22 Feb 1918; served in the Reichsmarine. Released 20 Aug 1920; taken as a Japanese prize; broken up 1922 at Dordrecht.

V 182 launched 1 Dec 1909, commissioned 4 May 1910; served in an escort flotilla 1918; renamed *T 182* 22 Feb 1918; served in the Reichsmarine; subsequent career as for *S 166*.

V 183 launched 23 Dec 1909, commissioned 12 May 1910; served in an escort flotilla 1918; renamed *T 183* 22 Feb 1918; subsequent career as for *S 166*.

V 184 launched 26 Feb 1910, commissioned 29 Jun 1910; served as a minesweeper flotilla flagship 1918; renamed *T 184* 22 Feb 1918; served in the Reichsmarine; subsequent career as for *S 166*.

V 185 launched 9 Apr 1910, commissioned 20 Sept 1910; served in an escort flotilla 1918; renamed *T 185* 22 Feb 1918; served in the Reichsmarine. Stricken 4 Oct 1932; converted to the fast tug and remote control boat *Blitz*; taken as a Soviet prize 1945, renamed *Vystrel*.

V 186 launched 28 Nov 1910, commissioned 21 Apr 1911; served in coastal defence and torpedo boat flotillas 1914; renamed *T 186* 22 Feb 1918; served in the Reichsmarine; subsequent career as for *S 166*.

V 187 launched 11 Jan 1911, commissioned 4 May 1911; served as a flagship. Sunk at 1000hrs on 28 Aug 1914 in the North Sea, position 54° 08N, 07° 31E, by gunfire from British cruisers and destroyers; 24 dead.

V 188 launched 8 Feb 1911, commissioned 20 May 1911. Sunk at 1400hrs on 26 Jul 1915 in the North Sea, position 54° 16N, 05° 35E, by a torpedo from the British submarine *E 16*; 5 dead.

V 189 launched 14 Mar 1911, commissioned 30 Jun 1911; renamed *T 189* 22 Feb 1918; served in the Reichsmarine; subsequent career as for *G 192*, but stranded in December 1920 on the English south coast.

V 190 launched 12 Apr 1911, commissioned 5 Aug 1911; renamed *T 190* 22 Feb 1918; served in the Reichsmarine and Kriegsmarine; renamed *Claus von Bevern* 29 Aug 1938; served as an experimental boat. Taken as a USA prize in 1945; scuttled 1946 at Skagerrak.

V 191 launched 2 Jun 1911, commissioned 28 Sept 1911. Sunk together with *Bremen* at 1745hrs on 17

Dec 1915 in the Baltic, position 57° 30N, 21° 34E, by a mine; 25 dead.

G 192 launched 5 Nov 1910, commissioned 8 May 1911; renamed *T 192* 22 Feb 1918; served in the Reichsmarine. Released 28 Apr 1920 at Cherbourg; taken as a British prize; broken up 1922 at Chatham.

G 193 launched 10 Dec 1910, commissioned 25 Jun 1911; renamed *T 193* 22 Feb 1918; served in the Reichsmarine; subsequent career as for *G 192*.

G 194 launched 12 Jan 1911, commissioned 2 Aug 1911; served in a torpedo boat flotilla. Sunk 26 Mar 1916 in the North Sea, position 55° 33N, 06° 05E, after being rammed by the British light cruiser *Cleopatra*; 93 dead.

G 195 launched 8 Apr 1911, commissioned 8 Sept 1911; renamed *T 195* 22 Feb 1918; served in the Reichsmarine; subsequent career as for *G 192*.

G 196 launched 24 May 1911, commissioned 2 Oct 1911; served in an escort flotilla 1918; renamed *T 196* 22 Feb 1918; served in the Reichsmarine and Kriegsmarine as a training boat, and as a flagship for the Minesweeper Command from 1938; taken as a Soviet prize 27 Dec 1945, renamed *Pronzitelnyy*; broken up.

G 197 launched 23 Jun 1911, commissioned 10 Nov 1911; served in an escort flotilla 1918; renamed *T 197* 22 Feb 1918; served in the Reichsmarine; subsequent career as for *G 192*, but broken up 1921 at Briton Ferry.

V 1 class

Construction
Transverse frame steel construction, in torpedo boat steels (twelve watertight compartments, ten in the *S* boats). Depth 4.10m.

Propulsion
Fitted with two sets of AEG Vulcan, Germania and Schichau turbines, direct (two 3-bladed screws, 2.08, 2.00 and 2.00m diameter) in 1 + 1 engine rooms. Three Marine-type boilers and one oil-fired Marine-type boiler (18.5, 18.0 and 18.5 atmospheres forced, 1580, 1602 and 1637sq m) [two oil-fired Marine-type boilers and one oil-fired Marine-type double boiler (18 atmospheres forced, 1923sq m)] in 1 + 1 + 1 boiler rooms. The *S* boats were fitted with a forward funnel of oval cross-section. Two 17kW 110V turbo-generators. One stern rudder, one retractable bow rudder [the latter removed later].

Armament
Two 8.8cm/30 torpedo guns (200 rounds) [after 1916 *V 1–G 11*, *S 15–20*, *23* and *24* were refitted with two 8.8cm/45 torpedo guns; after 1917 *S 15*, *18*, *20* and *24*, and after 1921 *S 23*, *V 1–3*, *5*, *6*, *G 7*, *8*, *10* and *11* were refitted with two 10.5cm/45 Utof guns]; four 50cm deck TT (5 rounds) [after 1921, two 50cm deck TT (4 rounds); *G 7*, *8*, *10* and *11* were finally fitted as *T 107–111* in April 1944 with one 10.5cm/45 Utof gun, two 2cm AA guns, one 50cm deck TT and two 50cm deck TT, as double V tubes]; eighteen mines.

Handling
Seakeeping was inferior to that of the class's predecessors, but characteristics were otherwise almost identical. The effect of the waist was especially bad (except on *V 6*). [The forecastle was extended and later the entire freeboard was raised considerably, which improved seakeeping, but increased leeway.]

Complement
Crew: 3/71 (half-flotilla 4/9) [4/86 (3/13); *G 7*, *8*, *10* and *11*, 4/88 (5/24); in 1940, 3/86]. Boats: one yawl, one dinghy.

Notes
Colour scheme and camouflage were approximately in the 1919–23 style. These vessels always appeared bow-heavy when at rest. Unless the weather was good, coal was always lost during transfer to the fireboxes. The class was nicknamed *Lanskrüppel* – Lans's Cripple – (after the Chief Inspector of Torpedoes, Admiral Lans). [The bridge (except on *V 6*) and forward funnel were raised by 1.2m; the *S* boats had a forward funnel only, with a cap.] *V 1–6* had a highly cambered forecastle [*S 15*, *18*, *20* and *24* in 1916–17, and the other vessels after 1919, had the forecastle extended, as shown in the drawing, but the *V* boats retained a curved main deck edge, while on the *S* boats the angular main deck edge continued up in a straight line. After 1919 the forward funnel was raised, as shown in the drawing, except on *S 23* which finally appeared as in the corresponding drawing of *T 23*. After

the extension of the forecastle the after mast was retained, but without a yard; the forward mast was as shown in the drawing of *G 7* (second form), but until 1925 it had a single yard, later a signal cross; after 1925 a short wireless telegraphy topmast was fitted to the after mast. After 1933 the stern was rebuilt as in the drawing of *T 23*.

Career
V 1 launched 11 Sept 1911, commissioned 12 Jan 1912; served in the Reichsmarine. Stricken 27 Mar 1939; broken up at Wilhelmshaven.

V 2 launched 14 Oct 1911, commissioned 28 Mar 1912; served in an escort flotilla 1918; served in the Reichsmarine. Stricken 18 Nov 1929; sold 25 Mar 1930 for 61,000M; broken up at Wilhelmshaven.

V 3 launched 15 Nov 1911, commissioned 2 May 1912. Stranded at Wollin; fate as for *V 2*, but sold for 71,000M.

V 4 launched 23 Dec 1911, commissioned 15 Jun 1912. Sunk at 0320hrs on 1 Jun 1916 in the North Sea, position 55° 36N, 06° 37E, by a dragging torpedo; 18 dead.

V 5 launched January 1912; released for sale; transferred to Greece in July 1912 as Greek destroyer *Nea Genea*. Broken up about 1927.

V 6 launched February 1912; career as for *V 5*, but named *Keravnos*.

Name	Builder	Built	Cost in Marks (000s)	Displacement (t = tonnes, T = tons)	Length (m)	Breadth (m)	Draught (m)	Power (hp)	Revs (rpm)	Speed (kts)	Range (nm/kts)	Coal (t)	Oil (t)
V 1–6	AG 'Vulcan', Stettin Construction nos 317-320, 335, 336 (322 and 323 for sale)	1911–13	1664	697t max 569t des	71.1 oa 70.2 cwl	7.6	3.11 fwd 3.06 aft	17,109shp max 17,000shp des	729	32.9 max 32.0 des	1190/17 490/29	107	78
	mod: Navy Dockyard, Wilhelmshaven (V 1–3, V 5, V 6)	1921–22		753t max 670t des			3.23 fwd 3.20 aft				1750/17	150	77
G 7–12	Germania Dockyard, Kiel Construction nos 170–175	1911–12	1682	719t max 573t des	71.5 oa 71.0 cwl	7.56	3.01 fwd 3.09 aft	16,406shp max 16,000shp des	678	33.0 max 32.0 des	1150/17	110	80
	mod: Reichs Dockyard, Wilhelmshaven (G 7, 8, 10, 11)	1920–21		775t max 660t des			3.21 fwd			31.5	1800/17	156	,,
	mod: Navy Dockyard, Wilhelmshaven (G 7, 8, 10, 11 as T 107...11)	1928–31		884t max 772t des	76.1 oa 75.7 cwl	7.58	3.11 fwd 3.13 aft			30.0	1900/17	—	220
S 13–24	F Schichau, Elbing Construction nos 864–875	1911–13		695t max 568t des	71.5 oa 71.0 cwl	7.43	2.77 fwd 3.15 aft	15,986shp max 15,700shp des	789	34.0 max 32.5 des	1050/17 600/29	108	72
	mod: Imperial Dockyard, Wilhelmshaven (S 15, 18, 20, 24)	1916–17		749t max 650t des			2.98 fwd 3.18 aft	15,986shp max 15,700shp des			1700/17	146	71
	mod: Navy Dockyard, Wilhelmshaven (S 19 and S 23 as T 123)	1923 and 1921											

476gt/155nt (V 1–3, 5, 6), 492gt/162nt (G 7, 8, 10, 11), 563gt/162nt (G 7, 8, 10, 11) as T 107...11), 472gt/158nt (S 15, 18, 19, 20 and S 23 as T 123)

V 5 launched 25 Apr 1913, commissioned 17 Jul 1913; career as for *V 2*.

V 6 launched 28 Feb 1913, commissioned 17 May 1913; served in the Reichsmarine. Stricken 27 Mar 1929; broken up at Wilhelmshaven.

G 7 launched 7 Nov 1911, commissioned 30 Apr 1912; served in a torpedo boat flotilla, and as a training boat from 1936; renamed *T 107* 23 Apr 1939. Taken as a Soviet prize in 1945, renamed *Porazaiuskyy*. Broken up about 1950.

G 8 launched 21 Dec 1911, commissioned 6 Aug 1912; served in torpedo boat flotilla, and as a training boat from 1936; renamed *T 108* 23 Apr 1939. Taken as a British prize 6 Jan 1946, and broken up.

G 9 launched 31 Jan 1912, commissioned 25 Sept 1912; served in a torpedo boat flotilla. Sunk at 0415hrs on 3 May 1918 in the North Sea, position 55° 14N, 06° 19E, by a mine; 31 dead.

G 10 launched 15 Mar 1912, commissioned 28 Aug 1912; served in torpedo boat flotilla, and as a training boat from 1936; renamed *T 110* 23 Apr 1939. Scuttled and sunk 5 May 1945 at Trave, Flender Werke.

G 11 launched 23 Apr 1912, commissioned 8 Aug 1912; served as a torpedo boat flotilla flagship, and as a training boat from 1936; renamed *T 111* 23 Apr

1939. Sunk 3 Apr 1945 at Kiel-Scheer harbour by an aircraft bomb.

G 12 launched 15 Jul 1912, commissioned 17 Oct 1912; served as a torpedo boat flotilla flagship. Sunk at 0600hrs on 8 Sept 1915 in the North Sea, position 55° 25N, 07° 28E, in a collision with *V 1* and subsequent torpedo explosion; 47 dead.

G 13 launched 7 Dec 1911, commissioned 2 Jul 1912. Sunk at 0858hrs on 6 Nov 1914 in the North Sea, position 54° 00N, 08° 22E, by an explosion (own torpedo); 9 dead.

S 14 launched 2 Mar 1912, commissioned 1 Nov 1912. Sunk 19 Feb 1915 in the Jade, position 53° 40N, 08° 05E, by an explosion in the stern; 11 dead. Raised 1915; broken up at Wilhelmshaven.

S 15 launched 23 Mar 1912, commissioned 1 Nov 1912; served in Flanders 1916. Severely damaged 21 Aug 1917 off the Flanders coast, position 51° 15N, 02° 55E, by a mine, and towed in; taken out of service 20 Sept 1917, broken up at Ghent.

S 16 launched 20 Apr 1912, commissioned 1 Oct 1912; served in a patrol flotilla 1917. Sunk at 1815hrs on 20 Jan 1918 in the North Sea, position 54° 41N, 06° 32E, by a mine; 80 dead.

S 17 launched 22 Jun 1912, commissioned 7 Dec

1912; served as a coastal defence vessel 1917. Sunk 16 May 1917 in the North Sea, position 53° 34N, 05° 56E, by a mine; 25 dead.

S 18 launched 10 Aug 1912, commissioned 12 Jan 1913; served in Flanders 1916, and in patrol and escort flotillas, 1917; served in the Reichsmarine; collided 23 May 1922 with the battleship *Hannover* in the vicinity of Rügen, and the bow was torn off; 10 dead. Repaired; stricken 31 Mar 1931; broken up 1935 at Wilhelmshaven.

S 19 launched 17 Oct 1912, commissioned 29 Mar 1913; served in patrol and escort flotillas 1917; served in the Reichsmarine. Stricken 31 Mar 1931; sold 4 Feb 1935; broken up at Deutsche Werke, Kiel.

S 20 launched 4 Dec 1912, commissioned 1 Nov 1913; served in Flanders 1916. Sunk at 0402hrs on 5 Jun 1917 off the Flanders coast, position 51° 28N, 02° 48E, by gunfire from British ships; 49 dead.

S 21 launched 11 Jan 1913, commissioned 20 Jun 1913. Sunk 21 Apr 1915 in the North Sea, position 53° 47N, 08° 09E, in a collision with the light cruiser *Hamburg*; 36 dead.

S 22 launched 15 Feb 1913, commissioned 23 Jul 1913. Sunk at 2135hrs on 26 Mar 1916 in the North Sea, position 53° 46N, 05° 04E, by a mine; 76 dead.

S 23 launched 29 Mar 1913, commissioned 1 Nov 1913; served in the escort flotilla 1918; served in the Reichsmarine and Kriegsmarine; renamed *T 23* 16 Mar 1932; served as a training boat; renamed *T 123* 23 Apr 1939, served as *Komet*, the remote control boat for *Hessen*, and as a *TF* boat from July 1943; taken as a Soviet prize in 1945; ultimate fate not known.

S 24 launched 28 Jun 1913, commissioned 27 Aug 1913; served in Flanders 1916, in patrol and escort flotillas 1917; served in the Reichsmarine. Stricken 5 Nov 1919; released 28 Apr 1920 at Cherbourg; taken as a British prize; stranded in December 1920 off the south coast of Britain.

T 23 (1936)

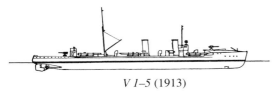

V 1–5 (1913)

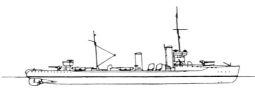

G 7, G 8, G 10, G 11 (before 1928), second form

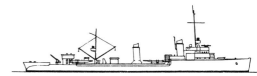

G 7, G 11 (1937), fourth form

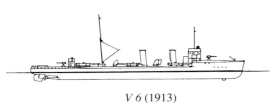

V 6 (1913)

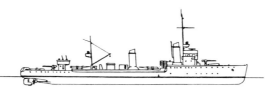

G 7, G 8, G 10, G 11 (1931), third form

T 107 (1944), *T 108, T 110, T 111*

V 25 class

Construction

Laid down as M (mobilisation) type boats, some extended by 3.5m on the stocks. Transverse frame steel construction, in torpedo boat steels (ten to twelve watertight compartments, *G* boats had a double bottom). Depth: *V 25–30*, *43–48* and *67–82*, 4.6m; *S 31–36* and *49–66*, 4.3m; *G 37–42* and *85–95*, 4.4m.

Propulsion

Details of the machinery in this class are given in the adjacent table. All vessels had two 28kW 110V turbogenerators, and one stern rudder and one retractable bow rudder.

Armament

Three 8.8cm/45 torpedo guns (300 rounds), but *S 60–66, V 82–84, G 92–95* at all times [and *G 42, 85–89, 91, V 47–48, 67–71, 73, 74, 77–81* and *S 53–56* after summer to winter 1916] had three 10.5cm/45 Utof or torpedo guns (210 rounds); six 50cm TT (8 rounds), two deck-mounted and two in a V mounting; 24 mines. [*V 25* was briefly fitted with one FF 33 B seaplane on the torpedo gun platform above the engine.]

Complement

Crew: 3/80, after *G 37*, 3/84 (half-flotilla staff 3/13–15); after *S 49–V 84*, only 3/82. Boats: one yawl, one dinghy.

Notes

Colour scheme no 10, 12. The *V* boats had loading gear central between the funnels, and the aft funnel was oval in cross-section; the *S* boats had loading gear on the forecastle near the forward funnel, and both funnels were oval in cross-section; the *G* boats had loading gear on the after funnel. Boats commissioned after winter 1916 generally had a low bridge and forward funnel as built [later both were raised]. *S 31–36* as built had a bridge as shown in the drawing of *V 25*; the other boats [and these vessels later] had a bridge as shown in the drawing of *S 49*, but initially with no

Vessel	Machinery	Screws, diam	Boilers	Pressure (atm forced) (sq m)	Area
V 25–30	2 sets AEG-Vulcan turbines, direct	2 3-bladed, 2.46m	3 oil-marine	18.5	2286
*V 43–48**	,,	2 3-bladed, 2.50m	2 oil-marine, 1 oil-marine double	,,	2381
*V 67–84**	,,	,,	1 oil-marine, 2 oil-marine double	,,	2286†
S 31–36	2 sets Schichau turbines, direct	,,	3 oil-marine	,,	2277
S 49–52	,,	,,	,,	,,	2311
S 53–66	,, , plus 1 cruise turbine on the starboard shaft	2 3-bladed, 2.60m	2 oil-marine, 1 oil-marine double	,,	2236
G 37–40	2 sets Germania turbines, direct	2 3-bladed, 2.50m	2 oil-marine, 1 oil-marine double or 1 oil-marine, 2 oil-marine double	18	2400
G 41, 42, G 85–95	,,	,,	1 oil-marine, 2 oil-marine double	,,	2403

All engines in 1 + 1 engine rooms; all boilers in 1 + 0 + 1 + 1 boiler rooms

* *V 46, 83* and *84* were also fitted with a Fottinger transformer
† *V83, 84*, 2311sq m

compass platform. *V 43–46* were similar to the drawing of *V 25* but the bridge was on short supports, the funnels 1m higher, the forecastle flat, the mainmast raked, the compass platform forward of the central gun and the searchlight on the after deckhouse. [The bridge, funnels (the after funnel with a short cap) and the mainmast with a searchlight platform were refitted as shown in the drawing of *S 49*.] [For *S 49–52* after refit see the drawing of *S 49*. *G 37–40* were fitted with a raised bridge (see the drawing of *G 85*), but the funnels were of the old shape and height.] *G 41–42* and *85–95* initially had a bridge with a searchlight, as

shown in the drawing of *G 37*, but 0.8m higher; the funnels were about 0.5m higher. For *S 53–66* see the drawing, but initially these had a low cap on the forward and after funnels (in some cases the forward cap was omitted). For *V 67–84* see the drawing, but *V 47–48* were formerly similar to *V 43–46*; in 1918 all boats had an upper bridge and searchlight similar to the drawing of *G 85*.

Career

V 25 launched 29 Jan 1914, commissioned 27 Jun 1914; served as a coastal defence vessel, etc. Sunk at

Name	Builder	Built	Cost in Marks (000s)	Displacement (t = tonnes T = tons)	Length (m)	Breadth (m)	Draught (m)	Power (hp)	Revs (rpm)	Speed (kts)	Range (nm/kts)	Coal (t)	Oil (t)
V 25–30	AG 'Vulcan', Stettin Construction nos 346–351	1913–14		975t max 812t des	78.5 oa 77.8 cwl	8.33	3.33 fwd 3.63 aft	24,800shp max 23,500shp des	612	36.3 max 33.5 des	1080/20	—	225
S 31–36	F Schichau, Elbing Construction nos 906–911	1913–15		971t max 802t des	79.6 oa 79.0 cwl	,,	2.80 fwd 3.64 aft	23,516shp max 24,000shp des	680	34.2 max 33.5 des	1100/20	—	220
G 37–40	Germania Dockyard, Kiel Construction nos 215–218	1914–15		1051t max 822t des	79.5 oa 78.6 cwl	8.36	3.74 fwd 3.45 aft	25.010shp max 24,000shp des	630	34.5 max 34.0 des	1685/17 1300/20	—	299
G 41–42	Germania Dockyard, Kiel Construction nos 219–220	,,		1147t max 960t des	83.0 oa 82.2 cwl	,,	3.40 fwd 3.50 aft	22,800shp max 24,000shp des	573	32.8 max 33.5 des	1950/17 1715/20	—	326
V 43–46	AG 'Vulcan, Stettin Construction nos 358–361	,,		1106t max 852t des	79.6 oa 78.8 cwl	8.32	3.96 fwd 3.61 aft	24,700shp max 24,000shp des	677	36.2 max 34.5 des	1750/17 1270/20	—	296
V 47–48	AG 'Vulcan, Stettin Construction nos 362–363	,,		1188t max 924t des	83.1 oa 82.3 cwl	,,	3.40 fwd 3.90 aft	25,200shp max 24,000shp des	579	34.4 max 33.5 des	2050/17 1810/20	—	338
S 49–52	F Schichau, Elbing Construction nos 939–942	,,		1074t max 802t des	79.6 oa 79.0 cwl	8.36	2.80 fwd 3.64 aft	25,015shp max 24,000shp des	669	36.6 max 34.0 des	1605/17 1270/20	—	252
S 53–66	F Schichau, Elbing Construction nos 943–956	1914–16		1170t max 919t des	83.1 oa 82.5 cwl	,,	3.90 fwd 3.60 aft	15,900shp max 24,000shp des	586	35.1 max 34.0 des	2450/14 1960/17	—	305
V 67, 68, 70, 75–77, 79, 83, 84	AG 'Vulcan', Hamburg Construction nos 11–18	,,		1188t max 924t des	82.0 oa 81.0 cwl	8.32	3.4 fwd 3.9 aft	24,400shp max 23,500shp des	563	36.6 max 34.0 des	2050/17 1810/20	—	306
V 69, 71–74, 78, 80–82	AG 'Vulcan', Stettin Construction nos 376–385	,,		,,	,,	,,	,,	,,	,,	,,	,,	—	308
G 85–95	Germania Dockyard, Kiel Construction nos 221–231	1915–16		1147t max 960t des	83.0 oa 82.2 cwl	8.36	3.4 fwd 3.5 aft	26,300shp max 24,000shp des	619	34.2 max 33.5 des	1760/20	—	326

0400hrs on 13 Feb 1915 in the North Sea, position 54° 22N, 07° 46E, by a mine; 79 dead.

V 26 launched 21 Feb 1914, commissioned 1 Aug 1914; served as coastal defence vessel, etc. Released 14 Jun 1920 at Cherbourg; taken as a British prize; broken up 1922 at Portishead.

V 27 launched 26 Mar 1914, commissioned 2 Sept 1914. Sunk at 1740hrs on 31 May 1916 in the North Sea, position 56° 43N, 05° 54E, by gunfire from a British cruiser; casualties not known.

V 28 launched 9 May 1914, commissioned 22 Sept 1914; subsequent career as for *V 26*.

V 29 launched 18 Aug 1914, commissioned 10 Oct 1914. Sunk at 1745hrs on 31 May 1916 in the North Sea, position 56° 43N, 05° 57E, by a torpedo from the British destroyer *Petard*; 43 dead.

V 30 launched 18 Sept 1914, commissioned 16 Nov 1914. Sunk en route to internment at Scapa Flow, on 20 Nov 1918 in the North Sea, position 54° 45N, 06° 15E, by a mine; 2 dead.

S 31 launched 20 Dec 1913, commissioned 9 Aug 1914. Sunk at 2300hrs on 19 Aug 1915 in Riga bay, position 57° 47N, 23° 05E, by a mine; 11 dead.

S 32 launched 28 Feb 1914, commissioned 10 Sept

1914; interned at Scapa Flow after 22 Nov 1918. Scuttled 21 Jun 1916; raised 19 Jun 1925; broken up at Granton.

S 33 launched 4 Apr 1914, commissioned 4 Oct 1914. Sunk at 1143hrs on 3 Oct 1918 in the North Sea, position 54° 44N, 05° 15E, by a torpedo from the British submarine *L 10*; 5 dead.

S 34 launched 13 Jun 1914, commissioned 5 Nov 1914. Sunk at 0305hrs on 3 Oct 1918 in the North Sea, position 54° 45N, 05° 43E, by a mine; 70 dead.

*S 35** launched 30 Aug 1914, commissioned 4 Dec 1914. Sunk at 2000hrs on 31 May 1916 in the North

Sea, position 56° 56N, 06° 04E, by heavy gunfire from British battleships; 87 dead.

*S 36** launched 17 Oct 1914, commissioned 4 Jan 1915; interned at Scapa Flow after 22 Nov 1918. Scuttled 21 Jun 1919; raised 18 Apr 1925; broken up at Scapa.

G 37 launched 17 Dec 1914, commissioned 29 Jun 1915; served as a flotilla flagship. Sunk at 0455hrs on 4 Nov 1917 in the North Sea, position 54° 19N, 04° 55E, by a mine; 4 dead.

G 38 launched 23 Dec 1914, commissioned 30 Jul 1915; interned at Scapa Flow after 22 Nov 1918. Scuttled 21 Jun 1919; raised 27 Sept 1924; broken up at Scapa.

G 39 launched 16 Jan 1915, commissioned 20 Aug 1915; interned at Scapa Flow after 22 Nov 1918. Scuttled 21 Jun 1919; raised 3 Jul 1925; broken up at Scapa.

G 40 launched 27 Feb 1915, commissioned 16 Sept 1915; interned at Scapa Flow after 22 Nov 1918. Scuttled 21 Jun 1919; raised 29 Jul 1925; broken up at Inverkeithing.

G 41 launched 24 Apr 1915, commissioned 14 Oct 1915; served as a flagship. Scuttled and sunk 3 Oct 1918 at Bruges, position 51° 13N, 03° 14E; raised and seaworthy at the evacuation of Belgium.

G 42 launched 20 May 1915, commissioned 10 Nov 1915. Sunk 21 Apr 1917 at night in the Straits of Dover, position 51° 09N, 01° 37E, by gunfire from the British destroyers *Swift* and *Broke*; 36 dead.

G 43 launched 27 Jan 1915, commissioned 28 May 1915; interned at Scapa Flow after 22 Nov 1918; stranded after a failed attempt at scuttling 21 Jun 1919. Raised in July 1919; taken as a USA prize 9 Oct 1920; sunk 15 Jul 1921 off Cape Henry (Virginia) by gunfire from the US battleship *Florida*.

G 44 launched 24 Feb 1915, commissioned 22 Jul 1915; career as for *V 43* but taken as a British prize, and broken up 1922 at Portsmouth.

V 45 launched 29 Mar 1915, commissioned 30 Sept 1915; interned at Scapa Flow after 22 Nov 1918. Scuttled 21 Jun 1919; raised September 1924; broken up at Liverpool-Troon.

V 46 launched 23 Dec 1914, commissioned 31 Oct 1915; career as for *V 43*, but taken as a French prize, and broken up 1924 at Cherbourg.

V 47 launched 10 Jun 1915, commissioned 20 Nov 1915; served in Flanders. Scuttled and sunk 2 Nov 1918 in the Terneuzen Canal, position 51° 14N, 03° 51E, during the evacuation of Belgium.

V 48 launched 6 Aug 1915, commissioned 10 Dec 1915. Sunk at 2150hrs on 31 May 1916 in the North Sea, position 57° 01N, 06° 00E, by gunfire from British destroyers, cruisers and battleships; 87 dead.

S 49† launched 10 Apr 1915, commissioned 12 Jul 1915; career as for *S 32*, but raised December 1924.

S 50† launched 24 Apr 1915, commissioned 15 Aug 1915; career as for *S 32*, but raised in October 1924 and broken up 1925 at Stranraer.

* Due to be sold to Greece June 1914, requisitioned 10 Aug 1914; planned as replacement boats *S 49* and *50*.

† Begun as replacements for *S 35–36*

S 51 launched 29 Apr 1915, commissioned 7 Sept 1915; interned at Scapa Flow after 22 Nov 1918. Scuttled 21 Jun 1919 and stranded while sinking; raised in July 1919; taken as a British prize; broken up 1922 at Rosyth.

S 52 launched 12 Jun 1915, commissioned 28 Sept 1915; career as for *S 32*, but raised 13 Oct 1924, and broken up at Inverkeithing.

S 53 launched 18 Sept 1915, commissioned 17 Dec 1915; career as for *S 32*, but raised 13 Aug 1924, and broken up 1927 at Scapa.

S 54 launched 11 Oct 1915, commissioned 30 Jan 1916; career as for *S 51*, but raised 7 Sept 1921; stranded on transfer to the breaking yard; refloated 5 Jun 1925, and broken up.

S 55 launched 6 Nov 1915, commissioned 6 Mar 1916; career as for *S 32*, but raised 29 Aug 1924, and broken up at Granton.

S 56 launched 11 Dec 1915, commissioned 16 Apr 1916; career as for *S 32*, but raised 5 Jun 1925, and broken up 1928 at Scapa.

S 57 launched 8 Jan 1916, commissioned 5 May 1916. Sunk at 2218hrs on 10 Nov 1916 in the Gulf of Finland, position 59° 21N, 22° 29E, by a mine; 2 dead.

S 58 launched 5 Feb 1916, commissioned 4 Jun 1916. Sunk at 0425hrs on 11 Nov 1916 in the Gulf of Finland, position 59° 22N, 22° 48E, by a mine; casualties not known.

S 59 launched 16 Feb 1916, commissioned 3 Jul 1916. Sunk at 0548hrs on 11 Nov 1916 in the Gulf of Finland, position 59° 21N, 22° 45E, by a mine; casualties not known.

S 60 launched 3 Apr 1916, commissioned 15 Aug 1916; career as for *S 51*, but taken as a Japanese prize, sold 1920 to a British company, and broken up in England.

S 61 launched 8 Apr 1916, commissioned 20 Sept 1916; served in Flanders 1917. Scuttled and sunk 2 Nov 1918 in the Terneuzen Canal, position 51° 14N, 03° 51E, during the evacuation of Belgium.

S 62 launched 13 May 1916, commissioned 7 Nov 1916; served as a flotilla flagship. Sunk at 2130hrs on 10 Jul 1918 in the North Sea, position 54° 47N, 04° 52E, by a mine; 27 dead.

S 63 launched 27 May 1916, commissioned 18 Dec 1916; served in Flanders 1917; served in the Reichsmarine. Stricken 5 Nov 1919; released 23 May 1920 at Cherbourg; taken as an Italian prize; renamed *Ardimentoso*. Stricken 1937; broken up.

S 64 launched 21 Aug 1916, commissioned 15 Mar 1917. Sunk at 0100hrs on 18 Oct 1917 in the northern Baltic, position 58° 43N, 23° 14E, by a mine; 6 dead.

S 65 launched 14 Oct 1916, commissioned 22 Apr 1917; career as for *S 32*, but raised 16 May 1922; ultimate fate not known.

S 66 launched 21 Nov 1916, commissioned 9 May 1917. Sunk at 2040hrs on 10 Jul 1918 in the North Sea, position 54° 47N, 04° 52E, by a mine; 76 dead.

V 67 launched 3 Aug 1915, commissioned 1 Nov 1915; served as a flotilla flagship in Flanders. Scuttled and sunk 2 Nov 1918 in the Terneuzen Canal, position 51° 13N, 03° 55E, during the evacuation of Belgium.

V 68 launched 24 Aug 1915, commissioned 3 Dec 1915; served in Flanders. Sunk at 1505hrs on 8 Aug 1918 off the Flanders coast, position 51° 33N, 03° 15E, by a mine; 18 dead.

V 69 launched 18 Aug 1915, commissioned 9 Jan 1916; served in Flanders 1917. Scuttled and sunk 2 Nov 1918 at Ghent, position 51° 04N, 03° 51E, during the evacuation of Belgium.

V 70 launched 14 Oct 1915, commissioned 6 Jan 1916; interned at Scapa Flow after 22 Nov 1918. Scuttled 21 Jun 1919; raised 1 Aug 1924; hulk salvaged; broken up 1929 at Scapa.

V 71 launched 1 Sept 1915, commissioned 10 Mar 1916; interned temporarily at Stockholm 1918; released 13 May 1920; taken as a British prize; broken up 1921 at Bo'ness.

V 72 launched 30 Dec 1915, commissioned 28 Mar 1916. Sunk at 0345hrs on 11 Nov 1916 in the Gulf of Finland, position 59° 23N, 22° 51E, by a mine; casualties not known.

V 73 launched 24 Sept 1915, commissioned 16 Feb 1916; career as for *V 43*, but taken as a British prize, and broken up 1922 at Grangemouth.

V 74 launched 29 Oct 1915, commissioned 28 Mar 1916; served in Flanders 1917. Sunk 25 May 1918 in Zeebrügge harbour, position 51° 20N, 03° 12E, during a mine transfer; 11 dead; raised in July 1918; scuttled and sunk 3 Oct 1918 at Bruges, position 51° 13N, 03° 14E, during the evacuation of Belgium.

V 75 launched 15 Jan 1916, commissioned 29 Apr 1916. Sunk at 2204hrs on 10 Nov 1916 in the Gulf of Finland, position 59° 23N, 22° 30E, by a mine; 3 dead.

V 76 launched 27 Feb 1916, commissioned 8 Jun 1916. Sunk at 0625hrs on 11 Nov 1916 in the Gulf of Finland, position 59° 20N, 22° 23E, by a mine; 1 dead.

V 77 launched 28 Feb 1916, commissioned 18 May 1916; subsequent career as for *V 67*.

V 78 launched 19 Feb 1916, commissioned 18 May 1916; served as a flagship; interned at Scapa Flow after 22 Nov 1918. Scuttled 21 Jun 1919; raised 7 Sept 1925; broken up at Granton.

V 79 launched 18 Apr 1916, commissioned 11 Jul 1916; served in the Reichsmarine; released 14 Jun 1920 at Cherbourg; taken as a French prize; renamed *Pierre Durand* until 15 Feb 1933; broken up.

V 80 launched 28 Apr 1916, commissioned 6 Jul 1916; career as for *V 43*, but taken as a Japanese prize, sold June 1920 to a British company, and broken up 1922 in England.

V 81 launched 27 May 1916, commissioned 29 Jul 1916; career as for *V 44*, but sunk en route to the breakers.

V 82 launched 5 Jul 1916, commissioned 30 Aug 1916; served in Flanders 1917; subsequent career as for *V 44*.

V 83 launched 10 Jun 1916, commissioned 3 Oct 1916; interned at Scapa Flow after 22 Nov 1918. Scuttled 21 Jun 1919; partially raised 1923; broken up 1928 at Scapa.

V 84 launched 17 Aug 1916, commissioned 6 Nov 1916. Sunk 26 May 1917 in the North Sea, position 53° 43N, 06° 21E, by a mine; 5 dead.

G 85 launched 24 Jul 1915, commissioned 14 Dec 1915. Sunk at night 21 Apr 1917 in the Straits of

Dover, position 51° 09N, 01° 37E, by gunfire from the British destroyers *Swift* and *Broke*; 35 dead.

G 86 launched 24 Aug 1915, commissioned 11 Jan 1916; career as for *G 38*, but raised 14 Jul 1925, and broken up at Granton.

G 87 launched 22 Sept 1915, commissioned 10 Feb 1916. Sunk at 0620hrs on 30 Mar 1918 in the North Sea, position 54° 54N, 06° 25E, by a mine; 43 dead.

G 88 launched 16 Oct 1915, commissioned 11 Mar 1916. Sunk at 0015hrs on 8 Apr 1917 off the Flanders coast, position 51° 22N, 03° 15E, by a torpedo from a British motor boat; 18 dead.

G 89 launched 11 Dec 1915, commissioned 10 May 1916; career as for *G 38*, but raised December 1922, and broken up 1926 at Scapa.

G 90 launched 15 Jan 1916, commissioned 15 Jun 1916. Sunk at 0352hrs on 11 Nov 1916 in the Gulf of Finland, position 59° 23N, 22° 48E, by a mine; 11 dead.

G 91 launched 16 Nov 1915, commissioned 22 Jul 1916; career as for *G 38*, but raised 12 Sept 1924, and broken up at Inverkeithing.

G 92 launched 15 Feb 1916, commissioned 25 Aug 1916; career as for *G 38*, but stranded while sinking, and broken up 1921–22 at Sunderland.

G 93 launched 11 Jul 1916, commissioned 27 Sept 1916; career as for *G 87*, but sunk at 0630hrs on 30 Mar 1918; 10 dead.

G 94 launched 1 Aug 1916, commissioned 26 Oct 1916; career as for *G 87*, but sunk at 0540hrs on 30 Mar 1918; 13 dead.

G 95 launched 29 Aug 1916, commissioned 25 Nov 1916; served as a flotilla flagship in Flanders. Released 5 Aug 1920; taken as a British prize, broken up 1921–22 at Sunderland.

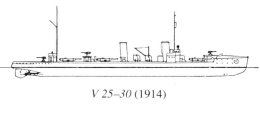

V 25–30 (1914)

V 67–84 (1917)

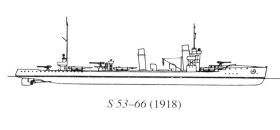

S 53–66 (1918)

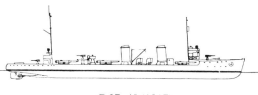

G 37–40 (1917)

S 49–52 (1918)

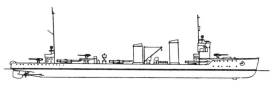

G 85–95 (1918)

G 96 class

Construction

Laid down as 1916 M (mobilisation) type boats, re-classified after *G 148* as the 1917 M (mobilisation) type, with 0.3m greater freeboard and a forecastle 0.5m higher. Transverse frame steel construction, in torpedo boat steels (ten to twelve watertight compartments, double bottom). The *H* boats and the *Ww* boat were built under licence to design by Germania at Kiel. Depth: *V 125–130* and *140–144*, 4.85m; *V 158–165*, 5.0m; *S 131–139*, 4.3m; *H 145–147*, 4.4m; *G 148–150* and *H 166–169*, 4.7m.

Propulsion

Two sets of Germania turbines with a cruise turbine for the starboard shaft on the *G*, *H* and *Ww* boats, but Schichau turbines on the *S* boats, and AEG-Vulcan turbines on the *V* boats, all direct (two 3-bladed screws, 2.6 and 2.6m diameter) in 1 + 1 engine rooms. One oil-fired Marine-type boiler and two oil-fired Marine-type double boilers (18 and 18.5 atmospheres forced, 2417, 2326 and 2286sq m) in 1 + 0 + 1 + 1 boiler rooms. Two 36kW 110V turbo-generators. One stern rudder; one retractable bow rudder.

Armament

Three 10.5cm/45 Utof guns (240 rounds); six 50cm TT (8 rounds), two deck-mounted and two in a V mounting; twenty-four mines (forty mines on the *G* boats).

Handling

The longer forecastle and greater freeboard forward improved the seakeeping qualities of the class, without any adverse affect on manoeuvrability or turning circle as compared with the class's predecessors; refer to *V 25–G 95*.

Complement

Crew: 4/101 (half-flotilla staff 3/14). Boats: one yawl, one dinghy.

Notes

Colour scheme no 12. For differences in loading gear, see *V 25–G 95*. On the *V* and *S* boats the after funnel was oval in cross-section. The *S* boats had tall (1.5m) funnel caps and no compass platform; they also had two large ventilators projecting sideways between the funnels, and the forecastle was 2m shorter; the distance between the funnels was as shown in the drawing of *V 125*. The *S* and *V* boats initially had a topmast only 10m long, with a wireless telegraphy yard. *G 96* had an upper bridge 1.5m shorter, a mast with a topmast and signal yard rather than a tall mast with a signal cross as on *H 145*.

The boats were nicknamed *Tannenbaumboote* – Christmas tree Boats – because the rigging of the foremast was reminiscent of a Christmas tree.

Career

G 96 launched 16 Sept 1916, commissioned 23 Dec 1916; served in Flanders. Sunk at 0130hrs on 26 Jun 1917 off the Flanders coast, position 51° 15N, 02° 38'6"E, by a mine; 4 dead.

V 125 launched 18 May 1917, commissioned 29 Aug 1917; interned at Scapa Flow after 22 Nov 1918; scuttled unsuccessfully 21 Jun 1919; raised July 1919; taken as a British prize; broken up 1922 at Newport.

V 126 launched 30 Jun 1917, commissioned 25 Sept 1917; career as for *V 125*, but taken as a French prize, and broken up 1925 at Lorient; the boilers were reused in *Intrepide*.

V 127 launched 28 Jul 1917, commissioned 23 Oct 1917; career as for *V 125*, but taken as a Japanese prize, and broken up 1922 at Dordrecht.

V 128 launched 11 Aug 1917, commissioned 15 Nov 1917; career as for *V 125*, but broken up 1922 at Grangemouth.

V 129 launched 19 Oct 1917, commissioned 20 Dec 1917; served as a flotilla flagship; interned at Scapa Flow after 6 Dec 1918. Scuttled 21 Jun 1919; raised 11 Aug 1925; broken up at Inverkeithing.

V 130 launched 20 Nov 1917, commissioned 2 Feb 1918; served in the Reichsmarine; released 3 Aug 1920 at Cherbourg; taken as a French prize; renamed *Buino* until 15 Feb 1933; broken up.

S 131 launched 3 Mar 1917, commissioned 11 Aug 1917; interned at Scapa Flow 22 Nov 1918. Scuttled 24 Jun 1919; raised 29 Aug 1924; broken up.

S 132 launched 19 May 1917, commissioned 2 Oct 1917; career as for *S 51*, but taken as a USA prize, and sunk 15 Jul 1921 in the vicinity of Cape Henry,

Name	Builder	Built	Cost in Marks (000s)	Displacement (t = tonnes T = tons)	Length (m)	Breadth (m)	Draught (m)	Power (hp)	Revs (rpm)	Speed (kts)	Range (nm/kts)	Coal (t)	Oil (t)
G 96	Germania Dockyard, Kiel Construction no 232	1915–16		1147t max 990t des	84.5 oa 82.3 cwl	8.36	3.4 fwd 3.5 aft	24,000shp des		32.0 des	2040/17 1760/20	—	326
V 125–130	AG 'Vulcan', Stettin Construction nos 470–475	1916–17 1917–18		1188t max 924t des	82.0 oa 81.7 cwl	8.32	3.49 fwd 4.12 aft	25.150shp max 23,500shp des	606	34.6 max 34.0 des	2050/17 1625/20	—	298
S 131–139	F Schichau, Elbing Construction nos 937, 938, 1006–1012	1916–18		1170t max 919t des	83.1 oa 82.5 cwl	,,	3.9 fwd 3.6 aft	23,690shp max 24,000shp des	589	33.4 max 32.0 des	2450/17 1960/20	—	300
V 140–141	AG 'Vulcan', Hamburg Construction nos 99–100	1917–		1188t max 924t des	82.0 oa 81.7 cwl	,,	3.4 fwd 3.9 aft	23,500shp des		34.0	2050/17 1625/20	—	298
V 142–144	AG 'Vulcan', Stettin Construction nos 493–495	,,		,,	,,	,,	,,	,,		,,	,,	—	,,
H 145–147	Howaldtswerke, Kiel Construction nos 607–609	1917–18 1917–20		1147t max 990t des	84.5 oa 83.5 cwl	8.35	3.4 fwd 3.5 aft	23,849shp max 24,500shp des	588	33.5 max 32.0 des	2780/14 2060/17 1840/20	—	326
G 148–150	Germania Dockyard, Kiel Construction nos 319–321	1917–		1216t max 1020t des	85.1 oa 83.6 cwl	8.35	3.46 fwd 3.48 aft	24,500shp	570	32.5	2170/17 1850/20	—	332
WW 151	Imperial Dockyard, Wilhelmshaven Construction no 37	,,		,,	,,	,,	,,	,,	,,	,,	—	—	,,
S 152–157	F Schichau, Elbing Construction nos 1013–1018	,,		1224t max 1020t des	83.0 oa 82.0 cwl	8.32	3.9 fwd 3.6 aft	22,000 shp	570	32.5	1440/20	—	324
V 158–165	AG 'Vulcan', Stettin Construction nos 541–548	,,		1236t max 1030t des	82.2 oa 81.2 cwl	,,	3.70 fwd 3.17 aft	26,500shp	620	32.5	1675/20	—	360
H 166–169	Howaldtswerke, Kiel Construction nos 618–621	,,		1291t max 1061t des	85.1 oa 83.4 cwl	8.35	3.53 fwd 3.21 aft	26,000shp	620	32.5	3255/17 1895/20	—	360

Virginia, by gunfire from the US battleship *Delaware* and the destroyer *Herbert*.

S 133 launched 1 Sept 1917, commissioned 21 Feb 1918; served in the Reichsmarine. Stricken 5 Nov 1919; released 20 Jul 1920 at Cherbourg; taken as a French prize; named *Chastang* until 18 Aug 1933; broken up.

S 134 launched 25 Aug 1917, commissioned 4 Jan 1918; career as for *S 133*, but commissioned 14 Jun 1920 as the French *Vesco* and served until 24 Jul 1935, then broken up.

S 135 launched 27 Oct 1917, commissioned 15 Mar 1918; career as for *S 133*, but became French *Mazare* until 24 Jul 1935, then broken up.

S 136 launched 1 Dec 1917, commissioned 30 Apr 1918; career as for *S 32*, but raised 3 Apr 1925, and broken up 1928 at Scapa.

S 137 launched 9 Mar 1918, commissioned 14 Jun 1918; career as for *S 51*, but broken up 1922 at Bo'ness.

S 138 launched 22 Apr 1918, commissioned 29 Jul 1918; career as for *S 32*, but raised 1 May 1925, and broken up 1926 at Inverkeithing.

S 139 launched 24 Nov 1917, commissioned 15 Apr 1918; career as for *S 133*, but became French *Deligny* until 18 Aug 1933, then broken up.

V 140 launched 22 Dec 1917, commissioned 18 Nov 1918. Stricken 3 Nov 1919; stranded 8 Dec 1920 in the vicinity of the Danish coast while under tow by the steam tug *Fairplay XII*; broken up.

V 141–144 launched 26 Mar 1918, 25 Sept 1918, 1(

Oct 1918, respectively; approx 60 to 40 percent complete when stricken 3 Nov 1919; sold 27 Oct 1921 to a south German company, and broken up at Kiel.

H 145 launched 11 Dec 1917, commissioned 4 Aug 1918; interned at Scapa Flow after 22 Nov 1918. Scuttled 21 Jun 1919; raised 14 Mar 1925; broken up 1928 at Scapa.

H 146 launched 23 Jan 1918, commissioned 3 Oct 1918; released 23 May 1920 at Cherbourg; taken as a French prize; served as *Rageot de la Touche* until 1935, then broken up.

H 147 launched 13 Mar 1918, commissioned 13 Jul 1920; released 29 Jul 1920 at Cherbourg; taken as a French prize; served as *Marcel Delage* until 15 Feb 1933, then broken up.

G 148–150 construction was started and completion planned by LMG at the Lübeck (for *G 148* and *149*) and Rendsburg dockyards when these boats were stricken 3 Nov 1919 and broken up on the stocks.

Ww 151 broken up on the stocks 1920, before launching.

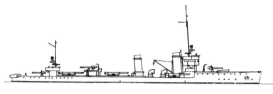
S 131–139 (1917)

S 152–157 all launched 1918 (exact dates not known) 50 to 40 percent complete when stricken 3 Nov 1919; sold 1920 and 1921 to companies in south Germany, Kiel and Berlin (*S 153* and *156* stranded at Neukrug in 1920, later raised); broken up at Kiel.

V 158–165 both launched 1 Nov 1918 about 40 percent or less complete. Stricken 3 Nov 1919; sold 4 Jul 1921; broken up at Hamburg. *V 160* launched as an incomplete hull 11 Mar 1921; stranded close to Bakenberg, west Arkona; towed to Sassnitz by the steam tug *Rügen*, broken up. *V 161–165* were broken up on the stocks.

H 166–169 launched 25 Oct 1919, 26 Oct 1918, 8 Nov 1919, 19 Oct 1918, respectively, approx 55 to 60 percent complete, without engines, boilers, etc. Stricken 3 Nov 1919; sold 1920; broken up at Kiel.

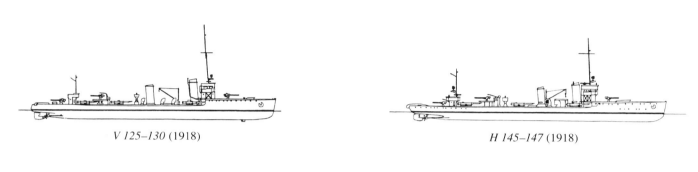

V 125–130 (1918)   *H 145–147* (1918)

Torpedo boat destroyers 1915–1919

B 97 class

Name	Builder	Built	Cost in Marks (000s)	Displacement (t = tonnes T = tons)	Length (m)	Breadth (m)	Draught (m)	Power (hp)	Revs (rpm)	Speed (kts)	Range (nm/kts)	Coal (t)	Oil (t)
B 97–98	Blohm & Voss, Hamburg Construction nos 238–239	1914–15		1843t max 1374t des	98.0 oa 96.0 cwl	9.35	3.42 fwd 3.87 aft	36,727shp max 40,000shp des	652	35.5 max 36.5 des	2600/20	—	527
V 99–100	AG 'Vulcan', Stettin Construction nos 384–385	,,		1847t max 1350t des	99.0 oa 98.0 cwl	9.36	3.60 fwd 4.05 aft	42,104shp max 40,000shp des	591	37.2 max 36.5 des	2250/20	—	519
B 109–112	Blohm & Voss, Hamburg Construction nos 242–245	,,		1843t max 1374t des	98.0 oa 96.0 cwl	9.35	3.39 fwd 3.83 aft	40,700shp max 40,000shp des	730	37.4 max 36.0 des	2620/20	—	527

Construction

Laid down as torpedo boat destroyers (dockyard designs under Russian contract, adapted). Transverse and longitudinal frame steel construction, in torpedo boat steels (twelve watertight compartments, double bottom). Depth: *B* boats, 5.7m; *V* boats, 5.6m.

Propulsion

Two sets of Marine-type turbines, direct, but *V 99–100* had AEG Vulcan turbines, direct (two 3-bladed screws, 2.6 and 2.9m diameter) in 1 + 1 engine rooms. Four oil-fired Marine-type double boilers (17 atmospheres forced, 18.5 atmospheres forced after *B 109*, 400sq m) in 1 + 1 + 1 + 1 boiler rooms. Two turbo-generators 110V (wattage not known). One rudder. Preparatory work on all engines began in 1914.

Armament

Four 8.8cm/45 torpedo guns (480 rounds) [after summer 1916 four 10.5cm/45 torpedo guns (320 rounds)]; six 50cm TT (8 rounds), two deck-mounted and two in a V mounting; twenty-four mines.

Handling

Excellent sea-boats, responsive but with a poor turning circle, though this was better with screw assistance. The *B* boats had Frahm roll tanks in the bunkers; roll period 6.6 seconds.

Complement

Crew: 4/110 (half-flotilla staff 4/12). Boats: two torpedo cutters.

Notes

Colour scheme no 10, 12. The *B* boats were fitted until 1916 with forward and after bridges and searchlight, as shown in the drawing of *V 99*; the forward funnel was the same height as the after funnel. *B109–112* had steampipes at the very edge of the sides of the centre funnel, rather than on its forward face. [On *V 100* the funnel was raised, and the bridges and searchlight platforms were rebuilt as shown in the drawing.] Various components, including the stem and stern and the turbine sets, were originally destined for the Russian destroyers *Leitenant Ilyin*, *Kapitan Kononzotov*, *Gavriil* and *Mikhail* (on the stocks in Russia); these were requisitioned in August 1914, and from then on the German boats were built to similar designs to those supplied by Blohm & Voss of Hamburg and AG 'Vulcan' of Stettin for the Russian destroyers in 1912. The funnel cross-sections were circular, elongated oval and short oval. The *V* boats had a central funnel only, oval in cross-section.

Career

B 97 launched 15 Dec 1914, commissioned 13 Feb 1915. Released at Cherbourg 23 May 1920; taken as an Italian prize; renamed *Cesare Rossarol*; broken up 1937.

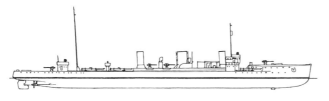

V 99, 100 (1915)

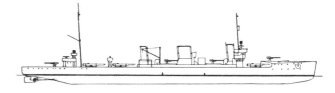

B 97–98 (1918); *B 109–112* were very similar.

B 98 launched 2 Jan 1915, commissioned 24 Mar 1915; requisitioned 22 Jun 1919 as a post boat for an internment group; taken as a British prize; broken up.

V 99 launched 9 Feb 1915, commissioned 20 Apr 1915. Scuttled and sunk at 0800hrs on 17 Aug 1915 in the Baltic, position 57° 37N, 21° 52E, after sustaining severe battle damage; 21 dead.

V 100 launched 8 Mar 1915, commissioned 17 Jun 1915; interned at Scapa Flow after 22 Nov 1918; un-

successful attempt at scuttling 21 Jun 1919; raised August 1919; taken as a French prize; broken up 1921. The boilers were reused in *Aventurier*.

B 109 launched 11 Mar 1915, commissioned 8 Jun 1915; interned at Scapa Flow after 22 Nov 1918. Scuttled 21 Jun 1919; raised 27 Mar 1926; broken up at Charleston.

B 110 launched 31 Mar 1915, commissioned 26 Jun 1915; interned at Scapa Flow after 22 Nov 1918. Scut-

tled 21 Jun 1919; raised 11 Dec 1925; broken up at Granton.

B 111 launched 8 Jun 1915, commissioned 10 Aug 1915; interned at Scapa Flow after 22 Nov 1918. Scuttled 21 Jun 1919; raised 8 Mar 1926; broken up at Granton.

B 112 launched 17 Jun 1915, commissioned 3 Sept 1915; interned at Scapa Flow after 22 Nov 1918. Scuttled 21 June 1919; raised 11 Feb 1926; broken up at Granton.

S 113 class

Name	Builder	Built	Cost in Marks (000s)	Displacement (t = tonnes T = tons)	Length (m)	Breadth (m)	Draught (m)	Power (hp)	Revs (rpm)	Speed (kts)	Range (nm/kts)	Coal (t)	Oil (t)
S 113–115	F Schichau, Elbing Construction nos 983–985	1916–19 1917–		2415t max 2060t des	106.0 oa 105.4 cwl	10.2	4.84 fwd 3.37 aft	56,000shp max 45,000shp des		36.9 max 34.5 des	2500/20	—	720
V 116–118	AG 'Vulcan', Stettin Construction nos 456–458	1916–18 1917–		2360t max 2060t des	107.5 oa 106.0 cwl	10.4	4.52 fwd 3.33 aft	55,300shp max 45,000shp des	570	35.2 max 34.5 des	,,	—	660
G 119–121	Germania Dockyard, Kiel Costruction nos 271–273	1916–		2405t max 2060t des	108.0 oa 106.5 cwl	10.3	4.15 fwd 3.65 aft	46,000shp des		34.5 des	,,	—	690
B 122–124	Blohm & Voss, Hamburg Construction nos 290–292	1916–		2354t max 2040t des	108.8 oa 107.5 cwl	,,	4.11 fwd 3.67 aft	,,		,,	,,	—	716

Construction
Laid down as destroyers or large torpedo boats (official design 1916). Transverse and longitudinal frame steel construction, in torpedo boat steels (thirteen watertight compartments, double bottom). Depth: *S 113–115*, 5.9m; *V 16–118*, 6.0m.

Propulsion
Two sets of Schichau/AEG-Vulcan/Germania/Marine-type turbines, direct (two 3-bladed screws, 3.2m diameter) in 1 + 1 engine rooms. Four oil-fired Marine-type double boilers (18.5 atmospheres forced, 4808/4805/4950/4800sq m) in 1 + 1 + 0 + 1 + 1 boiler rooms. Two 68kW 110V turbo-generators. One rudder.

Armament
Four 15cm/45 Utof guns (360 rounds); four 60cm TT (8 rounds), in two deck V mountings, power operated;

forty mines.

Handling
This class was far superior to all torpedo vessels built hitherto in size and combat worthiness. The *B* boats, because of their much greater freeboard forward, were expected to be particularly good sea-boats. The two units completed proved excellent in service in France and Italy.

Complement
Crew: 8/169 or 9/179 (half-flotilla staff 4/20). Boats: two torpedo cutters.

Notes
Colour scheme no 12. Differences were slight. The *V*, *G* and *B* boats had a projecting stern, as shown in the drawing. Some of the oil cells were fitted out as

Frahm-type roll tanks.

Career
S 113 launched 31 Jan 1918, commissioned 5 Aug 1919; served in the Reichsmarine. Stricken 5 Nov 1919; released 23 May 1920 at Cherbourg; taken as a French prize; served as *Amiral Senes* until 1936; sunk 19 Jul 1938 as a target ship for *Marseillaise, Jean de Vienne* and *La Galissonnière*.

S 114 launched 11 Apr 1918 approx 75 percent complete. Stricken 3 Nov 1919; sold and broken up 1919 at Bremerhaven.

S 115 launched 20 Jul 1918 approx 60 percent complete. Stricken 3 Nov 1919; sold and broken up 1919 at Bremerhaven.

V 116 launched 2 Mar 1918, commissioned 31 Jul

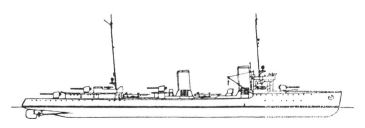

S 113–115 (1918)

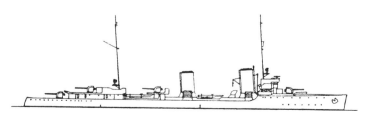

V 116–118 (1918)

1918; served in the Reichsmarine. Released 23 May 1920 at Cherbourg; taken as an Italian prize; renamed *Premuda*, stricken 1937; broken up.

V 117 launched 4 May 1918 approx 75–60 percent complete. Stricken 3 Nov 1919; sold 4 Jul 1921;

broken up 1921 at Hamburg.

V 118 launched 6 Jul 1918; fate as for *V 117*.

V 119 (launched 8 Oct 1918), *G 120* and *121* were 90, 75 and 68 percent complete when stricken 3 Nov

1919; the hulls were sold 8 Jul 1921 for 95,000M each, and broken up at Kiel.

B 122–124 launched 16 Oct 1917, 26 Oct 1918, 6 Jun 1919 65 to 40 percent complete. Stricken 3 Nov 1919; broken up 1921 at Kiel and Hamburg.

V 170 class

Name	Builder	Built	Cost in Marks (000s)	Displacement (t = tonnes T = tons)	Length (m)	Breadth (m)	Draught (m)	Power (hp)	Revs (rpm)	Speed (kts)	Range (nm/kts)	Coal (t)	Oil (t)
V 170–177	AG 'Vulcan', Stettin Construction nos 568–574	1918–		1563t max 1268t des	92.5 oa 90.8 cwl	9.10	3.60 fwd 3.21 aft	36,000shp des	650	35 des	2000/20 des	—	330
V 203–210	AG 'Vulcan', Stettin Construction nos 623–830	,,		,,	,,	,,	,,	,,	,,	,,	,,	—	345
S 178–185, S 211–223	F Schichau, Elbing Construction nos 1043–1063	,,		1523t max 1268t des	93.4 oa 92.0 cwl	,,	3.6 fwd 3.2 aft	34,000shp des	580	,,	,,	—	,,
H 186–202	Howaldtswerke, Kiel Construction nos 632–633... 4 hulls subcontracted to Stettin Oder- werke (697–700)	,,		1553t max 1268t des	92.5 oa 91.0 cwl	,,	3.70 fwd 3.12 aft	38,000shp des	690	,,	,,	—	,,

Construction
Laid down as 1918 M (mobilisation) type large torpedo boats (official design, 1917). Transverse frame longitudinal stringer steel construction, in torpedo boat steels (thirteen watertight compartments). Freeboard 5.4m.

Propulsion
Two sets of AEG-Vulcan/Schichau/Germania turbines with gear transmission (two 3-bladed screws, 2.85m diameter) in 1 + 1 engine rooms. Three oil-fired Marine-type double ended boilers (185 atmospheres forced, 3500sq m) in 1 + 0 + 1 + 1 boiler rooms. The funnels were oval in cross-section. Two 54kW 110V turbo-generators. One rudder.

Armament
Four 10.5cm/45 Utof guns (320 rounds); two deck-mounted TT and four 50cm TT (8 rounds) in two deck V mountings; forty mines.

Handling
Crew: 5/112 (half-flotilla staff 3/16). Boats: one Third Class cutter.

Career
V 170–177 did not complete the first stage of construction, (*V 176* and *V 177* were not begun) and were broken up on the stocks; the contracts were cancelled.

S 178 the incomplete hull minus the forecastle was sold 1919 and 1920 to Danzig then Bremen for conversion

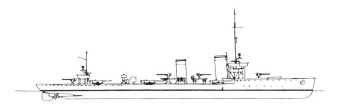

V 170–177 (design)

to a four-masted schooner with two auxiliary engines and two 3-bladed screws; entered service as *Franziska Kimme* for F Kimme, Bremerhaven; sold 1922 to Bremerhavener Reederei AG, then in 1926 to Atlantik Reederei, Hamburg, under the name *Kapitän J. Frobeen*; became the Brazilian *Capitan Alfredo Kling II* in 1926; sold to Oliveira de Almeida, Sao Paulo, and renamed *Ajuricaba*; renamed *Gonza* 1933, and continued in service until about 1936; ultimate fate not known.

S 179 career as for *178*, but named *Georg Kimme*; transferred to Addieks & Co, Bremen, 1927, as *Anneliese Rathjen*; sold 1928 to La Morue Francaise, St Pierre-Miquelon, renamed *Zazpiakbat*; requisitioned by Germany 1944; scuttled 21 Aug 1944 at Martigues, position 43° 24N, 05° 05E.

S 180–185 were vessels not completed, and broken up on the stocks.

H 186–202 generally reached only the first stage of construction or were not begun; the contracts were cancelled, and the materials broken up or reused for

other purposes; the hulls of *H 186* and *H 187* were sold 24 Nov 1919 for 81,000M each to Howaldtswerke, Kiel. *H 186* was converted in 1921, and renamed *Hansdorf* after 1921, for the Baltische Reederei KG (Baltic Shipping Company), Hamburg; sold 1924 to H Bohnekamp, Hamburg, and renamed *Dietrich Bohnekamp*; in 1928 she was sold again, to Handel und Transport GmbH, Hamburg; renamed *Peryneas II* in 1929; she was sold in 1931 to Comp Salinas Peryneas, Rio de Janeiro, and broken up in 1935. *H 187* was renamed *Hoisdorf* and sold to the Baltische Reederei KG, Hamburg, after 1921; she was sold to H Bohnekamp, Hamburg, in 1924, and renamed *Hermann Bohnekamp*; she was sold again to Handel und Transport GmbH, Hamburg, in 1928, renamed *Peryneas* in 1930; she was sold in 1931 to W Ogilvie, St Johns, Newfoundland, and in 1933 to P L Ogilvie, Belize (British Honduras); she was broken up the same year.

V 203–210 and *S 211–223* had their contracts cancelled before work had begun.

Foreign torpedo boats (up to 1919)

Taku

Name	Builder	Built	Cost in Marks (000s)	Displacement (t = tonnes T = tons)	Length (m)	Breadth (m)	Draught (m)	Power (hp)	Revs (rpm)	Speed (kts)	Range (nm/kts)	Coal (t)	Oil (t)
TAKU	F Schichau, Elbing Construction no 608	1897–98	c1000	284t max 243t des	59.0 cwl	6.40	1.40 fwd 2.55 aft	6000ihp max 5000ihp des	350 max	32.0 max 27.0 des mod	3000/12 2100/14 790/18	67 max 50 des	—

Construction Laid down as the Chinese destroyer *Hai-Jing*. Transverse frame steel construction, galvanised (nine watertight compartments). Depth not known.

Propulsion Two vertical 3-cylinder triple expansion engines (two 3-bladed screws, 1.85m diameter) in 1 + 1 engine rooms. Four Thornycroft boilers (16, [12] atmospheres forced, 1232sq m) in 1 + 1 + 1 + 1 boiler rooms. One 4kW 67V generator. One stern rudder; one bow rudder.

Armament Six 4.7cm/35 QF guns [two 5cm/40 torpedo guns after 1902]; two 45cm deck-mounted TT (4 rounds).

Complement Crew: 2/55. Boats: one yawl, one dinghy.

Notes The boat was designed for speed, and therefore built very light; in consequence her structure required continual reinforcement. [Refits resulted in horizontal funnel top edges, the installation of a wireless tele-

Taku (1901)

graphy booth at the front edge of the after funnel, and the fitting of torpedo guns on the conning tower forward and aft.] Her sister boats were named *Taku* (English), *Takou* (French) and *Leitenant Burakov* (Russian); as Chinese destroyers these were named *Hai-Niu, Hai-Lung and Hai-Hoah*.

Career
Taku launched March 1898, commissioned July 1898 as the Chinese destroyer *Hai-Jing*; captured 17 Jun 1900; served after 6 Dec 1900 as *Taku* with the cruiser squadron. Stricken 13 Jun 1914 as her boilers were unusable; scuttled and sunk 28 Sept 1914 at Kaoshu, position 36° 03N, 120° 16E.

V 105 class

Name	Builder	Built	Cost in Marks (000s)	Displacement (t = tonnes T = tons)	Length (m)	Breadth (m)	Draught (m)	Power (hp)	Revs (rpm)	Speed (kts)	Range (nm/kts)	Coal (t)	Oil (t)
V 105–108	AG 'Vulcan', Stettin Construction nos 353–356	1914–15		421t max 340t des	62.6 oa 62.0 cwl	6.22	2.54 fwd 2.07 aft	5670shp max 5500shp des	697	29.4 max 28.0 des	1400/17 460/20	60	16.2

Construction Laid down as Dutch torpedo boats *Z 1–4*. Transverse frame steel construction (six watertight compartments). Depth 3.50m.

Propulsion Two sets of AEG-Vulcan turbines, direct (two 3-bladed screws, 1.68m diameter) in 1 + 1 engine rooms. Two oil-fired Yarrow boilers and two Yarrow boilers (18.5 atmospheres forced, 750sq m) in

1 + 1 boiler rooms. The funnels were oval in cross-section. Two 8kW 110V turbo-generators. One stern rudder, one bow rudder.

Armament Two 8.8cm/45 torpedo guns, except for *V 106*, two 5.2cm/55 QF guns (200 rounds), and *V 108*, two 8.8cm/30 torpedo guns (120 rounds); two 45cm deck-mounted TT (2 rounds).

Complement Crew: 3/57. Boats: one torpedo cutter, one dinghy.

Notes Colour scheme no 10, 12.

Career
These boats were requisitioned 10 Aug 1914 at the dockyard; replacement boats were built in the Nether-

lands to German designs, under the names *Z 1–4* (launched 1918).

V 105 launched 26 Aug 1914, commissioned 5 Jan 1915 as a training boat and tender. Released 20 Aug 1920; taken as a Brazilian prize; bought by England; exchanged with Poland for *A 69* and renamed *Mazur*; sunk 1 Sept 1939 at Gdingen by an aircraft bomb; wreck broken up.

V 106 launched 26 Aug 1914, commissioned 25 Jan

V 105–108 (1915)

1915; career as for *V 105*, but broken up 1920.

V 107 launched 12 Dec 1914, commissioned 3 Mar 1915. Sunk 8 May 1915 at Libau, position 56° 33N, 20° 58E, by a mine; 1 dead.

V 108 launched 12 Dec 1914, commissioned 23 Mar 1915; served as a training boat 1916. Released 5 Aug 1920; taken as a Polish prize, and renamed *Kaszub*; sunk 20 Jul 1925 at Danzig Neufahrwasser after a boiler explosion; raised 29 Jul 1925 and broken up.

G 101 class

Name	Builder	Built	Cost in Marks (000s)	Displacement (t = tonnes T = tons)	Length (m)	Breadth (m)	Draught (m)	Power (hp)	Revs (rpm)	Speed (kts)	Range (nm/kts)	Coal (t)	Oil (t)
G 101–104	Germania Dockyard, Kiel Construction nos 211–214	1914–15	3300	1734t max 1116t des	95.3 oa 94.0 cwl	9.47	3.84 fwd 3.71 aft	29,400shp max 28,000shp des	556	33.7 max 33.5 des	2420/20	—	500

Construction Designed as Argentinian destroyers *Santiago*, *San Luis*, *Santa Fe* and *Tucuman*. Transverse and longitudinal frame steel construction, torpedo boat steels (twelve watertight compartments). Depth 5.82m.

Propulsion Two sets of Germania turbines, direct (two 3-bladed screws, 2.75m diameter) in 1 + 1 engine rooms. Three double-ended oil-fired boilers (18 atmospheres forced, 2785sq m) in 1 + 1 + 1 boiler rooms. Two 48kW 110V turbo-generators. One stern rudder; one retractable bow rudder.

Armament Four 8.8cm/45 torpedo guns (480 rounds) [four 10.5cm/45 torpedo guns after summer 1916; *G 102* had four 10.5cm/45 Utof guns (320 rounds)]; two 50cm deck-mounted TT, two 50cm deck double TT (8 rounds); twenty-four mines.

Complement Crew: 4/100 (half-flotilla staff 4/12). Boats: two torpedo cutters.

Notes Colour scheme no 10, 12. These were replacements for four ships laid down in England, not

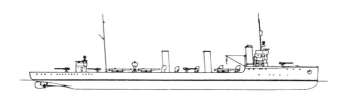

G 101–104 (1918)

delivered and subsequently sold to Greece, which were ordered from Germania at Kiel after that company's experience with *Catamarca* and *Jujui*. The torpedoes planned were 53.3cm, the guns 10.2cm from Bethlehem Steel Works. Cruise engines were included in the design for Argentina, consisting of two Germania 6-cylinder two-stroke diesel engines with a total output of 1800hp. Requisitioned 6 Aug 1914.

Career

G 101 launched 12 Aug 1914, commissioned 4 Mar 1915; interned at Scapa Flow, see *G 38*. Raised 13 Apr 1926; broken up at Charleston.

G 102 launched 16 Sept 1914, commissioned 8 Apr 1915; interned at Scapa Flow, see *G 38*; stranded. Raised 1919; taken as a USA prize; sunk 13 Jul 1921 in the vicinity of Cape Henry, Virginia, as a target for aircraft bombing.

G 103 launched 14 Nov 1914, commissioned 11 May 1915; interned at Scapa Flow, see *G 38*. Raised 30 Sept 1925; sunk in November 1925 in a storm off northern Scotland.

G 104 launched 28 Nov 1914, commissioned 5 Jun 1915; interned at Scapa Flow, see *G 38*. Raised 30 Apr 1926; broken up at Charleston.

R 01 class

Construction Laid down as Russian *eskadrennyy minonoski* (destroyers) of the *Novic* type, the first series built at Nikolaev, the second series at St Petersburg and Cherson.

Propulsion *Gnevnyy* was fitted with two Parsons turbines (two screws, diameter not known) and five Thornycroft boilers; *Bystryy* and *Schastlivyy* had two Curtiss AEG Vulcan turbines, and five Yarrow boilers.

Armament Three 10.2cm/60 QF guns (no of rounds

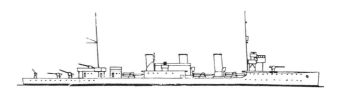

R 01 (1918); *R 02* and *R 03* were similar.

not known); two 4.7cm/44 AA guns (no of rounds not known); two machine guns; ten 45cm TT (no of rounds not known); eighty mines.

Notes The ships laid down at St Petersburg had round funnels, those at Nikolaev had oval funnels.

Name	Builder	Built	Cost in Marks (000s)	Displacement (t = tonnes T = tons)	Length (m)	Breadth (m)	Draught (m)	Power (hp)	Revs (rpm)	Speed (kts)	Range (nm/kts)	Coal (t)	Oil (t)
R 01	Putilov, St Petersburg	1912–15		1460t max 1110t des	98	9.3	3.2 fwd 2.8 aft	25,500shp max 23,000shp des	17 max 29 des		1600/17 540/30	—	350 max 255 des
R 02	Metallfabrik, St Petersburg assembly by Vaddon, Cherson	1913–15		1460t max 1050t des	,,	,,	,,	,,	,,		,,	—	,,
R 03	Obščestvo Mechanic. Zavod, Nikolaev	1913–14		1300t max 1088t des	,,	,,	,,	,,	30 des		,,	—	,,

Career

R 01 launched 29 Mar 1914, commissioned May 1915 as the Russian *Schastlivyy* into the Black Sea Fleet; taken as a German prize at Sevastopol 1 May 1918; commissioned 7 Aug 1918 as the German *R 01*; taken as an Allied prize at Sevastopol 24 Nov 1918; sunk in 1919 at Mudros in a storm, with a British crew.

R 02 launched 7 Jun 1914, commissioned 1 May 1915 as the Russian *Bystryy* into the Black Sea Fleet; taken as a German prize at Sevastopol 1 May 1918; saw no service as *R 02*; became the Soviet *Frunze* in 1925. Sunk 21 Sept 1941 off Tendra Island, East of Odessa, by a German aircraft bomb.

R 03 launched 31 Oct 1913, commissioned October 1914 as the Russian *Gnevnyy* into the Black Sea Fleet. Stranded 1 May 1918 at Sevastopol; taken as a German prize; raising was still in progress by 5 Jul 1918; saw no service as *R 03*; served in the White Russian Wrangel Squadron 1919; interned at Bizerta January 1921; broken up 1930.

R 04

Name	Builder	Built	Cost in Marks (000s)	Displacement (t = tonnes T = tons)	Length (m)	Breadth (m)	Draught (m)	Power (hp)	Revs (rpm)	Speed (kts)	Range (nm/kts)	Coal (t)	Oil (t)
R 04	Obščestvo Mechanic. Zavod, Nikolaev (Naval)	1906–09		780t max 605t des	73.4	7.5	2.5	6500ihp max 7300ihp des		18 max 25 des	600/25 1800/15	200 max 170 des	—

Construction Laid down as a Russian *eskadrennyy minonosets*.

Propulsion Two triple expansion engines (two screws, diameter not known). Four Normand boilers.

Armament Two 12cm/45 QF guns (no of rounds not known); two 4.7cm/44 QF guns (no of rounds not known); three 45cm TT (no of rounds not known); forty mines.

Complement Crew: 5/95. Boats not known.

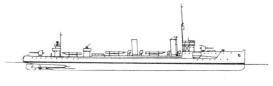

R 04 (1918)

Career

R 04 launched in 1907 as *Leitenant Pushkin*; renamed *Kapitan Saken* April 1907; served in the Russian Black Sea Fleet; taken as a German prize at Sevastopol 1 May 1918; commissioned 12 Oct 1918 as the German *R 04*; taken as an Allied prize at Sevastopol 24 Nov 1918; temporarily became the French *R 2*; served in the White Russian Wrangel Squadron 1919. Interned at Bizerta 29 Dec 1920; broken up in France 1930.

R 10 class

Construction Laid down as Russian *minonoski* (torpedo boats), Yarrow type.

Propulsion Two triple expansion engines (two screws, diameter not known). Four Yarrow boilers.

Armament Two 7.5cm/50 QF guns (no of rounds not known); four machine guns; two 45cm TT (no of rounds not known); eighteen mines.

Complement Crew: 70. Boats not known.

Career

R 10 launched October 1904, commissioned August 1905 as the Russian *Zorkyy* into the Black Sea Fleet; taken as a German prize at Sevastopol 1 May 1918; commissioned as the German *R 10* (as a dispatch boat for Poti) 7 May 1918; taken as an Allied prize at Sevastopol 24 Nov 1918; served in the White Russian

Wrangel Squadron 1919. Interned at Bizerta 29 Dec 1920; broken up in France 1930.

R 11 launched October 1904, commissioned August 1905 as the Russian *Zvonkyy* into the Black Sea Fleet; taken as a German prize at Sevastopol 1 May 1918; commissioned as the German *R 11* July 1918; taken out of service 1 Oct 1918 as the engine was unusable (crew transferred to *R 12*); taken as an Allied prize at

Name	Builder	Built	Cost in Marks (000s)	Displacement (t = tonnes T = tons)	Length (m)	Breadth (m)	Draught (m)	Power (hp)	Revs (rpm)	Speed (kts)	Range (nm/kts)	Coal (t)	Oil (t)
R 10	Obščestvo Mechanic, Zavod, Nikolaev (Naval)	1903–05		445t max 350t des	64	6.4	2.6 fwd 2.0 aft	5700ihp max 6000ihp des		24–25 max 26 des	300/25	80	
R 11	,,	1902–04	,,	,,	,,	,,	,,		,,	,,	,,	,,	
R 13	,,	,,									..		
R 12 (I)	Admiralty Dockyard, Nikolaev	1903–05					as above						
R 12 (II)	,,	,,											

Sevastopol 24 Nov 1918; temporarily transferred to Greece as a replacement for *Doxa*; served in the White Russian Wrangel Squadron 1919. Interned at Bizerta 29 Dec 1920; broken up in France 1930.

R 12 (I) launched May 1904, commissioned 1905 as the Russian *Zutkyy* into the Black Sea Fleet; taken as a German prize at Sevastopol 1 May 1918; checked for commissioning as *R 12* July 1918, but the results were negative, and she was not used; returned to Russia November 1918; broken up 1922.

R 12 (II) launched in 1904, commissioned 1905 as the Russian *Zivoy* into the Black Sea Fleet; taken as a German prize at Sevastopol 1 May 1918; commissioned as the German *R 12* 22 Oct 1918 (with the crew from *R 11*); taken as an Allied prize at Sevastopol 24 Nov 1918; served in the White Russian Wrangel Squadron 1919. Sunk 16 Nov 1920 in a storm in the Black Sea.

R 13 launched August 1903, commissioned 1904 as the Russian *Zavidnyy* into the Black Sea Fleet; taken as a German prize at Sevastopol 1 May 1918; checked for commissioning as *R 13* July 1918, but the results were negative, and she was not used; returned to Russia in November 1918; served with the Soviet forces 1921; broken up about 1925–26.

Torpedo boats (post-1923)

Möwe class

Construction

Laid down as 1923 and 1924 torpedo boats (official designs based on the *H 145* type, design officer MarOBrt Ehrenberg). Longitudinal frame longitudinal stringer construction, in torpedo boat steels (thirteen watertight compartments, double bottom 96 percent); the fittings were partly light alloy. Depth: *Möwe*, 5.10m; *Wolf* 5.20m. Immersion increased by 1cm per 15.3t; *Wolf* class 1cm per 5.8t. Trim moment for *Möwe* was 2330t. Official standard displacement 800 tons (see *Notes* under *Möwe*).

Propulsion

Two sets of geared turbines, in *Möwe* by Blohm & Voss, in *Greif*, *Falke*, *Iltis* and *Tiger* by Vulcan, in *Seeadler* by Germania, in *Albatros*, *Kondor*, *Jaguar* and *Luchs* by Schichau, and in *Wolf* and *Leopard* by Brown, Boveri & Co, (two 3-bladed screws, 2.50 [2.35m] diameter) in 1 + 1 engine rooms. *Möwe* and *Falke* had one oil-fired Marine-type boiler and two oil-fired Marine-type boilers; *Wolf* and *Tiger* had three oil-fired Marine-type double-ended boilers (18.5 atmospheres forced, 2241 and 2487sq m) in 1 + 0 + 1 + 1 boiler rooms. Two turbo-generators, one 75kW 115V diesel generator; one turbo-generator from *Wolf* onward, two 99kW 120V diesel generators. One rudder.

Armament

Three 10.5cm/45 Utof guns (300 rounds) [*Leopard* and *Luchs* were fitted with three 12.7cm/45 QF (300 rounds) in 1932]; four 3.7cm AA guns (8000 rounds) [four 2cm AA guns (8000 rounds) after 1941]; six 50cm TT in triple deck mountings [53.3cm TT after 1931]; thirty mines.

Handling

Comparable with *H 145* but drier, and with marked weather helm, almost impossible to hold on course in wind and at low speed; fuel consumption from forward tanks and consequent reduced forward draught reduced the weather helm. Considerable heel when turning in a crosswind, somewhat stiffer after the reduction in the bridge superstructure.

Complement

Crew: 4/116, [4/123–125 (5/25 as a flotilla flagship); *Wolf* as a gunnery training ship, 3/120; *Seeadler* as an experimental vessel, 4/113]. Boats: one motor cutter, one cutter.

Notes

Colour scheme no 10, 12 and grey; *Seeadler* was bottle green for trials in 1927. The original design was for 769t standard with three 12cm AA guns and four 50cm TT (twins); the first version of *Möwe* was 811t, 798 tons standard, with three 10.5cm AA guns and six 50cm TT (triple) giving 42t extra weight. *Möwe* originally had a rounded cruiser stern [after a torpedo strike on 8 May 1940, when the stern was blown off, she was fitted with a transom stern as on the other boats, thus improving stability and speed]; the superstructure as built was as shown in the drawing of

Möwe (1927)

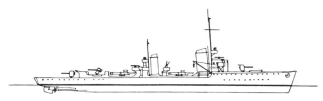

Greif (1930), *Seeadler*, *Albatros*, *Kondor*, *Falke*; *Möwe* was similar after 1940.

Wolf (1936), *Iltis*, *Jaguar*, *Leopard*, *Luchs*, *Tiger*

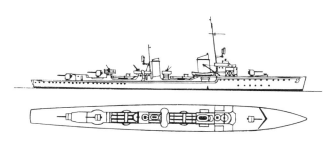

Wolf, *Iltis* (1941)

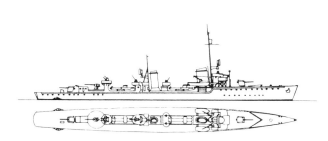

Möwe, *Greif*, *Kondor*, *Falke* (1944). *Mickel*

Jaguar (1944)

Name	Builder	Built	Cost in Marks (000s)	Displacement (t = tonnes T = tons)	Length (m)	Breadth (m)	Draught (m)	Power (hp)	Revs (rpm)	Speed (kts)	Range (nm/kts)	Coal (t)	Oil (t)
MÖWE	Naval Dockyard, Wilhelmshaven Construction 102	1924–27		1213T max 976t des 798T std	87.0 oa 84.7 cwl	8.30	3.65 max 3.33 des 2.81 std	22,100shp max 23,000shp des		32.0 max 33.0 des	3600/17 2000/20	—	321 max 150 des 340 mod
SEEADLER	Naval Dockyard, Wilhelmshaven Construction no 103	1925–27		1290T max 998t des 924T std	88.5 oa 85.7 cwl	,,	,,	24,829shp max 23,000shp des	521 max	33.6 max 33.0 des	,,	—	,,
GREIF	Naval Dockyard, Wilhelmshaven Construction no 104	1925–28		,,	,,	,,	,,	,,	,,	,,	,,	—	,,
ALBATROS	Naval Dockyard, Wilhelmshaven Construction no 105												
KONDOR	Naval Dockyard, Wilhelmshaven Construction no 106						as above						
FALKE	Naval Dockyard, Wilhelmshaven Construction no 107												
WOLF	Naval Dockyard, Wilhelmshaven Construction no 109	1927–28		1320T max 1045t des 933T std	92.6 oa 89.0 cwl	8.60	3.52 max 3.36 des 2.83 std	25,500 shp max 23,000 shp des	510 max	35.2 max 34.0 des	3900/17 2200/20	—	380 mod 338 max
ILTIS	Naval Dockyard, Wilhelmshaven Construction no 110	,,		,,	,,	,,	,,	,,	,,	,,	,,	—	,,
LUCHS	Naval Dockyard, Wilhelmshaven Construction no 111	1927–29		,,	,,	,,	,,	,,	,,	,,	,,	—	,,
TIGER	Naval Dockyard, Wilhelmshaven Construction no 112												
JAGUAR	Naval Dockyard, Wilhelmshaven Construction no 113						as above						
LEOPARD	Naval Dockyard, Wilhelmshaven Construction no 114												

Möwe (1927). After trials the *Möwe* class boats were modified in an effort to reduce their silhouette and to increase stability, the subject of criticism during trials. [In the *Wolf* class modifications were carried out during construction, including the repositioning or modification of many parts on the forecastle and upper deck, and the freestanding after mast was removed.] Some boats had two temporary parallel wind guide panels on the funnel caps, projecting slightly forward and aft beyond the funnel plate.

Career
Möwe (*MÖ**) launched 4 Mar 1926, commissioned 1 Oct 1926. Sunk together with *Falke*, *Jaguar*, *S 66*, *S 84*, etc, at 0300hrs on 15 Jun 1944 in the vicinity of Le Havre, position 49° 30N, 00° 07E, by a British aircraft bomb; 12 dead.

Seeadler (*SE*) launched 15 Jul 1926, commissioned 1 May 1927. Sunk together with the escort *HSK 6* (*Stier*) at 0409hrs on 13 May 1942 southwest of Gris Nez, position 50° 48N, 01° 32E, by torpedoes from British MTBs; 85 dead.

Greif (*GR*) launched 15 Jul 1926, commissioned 15

* Letter code cancelled after 7 Nov 1939.

Mar 1927. Sunk at 0632hrs on 23 May 1944 northwest of Ouistreham, position 49° 21N, 00° 19W, after being damaged by an aircraft bomb at 0252hrs and colliding with *Falke* while on tow; casualties unknown.

Albatros (*AT*) launched 15 Jul 1926, commissioned 15 May 1927. Sunk at 1318hrs on 10 Apr 1940 southeast of Søstren Bolaerne Island, position 59° 24N, 10° 35E, after running aground due to a navigational error.

Kondor (*KO*) launched 22 Sept 1926, commissioned 15 Jul 1928; taken out of service at Le Havre 28 Jun 1944, after being mined on passage from Cherbourg to Le Havre 23 Jun 1944; capsized in no 6 dock 31 Jun 1944 after an aircraft bomb hit; casualties unknown.

Falke (*FK*) launched 22 Sept 1926, commissioned 1

Aug 1927. Sunk at 0300hrs on 15 Jul 1944 (see *Möwe*); 26 dead.

Wolf (*WO, WL*) launched 12 Oct 1927, commissioned 15 Nov 1928. Sunk at 1150hrs on 8 Jan 1941 north of Dunkirk, position 51° 05N, 02° 08E, by a mine; 45 dead.

Iltis (*IT*) launched 12 Oct 1927, commissioned 10 Oct 1928. Sunk while escorting *Ship 23* at 0404hrs on 13 May 1942 north of Boulogne, position 50° 46N, 01° 34E, by torpedoes from British MTBs; 115 dead.

Luchs (*LU*) launched 15 Mar 1928, commissioned 15 Apr 1929. Sunk while escorting *Gneisenau* at 1550hrs on 26 Jul 1940 in the northern North Sea, position ap-

prox 60°N, 04°E, by a torpedo from the British submarine *Swordfish*; 89 dead.

Tiger (*TG*) launched 15 Mar 1928, commissioned 15 Jan 1929. Sunk at 0230hrs on 27 Aug 1939 southeast of Bornholm, position 54° 55N, 16°E, in a collision with *Max Schultz* (*Z 3*); 2 dead.

Jaguar (*JA, JR*) launched 15 Mar 1928, commissioned 1 Jun 1929. Sunk at 0600hrs in 15 Jun 1944 (see *Möwe*); 16 dead.

Leopard (*LP*) launched 15 Mar 1928, commissioned 15 Aug 1929. Sunk at 0155hrs on 30 Apr 1940 in the Skagerrak, position approx 58°N, 10°E, after breaking up in a collision with the mine ship and converted motor ferry *Preussen*; 1 dead.

T 1 class

Name	Builder	Built	Cost in Marks (000s)	Displacement (t = tonnes T = tons)	Length (m)	Breadth (m)	Draught (m)	Power (hp)	Revs (rpm)	Speed (kts)	Range (nm/kts)	Coal (t)	Oil (t)
T 1–4	F Schichau, Elbing Construction nos 1380–1383	1936–40	35,160*	1088T max 962t des 844T std	84.3 oa 82.2 cwl 87.1 oa mod	8.62	2.94 max 2.57 des 2.33 std	28,200shp max 31,000shp des	502 max 520 des	35.0 max 34.5 des	1070/19 600/35	—	200 max 85 des
T 5–8	Deschimag, Bremen Construction nos 934–937	1937–40	31,160*	,,	,,	,,	,,	,,	,,	,,	,,	—	,,
T 9–10	F Schichau, Elbing Construction nos 1393–1394	1936–40	17,579*	1082T max 839T des 844T std	,,	,,	,,	,,	,,	,,	,,	—	,,
T 11–12	Deschimag, Bremen Construction nos 938–939	1938–40	15,579*	,,	,,	,,	,,	,,	,,	,,	,,	—	,,
T 13–21	F Schichau, Elbing Construction nos 1401–1406, 1444–1446	1939–42	84,399*	1098T max 997t des 853T std	85.2 oa 82.0 cwl	8.87	3.14 max 2.51 des	34,110shp max 31,000shp des	493 max 520 des	36.6 max 34.5 des	1400/19 1650/16	—	216 max 90 des

* cost of series

Construction

Laid down as 1935 and 1937 torpedo boats (official designs, design officer MarOBrt Witte). Longitudinal frame longitudinal stringer construction in steel 52, superstructure mostly light alloy; flush deck vessels (twelve watertight compartments; eleven watertight compartments after *T 13*, no double bottom). Depth 5.14m.

Propulsion

Two sets of Wagner geared turbines (two 3-bladed screws, 2.45–2.60m diameter) in 1 + 1 engine rooms; primary revolutions at full load 7650rpm for high and medium pressure turbine, 4720rpm for low pressure turbine. Four Wagner boilers (70 [58] atmospheres forced, 460°) in 1 + 1 boiler rooms. Fuel oil consumption 0.340kg per shp/hr, steam consumption 23 to 30t per h. Two electricity plants with two turbo-generators, each 52kW, and one 60kW diesel generator, in a central generating room on two decks (after *T 13* the plant

was divided aft into turbine rooms), total output 164kW at 220V. One balanced rudder; smaller twin rudders after *T 13*.

Armament

One 10.5cm/45 torpedo gun (600 and 120 rounds), +80° –8°, range 17,600m; [five to twelve 2cm AA guns (each 2000 rounds)]; six 53.3cm TT (6 rounds), in triple deck mountings; thirty mines. [After November 1941 *T 13* and *18* had one additional 3.7cm AA gun on the forecastle; after June 1944 *T 4* and *19* had one 10.5cm/45 torpedo gun, four 3.7cm AA guns, twelve 2cm AA guns, and three 53.3cm TT; *T 8, 10, 12* and *17* had one 10.5cm/45 torpedo gun, two 3.7cm AA guns, twelve 2cm AA guns, and three 53.3cm TT; *T 11* had one 10.5cm/45 torpedo gun, one 4cm Bofors AA gun, two 3.7cm AA guns, twelve 2cm AA guns, and three 53.3cm TT (in each case the after TT set was removed).]

Handling

Excellent sea-boats, very manoeuvrable even in poor weather, and with a good turning circle. *T 1–12* initially had a very wet forecastle in spite of the knuckle [improved in 1941 by the Atlantic bow]. *T 2, 4* and *8–10* had a tendency to lee helm. Transverse metacentric height 0.72m.

Complement

Crew: 6/113 [6/149]. Boats: one motor yawl, one torpedo cutter, one dinghy.

Notes

Colour scheme no 9 and camouflage. The high pressure superheated steam installations were initially prone to breakdown and the range was always inadequate (maximum tactical fuel oil load 194t). After *T 11* the engine installation was more reliable. They were inadequately armed ships, of limited use for escort duties and categorised as 'large high speed boats' by the Commodore of Torpedo Boats. Originally the masts had no angled struts, with searchlights on the forward platform in place of the later rangefinder mattress; for the earlier stem see the supplementary drawing.

Career

T 1 launched in 1938, commissioned 2 Dec 1939. Sunk 10 Apr 1945 at Kiel, in the Deutsche Werke berth 7, by a US aircraft bomb; 9 dead.

T 2 launched in 1938, commissioned 9 Dec 1939. Sunk 29 Jul 1944 at Deschimag, Bremen, by a US aircraft bomb; casualties unknown. Raised; defunct at Cuxhaven 1945; broken up 1946.

T 3 launched in 1938, commissioned 3 Feb 1940. Sunk at 2330hrs on 18 Sept 1940 at Le Havre by a British aircraft bomb; 9 dead. Raised 1941, repaired 16 March; recommissioned 12 Dec 1943. Sunk 14 Mar 1945 north of Hela, position 54° 39N, 18° 47E, by a mine (see *T 5*); 300 dead.

T 4 launched in 1938, commissioned 27 Aug 1940; taken as a US prize 9 Jan 1946; transferred to Denmark 16 Apr 1948, laid up; [planned conversion as an MTB command ship, 1950, was not implemented]. Stricken 1951; sold in February 1952 to H I Hansen, Odensee, for breaking up.

T 5 launched 22 Nov 1937, commissioned 23 Jan 1940. Sunk 14 Mar 1945 north of Hela, position 54° 39N, 18° 47E, by a mine (see *T 3*); 20 dead.

T 6 launched 16 Dec 1937, commissioned 30 Apr 1940. Sunk at 0015hrs on 7 Nov 1940 east of Aberdeen, position 57° 08N, 01° 58W, by a mine; 48 dead.

T 7 launched 10 Aug 1938, commissioned 8 Oct 1939. Sunk 29 Jul 1944 at Bremen, in the Deschimag Industrial Harbour, basin F, by an aircraft bomb; casualties unknown. Raised; broken up December 1947 to June 1949.

T 8 launched 10 Aug 1938, commissioned 8 Oct 1939. Sunk 3 May 1945 at Strander Bay, position 54° 26N, 10° 10.5E; later broken up.

T 9 launched in 1939, commissioned 4 Jul 1940; subsequent career as for *T 8*.

T 10 launched in 1939, commissioned 5 Aug 1940. Sunk 18 Dec 1944 in the collapsing dock at Gotenhafen, position 54° 32N, 18° 34E, by a British aircraft bomb.

T 11 launched 1 Mar 1939, commissioned 7 May 1940. Taken as a British prize 1945; transferred to France February 1946; renamed *Bir Hakeim*. Stricken 7 Oct 1951; broken up.

T 12 launched 12 Apr 1939, commissioned 3 Jul 1940. Taken as a USSR prize 27 Dec 1945; transferred to Libau early 1946; renamed *Podviznyy*; subsequent career unknown; broken up.

T 13 launched 15 Jun 1939, commissioned 31 May 1941. Sunk 10 Apr 1945 in the Kattegat, position not known, by British fighter bombers; 20 dead.

T 14 launched in 1939, commissioned 14 Jun 1941. Taken as a USA prize 9 Jan 1946; transferred to France in October 1947; renamed *Dompaire*. Stricken 7 Oct 1951; broken up.

T 15 launched in 1939, commissioned 26 Jun 1941. Sunk at 1300hrs on 13 Dec 1943 at Kiel, in Deutsche Werke berth 9, by a US aircraft bomb.

T 16 launch date unknown, commissioned 24 Jul 1941. Bombed by British aircraft 13 Apr 1945 at Frederikshavn, Denmark, and taken out of service; broken up.

T 17 launch date unknown, commissioned 28 Aug 1941. Taken as a USSR prize 15 Jan 1946; transferred to Libau early 1946; renamed *Porivistyy*. Stricken 1957; broken up.

T 18 launch date unknown, commissioned 22 Nov 1941. Sunk at 0708hrs on 17 Sept 1944 northwest of Baltischport, position 59° 22N, 24° 03E, by British aircraft rockets; 30 dead.

T 19 launch date unknown, commissioned 18 Dec 1941. Taken as a USA prize 9 Jan 1946; transferred to Denmark 25 Nov 1947; laid up; [planned conversion to an MTB command ship, 1950, was not implemented]. Stricken 1951; sold February 1952 to H I Hansen, Odensee, for breaking up.

T 20 launch date unknown, commissioned 5 Jun 1942. Taken as a British prize 1945; transferred to France February 1946; renamed *Baccarat*. Stricken 7 Oct 1951; broken up.

T 21 launch date unknown, commissioned 11 Jul 1942; seriously damaged at Wesermünde in 1945 and taken as a USA prize. Scuttled 16 Dec 1946 (with *Leipzig*, see page 123.)

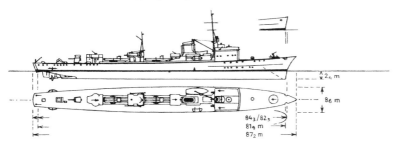

T 2 (1942); *T 4* and *T 8–12* were very similar. The supplementary drawing shows the original bow form of *T 1–12*.

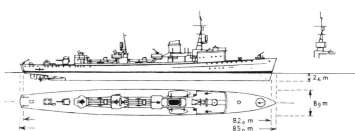

T 13–21 (1944)

Fleet torpedo boats 1942–1944

T 22 class

Name	Builder	Built	Cost in Marks (000s)	Displacement (t = tonnes T = tons)	Length (m)	Breadth (m)	Draught (m)	Power (hp)	Revs (rpm)	Speed (kts)	Range (nm/kts)	Coal (t)	Oil (t)
T 22–25	F Schichau, Elbing	1941–42	84,869*	1754T max 1512t des 1294T std	102.5 oa 97.0 cwl	10.0	3.22 max 2.60 std	32,560shp max 29,000shp des	463 max 470 des	34.0 max 32.5 des	5000/19	—	374 160
T 26–30	,,	1942–43		,,	,,	,,	,,	,,	,,	,,	,,	—	,,
T 31–36	,,	1943–44		,,	,,	,,	,,	,,	,,	,,	,,	—	,,
T 37–39	,,	1943–		2155T max 1782t des 1493T std	106.0 oa 102.0 cwl	10.7	3.72 max 2.94 std	40,000shp	520 des	34.0 des	6500/19 des	—	582 max 250 des
T 40–43	,,	1944–		,,	,,	,,	,,	,,	,,	,,	,,	—	,,
T 44–51	,,	,,		,,	,,	,,	,,	,,	,,	,,	,,	—	,,

* cost of series T 22–36

Construction

Designed as 1939 and 1941 fleet torpedo boats after T 37 (official designs). Transverse frame longitudinal stringer construction in steel 52, superstructure mostly light alloy; flush deck vessels (thirteen watertight compartments, double bottom 67 percent and 69 percent). Depth 5.80 and 6.25m.

Propulsion

Two power plants each with one set of Wagner turbines with gear transmission, in one engine room (two 3-bladed screws 2.50 to 2.65m in diameter). Two Wagner boilers (70 atmospheres forced, 400–450°) in one boiler room, a starboard installation forward of the engine room. Two electricity stations with two 80kW turbo-generators, and one 160kW diesel generator, giving a total output of 320kW at 220V. Two balanced rudders.

Armament

Four 10.5cm/45 torpedo guns (2400 and 480 rounds), +80° –8°, range 17,600m; four 3.7cm AA guns (8000 rounds); two to nine 2cm AA guns (4000–18,000 rounds); six 53.3cm TT (6 rounds) in triple deck tubes; fifty mines. [In some cases more 2cm AA guns were installed after 1943.] T 37 was armed in 1944 with four 10.5cm/45 QF guns (2400 rounds); three to six 3.7cm AA guns (12,000 rounds); eight 2cm AA guns (16,000 rounds); six 53.3cm TT (6 rounds); four depth charge launchers; six individual depth charge mounts (32 rounds).

Handling

Excellent sea-boats, with a tight turning circle, very manoeuvrable even in severe weather; tendency to lee helm. Transverse metacentric height 0.75/0.83m.

Complement

Crew: 8/198. Boats: one motor yawl, one torpedo cutter, one dinghy.

Notes

Colour scheme no 9 and camouflage. After T 31 the design was simplified for wartime, eg the angled forecastle bulkhead was deleted. [The searchlight on the after mast platform was later replaced by a rangefinder mattress.] For differences in the bridge layout, see the supplementary drawing.

Career

T 22 launched in 1941, commissioned 28 Feb 1942. Sunk at 0115hrs on 18 Aug 1944 in Narva Bay, position 59° 42N, 27° 44E, by her own mine; 143 dead.

T 23 launched November 1941, commissioned 14 Jun 1942. Taken as a British prize 1945; transferred to France February 1946; renamed L'Alsacien. Stricken 9 Jun 1954; named Q 11, and broken up.

T 24 launched in 1942, commissioned 17 Oct 1942. Sunk 24 Aug 1944 at Le Verdon Roads, position 45° 31N, 01° 05W, by a British aircraft bomb; 18 dead.

T 25 launched in 1942, commissioned 12 Dec 1942. Sunk at 1546hrs on 28 Dec 1943 near Biscaya (exact location unknown) during action with T 26 against the British cruisers Glasgow and Enterprise; 85 dead.

T 26 launched in 1942, commissioned 27 Feb 1943. Sunk at 1600hrs on 28 Dec 1943 with T 25; 90 dead.

T 27 launch date unknown, commissioned 17 Apr 1943. Sunk 29 Apr 1944 off the Breton coast in the vicinity of the Ile de Batz, position 48° 39N, 04° 21W, in battle with the Canadian destroyer Haida; left stranded and on fire, and finally destroyed on 4 May 1944 by torpedoes from British MTBs; 11 dead.

T 28 launched in November 1941, commissioned 19 Jun 1943. Taken as a British prize 1945; transferred to France February 1946; renamed Le Lorrain. Stricken 31 Oct 1955; stationary hulk named Q 59; broken up 1959.

T 29 launched in 1943, commissioned 21 Aug 1943. Sunk at 0330hrs on 26 Apr 1944 off the Breton coast in the vicinity of the Sept Iles, position 48° 53N, 03° 33W, by gunfire and torpedoes from the British cruiser Black Prince; 137 dead.

T 30 launched in 1943, commissioned 24 Oct 1943. Sunk at 0040hrs on 18 Aug 1944 in Narva Bay, position 59° 43N, 27° 44E, by her own mine; 114 dead.

T 31 launched in 1943, commissioned 5 Feb 1944. Sunk at 0003hrs on 20 Jun 1944 off Narvi Island, position 60° 16N, 28° 17E, by torpedoes from Soviet MTBs; 82 dead.

T 32 launched in 1943, commissioned 8 May 1944. Sunk at 0049hrs on 18 Aug 1944 in Narva Bay, position 59° 42N, 27° 43E, by her own mine; 137 dead.

T 33 launched in 1943, commissioned 16 Jun 1944. Taken as a USSR prize 1945; released in Libau in January 1946; renamed *Primernyy*. Used as a training hulk 1951; broken up 1958.

T 34 launched in 1942, commissioned 12 Aug 1944. Sunk at 1128hrs on 20 Nov 1944 east of Cape Arkona, position 54° 40N, 13° 29E, by a mine from the Soviet submarine *Frunzevez L 3*; 62 dead.

T 35 launched in 1944, commissioned 7 Oct 1944. Taken as a USA prize July 1945; transferred to USA July 1945; renamed *DD 935*; transferred to France 1948 and cannibalized. Stricken 3 Oct 1952; broken up.

T 36 launched in 1944, commissioned 9 Dec 1944. Sunk 4 May 1945 in the central Baltic, exact position unknown, after hitting a mine and being bombed by Soviet aircraft.

Contracts for main turbines and boilers for the following boats were granted in 1941, cancelled the same year and renewed 25 Nov 1942 under the same construction numbers for the fleet torpedo boats 1941.

T 37 launched in 1944, 96.5 percent complete; towed west from Elbing 8 May 1945 to the Weser estuary; fate unknown.

T 38 launched in 1944, 84 percent complete; towed west from Elbing 8 May 1945 to Kiel. Scuttled at 1745hrs on 10 May 1946 in the Skagerrak, position 58° 07N, 10° 46E.

T 39 launched in 1944, 76 percent complete; towed west from Elbing 8 May 1945 to Kiel. Scuttled at 1920hrs on 10 May 1946 in the Skagerrak, position 58° 08N, 10° 47E.

T 40 launched in 1944, 70 percent complete. Scuttled at Danzig-Brösen in March 1945 as further towing was impossible.

T 41 launched in 1944, 66.5 percent complete.

T 42 launched in 1944, 58.5 percent complete.

T 43 launched in 1944, 48 percent complete. Scuttled in March 1945 during the evacuation of Elbing.

T 44 launched in 1944, 40 percent complete.

T 45 launched in 1944, 35 percent complete.

T 46–50 respectively 26, 23, 20.5, 8.2 and 5.3 percent complete, were destroyed on the stocks at Elbing in March 1945 during the evacuation.

T 51 was cancelled before work began.

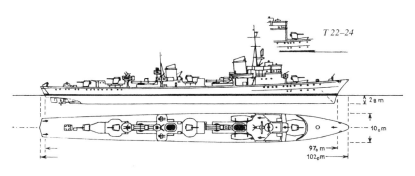

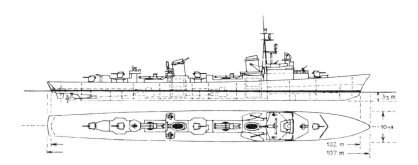

T 25–36 (1944); *T 22–44* were very similar (see the supplementary drawing).   *T 37–51* (design)

T 43 class

Name	Builder	Built	Cost in Marks (000s)	Displacement (t = tonnes T = tons)	Length (m)	Breadth (m)	Draught (m)	Power (hp)	Revs (rpm)	Speed (kts)	Range (nm/kts)	Coal (t)	Oil (t)
T 43–48	Deschimag, Bremen Construction nos 1109–1114	—		2675T max 2315t des 2075T std	108.0 cwl	11.0	3.20 des	6000shp des		36.5 des	6000/19 des	—	

Construction

Designed as 1942 fleet torpedo boats (official design, 1942). Transverse frame longitudinal stringer construction in steel 52, superstructure in light alloy; other details unknown. Depth unknown.

Armament

Four 12.7cm torpedo guns; eight 3.7cm AA guns; twelve 2cm AA guns; six 53.3cm TT.

Complement

Crew: 220.

Career

Contracts were granted 21 Nov 1942 and altered 25 Nov 1943 as follows:

Construction no 1109 became the 1942 destroyer *Z 51* (see page 210). Construction nos 1110–1114 became the 1942 A destroyers *Z 52–56* (see page 210). The contracts for *T 43–48* were renewed on 12 Jun 1943, reverting to the 1941 fleet torpedo boat design (see page 195).

T 52 class

Construction

Designed as 1944 fleet torpedo boats (official design, developed from the 1941 A design). Transverse frame longitudinal stringer construction in steel 52, superstructure in light alloy (twelve water-tight compartments, double bottom 70 percent). Depth 6.25m.

Propulsion

Engines and boilers were as for *T 22–51*, but using the so-called IS (Illies-Schichau) installation, in which all auxiliary machines were electrically powered (3-phase power with frequency control), and all motors simple 3-phase electric motors with central control system. Feed water pre-heating was by steam extracted from

Name	Builder	Built	Cost in Marks (000s)	Displacement (t = tonnes T = tons)	Length (m)	Breadth (m)	Draught (m)	Power (hp)	Revs (rpm)	Speed (kts)	Range (nm/kts)	Coal (t)	Oil (t)
T 52–60	F Schichau, Elbing Construction nos 1720–1725, 1447–1449	—		1794T max 1604t des 1418T std	103.0 oa 98.0 cwl	10.1	3.70 max 2.91 des	52,000shp		37.0	4500/19	—	300 max 130 des

the main turbine, and automatic in operation so that when the output of the main turbine varied or the fuel supply to the boiler altered, the pressure varied by the same amount without the need to operate the manoeuvre valve.

One boiler system built for installation in a ship (with components from the production series of 1939 fleet torpedo boats) was tested at Schichau, Elbing, under the supervision of Dipl-Ing Illies; a full-size wooden model of one turbine and one boiler room was also built.

Acceptance trials of the electrical auxiliary machine operation system was under the direction of the Chief of Staff, Navy; it was evidently decided not to implement the economical steam installation described above (which gave speeds up to about 25kts at a greatly reduced pressure of 19 atmospheres forced) until the 1944 fleet torpedo boat.

Armament

Four 10.5cm/52 AA guns (1600 rounds); ten 3.7cm AA guns (20,000 rounds); six 53.3cm TT (6 rounds), in triple deck tubes; thirty mines.

Complement

Crew: 8/214. Boats: one motor yawl, one torpedo cutter, one dinghy.

Notes

Colour scheme no 9 and camouflage.

Career

T 52–60 contracted 28 Mar 1944, but construction had not progressed beyond preliminary preparations when the contracts were cancelled.

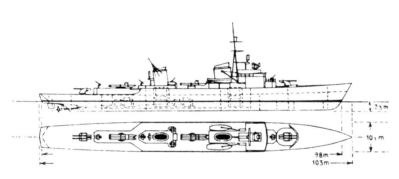

T 52–60 (design)

T 61 class

Name	Builder	Built	Cost in Marks (000s)	Displacement (t = tonnes T = tons)	Length (m)	Breadth (m)	Draught (m)	Power (hp)	Revs (rpm)	Speed (kts)	Range (nm/kts)	Coal (t)	Oil (t)
T 61, 62, 69 T 73–75	Wilton-Fijenoord, Schiedam Construction nos 691–693, —	1942–		2566T max 2249t des 1931T std	114.5 oa 110.0 cwl	11.3	3.81 max 3.24 des	49,500shp max 45,000shp des	475 des	35.0 max 34.8 des	2100/19	—	561 max 240 des
T 63, 64, 70 T 76–78	Rotterdamse Droogdok Mij, Construction nos 243–245, —	,,		,,	,,	,,	,,	,,	,,	,,	,,	—	,,
T 65, 66, 71 T 79–81	De Schelde, Vlissingen Construction nos 224–226, —							as above					
T 67, 68, 72* T 82–84	Nederl. Scheepsbouw, Amsterdam Construction nos 305, 306, 309, —												

* Changed in 1943 – *T 67* to De Schelde, *T 68* to Wilton, *T 72* to Rotterdamse Droogdok

Construction

Designed as 1940 fleet torpedo boats (the temporary designation Destroyer 40 was considered). Transverse frame longitudinal stringer construction in steel 52, superstructure mostly light alloy (thirteen watertight compartments, double bottom 90 percent). Freeboard 6.55m.

Propulsion

Two sets of Parsons turbines with gear transmission by N V Werkspoor of Amsterdam (two 3-bladed screws, 3.15m diameter) in 1 + 1 engine rooms. Three Yarrow-Werkspoor boilers (28.1 atmospheres forced, 350°) in 1 + 1 boiler rooms. Two balanced rudders.

Armament

Four 12.7cm/45 QF guns (600 rounds), +30° −10°, range 17,400m; four 3.7cm AA guns (8000 rounds); sixteen 2cm AA guns (16,000 rounds); eight 53.3cm deck TT (8 rounds), in quadruple mountings; fifty mines; four depth charge launchers; six individual depth charge mounts (32 rounds).

Complement

Crew: 8/223. Boats: one motor yawl, one torpedo cutter, one dinghy.

Notes

This class was originally designed with a low tripod mast (with a V-shaped double radar mattress), one rangefinder cupola of the Dutch type on the forward bridge and after director, and a searchlight platform on the after mast; the funnel had a fairly tall cap, and boat davits were omitted in favour of a starboard derrick.

The turbine sets and boilers from the Dutch destroyers *Tjerk Hiddes* and *Philips van Almonde* (see *ZH 1*), whose hulls were blown up in the dockyards in 1940 when the Germans invaded, formed the basis of the design for the 1940 fleet torpedo boat type. In consideration of the capabilities of the Dutch dockyards and engine factories, contracts were drawn up according to Dutch construction standards; the vessels can be considered as full-strength destroyers. Dutch designers were critical of the design.

Career

T 61 launched June 1944; towed to Germany incomplete. Stranded and destroyed 12 Sept 1944, northwest of Den Helder, by an aerial torpedo while on tow; wreck subsequently broken up.

T 63 launched 28 Oct 1944, commissioned 28 Oct 1944; towed to Wesermünde incomplete. Scuttled 2 May 1946; broken up.

*T 65** launched 8 Jul 1944, commissioned 8 Sept 1944; towed to Kiel incomplete. Scuttled 3 May 1946; broken up.

T 62, *64*, *69* and *70** destroyed on the stocks at Rotterdam and Schiedam, 1944.

*T 66** destroyed on the stocks at Vlissingen 1944, by an aircraft bomb.

T 67–68 and *71–72** construction contracts cancelled 1945.

T 73–84 construction contracts granted 27 Aug 1941 and cancelled the same year before construction numbers were allotted.

* Turbines and boiler installations for these boats were installed in the Dutch destroyers *Holland*, *Gelderland*, *Noordbrabant* and *Zeeland* after 1949/50.

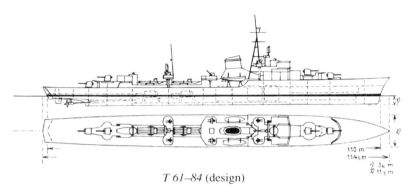

T 61–84 (design)

Destroyers 1937–1945

Z 1 class

Name	Builder	Built	Cost in Marks (000s)	Displacement (t = tonnes T = tons)	Length (m)	Breadth (m)	Draught (m)	Power (hp)	Revs (rpm)	Speed (kts)	Range (nm/kts)	Coal (t)	Oil (t)
Z 1, Z 2 Z 3, Z 4	Deutsche Werke, Kiel Construction nos 242–245	1934–37 1935–37	54,749*	3156T max 2619t des 2223T std	119.3 oa mod 119.0 oa 114.0 cwl 114.4 cwl mod	11.3	4.23 max 3.82 des	70,000shp max 70,000shp des	450 max 427 des	38.7 max 36.0 des	1825/19	—	715 max 299 des
Z 5 Z 6, Z 7 Z 8	Deschimag, Bremen Construction nos 899–902	1935–37 1935–37 1936–37	50,749*	3110T max 2474t des 2171T std	120.0 oa mod 119.0 oa 114.0 cwl 114.4 cwl mod	,,	,,	,,	,,	,,	,,	—	,,
Z 9, Z 10 Z 11 Z 12, Z 13	Germania Dockyard, Kiel Construction nos 535–539	1935–38 1935–38 1935–39	67,249*	3190T max 2270T des	,,	,,	,,	,,	,,	,,	,,	—	,,
Z 14–16	Blohm & Voss, Hamburg Construction nos 503–505	1935–38	42.249*	3165T max 2619t des 2239T std	,,	,,	,,	,,	,,	,,	,,	—	,,
1989gt/652nt (Z 1)													

* cost of series

Construction
Laid down as 1934 destroyers (1934 A after Z 5) (official design from a destroyer study, 1932). Longitudinal frame longitudinal stringer construction in steel 5l, superstructure partly light alloy (sixteen watertight compartments, double bottom 47 percent, ie under centre of ship [bow and stern designs were modified (see Notes) after the trials of Z 1–4]). Official standard displacement 1625 tons. Depth 6.40m.

Propulsion
Two sets of Wagner turbines with gear transmission (two 3-bladed screws, 3.25m diameter) in 1 + 0 + 1 engine rooms and a starboard turbine in the forward room. Six Wagner boilers (70 atmospheres forced, 460 [450]°); Z 9–16 had six Benson boilers (110 atmospheres forced, 510°) in 1 + 0 + 1 + 1 boiler rooms. Three electricity plants with two 200kW turbo-generators and two 60kW and 30kW diesel generators; after Z 9, three 50kW diesel generators with a total output of 550kW at 220V. One balanced rudder. Primary revolutions of high pressure turbine 7100rpm, medium pressure turbine 5760rpm, low pressure turbine 2826rpm. The cruise turbine was in a drum on some ships [later removed], producing 35 to 46t of steam per hour with natural circulation. Weight of complete power installation 13.8kg/shp.

Armament
Five 12.7cm/45 QF guns (600 rounds), +30° –10°, range 17,400m; four 3.7cm AA guns (8000 rounds); six [after mid-1942 up to eight] 2cm AA guns (12,000 [16,000] rounds); eight 53.3cm TT (16 rounds) in quadruple deck tubes; four depth charge launchers, etc; 60 mines. [In about 1939 Z 8 was temporarily fitted with four 15cm/45 Utof guns, etc. After the rearmament in 1944* Z 5, 10 and 15 had only four 12.7cm/45 QF guns (480 rounds), plus a total of ten (Z 5), twelve (Z 10) and fourteen (Z 15) 3.7cm AA guns (up to 28,000 rounds).]

Handling
All ships suffered from inadequate stability. A restriction had to be placed on fuel consumption (normal minimum 30 percent full) to maintain adequate ballast against extra weight high in the ship; this caused reduced freeboard and poor stability. All ships suffered from weather helm. With the original steep, rounder stem, spray at high speeds made the use of the forward QF guns dangerous, and spray reached as far aft as ie bridge [the stem conversion, etc, (see Notes) mean a considerable improvement]. Manoeuvred moderately, poor turning circle; [modification to the stern (see below) had little effect, making the ship bow-heavy in swell, with stiff movements]. All ships were fitted with active roll damping [later replaced by roll keels]. Metacentric height with full load 0.79m, with half-load 0.60cm (K-Office, 20 Nov 1940).

Complement
Crew: 10/315 (4/19 as flotilla flagship). Boats: two motor pinnaces, one torpedo cutter.

Notes
Colour scheme no 9 and camouflage; funnel caps on Z 1–6 were black in 1937, all others light (silvery) grey, as later. [The considerable weight added after

* Operation Barbara.

completion of the design was too much for the longitudinal strength of the boats, which had to be fitted
with extensive reinforcements to the keel and deck immediately after completion. To improve the turning
circle units already completed (1935–36) were fitted
with a Staukeil (a short keel with a shallow wedge-
shaped cross-section) under the transom; this was
removed in 1940–42. In 1938–39 a retractable bow
spar (bow guard device) was installed which increased
the bow length by 1m and raised it by about 0.5m. At
the same time an experiment was carried out to improve the turning circle by extending the deadwood,
beginning with *Z 7*.]

Differences in appearance are shown in the drawings
and supplementary drawings. *Z 1–4* had a forecastle
sheer strake on each side formed as a quadrant section
[after 1938 they were fitted with a narrow spray deflect-
or strake on the underside between the forwardmost
QF gun and anchor hawse. At the same time the stem
was reformed with a sharper entry, raising it by about
0.5m and extending it by 0.3m. *Z 2* had a wider spray
deflector strake on the foreship, 1937–38 only. Instead
of an upper bridge with a half-round front face, fitted
up to 1938, all four ships were fitted with a new shape
bridge, which became standard from then on (this also
applies to *Z 5* and *Z 7*, probably also to *Z 6* and *Z 8*)].
Z 5–16 had an angular forecastle sheer strake, and the
frames and outer plating of the bow had a slightly
more marked slope in consequence. The Benson boiler
destroyers *Z 9–16* had two steam pipes forward on the
after funnel; on the forward funnel (port) a rectangular
exhaust air shaft ran diagonally upward at around 45°,
rather than at a shallow angle as on the first destroyers.
There were slight differences in the Hance profile at
the end of the forecastle and on the after superstructure. [In 1941–42 quadruple 2cm AA guns were fitted
on the after deckhouse; FuMO 21/24/25 radar was installed on the bridge house in 1939–41 and degaussing
coils under the sheer strakes of the main and forecastle
decks. After mid-1940 there were angled struts on the
forward mast, and the searchlights and platform were
removed. *Z 4, 5, 6, 10, 14* and *15* had the forward funnel shortened by 0.7m as far as the plate, the forward
cap by 1.2m, the after cap by 0.7m. *Z 5, 10* and *15*
after 1944 had the lower main section of the forward
mast rebuilt as a gate mast as an experiment to provide
a full horizon for the forward radar. *Z 5* and *15* had a
curved bow without a deck hawse, no third 12.7cm QF

gun, new platforms for the twin 3.7cm AA guns forward and aft, and the after mast shifted forward, now
with two angled struts. *Z 5, 6* and *10* in 1944 had the
searchlight on the after mast replaced by an FuMG 63
Hohentwiel K/FuMO 24/25 radar. After autumn 1941
all boats were fitted with TT master seats with a Plexi-
glas shield]. As a result of the unreliability of the
ultra-high pressure hot steam installations the useful-
ness of this class in active service was limited,
especially for ships operating alone.

Career

Z 1 (*Leberecht Maass*) launched 18 Aug 1935, commissioned 14 Jan 1937; served as a destroyer flotilla
flagship. Sunk at 2018hrs on 22 Feb 1940 northwest of
Borkum (location unknown) when avoiding German
aircraft bombs dropped in error in a British minefield,
together with *Z 3*; 282 dead.

Z 2 (*Georg Thiele*) *13/1†* launched 18 Aug 1935, commissioned 27 Feb 1937. Sunk 13 Apr 1940 at
Rombaksbotten, position 68° 24N, 17° 35E, in action
with British destroyers; 27 dead. Wreck broken up
1963.

Z 3 (*Max Schultz*) *12/1†* undocked 30 Nov 1935, commissioned 8 Apr 1937. Sunk at 2050hrs on 22 Feb
1940 (see *Z 1*); 308 dead.

Z 4 (*Richard Beitzen*) *11/–†* undocked 30 Nov 1935,
commissioned 13 May 1937. Taken as a British prize
1945; laid up; broken up 1947.

Z 5 (*Paul Jacobi*) *21/1†* launched 24 Mar 1936, commissioned 29 Jun 1937. Taken as a British, then
French prize 15 Jan 1946; released February 1946; renamed *Desaix*. Stricken 17 Feb 1954; renamed *Q 02*
1958; broken up.

Z 6 (*Theodor Riedel*) *22/–†* launched 22 Apr 1936,
commissioned 6 Jul 1937. Taken as a British, then
French prize 28 Jan 1946; released February 1946; renamed *Kleber*. Stricken 21 Apr 1957; renamed *Q 86*;
broken up 1958.

Z 7 (*Hermann Schoemann*) *23/–†* launched 16 Jul
1936, commissioned 15 Sept 1937. Scuttled and sunk
at 0830hrs on 2 May 1942 in the North Sea, position
73° 30N, 35° 10E, by a torpedo from the German *Z 24*,
after action against the British cruiser *Edinburgh*, during which she suffered engine failure.

Z 8 (*Bruno Heinemann*) *63/61†* launched 15 Sept
1936, commissioned 8 Jan 1938. Sunk at 2315hrs on
25 Jan 1942 8nm north of Dunkirk (location unknown)
by a mine; 93 dead.

Z 9 (*Wolfgang Zenker*) *61/62/63†* launched 27 Mar
1936, commissioned 2 Jul 1938. Scuttled and sunk 13
Apr 1940 at Rombaksbotten, position 68° 25N, 17°
55E, undamaged but with fuel oil and ammunition exhausted after action; no of dead unknown. Wreck
broken up.

Z 10 (*Hans Lody*) *62/81†* launched 14 May 1936,
commissioned 17 Sept 1938. Taken as a British prize 6
Jan 1946; renamed *R 38*; used for experiments. Broken
up 1949 at Sunderland.

Z 11 (*Bernd von Arnim*) *81/62†* launched 8 Jul 1936,
commissioned 6 Dec 1938. Scuttled and sunk 13 Apr
1940 at Rombaksbotten, position 68° 25N, 17° 54E,
undamaged but with fuel oil and ammunition exhausted after action; 1 dead. Wreck broken up 1962.

Z 12 (*Erich Giese*) *82/82†* launched 12 Mar 1937,
commissioned 4 Mar 1939. Sunk at 1430hrs on 13 Apr
1940 west of Narvik, position 68° 24.5N, 17° 39E, in a
battle with six British destroyers; 83 dead.

Z 13 (*Erich Koellner*) *61/83†* launched 18 Mar 1937,
commissioned 28 Aug 1939. Sunk 13 Apr 1940 at
Ofotfjord in the vicinity of Djupviken, position 68°
24N, 16° 48E, in a battle with British destroyers; 31
dead. Raising was begun in 1963 prior to breaking up.

Z 14 (*Friedrich Ihn*) *32/33†* launched 5 Nov 1935,
commissioned 9 Apr 1938. Taken as a USSR prize 5
Feb 1946; renamed *Pospesnyy*. Broken up about 1961.

Z 15 (*Erich Steinbrinck*) *31/32†* launched 24 Sept
1936, commissioned 8 Jun 1938. Taken as a British
prize 1945; renamed *R 92*, then a USSR prize 2 Jan
1946; renamed *Pylkyy*. Broken up about 1961.

Z 16 (*Friedrich Eckoldt*) *33/31†* launched 21 Mar
1937, commissioned 2 Aug 1938. Sunk at 1155hrs on
31 Dec 1942 in the Barents Sea, position 77° 19N, 30°
47E, by gunfire from the British cruisers *Sheffield* and
Jamaica; destroyed by fire, all crew dead.

† In contrast to all other ships in the Kriegsmarine, these tactical
identification numbers were not a substitute for ship names; after 7
Nov 1939 they were removed from the ships' sides.

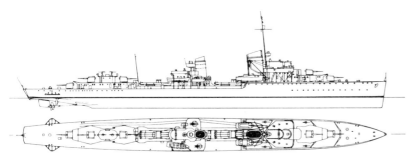

Z 2 bow, mid-1938. *Mrva*

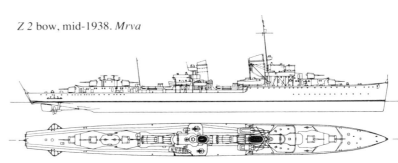

Z 1–4 (1937) at commissioning. *Mrva*

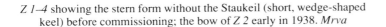

Z 1–4 showing the stern form without the Staukeil (short, wedge-shaped
keel) before commissioning; the bow of *Z 2* early in 1938. *Mrva*

Z 1–4 (1938) after conversion work to the bow and bridge. *Mrva*

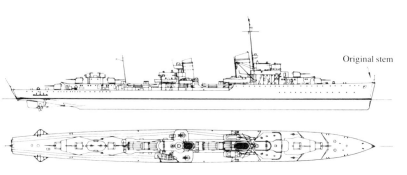

Z 5–8 (1938); Z 5–7 initially had a rounded bridge as on Z 1–4. *Mrva*

Z 9–13 (1938–39). *Mrva*

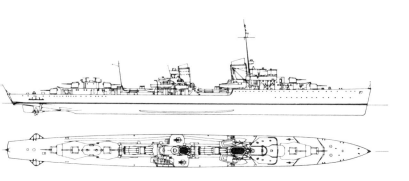

Z 14–16 (1938). *Mrva*

Z 4 (1942). *Mrva*

Z 16 (1942); Z 5–8, 10, 14 and 15 were similar. *Mrva*

Z 15 (1943); Z 5, 6 and 10–14 were similar. *Mrva*

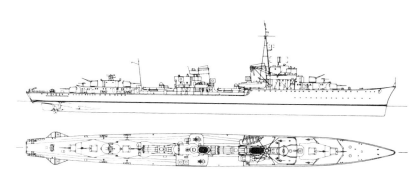

Z 4 (February 1945). *Mrva*

Z 5 (1945) with a gate mast. *Mrva*

Z 6 (1945). *Mrva*

Z 10 (1945) with a gate mast. *Mrva*

Z 17 class

Name	Builder	Built	Cost in Marks (000s)	Displacement (t = tonnes T = tons)	Length (m)	Breadth (m)	Draught (m)	Power (hp)	Revs (rpm)	Speed (kts)	Range (nm/kts)	Coal (t)	Oil (t)
Z 17, Z 18	Deschimag, Bremen Construction nos 919–920	1936–38	77,248*	3415T max 2806t des 2411T std	123.4 oa mod 123.0 oa 120.0 cwl	11.8	4.50 max 3.77 des 2.90 std	70,000shp max** 70,000shp des	427 des	28.5 max 36.0 des	2050/19	—	739 max 310 des
Z 19, Z 20–22	Deschimag, Bremen Construction nos 921–924	1936-39	,,	,,	125.1 oa 121.0 oa mod 120.6 cwl mod	,,	,,	,,	,,	,,	,,	—	,,

* cost of complete series

** *Z 17*: 74,482shp, 40.45kts

Construction

Laid down as 1936 destroyers (official design, 1936). Longitudinal frame longitudinal stringer construction as for *Z 1–16*, but with significant improvements compared with the 1934 destroyers including lower drag, adequate stability (and no consequent restrictions on fuel consumption) and better seakeeping. Official standard displacement 1811 tons. Depth 6.60m.

Propulsion

Two sets of Wagner turbines with gear transmission (two 3-bladed screws, 3.25m diameter) in 1 + 0 + 1 engine rooms, starboard engine in forward room. Six Wagner double-ended boilers (70 atmospheres forced, 450°, 2824sq m) in 1 + 0 + 1 boiler rooms (see *Z 1–16*). Three electricity plants with two 200kW turbo-generators, two 80kW diesel generators and one 40kW, total output 600kW at 220V. One balanced rudder.

Armament

Five 12.7cm/45 QF guns (600 rounds), +30° –10°, range 17,400m; four 3.7cm AA guns (8000 rounds); six [later nine] 2cm AA guns (12,000 [18,000] rounds); eight 53.3cm TT (16 rounds), in quadruple deck-mounted tubes; 60 mines.

Handling

Improved seakeeping, turning circle slightly better than for *Z 1–16* due to the altered position of the screws (closer to midships); nevertheless, this class remained difficult to control in a following sea, and all ships were still very crank. Metacentric height fully loaded 0.95m, with half load 0.81m.

Complement

Crew: 10/313. Boats: two motor pinnaces, two torpedo cutters.

Notes

Colour scheme no 9 and camouflage. [A bow spar system was installed in 1939. Initially all ships had an active roll damping system, later replaced by roll keels. *Z 20* only (for further testing) was fitted with an improved 3-circuit system. Differences include a curved bow shape after *Z 20–Z 20*; angled struts on the forward mast 1942–44; a FuMO 24 6m radar antenna on the bridge house; a FuMO 63 Hohentwiel K radar behind the after funnel; and a degaussing coil under the sheer strakes of the main and forecastle decks.]

Career

Z 17 (*Diether von Roeder*) 51* launched 19 Aug 1937, commissioned 29 Aug 1938. Scuttled and sunk 13 Apr 1940 at the Narvik Postpier, position 68° 25N, 17° 34E, after action against British destroyers; 16 dead.

Z 18 (*Hans Lüdemann*) 53* launched 1 Dec 1937, commissioned 8 Dec 1938. Scuttled and sunk 13 Apr 1940 at Rombaksbotten, position 68° 25N, 17° 54E, undamaged but with fuel oil and ammunition exhausted after action; 2 dead.

Z 19 (*Hermann Künne*) 52* launched 22 Dec 1937, commissioned 12 Jan 1939. Scuttled and sunk 13 Apr 1940 at Herjangsford, position 68° 31N, 17° 35E, undamaged but with fuel oil and ammunition exhausted

* Tactical identification number.

after action; no of dead unknown. Breaking up begun by Eisen & Metall 1941.

Z 20 (*Karl Galster*) 42* launched 15 Jun 1938, commissioned 21 Mar 1939. Taken as a USSR prize February 1946; renamed *Procnyy*; broken up about 1961.

Z 21 (*Wilhelm Heidkamp*) 43* launched 20 Aug 1938, commissioned 10 Jun 1939. Broken in two by a torpedo 10 Apr 1940 during a battle with British destroyers in Narvik bay, position 68° 25N, 17° 24E; the stern sank at 0530hrs on 10 April and the bow at 0610hrs on 11 April; 83 dead.

Z 22 (*Anton Schmitt*) 41* launched 20 Sept 1938, commissioned 24 Sept 1939. Sunk at 0535hrs on 10 Apr 1940 at Narvik bay, position 68° 25N, 17° 24E, by two torpedoes, during action against British destroyers; 52 dead.

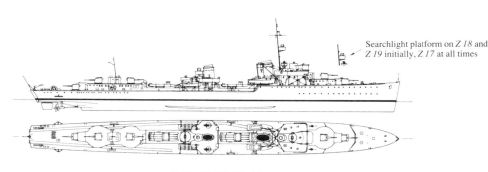

Searchlight platform on *Z 18* and *Z 19* initially, *Z 17* at all times

Z 17–19 (1940). *Mrva*

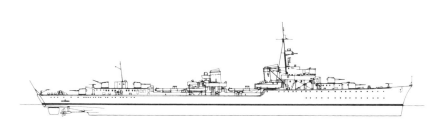

Z 20 (summer 1940). *Mrva*

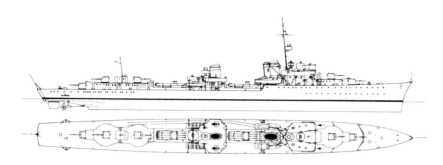

Z 21 and *Z 22* bridge

Z 20–22 (1940); *Z 21* and *22* were later fitted with roll keels. *Mrva*

Z 20 (1942). *Mrva*

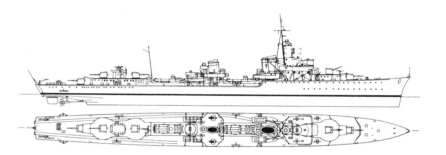

Z 20 (1945). *Mrva*

Z 23 class

Construction

Z 23–30 were laid down as 1936 A destroyers, *Z 31–34, 37–42* as 1936 A (Mob) destroyers, *Z 35–36* and *43–45* as 1936 B (Mob) destroyers and *Z 46–50* as 1936 C destroyers (improved official design, 1936). Longitudinal frame stringer construction, partially light alloy (sixteen watertight compartments, double bottom 47 percent, under midship section). Extended dead-wood aft. Bow bulge [later reduced or completely removed]. Bar hawses (see drawings). Depth: *Z 23–45*, 6.60m; *Z 46–50*, 6.65m.

Propulsion

Turbines and boilers as in *Z 17–22*, but *Z 31–36* and *43–50* had an improved Wagner-Deschimag engine installation; all ships had reconnaissance cruiser turbines (two 3-bladed screws, 3.35m diameter, but 3.22m in *Z 23*, 3.20m in *Z 24* and 3.30m in *Z 32–34* and *37–39*). One electricity plant with one 200kW turbo-generator and four 80kW diesel generators with a total output of 520kW at 220V. Two balanced rudders.

Armament

The armament demanded by the Fleet Command for the 1936 A destroyers, including 15cm guns, was judged too heavy and awkward in practice; thus the 1936 B destroyers were fitted with 12.7cm guns. For the 1936 C destroyers a newly developed 12.8cm double turret was planned.

1936 A Destroyers Armament when commissioned included four 15cm/48 torpedo guns (480 rounds), +48° –19°, range 23,500m; four 3.7cm AA guns (8000 rounds); five (six in *Z 28*, seven in *Z 29*) 2cm AA guns (10,000–14,000 rounds). [After 1942–43 *Z 23, 24* and

25 had two torpedo guns (in a turret) and three 15cm/48 torpedo guns (600 rounds); four 3.7cm AA guns (8000 rounds); twelve (sixteen in *Z 24*) 2cm AA guns (24,000–32,000 rounds). Operation Barbara armament, fitted 1944–45, (involving AA reinforcement) was as follows: *Z 25* and *Z 29*, two torpedo guns (in a turret), three 15cm/48 torpedo guns, ten (eleven in *Z 29*) 3.7cm AA guns and seventeen (twenty-nine in *Z 29*) 2cm AA guns; *Z 28* and *Z 30*, four 15cm/48 torpedo guns, ten (seven in *Z 30*) 3.7cm AA guns, and ten (fourteen in *Z 30*) 2cm AA guns.]

1936 A (Mob) Destroyers Two torpedo guns (in a turret) and three 15cm/48 torpedo guns (600 rounds); four 3.7cm AA guns (8000 rounds); ten 2cm AA guns (20,000 rounds); *Z 31* had only four 15cm/48 torpedo guns at first. [1945 armament was as follows: *Z 31*, three 15cm/48 torpedo guns, one 10.5cm/45 QF gun (200 rounds), +47° –19°, range 17,000m, fourteen 3.7cm AA guns and ten 2cm AA guns. *Z 33*, two torpedo guns (in a turret) and two 15cm/48 torpedo guns, six 3.7cm AA guns, and sixteen 2cm AA guns. *Z 34*, two torpedo guns (in a turret) and three 15cm/48 torpedo guns, six 3.7cm AA guns, eighteen 2cm AA guns and two 8.6cm RaG (rocket launchers).]

1936 B (Mob) Destroyers Five 12.7cm/45 QF guns (600 rounds), +30° –10°, range 17,400m; four 3.7cm AA guns (8000 rounds); fourteen to sixteen 2cm AA guns (14,000–16,000 rounds).

1936 C Destroyers (planned) Six 12.8cm/45 QF guns (720 rounds) +40° –10°, range 19,000m; four to six 3.7cm AA guns (8000–12,000 rounds); eight to fourteen 2cm AA guns (16,000–28,000 rounds).

All destroyers 1936 A to C had eight 53.3cm TT (8–12 rounds), in quadruple deck-mounted tubes; sixty

mines (Destroyers 1936 B had 32–36 mines); four depth charge launchers.

Handling

Relatively good sea-boats for their size, but with weather helm at low speed; somewhat crank. The sea-keeping of the type 1936 A, with approx 65t extra weight (because of their 15cm turret armament), was worse than the others, immersion was increased by 15cm at all loadings, and max speed was 32.8kts. All types were moderately handy. The arrangement of two rudders in the screw slipstream resulted in a marked improvement in turning capabilities, and the deadwood was extended aft to increase directional stability. An improved arrangement of oil cells and the lower positioning of the water cells improved stability and the restrictions on fuel oil consumption could be lifted. The sharply raked bow frames, compared with earlier destroyer types, gave no improvement in seakeeping. All vessels were fitted with roll keels. Metacentric height 0.88/0.78/0.83m. Maximum stability moment at 45° = 0 at >90°.

Complement

Crew: 11/321 [15/305]; *Z 31–34* and *46–50* /320 (other details unknown); *Z 28* 12/315 (plus 12 as a flotilla flagship). Boats: one motor pinnace, one motor yawl, one torpedo cutter, one dinghy.

Notes

Colour scheme no 9; later units were dark grey or light grey overall with camouflage; some units had black funnel caps for a time. [The bow spar on some units (*Z 25* and *Z 28*) was removed later, *Z 25* had a modi-

Name	Builder	Built	Cost in Marks (000s)	Displacement (t = tonnes T = tons)	Length (m)	Breadth (m)	Draught (m)	Power (hp)	Revs (rpm)	Speed (kts)	Range (nm/kts)	Coal (t)	Oil (t)
Z 23, Z 24	Deschimag, Bremen Construction nos 957–958	1938–40	13,175 each	3605T max 2603T des	127.0 oa 121.9 cwl	12.0	4.65 max 3.92 des	70,000shp des	390 des	37.5 max 36.0 des	2500/19	—	791 max 308 des
Z 25–27	Deschimag, Bremen Construction nos 959–961	1939–41	,,	3543T max 3079t des 2543T std	,,	,,	4.43 max 3.91 des	,,	,,	36.0 des	,,	—	,,
Z 28	Deschimag, Bremen Construction no 962	,,	13,106	3519T max 2596T des	,,	,,	4.38 max 3.72 des	,,	,,	,,	2900/19	—	804 max 321 des
Z 29, Z 30 Z 31, Z 32 Z 33, Z 34	Deschimag, Bremen Construction nos 963–964, 1001–1004	,, 1939–42 1940–42	,,	3691T max 3083t des 2657T std	,,	,,	4.62 max 3.92 des	71,915shp max 70,000shp des	388 max 390 des	36.1 max 36.0 des	2950/19	—	825 max 318 des
Z 35, Z 36	Deschimag, Bremen Construction nos 1005–1006	1941–43		3542T max 2954t des 2519T std	,,	,,	4.32 max 3.83 des 3.54 std	71,510shp max 70,000shp des	390 max 390 des	36.5 max 36.0 des	2600/19	—	835 max 341 des
Z 37, Z 38 Z 39 Z 40-42	Germania Dockyard, Kiel Construction nos 627–629, 642–644	1940–42 1940–43 —		3691T max 3083t des 2657T std	,,	,,	4.62 max 3.92 des	75,638shp max 70,000shp des	391 max 390 des	35.5 max 36.0 des	2950/19	—	825 max 318 des
Z 43 Z 44, Z 45	Deschimag, Bremen Construction nos 1029–1031	1942–44 1942–		3542T max 2954t des 2519T std	,,	,,	4.32 max 3.83 des 3.54 std	70,000shp des	390 des	36.0 des	,,	—	,,
Z 46–50	Deschimag, Bremen Construction nos 1071–1072, 1057–1159	1943–		3683T max 3071t des 2636T std	126.2 oa 121.5 cwl	12.2	4.45 max 3.88 des 3.62 std	,,	,,	37.5 des	2500/19	—	822 max 340 des

fied (rounded) bow shape. A FuMo 24/25 6m radar antenna was installed on *Z 25, 28, 29, 30, 33, 34, 35, 36* and *43*; in 1944–45 a FuMo 63 Hohentwiel K radar was installed in place of searchlights behind the after funnel on *Z 25, 28, 29, 30, 31, 33* and *34*.] There were some differences between the production series in respect of tripod masts and funnel caps (see the drawings); *Z 25, 28* and others had one extra degaussing coil forward on the bow temporarily, *Z 39* at all times and *Z 38* in her final form only. *Z 39* had a degaussing coil full-length in the main deck region, covered by a spray deflector strake forward. *Z 30* had a gangway over the forward *TT* set until 1943. *Z 28*'s after mast was initially at the after end of the deckhouse. These vessels were nicknamed *Schreibstubenzerstörer* – office destroyers – a reference to the staff office on the deckhouse.

Career

Z 23 launched 15 Dec 1939, commissioned 15 Sept 1940. Scuttled and sunk at 0930hrs on 21 Aug 1944 at La Pallice, position 46° 10N, 01° 12W, after being bombed by British aircraft; raised 1945; named *Leopard* by the French; not repaired. Stricken 7 Oct 1951; cannibalised.

Z 24 launched 7 Mar 1940, commissioned 26 Oct 1940. Sunk 25 Aug 1944 at Le Verdon roads, position 45° 31N, 01° 06W, by a British aircraft bomb; broken up 1946.

Z 25 launched 16 Mar 1940, commissioned 30 Nov 1940; taken as a British prize 6 Jan 1946; transferred to France February 1946; renamed *Hoche*. Stricken 2 Jan 1958 as *Q 102*; broken up.

Z 26 launched 2 Apr 1940, commissioned 11 Jan 1941. Sunk at about 1020hrs on 29 Mar 1942 in the North Sea north of Murmansk, position 72° 07N, 32° 15E, in battle with the British cruiser *Trinidad* and the destroyers *Fury* and *Eclipse*; 243 dead.

Z 27 launched 1 Aug 1940, commissioned 26 Feb 1941. Sunk together with *T 25* and *T 26* at 1625hrs on 28 Dec 1943 in the Bay of Biscay (position unknown) in battle with the British cruisers *Glasgow* and *Enterprise*; 220 dead.

Z 28 launched 20 Aug 1940, commissioned 9 Aug 1941. Sunk at 2300hrs on 6 Mar 1945 in the vicinity of Sassnitz roads, position 54° 30N, 19° 40E, by a British aircraft bomb; 150 dead. The wreck was broken up later.

Z 29 launched 15 Oct 1940, commissioned 25 Jun 1941; taken as a USA prize 1945; cannibalised at Bremerhaven. Scuttled 16 Dec 1946 in the Skagerrak (with *Leipzig*, see page 123).

Z 30 launched 8 Dec 1940, commissioned 15 Nov 1941; taken as a British prize 1945; used finally in underwater explosives experiments.

Z 31 launched 15 Apr 1941, commissioned 11 Apr 1942; taken as a British prize 20 Dec 1945; transferred to France February 1946; renamed *Marceau*. Stricken 2 Jan 1958 as *Q 103*; broken up.

Z 32 launched 15 Aug 1941, commissioned 15 Sept 1942. Sunk at 0520hrs on 9 Jun 1944 north of the Ile de Batz, position 48° 47N, 04° 07W; 26 dead (see *ZH 1*, page 212).

Z 33 launched 15 Sept 1941, commissioned 6 Feb 1943; taken as a USSR prize February 1946; renamed *Provornyy*. Broken up in about 1964.

Z 34 launched 5 May 1942, commissioned 5 Jun 1943; taken as a USA prize 1945. Scuttled and sunk 26 Mar 1946 in the Skagerrak.

Z 35 launched 2 Oct 1942, commissioned 22 Sept 1943. Sunk at 0151hrs on 12 Dec 1944 north-northeast of Reval, position 59° 34N, 24° 49E, by two mines in a German Nashorn barrage, followed by a boiler and munitions explosion.

Z 36 launched 15 May 1943, commissioned 19 Feb 1944. Sunk at 0215hrs on 12 Dec 1944 north-northeast of Reval, position 59° 37N, 24° 51E, by a mine in a German Nashorn barrage, followed by a boiler and munitions explosion.

Z 37 launched 24 Feb 1941, commissioned 16 Jul 1942; damaged in a collision with *Z 32* in the vicinity of Bilbao 30 Jan 1944; towed in, defunct. Scuttled and sunk 24 Aug 1944 in the Bordeaux docks, position 44° 50N, 00° 34W; broken up 1949.

Z 38 launched 5 Aug 1941, commissioned 20 Mar 1943; taken as a British prize 22 Sept 1945; renamed *Nonsuch*; used in experiments. Broken up 1949.

Z 39 launched 2 Dec 1941, commissioned 21 Aug 1943; taken as a USA prize July 1945; renamed *DD 939*; used for materials experiments; transferred from Annapolis to France late 1947; used as replacement parts reserve for French prize destroyers 1951. Stricken 1953 as *Q 128* 1954; used as a pontoon 1958, broken up February 1964.

Z 40–42 Mob construction contracts were granted in September 1939 to the Germania dockyard at Kiel but cancelled 14 Mar 1940; new contracts were granted for the reconnaissance cruisers *SP 1–3* in their place in January 1941.

Z 43 launched September 1943, commissioned 31 May 1944. Scuttled and sunk on 3 May 1945 in Geltinger bay, position 54° 48N, 09° 47E, after mine and aircraft bomb hits; broken up 1953.

Z 44 launched 20 Jan 1944 before commissioning. Sunk 29 Jul 1944 at a fitting-out wharf in the dockyard by British aircraft bombs; broken up April 1948 to February 1949.

Z 45 launched 1944, not completed. Broken up in the dockyard in 1946.

Z 46, 47 contract granted 8 Oct 1941; work halted 1942; construction begun again in 1943; damage by aircraft bombs, delays in material supplies, shortage of copper and other problems resulted in slow progress. Vessels were broken up after 1945.

Z 48–50 contracted 12 Jun 1943, construction not begun; fate as for *Z 46*.

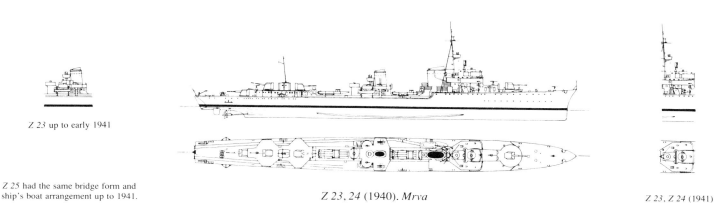

Z 23 up to early 1941

Z 25 had the same bridge form and ship's boat arrangement up to 1941.

Z 23, 24 (1940). *Mrva*

Z 23, Z 24 (1941)

Z 25 screw guard

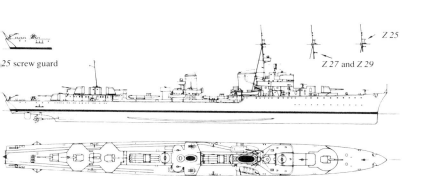

Z 25
Z 27 and Z 29

Z 25–27 (1941–42); Z 24 was similar, but her boat arrangement remained as in 1940. *Mrva*

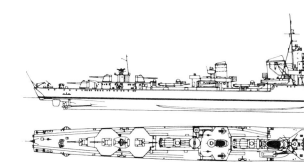

Z 31 (1941–42). *Mrva*

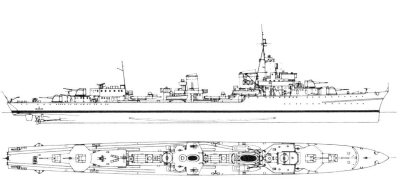

Z 28 (1941). *Mrva*

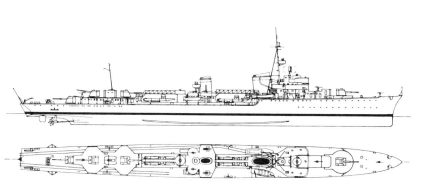

Z 30 (1941–43). *Mrva*

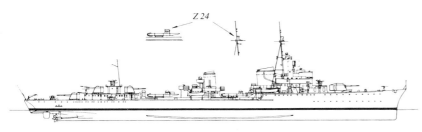

Z 23, 24 1942). *Mrva*

Z 32–34 (1943), *Z 31* after January 1944; the supplementary
drawing shows *Z 32* (1942); *Z 23* and *37* were similar. *Mrva*

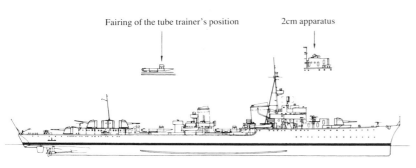

Z 25–27, 29 (1942). *Mrva*

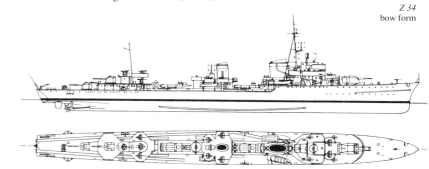

Z 25 (1944–45). *Mrva*

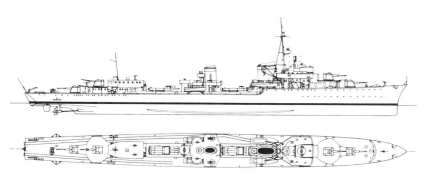

Z 28 (1943). *Mrva*

Z 34 (1944–45). *Mrva*

Z 24 (1944). *Mrva*

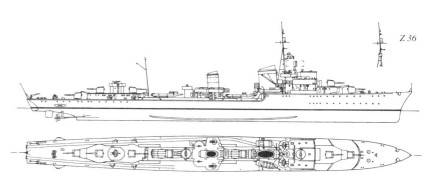

Z 35–36 (1944). *Mrva*

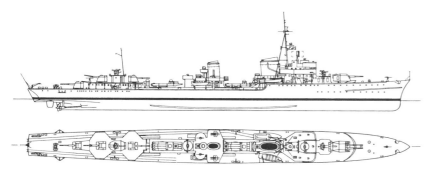

Z 25 (1944). *Mrva*

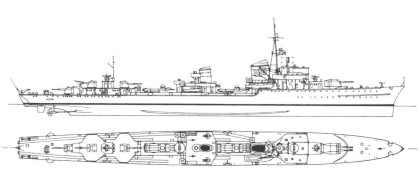

Z 37 (1944); initially she was not fitted with the spray deflector
strake, and the forward turret was 0.7m higher. *Mrva*

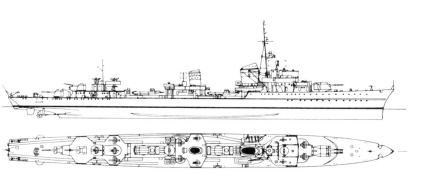

Z 39 (1944). *Mrva*

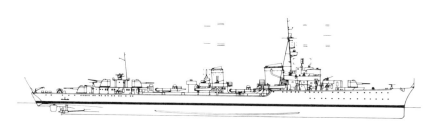

Z 30 (1945). *Mrva*

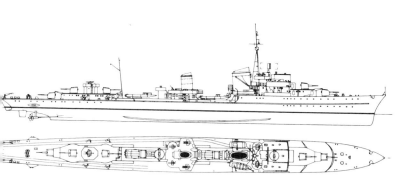

Z 43 (1944). *Mrva*

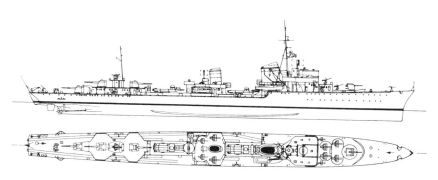

Z 31 (1945). *Mrva*

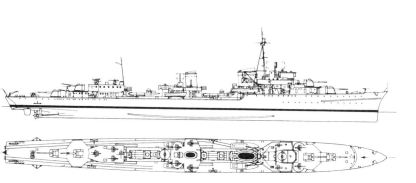

Z 28 (1945). *Mrva*

Platform for planned AA
weapons reinforcement

Z 33 (1945). *Mrva*

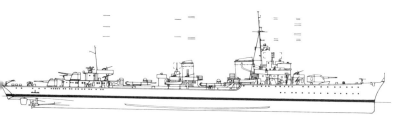

Z 29 (1945). *Mrva*

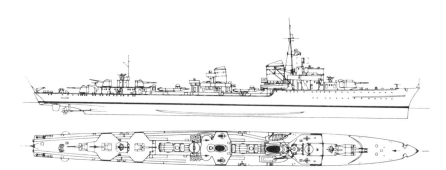

Z 38 (1945); initially she was not fitted with the spray deflector strake. *Mrva*

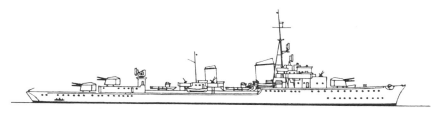

Z 46–50 (as planned)

Z 31 class

Name	Builder	Built	Cost in Marks (000s)	Displacement (t = tonnes T = tons)	Length (m)	Breadth (m)	Draught (m)	Power (hp)	Revs (rpm)	Speed (kts)	Range (nm/kts)	Coal (t)	Oil (t)
Z 31–36	Deschimag, Bremen Construction nos 663–668	—		2747T max 2200t des 1969T std	111.7 oa 108.0 cwl	11.3	4.03 max 3.40 des 3.19 std	50,000shp des	390	36.0 des	3350/19	—	594 max 152 des
Z 37–42	Stettiner Oldewerke Construction nos 822–827	—		,,	,,	,,	,,	,,	,,	,,	,,	,,	,,

Construction
Designed as 1938 B destroyers (official design, 1938). Transverse frame longitudinal stringer construction in steel 52; superstructure partly in light alloy (thirteen watertight compartments, double bottom 77 percent); flush deck vessels; no roll damping. Depth 6.75m.

Propulsion
Two power plants, the starboard installation forward, each with one set of Wagner turbines with geared transmission (two 3-bladed screws, 2.8m diameter) in an engine room directly aft of a boiler room with two Wagner boilers (70 atmospheres forced, 450°). Two 500kW electricity plants. One rudder.

Armament
Four 12.7cm/45 QF guns (480 rounds); two 3.7cm AA guns (2000 rounds); two 2cm AA guns (4000 rounds; eight 53.3cm TT (no of rounds unknown) in quadruple deck-mounted tubes; no of mines unknown.

Complement
Crew: 8/231. Boats: one motor pinnace, one torpedo cutter.

Career
On the outbreak of war the contracts for *Z 37–42* granted on 28 Jun 1939 to Deschimag and 21 Jul 1939 to Oderwerke were suspended; the type was replaced by a larger Destroyers 1936 A (Mob).

1937 destroyer projects

Name	Builder	Built	Cost in Marks (000s)	Displacement (t = tonnes T = tons)	Length (m)	Breadth (m)	Draught (m)	Power (hp)	Revs (rpm)	Speed (kts)	Range (nm/kts)	Coal (t)	Oil (t)
Destroyer 1937–J_1	Project	—	—	4984T max 4427t des 3776T std	137.25 oa	14.20	4.34 des	90,360shp		36	4450/19	—	1052 max 501 des
Destroyer 1937–I	Project	—	—	4522t des						37.9		—	
Destroyer 1937–II	Project	—	—	4797t des						35.3		—	
Destroyer 1937–III	Project	—	—	5449T max 4720t des 4167T std	140.0 cwl	14.5	4.64 des	90,360shp		,,	4420/19	—	1127 max 396 des
Destroyer 1937–IV	Project	—	—	,,	,,	,,	,,	,,		,,	,,	—	,,

Construction
Originated as a series of destroyer designs in 1937 for ocean-going escorts, capable of service in tropical conditions and for convoy attack and defence in the Atlantic (similar to the French flotilla leaders); planned as replacements for Destroyers 1936/1936 A. Depth: J_1 7.60m, IV 7.90m.

Propulsion
Electricity plants were as follows: J_1, 760kW; IV, 940kW.

Armament
J_1 and I, five 15cm QF guns, one 10.5cm AA gun, four 3.7cm AA guns, eight 53.3cm TT in two double sets and one quadruple set of deck tubes; II, III and IV, six 15cm QF guns, one 10.5cm AA gun, four 3.7cm AA guns, eight 53.3cm TT in two quadruple sets of deck tubes.

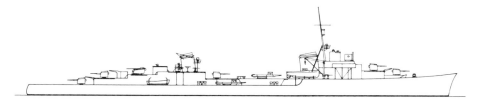

Destroyer 1937-J_1 (1937 project). *Mrva*

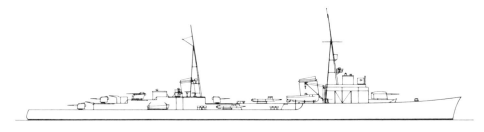

Destroyer 1937-I (1937 project). *Mrva*

Complement

Crew: J_1, 360; IV, 360.

Career

The April 1938 design was unsatisfactory because the vessels were slower than all French light cruisers and their range was too restricted, even though they were almost of cruiser size. No further development of this design series was undertaken; a fresh start was made in June 1938 with two new series: the Destroyer 1938 A long- range Atlantic destroyers, and the Destroyer 1938 B small destroyers for home use (in the North Sea and Baltic).

1938–39 destroyer projects

Name	Builder	Built	Cost in Marks (000s)	Displacement (t = tonnes T = tons)	Length (m)	Breadth (m)	Draught (m)	Power (hp)	Revs (rpm)	Speed (kts)	Range (nm/kts)	Coal (t)	Oil (t)
Destroyer 1938 Ac	Project	—	—	4902T max 3914T std	144.5 oa 138.0 cwl	13.9	4.35 des	75,000shp + 12,450 shp		37.5 20.0	8000/17	—	860 max 330 des
Destroyer 1938 Ad	Project	—	—	4638t des 4205T std	140.0 cwl	14.1	4.48 des	73,000shp + 14,500shp		35.5	,,	—	800 max
SP 1–3	Germania Dockyard, Kiel	1941–		5900T max 5037t des 4589T std	152.2 oa 145.0 cwl	14.6	4.6 des	77,500shp + 14,500shp	,,	,,		—	820 max
Reconnaissance cruiser 1939	Project	—	—	7550T max 6300t des 5810T std	169.0 oa 162.0 cwl	16.0	4.9 des	80,000shp + 32,000shp		35.0	7000/17	—	800 max
Reconnaissance cruiser 1940	Project	—	—	7500T max 6500t des 5800T std	,,	,,	,,	110,000 shp		36.0		—	,,

Construction

Designed as 1938 A destroyers (official design, 1938). Transverse frame longitudinal stringer construction in steel 52, splinter-proof longitudinal bulkheads and deck around the machinery compartment and magazines, and on the bridge and directors. After March 1940 the design was expanded to following types *Spähkreuzer* (reconnaissance cruisers) 1938–40 (1938 design by Blohm & Voss and 1939–1940 official designs). Superstructure partly in light alloy (seventeen watertight compartments, double bottom 81 percent). Light armour (Wh): deck 10mm, slopes 12mm; upper deck 15mm; funnel throats 10mm; bridge forward and aft roof 15mm, sides 10mm; turrets roof 20mm, face 30mm, sides 20mm; substructure and magazines 15mm, slopes 12mm; (Ww): torpedo bulkhead 15mm, slopes 12mm. The official designs for reconnaissance cruisers included CWL armour. All designs had active roll damping. Depth: 1938 A destroyers, 7.60m; reconnaissance cruisers, 9.90m.

Propulsion

Three power plants comprising one geared turbine for each of the two outer shafts and four diesel engines for the central shaft. The reconnaissance cruiser version had the starboard turbine installation forward, each power plant with one set of Wagner turbines with gear transmission (two 3-bladed screws, 4.25m diameter) in an engine room directly abaft the boiler room with two Wagner boilers (70 atmospheres forced, 450°); the diesel engines were four MAN double-acting 6-cylinder 2-stroke diesels with one Vulcan gearbox on the central shaft (one 3-bladed screw, 3.25m diameter) in 1 + 1 engine rooms forward of the forward funnel. Four electricity plants, 880kW at 220V. One balanced rudder with a skeg each side of the central screw.

Armament

1938 destroyer six 15cm/48 torpedo guns (720 rounds) +47° –19°, range 23,500m; two 8.8cm AA guns (580 rounds); two 3.7cm AA guns (8000 rounds); eight 2cm AA guns (32,000 rounds); ten 53.3cm TT (10 rounds) in quintuple deck tubes; 100 mines.

Reconnaissance cruisers six 15cm/48 torpedo guns (720 rounds); two to four 8.8cm AA guns (580–1160 rounds); eight 3.7cm AA guns (8000 rounds); twelve 2cm AA guns (24,000 rounds); ten 53.3cm TT (10 rounds) in quintuple deck tubes; 50 mines; one seaplane.

Destroyer 1938 Ac (1938 design)

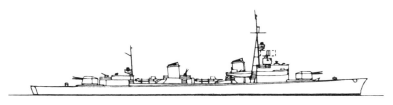

Destroyer 1938 B (*Z 31–42*) (1938 design)

Complement

Crew: Ac 13/335; Ad 13/335; reconnaissance cruisers 18/520. Boats: two motor pinnaces, two torpedo cutters; the reconnaissance cruisers had one additional dinghy.

Notes

Note that all designs retained the basic destroyer form despite the increase in size up to cruiser dimensions.

Career

The official designation for the 1938 destroyers planned by the Naval Command Office in July 1939 was *N* plus the running number, ie no Z numbers.

Contracts for the first 1938 reconnaissance cruisers were granted to the dockyard to take up the vacant capacity after the cancellation of *Z 40–42* (type 1936 B Mob) on 17 Feb 1941. The designations *SP 1–3* were applied after December 1941 in place of the previous designations *Z 40–42* initially carried over for the reconnaisance cruisers. In early 1941 construction was delayed through the destruction of design documents in an air attack. Construction work on *SP 1* was halted in mid-1942; she was broken up in 1943.

Contracts for the main turbines for *SP 4–6* were granted in December 1941. Further development work on the official 1939/40 designs halted in August 1940 as ships of this size (*M* cruisers) already existed.

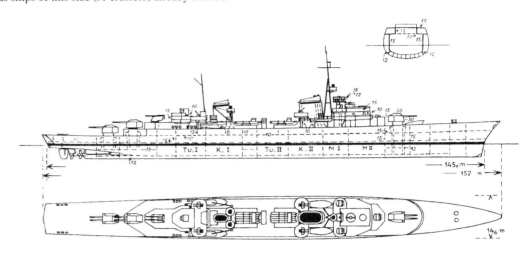

SP 1–3 (1940–41 design)

Z 51

Name	Builder	Built	Cost in Marks (000s)	Displacement (t = tonnes T = tons)	Length (m)	Breadth (m)	Draught (m)	Power (hp)	Revs (rpm)	Speed (kts)	Range (nm/kts)	Coal (t)	Oil (t)
Z 51	Deschimag, Bremen Construction no 1109	1943–		2720T max 2330t des 2041T std	114.3 oa 108.0 cwl	11.0	4.37 max 3.98 des 3.72 std	57,000ehp		36.0	5500/19	—	553 max 214 des

Construction

Laid down as an experimental type with pure diesel propulsion for the 1944 destroyer design series (official design 1942 destroyer, designated 'fleet torpedo boat 1942' – *T 43–48* – until contracts were granted on 25 Nov 1942 together with *Z 52–56*). Longitudinal frame longitudinal stringer construction in steel 52 (fifteen watertight compartments, double bottom approx 40 percent extended up to CWL). Active roll damping. Freeboard 6.50m.

Propulsion

Six MAN double-acting 2-stroke diesel engines, initially without supercharging, on three shafts (three 3-bladed screws, diameter unknown) arranged as follows: each outer shaft was coupled to one 5620shp diesel engine (direct), both diesels accommodated together in one engine room under the after TT position. On the central shaft four MAN 24-cylinder V

diesels were arranged in pairs, with a Vulcan transmission in between, in 1 + (1) + 1 engine and (transmission) rooms, each engine 11,650shp. Electricity plant unknown. Three rudders in the screw slipstream.

Armament

Four 12.7cm/45 QF guns (720 rounds) +30° –10°, range 17,400m; eight 3.7cm AA guns (16,000 rounds); twelve 2cm AA guns (24,000 rounds); six 53.3cm TT (18 rounds) in triple deck tubes; 50 mines.

Complement

Crew: 12/235. Boats: one motor pinnace, one torpedo cutter.

Career

Z 51 construction not completed; severely damaged 21 Mar 1945 at the Bremen industrial harbour by an aircraft bomb; broken up December 1947 to February 1949.

Z 51 (as planned)

Z 52 class

Construction

1944 destroyer design, designated 1942 A destroyer until September 1943, then 1942 B destroyer until February 1944 (official design) intended for escorting battle groups in Atlantic actions; fitted with newly developed engines as standard, in an effort to achieve the maximum possible range. Longitudinal frame longitudinal stringer construction in steel 52 (fourteen watertight compartments, double bottom approx 57

Name	Builder	Built	Cost in Marks (000s)	Displacement (t = tonnes T = tons)	Length (m)	Breadth (m)	Draught (m)	Power (hp)	Revs (rpm)	Speed (kts)	Range (nm/kts)	Coal (t)	Oil (t)
Z 52–56	Deschimag, Bremen Construction nos 1110–1114	1943–		3703T max 3170t des 2818T std	132.1 oa 126.0 cwl	12.6	4.92 max 4.14 des	76,000shp		37.5 des des	6800/19	—	640 max 280 des

percent). Active roll damping. Depth 7.00m.

Propulsion

Eight MAN double-acting 2-stroke diesel engines of the same type as in *Z 51*, acting on two shafts with two Vulcan transmissions (two 3-bladed screws, 3.45m diameter) in 1 + (1) + 1 + 1 + (1) engine and (transmission) rooms, offset to port aft for the port shaft and starboard forward for the starboard shaft, with Vulcan transmissions in each case between two pairs of diesels. Electricity plant unknown. Two rudders.

Armament

Six 12.8cm/45 QF guns (1080 rounds) +40° –10°, range 19,000m; three 5.5cm AA guns (1500 rounds); fourteen 3cm AA guns (28,000 rounds); eight 53.3cm TT (16 rounds) in quadruple deck tubes; 60 mines.

Complement

Crew: 12/308. Boats: two motor pinnaces, one torpedo cutter, one dinghy.

Career

Z 52–56 construction contract granted 1943; construction was halted because of shortage of materials. Cancelled 6 Jul 1944 and later broken up.

Z 52–56 (as planned)

1945 destroyer project

Name	Builder	Built	Cost in Marks (000s)	Displacement (t = tonnes T = tons)	Length (m)	Breadth (m)	Draught (m)	Power (hp)	Revs (rpm)	Speed (kts)	Range (nm/kts)	Coal (t)	Oil (t)
Destroyer 1945	Project	—	—	3700T max 3100t des 2700T std	120.0 oa	12.0	3.88 des	80,000shp		39	8000/19	—	800

Construction

1945 destroyer design (official design based on the 1936 D and E destroyer studies later destroyed by fire). Depth 6.80m.

Propulsion

Two sets of Wagner turbines with transmission (two 3-bladed screws), machinery disposition not known, with four Wagner-Deschimag boilers (70 atmospheres forced, 400°) intended to ensure 80,000shp, and 42.5kts/39.5kts/37kts depending on load. Calculated at 12kg/shp for entire power installation.

Armament

Eight 12.8cm/45 QF guns (1440 rounds); four 5.5cm AA guns (5000 rounds); twelve 3cm AA guns (24,000 rounds); eight 53.3cm TT (16 rounds) in quadruple deck tubes; 100 mines.

Complement

Crew: 350 (other details unknown). Boats: two motor pinnaces, one torpedo cutter, one motor dinghy.

Notes

This design gave 12 percent higher performance than the original design, and more powerful main armament in a shorter hull, all with a lighter machinery installation.

Destroyer 1945 (design). Mrva

Foreign destroyers 1940–1945

ZH 1 class

Name	Builder	Built	Cost in Marks (000s)	Displacement (t = tonnes T = tons)	Length (m)	Breadth (m)	Draught (m)	Power (hp)	Revs (rpm)	Speed (kts)	Range (nm/kts)	Coal (t)	Oil (t)
ZH 1	Rotterdamse Droogdok Mij, Rotterdam Construction no 208 completed by Blohm & Voss, Hamburg	1938–40 1940–42		2228T max 1864t des 1604T std	106.7 oa 105.2 cwl	10.6	3.52 max 3.11 des 2.82 std	49,500shp max 45,000shp des	475 max 470 des	37.5 max 36.0 des	2700/19		520
ZH 2	Rotterdamse Droogdok Mij, Rotterdam Construction no 207	1938–		,,	,,	,,	,,	,,	,,	,,	,,		,,

Construction

Laid down as Dutch torpedo boat hunters of the *Isaac Sweers* type (official Dutch design 1936–37 on an earlier plan by Yarrow). Transverse frame steel construction, welded (eleven watertight compartments, double bottom 43 percent). Depth 6.17m.

Propulsion

Two sets of Werkspoor-Parsons turbines with gear transmission (two 3-bladed screws, 3.25m diameter) in 1 + 1 engine rooms, starboard forward, port aft. Three Yarrow boilers (28 atmospheres forced 350°, size unknown) in 1 + 1 boiler rooms. Electricity plant and total output are unknown. One rudder.

Armament

Five 12cm/45 QF guns (750 rounds); four 3.7cm AA guns (8000 rounds); eight 53.3cm TT (8 rounds) in quadruple deck tubes; twenty-four mines; four depth charge launchers (40 rounds).

Handling

Excellent sea-boats, manoeuvrable and with a moderate turning circle; use of the armament was almost impossible above wind Force 9.

Complement

Crew: originally 14/143; German 12/218. Boats: two motor pinnaces, one torpedo cutter.

Notes

Colour scheme no 9. Trials were completed with a simple destroyer mast with a signal cross forward, and a topmast with wireless telegraphy yards on the rear side of the after funnel; a gunnery director with a rangefinder in the form of a round cradle was fitted forward; a flagstaff was fitted on the forward edge of the after searchlight platform.

Career

ZH 1 launched 9 May 1940 as the Dutch *Gerard Callenburgh*. Scuttled 15 May 1940 by her Dutch crew; raised 14 Jul 1940; placed under German command and transferred to Hamburg 11 Oct 1940; completed 5 Oct 1942. Scuttled at 0235hrs on 9 Jun 1944, 20nm northwest of the Ile de Batz, position 48° 55N, 04° 22W, after shell and torpedo hits from the British destroyers *Tartar* and *Ashanti*, together with *Z 32*; 33 dead.

ZH 2 launched 12 Oct 1939 as the Dutch *Tjerk Hiddes*. Scuttled at Nieuwe Waterweg 15 May 1940. Raising and completion as *ZH 2* were planned by the German authorities, but the plan was abandoned in August 1941. Raised 12 Jun 1942, broken up at Hendrik-Ido-Ambadt.

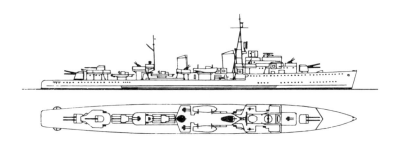

ZH 1 (ex *Gerard Callenburgh*) (1943); ZH 2 (ex *Tjerk Hiddes*) was similar as planned.

ZH 3

Name	Builder	Built	Cost in Marks (000s)	Displacement (t = tonnes T = tons)	Length (m)	Breadth (m)	Draught (m)	Power (hp)	Revs (rpm)	Speed (kts)	Range (nm/kts)	Coal (t)	Oil (t)
ZH 3	Fijenoord, Rotterdam	1927–29		1650T max 1316T des	98.14 oa 93.57 bp	9.53	3.20 max 2.97 des	31,000shp des	—	36 max 32 des	3300/15	—	330

Construction

Laid down as a Dutch torpedo boat hunter of the 'Admiralen' class, 2nd group (official Dutch design based on a Yarrow plan, 1925). Transverse frame steel construction (no of watertight compartments unknown). Depth unknown.

Propulsion

Two sets of Yarrow turbines with transmission (two 3-bladed screws, diameter unknown) in 1 + 1 engine rooms. Three Yarrow 3-drum boilers (17.8 atmospheres forced, temperature and size unknown) in 1 + 1 + 1 boiler rooms. One rudder.

Armament

Four 12cm/45 QF guns (no of rounds unknown); one 7.5cm AA gun (no of rounds unknown); four 1.3cm AA guns (no of rounds unknown); six 53.3cm TT (6 rounds); four depth charge launchers (40 rounds).

Complement

Crew: 149 in total. Boats: one motor pinnace, two cutters.

Notes

Colour scheme no unknown.

Career

ZH 3 launched 28 Jun 1928, commissioned 22 Oct 1929 as the Dutch *Van Galen*. Sunk 10 May 1940 at Rotterdam-Merwehaven by a German aircraft bomb (near miss); it was planned to raise and repair the vessel as *ZH 3* after the completion of *ZH 2*, but the plan was abandoned in August 1941. Raised 24 Oct 1941; broken up at Hendrik-Ido-Ambadt.

ZF 4

Name	Builder	Built	Cost in Marks (000s)	Displacement (t = tonnes T = tons)	Length (m)	Breadth (m)	Draught (m)	Power (hp)	Revs (rpm)	Speed (kts)	Range (nm/kts)	Coal (t)	Oil (t)
ZF 4	F et Chant de la Méditeranée	1923–27		1800T max 1500t des 1319T std	105.77 oa 99.33 cwl	9.64	4.30 max 4.00 des	31,000shp des	—	33 max 29 des	1500/15	—	340

Construction

Laid down as a French 1500t *torpilleur* of the *Bourrasque* class, 1922 series (official French design 1920–21). Transverse frame steel construction (no of watertight compartments unknown). Depth 6.32m.

Propulsion

Two sets of Parsons turbines (two screws, diameter unknown) in 1 + 1 engine rooms. Three Du Temple boilers (18 atmospheres forced, 216°, 925sq m) in 1 + 1 + 1 boiler rooms. No of rudders unknown.

Armament

Four 13.0cm QF guns (no of rounds unknown); two 3.7cm AA guns (no of rounds unknown); four machine guns; six 55.0cm TT in triple deck- mounted tubes (no of rounds unknown).

Complement

Crew: (7/131). Boats: one motor pinnace, two cutters.

Notes

Colour scheme unknown.

Career

ZF 4 launched 24 Jan 1925, commissioned 1927 as the French *Cyclone*. Scuttled 18 Jun 1940 at Brest while under repair after a torpedo hit from *S 24*; it was planned to repair the vessel as *ZF 4* in October 1940, but the plan was abandoned in August 1941; broken up.

ZF 5 For a short period in the fourth quarter of 1940, completion of the French torpilleur léger *Le Tunisien* (*Le Fier* class, under construction by Chantiers de la Loire) as *ZF 5* was planned; the vessel was 13 percent complete. The plan was abandoned in December 1940, and the materials were used for the completion of other, further advanced vessels of the class, as *TA 1–6* (see page 220).

ZF 2 class

Construction

Laid down as French 1772t *torpilleurs d'escadre* of the *Le Hardi* class, series 1939–1938b–1936 (official French design 1932, modified 1938–39). Transverse frame steel construction, partially welded (fourteen watertight compartments). Depth 7.00/6.65m.

Propulsion

Two sets of Rateau-Bretagne turbines with gear transmission (two screws, diameter unknown) in 1 + 1 engine rooms, starboard forward, port aft. Four Sural-Panhoet boilers (35 atmospheres forced, 358°, size unknown) in 1 + 1 + 1 + 1 boiler rooms. Electricity plant and total output unknown. No of rudders unknown.

Armament

French design: six 13.0cm AA guns in double shields, of which the two after units were raised (1350 + 60

Name	Builder	Built	Cost in Marks (000s)	Displacement (t = tonnes T = tons)	Length (m)	Breadth (m)	Draught (m)	Power (hp)	Revs (rpm)	Speed (kts)	Range (nm/kts)	Coal (t)	Oil (t)
ZF 2	F et Chant de la Gironde, Bordeaux Construction no 207	1939–		2910T max 2351t des 2070T std	118.8bp	11.9	3.62 des	62,000shp des		36 des	1700/20	—	
ZF 7	F et Chant de la Gironde, Bordeaux Construction no 208	1939–47		,,	,,	,,	,,	,,		,,	,,	—	
TA 34 (II)	F et Chant de la Gironde, Bordeaux Construction no 209	1936–40		2417T max 1982t des 1772T std	117.20 oa 111.59 bp	11.1	4.20 max 2.99 des	66,000shp max 58,000shp des	400 des	38 des	2760/20	—	470

rounds); two 3.7cm AA guns (2960 rounds); two 2.5cm AA guns (no of rounds unknown); eight 1.3cm AA guns (18,000 rounds); seven 55cm TT in triple deck-mounted tubes midships, double deck tubes on each side of the after fidley. [German design: five 12.7cm QF guns (400 rounds); four 3.7cm AA guns (6000 rounds); ten 2cm AA guns (20,000 rounds); eight 53.3cm TT (16 rounds) in quadruple deck-mounted tubes.]

Complement
Crew: 10/235. Boats: two motor pinnaces, one torpedo cutter.

Notes
Colour scheme unknown.

Career
ZF 2 laid down 1 Sept 1939 as the French *L'Opiniatre*; taken as a German prize in June 1940, 16 percent complete. After February 1941 work continued on the vessel as *ZF 6*; after 26 Aug 1941 further construction was undertaken using materials from *ZF 7* and she was renamed *ZF 2*. Stricken in July 1943, be-

fore launching; scuttled during the evacuation of France; broken up after 1945.

ZF 7 laid down 4 Aug 1939 as the French *L'Aventurier*; taken as a German prize in June 1940, 13 percent complete. After February 1941 construction as *ZF 7* continued, but further construction was abandoned in June 1941 in favour of *ZF 6*; construction was resumed 1945–46 for the French Navy, and she was launched 20 Apr 1947 as an experimental hulk; still in existence in 1960 as a floating landing vessel at Brest.

TA 34 (II) launched 20 May 1936, temporarily commissioned 17 Jun 1940 as the French *Lansquenet*; transferred to Casablanca; transferred 8 Nov 1940 with *Provence* to Toulon for further dockyard work. Scuttled 27 Nov 1942 at La Seyne; raised in 1943 by Italy, towed to Imperia for repairs as *F.R. 34*; taken as a German prize 9 Sept 1943; construction continued after June 1944 as *TA 34 (II)*; work was halted 13 Apr 1945, and she was scuttled in May 1945 at Genoa. Raised 19 Mar 1946; towed to Toulon; not repaired; broken up in 1946.

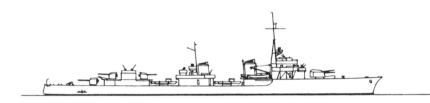

ZF 2, ZF 7 (as planned to German designs); *TA 34 (II)* was similar.

ZG 3/Hermes

Name	Builder	Built	Cost in Marks (000s)	Displacement (t = tonnes T = tons)	Length (m)	Breadth (m)	Draught (m)	Power (hp)	Revs (rpm)	Speed (kts)	Range (nm/kts)	Coal (t)	Oil (t)
ZG 3 (HERMES)	Yarrow & Co, Glasgow mod: Germania Dockyard, Piraeus	1937–39 1941		2088T max 1414T des	101.2 oa 98.5 cwl	10.4	3.23 max 2.34 des	34,000shp des		32.0 des	4800/19		465

Construction
Laid down as a Greek destroyer of the *Vasileus Georgios* class (British design, Admiralty *H* class 1934–35, Yarrow type). Transverse frame steel construction (nine watertight compartments, double bottom approx 30 percent). Depth unknown.

Propulsion
Two sets of Parsons turbines with gear transmission (two 3-bladed screws, diameter unknown) in 1 + 1 engine rooms, starboard forward, port aft. Three Yarrow 3-drum boilers (16 atmospheres forced, size unknown) in 1 + 1 + 1 boiler rooms. One rudder.

Armament
Four 12.7cm QF guns (400 rounds); four 3.7cm AA guns (6000 rounds); four 2cm AA guns (12,000 rounds); eight 53.3cm TT (16 rounds) in quadruple deck tubes.

Handling

Excellent sea-boat, with gentle motion; manoeuvrable with a good turning circle. Very wet forward in a head sea.

Complement

Crew: 10/215. Boats: one motor pinnace, two torpedo cutters.

Notes

Colour scheme no 9 and camouflage.

Career

ZG 3 laid down as the Greek *Vasileus Georgios*, launched 3 Mar 1938, commissioned 15 Feb 1939; sunk 20 Apr 1941 in the floating dock at Salamis-Skaramanga by German dive-bombers. After the German occupation of Greece she was raised and repaired at the Germania dockyard, Skaramanga; commissioned 21 Mar 1942; renamed *Hermes* (*ZG 3*) after 22 Aug 1942. Badly damaged 30 Apr 1943 southwest of Trapani, suffering failure of the drive shafts after being struck by an aircraft bomb; 23 dead. She was towed to Tunis, and scuttled at 0925hrs on 7 May 1943 in the entrance to La Goulette, position 36° 46N, 10° 21E, during the evacuation of Tunisia.

ZG 3 (*Hermes*) (1942)

Foreign torpedo boats 1940–1945

ZN 4 class

Name	Builder	Built	Cost in Marks (000s)	Displacement (t = tonnes T = tons)	Length (m)	Breadth (m)	Draught (m)	Power (hp)	Revs (rpm)	Speed (kts)	Range (nm/kts)	Coal (t)	Oil (t)
ZN 4, ZN 5	Marinens Hovedverft, Horten Construction nos 129–130	1939–		1694T max 1478t des 1278T std	100.6 oa 94.5 cwl	10.6	3.20 max 2.70 des	30,000shp des		32.0 des	1375/19		300

Construction

Laid down as the Norwegian *større jagare I* and *II* (official Norwegian design, 1937). Transverse frame steel construction (twelve watertight compartments, double bottom 55 percent). Depth 5.47m.

Propulsion

Two sets of De Laval turbines with gear transmission (two 3-bladed screws, 2.45m diameter) in one engine room. Three Yarrow boilers (32 atmospheres forced, size unknown) in 1 + 1 + 1 boiler rooms. Electrical installation unknown. One rudder.

Armament

Norwegian design: four 12cm QF guns, two of them in a double shield on the forecastle; four 4cm AA guns; four 53cm TT, in double deck tubes midships (type M XV). The German planned armament was three 10.5cm/45 torpedo guns (approx 1800 rounds) +80° –8°; two 3.7cm AA guns (8000 rounds); six 2cm AA guns (12,000 rounds); 53.3cm TT (4 rounds) in quadruple deck tubes.

TA 7–8 (ZN 4–5) (as planned to German designs)

Complement

Crew: 8/154. Boats: one motor yawl, one torpedo cutter, one dinghy.

Career

TA 7 captured on the stocks at Horten state dockyard; after the German occupation of Norway construction continued as *ZN 4* and *5*, after early 1942 as *TA 7* and *8*, but this was seriously delayed through sabotage; still not complete in 1945. *TA 7* launched 29 May 1941; sunk 0518hrs on 27 Sept 1944 at Horten by an explosion (sabotage). *TA 8* launched 30 Jun 1943; sunk 23 Feb 1945 at the fitting out stage by a British aircraft bomb; she was raised in 1945, and it was planned to resume her construction as *Aalesund* for Norway; the plan was subsequently abandoned.

Löwe class

Construction

Laid down as Norwegian *kustjagare* of the six-unit *Sleipner* class (design approx 1935). Transverse and longitudinal frame steel construction (twelve watertight compartments, no double bottom). Depth 4.87m.

Propulsion

Two sets of De Laval turbines with gear transmission (two 3-bladed screws, 1.65m diameter) in 1 + 1 engine rooms (port forward, starboard aft). Three Yarrow boilers (32 atmospheres forced) in 1 + 1 + 1 boiler rooms. One rudder.

Armament

Two 10cm/40 Bofors QF guns (no of rounds unknown); two 2cm AA guns (4000 rounds); two (*Löwe* four) 53.3cm TT (4 rounds); twenty-four mines. [Fitted after January 1941 with one 10.5cm/45 torpedo gun (no of rounds unknown); one 3.7cm AA gun (no of rounds unknown); two (*Panther* four) 2cm AA guns (4000–8000 rounds).]

Complement

Crew: 86–88 in total. Boats: one motor-, one cutter.

Notes

Colour scheme no 9. [In about 1943 a short mast with a wireless telegraphy topmast was fitted aft of the former position of the TT.]

Career

Löwe launched 7 Jul 1938 as the Norwegian *Gyller*; transferred intact 11 Apr 1940 to the Kriegsmarine at

Name	Builder	Built	Cost in Marks (000s)	Displacement (t = tonnes T = tons)	Length (m)	Breadth (m)	Draught (m)	Power (hp)	Revs (rpm)	Speed (kts)	Range (nm/kts)	Coal (t)	Oil (t)
LÖWE, PANTHER	Marinens Hovedverft, Horten Construction nos 125–126	1937–39		708T max 590T des	74.1 oa 72.0 cwl	7.75	2.82 max 2.10 des	12,500shp des		30.0 des	3500/15	—	100 max
LEOPARD, TIGER	Marinens Hovedverft, Horten Construction nos 127–128	1938–40		,,	,,	,,	,,	,,		,,	,,	—	,,

Kristiansand; commissioned 20 Apr 1940 as the German *Löwe*; served as a torpedo recovery boat 1 Jan 1942, in the 27th U-boat flotilla. Returned to Norway 1945 as *Gyller*; refitted as an escort boat 1949. Stricken 1962, broken up.

Panther launched 24 Jan 1939 as the Norwegian *Odin*; transferred intact 11 Apr 1940 to the Kriegsmarine at Kristiansand; commissioned 23 Apr 1940 as the German *Panther*; served as a torpedo recovery boat 1 Jan 1942, in the 27th U-boat flotilla; returned to Norway 1945 as *Odin*; refitted as an escort boat. Stricken 1962, broken up.

Leopard launched 11 Oct 1939 as the Norwegian *Balder*; taken as a German prize incomplete at Horten

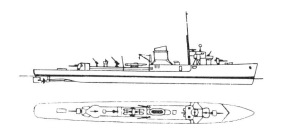

Panther (1940); *Leopard*, *Tiger* and *Löwe* were similar.

April 1940; completed at Drammen after 22 Apr 1940; commissioned 26 Jul 1940 as the German *Leopard*; served as a torpedo recovery boat 1 Jan 1942, in the 27th U-boat flotilla; returned to Norway 1945 as *Balder*; refitted as an escort boat 1949. Stricken 1962, broken up 1962 at Stavanger.

Tiger launched 7 Sept 1939 as the Norwegian *Tor*; scuttled 9 Apr 1940 at Fredrikstad at the fitting out stage; settled in shallow water. Taken as a German prize; raised 16 Apr 1940; repaired at Drammen after 22 Apr 1940; commissioned as the German *Tiger* 13 Jun 1940; served as a torpedo recovery boat 1 Jan 1942, in the 27th U-boat flotilla; returned to Norway 1945; renamed *Tor*; refitted as an escort boat. Stricken 1962, broken up.

Troll

Name	Builder	Built	Cost in Marks (000s)	Displacement (t = tonnes T = tons)	Length (m)	Breadth (m)	Draught (m)	Power (hp)	Revs (rpm)	Speed (kts)	Range (nm/kts)	Coal (t)	Oil (t)
TROLL	Marinens Hovedverft, Horten Construction no 104	1908–10		578t max 468t des	69.0	7.2	2.7 fwd 2.1 aft	8000ihp max 7500ihp des		27 des	2800/10	105	—

Construction
Laid down as a Norwegian *jagare* (navy design, 1906). Transverse frame steel construction (no of watertight compartments unknown). Freeboard unknown.

Propulsion
Two vertical 3-cylinder triple expansion engines (two screws, diameter unknown) in one engine room. No of boilers and details unknown.

Armament
(In Norwegian service) six 7.6cm/50 guns (no of rounds unknown); three 45.6cm individual TT (no of rounds unknown).

Complement
Crew: 76 in total. Boats unknown.

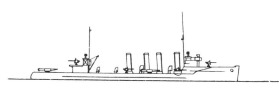

Troll (1940)

Notes
[Converted 1941 to a condensate production ship.]

Career
Troll launched 7 Jul 1910, commissioned 1910 as the Norwegian *Troll*; captured 4 May 1940 at Florø by *Ship 18*; commissioned 18 May 1940 as the German *Troll*; equipment landed 1940 at Bergen; [converted 1941]; served as a steam supply barge at Laksevaag dockyard; returned to Norway 1945. Stricken 1947, sold.

Zick class

Name	Builder	Built	Cost in Marks (000s)	Displacement (t = tonnes T = tons)	Length (m)	Breadth (m)	Draught (m)	Power (hp)	Revs (rpm)	Speed (kts)	Range (nm/kts)	Coal (t)	Oil (t)
ZICK, ZACK	Marinens Hovedverft, Horten Construction nos 109–110	1917–20		256t max 220t des	53.00 oa 52.00 cwl	5.50	2.00 aft	3600ihp max 3500ihp des		17 max mod 25 des		—	30
KT 1 GAZELLE NH 02	Marinens Hovedverft, Horten Construction nos 106, 101, 102	1911–13 1906–08 1907–08		103t max 92t des	41.10 oa 41.00 cwl	4.50	2.50 fwd 2.15 aft	1800ihp max 1700ihp des		20 max mod 25 des		16	—
NH.. (ex *Hval*) KÜRASSIER	Schichau, Elbing Construction nos 588–589	1895–96		94t max 84t des	39.90 oa 38.60 cwl	4.80	2.15 fwd 1.10 aft	1300ihp max 1100ihp des		17.0 max mod 24.5 des		17	—
NH.. (ex *Storm*), TARANTEL NH 01, NH 03 BALTE, ADMIRAL DEINHARD	Marinens Hovedverft, Horten Construction nos 79, 80, 86, 85, 84, 83	1898–1900 1901–02 1900		107t max 80t des	40.00 oa	4.90	2.10 fwd	650ihp des		17.5 max mod 21 des		,,	—
SCHLANGE EIDECHSE	Marinens Hovedverft, Horten Construction nos 94, 100	1903–05 1905–06		75.0t max 67.4t des	36.15 oa 35.20 cwl	4.50	1.90 fwd 1.89 aft	1000ihp des		23 des	900/	13	
SCHILDKRÖTE, SEESTERN		1900–01		63.8t des	34.50 cwl	4.40	1.80 for 1.60 aft	700ihp des		12 max mod 19 des	,,	12	—
QUALLE, KROKODIL	Marinens Hovedverft, Horten Construction nos 88, 87	1902–04		,,	,,	,,	,,	,,		,,	,,	,,	
KT 2 KT 3, KT 4		1887 1896		45.0t des	35.00 cwl	3.80	1.70 aft	650ihp des		15 max mod 18 des	,,	13	—
SEEPFERD	Carljohansvaerns Vaerft, Horten Construction no 74	1894		65.0t max 43.0t des	34.00 cwl	3.75	1.75 aft	,,		12 max mod 19 des		11	

Zick group

Construction

Laid down as Norwegian *torpedobater*, first class (navy design, 1916). Transverse frame steel construction (no of watertight compartments unknown). Depth unknown.

Propulsion

Two vertical 3-cylinder triple expansion engines (two screws, diameter unknown) in 1 + 1 engine rooms. Two boilers (details unknown) in 1 + 1 boiler rooms. One rudder.

Armament

One 7.6cm QF gun (no of rounds unknown); one or two 2cm AA guns (no of rounds unknown); two machine guns; four or two 45.6cm TT (no of rounds unknown); eight to ten depth charge launchers.

Complement

Crew: 2/35. One boat.

Notes

Colour scheme: camouflage (after January 1942 the hull sides were different, the starboard being predominantly flecked white for a snow covered background, the port dark grey-brown for a steep rock background). [Fitted with a new bridge and mast 1941.]

Career

Zick launched 31 May 1919, commissioned 1919 as the Norwegian *Trygg*; stranded 25 Apr 1940 at Isfjorden near Andalsnes after aircraft bomb damage; guns salvaged. Sunk 26 Apr 1940; raised by the Kriegsmarine between May and July 1940; commissioned 1 Aug 1940 as *Zick* (*V 5501*); renamed *V 5506* in September 1943. Ran aground and capsized at 1235hrs on 23 Oct 1944 at Hjeltefjord after being bombed by aircraft; 3 dead.

Zack launched 2 Sept 1920, commissioned 1920 as the Norwegian *Snøgg*; taken as a prize 4 May 1940 at Florø by *Ship 18*; commissioned 18 May 1940 as the German *Zack*; renamed *V 5504* 1 May 1942, and *V 5502* 20 May 1942; run aground at Bergen 1 Sept 1943. Sunk during a salvage attempt 6 Sept 1943; raised, broken up.

KT 1 group

Construction

Laid down as Norwegian *torpedobater*, second class (navy design, 1905). Transverse frame steel construction. Depth unknown.

Propulsion

One vertical 3-cylinder triple expansion engine (one screw, diameter unknown), two water tube boilers. One rudder.

Armament

KT 1, one 7.6cm QF gun (no of rounds unknown); one 3.7cm machine cannon (no of rounds unknown); one heavy machine gun; one 45.7cm TT (1 round), in the bow. *Gazelle* and *NH 02*, two 4.7cm guns (no of rounds unknown); one 2cm AA guns (no of rounds unknown); one heavy machine gun; twelve depth charges.

Complement

Crew: 21 in total. One boat.

Notes

[The bow TT was later sealed on *Gazelle* and *NH 02*. *Dragoner* was fitted with a new 1000shp engine.]

Career

KT 1 launched 12 Mar 1912, commissioned 1913 as the Norwegian *Kjell*; taken as a German prize while under repair at Kristiansand 9 Apr 1940; commissioned 19 Apr 1940 as the German torpedo boat *Tiger*; served as the Küstentorpedoboot – coastal torpedo boat – *KT 1* from 23 Apr 1940; served as *Dragoner* (*NK 02*) in the Kristiansand South Convoy Flotilla Group from 27 Jun 1940. Sunk at 1729hrs on 28 Sept 1944 at Schaeren, west of Kristiansand South, near Ryvingen, during a bomb and gunfire attack by six Mosquitos.

Gazelle launched 14 Dec 1906, commissioned 1908 as the Norwegian *Skarv*; taken as a prize 9 Apr 1940 at Egersund by *M 1*; commissioned 11 Apr 1940 as the German *Skarv*; served as a harbour defence vessel at Stavanger; renamed *Skarv* (*NS 01*) 20 May 1940, and *Gazelle* (*NS 28*) 1941. Sunk 27 Sept 1942 at Lervik, position 59° 46N, 05° 30E, in a collision with an unknown Norwegian boat.

NH 02 launched 18 Feb 1907, commissioned 1 Jul 1908 as the Norwegian *Teist*. Scuttled 14 Apr 1940 at Drauge, approx 7nm northeast of Rarsund; raised 1940 by the Kriegsmarine; repaired; commissioned 1940 as *NH 02* (identification *TI*); further details unknown.

Ex *Hval* group

Construction

Laid down as Norwegian *torpedobater*, second class (Schichau design, 1895 and later revisions). Transverse frame steel construction. Depth unknown.

Propulsion

One vertical 3-cylinder triple expansion engine (one screw, diameter unknown). Two water tube boilers, details unknown. One rudder.

Armament

Two 3.7cm/45 QF guns (no of rounds unknown); one or two heavy machine guns; (originally two 45.6cm TT); six depth charges.

Complement

Crew: 0/23–0/32. No boats.

Career

NH (?) launched 1895, commissioned 1895 as the Norwegian *Hval*. Stricken 1931. Still in existence 9 Apr 1940 at Marineholmen, Bergen; taken as a German prize; transferred to the Hammerfest Convoy Flotilla 1940 as *NH (?)* (service unknown); returned to Norway 1945; sold.

Kürassier launched 1895, commissioned 1896 as the Norwegian *Delfin*. Stricken 1927. Still in existence 9 Apr 1940 at Marvika naval depot, Kristiansand; taken as a German prize; commissioned 6 Nov 1940 as *Kürassier* (*NK 04*); returned to Norway 1945; sold.

NH (?) launched 1 Jun 1898, commissioned in 1900 as the Norwegian *Storm*; taken as a German prize 9 Apr 1940; planned for the Hammerfest Convoy Flotilla; stranded 13/14 Apr 1940 in the vicinity of Bremnesöaran Hardanger. Sunk.

Tarantel launched 22 Sept 1898, commissioned in 1900 as the Norwegian *Brand*; taken as a German prize 9 Apr 1940 during basic repairs at Bergen; commissioned 21 Sept 1940 as *Tarantel* (*NB 19*, subsequently renamed *V 5519*; in service May 1945 at Bergen; returned to Norway. Stricken.

NH 01 launched 31 Oct 1901, commissioned in 1902 as the Norwegian *Skrei*. Sunk 8 May 1940 at Freifjorden, near Kristiansand; raised 1940 by the Kriegsmarine; repaired; commissioned later in 1940 as *NH 01*; subsequently renamed *V 6501*; returned to Norway 1945.

NH 03 launched 25 Sept 1901, commissioned in 1902 as the Norwegian *Sael*. Sunk 18 Apr 1940 at Lukksundet after running aground after a battle with two S boats; raised 1940; commissioned later in 1940 as *NH 03*; further details unknown.

Balte launched 30 Jul 1900, commissioned in 1901 as the Norwegian *Sild*; scuttled 5 May 1940 at Fraenfjord Molde; raised later in 1940 by the Kriegsmarine; commissioned 26 Aug 1940 as *Balte* (*NM 16*); further details unknown.

Admiral Deinhard launched 12 Jul 1900, commissioned in 1901 as the Norwegian *Laks*; taken as a German prize 9 Apr 1940 while under repair at Trondheim; commissioned 13 Apr 1940 as *Admiral Deinhard* for the Trondheim Harbour Group; subsequently became the steam supply boat *ND (?)*; returned to Norway in May 1945; stricken.

Schlange group

Construction

Laid down as Norwegian *torpedobater*, second class (navy design, 1903?). Transverse frame steel construction (no of watertight compartments unknown). Depth unknown.

Propulsion

One vertical 3-cylinder triple expansion engine (one screw, diameter unknown). Two Thornycroft boilers, details unknown. One rudder.

Armament

Two 3.7cm Hotchkiss QF guns (no of rounds unknown); one heavy machine gun; six depth charges.

Complement

Crew: 1/16–1/18. No boats.

Career

Schlange launched 8 Dec 1903, commissioned in 1905 as the Norwegian *Oern*; under repair 9 Apr 1940 at Horten; requisitioned by Germany; commissioned 19 Apr 1940 as *Schlange* (*NO 21*); deserted to Sweden 16 Apr 1945; returned to Norway in May 1945. Stricken 1946; sold.

Eidechse launched 14 Sept 1905, commissioned 1 Jul 1906 as the Norwegian *Lom*; under repair 9 Apr 1940 at Horten; requisitioned 17 Apr 1940 by Germany; commissioned 12 Jun 1940 as *Eidechse* (*NO 22*); in service at Horten; returned to Norway 1946. Stricken 1946; sold.

Schildkröte group

Construction

Laid down as Norwegian *minsvepare*, formerly *torpedobater*, second class (navy design 1899?). Transverse frame steel construction (no of watertight compartments unknown). Depth unknown.

Propulsion

Two vertical 3-cylinder triple expansion engines (one screw, diameter unknown). Two water tube boilers, details unknown. One rudder.

Armament

Two 3.7cm Hotchkiss QF guns (no of rounds unknown); four to six depth charges.

Complement

Crew: 1/15–1/17. One boat.

Career

Schildkröte launched in 1900, commissioned in 1901 as the Norwegian *Kjaek*; taken as a German prize 14 Apr 1940 in dock at Tønsberg; commissioned 19 Apr 1940 as *Schildkröte* (*NO 24*); transferred to Horten in May 1945, for service; returned to Norway 1948. Stricken 1946; sold.

Seestern launched in 1900, commissioned in 1901 as the Norwegian *Hvas*; taken as a German prize 12 Apr 1940 at Stavern, Oslofjord; commissioned 14 Apr 1940 as *Seestern* (*NO 25*); under repair May 1945 in Fredrikstad, returned to Norway. Stricken 1946; sold.

Qualle launched 26 Jun 1902, commissioned 1904 as the Norwegian *Falk*; taken as a German prize 14 Apr 1940 at Tønsberg; commissioned 15 Apr 1940; renamed *Qualle* (*NO 26*); under repair in May 1945 in Fredrikstad, returned to Norway. Stricken 1946; sold.

Krokodil launched 3 Jun 1902, commissioned 1904 as the Norwegian *Hauk*; under repair 9 Apr 1940 at Horten; requisitioned 15 Apr 1940 by Germany; commissioned 19 Apr 1940 as *Krokodil* (*NO 23*); under repair May 1945 at Horten, returned to Norway. Stricken.

KT 2 group

Construction

Laid down as Norwegian *patrulbater*, formerly *torpedobater*, second class (navy design 1885?). Transverse frame steel construction (no of watertight compartments unknown). Depth unknown.

Propulsion

One vertical 3-cylinder triple expansion engine (one screw, diameter unknown). Two water tube boilers, details unknown. One rudder.

Armament

Two 3.7cm Hotchkiss QF guns; one heavy machine gun; six depth charges.

Complement

Crew: 0/21–0/22.

Career

KT 2 launched in 1897, commissioned in 1898 as the Norwegian *Kvik*; taken as a German prize 11 Apr 1940 at Vigebukta/Kristiansand; commissioned 24 Apr 1940 as the coastal torpedo boat *KT 2*; after 15 Jul 1940 renamed *Musketier* (*NK 03*); taken out of service; returned to Norway May 1945; stricken and sold.

KT 3 launched in 1896, commissioned in 1897 as the Norwegian *Lyn*; taken as a German prize 11 Apr 1940 at Vigebukta/Kristiansand; commissioned 23 Apr 1940 as *KT 3*; subsequently renamed *Musketier* (*NK 03*) (as a replacement for *Kvik*); in service May 1945 at Kristiansand South; returned to Norway, stricken.

KT 4 launched in 1896, commissioned in 1897 as the Norwegian *Blink*; taken as a German prize 11 Apr 1940 at Vigebukta/Kristiansand; commissioned 23 Apr 1940 as *KT 4*; after 15 Jul 1940 renamed *Husar* (*NK 05*); in service May 1945 at Kristiansand South; returned to Norway, stricken.

Zick, Zack (1940), before their conversion

Seepferd

Construction

Laid down as a Norwegian *transportbat*, formerly *torpedobat*, second class (navy design, 1892?). Transverse frame steel construction (no of watertight compartments unknown). Depth unknown.

Propulsion

One vertical 3-cylinder triple expansion engine (one screw, diameter unknown). Two Thornycroft boilers, details unknown. One rudder.

Armament

Two 0.8cm heavy machine guns; six depth charges.

Complement

Crew: 1/8. No boats.

Career

Seepferd launched 17 May 1894, commissioned in 1895 as the Norwegian torpedo boat *Varg*; subsequently served as a transport ship; requisitioned 21 Oct 1940 by Germany; commissioned 2 Dec 1940 as *Seepferd* (*NO 27*); under repair May 1945 at Horten; returned to Norway, stricken.

TA 1 class

Name	Builder	Built	Cost in Marks (000s)	Displacement (t = tonnes T = tons)	Length (m)	Breadth (m)	Draught (m)	Power (hp)	Revs (rpm)	Speed (kts)	Range (nm/kts)	Coal (t)	Oil (t)
TA 1–3	Ateliers et Chantiers de la Bretagne, Nantes	1939–		1443T max 1245t des 1087T std	93.2 oa 90.0 cwl	9.28	3.91 max 3.08 des	30,800shp max 28,000shp des	600 des	34 max 33.0 des	2170/19	—	290 max
TA 4–6	Ateliers et Chantiers de la Loire, Nantes	″		″	″	″	″	″	″	″	″	—	″

Construction

Laid down as French *torpilleurs légers* of the fourteen-unit, 1010t, *Le Fier* class (design 1937–38). Transverse frame steel construction (twelve watertight compartments, no double bottom). Depth 5.20m.

Propulsion

Two sets of Rateau-Bretagne (*T 4–T 6*, Parsons) turbines with gear transmission (two 3-bladed screws, 3.75m diameter) and 2 + 1 oil-fired water tube boilers (35 atmospheres forced, 375°, 503–530sq m) in 1 + 1 power plants, each with one engine and one boiler room. One rudder.

Armament

Three 10.5cm/45 QF guns (420 rounds); three 3.7cm AA guns (4500 rounds); nine 2cm AA guns (18,000 rounds); *TA 1, 2* and *5* had six 53.3cm deck TT (6 rounds).

Complement

Crew: 9/158. Boats: two motor boats.

Notes

Colour scheme approx no 9.

Career

TA 1 launched 12 Mar 1940 as the French *Le Fier*; stranded near the Ile d'Oleron on 22 Jun 1940 after being hit by a German aircraft bomb while under tow; taken as a German prize; raised in October 1940; towed back to Nantes for completion. Scuttled 11 Aug 1944 at Nantes, position 47° 13N, 01° 34W, during fitting out; broken up after 1945.

TA 2 launched 23 May 1940 as the French *l'Agile*; scuttled and stranded incomplete on 22 Jun 1940 at Le Verdon roads; taken as a German prize; raised 3 Sept 1940; transferred to Nantes for completion 23 Oct 1940; power installation approx 95 percent complete February 1943. Destroyed before commissioning 16 Sept 1943, position 47° 13N, 01° 34W, by a US aircraft bomb; wreck scuttled 11 Aug 1944.

TA 3 launched (date unknown) as a new French vessel (planned name *L'Alsacien*); taken as a German prize on the stocks at Nantes in June 1940; underwent fur-

ther construction as *TA 3* but progress was slow; her power installations were only about 38 percent complete by February 1943; work was halted in April 1942, and the vessel was released for cannibalisation on 16 Jul 1943 to provide replacement parts for other ships of the class. The hull was sunk in March 1944 at Nantes by a British aircraft bomb.

TA 4 launched 25 May 1940 as the French *L'Entreprenant*; scuttled incomplete on 22 Jun 1940 in the Gironde estuary; taken as a German prize; raised in October 1940; transferred 23 Oct 1940 from Rochefort to Nantes for completion. Sunk 16 Sept 1943 at Nantes, position 47° 13N, 01° 34W, (before commissioning) by a US aircraft bomb; raised 17 May 1946, broken up.

TA 5 laid down as a new French vessel (planned name *Le Farouche*); taken as a German prize on the stocks at Nantes in June 1940; renamed *TA 5*; 50 percent complete by 19 Oct 1940; power installation 97 percent complete by February 1943. Scuttled 11 Aug 1944 at Nantes, position 47° 13N, 01° 34W, before commissioning; raised 24 Aug 1945, broken up.

TA 1–6 (as planned); *ZF 5* was similar.

TA 6 laid down as a new French vessel (planned name *Le Corse*); taken as a German prize on the stocks at Nantes in June 1940; renamed *TA 6*; 15 percent complete by 4 Apr 1942; stranded 7 May 1942 after being bombed by British aircraft; her power installation was approx 80 percent complete by February 1943, and she was released for cannibalisation on 16 Jul 1943 to provide replacement parts for other ships of the class. The hull was scuttled 11 Aug 1944 at Nantes, position 47° 13N, 01° 34W.

TA 9 class

Name	Builder	Built	Cost in Marks (000s)	Displacement (t = tonnes T = tons)	Length (m)	Breadth (m)	Draught (m)	Power (hp)	Revs (rpm)	Speed (kts)	Range (nm/kts)	Coal (t)	Oil (t)
TA 9, TA 10, TA 11	Ateliers et Chantiers de la Loire, Nantes	1933–37		846T max 709t des 680T std	80.70 oa 76.00 cwl	7.96 max	3.50 max 2.48 des	22,000shp des	604 max 585 des	35.5 max 34.5 des	650/25 1000/20 1200/12.5	—	175 max 140 des
TA 12	Ateliers et Chantiers de France, Dunkirk	1934–38		,,	,,	,,	,,	,,	,,	,,	,,	—	,,
TA 13	Chantiers Maritimes du Sud-Ouest, Bordeaux	1934–38		,,	,,	,,	,,	,,	,,	,,	,,	—	,,

Construction

Laid down as French *torpilleurs légers* of the 600t *La Pomone* class (1931–32 design). Transverse and longitudinal frame steel/light alloy construction (fourteen watertight compartments). Depth 4.50m.

Propulsion

Two sets of Parsons turbines with gear transmission (two 3-bladed screws, diameter unknown) in 1 + 1 engine rooms. Two water tube boilers for oil firing (27 atmospheres forced, 350°, 1449sq m) in 1 + 1 boiler rooms. Two 115V 52kW diesel generators. One rudder.

Armament

Two 10.0cm/40 QF guns (150 rounds) +34° –10°, range 15,800m; two 3.7cm AA guns (3000 rounds); four 2cm AA guns (8000 rounds); originally two 55.0cm deck TT (2 rounds) [later removed].

Handling

Stability was inadequate, with heel up to 60°. At full fuel oil load the class were bow-heavy, and very wet in poor weather. The rudder installation, electrical system and conning controls were unreliable, and the engines prone to breakdown. Metacentric height 0.80m.

Complement

Crew 5/100. Boats: one motor boat, one steam pinnace, one cutter, one dinghy.

Notes

Colour scheme no 9 and camouflage. These vessels were fragile due to the excessive use of light alloy in their construction. The engine and boiler rooms were very hot, no submarine detection equipment was carried, and no command transfer system for the AA guns was fitted.

Career

TA 9 launched 23 Mar 1936, commissioned in April 1937 as the French *Bombarde*; taken as an Italian prize at Bizerta 8 Dec 1942; transferred to La Spezia; commissioned as the Italian *F.R. 41* in March 1943; became the German *SG 48* on 5 Apr 1943 in the 4th Escort Flotilla; renamed *TA 9* 15 May 1943; taken out of service at Toulon 27 Sept 1944; Sunk on 23 Aug 1944 at Toulon, position 43° 07N, 05° 56E, by a US aircraft bomb.

TA 10 launched 25 Jan 1935, commissioned in March 1936 as the French *La Pomone*; taken as an Italian prize at Bizerta 8 Dec 1942; transferred to La Spezia; commissioned in March 1943 as the Italian *F.R. 42*; became the German *SG 47* on 7 Apr 1943, in the 4th Escort Flotilla; renamed *TA 10* 15 May 1943. Badly damaged 23 Sept 1943 10nm south of Rhodos, approx position 36° 25N, 28° 14E, by gunfire from the British destroyer *Eclipse* (both engines destroyed, 5 dead); brought in to Rhodos. Sunk in 9m of water at 1700hrs on 25 Sept 1943 by forty Teller mines; broken up.

TA 11 launched 18 Apr 1935, commissioned August 1936 as the French *L'Iphigenie*; taken as an Italian prize at Bizerta 8 Dec 1942; transferred to La Spezia; commissioned as the Italian *F.R. 43* in March 1943; became the German *SG 46* on 5 Apr 1943 in the 4th Escort Flotilla; renamed *TA 11* 15 May 1943. Sunk at 0042hrs on 11 Sept 1943 at Piombino, position 42° 55N, 10° 32E, by gunfire from Italian tanks, after an engine failure on 10 Sept 1943; 2 dead.

TA 12 launched 17 Mar 1937, commissioned October 1938 as the French *Baliste*; scuttled 27 Nov 1942 at the Vieille basin, Toulon; taken as an Italian prize; raised; became *F.R. 44*; commissioned as the German *TA 12* 5 Apr 1943. Badly damaged on 22 Aug 1943 by gunfire from the British destroyer *Eclipse* near Cape Prasonesi, position 35° 08N, 27° 53E, and stranded; subsequently destroyed by an aircraft bomb.

TA 13 launched 28 Jan 1936 as the French *La Bayonnaise*; scuttled 27 Nov 1942 at Toulon, La Seyne; taken as an Italian prize; repairs begun as *F.R. 45*; transferred to the Kriegsmarine 5 Apr 1943 as *TA 13*; not completed. Scuttled 25 Aug 1944 at Toulon, position 43° 07N, 05° 56E.

TA 9–13 (1943)

TA 14 class

Name	Builder	Built	Cost in Marks (000s)	Displacement (t = tonnes T = tons)	Length (m)	Breadth (m)	Draught (m)	Power (hp)	Revs (rpm)	Speed (kts)	Range (nm/kts)	Coal (t)	Oil (t)
TA 14	Nicolo Odero, Sestri-Ponente	1925–27		1356T max 1073T des	94.1 oa 93.7 cwl	9.20	3.64 max 3.28 des	40,000shp des		27 max mod 36.0 des	2150/15 mod	—	400 mod
TA 15	C & T T Pattison, Naples-S Giovanni	,,		1261T max 965T des	84.9 oa 84.0 cwl	8.60	3.35 max 2.98 des	35,540shp max 36,000shp des		28 max mod 35.0 des	1309/15 mod	—	233 mod

Construction

Laid down as Italian *cacciatorpediniere* of the *Turbine* and *Quintino Sella* class (dockyard designs, approx 1926–27). Transverse and longitudinal frame steel construction (twelve watertight compartments).

Propulsion

Two sets of Parsons/Belluzzo turbines with gear transmission (two 3- bladed screws, 2.9/2.2m diameter) in 1 + 1 engine rooms. Three Yarrow/Thornycroft oil-fired boilers, details not known, in 1 + 1 + 1 boiler rooms. One rudder.

Armament

One 12cm/45 QF gun (no of rounds unknown); two 3.7cm Breda AA guns (no of rounds unknown); eight 2cm/65 Breda AA guns (no of rounds unknown); three or two 53.3cm deck-mounted TT (no of rounds unknown); thirty mines.

Handling

Both vessels were very crank; the metacentric height of *TA 14* was only 0.10m, and *TA 15* only 0.29m. Seagoing capabilities were limited, transfer of mines was impossible, and neither could carry a full load of torpedoes and depth charges.

Complement

Crew: 120–150. Boats: two.

Notes

Colour scheme approx no 9, plus camouflage. *TA 15*'s after funnel was thicker by about 1m; the forward funnel had an angled cap. [After November 1943 *TA 14*'s upper (training) cross gun director was removed; the after mast was removed, and the forward mast was shortened; FuMG and FuMB radar, and quadruple 2cm guns were installed on *TA 15*.]

Career

TA 14 launched 12 Apr 1927, commissioned 27 Aug 1927 as the Italian *Turbine*; taken over on 9 Sept 1943 at Piraeus; commissioned 28 Oct 1943. Sunk with *KT 29* at about 1000hrs on 15 Sept 1944 at Salamina, position 37° 57N, 23° 32E, by a US aircraft bomb; 6 dead.

TA 15 launched 12 Sept 1925, commissioned 1 May 1927 as the Italian *Francesco Crispi*; taken over by Germany on 9 Sept 1943 in the Aegean; commissioned 20 Oct 1943 as *TA 17*, renamed *TA 15* 16 Nov 1943. Sunk at 1900hrs on 8 Mar 1944 at Heraklion, position 35° 28' 4"N, 25° 07' 7"E, by a British aircraft rocket; 15 dead. Raised; transferred to Piraeus; sunk 12 Oct 1944 by an aircraft bomb.

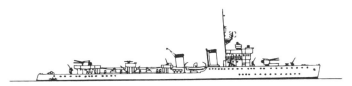

TA 14 (1944); *TA 15* was similar.

TA 16 class

Name	Builder	Built	Cost in Marks (000s)	Displacement (t = tonnes T = tons)	Length (m)	Breadth (m)	Draught (m)	Power (hp)	Revs (rpm)	Speed (kts)	Range (nm/kts)	Coal (t)	Oil (t)
TA 16, TA 19	Fratelli Orlando, Livorno	1920–24		1073T max 863T des	84.9 oa 84.7 cwl	8.02	2.76 max 2.46 des	22,000shp des		24.0 max mod 32.0	900/8 mod 600/12 mod	—	206 max mod 190 des mod
TA 17, TA 18	,,	1917–21, 1917–22		1046T max 822T des	80.3 oa 80.3 cwl	7.52	2.39 des	,,		25.0 max mod 32.0 des	910/9 mod 699/20 mod	—	208 max mod 186 des mod

Construction

Laid down as Italian *cacciatorpediniere* of the *Curtatone* and *Palestro* class (dockyard design 1915 based on *Audace*, and naval modifications 1919–20). Transverse frame steel construction (twelve watertight compartments).

Propulsion

Two sets of Zoelly turbines, direct (two 3-bladed screws, 1.58m/1.50m diameter) in 1 + 1 engine rooms. Four Thornycroft oil-fired boilers (18 atmospheres forced) in 1 + 1 + 1 + 1 boiler rooms. One rudder.

Armament

TA 16, four 10.2cm/45 QF guns (no of rounds unknown), four 2cm/45 AA guns (no of rounds unknown), six 45cm deck-mounted TT (6 rounds); *TA 19*, two 10.2cm/45 QF guns (no of rounds unknown), one 3.5cm Utof AA gun (no of rounds unknown), five 2cm/45 AA guns (no of rounds unknown), two 53.3cm deck-mounted TT (2 rounds); *TA 17*, three 10.2cm/45 QF guns (no of rounds unknown), six 2cm/45 AA guns (no of rounds unknown), four 45cm deck-mounted TT (4 rounds); *TA 18*, four 10.2cm/45 QF guns (no of rounds unknown), two 2cm/45 AA guns (no of rounds unknown).

Complement

Crew: 105. Boats: two.

Notes

Colour scheme approx no 9. *TA 17–18* had slightly narrower funnels. [The original vertical after mast with a topmast was shortened by the removal of the topmast or removed altogether in about 1942–43, and replaced by wireless telegraphy yards on the after funnel.]

Career

TA 16 launched 4 Jun 1922, commissioned 7 Mar 1924 as the Italian *Castelfidardo*; served after 1 Oct 1938 as a *torpediniera*; taken over by Germany at about 0200hrs on 9 Sept 1943 at Suda Bay; commissioned 14 Oct 1943. Sunk at 2015hrs on 2 Jun 1944 at Heraklion, position 35° 20N, 25° 10E, after being hit by sixteen British aircraft rockets; 3 dead. An attempt at raising her was abandoned on 13 Jun 1944.

TA 17 launched 8 Sept 1920, commissioned 20 Jun 1922 as the Italian *San Martino*; served after 1 Oct 1938 as a *torpediniera*; taken over by Germany at 1200hrs on 9 Sept 1943 at Piraeus; commissioned 28 Oct 1943 as *TA 18*; renamed *TA 17* 16 Nov 1943; damaged 18 Sept 1944 at Piraeus by an aircraft bomb; irreparable, taken out of service. Scuttled 12 Nov 1944 after further damage from British aircraft bomb.

TA 18 launched 28 Apr 1920, commissioned 31 Oct 1921 as the Italian *Solferino*; served after 1 Oct 1938 as a *torpediniera*; taken over by Germany at about 2100hrs on 9 Sept 1944 at Suda Bay; initially cannibalised, later repaired; commissioned 25 Jul 1944. Sunk on 19 Oct 1944 south of Volos, position 37° 45N, 26° 59E, in action against the British destroyers *Termagant* and *Tuscan*.

TA 19 launched 17 Mar 1923, commissioned 24 May 1924 as the Italian *Calatafimi*; served after 1 Oct 1938 as a *torpediniera*; taken over at about 1200hrs on 10 Sept 1943 at Piraeus; commissioned 13 Sept 1943 as *Achilles* in the 21st Submarine-Hunting Flotilla; renamed *TA 15* 28 Oct 1943, and *TA 19* 16 Nov 1943. Sunk at 1702hrs on 9 Aug 1944 at Vathi, position 37° 45N, 26° 59E, by a torpedo from the Greek submarine *Pipinos*; 5 dead.

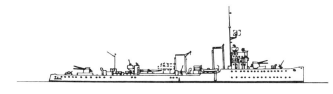

TA 16 (1944); *TA 17* and *TA 18* were similar.

TA 20

Name	Builder	Built	Cost in Marks (000s)	Displacement (t = tonnes T = tons)	Length (m)	Breadth (m)	Draught (m)	Power (hp)	Revs (rpm)	Speed (kts)	Range (nm/kts)	Coal (t)	Oil (t)
TA 20	Yarrow & Co Glasgow – Scotstoun Construction no 1349	1914–16		1011T max 829T des	87.6 oa 85.3 cwl	8.38	2.89 max 2.50 des	22,000shp des		27.0 max mod 31.0 des	2180/15 560/31	—	252 max 170 des

Construction

Laid down as the Japanese destroyer *Kawakaze* (Yarrow design, 1914–15). Transverse frame steel construction (no of watertight compartments unknown).

Propulsion

Two sets of Brown-Curtis turbines, direct (two 3-bladed screws, 1.90m diameter) in 1 + 1 engine rooms. Three Yarrow oil-fired boilers (18 atmospheres forced) in 1 + 1 + 1 boiler rooms; one rudder.

Armament

Two (originally six) 10.2cm/45 QF guns (no of rounds unknown); eight 2cm/65 AA guns; no TT (originally four 45cm deck-mounted TT (4 rounds)); twenty mines.

Complement

Crew: approx 138. Boats: four.

Notes

Colour scheme approx no 9, plus camouflage.

Career

TA 20 launched 26 Oct 1915 as the Japanese *Kawakaze*; taken over 5 Jul 1916 by Italy as *Intrepido*; commissioned 23 Dec 1916 as the Italian *Audace*; served as a *torpediniera* after 1 Oct 1929; taken over by Germany 12 Sept 1943 at Venice; commissioned 21 Oct 1943. Sunk at 2230hrs on 1 Nov 1944 north of Zara, Pago island, position 44° 24N, 15° 02E, by gunfire from the British *Avon Vale* and *Wheatland* (from about 1938 she had served as a remote control vessel for the Italian target ship *San Marco*).

TA 21 class

Construction

Laid down as an Italian *cacciatorpediniere* of the *Indomito–Giuseppe Abba* class (design by Pattison on the basis of a Thornycroft design of 1912–13, adapted by Odero). Transverse frame steel construction (eleven watertight compartments).

Propulsion

Two sets of Tosi turbines, direct (two 3-bladed screws, 1.30m diameter) in 1 + 1 engine rooms. Four Thornycroft oil-fired boilers (18 atmospheres forced) in 1 + 1

Name	Builder	Built	Cost in Marks (000s)	Displacement (t = tonnes T = tons)	Length (m)	Breadth (m)	Draught (m)	Power (hp)	Revs (rpm)	Speed (kts)	Range (nm/kts)	Coal (t)	Oil (t)
TA 21	C & T T Pattison, Naples-S Giovanni	1912–14		780T max 686T des	73.0 oa 73.0 cwl	7.32	2.78 fwd 2.33 aft	16,000shp des		24.0 max mod 30.0 max 35.0 des	1700/15 440/32	—	150 max 110 des
TA 22	Nicolo Odero & Co, Genoa-Sestri Ponente	1913–16		863T max 686T des	"	"	"	"		"	"	—	"
TA 35	"	1914–16		"	"	"	"	"		"	"	—	"

boiler rooms; one rudder.

Armament

Two (originally five) 10.2cm/35 QF guns (no of rounds unknown); *TA 21* had nine AA guns, *TA 22* had ten AA guns, *TA 35* had fifteen 2cm/65 AA guns, *TA 21* had only two 1.3cm Breda AA guns; two 45cm deck-mounted TT; ten mines.

Complement

Crew: 130. Boats: two.

Notes

Colour scheme approx no 9. [*TA 21* after 1 Mar 1941 had no forward funnel and boiler; the forward boiler compartment was reduced in size to provide space for a training room for the *Scuola sommergibili* (submarine training school) at Pola].

Career

TA 21 launched 30 Sept 1913, commissioned 6 Jul 1914 as the Italian *Insidioso*, served as a *torpediniera* after 1 Oct 1929; stricken 18 Sept 1938; converted to an escort boat; commissioned 1 Mar 1941. Scuttled 10 Sept 1943 at Pola; raised; recommissioned 8 Nov 1943 as the German *TA 21* (*Wildfang*; transfer to the Croat navy was briefly planned; damaged 9 Aug 1944 west of Cap Salvore (Istria) by gunfire from aircraft; transferred to Trieste for repair. Sunk 5 Nov 1944 at Fiume,

TA 22 (1943), *TA 35*, *SG 20*; *TA 21* was similar, but without the first funnel.

position 42° 21N, 14° 26E, by a US aircraft torpedo; broken up 1947.

TA 22 launched 20 Dec 1915, commissioned 21 Jun 1916 as the Italian *Giuseppe Missori*; served after 1 Oct 1929 as a *torpediniera*; captured by Germany 10 Sept 1943 at Durazzo; commissioned 3 Dec 1943 as *TA 22*; underwent trials 14 Dec 1943; hit by two aircraft bombs southeast of Trieste, and towed on fire to Trieste; 15 dead. Taken out of service 11 Aug 1944; scuttled 3 May 1945 at Muggia-Trieste, position 45° 29N, 13° 34E, broken up in 1949.

TA 35 launched 26 Oct 1915, commissioned 15 Dec 1915 as the Italian *Pilade Bronzetti*; renamed *Giuseppe Dezza* 16 Jan 1921; served as a *torpediniera* after 1 Oct 1929; scuttled 16 Sept 1943 at Fiume; repaired; commissioned 9 Jun 1944 as the German *TA 35*; transfer to the Croat navy was temporarily planned. Sunk at 0458hrs on 17 Aug 1944 in the Fasana canal, position 44° 53N, 13° 47E, by a mine; 71 dead.

TA 23 class

Name	Builder	Built	Cost in Marks (000s)	Displacement (t = tonnes T = tons)	Length (m)	Breadth (m)	Draught (m)	Power (hp)	Revs (rpm)	Speed (kts)	Range (nm/kts)	Coal (t)	Oil (t)
TA 23, TA 26	Cant del Tirreno, Riva Trigosa	1941–43		1683T max 1185T des 925T std	98.3 oa 86.1 cql	9.90	3.70 max 2.90 des	15,500shp max mod 16,000shp des	430 des	22.0 max mod 25.0 des	800/22 mod 2800/14 mod	—	430 max 280 des
TA 25	Gio Ansaldo & Co, Sestri-Ponente	1941–42		"	"	"	"	"	"	"	"	—	"

Construction

Laid down as Italian *torpediniere di scorta* (originally *avviso-scorta*) of the sixteen-unit *Ciclone* class (navy design, improved *Pegaso* type, 1940). Transverse frame steel construction (thirteen watertight compartments).

Propulsion

Two sets of Tosi turbines with gear transmission; each set had one high pressure turbine, one medium pressure turbine/cruise turbine and one low pressure turbine combined with an astern turbine (two 3-bladed screws,

2.39m diameter) in 1 + 1 engine rooms. Two Yarrow oil-fired boilers (25 atmospheres forced, 350°) in 1 + 1 boiler rooms. One rudder.

Armament

Three (*TA 25*, only two) 10cm/47 AA guns (no of rounds unknown); ten 2cm/65 AA guns (no of rounds unknown); four 45cm deck-mounted TT (4 rounds); twenty mines.

Complement

Crew: 175–200 in total. Boats: four.

Notes

Colour scheme approx no 9, with camouflage.

Career

TA 23 launched 24 Feb 1943, commissioned 30 Apr 1943 as the Italian *Impavido*; taken over 18 Sept 1943 at Portoferraio; commissioned 9 Oct 1943 as the German *TA 1*; renamed *TA 23* in October 1943.

Badly damaged at 0645hrs on 25 Apr 1944 east of Capraia, position 43° 02N, 10° 12E, by a mine; later scuttled by *TA 29* after an attempt to tow her had failed.

TA 25 launched 16 Mar 1942, commissioned 30 Jun 1942 by the Italian *Ardito*; taken over 18 Sept 1943 at Portoferraio; commissioned 18 Dec 1943 as the German *TA 25*; underwent trials 2 Feb 1944. Badly damaged at 0430hrs 21 Jun 1944 southwest of Viareggio, position 43° 49N, 10° 12E, by two torpedoes from a US PT-boat; scuttled at about 0230hrs by gunfire from *TA 29*; approx 60 dead.

TA 26 launched 8 Sept 1943 as the Italian *Intrepido*; taken as a German prize 9 Sept 1943 at Genoa; commissioned 16 Jan 1944 as *TA 26*; undersent trials 9 Feb 1944. Sunk with *TA 30* at 0416hrs on 15 Jun 1944 17nm west of la Spezia, position 43° 58N, 09° 29E, by torpedoes from the US *PT 552, 558* and *559*; 90 dead.

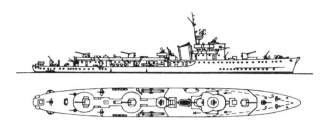

TA 23 (1944); *TA 26* was similar.

TA 25 (1944)

TA 24 class

Name	Builder	Built	Cost in Marks (000s)	Displacement (t = tonnes T = tons)	Length (m)	Breadth (m)	Draught (m)	Power (hp)	Revs (rpm)	Speed (kts)	Range (nm/kts)	Coal (t)	Oil (t)
TA 24, TA 27–30	Gio Ansaldo & Co, Sestri-Ponente	1942–44		1130T max 783T des	83.5 oa 79.1 cwl	8.62	3.45T max 2.87T des	20,000shp max mod 22,000shp des		28 max mod 31.5 des	630/30 mod 1400/20 mod	—	250 max 110 des
TA 36, TA 45–47	C Navale del Quarnaro, Fiume Construction nos ..., 234–236	1942–45		''	''	''	''	''		''	''	—	''
TA 37–42	C Riuniti dell'Adriatico, Trieste Construction nos 1407–1412	1943–44		''	''	''	''	''		''	''	—	''

Construction
Laid down as Italian *torpediniere* of the forty-two-unit *Ariete* class, of which twenty-six contracts were cancelled in 1943 (improved *Spica* type by the Ansaldo dockyard, 1940). Transverse frame steel construction (twelve watertight compartments).

Propulsion
Two sets of Tosi turbines with gear transmission; one high pressure, one medium pressure and one low pressure turbine per set, the last coupled with an astern turbine (two 3-bladed screws, 2.30m diameter) in 1 + 1 engine rooms. Two Regale-Marina oil-fired boilers (25 atmospheres forced, 350°, size unknown) in 1 + 1 boiler rooms. One rudder.

Armament
The original design was for two 10cm/47 AA guns (no of rounds unknown), ten 2cm/65 AA guns (no of rounds unknown), six 45cm deck TT (six rounds), twenty-eight mines. The vessels were completed with the following TT and AA armament: *TA 27*, three 3.7cm AA guns, six 2cm AA guns; *TA 28*, two 3.7cm AA guns; *TA 37*, five TT, and fourteen 2cm Breda AA

guns; *TA 38*, three TT, three 3.7cm AA guns, eight 2cm AA guns and three 1.3cm AA guns; *TA 39*, three TT, two 3.7cm AA guns, eight 2cm AA guns and four 8.6cm Rag; *TA 40*, one 4cm AA gun, two 3.7cm AA guns and eight 2cm AA guns.

Complement
Crew: 145. Boats: one yawl, one dinghy, fourteen rafts.

Notes
Colour scheme approx no 9, with camouflage. [*TA 29* was fitted with FuMO radar after October 1944.]

Career
TA 24 launched 27 Mar 1943, commissioned 7 Oct 1943. Sunk 18 Mar 1943 in the Gulf of Genoa, northeast of Corsica, position 43° 40N, 09° 40E, by a torpedo from the British destroyer *Meteor*, together with *TA 29*, while laying a mine barrage; approx 30 dead.

TA 27 launched 15 Apr 1943, commissioned 29 Dec 1943; underwent trials 9 Feb 1944. Sunk at 2245hrs on 9 Jun 1944 at Portoferraio, position 42° 49N, 10° 20E, after being bombed by US aircraft; 2 dead. The wreck

was blown up 14 Jun 1944.

TA 28 launched 22 May 1943, commissioned 23 Jan 1944; underwent trials 9 Feb 1944. Sunk at approx 1910hrs on 4 Sept 1944 in Genoa dock, position 44° 23N, 08° 51E, by three US aircraft bombs; approx 100 dead.

TA 29 launched 12 Jul 1943, commissioned 6 Mar 1944. Sunk 18 Mar 1945 in the Gulf of Genoa, northeast of Corsica, approx position 43° 30N, 09° 30E, by gunfire from the British destroyer *Lookout*, together with *TA 24*, while laying a mine barrage; 20 dead.

TA 30 launched 14 Aug 1943, commissioned 15 Apr 1944. Sunk at 0433hrs on 15 Jun 1944, 17nm west of La Spezia, position 43° 58N, 09° 29E, by torpedoes from the US *PT 552, 558* and *559*, together with *TA 26*; 20 dead.

TA 36 launched 11 Jul 1943, commissioned 13 Jan 1944. Sunk at 2025hrs on 18 Mar 1944, 15nm south-southwest of Fiume, position 45° 07N, 14° 21E, by her own mine.

TA 37 launched 15 Jun 1943, commissioned 8 Jan 1944. Sunk 7 Nov 1944 in the Gulf of Saloniki, position 40° 36N, 22° 46E, in a battle with the British destroyers *Termagant* and *Tuscan*; 103 dead.

TA 38 launched 1 Jul 1943, commissioned 12 Feb 1944. Scuttled at 1930hrs on 13 Oct 1944 at Volos harbour entrance, position 39° 21N, 22° 56E, after becoming unserviceable after grounding in action on 8 Oct 1944.

TA 39 launched 15 Jul 1943, commissioned 27 Mar 1944. Sunk at 0142hrs on 16 Oct 1944 45nm south of Cape Dermata by a mine; 1 dead.

TA 40 launched 18 Aug 1943, commissioned 17 Oct 1944; damaged by an aircraft bomb at Trieste 20 Feb 1945. Scuttled at Monfalcone 4 May 1945.

TA 41 launched 7 May 1944, commissioned 7 Sept 1944. Destroyed 17 Feb 1945 at San Rocco-Trieste by

an aircraft bomb; the wreck was scuttled 1 May 1945, then broken up in 1949.

TA 42 launched 7 May 1944, commissioned 30 Jan 1945. Sunk 21 Mar 1945 at Venice by an aircraft bomb; 9 dead. Later broken up.

TA 45 launched 30 Jan 1944, commissioned 6 Sept 1944. Sunk 13 Apr 1945 in the Morlacca channel (Dalmatia) in a battle with British MGBs.

TA 46 launched 31 Jan 1944, commissioned 20 Feb 1945; severely damaged at Fiume by an aircraft bomb, and scuttled there 3 May 1945; she was raised, but the planned repair as the Yugoslavian *Velebit* was not carried out.

TA 47 was taken over incomplete; she was completed 1948–49 as *Ucka* for the Yugoslavian Navy using parts from *TA 46*. Stricken 1971.

TA 24, 27–30, 36–42, 45–47, showing the armament arrangement as originally planned, 1943.

TA 31

Name	Builder	Built	Cost in Marks (000s)	Displacement (t = tonnes T = tons)	Length (m)	Breadth (m)	Draught (m)	Power (hp)	Revs (rpm)	Speed (kts)	Range (nm/kts)	Coal (t)	Oil (t)
TA 31	Nicolo Odero, Sestri-Ponente	1929–32		1570T max 1206T des	96.0 oa 95.3 cwl	9.75	3.21 max 2.89 des	44,000shp des	—	30 max mod 38.0 des	2800/15	—	310 max 225 des

Construction
Laid down as an Italian *cacciatorpediniera* of the four-unit *Freccia* class (improved *Turbine* type, 1929). Transverse frame steel construction (eleven watertight compartments).

Propulsion
Two sets of Parsons turbines with gear transmission (two 3-bladed screws, 2.95m diameter) in 1 + 1 engine rooms. Three Thornycroft oil-fired boilers (pressure unknown) in 1 + 1 + 1 boiler rooms. One rudder.

Armament
Four 12cm/45 QF guns (no of rounds unknown); four 3.7cm Breda AA guns (no of rounds unknown); eleven 2cm/65 Breda AA guns; six 53.3cm deck- mounted TT (no of rounds unknown); thirty mines.

Handling
This boat was seriously crank, and later capsized while

TA 31 (1944)

under the Italian flag; she became a 'dockyard ship' because of her unsuitability for active service.

Complement
Crew: 6/189. Boats: two.

Notes
Colour scheme approx no 9. The original 1932 design retained a tripod mast; she was the world's first single-funnel destroyer.

Career
TA 31 launched 6 Sept 1930, commissioned 25 Jan 1932 as the Italian *Dardo*; taken over by Germany 9 Sept 1943 while under repair at Genoa; commissioned 17 Jun 1944; taken out of service at Genoa 25 Oct 1944 (unserviceable). Scuttled 24 Apr 1945; wreck later broken up.

TA 32

Construction
Laid down as the Yugoslavian *razarač Dubrovnik* (designed by Yarrow as flotilla leader, approx 1929–30). Transverse frame steel construction (no of watertight compartments unknown). A sister ship was planned in 1939 (keel laid at Split 1939, completed as

Split 1958).

Propulsion
Two sets of Parsons turbines with gear transmission plus one Curtiss cruise turbine (two 3-bladed screws,

diameter unknown) in 1 + 1 engine rooms. Three Yarrow oil-fired boilers (atmospheres forced unknown) in 1 + 1 + 1 boiler rooms; maximum speed under ideal conditions in 1934 was 40.3kts. One rudder.

Name	Builder	Built	Cost in Marks (000s)	Displacement (t = tonnes T = tons)	Length (m)	Breadth (m)	Draught (m)	Power (hp)	Revs (rpm)	Speed (kts)	Range (nm/kts)	Coal (t)	Oil (t)
TA 32	Yarrow & Co, Glasgow – Scotstoun	1929–32		2400T max 1850T des	113.2 oa 111.1 cwl	10.7	4.10 max 3.59 des	42,000shp des + 900shp		30 max mod 37.0 des	(7000/15) (1700/20)	—	590 max

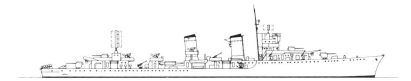

TA 32 as a night fighter direction ship (1943, incomplete). *Mrva*

TA 32 (1944)

Armament

Four 10.5cm/45 QF guns (no of rounds unknown); ten 3.7cm AA guns (no of rounds unknown); thirty-two 2cm AA guns (no of rounds unknown); two 1.5cm AA guns (no of rounds unknown); three 53.3cm TT (no of rounds unknown).

Complement

Crew: approx 220. Boats: four, later two.

Notes

Colour scheme approx no 9. As built, she had an after mast of about 27m, at the rear edge of the former deckhouse on the poop. [Conversion was begun in 1943 to a night-fighting director ship; she was rebuilt as a destroyer early in 1944.]

Career

TA 32 launched 11 Mar 1931, commissioned 1932 as the Yugoslavian *Dubrovnik*; taken over by Italy at Kotor 17 Apr 1943; commissioned as the Italian *Premuda* 25 Apr 1941. Taken over by Germany 9 Sept 1943 while under repair at Genoa; commissioned 18 Aug 1944. Scuttled 24 Apr 1945 at Genoa; raised 1950; broken up.

TA 33

Name	Builder	Built	Cost in Marks (000s)	Displacement (t = tonnes T = tons)	Length (m)	Breadth (m)	Draught (m)	Power (hp)	Revs (rpm)	Speed (kts)	Range (nm/kts)	Coal (t)	Oil (t)
TA 33	Odero-Terni-Orlando, Livorno	1941–		2422T max 1800T des 1620T std	106.7 oa 104.0 cwl	10.2	3.98 max 3.56 des 3.30 std	55,000shp max 52,000shp des	380	39 max 38.5 des	2450/14 1800/20	—	525 max 210 des

Construction

Laid down as an Italian *cacciatorpediniera* of the seven-unit *Soldati* class, second series (enlarged and improved *Maestrale/Soldati* type, first series). Transverse frame steel construction (no of watertight compartments unknown).

Propulsion

Two sets of Tosi turbines with gear transmission (two 3-bladed screws, diameter unknown) in 1 + 1 engine rooms. Three Regale-Marina oil-fired boilers (25 atmospheres forced) in 1 + 1 boiler rooms. One rudder.

Armament

Three 10.5cm/45 torpedo guns (no of rounds unknown); one 8.8cm AA gun (no of rounds unknown); four 3.7cm Breda AA guns (no of rounds unknown); twenty-four 2cm AA guns (no of rounds unknown); three 53.3cm deck-mounted TT (no of rounds unknown); eighty mines.

Complement

Crew: 230. Boats: two.

Notes

Colour scheme approx no 9. [Converted to a night-hunting director ship early 1944; rebuilt as a destroyer after June 1944.]

Career

TA 33 launched 12 Sept 1942 as *Squadrista*; renamed *Corsaro* 31 Jul 1943, not completely fitted out, and underwent engine trials only; taken over by Germany 9 Sept 1943 in the Livorno dockyard; towed to Genoa in November 1943. Sunk 4 Sept 1944, during fitting out at Genoa, by a US aircraft bomb; 14 dead. The wreck was later broken up.

A second unit, named **Carrista**, was requisitioned before launching at Livorno 9 Sept 1943, but construction was not continued as completion was unlikely; a *TA* number was never allotted.

TA 33 as a night fighter direction ship (1943, incomplete). *Mrva*

TA 33 (1944, incomplete)

TA 34 class

Name	Builder	Built	Cost in Marks (000s)	Displacement (t = tonnes T = tons)	Length (m)	Breadth (m)	Draught (m)	Power (hp)	Revs (rpm)	Speed (kts)	Range (nm/kts)	Coal (t)	Oil (t)
TA 34	Ganz-Danubius, Fiume	1915–16		289T max 237T des	58.5 oa 58.2 cwl	5.7	1.98 max 1.75 des	5000shp des		20.0 max mod 28.0	220/20 310/10	18 max	24 max
TA 48	Stabilimento Tecnico Triestino, Trieste	1912–14		,,	,,	,,	,,	,,		,,	,,	,,	,,

Construction
Laid down as Austro-Hungarian torpedo boats of 250t, *F* and *T* classes (1912–13 design). Transverse frame steel construction.

Propulsion
Two Curtiss-AEG/Parsons turbines, direct (two 3-bladed screws, diameter unknown) in two engine rooms. Two Yarrow boilers (one coal-fired, one oil-fired) (16 atmospheres forced) in 1 + 1 boiler rooms. One rudder.

Armament
Two 6.6cm/30 AA guns (no of rounds unknown); four 45cm deck-mounted TT (4 rounds); ten mines.

Complement
Crew: 35. Boats: two.

Notes
Colour scheme approx no 9, with camouflage. [Maximum speed was 24kts after about 1920; modifications are not known, but these vessels were constantly under repair, and virtually defunct.]

Career
TA 34 launched 8 Jul 1916, commissioned 23 Nov 1916 as the Austro-Hungarian *96 F*; transferred to

TA 34, TA 48 (1943)

Yugoslavia in 1918 as *T 7*; taken as an Italian prize at Divulje 21 Apr 1941, renamed *T 7*; taken as a German prize at Gruz 8 Sept 1943, renamed *TA 34*; transferred to the Croat navy as *T 7* 17 Jun 1944. Stranded at 2230hrs on 24 Jun 1944 off Murter Island, position 43° 47' 8"N, 15° 36E, after an attack by *MGB 659, 662* and *MTB 670*, and burned out; 14 dead.

TA 48 launched 4 Mar 1914, commissioned 23 Aug 1914 as the Austro-Hungarian *78 T*; transferred to Yugoslavia in 1918 as *T 3*; taken over by Italy at Cattaro 17 Apr 1941, together with *T 8*; taken over by Germany at Fiume 16 Sept 1943; commissioned 16 Oct 1943 as *TA 48*; transferred to the Croat navy 15 Aug 1944; taken over again after an attempt at desertion 13 Dec 1944. Sunk 20 Feb 1945 at Trieste by an aircraft bomb; raised by AMG 10 May 1946; taken to Tomsic & Co, Ilva, 1947; broken up 1948–49 at Trieste.

TA 43

Name	Builder	Built	Cost in Marks (000s)	Displacement (t = tonnes T = tons)	Length (m)	Breadth (m)	Draught (m)	Power (hp)	Revs (rpm)	Speed (kts)	Range (nm/kts)	Coal (t)	Oil (t)
TA 43	Ateliers et chantiers de la loire, St Nazaire	1936–39		1210t des	98.0 oa 95.4 cwl	9.54	3.30 fwd 2.95 aft	44,000shp des		38.0 des		—	120 max

Construction
Laid down as a Yugoslavian *razarač* of the three-unit *Beograd* class, (design by a French dockyard as a smaller, more modern form of the *Simoun* type, in approx 1935–36). Transverse frame steel construction (no of watertight compartments unknown).

Propulsion
Two sets of Curtiss turbines with gear transmission (two 3-bladed screws, diameter unknown) in 1 + 1 engine rooms. Three Yarrow oil-fired boilers (28.5 atmospheres) in 1 + 1 + 1 boiler rooms. One rudder.

Armament
Four 12cm/46 Skoda QF guns (2400 rounds); four 4cm Bofors AA guns (1000 rounds) [four 2cm/65 AA guns (15,000 rounds)]; three (originally six) 55.0cm deck-mounted TT (no of rounds unknown); thirty mines.

Complement
Crew: 10/135. Boats: two.

Notes
Colour scheme approx no 9. The after mast as built was approx 1.5m aft of the after funnel. [The after triple TT were replaced by 2cm AA guns in diagonally offset cradles; further modifications are not known.]

Career
TA 43 launched 23 Dec 1937, commissioned January 1939 as the Yugoslavian *Beograd*; taken over by Italy at Kotor 17 Apr 1941; renamed *Sebenico*; taken over by Germany at Venice 11 Sept 1943; commissioned 22 Feb 1945; served in the First Escort Flotilla. Scuttled at Trieste 1 May 1945; raised in June 1946; scuttled again 19 Jul 1946; wreck raised 1948; broken up 1949.

TA 43 (1943)

TA 44

Name	Builder	Built	Cost in Marks (000s)	Displacement (t = tonnes T = tons)	Length (m)	Breadth (m)	Draught (m)	Power (hp)	Revs (rpm)	Speed (kts)	Range (nm/kts)	Coal (t)	Oil (t)
TA 44	Cantieri Navali del Quarnaro, Fiume	1928–31	20,650 Lire	2538T max 1912T des	107.7 oa 107.0 cwl	10.2	3.87 max 3.31 des	55,000shp des	380 des	32 max mod 38.0	2132/16 1450/26	—	405 max 230 des

Construction
Laid down as an Italian *cacciatorpediniera* of the twelve-unit 'Navigatori' class, reclassified as *esploratori* in July 1929 (designed 1926–27). Transverse frame steel construction (thirteen watertight compartments).

Propulsion
Two sets of Belluzzo turbines with gear transmission (two 3-bladed screws, 3.56m diameter). Four adapted Yarrow oil-fired boilers (22 atmospheres forced) in 1 + 1 power plants each in 1 engine room + 1 + 1 boiler rooms. Three 30kW turbo-generators, total 90kW at 110V. One rudder.

Armament
Six 12cm/50 QF guns (1200 + 100 rounds); two 3.7cm/54 AA guns (3060 rounds); nine 2cm/70 AA guns (16,000 rounds); four 53.3cm deck-mounted TT (four rounds); fifty-two mines.

Complement
Crew: 170. Boats: two.

Notes
Colour scheme approx no 9, with camouflage.

Career
TA 44 launched 10 Nov 1929, commissioned 1 May 1931 as the Italian *Antonio Pigafetta*; reclassified as a *cacciatorpediniera* 5 Sept 1938; taken over by Germany at Fiume 10 Sept 1943, serviceable despite sabotage to the engine; commissioned 14 Oct 1944; served in the First Escort Flotilla. Sunk 17 Feb 1945 at Trieste by a British aircraft bomb; wreck broken up 1949 together with *Conte di Cavour* and *Impero*.

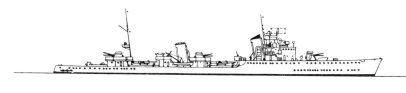
TA 44 (1944)

TA 49

Name	Builder	Built	Cost in Marks (000s)	Displacement (t = tonnes T = tons)	Length (m)	Breadth (m)	Draught (m)	Power (hp)	Revs (rpm)	Speed (kts)	Range (nm/kts)	Coal (t)	Oil (t)
TA 49	Cantieri Navali del Quarnaro, Fiume	1936–38		967T max 785T des	81.4 oa 78.0 cwl	7.92	2.93 max 2.55 des	19,000shp des		34.0 des	1700/15 1260/20	—	207 max 90 des

Construction
Laid down as an Italian *torpediniera* of the thirty-two-unit *Spica* class (navy design by Chief Engineer Gustavo Bozzoni, 1935–36). Transverse frame steel construction (twelve watertight compartments).

Propulsion
Two sets of Tosi turbines with gear transmission (two 3-bladed screws, 2.30m diameter) in 1 + 1 engine rooms. Two Regale-Marina oil-fired boilers (pressure unknown) in 1 + 1 boiler rooms. One rudder.

Armament
Two 10cm/47 AA guns (no of rounds unknown); one 3.7cm AA gun (no of rounds unknown); nine 2cm/65 AA guns (no of rounds unknown); four 45cm deck-mounted TT (4 rounds); twenty mines.

Complement
Crew: 94, originally 6/110. Boats: one, initially two.

Notes
Colour scheme approx no 9, with camouflage.

Career
TA 49 launched 12 Sept 1937, commissioned 1 Jan 1938 as the Italian *Lira*. Scuttled at La Spezia 9 Sept 1943 after becoming unserviceable; raised after 15 Mar 1944. Sunk 4 Nov 1944 at La Spezia by an aircraft bomb while under repair; never commissioned by Germany; wreck broken up.

TA 49 (1944)

Summary of TA boats taken over from Italy (1943)

German designation	Italian designation	Notes	German designation	Italian designation	Notes	German designation	Italian designation	Notes
TA 9 (ex SG 48)	F.R. 41	ex-French Bombarde	TA 19	Calatafimi	after 16 Nov 1943	TA 35	Giuseppe Dezza	
TA 10 (ex SG 47)	F.R. 42	ex-French La Pomone	TA 20	Audace		TA 36	Stella Polare	
TA 11 (ex SG 46)	F.R. 43	ex-French L'Iphigénie	TA 21	Insidioso		TA 37	Gladio	
TA 12	F.R. 44	ex-French Baliste	TA 22	Giuseppe Missori		TA 38	Spada	
TA 13	F.R. 45	ex-French La Bayonnaise	TA 23	Impavido		TA 39	Daga	
TA 14	Turbine		TA 24	Arturo		TA 40	Pugnale	
TA 15	Calatafimi	28 Oct – 16 Nov 1943	TA 25	Ardito		TA 41	Lancia	
	Francesco Crispi	after 16 Nov 1943	TA 26	Intrepido		TA 42	Alabarda	
TA 16	Castelfidardo		TA 27	Auriga		TA 43	Sebenico	ex-Yugoslav Beograd
TA 17	Francesco Crispi	30 Oct – 16 Nov 1943	TA 28	Rigel		TA 44	Antonio Pigafetta	
	San Martino	after 16 Nov 1943	TA 29	Eridano		TA 45	Spica	
TA 18	San Martino	28 Oct – 16 Nov 1943	TA 30	Dragone		TA 46	Fionda	
	Solferino	after 16 Nov 1943	TA 31	Dardo		TA 47	Balestra	
			TA 32	Premuda	ex-Yugoslav Dubrovnik	TA 48	T 3	ex-Yugoslav T 3, ex Austro-Hungarian 78 T
			TA 33	Corsaro		TA 49	Lira	
			TA 34	T 7	ex-Yugoslav T 7, ex Austro-Hungarian 96 F			
			(after June 1944)	F.R. 34	ex-French Lansquenet			

Fleet escorts 1936–1942

F 1 class

Name	Builder	Built	Cost in Marks (000s)	Displacement (t = tonnes T = tons)	Length (m)	Breadth (m)	Draught (m)	Power (hp)	Revs (rpm)	Speed (kts)	Range (nm/kts)	Coal (t)	Oil (t)
F 1–6	Germania Dockyard, Kiel Construction nos 526–531	1934–36		1028T max 803t des 712T std	75.94 oa 73.50 cwl	8.8	3.24 max 2.59 des	16,993shp max 14,000shp des	480 max	27.9 max 28.0 des	1500/20	—	216 max 60 des
	mod: KM Dockyard, Wilhelmshaven (F 1–4, F 6)	1938–39		1147 1065 max 768 des	80.20 oa 77.74 cwl	,,	,,	,,			21.0		—	240
F 7, F 8	Blohm & Voss, Hamburg Construction nos 498–499	,,		,,	,,	,,	,,	,,	,,	,,	,,	—	,,
F 9, F 10	KM Dockyard, Wilhelmshaven Construction nos 126–127	1934–38		,,	,,	,,	,,	,,	,,	,,	,,	—	,,

Construction

Laid down as so-called *Flottenbegleiter* – Fleet Escorts – A–K, intended to serve also as fast minesweepers (official designs, 1932–34). Transverse frame longitudinal stringer construction in steel 52 (fourteen watertight compartments, double bottom 86 percent), superstructure partially light alloy. Depth unknown. Immersion increase unknown. Trim moment unknown. Official standard displacement 600T.

Propulsion

Two Brown, Boveri & Cie geared turbines by Germania dockyard, G–K by Blohm & Voss (two 4-bladed screws, 2.45m diameter) in 1 + 0 + 1 engine rooms. Two ultra-high pressure boilers, La Mont system (450°, 80 [later 45] atmospheres forced, 35t/hr); after F 7 Velox-Benson (480°, 80 atmospheres forced, 41t/hr) in 1 + 0 + 1 boiler rooms. Two 230V 200kW turbo-generators. Two rudders.

Armament

Two 10.5cm/45 QF AA guns (400 rounds); four 3.7cm AA guns (6000 rounds); four 2cm AA guns (8000 rounds) or variations as shown in the drawings; thirty-six depth charges. [*Hai* was fitted in May 1942 with one 10.5cm/45 QF gun, two 3.7cm AA guns, four 2cm AA guns and five heavy machine guns; F 2 was refitted in July 1942 with one 10.5cm/45 QF gun.]

Handling

[The active Frahm-type roll damping was disconnected after about 1939, due to the danger of additive effects if incorrectly operated, and later removed.] All vessels were particularly sensitive and unpredictable to handle in a swell, depending on the methods of control adopted. All suffered from severe roll and severe speed loss in a head sea. The class was unsuitable for the North Sea.

Complement

Crew: 4/117; F 1 3/110; F 3 and 6 3/114 (plus 4/21 as a flotilla flagship). Boats: two motor cutters, one dinghy or similar.

Notes

Colour scheme no 10, 12 or similar. [See drawings for conversions, etc. The type was fatally flawed in terms of construction and engines (with weaknesses in the bow and bridge layout, inadequate main structural members, and a lack of roll keels) because of the difficulty of combining the requirements of a high speed escort boat, mineseeker and submarine hunter; they were finally used for other purposes.] The power installation was unreliable, necessitating frequent dockyard repairs (which took place near the Kiel railway station, hence the nickname *Bahnhofs Flotilla* – Station Flotilla) and periods laid up (they were also known as the Horst-Wessel flotilla, 'cruising with you ... in spirit', in the words of the song). F 1–4 and 6 had the bow extended in 1940–41.

Career

F 1 launched 1 Mar 1935, commissioned 15 Dec 1935; served in the Escort Flotilla; served from 23 May 1941 as fleet tender *Libelle*, and from January 1945 as fleet tender *Jagd*; taken as a USA prize in 1945, and used in the German Minesweeping Administration; transferred to France in 1947, and broken up.

F 2 launched 2 Apr 1935, commissioned 27 Feb 1936; served in the Escort Flotilla; [converted to a TF-boat 6 Apr to 22 May 1940]; taken as a British prize 20 Dec 1945. Scuttled at Scapa Flow in 1946; broken up in 1967.

F 3 launched 1 Jun 1935, commissioned 7 Mar 1936; served as the fleet tender *Königin Luise* from 29 Aug 1938; renamed *Hai* in May 1939, and became flagship of the Commodore Minesweepers, East. Sunk 3 May 1945 in Kiel Bay, position 54° 31N, 10° 11E, by a British aircraft bomb; no of dead unknown. Raised in 1948 and broken up.

F 4 launched 2 Jul 1935, commissioned 5 Apr 1936; served in Escort Flotilla 193 and as an experimental boat with the Experimental Barrage Group; taken as a British prize 16 Jan 1946; broken up.

F 5 launched 14 Aug 1935, commissioned 1 May 1936; [converted to a torpedo recovery boat 18 Dec 1939 until 1 Apr 1940]. Sunk 29 Jan 1945 in the central Baltic, position 54° 20N, 15°E, by a mine.

F 6 launched 1 Oct 1935, commissioned 25 Mar 1936; served as a flagship in the Escort Flotilla; became the fleet tender *Hai* 29 Aug 1938 and *Königin Luise* 15 Apr 1939. Sunk 30 Mar 1945 at Wilhelmshaven (location unknown) by a British aircraft bomb; no of dead unknown.

F 7 launched 25 May 1936, commissioned 15 Feb 1937; served in the Escort Flotilla; [converted to a torpedo recovery boat 1 Apr to 22 May 1940]; taken as a Soviet prize 15 Jan 1946; used as the target ship *V-225* in 1957.

F 8 launched 27 Jul 1936, commissioned 8 Apr 1937; served in the Escort Flotilla; [converted to a torpedo recovery boat 1 Apr to 22 May 1940]; taken as a British prize 23 Dec 1945. Broken up in the Netherlands in 1950.

F 9 launched 11 May 1936, commissioned 21 Aug 1937; served as a flagship in the Escort Flotilla. Sunk at 1230hrs on 14 Dec 1939 in the vicinity of Helgoland (location unknown) by a torpedo from the British submarine *Ursula*; approx 120 dead.

F 10 launched 11 May 1936, commissioned 12 Mar 1938; served in the Escort Flotilla; [converted to a torpedo recovery boat 1 Apr to 22 May 1940]; taken as a British prize 21 Dec 1945. Broken up in the Netherlands in 1950.

F 1–6 (1936)

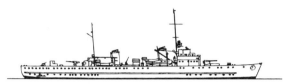

Hai (1941); *Libelle* and *Königin Luise* were very similar.

F 2 as a TF boat (1940); *F 4* was similar.

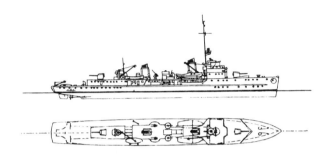

F 7 as an escort boat (1939); *F 5, 8, 9* and *10* were very similar.

G 1 class

Name	Builder	Built	Cost in Marks (000s)	Displacement (t = tonnes T = tons)	Length (m)	Breadth (m)	Draught (m)	Power (hp)	Revs (rpm)	Speed (kts)	Range (nm/kts)	Coal (t)	Oil (t)
G 1–4	Stülcken Sohn, Hamburg Construction nos 789–792	1941–	4800	1793T max 1542t des 1372T std	87.0 oa 84.0 cwl	11.0	3.85 max 3.43 des 3.18 std	6750shp des		21.0 des	6000/20	—	465 max 238 des
G 5–8	Wilton-Fijenoord, Rotterdam Construction nos 702–703,....	1942–	,,	,,	,,	,,	,,	,,		,,	,,	—	,,
G 9–12	P Smit jr, Rotterdam	—											
G 13–15	de Schelde, Vlissingen	—											
G 16–18	Gusto, Schiedam	—					as above						
G 19–20	J & K Smit, Kinderijk	—											
G 21–22	Nederlandse Droogdok Mij, Amsterdam	—											
G 23–24	Boele, Bolnes	—											

Construction

Designed as *Schnelle Geleitboote* – Fast Escort Boats – (official designs, 1941–42, based on the 1938 gunboats). Transverse frame longitudinal stringer construction in steel 52 (twelve watertight compartments, double bottom 78 percent), superstructure partially light alloy. Depth 5.70m.

Propulsion

Three Lentz uniform expansion engines with exhaust steam turbines (three 4-bladed screws, 2.12m diameter) in 1 + 0 + 0 + 1 engine rooms. Three Benson boilers (28 atmospheres forced, six fireboxes, size unknown) in 1 + 0 + 0 + 1 + 1 boiler rooms; one 220V diesel generator. One rudder.

Armament

Four [later two] 10.5cm/45 AA guns (800 [400] rounds); four [five with the elimination of the helicopter] 3.7cm AA guns (6000 [7500] rounds); eight 2cm AA guns (16,000 rounds); up to fifty mines; one helicopter; four depth chargers and eleven individual depth charge mounts.

Handling

No roll damping fitted.

Complement

Crew: 6/152. Boats: two motor cutters, one dinghy or similar.

Notes

Colour scheme no 10, 12 or similar. An alternative version with MAN diesel engine (10,200shp) was designed in detail but not built due to a shortage of engines.

Career

G 1 construction began 15 Nov 1942; work was halted in favour of the Hansa programme in May 1943. Destroyed 27 Jul 1943 on the stocks by a British aircraft bomb; broken up December 1943 to June 1944.

G 2, *5* and *6* preparations were made for construction, but work was halted after 15 Apr 1942.

G 3, *4* and *7–24* construction was not begun; contracts were cancelled 28 Oct 1943.

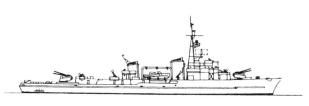

G 1–24 (1941–42 design)

Fast escort vessels 1942–1945

Most of the information printed in previous publications regarding the fast escort vessels (*SG* – Schnelle Geleitfahrzeuge) and the vessels under construction in western and southern Europe which were taken as prizes has not been confirmed by the Official War Diaries of the Naval War now being published in Germany. The following summary lists all the *SG* numbers and all the prize vessels for which we have been able to find evidence:

SG 1 ex *Sans Peur*

SG 2 ex *Sans Reproche*

SG 3 ex *Sans Souci*

SG 4 ex *Sans Pareil*

SG 5 planned February/March 1943 as *Felix Henri*, not allotted (see *SG 10*)

SG 6 planned February/March 1943 as *Alice Robert*, not allotted (see *SG 11*)

SG 7 planned February/March 1943 as *Belain d'Esnambuc*, see mine ship *Pommern*

SG 8 planned February/March 1943 as *Kita*, see mine ship *Brandenburg*

SG 9 planned February/March 1943 as *Cyrnos*, not allotted (see *SG 13*)

SG 10 ex *Felix Henri*

SG 11 ex *Alice Robert*

SG 12 ex *Djebel Dira**

SG 13 ex *Cyrnos*

SG 14 ex *Aviso I (Matelot Leblanc*

SG 15 ex *Aviso II (Rageot de la Touche*

SG 16 ex *La Curieuse*

SG 17 ex *L'Impetueuse*

SG 18 ex *Le Gladiateur*

SG 19 ex *Kilissi**

SG 20 ex *Generale Achille Papa*

SG 21 ex *Aviso III = Amiral Senes*

SG 22 ex *Aviso IV = Enseigne Ballande*

SG 23 planned early 1944 as *La Batailleuse*, see *UJ 2231*

SG 24 ex *Ampere*

SG 25 ex *Les Eparges*

SG 26 planned July/August 1943 as *Granit*, see escort ship *Krebs*

SG 41 ex *Aviso I = Matelot Leblanc*, see *SG 14*

SG 42 ex *Aviso II = Rageot de la Touche*, see *SG 15*

SG 46 ex *Iphigenie*, see *TA 11*

SG 47 ex *Pomone*, see *TA 10*

SG 48 ex *Bombarde*, see *TA 9*

*Proof exists that these three units were prepared and fitted out as *SG*; the number allotment was deduced from circumstantial evidence.

SG 1 class

Name	Builder	Built	Cost in Marks (000s)	Displacement (t = tonnes T = tons)	Length (m)	Breadth (m)	Draught (m)	Power (hp)	Revs (rpm)	Speed (kts)	Range (nm/kts)	Coal (t)	Oil (t)
SG 1	Chant et At de Nazaire (Penhoet), St Nazaire, S 9, T 9	1940–42		2100T max 1500t des 1372T std	95.00 oa 92,00 cwl	11.76	3.64 max 3.20 des	4140shp max 4200shp des		16.72 max 18.00 des	6000/16 12,000/10	—	256 max
SG 2	,,	,,											
SG 3	At et Chant de la Loire, St Nazaire Construction nos 311–312	1940–43						as above					
SG 4	,,	,,											

Construction
Laid down as French *ravitailleurs d'hydroavions* (1937 programme).

Propulsion
Two Sulzer 6-cylinder 2-stroke diesel engines (two 3-bladed screws, diameter unknown).

Armament
Three 10.5cm/45 AA guns (600 rounds); four 3.7cm AA guns (400 rounds); ten to fourteen 2cm AA guns (20,000–28,000 rounds), except *SG 2*, two 10.5cm/45 AA guns (400 rounds); four grenade launchers (no of rounds unknown); twelve 2cm AA guns (24,000 rounds); two heavy machine guns. *SG 4* had two 10.5cm/45 AA guns (400 rounds), four 3.7cm AA guns (4000 rounds), and twelve 2cm AA guns (24,000 rounds).

Handling
Very lightly built ships, with poor seakeeping.

Complement

Crew: 178. Boats: two or three.

Notes

Colour scheme no unknown. All these vessels were taken over at St Nazaire in June 1940 at various stages of completion; construction resumed in October 1940, and they were offered to the Luftwaffe for use as air support ships. After February 1941 building continued to the account of the RLM, with work supervised by the Kriegsmarine. Provisional names were *Jupiter*, *Saturn*, *Uranus* and *Merkur*, later changed to *Merkur*, *Uranus*, *Jupiter* and *Saturn*. A shortage of cranes after April 1942 led to the transfer of all vessels back to the Kriegsmarine as fast escort boats, completed as *SG 1–4*. [The after masts on *SG 2* and *SG 4* were removed in February 1943.]

Career

SG 1 taken over 34 percent complete; launched 2 Oct 1940, commissioned 9 Aug 1942 as *SG 1* in the 4th Patrol Flotilla, and from 1 Jan 1943 in the 6th Patrol Flotilla/A Group; taken out of service at St Nazaire 22 Aug 1944, partially disarmed in May 1945, and returned to France; commissioned as the survey vessel *Beautemps Beaupré* 8 May 1947. Stricken in 1969; renamed *Q 456*; broken up in 1973.

SG 2 taken over 41 percent complete; launched 30 Oct 1940, commissioned 7 Sept 1942 as *SG 2* in the 4th Patrol Flotilla, and from 1 Jan 1943 in the 6th Patrol Flotilla/A Group; severely damaged at 1327hrs on 8 May 1943 at the harbour entrance, St Jean de Luz, position 43° 23N, 01° 39W, by a mine, towed in by *SG 1*. Sunk at 1000hrs on 23 Sept 1943 at Nantes, position 47° 13N, 01° 34W, by three aircraft bombs which penetrated the entire ship; 2 dead.

SG 3 taken over 32 percent complete; launched 28 Nov 1940, commissioned 22 Nov 1942 as *SG 3* in the 4th Patrol Flotilla, and from 1 Jan 1943 in the 6th Patrol Flotilla/A Group. Burned out and sunk at 2157hrs on 6 Aug 1944 at Les Sables d'Olonne, position 46° 30N, 01° 47W, by an aircraft bomb; 40 dead.

SG 4 taken over 42 percent complete; launched 28 Nov 1940, commissioned 2 Sept 1943 as *SG 4* in the 6th Patrol Flotilla/A Group; taken out of service at St Nazaire 22 Aug 1944, partially disarmed in May 1945; returned to France, commissioned as the survey vessel *La Perouse* 23 Apr 1947. Stricken 1969.

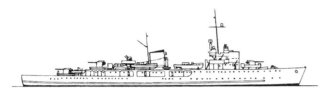
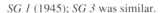

SG 1 (1945); *SG 3* was similar.

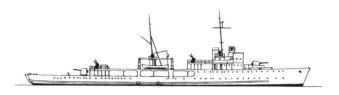

SG 2, *SG 4* (1943)

SG 10 class

Name	Builder	Built	Cost in Marks (000s)	Displacement (t = tonnes T = tons)	Length (m)	Breadth (m)	Draught (m)	Power (hp)	Revs (rpm)	Speed (kts)	Range (nm/kts)	Coal (t)	Oil (t)
SG 10	AS Fredrikstad Mek V, Fredrikstad mod: Marseille	1933 1943		3750t max	96.00 oa 91.28 cwl	14.17	5.5	1900ihp max	100 max	12 max 15 des		—	515
SG 11	Nakskov Skibsv, Nakskov Construction no 59 mod: Marseille	1934 1943			95.00 oa 88.39 cwl	14.63	5.5	1900ihp max 1700ihp des	117 max	13.1 max 12.0 des		—	497
SG (12)	Swan, Hunter & Wigham Richardson, Walker yard Construction no 1370 mod:	1930 1944			99.05 oa	13.59	5.6	2400shp des	100 des	14.3 max		70	372
SG 13	AG Weser, Bremen Construction no 873 mod: Ch Nav Ciotat, Marseille	1928–29 1943		3230 max	94.50 oa 89.20 cwl	12.52	5.8 max 5.2 des	3700ehp max 3300ehp des	175 max 165 des	16.1 max 15 des		—	101
SG (19)	Chant et At de Provence, Port de Bouc Construction no 226	1934			99.01 oa	14.82	5.5	3600ihp des	112 des	13 max 15 des		—	768

2526gt (*SG 10*), 2588gt (*SG 11*), 2835gt (*SG (12)*), 2406gt (*SG 13*), 3723gt (*SG (19)*)

SG 10

Construction

Laid down as a fruit carrier. Transverse frame steel construction (five watertight compartments) shelter deck vessel with two decks, four hatches and a refrigeration system. Depth 7.54m.

Propulsion

One vertical 4-cylinder double compound engine (one screw, diameter unknown) in an engine room. Two cylindrical boilers (15.5 atmospheres forced, 455sq m) in a boiler room, projecting through the main deck into the deckhouse. Electrical system details unknown. One rudder.

Armament

Two 10.5cm/65 QF guns (no of rounds unknown); four 3.7cm AA guns (no of rounds unknown); eighteen 2cm AA guns (no of rounds unknown); six depth charge launchers; six individual depth charge mounts (100 rounds).

Handling

Maximum permissible continuous speed 11.5kts.

Complement

Crew: 194. Boats unknown.

Notes

[Fu.MB radar, S apparatus was installed in 1943.]

Career

SG 10 launched in 1933 in France as S/B *Felix-Henri*, for L Martin, at Nantes; became a French auxiliary in 1940; taken as the German prize 'Frida 7' in November 1942; [refitted after February 1943]; commissioned into the 3rd Escort Flotilla 1 May 1943. Sunk at 0705hrs on 28 Aug 1943 west of Corsica, position 42° 24N, 09° 41E, by two submarine torpedoes; 85 dead.

SG 11

Construction

Laid down as a fruit carrier. Transverse frame steel construction (seven watertight compartments) with forecastle, two decks, four hatches and a refrigeration system. Depth 8.13m.

Propulsion

One vertical 4-cylinder double compound engine (one screw, diameter unknown) in an engine room. Two Falmmrohr oil-fired boilers (15.5 atmospheres forced, 271sq m) in a separate boiler room. Electrical installation details unknown. One rudder.

Armament

Three 10.5cm/65 QF guns (no of rounds unknown); four 3.7cm AA guns (no of rounds unknown); sixteen 2cm AA guns (no of rounds unknown); six depth charge launchers with three ramps and six individual depth charge mounts (100 rounds).

Handling

Continuous steaming at speeds above 12kts threatened damage to the entire propulsion system.

Complement

Crew: approx 200. Boats unknown.

Notes

[Conversion to a minelayer was temporarily planned in January 1943 because of the full-length tweendeck. S apparatus was installed in 1943.]

Career

SG 11 launched 1934 as the French S/B *Alice Robert*, for Cie Franco Coloniale de Navigation, Nantes; served as a French auxiliary guard ship from 1939; taken as the German prize 'Frida 1' in November 1942; [refitted after 11 Feb 1943]; commissioned 1 May 1943 as *SG 11* into the 3rd Escort Flotilla. Sunk at 0905hrs on 2 Jun 1944 at Port Vendres, position 42° 30N, 03° 07E, by a torpedo from the British submarine *Ultor*.

SG (12)

Construction

Laid down as a freighter. Transverse frame steel construction (seven watertight compartments) with a forecastle, three decks, four hatches, fitted out for thirty-four passengers. Depth 8.38m.

Propulsion

One set of Parsons geared turbines (one screw, diameter unknown) in an engine room. Three Prudhon-Capus boilers (16.0 atmospheres forced, 600sq m) in a separate boiler room. Electrical installation details unknown. One rudder.

Complement

Crew: approx 200. Boats unknown.

Career

SG (12) launched in 1930 as the French T/S *Djebel Dira*, for the Cie de Navigation Mixte, Marseille; taken as the German prize 'Felix 21' in November 1942; adapted as an AA corvette and mineship *SG 12* (?) in early 1944; commissioned as *M 6062* 21 Jun 1944. Scuttled at Marseille 28 Aug 1944; raised 1947; broken up.

SG 13

Construction

Laid down as a passenger ship. Transverse frame steel construction (nine watertight compartments) with a forecastle, two decks plus a shelter deck, three hatches, fitted out for 152 passengers. Depth 7.64m.

Propulsion

Two MAN 6-cylinder 2-stroke diesel engines (two 4-bladed screws, diameter unknown) in an engine room. Three 110V 225kW diesel generators; no of rudders unknown.

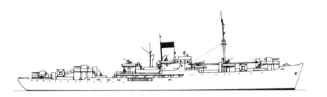

SG 11 (1944). *Mickel*

Armament

Three 10.5cm/65 guns (no of rounds unknown); four 3.7cm AA guns (no of rounds unknown); sixteen 2cm AA guns (no of rounds unknown); six depth charge launchers, with two ramps and six individual depth charge mounts (100 rounds); 220 mines (planned as a mineship).

Complement

Crew: approx 200. Boats unknown.

Notes

[Fu.MB radar, S apparatus installed in 1943.]

Career

SG 13 launched 21 Mar 1929 as the French M/P *Cyrnos*, for the Cie de Navigation Fraissinet, Marseille; became

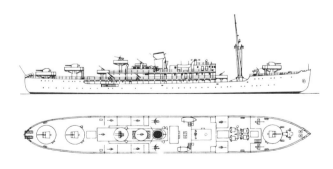

SG 13 (1943). *Mickel*

the French guard ship *P 2* in 1940; taken as a German prize in August 1940; [conversion started 10 Mar 1943]; commissioned 1 May 1943 as *SG 13* into the 3rd Escort Flotilla; hit at 1820hrs on 11 Jul 1943 83nm south of Naples, position 39° 29'5"N, 14° 21'6"E, by an aircraft torpedo; bow torn off, 10 dead. Stranded at 0558hrs on 12 Jul 1943 3.5nm east of La Ponta; raised

23 Jul 1943; towed to La Ciotat 4 Aug 1943; taken out of service 13 Oct 1943 [for conversion to the mine-layer *M 6063*]. Scuttled at Marseille in August 1944; raised in April 1945; repaired; renamed *Cyrnos* in 1947; broken up in November 1966.

SG (19)

Construction

Laid down as a fruit carrier. Transverse frame steel construction (eight watertight compartments) with a forecastle, three decks, four hatches and a refrigeration system. Depth 9.26m.

Propulsion

One vertical 3-cylinder triple expansion engine (one screw, diameter unknown) in an engine room. Three Prudhon-Capus boilers (16 atmospheres forced, 825sq m) in a separate boiler room. Electrical system details unknown. One rudder.

Complement

Crew: 200. Boats unknown.

Career

SG (19) launched in 1934 as the French S/B *Kilissi*, for the Cie de Chargeurs Reunis, Bordeaux; taken as a German prize at Marseille 7 Nov 1942; [adapted after January 1944 as the escort and AA corvette *SG 19* (?), planned for the 6th Security Flotilla]. Sunk in the Ebro estuary 12 Sept 1944 by an aircraft bomb.

SG 14 class

Name	Builder	Built	Cost in Marks (000s)	Displacement (t = tonnes T = tons)	Length (m)	Breadth (m)	Draught (m)	Power (hp)	Revs (rpm)	Speed (kts)	Range (nm/kts)	Coal (t)	Oil (t)
SG 14, SG 15 SG 21, SG 22	At et Chant de Provence, Port de Bouc	1939–42		917t max 647T std	78.30 oa 73.81 cwl	8.70 max 8.48 des	2.88	4000ehp des		20 des	3000/18 5200/15 10,000/9	—	105
SG 16	Chant Nav Lorient	1938–40		890t max 750t des 639T std	78.30 oa 73.81 pp	8.5	3.20 max 2.40 des	4600ehp max 4000ehp des		20 des	4000/15 10,000/9	—	95
SG 17	At et Chant de France, Dunkirk	1938–40		,,	,,	,,	,,	,,		,,	,,	—	,,
(SG 23)	At et Chant de Provence, Port de Bouc	1937–40		,,	,,	,,	,,	,,		,,	,,	—	,,

SG 14, 15, 21 and 22

Construction

Laid down as *avisos drageurs de mines* of the 'Colonial' series of 647t. Depth 3.28m.

Propulsion

Two Sulzer 6-cylinder 2-stroke diesels (two screws, diameter unknown).

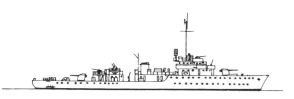

SG 14 (1943), SG 15, SG 21, SG 22

Armament

Two 10.5cm/65 guns (no of rounds unknown); one 3.7cm AA gun (no of rounds unknown); fourteen to eighteen 2cm AA guns (no of rounds unknown).

Handling

Unstable in heavy seas.

Complement

Crew: approx 125. Boats: four.

Career

SG 14 launched 10 Jul 1942 as the French *Aviso I* (planned name *Matelot Leblanc*); requisitioned and fitted out by Germany in November 1942; commissioned 5 Jun 1943 as *SG 41* into the 4th Escort Flotilla; renamed *SG 14* 15 May 1943. Sunk at 1650hrs on 24 Aug 1983 in the Bay of Acqua Fredda, south of Capri, position 40° 35N, 14° 12E, by two aircraft bombs; 8 dead.

SG 15 launched 2 Sept 1942 as the French *Aviso II* (planned name *Rageot de la Touche*); requisitioned and fitted out as *SG 42* by Germany in November 1942; commissioned 3 Oct 1943 as *SG 15* into the 3rd Escort Flotilla; transferred to the 10th Torpedo boat Flotilla 15 Jan 1944; renamed *UJ 2229* 16 May 1944; hit at Genoa 5 Sept 1944 by an aircraft bomb and severely damaged; repaired. Sunk 26 Apr 1945 at Genoa, position 44° 24N, 08° 56E, by a torpedo from the British submarine *Universal*.

SG 21 launched in 1942 as the French *Aviso III* (planned name *Amiral Senes*); requisitioned and completed by Germany in November 1942; commissioned 28 Mar 1944 as *SG 21* (*Bernd von Arnim*) into the 6th Security Flotilla. Sunk at 0428hrs on 15 Aug 1944 in the vicinity of St Tropez after a battle with the invasion fleet, together with *UJ 6082*.

SG 22 launched as the French *Aviso IV* (planned name *Enseigne Ballande*); under construction in November 1942 when requisitioned by Germany for further construction work as *SG 22*; not completed. Scuttled at Port de Bouc 20 Aug 1944.

SG 16, 17 and 23

Construction

Laid down as *avisos drageurs de mines* of the 630t series. Depth unknown.

Propulsion

Two Sulzer 6-cylinder 2-stroke diesel engines (two screws, diameter unknown).

Armament

Two 10.5cm/65 guns (no of rounds unknown); four 3.7cm AA guns (no of rounds unknown); ten 2cm AA guns (no of rounds unknown). *SG 23* however had only one Italian 10.5cm/65 gun aft, two 3.7cm AA guns (no of rounds unknown), four 2cm AA guns (no of rounds unknown), and seven Breda 1.3cm AA guns (no of rounds unknown).

Complement

Crew: 6/120. Boats unknown.

Notes

As a submarine hunting training ship *SG 23* was fitted with German S and NHG (L) apparatus; two Italian Menon 42 depth charge launchers; two German B depth charges ramps; and six individual depth charge mounts.

Career

SG 16 launched 11 Nov 1939, commissioned in 1940 as the French aviso *La Curieuse*; scuttled at Toulon 27 Nov 1942. Raised, transferred to Italy, reconstruction as *F.R. 55* begun; taken incomplete at Toulon 9 Sept 1943 as a German prize; under repair 24 Nov 1943 when severely damaged by an aircraft bomb; commissioned in May 1944 as *SG 16*; docked at Marseille 22 Jul 1944 on account of shaft damage; undocked incomplete at the start of the invasion 14–15 Aug 1944; taken out of service 19 Aug 1944; scuttled at Marseille 22 Aug 1944; broken up in 1945.

SG 17 launched 15 Jan 1940, commissioned May 1940 as the French aviso *l'Impetueuse*; scuttled at Toulon 27 Nov 1942. Raised; transferred to Italy; reconstruction begun to *F.R. 54*; taken incomplete as a German prize at Toulon 9 Sept 1943; under repair 24 Nov 1943 when severely damaged by an aircraft bomb; still under repair 7 Aug 1944; scuttled at Marseille; broken up 1945.

(*SG 23*) launched 22 Aug 1939, commissioned March 1940 as the French aviso *La Batailleuse*; taken as an Italian prize at Bizerta November 1942; commissioned 28 Jan 1943 as the Italian *F.R. 51* into the 11th Corvette Squadron. Scuttled at La Spezia 9 Sept 1943, the destroyer wharf; raised in February 1944 for planned conversion to the submarine training ship *SG 23*(?) for acoustic detection training; reconstructed after July 1944 as *UJ 2231* in Genoa. Scuttled 25 Apr 1945 at Genoa, position 44° 24N, 08° 54E.

SG 16 (1944); *SG 17*; *SG 23* was similar.

SG 18 class

Name	Builder	Built	Cost in Marks (000s)	Displacement (t = tonnes T = tons)	Length (m)	Breadth (m)	Draught (m)	Power (hp)	Revs (rpm)	Speed (kts)	Range (nm/kts)	Coal (t)	Oil (t)
SG 18	Chant Nav Lorient	1932–33		2293T max 1858T std	113.0 cwl	12.70	3.50	6000shp		18		—	399
SG 20	Soc Odero, Sestri	1919–22		890t max 832t des	73.54 oa	7.32	3.01 max 2.46 des	16,000shp		25 max 30 des	400/30	—	157
(SG 24)	Soc Provencales de Constr Nav, La Ciotat	1930		3920t max	91.50 oa 87.86 cwl	12.53	5.50	2400ihp des	120 des	12.5 max 10 des		700	—
(SG 25)	Chant Nav Brest	1919		850T max 644T des	74.91 oa 72.00 cwl	8.71	3.20	5000shp		19	3000/11	—	
2435gt (SG 24)													

SG 18

Construction

Laid down as a *mouilleur de filets* (net layer).

Propulsion

Two sets of Parsons geared turbines (two screws, diameter unknown). Two Indret boilers.

Armament

Four 10.5cm/65 guns (no of rounds unknown); six 2cm AA guns (no of rounds unknown).

Complement

Crew: about 132 in total. Boats unknown.

Career

SG 18 launched 10 Apr 1933, commissioned as the French net layer *Le Gladiateur*. Scuttled 27 Nov 1942 at Toulon; raised 30 Mar 1943; adapted after January 1944 as the AA corvette *SG 18* and as a mine ship for the 6th Security Division. Sunk 4 Feb 1944 at Toulon by an aircraft bomb.

SG 20

Construction

Laid down as an Italian *cacciatorpediniera* of the *Cantore* class (La Masa type, an improved version of the *Indomito* design, fourth series). Transverse frame steel construction (subdivision unknown). Freeboard unknown.

Propulsion

Two sets of Tosi turbines, direct (two 3-bladed screws, diameter unknown) in 1 + 1 engine rooms. Four Thor-

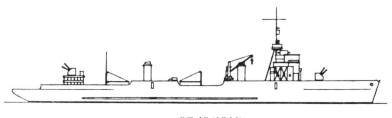

SG 18 (1944)

nycroft oil-fired boilers (18 atmospheres forced, size unknown) in 1 + 1 + 1 + 1 boiler rooms. One rudder.

Armament

Two 3.7cm AA guns (no of rounds unknown); six 2cm Oerlikon AA guns (no of rounds unknown); ten 2cm Breda AA guns (no of rounds unknown); four 8.4cm Rag (no of rounds unknown).

Complement

Crew: approx 100. Boats: three.

Notes

Unsuited to mine use. The weight of the mines led to irreparable distortion and leaks throughout the hull, which led to its sinking at Genoa.

Career

SG 20 launched 8 Dec 1921, commissioned 10 Feb 1922 as the Italian torpedo boat *Generale Achille Papa*; taken as a German prize at Genoa 9 Sept 1943; commissioned 17 Oct 1943 as *TA 7*; renamed *SG 20* 18 Oct 1943; severely damaged 1 Nov 1943, with hull distortion due to mine use. Sunk at Genoa's North Wharf, after springing a leak; further damaged there by an aircraft bomb 12 Jan 1944. Raised and scuttled 25 Apr 1945 as a block ship in Oneglia harbour, position 43° 53N, 08° 03E.

(SG 24)

Construction

Laid down as a French cable layer. Transverse frame steel construction (twelve watertight compartments), one deck, five hatches. Freeboard 8.00m.

Propulsion

Two vertical 3-cylinder triple expansion engines (two screws, diameter unknown). Three Prudhon-Capus boilers (14 atmospheres forced, 816sq m). Electrical installation details unknown.

Complement

Crew: approx 100. Boats unknown.

Career

(SG 24) launched in 1930 as the French cable layer *Ampere*, for the Postes et Telegraphes, Paris; became the French auxiliary *X 81* in 1940; requisitioned in November 1942 by Germany; converted after January 1944 to an AA corvette (*SG 24*) for the 6th Security Flotilla. Scuttled at Marseille in August 1944, incomplete; raised; stricken; broken up.

(SG 25)

Construction

Laid down as a French *aviso de 1er-classe* of the *Arras* class freighter type design.

Propulsion

Two sets of Parsons geared turbines (two screws, diameter unknown). Two Normand (?) boilers (pressure and size unknown) in 1 + 1 boiler rooms. One rudder.

Complement

Crew: 100. Boats unknown.

Career

SG 25 launched in September 1919 as the French aviso *Les Epargues*, 193rd Survey Vessel. Scuttled 27 Nov 1942 at Toulon, Vieille Bay; raised; commissioned 5 May 1943 as the German *M(L) 6060*; adapted in January 1944 as an escort boat (*SG 25*) for the 6th Security Flotilla; burnt out and severely damaged at about 0200hrs on 1 Mar 1944 at Marseille; scuttled there on 3 Aug 1944.

Use of the following units as Fast Escort Vessels was considered; the assignment of numbers for these vessels so far not been confirmed:

T/P *Altamura* (launched in 1931, 3900t): in January 1943 use as *SG 11* instead of *Alice Robert* was considered; scuttled at La Spezia 15 September 1943; raised 7 July to 25 Dec 1943, usable thereafter only as a block ship.

T/P *Sampiero Corso* (launched 1936, 3823 gross tons): planned 30 Jan 1943 as a target ship for the OKM Torpedo Department; considered in May 1943 for fitting out as an AA corvette to replace *Belain d'Esnambuc*. Sunk 22 Jun 1944 in the vicinity of Cassis by the torpedo British submarine *Universal*; raised 18 Nov to 14 Dec 1945; taken over by the French navy in 1956.

Destroyer *l'Indomptable* (launched 1933, 2569t): scuttled at the coal jetty at Toulon, 27 Nov 1942; use as an *SG* was considered after raising. Sunk again 7 Mar 1944 following the interruption of salvage work by a US air attack between 1112hrs and 1133hrs; further attempts to raise the ship were abandoned; eventually raised 1950; broken up.

Aviso *Chamois* (launched 1938, 647t): scuttled at Toulon, Vieille Basin, 27 Nov 1942; raised 1943; planned as the Italian corvette *F.R. 53*; scuttled incomplete 9 Sept 1943. Raised by the German navy but sunk before repair at Toulon 30 Nov 1943 by an aircraft bomb; raised; broken up.

Aviso *Commandant Riviere* (launched 1939, 647t): taken as an Italian prize at Bizerta 8 Dec 1942; commissioned 1 Feb 1943 as the Italian *F.R. 52*. Sunk at 1230hrs on 28 May 1943 at Livorno by an aircraft bomb; raising was considered in 1944; raised after April 1945; broken up.

Aviso *Yser* (launched 1917, 576t): taken as a German prize 27 Nov 1942 at Toulon, Vieille Basin; service for the 6th Security Division was considered; found to be completely unserviceable 2 Apr 1943. Stricken.

The following French units were *not* included in considerations for fitting out as Fast Escort Vessels:

Survey ship *Chimere* (launched 1901, 613t); became the harbour defence boat *FMa 09*.

Flight security boats *Petrel 2–Petrel 4* (launched 1932, 80t).

Aviso *Elan* (launched 1938, 630t); after use in Syria until 23 Dec 1944 the ship was interned in Turkey, hence not available to Germany.

Index

A, 156
A, see *Bayern* (1881), 7–8
A, see *Brandenburg*, 13–14
A, see *Emden* (1925), 118–9
A, see *Graf Zeppelin*, 71–2
A, see *Kaiser Karl Barbarossa*, 14–16
A, see *Königsberg* (1916), 113
A, see *Lützow* (1933), 60–1
A, see *Nautilus*, 134
A, see *Nymphe* (1900), 99–101
A, see *Panther*, 142–3
A, see *Prinz Adalbert* (1877), 43
A, see *Prinz Heinrich*, 49–50
A, see *Tsingtau*, 145
A, see *Wespe* (1876), 138
A 1 class, 161–2
A 1–25, 161–2
A 26 class, 162–3
A 26–55, 162–3
A 56 class, 163–5
A 56–113, 163–5
Acheron, see *Moltke* (1878), 44–5
Adler (1880), 139–40
Adler, see *Pommerania*, 88
Admiral Deinhard, 218–20
Admiral Graf Spee, 60–3
Admiral Hipper, 65–7
Admiral Makarov, see *Nürnberg* (1935), 122–3
Admiral Nevelskoy, see *Elbing*, 110–11
Admiral Scheer, 60–2
Adolf Sommerfeld, see *Gefion* (1893), 98–9
Ägir, 11–12
Ajuricaba, see *S 178*, 186
Alabarda, see *TA 42*, 225–6, 230
Albatros, 191–3
Albatross, 134
Albatross class, 134
Alexandrine, 89–91
Alice Robert, see *SG 6* & *SG 11*, 234, 236, 239
Alice Roosevelt, see *D 2*, 167
Almirante Aguirre, see *KH 2*, 126
Almirante Grau, see *KH 1*, 126
Altamura, 239
Amazone (1844), 78–9
Amazone (1901), 99–102
Ametist, see *A 32*, 162
Amiral Senes, see *S 113*, 185
Amiral Senes, see *SG 21*, 234, 237
Ampere, see *SG 24*, 234, 239
Annelise Ruthjen, see *S 179*, 186
Anton Schmitt, see *Z 22*, 202
Antonio Pigafetta, see *TA 44*, 229, 230
Arcadia, see *Erzherzog Johann*, 39–40
Arcona (1859), 42–3
Arcona (1886), 89–91

Arcona (1903), 99–102
Arcona class, 42–3
Arcona, see *Graudenz* (1914), 109–10
Ardimentoso, see *S 63*, 180
Ardito, see *TA 25*, 225, 230
Ariadne (1872), 86–7
Ariadne (1901), 99–101
Ariadne class, 86–7
Arminius, 1–2
Arnis, 129
Artevelde, see *K4/ Lorelei*, 147–8
Arturo, see *TA 24*, 225, 230
Audace, see *TA 20*, 223, 230
Augsburg, 106–7
Augusta, 86
Augusta class, 86
Auriga, see *TA 48*, 228, 230
Ausonia, see *I* (1915), 70
ex *Avantgarde*, 134–5
Aviso I–II, 234, 237
Aviso III–IV, 237
Azuma, see *Sphinx*, 1

B (1938), 71–2
B, see *Admiral Scheer*, 60–2
B, see *Bismarck* (1878), 44
B, see *Eber* (1903), 42–3
B, see *Habicht* (1880), 139
B, see *Kaiser Karl der Grosse*, 14–16
B, see *Königsberg* (1929), 119–21
B, see *Niobe* (1900), 99–101
B, see *Prinz Adalbert* (1901), 50–1
B, see *Sachsen* (1878), 7–8
B, see *Vaterland*, 145
B, see *Viper*, 138
B, see *Wörth* (1893), 13–14
B 97 class, 184–6
B 97–98, 184–5
B 109–112, 184–5
B 122–124, 185–6
Baccarat, see *T 20*, 194
Baden (1883), 7–8
Baden (1915), 28–9
Balder, see *Leopard*, 216–7
Balestra, see *TA 47*, 225–6, 230
Baliste, see *TA 12*, 221, 230
Balte, 218–20
Barbaros Hayreddin, see *Kurfürst Friedrich Wilhelm*, 13–14
Barbarossa, 39–40
Barbarossa class, 39–40
Bari, see *Pillau*, 110–11
Basilisk (*1862*), 133–4
Basilisk (1880), 137–8
Bayern (1881), 7–8
Bayern (1915), 28–30
Bayern class, 28–30
Beautemps Beaupré, see *SG 1*, 235
Belain d'Esnambuc, see *SG 7*, 234
Belgium, see *Grossherzog von Oldenburg*, 80

Beograd, see *TA 43*, 228, 230
Beowulf, 10–12
Berlin, 102–4
Bernd von Arnim (1938), see *Z 11*, 200
Bernd von Arnim (1944), see *SG 21*, 237
Biene, 137–8
Bir Hakeim, see *T 11*, 194
Bismarck (1878), 44–5
Bismarck (1940), 33–5
Bismarck class (corvettes), 44–5
Bismarck class (battleships), 33–5
Blink, see *KT 4*, 218–20
Blitz (1862), 133–4
Blitz (1883), 91
Blitz class, 91
Blitz, see *S 141*, 174
Blitz, see *V 185*, 174
Blücher (1878), 2, 44–5
Blücher (1909), 53
Blücher (1939), 65–7
Blücher class, 65–7
Blücher, see *Wolf* (1860), 132–3
Bombarde, see *TA 9*, 221, 230, 234
Bonin, 130
Borets za Svobodu, 30
Borussia, see *Preussen*, 5–6
Brand, see *Tarantel*, 218–20
Brandenburg, 13–14
Braunschweig, 18–20, 21
Bremen (1842), 81
Bremen (1904), 102–4
Bremen class (light cruisers), 102–4
Bremen class (steamers), 81
Bremse (1884), 140–1
Bremse (1916), 112–3
Bremse, see *V 156*, 174
Breslau, 107–8
Brest, 134–5
Britannia, see *Barbarossa*, 39–40
Brummer (1884), 140–1
Brummer (1916), 112–3
Brummer class (gunboats), 140–1
Brummer class (light cruisers), 112–3
Bruno Heinemann, see *Z 8*, 200
Buino, see *V 130*, 181–2
Bussard, 97–8
Bussard class, 97–8
Bystryy, see *R 02*, 188–9

C, see *Admiral Graf Spee*, 60–3
C, see *Baden* (1883), 7–8
C, see *Biene*, 138
C, see *Blücher* (1878), 44
C, see *Brummer* (1916), 112–13
C, see *Bussard*, 97–8
C, see *Gneisenau* (1908), 52
C, see *Karlsruhe* (1929), 119–21
C, see *Möwe*, 139–40
C, see *Thetis* (1901), 99–101
C, see *Weissenburg*, 13–14

C, see *Wittelsbach*, 16–17
C.T.B. 9, see *Schichau experimental boat*, 160–1
Calatafimi, see *TA 15* & *TA 19*, 223, 230
Camäleon (1860), 133–4
Camäleon class, 133–4
Camaeleon (1879), 137–8
Capitan Alfredo Kling II, see *S 178*, 186
Carl Schurz, see *Geier*, 97–8
Carmen, see *D 1*, 167
Carola, 89–91
Carola class, 89–91
Castelfidardo, see *TA 16*, 223, 230
Cattaro, see *Niobe* (1900), 99–101
Cazique, see *Frankfurt* (1849), 79–80
Cesare Rossarol, see *B 97*, 184
Chamois, 239
Charlotte, 45
Cheops, see *Prinz Adalbert*, 1
Chimere, 239
Christian VIII, see *Bonin*, 130
Clara, see ex *Garde Mobile*, 134–5
Claus von Bevern, see *V 190*, 176
Clemenceau, 38
Colmar, see *Kolberg* (1910), 106–7
Cöln (1911), 106–7
Cöln (1918), 114–15
Cöln class, 114–15
Comet (1860), 133–4
Comet (1893), 96
Comet, see *V 151*, 174
Commandant Riviere, 239
Concordia, see Gun yawl *No 4*, 130–1
Condor, 97–8
Cora, see *Der Königliche Ernst August*, 79–80
Cormoran, 97–8
Corsaro, see *TA 33*, 227, 230
Crocodill (1860), 132–3
Crocodill (1880), 137–8
La Curieuse, see *SG 16*, 234, 238
Cyclone, see *ZF 4*, 213
Cyclop, (1860), 133–4
Cyclop (1875), 137
Cyrnos, see *SG 9* & *SG 13*, 234, 236

D (1934), 63
D, see *Ariadne* (1901), 99–101
D, see *Blitz* (1883), 91
D, see *Brummer* (1916), 112–13
D, see *Falke* (1865), 87–8
D, see *Falke* (1891), 97–8
D, see *Gneisenau* (1880), 44–5
D, see *Köln* (1930), 119–21
D, see *Kurfürst Friedrich Wilhelm*, 13–14

D, see *Mücke*, 138
D, see *Scharnhorst* (1907), 52
D, see *Scharnhorst* (1939), 31–2
D, see *Wettin* (1902), 16–17
D, see *Württemberg* (1881), 7–8
D 1 class, 166–7
D 1–6, 166–7
D 7 class, 167
D 7–8, 167
D 9, 168
D 10, 168
DD 935, see *T 35*, 196
Daga, see *TA 39*, 225, 230
Dalmacija, see *Niobe* (1900), 99–101
Danzig (1825), 127
Danzig (1853), 41
Danzig (1907), 102–4
Dardo, see *TA 31*, 226, 230
De Grasse, see *B 97*, 184
De Grasse, see *II* (1938), 76–7
De Ruyter, see *KH 1*, 126
De Zeven Provincien, see *KH 1* & *KH 2*, 126
Delfin, see *Kürassier*, 218–20
Delphin, 133–4
Denmark, see *Hamburg* (1841), 81
Der Königliche Ernst August, 79–80
Der Urwähler, see *Hela* (1854), 82–3
Derfflinger, 56–7
Derfflinger class, 56–7
Destroyer 1937 J, 208
Destroyer 1937 I–IV, 208
Destroyer 1938 Ac, 209–10
Destroyer 1938 Ad, 209–10
Destroyer 1945, 211
Deutschland (1875), 6–7
Deutschland (1906), 20–2
Deutschland, see *Lützow* (1933), 60–1
Deutschland class, 20–2
Deutschland/ Lützow class, 60–3
Devrient boats *Nos I–III*, 149
Diether von Roeder, see *Z 17*, 202
Dietrich Bohnekamp, see *H 186*, 186
Djebel Dira, see *SG 12*, 234, 236
Drache, 133–4
Dragone, see *TA 30*, 225, 230
Dragoner, see *KT 1*, 219
Dresden (1908), 105–6
Dresden (1917), 114–15
Dresden class, 105–6
Dubrovnik, see *TA 32*, 226–7, 230

E (1934), 63
E, see *Blücher* (1909), 53
E, see *Carola* (1881), 89–91
E, see *Cormoran* (1893), 97–8
E, see *Gneisenau* (1938), 31–3
E, see *Graudenz* (1914), 109–10
E, see *Leipzig* (1931), 122–3

E, see *Medusa*, 99–102
E, see *Oldenburg* (1886), 8–9
E, see *Scorpion*, 138
E, see *Wacht* (1888), 95
E, see *Zähringen* (1902), 16–17
Eagle, see *Danzig* (1853), 41
Eagle, see *Kiel* (1810), 130
Eber (1887), 141
Eber (1903), 142–3
Eckernförde (1849), 129
Eckernförde, see *Gefion* (1843), 39
Edinburgh, see *Der Königliche Ernst August*, 80
Eduard Jungmann, see *V 153*, 174
Eendracht, see *KH 2*, 126
Eidechse, 218–20
Ekvator, see *Meteor* (1924), 143–4
Elan, 239
Elbe (1848), 80
Elbe (1935), 74–5
Elbing, 110–11
'*Electric Anna*', see *Ägir*, 11–12
Elisabeth, 42–3
Elmshorn, 129
Elmshorn/ No 2 class, 129
Elsass, 18–20, 21
Emden (1908), 105–6
Emden (1916), 113
Emden (1925), 118–19
Emden, see *Falke* (1865), 87–8
Empire Fowey, see *Elbe* (1935), 74
Enseigne Ballande, see *SG 22*, 234, 237
Erich Giese, see *Z 12*, 200
Erich Koellner, see *Z 13*, 200
Erich Steinbrinck, see *Z 15*, 200
Eridano, see *TA 29*, 225, 230
Ersatz A, 58
  Adler, see *Seeadler* (1892), 97–8
  Ägir, see *König Albert*, 25–6
  Albatross, see *Eber* (1887), 141
  Alexandrine, see *Danzig* (1907), 102–4
  Amazone, see *Leipzig* (1931), 122–3
  Arcona, see *Köln* (1930), 119–21
  „ *Moltke* (1878), 44–5
  Ariadne, see *Cöln* (1918), 114–15
  „ *Prinzess Wilhelm*, 94
  Augusta, see *Olga* (1881), 89–91
  Baden, see *Posen*, 23–4
  Bayern, see *Nassau* (1909), 23–4
  Beowulf, see *Thüringen*, 24–5
  Berlin, see *Blücher* (1939), 65–7
  Blitz, see *Nürnberg* (1908), 104–5
  Brandenburg, see *Kronprinz Wilhelm*, 27–8
  Braunschweig, see *Admiral Graf Spee*, 60–3
  Brinio class, see *K1* class (ex-Dutch), 147
  Bussard, see *Magdeburg* (1912), 107–8
  Cöln (1919), 114–15
  Comet, see *Adler* (1885), 139–40
  „ *Dresden* (1908), 105–6
  Condor, see *Strassburg*, 107–8
  Cormoran, see *Stralsund* (1912), 107–8

Ersatz Crocodill, see *Albatross* (1871), 134
  Deutschland, see *Yorck* (1905), 51–2
  Dresden, see *Dresden* (1917), 114–15
  Eber, see *Condor* (1894), 97–8
  Elisabeth, see *Irene*, 94
  Elsass, see *Scharnhorst* (1939), 31–2
  Emden (1919), 114–15
  „ see *KH1* (1939), 126
  Falke, see *Breslau*, 107–8
  Freya, see *Freya* (1898), 47–8
  Friedrich der Grosse, see *Kaiser Wilhelm II*, 14–16
  Frithjof, see *Oldenburg* (1912), 24–5
  Gazelle, see *Königsberg* (1916), 113
  „ *Stosch*, 44
  Gefion, see *Wiesbaden* (1915), 111–12
  Geier, see *Rostock* (1914), 109
  Gneisenau (1915), 59
  Greif, see *Kolberg* (1910), 106–7
  Grille, see *Pfeil* (1884), 91
  Habicht, see *Hay* (1882), 140
  „ *Luchs* (1900), 142–3
  Hagen, see *Kaiser*, 25–6
  Hamburg, see *Admiral Hipper*, 65–7
  Hannover, see *Bismarck* (1940), 33–5
  Heimdall, see *Friedrich der Grosse*, 25–6
  Hela, see *Frankfurt* (1915), 111–12
  Hertha, see *Hindenburg*, 56–7
  „ *Stein*, 44–5
  Hessen, see *Gneisenau* (1938), 31–3
  Hildebrand, see *Kaiser* (1912), 25–6
  Hyäne, see *Jaguar*, 142–3
  Iltis, see *Iltis* (1898), 142–3
  Jagd, see *Mainz*, 106–7
  Java, see *KH 2*, 126
  Kaiser, see *Roon*, 51–2
  Kaiser Friedrich III, see *Sachsen* (1916), 28–30
  Kaiser Wilhelm II, see *Württemberg* (1917), 28–30
  Kaiserin Augusta, see *Lützow* (1915), 56–7
  Karlsruhe (A) (1915), 114–15
  König Wilhelm, see *Friedrich Carl*, 50–1
  „ „ *Kaiser Wilhelm der Grosse*, 14–16
  Königsberg, see *Frauenlob* (1918), 114–15
  Königsberg (?), see *KH 2*, 126
  Kurfürst, see *König*, 27–8
  Leipzig, see *Fürst Bismarck*, 48–9
  „ *Leipzig* (1918), 114–15

Ersatz Loreley, see *Greif*, 93
  „ *Loreley* (1896), 141–2
  Lothringen, see *Admiral Scheer*, 60–2
  Magdeburg, see *Magdeburg* (1917), 114–15
  Mainz, see *Rostock* (1918), 114–15
  Medusa, see *Karlsruhe* (1929), 119–21
  „ *Nixe*, 92
  Mercur, see *Lübeck* (1905), 102–4
  Meteor, see *Hyäne* (1879), 139
  „ *Königsberg* (1907), 104–5
  Natter, see *Jäger* (1883), 153
  Niobe, see *Emden* (1925), 118–19
  „ *Karlsruhe* (1916), 113
  Nürnberg, see *Wiesbaden* (1917), 114–15
  Nymphe, see *Arcona* (1886), 89–91
  „ *Emden* (1916), 113
  „ *Nürnberg* (1935), 122–3
  Odin, see *Prinzregent Luitpold* (1913), 25–26
  Oldenburg, see *Ostfriesland*, 24–5
  Pfeil, see *Emden* (1908), 105–6
  Pommerania, see *Jagd*, 95
  Preussen, see *Kaiser Friedrich III*, 14–16
  Preussen, see *Lützow* (1933), 60–1
  Prinzess Wilhelm, see *Graudenz* (1914), 109–10
  Sachsen, see *Westfalen*, 23–4
  Salamander, see *Wolf* (1878), 139
  Scharnhorst (1915), 59
  Schleswig-Holstein, see *Tirpitz*, 33–5
  Schwalbe, see *Cöln* (1911), 106–7
  Seeadler, see *Karlsruhe* (1914), 109
  Siegfried, see *Helgoland*, 24–5
  Sperber, see *Augsburg* (1910), 106–7
  Sumatra, see *KH 1*, 126
  Thetis, see *Königsberg* (1929), 119–21
  „ *Nürnberg* (1917), 113
  Tiger, see *Iltis* (1880), 139
  Victoria, see *Charlotte*, 45
  Vineta, see *Marie*, 89–91
  Wacht, see *Stettin*, 104–5
  Weissenburg, see *Markgraf*, 27–8
  Wolf, see *Tiger* (1900), 142–3
  Wörth, see *Baden* (1915), 28–30
  Württemberg, see *Rheinland*, 23–4
  Yorck (1916), 59
  Zieten, see *Berlin*, 102–4
  Zinnia, see *Lorelei/ K4*, 147–8
Erzherzog Johann, 39–40
Europa, see *I* (1928), 73–4

F, see *Amazone* (1901), 99–102
F, see *Basilisk* (1880), 138
F, see *Bismarck* (1940), 33–5
F, see *Geier*, 97–8
F, see *Mecklenburg*, 16–17
F, see *Meteor* (1891), 96
F, see *Nürnberg* (1935), 122–3
F, see *Sophie*, 89–91
F, see *Von der Tann* (1911), 53–4
F 1 class, 231–2
F 1–10, 231–2
FK1–7, 116–17
F.R. 34, see *TA 34*, 230
F.R. 41–45, see *TA 9–13*, 221, 230
Falk, see *Qualle*, 218–20
Falke (1865), 87–8
Falke (1891), 97–8
Falke (1927), 191–3
Fatikh, see *König Wilhelm*, 3
Felix Henri, see *SG 5 & SG 10*, 234, 236
Fionda, see *TA 46*, 225–6, 230
Flink, 152
Flora Sommerfeld, see *Victoria Louise*, 48
Forelle, see *V 6*, 155
Francesco Crispi, see *TA 15 & TA 17*, 227, 230
ex *Franctireur*, 134–5
Frankfurt (1849), 79–80
Frankfurt (1915), 111–12
Franziska Kimme, see *S 178*, 186
Frauengabe, see *Frauenlob* (1856), 82–3
Frauenlob (1856), 82–3
Frauenlob (1903), 99–102
Frauenlob (1918), 114–15
Freya (1876), 86–7
Freya (1898), 47–8
Friedrich Carl (1867), 2
Friedrich Carl (1903), 50–1
Friedrich der Grosse (1877), 5–6
Friedrich der Grosse (1912), 25–6
Friedrich Eckoldt, see *Z 16*, 200
Friedrich Ihn, see *Z 14*, 200
Friedrich Wilhelm, see *Grosser Kurfürst*, 27–8
Frithjof, 10–12
Frunze, see *R 02*, 188–9
Fuchs, 132–3
Fürst Bismarck, 48–9

G (1885), 154–5
G, see *Alexandrine*, 89–91
G, see *Blücher* (1939), 65–7
G, see *Camaeleon* (1879), 138
G, see *Comet* (1891), 96
G, see *Frauenlob* (1903), 99–102
G, see *Gazelle* (1901), 99–101
G, see *Moltke* (1911), 54–5
G, see *Schwaben* (1904), 16–17
G, see *Tirpitz*, 33–5
G 1 class, 232–3
G 1–24, 232–3
G 7–12, 176–8
G 37–44, 178–80
G 85–95, 178–81
G 96, 181–2
G 96 class, 181–3
G 101 class, 188
G 101–104, 188
G 119–121, 185–6
G 132–137, 171
G 148–150, 181–3
G 169–175, 172–5
G 192–197, 173–6
ex *Garde-Mobile*, 134–5
Gascogne, 38
Gayret-ı-Vataniye, see *S 168*, 174
Gazelle (1862), 42–3

Gazelle (1901), 99–101
Gazelle (1908), 218–20
Gazelle class, 99–102
Gefion (1843), 39
Gefion (1893), 98–9
Geier, 97–8
Generale Achille Papa, see *SG 20*, 234, 239
General Alexeev, see *Volya*, 30
Georg Thiele, see *Z 2*, 200
Georg Kimme, see *S 179*, 186
Georgi Pobiedonosets, 30
Gerard Callenburgh, see *ZH1*, 212
Germania, see *Erzherzog Johann*, 39–40
Germania, see *Gun yawl No 3*, 130–1
Giuseppe Dezza, see *TA 35*, 224, 230
Giuseppe Missori, see *TA 22*, 224, 230
Gladio, see *TA 37*, 225, 230
Glückstadt, 129
Gneisenau (1880), 44–5
Gneisenau (1908), 52
Gneisenau (1938), 31–3
Gneisenau, see '*Jade*', 74–5
Gnevnyy, see *R 03*, 188–9
Goeben, 30, 54–5
Gonza, see *S 178*, 186
Goral, see *A 80*, 164
Graf Spee, 58
Graf Zeppelin, 71–2
Granit, see *SG 26*, 234
Graudenz, 109–10
Graudenz class, 109–10
Greif (1887), 93
Greif (1927), 191–3
Grille, 84
Grosser Kurfürst (1878), 5–6
Grosser Kurfürst (1914), 27–8
Grossherzog von Oldenburg, 79–80
Gun sloop No 1 class (1848–9), 131–2
Gun sloops Nos 1–36, 131–2
Gun sloop No 10 class (1805–8), 127
Gun sloops Nos 10, 17, 45, 48, 51, 116; 127
Gun yawl No 1 class, 130–1
  Nos 1 & 2 (1840–1), 130–1
  Nos 3, 4, 5 & 6 (1848), 130–1
  Nos 7 & 8 (1849), 130–1
Gunboat No 3 class, 128
  Nos 3, 6, 9, 12 (1848), 128
  Nos 8, 11 (1849), 128
Gyller, see *Löwe*, 216–17

H (1886), 155–6
H (1939), 37
H, see *Admiral Hipper*, 65–7
H, see *Arcona* (1903), 99–102
H, see *Braunschweig*, 18–20
H, see *Crocodill* (1880), 138
H, see *Goeben* (1912), 54–5
H, see *Hela* (1896), 99
H, see *Kaiserin Augusta*, 46
H41 (1940), 37–8
H42–44, 38
H 145–147, 181–3
H 166–169, 181–3
H 186–202, 186
H class, 35, 155
Habicht (1860), 132–3
Habicht (1880), 139–40
Habicht class, 139–40
Haci Pasa, see *Loreley* (1896), 141–2
Hagen, 10–12
Hai, see *F 3 & F 6*, 231
Hai-Jing, see *Taku*, 187

Hamburg (1841), 81
Hamburg (1904), 102–4
Hannover (1907), 20–2
Hannover, see *Bremen* (1842), 81
Hansa (1847), 40
Hansa (1875), 4–5
Hansa (1899), 47–8
Hansdorf, see *H 186*, 186
Hans Lody, see *Z 10*, 200
Hans Lüdemann, see *Z 18*, 202
Hauk, see *Krokodil*, 218–20
Hay (1860), 132–3
Hay (1882), 146
Heimdall, 10–12
Heinrich Heister, see *Falke* (1865), 87–8
Hela (1854), 82–3
Hela (1896), 99
Hela class, 82–3
Helgoland, 24–5
Helgoland class, 24–5
Hermann Bohnekamp, see *H 187*, 186
Hermann Kühne, see *Z 19*, 202
Hermann Schoemann, see *Z 7*, 200
Hertha (1865), 42–3
Hertha (1898), 47–8
Hessen 18–20, 21
Hildebrand, 10–12
Hindenburg, 56–7
Hoche, see *Z 25*, 204
Hoisdorf, see *H 187*, 186
Holland, see *Frankfurt* (1849), 80
Hulk C, see *Nixe*, 92
Hummel, 137–8
Husar, see *KT 4*, 218–20
Hval, see *NH (?)* (ex *Hval*), 218–20
Hvas, see *Seestern*, 218–20
Hyäne (1860), 132–3
Hyäne (1879), 139

Iltis (1880), 139
Iltis (1898), 142–3
Iltis (1928), 191–3
Iltis class, 142–3
Impavido, see *TA 23*, 224, 230
Imperator, see *Volya*, 30
Imperator Alexander III, see *Volya*, 30
Inca, see *Grossherzog von Oldenburg*, 79–80
Indomitable, 239
Insidioso, see *TA 21*, 224, 230
Intrepido, see *TA 20*, 223, 230
Intrepido, see *TA 26*, 225
Ioann Zlatoust, 30
Iphigenie, see *SG 46*, 234
Irene (1887), 94–5
Irene, see *Regensburg* (1915), 109–10
Irene class, 94–5

J (1939), 37
J, see *Elsass*, 18–20
J, see *Prinz Eugen*, 65–7
J, see *Regensburg* (1915), 109–10
J, see *Salamander* (1880), 138
J, see *Seydlitz* (1913), 55–6
J, see *Undine* (1904), 99–102
'*Jade*', 74–5
Jagd (1889), 95–6
Jagd, see *F 1*, 231
Jäger (1860), 132
Jäger (1883), 153
Jäger class, 132–3
Jaguar (1898), 142–3
Jaguar (1929), 191–3
Jawus Sultan Selim, see *Goeben* (1911), 54–5

Jupiter, see *Deutschland*, 7
Jupiter, see *SG 1* & *SG 3*, 235

K (1889), 155–6
K (1939), 37
K, see *Derfflinger*, 56–7
K, see *Hamburg* (1904), 102–4
K, see *Hertha* (1898), 47–8
K, see *Natter* (1881), 138
K, see *Preussen*, 18–20
K, see *Seydlitz* (1936), 65–7
K1 class (ex-Dutch), 147
K1 class (1938 design), 146
K1 class (1939 design), 146
K1–3 (1941–3), 147
K1–4 (1941–2), 146
K1–IV (1938–39), 146–7
K4/ Lorelei (1940), 147–8
KH 1 (1939), 126
KH 2 (1939), *126*
KT 1–4, 218–20
Kaiser (1875), 6–7
Kaiser (1912), 25–6
Kaiser class, 6–7, 25–6
Kaiser Friedrich III, 14–16
Kaiser Karl Barbarossa, 14–16
Kaiser Karl der Grosse, 14–16
Kaiser Wilhelm der Grosse, 14–16
Kaiser Wilhelm II, 14–16
Kaiseradler, see *Seeadler*, 97–8
Kaiserin, 25–6
Kaiserin Augusta, 46
Kapitän J Frobeen, see *S 178*, 186
Kapitan Saken, *R 04*, 189
Karl Galster, see *Z 20*, 202
Karlsruhe (1914), 109
Karlsruhe (1916), 113
Karlsruhe (1929), 119–21
Karlsruhe class, 109
Kawakaze, see *TA 20*, 223
Keravnos, see *V 6*, 176
Kiel, 130
Kijkduin, see *KH 2* (1939), 126
Kilissi, see *SG 19*, 234, 237
Kita, see *SG 8*, 234
Kjach, see *Schildkröte*, 218–20
Kjell, see *KT 1*, 218–20
Kolberg, 106–7
Kolberg class, 106–7
Köln, 119–21
Komet, see *S 23*, 177–8
Kondor, 191–3
Kongens Skib, see *Kiel*, 130
König, 27–8
König class, 27–8
König Albert, 25–6
König Wilhelm, 3–4, 6, 45, 102
Königin Luise, see *F 3* & *F 6*, 231
Königsberg (1907), 104–5
Königsberg (1916), 113
Königsberg (1929), 119–21
Königsberg class (1903–5), 104–5
Königsberg class (1913), 113
Königsberg class (1924–5), 119–21
Kotetsu-Kan, see *Sphinx*, 1
Krakowiak, see *A 64*, 164
Krokodil, 218–20
Kronprinz, 3
Kronprinz (Wilhelm) (1914), 27–8
Kühn (1883), 152
Kujawiak, see *A 68*, 164
Kürassier, 218–20
Kurfürst Friedrich Wilhelm, 13–14
Kvik, see *KT 2*, 218–20
Kwaiten, see *Danzig* (1853), 41

L (1939), 37
L, see *Bremen* (1904), 102–4
L, see *Hessen* (1905), 18–20

L, see *Hummel* (1881), 138
L, see *Lützow* (1937), 65–7
L, see *Victoria Louise*, 47–8
La Batailleuse, see *SG 23*, 234, 238
La Bayonnaise, see *TA 13*, 221, 230
La Perouse, see *S 94*, 235
La Pomone, see *TA 10*, 221, 230
L'Agile, see *TA 2*, 220–1
Laks, see *Admiral Deinhard*, 218–20
L'Alsacien, see *T 23*, 195
Lancia, see *TA 41*, 225–6, 230
Landesvater, see *Vaterland*, 145
Lansquenet, see *TA 34*, 228–9, 230
L'Aventurier, see *ZF 7*, 213–14
Le Fier, see *TA 1*, 220–1
Le Gladiateur, see *SG 18*, 234, 238
Leberecht Maass, see *Z 1*, 200
Leeds, see *Bremen* (1842), 81
Leipzig (1877), 43
Leipzig (1906), 102–4
Leipzig (1918), 114–15
Leipzig (1931), 122–3
Leipzig class (1871–2), 43
Leipzig class (1927–33), 122–3
Leitenant Pushkin, see *R 04*, 189
L'Entreprenant, see *TA 4*, 220–1
Leopard (1929), 191–3
Leopard (1940), 216–17
Leopard, see *Z 23*, 204
Les Eparges, see *SG 25*, 234, 239
Libelle, see *F 1*, 231
Liberté, see *I* (1928), 73–4
L'Iphigenie, see *TA 11*, 221, 230
Lira, see *TA 49*, 229, 230
Li-Sui, see *Vaterland*, 145
Li-Tsieh, see *Otter* (1910), 145–6
L'Impeteuese, see *SG 17*, 234, 238
Lom, see *Eidechse* 218–20
L'Opiniatre, see *ZF 2*, 213–14
Lorelei/ K4 (1940), 147–8
Loreley (1859), 84–5
Loreley (1896), 141–2
Lothringen, 18–20, 21
Löwe, 216–17
Lübeck (1844), 81
Lübeck (1905), 102–4
Luchs (1900), 142–3
Luchs (1929), 191–3
Luise, 86–7
Lützow (1915), 56–7
Lützow (1933), 60–1
Lützow (1937), 65–7
Lyn, see *KT 3*, 218–20

M (1938), 124–5
M (1939), 37
M class, 124–5
M, see *Brummer* (1884), 140–1
M, see *Lothringen* (1906), 18–20
M, see *München* (1905), 102–4
M, see *Vineta* (1899), 47–8
Mackensen, 58
Mackensen class, 57–8
Magdeburg (1912), 107–8
Magdeburg (1917), 114–15
Magdeburg class, 107–8
Mainz, 106–7
Muraviev Amurskyy, see *Pillau* (1914), 110–11
Marceau, see *Z 31*, 204
Marie, 89–91
Markgraf, 27–8
Matelot Leblanc, see *SG 14* & *SG 41*, 234, 237
Max Schultz, see *Z 3*, 200

Mazur, see *V 105*, 188
Mecklenburg, 16–17
Medusa (1867), 85
Medusa (1901), 99–102
Mercur (1847), 81–2
Mercur, see *Bonin*, 130
Merkur, see *SG 1* & *SG 4*, 235
Meteor (1869), 133–4
Meteor (1891), 96
Meteor (1924), 143–4
Meteor class, 96
Metz, see *Königsberg* (1916), 113
Miantonomoh, 2
Midilli, see *Breslau* (1912), 107–8
Mine barge *No 2*, see *Pfeil* & *Wolf* (1860), 132–3
Mine barge *No 4*, see *Tiger* (1860), 132–3
Mohican, see *Loreley* (1896), 141–2
Moltke (1878), 44–5
Moltke (1911), 54–5
Moltke class, 54–5
Mosel, 136
Möwe (1880), 139–40
Möwe (1926), 191–2
Möwe class, 191–3
Muavenet-i-Milleye, see *S 165*, 174
Mücke, 137–8
Mulhouse, see *Stralsund* (1912), 107–8
München (1905), 102–4
München, see *Otter* (1910), 145–6
Musketier, see *KT 2*, 218–20
Musquito, 83

N (1939), 37
N, see *Bremse* (1884), 140–1
N, see *Deutschland* (1906), 20–2
N, see *Hansa* (1899), 47–8
N, see *Leipzig* (1906), 102–4
NH (?) (ex *Hval*), 218–20
NH (?) (ex *Storm*), 218–20
NH 01–03, 218–20
Nassau, 23–4
Natter (1860), 132–3
Natter (1881), 137–8
Nautilus, 134
Nea Genea, see *V 5*, 176
Neptun, see *Friedrich Carl*, 2
Newcastle, see *Lübeck* (1844), 81
Niobe (1849), 41
Niobe (1900), 99–101
Nix (1851), 82
Nixe (1886), 92
Nonsuch, see *Z 38*, 205
Notus, 150
Numune-i-Hamiyet, see *S 167*, 174
Nürnberg (1908), 104–5
Nürnberg (1917), 113
Nürnberg (1935), 122–3
Nymphe (1863), 85
Nymphe (1900), 99–101
Nymphe class, 85

O (1937), 68–9
O (1938), 124–5
O class, 68–9
O, see *Pommern*, 20–2
O, see *Siegfried* (1890), 10–12
O, see *Strassburg* (1912), 108
O, see *Stuttgart* (1908), 104–5
Oared gunboat *No 1* class, 131
Nos 1–27 (1848–9), 131
Odin, 11–12
Odin class, 11–12
Odin, see *Panther*, 216–17
Oern, see *Schlange*, 218–20
Oldenburg (1886), 8–9

Oldenburg (1912), 24–5
Olga, 89–91
Osakka, see *Victoria*, 86
Ostfriesland, 24–5
Otter (1878), 138
Otter (1910), 145–6

P (1937), 68–9
P (1938), 124–5
P, see *Beowulf*, 10–12
P, see *Hannover*, 20–2
P1–12, 63–4
PKZ-34, see *Meteor* (1924), 143–4
Panther (1902), 142–3
Panther (1940), 216–17
Paul Jacobi, see *Z 5*, 200
Peryneas, see *H 187*, 186
Peryneas II, see *H 186*, 186
Petrel 2 – Petrel 4, 239
Petropavlovsk, see *Lützow* (1937), 67
Pfeil (1860), 132–3
Pfeil (1884), 91
Pfeil, see *S 139*, 174
Pierre Durand, see *V 79*, 180
Pilade Bronzetti, see *TA 35*, 224
Pillau, 110–11
Podhalanin, see *A 80*, 164
Podriznyy, see *T 12*, 194
Pommerania, 88
Pommern, 20–2
Pomone, see *SG 47*, 234
Porivistyy, see *T 17*, 194
Posen, 23–4
Potsdam, see *Elbe* (1935), 74–5
Premuda, see *TA 32*, 227, 230
Premuda, see *V 116*, 185–6
Preussen (1876), 5–6
Preussen (1905), 18–20, 21
Preussen class, 5–6
Preussischer Adler, 79
Primernyy, see *T 33*, 196
Prince Charles, see *A 12*, 161
Prince Leopold, see *A 14*, 161
Princesse Marie-José, see *A 4*, 161
Prinz Adalbert (1864), 1
Prinz Adalbert (1877), 43
Prinz Adalbert (1901), 50–1
Prinz Adalbert class, 50–1
Prinz Eitel Friedrich, 58
Prinz Eugen, 65–7
Prinz Heinrich, 49–50
Prinzess Wilhelm, 94–5
Prinzregent Luitpold, 25–6
Procnyy, see *Z 20*, 202
Pronzitelnyy, see *G 196*, 176
Provornyy, see *Z 33*, 204
Prozorlivyy, see *V 158*, 174
Pugnale, see *TA 40*, 225, 230

Q (1937), 68–9
Q (1938), 124–5
Q, see *Frithjof* (1893), 10–12
Q, see *Schleswig-Holstein*, 20–2
Qualle, 218–20

R (1938), 124–5
R, see *Hildebrand* (1893), 10–12
R, see *Schlesien* (1908), 20–2
R 01 class, 188–9
R 01–04, 188–9
R 10 class, 189–90
R 10–13, 189–90
Rageot de la Touche, see *SG 15* & *SG 42*, 234, 237
Reconnaissance cruiser 1939, 209–10
Reconnaissance cruiser 1940, 209–10
Recruit, see *Nix* (1851), 82

Regensburg, 109–10
Reiher, see *A 20*, 162
Rhein, 136
Rheinland, 23–4
Richard Beitzen, see *Z 4*, 200
Rigel, see *TA 28*, 225, 230
Risui, see *Vaterland*, 145
Rival, 150
Robert Napier, see *Lübeck* (1844), 81
Rolf Krake, 2
Roon, 51–2
Rostislav, 30
Rostock (1914), 109
Rostock (1918), 114–15
Rover, 83

S, see *Hagen* (1894), 10–12
S 1–6, 154–5
S 7 class, 156–9
S 7–65 (1885), 157–9
S 13–24 (1912–13), 176–8
S 31–36 (1914), 178–80
S 49–66 (1915–17), 178–80
S 66 class, 159–60
S 66–81, 159–60
S 82 class, 160–1
S 82–89, 160–1
S 90 class, 169–71
S 90–131, 169–71
S 113 class, 185–6
S 113–115 (1919), 185
S 131–139 (1917–18), 181–2
S 138–149 (1907–08), 172–5
S 152–157 (1918), 181–3
S 165–168 (1910–11), 172–5
S 176–179 (1910–11), 172–6
S 138 class, 172–6
S 211–223, 186
SG 1–26, 234–9
SG 41, 42, 46, 47, 48; 234
SG 46–48, see *TA 9–11*, 221, 230
SP 1–3 (1941), 209–10
Sachsen (1878), 7–8, 96
Sachsen (1916), 28–30
Sachsen class, 7–8
Sael, see *NH 03*, 218–20
Safina-E-Hujjaj, see *Elbe* (1935), 74
St Pauli, see Oared gunboat *No 27*, 131
Salamander (1851), 82
Salamander (1860), 132–3
Salamander (1880), 137–8
Sampiero Corso, 239
San Luis, see *G 102*, 188
San Martino, see *TA 17* & *TA 18*, 223, 230
Sans Pareil, see *SG 4*, 234
Sans Peur, see *SG 1*, 234
Sans Reproche, see *SG 2*, 234
Sans Souci, see *SG 3*, 234
Santa Fe, see *G 103*, 188
Santiago, see *G 101*, 188
Saturn, see *Preussen*, 6
Saturn, see *SG 2* & *SG 4*, 235
Schamien, 144–5
Scharf, 152
Scharnhorst (1907), 52
Scharnhorst (1939), 31–2
Schastlivyy, see *R 01*, 188–9
Schichau experimental boat, 160–1
Schildkröte, 218–20
Schlange, 218–20
Schlesien, 20–2
Schleswig-Holstein, 20–2
Schneewittchen, see *A* (1889), 156

Schütze, 152
Schwaben, 16–17
Schwalbe (1860), 132–3
Schwalbe (1888), 94
Schwalbe class, 93–4
Scorpion (1860), 132–3
Scorpion (1877), 137–8
Sebenico, see *TA 43*, 228, 230
Sédan, see *Prinz Adalbert*, 43
Seeadler (1892), 97–8
Seeadler (1927), 191–2
Seebär, see *Th 2*, 153
Seepferd, 218–20
Seestern, 218–20
Seewolf, see *Hyäne* (1879), 139
Seydlitz (1913), 55–6
Seydlitz (1936), 65–7
Seydlitz, see *Weser* (1939), 75–6
Sicher, 152
Siegfried, 10–12
Sild, see *Balte*, 218–20
Sinop, 30
Skarv, see *Gazelle* (1908), 219
Skrei, see *NH 01*, 218–20
Slazak, see *A 59*, 164
Sleipner, see *S 97*, 169
Snøgg, see *Zach*, 219
Solferino, see *TA 18*, 223, 230
Somers, see *Schichau experimental boat*, 160–1
Sophie, 89–91
Sophie, see ex *Brest*, 134–5
Sovietskaya Ukraina, 38
Spada, see *TA 38*, 225–6, 230
Sperber (1860), 132–3
Sperber (1889), 94
Sphinx, 1
Spica, see *TA 45*, 225–6, 230
Squadrista, see *TA 33*, 227
Stein, 44–5
Stella Polare, see *TA 36*, 225, 230
Stettin, 104–5
Stjerckodder, see *Sphinx*, 1
Stonewall Jackson, see *Sphinx*, 1
Støren, see *Von der Tan* (1849), 129
Storm, see *NH* (?) (ex *Storm*) (1900), 218–20
Stosch, 44–5
Stralsund (1817), 78
Stralsund (1912), 107–8
Strasbourg, see *Regensburg* (1915), 109–10
Strassburg (1912), 107–8
Strelasund, see Gun sloop *No 1* (1848), 132
Stuttgart, 104–5
Sulev, see *A 32*, 162

T, see *Bayern* (1915), 28–30
T 1 class, 193–4
T 1–4, 193–4
T 2, see *S 2* (1884), 155
T 3, see *TA 48* (1914), 228, 230
T 5–8, 193–4
T 7, see *TA 34* (1916), 228, 230
T 9–10, 193–4
T 11–12 (1940), 193–4
T 11–65, see *S 11–65* (1885), 157
T 13–21, 193–4
T 22 class, 195–6
T 22–25, 195–6
T 23, see *S 23* (1913), 177–8
T 26–51, 195–6
T 43 class, 196
T 43–48, 196
T 52 class, 196–7

T 52–60, 196–7
T 61 class, 197–8
T 61–84, 197–8
T 66–89, see *S 66–89*, 169–61
T 91–131, see *S 91–131*, 169–71
T 107–108, see *G 7–8* (1912), 176–8
T 110–111, see *G 10–11* (1912), 176–8
T 123, see *S 23* (1913), 177–8
T 132–137, see *G 132–137*, 171
T 138–149, see *S 138–149* (1907–08), 172–5
T 151–161, see *V 151–161* (1908), 172–5
T 163–164, see *V 163–164* (1909), 174
T 165–169, see *S 165–169*, 172–5
T 170, see *G 170* (1909), 175
T 172–175, see *G 172–75*, 175
T 176, see *S 176* (1910), 175
T 178–179, see *S 178–179* (1911), 176
T 180–186, see *V 180–186* (1910–11), 172–6
T 189–190, see *V 189–190* (1911), 172–6
T 192–193, see *G 192–193* (1911), 172–6
T 195–197, see *G 195–197* (1911), 172–6
TA 1 class, 220–1
TA 1–6, 220–1
TA 9 class, 221
TA 9–13, 221, 230
TA 14 class, 222
TA 14–15, 222, 230
TA 16 class, 222–3
TA 16–20, 222–3, 230
TA 21 class, 223–4
TA 21–22, 223–4, 230
TA 23 class, 224–5
TA 23, 224–5, 230
TA 24 class, 225–6
TA 24–33, 225–7, 230
TA 34 class, 228
TA 34–49, 228–9, 230
Taku, 187
Tallinn, see *Lützow* (1937), 67
Tapfer, 152
Tarantel, 218–20
Taranto, see *Strassburg* (1912), 107–8
Teist, see *NH 02*, 218–20
Th 1–2, 154–5
Theodor Riedel, see *Z 6* (1937), 200
Thetis, 41
Thetis (1901), 99–101
Thetis class, 41
Thorn (1823), 128
　No 1 (1826), 128
　No 2 (1827), 128
Thüringen, 24–5
Thusnelda, see *Leipzig* (1877), 43
Tiger (1860), 132–3
Tiger (1900), 142–3
Tiger (1929), 191–3
Tiger (1940), 216–17
Tiger, see *KT 1* (1940), 219
Tirpitz, 33–5
Tjerk Hiddes, see *ZH 2* (1939), 212
Tong Cheong, see *Schamien* (1899), 144–5
Tönning, 129
Tor, see *Tiger* (1940), 216–17

Torgut Reis, see *Weissenburg*, 13–14
Torpedo boats *Nos V–XI*, 152
Torpedo steamers *Nos I, II, III*, 150
　IV, see *Ulan* (1876), 150–1
Tri Sviatitelia, 30
Troll, 217
Trugg, see *Zick*, 218–19
Tsel, see *Hessen*, 18–19
Tsingtau, 145
Tucuman, see *G 104* (1915), 188
Turbine, see *TA 14* (1927), 222, 230

U, see *Bremen*, 28
U, see *Heimdall* (1892), 10–12
U, see *Pillau* (1914), 110–11
U9, 105–6
U151, 28
U156, 28
U157, 28
UJ 2229, see *SG 15*, 237
UJ 2231, see (*SG 23*), 238
Ulan, 150–1
Undine (1869), 83
Undine (1904), 99–102
United Sates, see *Hansa* (1847), 40
Uranus, see *Kaiser*, 7
Uranus, see *SG 2* & *SG 3*, 235

V 1 class, 176–7
V 1–10 (1884), 154–5
V 11–19, see *V 1–10* (1884), 154–5
V 1–6 (1912–13), 176–7
V 25 class, 178–81
V 25–30, 178–80
V 47–48, 178–80
V 67–85, 178–81
V 99–100, 184–5
V 105 class, 187–8
V 105–108, 187–8
V 116–118, 185–6
V 125–130, 181–2
V 140–144, 181–3
V 150–164 (1907–8), 172–5
V 158–165 (1918), 181–3
V 170 class, 186
V 170– 177, 186
V 180–191, 173–6
V 203–210, 186
Van Galen, see *ZH 3* (1929), 213
Van Speyk, see *K 3*, 147
Varg, see *Seepferd*, 218–20
Vasileus Georgios, see *ZG 3* (*Hermes*) (1939), 215
Vaterland, 145
Victoria (1864), 86
Victoria Louise (1899), 47–8
Vineta (1864), 42–3
Vineta (1899), 47–8
Viper, 137–8
Volya, 30
Von der Tann (1849), 129
Von der Tann (1911), 53–4
Vorwärts (1883), 152
Vorwärts (1901), 144
Vulcan, see *Bonin*, 130

W 1–6, 154–5
WW 151, 181–3
Wacht, 95–6
Waltjen boats *Nos I–III* (1872), 149
Warendorp, see *A 20*, 162
Weissenburg, 13–14

Weser (1939), 75–6
Weser, see *Salamander*, 82
Wespe (1860), 132–3
Wespe (1876), 137–8
Wespe class, 137–8
Westfalen, 23–4
Wettin, 16–17
White type torpedo boats, 153–4
Wiesbaden (1915), 111–12
Wiesbaden (1917), 114–15
Wiesbaden class, 111–12
Wilhelm I, see *König Wilhelm*, 3
Wilhelm Heidkamp, see *Z 21* (1939), 202
Wittelsbach, 16–17
Wolf (1860), 132–3
Wolf (1878), 139
Wolf (1928), 191–3
Wolf class, 139
Wolfgang Zenker, see *Z 9*, 200
Wörth, 13–14
Wuchow, see *Vorwärts* (1910), 144
Württemberg (1881), 7–8
Württemberg (1917), 28–30

Y, 154, 155
Yadagar-i-Millet, see *S 166* (1910), 174
Yeddo, see *Augusta*, 86
Yorck, 51–2
Yser, 239

Z, see *Stralsund* (1912), 107–8
Z 1 class, 199–201
Z 1–16 (1937–38), 199–201
Z 1–4, see *V 105–108* (1915), 187–8
Z 17 class, 202–3
Z 17–22 (1938–39), 202–3
Z 23 class, 203–7
Z 23–43 (1940–44), 203–7
Z 31 class, 208
Z 31–42 (1938), 208
Z 44–50 (1944), 203–7
Z 51 (1943), 210
Z 52 class, 210–11
Z 52–56 (1943), 210–11
ZF 2 class, 213–14
ZF 2, ZF 4, ZF 5, ZF 7; 213–14
ZG 3 (*Hermes*), 214–15
ZH 1 class, 212
ZH 1–3, 212–13
ZN 4 class, 216
ZN 4–5, 216
Zack, 218–20
Zähringen, 16–17
Zand, see *A 42*, 163
Zavidnyy, see *R 13*, 189–90
Zazpiakbat, see *S 179* (1918), 186
Zephir, 150
Zick, 218–20
Zick class, 218–20
Zieten, 88–9
Zivoy, see *R 12 II*, 189–90
Zorkyy, see *R 10*, 189–90
Zutkyy, see *R 12 I*, 189–90
Zvonkyy, see *R 11*, 189–90

I (ex *Ausonia*), 70
I (ex *Europa*), 73
I class (White type), 153–4
II, 76–7
XII class, 154

78 T, see *TA 48*, 228, 230
96 F, see *TA 34*, 228, 230